2/08

95.00

THE LEGISLATIVE BRANCH OF STATE GOVERNMENT

People, Process, and Politics

Other Titles in ABC-CLIO's
ABOUT
STATE GOVERNMENT
Set

The Executive Branch of State Government: People, Process, and Politics, Margaret R. Ferguson
The Judicial Branch of State Government: People, Process, and Politics, Sean O. Hogan

THE LEGISLATIVE BRANCH OF STATE GOVERNMENT

People, Process, and Politics

Thomas H. Little
and
David B. Ogle

A B C · C L I O

Santa Barbara, California   Denver, Colorado   Oxford, England

Library of Congress Cataloging-in-Publication Data

Little, Thomas H.
  The legislative branch of state government : people, process, and politics / Thomas H. Little and David B. Ogle.
      p. cm. -- (ABC-CLIO's about state government)
  Includes bibliographical and references and index.
    ISBN 1-85109-761-9 (hardcover : alk. paper) -- ISBN 1-85109-766-X (ebook) 1. Legislative bodies--United States--States. 2. Legislation--United States--States. 3. Legislators--United States--States. I Ogle, David B. II. Title. III. Series.
JK2488.L58 2006
328.73--dc22
                              2006001699

09 08 07 06 05 10 9 8 7 6 5 4 3 2 1
This book is also available on the World Wide Web as an eBook. Visit abc-clio.com for details.

ABC-CLIO, Inc.
130 Cremona Drive, P.O. Box 1911
Santa Barbara, California 93116–1911

Production Team
    Acquisitions Editor: Alicia Merritt
    Media Editor: Ellen Rasmussen
    Media Resources Manager: Caroline Price
    Production Editor: Martha Ripley Gray
    Editorial Assistant: Alisha Martinez
    Production Manager: Don Schmidt
    Manufacturing Coordinator: George Smyser

Text Design: Darice Zimmermann, ZimmServices LLC

This book is printed on acid-free paper ∞ .
Manufactured in the United States of America

To my parents and grandparents, who encouraged and supported my education, even when the end was nowhere in sight. Thank you!
—T. H. L.

To Kathy, Stephanie, Greg, Mo, and my dad.
—D. B. O.

CONTENTS

FOREWORD

Most Americans have some familiarity with the role and structure of the federal government. At an early age, we are taught in school about the president of the United States and the roles performed by the three branches of the federal government: the legislative, the executive, and the judicial. In civics classes, we are often given a skeletal picture of how the nation's government works; we are told that Congress writes the laws, the president executes them, and the Supreme Court acts as the interpreter of the U.S. Constitution. Outside of the classroom, the media repeatedly remind us of the important duties that all three branches play in the nation's political system. Through television news, radio talk shows, newspapers, magazines, and web blogs, the media draw our attention to the major political battles in Washington, D.C., building our knowledge of the president, Congress, and the U.S. Supreme Court.

While most Americans have some knowledge of the federal government, they tend to know far less about their state governments. Our schools frequently teach us about the governments in our own states, yet what we learn about state government does not become as deeply ingrained as what we learn about the federal government. The media do little to improve our knowledge about the states. With their attention primarily drawn to conflict in the nation's Capitol, the media tend to devote little attention to the politics in our state capitols.

The lack of knowledge about state government is unfortunate because state governments today play a major role in American politics. Certainly, one cannot dismiss the importance of the federal government. The president, Congress, and the Supreme Court routinely address some of the most vital political issues confronting the nation today, from the health of the economy to the advancement of civil rights to whether the nation will go to war or seek peace. Yet on a day-to-day basis, the state governments may have an even greater effect on our lives, for they tend to be directly responsible for establishing most of the laws under which we live and for providing the everyday services that we need to survive. The importance of state governments can be seen by simply noting three facts.

- State legislatures produce more laws than the U.S. Congress. Combined, more than 20,000 new laws are passed each year across the states, with an average of more than 400 new laws per state. Congress tends to adopt fewer than 300 laws in a given year. State laws are essential because they constitute most of the rules governing criminal behavior in the nation and help shape such things as the character of our schools, the strength of the states' economies, the type of help that is provided to the needy, the quality of our roads, and the health of the environment.

- State governments are large and growing. Their growth has been outpacing that of the federal government for the past several decades. In fact, the expansion of government bureaucracy over the past three decades has come primarily at the state and local level, while the number of federal employees has seen little change. As of 2004, more than 5 million people were working for state governments compared with 2.7 million for the federal government. Another 11 million people are employed by local governments, many of whom handle responsibilities determined by the state government.
- Far more cases are heard in state courts each year than in the federal courts. In an average year, more than 93 million cases are filed in state courts. This compares with approximately 2.6 million cases filed in the federal courts.

Not only does state politics matter, but state governments are in many ways different from the federal government. The three branches of government are common to both the national and the fifty state governments, yet beyond this rather cosmetic similarity, significant differences exist. One of the most central is that while the executive branch of the national government is led by one individual—the president—the executive branch of state governments is led by several executives. Beyond the governor, who is the state's chief executive, the fifty states have other elected executives who have their own independent responsibilities and sources of power, including such figures as the lieutenant governor, the secretary of state, the attorney general, the treasurer, and the superintendent of public instruction.

The state legislatures also vary considerably from Congress. Some of them, most notably the California and New York legislatures, look a lot like Congress, meeting year-round, with full-time staff and well-paid members. Yet other legislatures, such as those in Wyoming and South Dakota, meet only briefly every year or every other year, have minimal staff support, and pay members very little. The legislature in Nebraska, unlike Congress or any other state, has only one chamber and is the only nonpartisan legislature in the nation. With 400 representatives, the house of representatives in the state of New Hampshire has almost as many members as the 435-seat U.S. House. The boundaries for all state senate districts in the nation are based on population so that each district in a given state has approximately the same number of residents, whereas population does not affect the number of members each state elects to the U.S. Senate. All states elect two U.S. senators, even though the states vary widely in population.

The state courts are similarly distinctive. One of the most significant differences between the state and federal courts is that all state court judges are selected through some type of election, whereas federal judges are appointed by the president with senate approval. Thus, state court judges are more directly beholden to the public. State courts are also affected by variations in state constitutions, some of which grant more extensive rights and liberties than what is set forth in the U.S. Constitution. Thus, important differences may exist across the states in what the state supreme courts will consider constitutional and unconstitutional.

These differences across the states and between the states and federal government affect how politics is practiced, who wins and who loses, the substance of state laws, the extent to which government pays attention to voters, the ability of government to fulfill its responsibilities, the types of rights and liberties we enjoy, and the type of people who are elected to public office. Learning about state government provides a means for understanding different ways in which democratic government can be structured and how those differences affect us.

Part of the reason that Americans know so little about state government is likely a result of the strong emphasis placed on the federal government by the media and the schools, but some of it also reflects the lack of available resources on state governments. Numerous books are devoted to the national government generally and to each of the three branches of the national government, yet there are very few places where you can turn to find information about the structure and character of state governments. If you want to understand how government and politics works in the states, it is just not easy to do so. The few scholarly books available on state governments can be difficult to locate, narrow in scope, or hard for someone unfamiliar with government studies to understand. A few general reference books on American politics touch on topics related to state government, but these often provide only a bit of the picture of how state government works. You can also find books on the governments of individual states, but these tell you little as to how the structure of government and character of politics in those states compare with the government and politics in other states. Simply put, there is no reference work available that focuses solely on explaining the workings of state government across the nation.

About State Government is designed to help fill this gap by providing a comprehensive source of information on state government for high school students, college undergraduates, and the general public. The *About State Government* reference set consists of three volumes, with each volume devoted to a different branch of state government: the legislative, the executive, and the judiciary. All three volumes provide general information about the states, explaining major trends found across the states, while also pointing out important differences that make some states unique or unusual. The books explain how each branch of state government has changed over time, what roles the three branches play in state politics, how the three branches are structured, who serves in them, and how these individuals are selected. The books also describe the character of politics in the states today, the relationship among the different branches of government, some of the major problems confronting state government, and modern proposals for political reform. Each volume also includes a lengthy chapter providing information on the governments state by state, including a description of how each state government is structured, an overview of how the elected officials are selected, and some insights into the character of politics in each state. All three books include a glossary of terms, a comprehensive index, and an annotated bibliography to provide direction for further study.

This set will not make everyone in the nation as familiar with state government as they are with the federal government. But it should provide a good starting place for those who have questions about government in the nation's fifty states and are looking for a book to provide them with answers.

Richard A. Clucas
Portland State University

Preface and Acknowledgments

State governments are the linchpin of American democracy. They were around long before there was a national government, the Virginia General Assembly having been first called to order more than 150 years before the national government was created. Today, state governments propose, consider, debate, and pass most of the laws that determine how we live, the safety of the food we eat, the quality of the education our children receive, and the content of the air we breathe. While the political leaders in Washington get the bulk of the press coverage, it is the people in state capitols across the United States who develop most of the policies that address the challenges we face today and will be facing tomorrow.

State governments are important, and state legislatures are the central part of these governments. It is because of their importance—and the unique qualities that define state legislatures—that this book is dedicated to exploring the fifty state legislative bodies of the United States, and the people, processes, policies, and powers that compose them. While all state legislatures are similar in structure (except for that of unicameral Nebraska) and objective, each bears unique traits and qualities that set it apart from the others—and even more so, from the U.S. Congress. Some state legislatures are small; others are large. Some legislators are paid a full-time salary; others are not paid enough to cover even a small apartment during session. As in the U.S. Congress, in some state legislatures seniority is the primary factor in determining a senator's influence. In others, decisions are made more on the basis of relationships with leadership than upon seniority. In a few states, legislators have a full-time professional staff, similar to that of a member of the U.S. Congress; most, however, make do with at most one or two staff people, who may work only when the legislature is in session.

While politics in the U.S. Congress has been, of late, defined almost exclusively by partisanship, dissension in some state legislatures is more a reflection of regionalism, ideology, and economic differences. In some states a campaign for the state legislature can cost as much as a contested congressional race, while in others it is still possible to win a contested seat with less than $10,000. Lobbyists are important in all state legislatures, whether they are a primary source of information or of campaign support. In the end, each state legislature is unique; each is different from that of every other state body, and each is uniquely different from the U.S. Congress.

Chapter 1 of this volume is dedicated to an exploration of the fundamental qualities that define state legislatures and to a brief history of these legislatures, including a look at their evolution, the general functions they perform, and the challenges they face in the modern world. Chapter 2 examines the particular functions and responsibilities associated with the legislative branch of government (lawmaking, budget-making, education, and oversight). While each legislature is responsible for performing all of these functions, the priority given to the various functions and the methods used to achieve them vary significantly from state to state.

In Chapter 3, we turn to the structures and processes that state legislatures use to achieve their goals. While all state legislatures have similar structures (leadership, party organizations, committees, staff, and so forth), the importance and specific qualities of those structures may vary greatly from one state to the next. Chapter 4 focuses on the people who make up the legislature. Who runs for the legislature? Why do they run? What qualities do they possess? How and why do certain people win, and others lose? In Chapter 5 we examine legislatures in the context of the other branches of government (the judicial and executive), nongovernmental groups (interest groups, political parties, and the news media), and federal players (the national government and other state governments). In the case of each, we examine the nature of the relationship, the sources of influence or interaction, and the current balance between those entities and the legislature. We also look at the conditions under which that relationship may vary from state to state.

Finally, while all state legislatures share common responsibilities, powers, institutions, and organizations, no two state legislatures are exactly alike. Chapter 6 is dedicated to providing a summary description of each state legislature in the United States. It includes a section on each state, explaining important characteristics of the membership, organization, leadership, campaign practices, and political environments that define the state and its legislature. This section allows the reader to see how each differs from its neighbors. In short, Chapters 1 through 5 focus on what makes state legislatures similar, while Chapter 6 brings attentions to what makes each state legislature unique.

Throughout the book, we have included a series of anecdotal sidebars and tables that are intended to provide a fuller insight into the dynamics and nuances of the American state legislative process. In most instances, these have direct relevance to the text of the chapter in which they appear. In a few instances, however, we have chosen to include tabular information that relates only indirectly to the text, but which provides additional information about state legislatures that we believed the reader might find interesting and useful.

This book would not have been possible without the diligent efforts of many people. First, our thanks go to Richard Clucas, set editor and the person who came up with the idea for this volume. Without him, the project would never have gotten off the ground. Second, we want to thank several students who gathered data for the project, including Jessica Phelan, Andrew Weisbecker, Justin Outling, and Ben Anderson. Our gratitude also goes to the folks at ABC-CLIO, especially Martha Gray, and also Peter Westwick and Alicia Merritt, whose patience in working with authors not too good at meeting deadlines we applaud.

This book took a great deal of time that might have been spent doing other things. For letting us dedicate time to this project, we thank our colleagues at the State Legislative Leaders Foundation, especially President Stephen G. Lakis, who signs the checks. We also thank our families, who put up with the late nights and early mornings we spent at the word processor or poring over websites or the *Book of the States.* Finally, we must thank the many members of the legislature and staffers who took time to read parts of this manuscript, correcting our mistakes and sharing insights and stories that help bring this volume to life. Without the support of all these people there would be no book, and we thank them all, reserving to ourselves any blame that may be due for omissions or errors.

Thomas H. Little
David B. Ogle

1

FUNDAMENTALS OF
STATE LEGISLATURES

The people's branch of government: That is what a state legislature is often called in the American form of government. It has earned that moniker for a variety of reasons. While the appellation is far from perfect, the state legislative bodies of the United States are much more likely to "look like the people" than are their sister executive or judicial branches. About a quarter of all state legislators are women, with the proportion approaching 40 percent in some states. About 10 percent are African Americans—a bit below the proportion of blacks in the national population, but more reflective than are either of the other two branches of government. Many legislators are lawyers and businesspeople, but many others are teachers, farmers, students, retirees, doctors, ranchers, ministers, and real estate agents. As a whole, legislators are more representative of the diversity of the general population than is the judiciary, whose members must be attorneys, or than are governors, who are most often white men with backgrounds in law, government, or business.

State legislatures are also called the people's branch of government because their members generally work and live with the people. Governors usually reside in their state capital. The decisions of judges, who are generally full-time judicial employees, are made in private and are announced from the bench, setting both the judges and their decisions far apart from "the people." Most state legislators live for much of the year in the districts they represent. More than two-thirds have a job outside of the legislature that requires them to spend most of the year in their district, with the people they represent. In some smaller Northeastern states, legislators may live in the district year-round and commute to their state capital as necessary. Even so-called full-time legislatures generally take extended recesses and meet no more than three days a week when they are in session, so that members may spend most of their time among their constituents.

Citizens have access to their state legislature in a way they do not to the other branches of state government. Very few ever meet personally with their state's governor or, voluntarily, with a judge. But state legislators continually meet with all kinds of people, from both within and without the districts they represent. The halls of state capitol and legislative buildings are always full of citizens coming to meet with legislators; school children headed to the legislative gallery to watch their legislators in action; or people preparing to speak at a public hearing. A number of states require that no bill be approved by the legislature unless it has received a public hearing at which any interested citizen may speak. In Delaware, for example, citizens are allowed and even encouraged to speak on the floor of the state Senate or House of Representatives when a bill is being debated. Delaware is one of several states in which every vote cast by a legislator in a committee and on the floor of the legislature is recorded for public record and public inspection.

Still another reason that state legislatures are called the people's branch of government is that they are expected to be responsive to the needs and wishes of the people in ways that governors and judges are not. Governors are expected to look at problems from a statewide perspective. Citizens look to their governors to lead their states, to do what they consider right and in the best interests of the state as a whole. Judges are expected only to dispense justice and uphold the law. They are responsible to their state's constitution and laws, not to the people. While legislators are expected to protect the interests of the state, they are, however, also expected to represent, to work in behalf of, and to protect the interests of the people in their districts. Unlike governors and judges, state legislators are constantly being asked to see that a pothole is filled, to find out why someone's son or daughter did not get into the state university, or to help get a skunk out of a constituent's yard. They are expected to serve the people they represent in personal and direct ways.

A Note on the Importance of State Governments

Legislatures are the centerpiece of representative democracy. The U.S. Congress plays a central role in national politics and policy. County commissions or city councils are important within their jurisdictions. But state legislatures are particularly important, because of the unique and significant role that state governments play in U.S. politics. Unlike most countries, in which state or subnational units of government are clearly secondary to the national government, in the United States, state government—in the form of the original Thirteen Colonies—preceded the national government. Indeed, it was delegates from the state governments who created the national government—first in 1783 (the Articles of Confederation) and then again in 1789 (the U.S. Constitution).

State governments are vitally important partners in the U.S. system of government. The vast majority of laws that affect the daily lives of Americans are passed not in Washington, D.C., but in places such as Bismarck, North Dakota; Springfield, Illinois; Columbus, Ohio; Sacramento, California; and Montgomery, Alabama. States are responsible for governing how people drive, what students learn in school, the quality of the air they breathe, the quality of the food they eat, and the safety of the buildings in which they work. Most of crimes are violations of state, rather than national, law: more than 99 percent of all crimes are state or local offenses, including most murders, assaults, and burglaries. National politicians may talk about "getting tough on crime," but it is state officials who are really in a position to do so.

George Washington presiding at the signing of the Constitution of the United States in Philadelphia on September 17, 1787. Authors of the U.S. Constitution were keenly aware of the importance of state's rights. (Library of Congress)

The balance of power between the states and the national government has always been constantly changing. The U.S. Constitution, which established the national government, muddied the waters right from the beginning by indicating that, while the national government should be "supreme" (Article VI), powers not specifically granted to the national government are reserved to the states or to the people (Amendment X). This leaves significant room for interpretation regarding what powers are granted by the Constitution and what is "left to the states." This intergovernmental tug-of-war continues daily in the courts, in the legislatures, and in the minds of the public. But it does not alter the fact that state governments are, and have always been, a central and important component of U.S. government.

WHY LEGISLATURES MATTER

Legislative branches were the first units of government, established by the founders of both the national and state governments in the 1770s. In fact, many of the states (as well as the Articles of Confederation, which established the first national government, operating from 1783 to 1789) created only a legislative government. While it soon became clear that there was a need for executive and judicial branches of government as well, legislatures have, from the very outset of the country's history, played a vital and unique role in U.S. government. They remain critical because of their essential relationship with the people, and what that relationship enables and requires them to do.

The Will of the Constituency

As noted above, legislatures are in a unique position to represent the will of the people. At the state level, legislators have always been elected by the people, unlike governors (many of whom were initially appointed by the legislature) and judges (many of whom are still appointed by governors, legislatures, or some combination of the two). State legislators know what their constituents want because, far more than governors or judges, they work, live, play, and worship among them. Legislators often represent relatively small units of population, especially in states like Delaware, Rhode Island, or New Hampshire, where the average House of Representatives district contains fewer than twenty thousand people. Legislators often introduce legislation because someone in their district requested it, or because the legislation would help a constituent to resolve a problem. When a state legislator votes on a matter of public policy, one of the primary concerns on that legislator's mind is: "What do the people in my district want?"

The Collective Will of the People

A state's legislature, like the state itself, is made up of rural and urban members, Republicans and Democrats, liberals and conservatives, men and women, blacks, whites, and Hispanics. That enables a legislative chamber, acting as a body, to reflect the collective needs and interests of the people of its state in a way that a single executive or a handful of Supreme Court judges never could. Through the debate and discussions that are central to the legislative process, the many diverse constituencies of a state are given voice. Those voices are reflected in the laws passed by the legislature.

The Interests of the People

While a state legislature is a representative body, it is also a deliberative body. Its members are expected to listen to their constituents, but its decisions need to reflect more than just the will of those people. Representative democracy means that legislators should listen to the arguments and perspectives of their colleagues, as well as the concerns of their constituents, and then cast a vote that is in the best interests of their constituency, the state, and even the nation. As a deliberative body, a state legislature debates and discusses ideas, sharing thoughts and concerns among its members. Its members gather information and understanding from these exchanges that enable them to cast informed votes designed to protect the interests of the people of their state.

Institutional Balance

In the U.S. system, the legislature is the branch of government that is supposed to make law. The executive branch is charged with implementing or executing the laws, and the judicial branch with applying and interpreting them. This system, known as "checks and balances," works well when each of the branches is independent and informed. However, if one of the three branches becomes weak, ceding power to one or both of the others, that fragile balance is in jeopardy. One important role of a state legislature is to provide an effective counterbalance to the other two branches, but particularly to the executive. The legislature does this by remaining strong enough to initiate and enact its own agenda, by being informed and autonomous enough to challenge executive branch initiatives when necessary, and by enacting laws for the state, in some cases over the objection of the executive. In a similar manner, although not nearly to the same degree as with the executive, the legislature provides a balance to the judiciary, reprimanding judges when they act illegally, modifying laws or even amending the constitution in light of judicial decisions, and, in some states, approving and reapproving the appointment of judges.

Consensus out of Conflict

People disagree about things every day. If a disagreement cannot be resolved, those involved usually walk away with no solution and "agree to disagree." People who are "pro-life" go their own way from those who are "pro-choice," as do those who support the death penalty from those who oppose it. Every day, people walk away from disagreements without resolving them. Governments, however, do not have that luxury. With every issue or problem, there is a decision that reflects one side or the other—or, most often in a democracy, a combination of the two, even if that decision results in no policy. Through a series of institutional norms, structures, processes, and relationships, state legislatures are able to fashion consensus from very divergent points of view. Governors, because they generally reflect one party or perspective, seldom promote consensus but, rather, promote their own perspective, which the legislature may have to balance. Judges seldom reflect or seek consensus, because their objective is justice, not representation.

THE COMMON CHARACTERISTICS OF STATE LEGISLATURES

While every state legislature has unique characteristics that set it apart from the legislatures of the other forty-nine states, most share some common characteristics in terms of basic organization. With a few exceptions, every state legislature is bicameral, partisan, hierarchical, and decentralized.

TABLE 1.1   MEMBERSHIP OF STATE HOUSES OF REPRESENTATIVES, 2005

Top 5		Bottom 4	
New Hampshire	400		
Pennsylvania	203	Hawaii	51
Georgia	180	Nevada	42
Missouri	163	Delaware	41
Massachusetts	160	Alaska	40

Source: National Conference of State Legislatures (http://www.ncsl.org).

Bicameralism

Every state legislature, except that of Nebraska, is bicameral, meaning that it consists of two independent chambers. Every legislature has a Senate, while forty-nine have either a House or Assembly as a counterpart to the Senate. In order for a bill to become law, it must pass both chambers in identical form.

In the forty-nine states that have two houses, Senates have fewer members and larger district sizes than the House or Assembly. Usually, a Senate has a few responsibilities that are not granted the House or Assembly, and the House has some responsibilities not granted the Senate. For example, many state Senates must approve appointments made by the governor; in some states, legislation appropriating funds must originate in the House.

Partisanship

All fifty state legislatures organize themselves along party lines, with the party having the most members (the majority party), controlling key leadership positions and making important decisions. Even the Nebraska legislature, which is officially nonpartisan, has members who are listed outside the legislature as Republicans holding all key leadership posts.

Party affiliation generally determines who will preside over a chamber, who will assign bills to committee, and who will chair legislative committees. While Nebraska legislators run in nonpartisan elections (that is, the candidates do not declare their party), they generally organize along party lines once in session. Even in states in which the minority party participates in key decisions, the choice to allow such participation is in the hands of the majority party. When there is a dead even split in partisan balance between Democrats and Republicans (at least one state legislative chamber has been tied every session since 1984), the two parties find a way to share power.

Hierarchical Leadership

Every state legislature has a hierarchical leadership structure, meaning that there are levels of leadership. One person is chosen to serve as the top leader of the body. In every state except North Dakota, the primary leader of the House or Assembly is the speaker. In state Senates, the position of president, president pro tempore, or majority leader will be considered the chamber's number one position. A chamber's top leader generally has assistants, often called floor leaders and assistant floor leaders, who in some cases are elected by the legislative members from their party and in other cases are appointed by the top leader. They assist in the daily administration and operation of the chamber and provide support to their fellow party members. Below those leaders there are often other leaders, sometimes called "whips," because they are to "whip" the members into line when votes are cast. In some state legislatures, as many as a third of the members are assigned some leadership title.

The minority party membership elects a minority leader who serves as its leader in the chamber. The minority leader is assisted by a series of either elected or appointed deputy and assistance leaders, just as is the case with the majority party.

Decentralized Committee Structures

While it might in theory be possible for every member of a legislative chamber to discuss every bill (that is, every piece of proposed legislation) that is introduced into the body, it would not be very practicable. In order to give these proposals a careful and detailed examination, each legislature organizes itself into smaller working groups called committees, ranging from a handful (six in the Maryland Senate) to a large number (more than forty in the Wisconsin Assembly). In most state legislatures, committees have the power to determine the fate of bills sent to them for review. In most states, a committee can defeat a bill simply by deciding that it not be considered by the whole body. In the few states in which every bill must be voted upon by the committee to which it has been assigned, the committee's recommendation (to pass or reject a bill) will usually determine its fate. Through their power to review proposed legislation that falls within their jurisdiction, legislative committees thus have a great deal of power and influence.

WHAT STATE LEGISLATURES DO

State legislatures perform specific constitutionally assigned activities that are necessary to government and that promote the achievement of the objectives outlined in the previous section. The five basic responsibilities of a legislative body under the U.S. system of government are lawmaking, budgeting, representation, oversight, and education. Each state legislature may perform these responsibilities a bit differently, depending on the state's rules, its norms, history, and traditions, and the nature of the state's population.

Lawmaking

In theory, legislatures make laws, governors carry them out, and courts apply or interpret them. While the reality is never as tidy as the theory (governors and judges, in their own ways, also make laws), legislatures are at the center of the lawmaking process. Political scientist William J. Keefe emphasizes the importance of this function:

> The burden of settling conflict and making authoritative rules in American society has always been lodged essentially within legislative jurisdiction. . . . [In] legal, constitutional terms lawmaking is mainly, if not purely, a legislative task. Lawmaking is by no means the only function of the state legislature but, measured by the activity that is allotted, it is plainly the most important. (Keefe and Ogul 1968, 38)

During their 2003 sessions, the fifty state legislatures approved more than 23,000 bills and resolutions, ranging from the symbolic (recognizing the local high school soccer team for winning the state championship) to the monumental (reforming criminal justice or placing a moratorium on the death penalty).

The lawmaking process is complex and dynamic. A bill is introduced by a legislator or legislators and assigned to a committee either by the presiding officer of the legislator's chamber or by a committee of its members. The bill is debated and discussed by the legislators who serve on the committee, and citizens often are given an opportunity to express their thoughts about it directly to the members by means of a public hearing. If a majority of the members of the committee support the bill, it is considered by the full membership of the chamber in which it was introduced. If a majority of the members of that chamber agree, the bill is sent to the other chamber, where the process begins anew. If the second chamber approves the bill in identical form, the bill is sent to the governor, who can choose to sign it into law or to veto (reject) it. If the governor vetoes the bill, it is sent back to the legislature, which may nevertheless make it law and override the governor's veto by repassing the bill in each chamber. In most states,

---

DID YOU KNOW?

South Carolina Legislators Told the Governor "No" 106 Times in Less than an Hour

The South Carolina House of Representatives overrode their governor's vetoes of 106 bills in less than an hour. In the final weeks of South Carolina's 2003–2004 legislative session, Governor Mark Sanford vetoed 107 bills that had been passed by the legislature.

On May 26, 2004, the members of the House took just 55 minutes to override 106 of Governor Sanford's 107 vetoes.

Source: *The State*, Valerie Baeurlein. May 27, 2004. Columbia, South Carolina

legislative override of a gubernatorial veto requires that repassage of the bill be accomplished by more than a simple majority in each chamber (usually the requirement is 60 percent or two-thirds). If the bill is defeated at any point in this complex process, it does not become law.

Budgetmaking

Probably no single legislative responsibility is more important to the state and its citizens than the passage of the state's budget. The budget indicates not only how much money the state will raise and spend on its operations and policies but also which of those operations and policies are going to be deemed the most important. That one state spends twice as much on education per student as another, or that one state taxes wealthy citizens at a significantly higher rate than another, says a great deal about the relative priorities of those states. State legislatures spend a great deal of time and effort trying to devise budgets that will meet their states' financial obligations without requiring tax increases to levels that voters will find unacceptable.

Legislatures rely on a variety of means to produce revenue to cover their state's budget. The most common are sales taxes (taxes on goods and, sometimes, purchased services), income taxes, property taxes (taxes on homes, land, and, in some states, automobiles), and so-called sin taxes (additional sales taxes on such things as gasoline, alcohol, and cigarettes). Legislators know that they have to raise enough revenue from these sources to satisfy voter demands for services by the government, including the education of their children, the paving of their streets, the maintenance of a capable state police force, and the imprisonment of criminals. The difficult balancing act that legislators must perform is to develop a budget that will satisfy the public's demand both for services and for an acceptable level of taxation (Garand and Baudoin 2003, 305).

Representation

Legislatures are, by definition, representative institutions. Citizens vote to determine who will represent them and enact laws on their behalf. Representing the interests of the citizens is a fundamental part of what a legislator does. Legislators who do not keep an eye on the needs and desires of the people they represent will be in serious danger of losing their seats in the next election. The viewpoints and possible response of the voters are always in the back of any legislator's mind. A legislator seldom casts a vote on an important issue that is counter to the clear sentiment and interests of that legislator's district (Jewell 1980).

Legislators generally introduce legislation that reflects the desires, needs, and interests of their districts. The committees that a legislator asks to serve on are usually reflective of the political, economic, and geographic interests of those who voted the legislator into office. When legislators speak on the floor of their chamber or in a committee, they always cast a watchful eye toward the probable response of their constituents. Finally, a critical component of the electoral success of any legislator is the ability to respond effectively to letters, phone calls, faxes, and e-mails from constituents. Citizens having trouble securing help from a state agency or simply wanting a tour of the capitol building may well call upon their legislator for assistance.

The link between a legislator and his or her constituents is the legislator's most important relationship. A legislator who loses touch with the people of the district being represented is failing to meet the obligations of representative democracy. To represent the needs and wishes of their constituents effectively, and to represent the interests of their state, legislators must have a strong grasp of the attitudes, positions, interests, needs, and desires of voters in their districts. Therefore, most try to remain in constant contact with their constituents, speaking at civic organizations, schools, and churches, meeting with constituents who visit the capitol, answering constituent mail, and issuing newsletters and press releases. Legislators who neglect the citizens they have been elected to represent often find those citizens voting for their opponent at the next election.

Education

A less prominent, but no less important, responsibility of the legislature is education. Whereas representation focuses on two-way communications between legislators and their constituents concerning issues under consideration by the legislature, the education function means keeping their constituents informed about their activities and their positions on important matters of public policy. Citizens are often confused by the legislative process, and by much of the legislation that is considered by their legislature. That confusion often leads to distrust and loss of support, because people seldom have a great deal of trust in that which they cannot understand. Legislators need to explain to citizens both the complexities of the legislative process and the specifics of important public policy matters. With a few notable exceptions (Goehring 2000), most U.S. state legislators do not take enough time or put forth enough effort in this area, which is contributing to a decline in public support of state legislatures and of government in general (Hibbing and Theiss-Morse 2001; Rosenthal 1998).

In the twenty-first century, state legislators have numerous tools at their disposal to assist them in educating and informing the public about the workings of the legislature and about issues under its consideration (Lassman 2002; Mechling and Applegate 2003). Traditionally, legislators have relied upon such things as newsletters, newspaper columns, direct mailings, responses to constituent letters, and, more recently, electronic mail. However, the communications revolution of the last decade has opened up many additional avenues for public education. Legislators can now participate in chat rooms or answer questions live on the Internet. Many state legislators have their own websites, and every state legislature in the country has a legislative website where citizens can access information about bills, processes, votes, schedules, hearings, committee meetings, and other legislative activities. Many websites offer citizens an opportunity to listen to live debates on the floor of the legislature and some-times even in committee. With little financial investment, legislators can conduct "town meetings" with video streaming from their office or hold video conferencing, to work with constituents all across the state at the same time. With modern technology, it really is possible to be in two (or three or four or five) places at the same time (Rosen-thal 2000).

Oversight

Finally, a critical—but often the least appreciated and most poorly performed—function of the legislature is that of oversight: ensuring that the laws passed by the legislature and signed by the governor are effectively implemented and administered. It is not enough that a legislature passes an education reform bill. It is arguably even more im-portant that the reforms be implemented in such a way as to have the desired positive effect on public policy. That is a critical responsibility of legislatures and one that leg-islatures must undertake aggressively, because it is only through effective legislative oversight that they can ensure there will be adequate checks and balances on the other branches of government (Rosenthal 1990).

The legislature has several tools at its disposal through which it can fulfill this ob-ligation. Legislative committees often hold hearings and sometimes conduct investi-gations to try to determine if a particular agency is administering a program effec-tively—that is, in accordance with the provisions of the legislation that established it, and in the manner intended by the legislature when it enacted the legislation. For example, an education committee will hold hearings to determine whether the money allocated to implement a reading enhancement program is indeed being spent in that manner, and to see if students are showing the intended gains in reading skills. Further, given its budgetmaking responsibility, the legislature is the primary source of revenue for most state agencies, and all government agencies regularly go before its committees to justify their budget requests. These regular meetings provide the leg-islators with opportunities to engage in oversight of the executive branch. Because the legislative committee system generally mirrors the state bureaucracy (for most government agencies, there is a corresponding legislative committee), the legislature is organizationally structured to conduct oversight, with legislators and staff mem-bers in each policy area possessing the knowledge and expertise necessary to hold members of the corresponding executive branch agency accountable for their actions and performance.

THE NATURE OF LEGISLATIVE INFLUENCE

The nation's Founding Fathers saw the legislative as the most important branch among the three branches of government. James Madison, Alexander Hamilton, James Mon-roe, and the other authors of the U.S. Constitution granted the legislative branch much stronger formal powers than the other two, and the authors of the earliest state consti-tutions followed their lead when writing constitutions for their respective states. Re-acting to the concern of the Founding Fathers to ensure against the establishment of an American monarchy, all of the colonies placed strict limitations on the powers of their executive branches, often limiting their terms to a single year and forbidding more than two or three successive terms. The longest gubernatorial terms were two years. Just as did the national constitution, state constitutions poorly defined the judicial branch, in both structure and role.

And yet, state legislatures have often neglected to accept the full mantle of responsi-bility assigned them by the early state constitutions. Throughout the nation's history, many scholars, politicians, and voters have found U.S. state legislatures falling short of this grand ideal and neglecting to take responsibility and control over policymaking within the states. Too often, when challenges have arisen, state legislatures have not risen to the occasion, by failing to act, ceding power to another player (most often the executive or the courts), or making ill-advised decisions based on limited or biased in-formation.

If state legislatures have the power to act as effective policymaking institutions, why have they so often fallen short? The answer is that, while constitutional powers are a necessary component of institutional power, they are not in and of themselves suffi-cient to make that power a reality. In order for state legislatures, or any governmental institution, to successfully wield the power formally granted it, three prerequisites—beyond constitutional authorization—must be fulfilled: opportunity, capacity, and leadership.

Opportunity

In the U.S. separation of powers system of government, the legislative, judicial, and ex-ecutive branches are each responsible for distinct parts of the governing process. And under the U.S. system of federalism, power is shared by state and national governments (with local governments exercising such powers and authority as are granted them by their state governments). At the state level, state legislatures have to share power with governors, judges, and the public (in states in which citizens have the power to initiate proposed legislation by placing it on the election ballot through a petition process). State governments as a whole have to share power with the national government. A state legislature faced with a powerful and popular governor, an aggressive and inde-pendent judiciary, or heavy citizen use of the citizen initiative process is likely to find its opportunity to lead restricted. Likewise, when expectations for government in gen-eral are limited, as they were throughout much of the eighteenth and nineteenth cen-turies, state legislatures will find their opportunities to lead curtailed. However, when other officials are weak and the public demand for state government action is high, state legislatures have the opportunity to make a significant and positive impact in the lives of the citizens they represent and serve.

Capacity

The opportunity to lead must be buttressed by a capacity to make informed and independent decisions. A weak governor and an inactive court competing with an even weaker and less active legislature can still win a battle of the weak. An inept or poorly functioning state government may waste an opportunity to lead that is presented to it when the national government decides—for economic, ideological, or political reasons—to restrict its activities. While legislative capacity will be addressed in more detail in a later chapter, it can be said here that, at a minimum, an effective legislature must have a knowledgeable and competent staff to provide it with its own independent source of information, an intelligent and concerned membership and leadership, and sufficient resources—that is, time, information, and money—to make informed decisions. Lacking those, a legislature can seldom reach its potential (Rosenthal 1981).

Leadership

Neither opportunity nor capacity can compel a legislature to exert influence unless it also has capable leadership. Having a legislature with only opportunity and capacity is like having a sports car with a powerful engine, a full tank of gas, but no one behind the wheel: the speed and power are merely potential. Just as someone has to put the car into gear and take control of the steering wheel, a legislator or a group of legislators must drive the legislature if it is to achieve its full capacity. The most effective legislatures are those that have leaders with both vision and skill—the vision to see how things can be made better in their state, and the skills to turn that vision into reality (Rosenthal 2004, 209–229).

The reason that state legislatures have so often failed to meet the goals set out by the Founding Fathers is that it is rare for the three components of opportunity, capacity, and leadership to come together in a single legislature at the same time. Too often, a weak governor has been met by an even weaker legislature that has lacked both the capacity and the leadership to take advantage of the opportunity presented them. At other times, strong leaders have found themselves up against strong and popular governors or aggressive courts. Sometimes, fully capable legislatures have been unable to take advantage of weak executives because their leaders have lacked vision or managerial skill. Powerful legislatures exist when these three pieces of the puzzle come together. An examination of the historical development of U.S. state legislatures shows how infrequently that occurs.

THE HISTORICAL DEVELOPMENT OF STATE LEGISLATURES

Legislative or representative bodies have been a part of the governance structure of this land for almost four hundred years, beginning with the legislative assembly of colonial Virginia in 1619. Throughout the course of the nation's history, they have taken on a variety of forms and fashions, with varying degrees of success and influence.

Colonial Legislatures: Limited Opportunity, Capacity, and Leadership

The first so-called legislatures in the new world were not legislatures in the modern sense of that word. That is, they were not representative bodies directly responsible to the people and also were relatively independent of the executive and the courts. Colonial legislatures included (in some cases, almost exclusively) members of the executive branch, and they were beholden not to the people but to the executive, the British Crown, or the company that funded the establishment of the colony. Their members acted primarily as trustees and boards of directors for either the king or the companies created to finance exploration of the colonies, not as representative legislative bodies. Their concerns focused on the financial interests of the Crown or the company, rather than on the economic and political interests of the people. They exercised what today would be considered executive and judicial as well as legislative responsibility and power.

According to noted historian Robert Luce, the first representative body in the colonies can be traced to the "Articles, Instructions and Orders" of 1606 from the Virginia Companies: "[T]he said President and Council of each of the said colonies and the

TABLE 1.2   AMERICAN COLONIAL ASSEMBLIES

Colony	Year of First Meeting	Number of Representatives	Year Assembly Became Bicameral
Virginia	1619	22	Pre-1660
Massachusetts Bay	1634	24	1644
Connecticut	1637	12	1698
Maryland	1638	24	1650
Rhode Island	1647	24	1696
North Carolina	1665	12	1691
South Carolina	1671	20	1691
East Jersey	1668	10	1672
West Jersey	1681	34	1696
New Hampshire	1680	11	1692
Pennsylvania	1682	42	1682
New York	1683	18	1691
Delaware	1704	18	1704
Georgia	1755	18	1755

Source: Squire, Peverill, and Hamm. 2005. *101 Chambers: Congress, State Legislatures and the Future of Legislative Studies.* Columbus: Ohio State University Press.

more part of them, respectively, shall, and may lawfully from time to time, constitute, make and ordain such Constitutions, Ordinances, and Officers, for the better order, government and peace of the people of the several colonies" (Luce 1971). By 1621, the order had been refined to include the Assembly, in addition to the Council of State: two persons elected from every town, every one hundred people, or particular plantations, to be chosen by the people in that unit. Laws could be enacted by a majority of this body, but the governor had a negative vote, giving him the power to overrule any action. Further, the governor had the power to convene and dissolve the Assembly. By 1659, the General Assembly had established its position as the representatives of the people and its right to determine its own session; however, it still remained very much secondary in influence to the executive (ibid.).

Colonial legislatures developed along similar patterns in the rest of the colonies. In 1629, the charter establishing the Massachusetts Bay Colony declared that an assembly shall meet regularly consisting of the governor or deputy governor "of said company" and seven or more assistant governors. The members of the General Court were to be chosen directly by the "freemen." By the 1630s it was evident that it was too difficult and expensive for every freeman to travel to the capital to vote, and so it was determined that each town should elect two members to send to the capital to assist in the enactment "of all such laws and ordinances for the good and welfare of the said company" (1629 Massachusetts Bay Charter, as quoted in Luce 1971, 99) Despite the presence of some colonial assemblies during the first half of the seventeenth century, the earliest truly representative bodies were established in Maryland in 1650, Connecticut in 1666, Rhode Island in 1667, and New Jersey in 1681. The charters establishing New Hampshire (1679) and Pennsylvania (1681) each provided for a representative assembly. Delaware declared its independence from Pennsylvania in 1701 and established its own representative assembly. Farther to the south, while it appears that representative democracy was in place by the late seventeenth century in the single colony that would eventually become North and South Carolina, it cannot be traced to a particular event or document. When King George II issued the charter to establish the colony of Georgia in 1732, he issued a simple and direct corporation charter, with no provision for self-government or representative assemblies. Twenty years later, in 1752, the original charter was surrendered for a provincial government with a government and council similar to those well established in other colonies (ibid., 112–115).

While legislative bodies grew more representative as the colonial period progressed, their powers and support remained very limited. Governors remained powerful, possessing what one historian has called "unqualified veto power." Although the representative body was to have full power over the government of the colonies, there was little or no distinction between the legislative, executive, and judicial branches. These colonial legislative bodies met irregularly and generally functioned at the discretion of the executive (Squire and Hamm 2005).

The first meeting of the Assembly in Virginia. (Library of Congress)

The "Supreme" Legislature (Late 1770s–1840s): Opportunity, but Limited Capacity and Leadership

Reacting against the often oppressive power exercised by many colonial governors and wanting to ensure that there would be no executive monarchy in the new country, most of the original states severely restricted executive influence in the constitutions that established their state governments in the 1770s. Having struggled so long against what it regarded as an oppressive executive, the new country preferred to have power vested in elected representative bodies rather than in an appointed or even elected executive (Crane and Watts 1968, 2). The governors of all but two of the thirteen original states were appointed by their legislature, and only the governors of Massachusetts and South Carolina were granted the power to veto legislation. The constitutional restrictions on the governor of Virginia were typical. He was to be elected for a one-year term, could serve no more than three successive terms, and had no power to convene the legislature, recommend action, or veto legislation. An eight-member council of legislators elected by the legislature further checked him. In a similar manner, the governor of Massachusetts was elected for a one-year term but was provided with a nine-member "council for advising the Governor in the Executive part of governing" (Lipscomb 1968, 12–13). It should also be noted that during this period, the expectations for government, both state and national, were very low.

While the constitutional structures of government in the postrevolutionary era may have provided the opportunity for state legislatures to be very influential in the policy-making area, most lacked either the institutional capacity or the stable leadership to take advantage of it. They had virtually no staff, seldom met, and were often composed of an unimpressive group of members with little education and experience and with limited interest. Governor Elbridge Gerry of Massachusetts described his state's legislature in 1787: "In Massachusetts, the worst men get into the legislature. Several members of the body had lately been convicted of infamous crimes. [They are men] of indigence, ignorance and baseness" (Luce 1971). Scandals and overspending began to take their toll on the "potentially dominant legislature" in the 1820s and 1830s, and the people of the United States began to take a second look at the benefits of a strong executive. Gradually, taxing and spending decisions came to be a shared responsibility between the legislature and the governor, and voters began to place limitations on the length of legislative sessions and the amount of financial support provided to their legislatures (Crane and Watts 1968, 5). State legislatures of this era also found themselves with rapid turnover of membership and leadership, which allowed them little opportunity to develop cohesive need and action agendas.

DID YOU KNOW?
State Legislatures Have Two Chambers because of a Pig

A lost pig was the reason why an American legislative body first voted as two separate and independent chambers (bicameralism). In 1643, the General Court of the Massachusetts Bay Colony was compelled to settle a disagreement over the ownership of a sow that had disappeared. In reaching its decision, the magistrates (upper house) and the deputies (lower house) reached a different conclusion, with each chamber meeting independently and siding with a different party. Prior to that disagreement, the two chambers, while technically separate, had sat and voted as one.

The bicameral legislature, with two chambers independent and autonomous of each other, was thus established in the colonies as a result of a runaway pig. While bicameralism was not expressed in the constitution of the colony and would later be challenged, it became the practice in Massachusetts and was eventually emulated in all American legislatures (including the nation's only unicameral state, Nebraska, which had a bicameral legislature until 1937).

Source: Luce 1971.

THE LEGISLATURE IN ACTION
The More Things Change, the More They Stay the Same

In 1992, the state of Michigan completed a five-year restoration of its historic capitol building. In preparing his remarks for the occasion, House of Representatives speaker Lewis Dodak decided to research the problems that had concerned the legislature at the time the building was originally dedicated, in 1879. He found that the speaker at that time, John T. Rich, a Michigan farmer, had convened the first session in the new capitol building for the purpose of focusing on three bills, concerning road construction and maintenance, prison overcrowding, and education reform. More than a century later, Speaker Dodak suggested, those three issues were as likely to dominate the legislative agenda as they had been 113 years earlier. The more things change, the more they stay the same!

Source: Interview by Thomas Little (April 23, 2005) with Lewis Dodak, former speaker of the Michigan House of Representatives.

The Declining Legislature (1850s–1900): Minimal Opportunity, Capacity, and Leadership

While the last half of the nineteenth century represents what most consider the Golden Age of the U.S. Senate, it also represents the darkest of times for most state legislatures. Their opportunities for influence over policy and governance, which had begun to be restricted by the increased constitutional powers of state governors in the 1820s and 1830s, were further restricted with the onset of so-called Jacksonian Democracy in the 1830s. Taking its name from America's first populist leader, Andrew Jackson, who served as president of the United States from 1829 to 1837, Jacksonian Democracy reforms strove to take power from the hands of wealthy, established political leaders (namely, legislators and state party officials) and put it into the hands of voters. The reforms in those years included lifting the landholding and wealth restrictions on voting, and greatly expanding the number of offices filled by popular election rather than by legislatures or governors (Lipscomb 1968; Key 1956).

However, it may have been fortunate that expectations and opportunities for legislative influence were low as the United States reached the midpoint of the nineteenth century, because the capacity of state legislatures to operate as effective policymaking bodies was also low. Many historians consider this period the low point in U.S. history in both the integrity and capability of state legislatures. Most legislatures and most individual legislators were controlled almost exclusively by the moneyed interests of their state during this era. As the agricultural economy of the early part of the century was replaced by a much more industrial economy, state legislatures found themselves doing the bidding of the rapidly expanding industrial interests, often at the expense of the public interest (Crane and Watts 1968, 4). For the most part, state legislatures during the second half of the nineteenth century found themselves hostages to outdated structures, unethical practices, incompetent and often corrupt membership, and un-scrupulous lobbyists. Author Henry Reed, a late nineteenth-century political journal-ist, may have summed up the legislatures of this era best: "[M]ost state legislatures are composed of men of low tone, ignorant, selfish and easily debauched" (as quoted in Luce 1971, 299).

The Potential Legislature (1900–1960s): Potential Opportunity, Increasing Capacity, and Sporadic Leadership

In response to the many failings and weaknesses of state government during the second half of the nineteenth century, the first years of the twentieth century gave rise to two political movements that had a significant impact on the opportunities and capacity of state legislatures. The Populist Movement, which took hold in the 1890s, altered the political landscape across the United States by instituting such reforms to the electoral process as primary elections (voters, rather than politicians, choosing a political party's candidates for office), voter registration requirements, female suffrage, and what is sometimes called direct democracy (that is, permitting citizens to initiate and approve legislation by bypassing normal political and governmental processes and allowing the people to vote for or against a law in a referendum). The Progressive Era, which is gen-erally considered to have begun with the presidency of Theodore Roosevelt (1901–1908), ushered in a new period of government activism in which the people called on govern-ment to take expanding roles in regulatory, economic, and social policy.

These populist and progressive movements, which arose almost simultaneously, were a mixed blessing for state legislatures. On the negative side, many of the populist reforms further restricted the relative influence of state legislative and party leaders by limiting their ability to influence elections. As states began to provide for primary elections, voters rather than political leaders would determine which candidates would run in the general election. The power of political leaders and legislatures was further eroded in the twenty-three states that, between 1895 and 1915, granted their citizens the right to bypass both the legislative and executive branches of government by initiating and enacting their own laws through a public referendum. On the posi-tive side for state legislatures, some of the ethical reforms spawned by these two movements provided legislatures with the opportunity to implement changes that would improve the quality of their membership and their public standing as an insti-tution of government.

The Progressive Era also brought an increased public demand for government ser-vices to which the national government did not fully respond, leaving the door open for state legislatures to step in (Sanford 1967). In most cases, however, it was governors rather than legislatures that took advantage of these new opportunities. In the first two decades of the twentieth century, governors were making their marks through the successful reform agendas of governors Woodrow Wilson (New Jersey), Theodore Roo-sevelt and Alfred E. Smith (New York), and Frank O. Lowden (Illinois), as well as the progressive policy proposals of governors Robert La Follette (Wisconsin) and Franklin Roosevelt (New York) (ibid.). During this same period, state legislative membership was gradually becoming more stable. While turnover in some bodies remained high, the average turnover in the first half of the century was about 40 percent for houses of representatives and around 20 percent for state senates. By the mid-1960s, an average of about two-thirds of the previous term's membership of a state legislative chamber was returning to that chamber for the new term (Lockard 1966). However, rapid leadership turnover continued to remain the norm in most states through the 1960s and into the early 1970s (Jewell 1980).

The Professional Legislature (1960s–Present): Increasing Opportunity, Capacity, and Leadership

The 1960s dawned with a renewed vision of the possibilities of government. Voters, scholars, and political leaders alike began to believe that government was more a solution than a problem. And most governing officials were ready. The country had a young, dynamic president and an activist Supreme Court, and the states had a cadre of new, educated, and progressive governors ready to tackle problems. However, state legislatures seemed to have missed the boat. Almost all of them were still poorly staffed, poorly funded, poorly informed, and poorly led. While state populations were shifting to the cities, legislative power in most states remained tightly in the grip of rural, conservative legislators who saw little need for a progressive and aggressive legislature. For the most part, states continued to compensate their state legislators very inadequately. Legislatures had minimal staff support, often from unqualified, politically appointed patronage employees. The majority continued to meet only once every two years, and even then they were usually restricted in the number of days they could meet in formal session.

This time, state legislatures responded with action rather than passivity. Stung by criticisms on all fronts and forced to act by decisions of the U.S. Supreme Court, legislatures began an unparalleled transformation. They took steps to enhance their capacities to operate as policymaking institutions and make themselves more representative of and responsive to the people. Most states began to implement reforms and changes to move them in the direction of a more professional institution by focusing on increasing staff, salaries, and sessions.

Two particular Supreme Court decisions served as the catalyst for these changes. In its 1962 decision in the case of *Baker vs. Carr*, the Court ruled that state legislative districts that were significantly unequal in size constituted a "denial of equal protection," as required by the U.S. Constitution; the Court permitted voters to sue the government to correct such situations. In *Reynolds vs. Simms* (1964), the Court confirmed that state legislative districts must be as similar in population as "practicable," establishing the constitutional principle of "one voter, one vote" and requiring that state legisla-

THE LEGISLATURE AND DIVERSITY
Courts Blow the Legislative Doors Open

Up through the 1950s, state legislatures were very much the dominion of white men. For a variety of reasons, few women or persons of color were elected to serve. One of the primary reasons for this disparity was the fact that most legislatures were dominated by rural constituencies that had few minorities and were less likely to elect women. With two decisions in the early 1960s (*Baker vs. Carr*, 1962, and *Reynolds vs. Simms*, 1964), the U.S. Supreme Court changed that situation. By requiring all districts within a state legislative chamber to be of similar population, the Court opened the doors of U.S. state legislatures to women and minorities. For most legislative chambers, these decisions dramatically in-creased the number of legislators elected from urban districts, in which minorities are most heavily concentrated. Urban and suburban voters also tend to be more receptive to electing women to represent them in their legislature, so the number of women legislators also increased dramatically. In 1970, only 4 percent of all state legislators were female. By the 1990s, that percentage had increased fivefold, to 20 percent.

Sources: Center for American Women and Politics, Eagleton Institute of Politics, Rutgers University Haynie, Kerry L. 2001. *African American Legislators in the American States* (New York: Columbia University Press).

tures reapportion their districts every ten years after each national census and draw legislative districts such that every member of a given legislative chamber represents a similar number of citizens.

At the beginning of the 1960s, few state legislators had even part-time clerical staff assistance, and no legislature provided for its members a fully professional support staff for legal and fiscal research, bill drafting, or constituent services. By the end of the 1970s, however, almost all state legislatures provided clerical support for their members, as well as full-time research, bill drafting, and fiscal support services to both their committees and members. Several also had begun to provide office staff for constituent services, and a few of the most populous states even provided support for district offices. Compensation was increased in most states—significantly in many—and by the early 1980s, it was possible to make a modest living as a full-time legislator in several of the nation's larger states (California, Illinois, Michigan, New York, and Ohio). In most states, salaries and expense allowances reached levels high enough to enable legislators to survive during legislative sessions. Finally, by the end of the 1970s, the vast majority of states had abandoned the practice of having their legislature meet only every other year (biennially) and provided for annual sessions, in some cases with no constitutional limitation on length.

As a result of these reforms, the state legislatures that convened in their state capitol buildings as the decade of the 1980s dawned were markedly different from their counterparts of only ten to fifteen years earlier. Their memberships were more stable, with an average annual turnover of less than 20 percent in most states, and several chambers returning more than 90 percent of their members after each election cycle. Membership was much more diverse and representative of state populations in terms of geography, race, gender, and economic status. Legislators were also better educated than their predecessors of earlier decades, and were much more likely to identify themselves as full-time legislators.

LEADERS IN ACTION
The "Father" of the Modern State Legislature

What is known as the era of state legislative modernization began in the mid-1960s and continued into the early 1980s. During that time U.S. state legislatures underwent more change and transformation than they had in the almost two hundred years prior.

The so-called father of the legislative modernization movement was Jesse Unruh, who served as Democratic speaker of the California State assembly from 1961 to 1969. Born in rural Kansas in 1922, Unruh moved to southern California with his family as a child. When he arrived in Sacramento as a 300-pound freshman legislator in the 1950s, he was appalled at the control he saw special interests wielding within the

Jesse Unruh (Bettmann/Corbis)

During the 1980s, the growing stability in state legislative membership helped to produce a corresponding increase in the stability of the leadership of those bodies. Many states had followed long-standing practices of rotating leaders every two or four years. Such traditions were often ended in favor of longer terms that reflected the increased tenure potential of governors. Not only could more stable and longer-established legislative leaders now compete with governors in terms of experience and leadership

California Legislature. He concluded that California's state government, and particularly its legislature, were ill equipped to cope with the myriad of new problems that were emerging in the second decade following World War II; he determined to get himself into a position where he could do something about it.

Upon becoming Assembly speaker at the age of thirty-nine, Unruh was immediately tagged by legislative reporters in Sacramento with the nickname "Big Daddy" because of his weight. Realizing that he had to change his image if he wanted to be taken seriously as a reformer, he went on a crash diet and dropped the *e* at the end of his first name, thereafter being known as Jess rather than Jesse. Unruh then dove into transforming the California Assembly into a modern and independent legislative body, free from the undue influence of lobbyists and capable of serving as a coequal branch of government with the state's governor. He developed a professional legislative staff to provide legislators with their own independent sources of information, streamlined the Assembly's rules of procedure and its committee system, expanded the time that the Assembly spent in session, increased legislator salaries, improved the Assembly's office and meeting facilities, forced special interest campaign contributions to members of his Democratic caucus to be funneled through him, and instituted new ethics and conflict of interest laws. Unruh's reputation spread to every state legislature, and he was often referred to as "the most famous state legislator in the United States."

The California legislature was hardly unique in its weakness and ineffectiveness. Throughout the country, supporters of the U.S. federal system were becoming increasingly concerned that more and more decisionmaking authority was gravitating to Washington because state governments, and particularly state legislatures, were proving incapable of addressing societal problems. All of the other forty-nine state legislatures took note of Unruh's accomplishments, and eventually every one of the fifty state legislatures was changed and strengthened as a result of the modernization movement. By the mid-1980s it was pretty much impossible to find any state legislature that resembled in any way, shape, or form its predecessor body of two decades earlier. Most had achieved, or at least approached, a status of coequality with their executive branches in the policymaking process, and state governments had become the laboratories and testing grounds of democracy that had been envisioned by the Founding Fathers.

Jess Unruh went on to enjoy further success in his political career. His reputation as the reform Speaker of the California Assembly propelled him to the state's 1970 Democratic gubernatorial nomination where he was defeated by Ronald Reagan in a race that the future president called one of his toughest. Unruh was later elected to four terms as California state treasurer. But nothing that he or any other state legislator ever did had the historic impact on American government and politics as his successful effort to modernize and streamline the California Assembly. When he died in 1987 following election to his fourth term as treasurer, Jess Unruh was still best known, not just in California but throughout the United States, as the "father of the American legislative reform movement."

but many were also able to compete in terms of information, relying on their own highly professional staffs for policy and political information rather than on information provided by the executive branch or by lobbyists (Rosenthal 1981).

THE LEGISLATURE TODAY: OPPORTUNITY, CAPACITY, AND LEADERSHIP UNDER SIEGE

As the nation entered the last decade of the twentieth century, most state legislatures appeared to be poised to accomplish great things. As deficits rose in Washington, voters and federal officials began to look to the states to do more, and many states had governors, legislatures, and judges who were more than eager to take on that role. To a greater extent than ever before, the membership of state legislatures consisted of individuals who were capable, experienced, educated, professional, and eager to design solutions to difficult problems. Just as important, they had at their disposal professional, informed, and well-organized staff to assist them in that effort. They seemed poised for greatness.

But something happened on the way to greatness. The reforms of the 1970s that so many had predicted would lead to great accomplishments instead led to legislatures that large numbers of citizens came to see in a negative light. Where scholars and politicians saw a professional and active legislature, voters and critics in the news media saw a legislature that was more interested in politics than policy. Where advocates of professional legislatures saw stable and experienced membership, critics saw legislators who were isolated from the real world and insulated from real electoral competition. Where political scientists saw well-organized, increasingly democratic institutions, the voters saw partisan legislatures whose lengthy debates often ended either in gridlock or in policies that were seen as benefiting special interest groups more than the public (Boulard 2000). The final years of the twentieth century and the first decade of the twenty-first have been marked by several trends in government and politics that significantly altered the opportunity, capacity, and leadership of state legislatures.

The Modern Legislature and Its Opportunities to Lead

While the legislative branch of government is designed to be its primary lawmaking arm, it is far from alone in its ability and power to influence public policy. Governors, citizens, and the federal government all have certain constitutional and legal powers to make public policy—or at least to exert a significant impact on the ability of the legislatures to make it. Any changes or trends that decrease the influence of a state legislature relative to these other power centers limits the opportunity of that legislature to influence public policy. While the 1990s witnessed a general shift toward more active state governments, three trends during the 1990s and the early twenty-first century tended to restrict the activities and influence of legislatures relative to governors, the citizenry, and the federal government.

Powerful Governors

Throughout much of U.S. history, governors, with a few exceptions, played second fiddle to legislatures when it came to making public policy. While many of these legislatures were poorly equipped to manage their states, the executive offices of most states were in worse shape. Governors often served only part time in their positions, were often limited to one term, and had very small staffs. Their managerial and administrative experience prior to becoming governor was often unimpressive, and their power over the state budget was limited. That all began to change in the latter part of the twentieth century as state gubernatorial responsibilities, powers, visibility, and staff all began to grow. In the early twenty-first century, many legislatures find themselves competing with governors who are well educated, professionally staffed, articulate, and possessing growing arsenals of both formal powers (appointive, budgetary, and veto) and informal powers (access to the news media, ability to mobilize the public, and control of well-financed professional campaign machines) (Rosenthal 2004, 165–183).

Increasing Use and Effect of Initiatives

For most of the twentieth century, so-called direct democracy (laws initiated by citizens and approved by the voters in public referenda) was used rather sparingly. After a flurry of activity between 1911 and 1920, its use remained relatively low for decades. However, that began to change in the 1970s, and the use of voter-initiated referenda has become rather commonplace in the new century in those nineteen states that provide their voters with this right. More state initiatives were proposed (389) and adopted (188)—with a higher passage rate (48 percent)—from 1991 to 2000 than during any other decade in the country's history. The next closest decade was 1911–1920, during which almost a hundred fewer initiatives (293) were introduced and 72 fewer passed into law (116). Perhaps more important than the number of initiatives passed during this era, however, was the nature of those initiatives. Political scientist Linda Fowler has noted: "Not since the Progressive Era has there been a grassroots movement so profoundly hostile to the practice of politics and so successful in pushing an agenda of procedural reform" (Fowler 1995).

Many of the states that permit citizen-initiated legislation have experienced a reduction in the ability of their legislatures to govern effectively. Citizen enactment of laws has placed limitations on legislative service by imposing legislative term limits; by requiring more than simple legislative majorities to approve tax increases (sometimes even approval in a public referendum for a tax increase to take effect); by limiting the ability of legislatures to manage or control spending through dedicating funds to particular policy areas; and by limiting budgetary growth while also creating new programs that require legislative funding.

The Legislature and the Public

The Consequences of an Initiative in Colorado

In 1992, the voters of Colorado overwhelmingly approved a citizen-initiated set of amendments to the state's constitution that came to be known as the Taxpayers' Bill of Rights (TABOR). The amendments placed limitations on how much money Colorado's state and local governments could expend, and on the types of taxes they could impose. The law also required that tax increases be submitted to voters for approval in a referendum before they could take effect.

Depending on how individual citizens feel about these voter-initiated limitations, the effects of the changes they have brought about can be seen as either positive or negative. Advocates of the limitations point out that taxes in Colorado have decreased under TABOR, with the state now ranked forty-third in terms of the percentage of income taxed by state and local government. For advocates of smaller government, the results also have been positive, with budget growth in Colorado equal to about half of that in similar states during the ten years since TABOR was enacted. On the other hand, opponents of the limitations argue that TABOR has significantly reduced the legislature's flexibility when it comes to determining how Colorado spends its money, and it has created a gap between spending and revenues that was the third largest in the country in 2002. Opponents further point out that TABOR has made it more difficult for legislators and policy-makers to respond to the increased needs of Colorado's citizens during economic downturns. By 2005, TABOR had created a situation in which legislators looking for ways to close a $230 million budget deficit were required to refund $385 million to the state's taxpayers.

Source: *Ten Years after TABOR*, Bell Policy Center, February 2003; "Budget Bargain Struck," *The Denver Post*, March 17, 2005.

Increasing Mandates and Financial Obligations

In 1994 the Republican Party took control of the U.S. House and Senate, a majority of the governorships, and a majority of state legislatures, with a promise to scale back government and to relieve financial burdens on the states by ending the increasing tendency of the federal government to adopt unfunded mandates that require states to do something without providing the money with which to do it. However, that promise was not fulfilled. With the economic difficulties of the late 1990s and the first years of the twenty-first century, federally mandated programs such as Medicare and Medicaid continue to take up larger and larger portions of state revenues. Furthermore, recent programs such as President Clinton's Personal Responsibility Act (1995) and President Bush's 2002 education reform package, No Child Left Behind (Matthews 2004), generally restrict the activity and influence of states while moving national policymakers into areas that have historically been reserved to the states. Almost one out of every four dollars of state and local expenditures comes from the federal government—

usually with strings attached (Hanson 2004). Without question, the ability of state legislatures to control their own budgets has been significantly curtailed by the growth of imposed mandates by the federal government

THE MODERN LEGISLATURE AND LEGISLATIVE CAPACITY

A legislative body that has the capacity to initiate and enact good public policy, represent its constituents, and provide an appropriate balance with the executive and judicial branches is usually characterized by three qualities: stable membership, professional staffing, and adequate time in formal session. Recent changes in government and state politics have contributed to significant decreases in two of these three: membership stability and professional staffing.

Legislative Term Limits

While there have been disagreements over the years with regard to the exact definition of a well-functioning legislature, one characteristic has remained constant: an effective legislature must include experienced legislators (Rosenthal 1998). Legislative term limits strike right at the heart of this quality, placing legal limits on how much experience a legislator may acquire. During the 1990s, more than twenty states established term limits for their legislatures, restricting members to a maximum number of consecutive years of service or to a total limit of service. In some states, in which legislative turnover was already relatively high before the institution of term limits, annual turnover now averages around 40 percent. In the California Assembly, Arkansas House, and Maine House, the three chambers with the most restrictive term limits, members are limited to three two-year terms of service. Legislators with one term of service in these chambers are considered to be veteran members. Institutional memory is a thing of the past in the California Assembly and the Arkansas and Maine houses, whose inexperienced members operate at great disadvantage in trying to respond to experienced and savvy bureaucrats or lobbyists—none of whom are constrained by term limits on their service. By the time that most members of these chambers are able to develop a decent understanding and mastery of the subtleties and complexities of the legislative process and the operations of their state government, they are likely to be in their final term. Furthermore, their service tenures are so brief that they do not have sufficient time to develop the personal relationships with colleagues that help to make the legislative process operate more efficiently and effectively. In short, the capacity of the legislative branch in these states, and in the other states that have adopted somewhat less restrictive term limits, makes it extremely difficult if not impossible for the legislature to uphold its end of the checks and balances system (Greenblatt 2005; State Legislative Leaders Foundation 2005).

More Partisan and Less Nonpartisan Professional Staff

In addition to a stable and experienced membership, most scholars agree that a capable legislature must have its own nonpartisan professional staff. While such staff was the norm in the 1980s, recent budget cuts and changes in partisanship have altered the nature, size, and impact of legislative staffing in many states. The same movement that led to legislative term limits also led to significant cuts in legislative staffing in California and Colorado. Furthermore, budget difficulties experienced by most states beginning in the late 1990s forced several states to make cuts in their own operating budgets, sometimes at the expense of information services and staff support.

In many legislatures, the percentage of partisan and political patronage staff is increasing at the expense of expert nonpartisan professionals. Approximately one-third of current state legislative staffers is classified as partisan staff, meaning that they work exclusively for legislators of one political party. These staff members are often hired as much or more for their partisan credentials (they may have worked on a member's campaign or have raised money for the party's candidates) as for their professional abilities. They perform their duties and responsibilities with at least as much of an eye cast toward the effect of a proposed law on the upcoming election as its effect on public policy. This partisan focus often takes place at the expense of sound bipartisan cooperation in the development of public policies.

Restricted Legislative Sessions

As previously indicated, many states have increased the frequency and length of their legislative sessions by moving from biennial to annual sessions in the 1960s and 1970s.

LEGISLATURES IN ACTION

Georgia Legislature Adjourns before the Bell Tolls

With dramatic gains in the 2004 elections, Republicans took control of the Georgia House of Representatives for the first time in more than a century. Working with a Republican Senate and a Republican governor, they promised a "new and improved" legislature, with new rules, stronger leadership, and a more efficient process. They also promised to complete legislative business and adjourn their 2005 regular session before it reached its constitutional forty-day limit. On day thirty-nine, one day before they were required to adjourn, Republican leaders in both chambers planned to adjourn the session by early evening. However, a conflict on ethics legislation stalled the effort and threatened the early ending. A last minute compromise allowed the legislators to adjourn minutes before midnight, keeping their promise to adjourn their session prior to its constitutional adjournment date—if only by a few minutes.

Source: Interview with Glenn Richardson, speaker of the Georgia House of Representatives, May 2, 2005.

It was believed that more frequent and longer sessions would enable legislators to consider proposed legislation more carefully and more thoroughly. That proved to be the case as legislatures became more effective policymaking institutions in the 1970s and 1980s. But the pressures and workload on state legislatures have increased dramatically over the past quarter-century, and legislative session length has not increased proportionately in the majority of legislatures that have constitutional restrictions on how long they can meet in regular session. These restrictions have led to an increasing number of special sessions in many states. During 2002, thirty-three states were forced to meet in at least one special session, with six states meeting at least five different times. Special sessions are, in many states, restricted to agendas set by the governor; they are almost always more chaotic and disorganized than regularly scheduled sessions, and are generally viewed with considerable suspicion by the voting public.

LEADERSHIP IN THE MODERN STATE LEGISLATURE

If a state legislature is to meet its many responsibilities, it must have strong leaders who are capable, willing, and able to lead their chambers. Effective leadership of a legislative body requires not just capable and willing leaders but also a membership that has an interest in following those leaders. Recent trends in state legislatures have made it more difficult for leaders to lead effectively and less likely that members will be inclined to follow them.

Increasing Leadership Turnover

While the 1970s and 1980s were generally marked by an increase in leadership tenure, a number of states have recently undergone institutional and political changes that have led to shortened leadership tenure in their legislatures (see T 1.3). First and foremost among these changes are the previously noted limitations that a number of states have placed on the number of terms that a legislator may serve. In limiting the tenure of members of their legislature, states are, by definition, limiting the potential tenure of their legislatures' leaders. Mathematically, six-year membership limits mean six-year leadership limits. Realistically, they mean a two-year leadership limit, as it almost always requires the first four of the six years for a leader to demonstrate leadership potential to colleagues and then to garner their support to secure election to the leadership position. In 2005 almost half of the presiding officers of the nation's ninety-nine state legislative chambers were in their first term in their positions, and in more than a dozen states that person had four or fewer years of previous service in the legislative chamber. Not only does limited tenure reduce the amount of time that potential leaders have to develop leadership skills, it also limits their ability to cultivate personal relationships. And it is through such personal relationships that effective legislative leaders are most able to engage in the consensus-building that is such an important and necessary element of success of a democratic legislative body.

TABLE **1.3**   EXPERIENCE OF LEGISLATIVE LEADERS, **2005**

Current 2-year Terms as Leader	*Senate Leader	House Leader
First Term	19	21
Second Term	15	12
Third Term	7	3
Fourth Term	2	6
Fifth Term	2	0
More than 5 terms	6	7

Source: Compiled by author from Duane, Roberta, ed. 2005. *The Handbook of State Legislative Leaders.* Centerville, MA: State Legislative Leaders Foundation.

* Senate leaders include Nebraska unicameral leader and two leaders in Iowa Senate because that chamber is tied.

Increasing Partisan Competition

Over the past decade state legislatures have become significantly more partisan, and partisan competition has in turn become more fierce. In 2005 fewer than five seats separated Democrats and Republicans in more than half of the ninety-nine state legislative chambers, with three chambers in flat ties. There was at least one evenly divided chamber in each of the twenty years between 1985 and 2005. These numbers make partisanship more important and forces legislative leaders to focus more of their attention on campaign and election-related activities—generally at the expense of running the legislature. Alan Rosenthal, a longtime observer of U.S. state legislatures, notes: "The new role of legislative parties has made maintaining the institutions' well-being an even harder job. Leaders are more preoccupied with campaigns and elections. . . .[T]he institution is relevant insofar as it serves party purposes" (Rosenthal 2003). Partisan agendas are forced through, often with more attention paid to their effects on the upcoming election than their long-term benefits to the state.

Growth of Candidate-Centered Campaigns and Independent Members

There was a time when state legislative campaigns were characterized by limited voter interest, strong party control, and low expenditures. In many states, those days are gone. In large, competitive states such as California, New York, Ohio, Michigan, or Illinois, it is not unusual for expenditures to exceed $1 million for a state Senate seat; in California, campaigns for some state assembly seats have climbed to that level. Furthermore, most candidates hire their own campaign consultants, raise their own money, select their own issues, and develop their own themes, apart from those of their party or legislative caucus (Bibby 1999, 196–198). Once elected, they feel little or no obligation to their legislative leaders or their party caucus. Such legislators may feel a much stronger loyalty to the voters who elected them from their district than they do their party or legislative caucus. This creates just one more obstacle that today's legislative leaders have to battle in trying to build coalitions within their party caucuses (Rosenthal 1998).

A DYNAMIC INSTITUTION

To many people, state legislatures seem static, almost motionless. They move slowly. They often meet in old buildings with archaic designs that reflect the rules and norms that govern them. They operate according to rules and precedents that were established decades ago, and they seem to address the same issues of education, public safety, transportation, public health, and the environment every year. Each year, they have the same debates and approve policies and budgets that bear remarkable resemblance to those passed the year before—and the year before that.

However, those willing to look more closely at state legislatures find that they are anything but static. Indeed, they are arguably the most dynamic and responsive branches of government. More than 20 percent of their members are new every two years, as are almost half of their leaders. New committee chairs and new leaders bring fresh ideas and solutions to the table. Legislatures remain a primary source of new ideas and innovative policy solutions. In addition, they show an amazing ability to adapt to the changing world around them, incorporating new technologies such as the world wide web, video streaming, and e-mail, and adjusting to new challenges such as term limits and direct democracy. While the basic responsibilities and functions of state legislatures may not change, the methods that they use to perform those responsibilities and functions are a reflection of the world around the legislature and the people who serve in it.

REFERENCES

Bibby, John. 1999. "State and Local Parties in a Candidate-Centered Age." In *American State and Local Politics*, edited by Ronald Weber and Paul Brace. New York: Chatham House/Seven Bridges.

Boulard, Gary. 2000. "Challenges of a New Century." *State Legislatures*, Volume 26 (January): 12–13, 15–16.

"Center for American Women and Politics Fact Sheet." Eagleton Institute of Politics, Rutgers University.

Crane, Wilder, Jr., and Meredith W. Watts, Jr. 1968. *State Legislative Systems*. Englewood Cliffs, NJ: Prentice-Hall.

Drage, Jennifer, et al. 2003. "The Impact of Term Limits on Legislative Leadership." In *The Test of Time: Coping with Legislative Term Limits*, edited by Rick Farmer, John David Rausch, Jr., and John C. Green. Lanham, MD: Lexington.

Fowler, Linda. 1995. *State Government News*, Volume 38 (May): 14–16.

Garand, James C., and Kyle Baudoin. 2003. "Spending, Taxes and Deficits: Fiscal Policies in the American States." In *Politics in the American States: A Comparative Analysis*, 8th ed., edited by Virginia Gray and Russell L. Hanson. Washington, DC: Congressional Quarterly Press.

Goehring, Jan. 2000. "Legislators Teach Real World Civics." *State Legislatures*, Volume 26 (March): 28–29.

Greenblatt, Alan. 2005. "Term Limits Aren't Working." *Governing Magazine*, Volume 18 (April): 13–14.

Hanson, Russell. 2004. "Intergovernmental Relations." In *Politics in the American States: A Comparative Analysis*, 8th ed., edited by Virginia Gray and Russell L. Hanson, 43. Washington, DC: Congressional Quarterly Press.

Hibbing, John R., and Elizabeth Theiss-Morse, eds. 2001. *What Is It About Government That Americans Dislike?* Cambridge and New York: Cambridge University Press.

Jewell, Malcolm. 1980. "Survey on the Selection of State Legislative Leaders." *Comparative State Politics Newsletter* 1: 7–21.

Kammen, Michael. 1969. *Deputyes and Libertyes: The Origins of Colonial Government in America*. New York: Knopf.

Keefe, William J., and Morris Ogul. 1968. *The American Legislative Process and the States*. Englewood Cliffs, NJ: Prentice-Hall.

Key, V. O., Jr. 1956. *American State Politics: An Introduction*. New York: Knopf.

Lassman, Kent. 2002. *The Digital State: How State Governments Use Digital Technologies*. Washington, DC: Progress and Freedom Foundation.

Leonard, Cynthia Miller. 1978. *The General Assembly of Virginia, July 30, 1619–January 11, 1978*. Richmond: Virginia State Library.

Lipscomb, Leslie. 1968. *The American Governor: From Figurehead to Leader*. New York: Greenwood.

Lockard, Duane. 1966. "The State Legislator." In *American Assemblies: State Legislatures in American Politics*, edited by Alexander Heard. Englewood Cliffs, NJ: Prentice-Hall.

Luce, Robert. 1971 [1930]. *The Legislative Principles: The History and Theory of Lawmaking by Representative Government*. New York: DaCapo.

Matthews, Dewayne. 2004. "No Child Left Behind: The Challenge of Implementation." In *Book of the States, 2003*, 493–496. Lexington, KY: Council of State Governments.

Mechling, Jerry, and Lynda Applegate. 2003. *Eight Imperatives for Leaders in a Networked World. Imperative 1: Focus on How It Can Reshape Work and Public Sector Strategies*. Cambridge, MA: Harvard Policy Group on Network-Enabled Services and Government.

Rosenthal, Alan. 1981. *Legislative Life: People, Process, and Performance in the States*. New York: Harper and Row.

———. 1990. *Governors and Legislatures: Contending Powers*. Washington, DC: Congressional Quarterly Press.

———. 1998. *The Decline of Representative Democracy: Process, Participation, and Power in State Legislatures*. Washington, DC: Congressional Quarterly Press.

———. 2000. "Getting the Word Out." *State Legislatures*. July/August: 28–29, 31, 33, 35.

———. 2003. "Trends in State Legislative Parties." In *Book of the States, 2003*. Lexington, KY: Council of State Governments.

———. 2004. *Heavy Lifting: The Job of the American Legislature*. Washington, DC: Congressional Quarterly Press.

Rosenthal, Alan, et al. 2002. *Republic on Trial: The Case for Representative Democracy*. Washington, DC: Congressional Quarterly Press.

Sanford, Terry. 1967. *Storm over the States*. New York: McGraw-Hill.

Squire, Peverill, and Keith Hamm. 2005. *101 Chambers: Congress, State Legislatures and the Future of Legislative Studies*. Columbus: Ohio State University Press.

State Legislative Leaders Foundation. 2005. *Restoring the Balance: Repealing the Failed Experiment of Legislative Term Limits*. Centerville, MA: State Legislative Leaders Foundation.

2

POWERS AND RESPONSIBILITIES OF STATE LEGISLATURES

State legislatures were originally established to accomplish particular objectives that the nation's Founding Fathers deemed critical to the effective functioning of the states and their governments. Each state constitution outlines the basic structure of its state's government and assigns specific authority and responsibilities to each of the three branches of the government. However, from the time of the nation's founding, constitutional writers and experts have usually concluded that the unique nature of legislatures and the complexities of their processes require longer and more explicit provisions concerning the authority of the legislative branch than for the executive or judicial branches.

EXPRESSED POWERS OF STATE LEGISLATURES

Expressed powers are responsibilities specifically assigned or delegated to a branch of government in a constitution. In the case of legislatures, the federal Constitution and most state constitutions also allow some discretion for the legislature to exceed its expressed authority and to exercise authority not specifically stated in the constitution, if it finds it necessary to do so to carry out its expressed powers. The expressed powers of state legislatures fall within one of five distinct categories: the power of institutional regulation, the power to propose legislation, the power of removal, the power of taxation, and the power of creation.

The Power of Institutional Regulation

Every state legislature has the power—within the boundaries established by its state constitution—to organize itself and to establish rules of procedure under which it will operate. All state constitutions include specific requirements concerning the size and powers of each legislative chamber, qualifications for legislative membership, and, in some states, a general framework for organization. The members of each legislative chamber decide who will fill its leadership positions. With the exception of Nebraska's single-chamber unicameral legislature, which is officially a nonpartisan body, all state legislatures have two chambers and are organized along partisan lines; the party with the greatest number of members in a chamber determines that chamber's agenda. State legislatures also possess the power, and responsibility, to punish their members for inappropriate conduct or behavior. The right of a legislature to control its own internal operations and organization is an essential element in its ability to operate independently of the executive and judicial branches.

The Power to Propose Legislation

The single most important power of state legislatures is their power to propose and enact legislation. Except for the small proportion of laws that are proposed and passed in a public referendum by direct vote of the people through the initiative process, every state law must be approved by the state's legislature. To be enacted into law, each piece of legislation must be approved in identical form by a majority (and in some cases, 60 percent or two-thirds) of the members of each legislative chamber. With a few exceptions in a handful of states (those exceptions having to do with legislation signed by the governor after the legislature has adjourned), a state legislature can enact legislation over the veto (refusal to approve) of their governor if a sufficient number of members (usually two-thirds) agree to repass the legislation and "override" the governor's veto.

The Power of Removal

In every state, the legislature is granted the power to remove members of the judicial or executive branch of government through a process known as impeachment. This process occurs in two stages. First, it must be determined if sufficient evidence exists to proceed with a trial (similar to a grand jury in the judicial system), which requires a majority vote in twenty states, a two-thirds majority in nine states, and is not specified in the others. The initial investigation takes place in the House of Representatives or Assembly—except in Nebraska, which has only one legislative chamber, and in Alaska, where the process takes place in the Senate. If sufficient evidence is found to warrant impeachment, a trial is then held in the other legislative chamber—except in Alaska and Missouri, where the chamber that brings the impeachment charges also conducts the trial. A vote of two-thirds of the chamber's membership is then required to remove the impeached official from office.

The Power of Taxation

Governors can propose new revenues and promote new programs, but only legislatures have the power to enact them. Governments cannot govern without sufficient and reliable sources of revenue, and it is the responsibility of the legislature to ensure that such revenue is generated. Legislatures may tax individuals, corporations, property, purchases, or services. The largest source of revenue for states comes from taxes on the sale of goods and on income earned by state residents (Willoughby 2004). A few states now require that new taxes be approved by a supermajority (three-fifths or two-thirds) of the legislators. In some states, revenue bills must originate in the House or Assembly. For example, the Texas constitution states: "All bills for raising revenue shall originate in the House of Representatives" (Article 3, Section 33).

The Power of Creation

In addition to the power to tax, legislatures also have the power to spend and, in so doing, to create and fund the agencies that are responsible for administering the laws they enact. For example, if a legislature enacts legislation to regulate and tax Internet commerce in its state, it will in all likelihood create a new executive branch agency to implement and administer the law. Likewise, most state legislatures are empowered to create additional courts, as they see necessary, for the effective and efficient functioning of the state's judicial system. For example, the Maine Constitution stipulates: "The judicial power of this State shall be vested in a Supreme Judicial Court, and such other courts as the Legislature shall from time to time establish" (Article VI, Section I).

THE LEGISLATURE IN ACTION
Connecticut Governor John Rowland and the Impeachment Process

In January of 2004, following a year-long investigation by the FBI and federal prosecutors that originally focused on bid-rigging and bribery in the award of state contracts, Connecticut's Democratic House speaker, Moria Lyons, appointed a ten-member investigative committee to determine if sufficient cause existed to bring impeachment charges against Republican governor John Rowland. When Rowland publicly admitted that he had lied to the FBI when denying that state contractors and friends had picked up all or part of the costs of repairs to his summer cottage, Speaker Lyons felt compelled to act. Lyons and the House minority leader, Robert Ward, each appointed five members to the investigative committee.

New revelations uncovered during the legislative committee's investigation included a state contractor and campaign contributor who rented and then purchased a Washington, D.C., condominium owned by Rowland at rates far in excess of the market, and also payment of a $15,000 honorarium to his wife for a speech at a Florida convention to which Rowland accompanied his wife. Rowland claimed that he attended the convention on official business, which would have made it illegal for his wife to receive the honorarium.

The consensus among reporters and close observers of the committee's five-month investigation was that the committee members were heading toward a unanimous or near-unanimous recommendation for impeachment. Eleven of the fifteen Republican senators had publicly called for Rowland to resign even before the House committee completed its work. On July 1, following an order by the state's supreme court that Governor Rowland testify under oath before the House impeachment committee, Rowland resigned from office.

The specific nature of legislative powers and a legislature's use of the powers assigned to it can vary from state to state, and within a state from year to year—and sometimes even from day to day. Legislators and legislative leaders exercise their powers to carry out the responsibilities assigned to them by their respective state constitutions.

What a State Legislature Does and How It Does It

Trying to organize the array of activities in which a legislature engages into a manageable list of responsibilities and functions is no easy task, but various scholars have tried. Wahlke, Eulau, Buchanan and Ferguson (1962) suggested that state legislatures engage in representing the public, allocating the values of society, providing legitimacy for the government, working both with and against the executive, and building a common policy out of diverse positions. Keefe and Ogul (1968) offered a more concrete list of functions, indicating that state legislatures are involved in lawmaking, as well as representational and oversight activities. Crane and Watts (1968) suggested that state legislative activities could be divided into the following: lawmaking, administrative, electoral, judicial, constituent, and investigatory. More recently, Hamm and Moncrief (2002) have indicated that state legislatures engage in four types of activities: making policy, appropriating revenue, constituent service, and administrative oversight. Finally, Alan Rosenthal (2004) argues that legislative activities can be distilled to three basic functions: representation, lawmaking, and balancing the power of the executive.

Looking at and building on the lists of responsibilities that have been suggested by these scholars, it is possible to examine a state legislature's responsibilities in five basic categories: representation, lawmaking, appropriations/budgeting, balancing the executive, and public education. While each of these may be listed as a separate activity, they all overlap and relate to one another. It may be argued, for example, that appropriations/budgeting is just a particular type of lawmaking, that educating and informing the public on the issues and process of the legislature is really just an extension of representation, or that lawmaking is a way through which legislatures balance the power of the executive. While there is clear and obvious overlap among these five basic responsibilities, each is also unique and distinct from the others and deserves examination as an independent activity.

Representation

Without question, the single most important relationship for all state legislators is with their constituents, the people who reside in the districts. If that relationship is broken, the legislator is likely to be looking for another job, as voters will seek someone they feel is more interested in and attuned to their needs. In order to remain in office, legislators must maintain an effective link between their actions in the legislature and the desires and interests of the voters in their districts. Furthermore, for the legislature to remain a legitimate representative body in the eyes of the public, its members must have the support of the voters. That support is comprised of four components: policy responsiveness, symbolic responsiveness, service responsiveness, and allocative responsiveness.

Most often, representation is defined as a legislator acting on behalf of the citizens in the legislator's district when deciding how to vote on a bill. This is often referred to as policy responsiveness. Legislators are considered to be effective policy representatives when they vote in accordance with the interests and desires of the people they have been elected to represent. However, in reality, the relationship between the representative and the represented is much more complex. Given the low level of support in which most state legislators (and also members of Congress) are held, if representation were to be defined as simply a belief by the people that their legislators are acting on their behalf, few legislators would be reelected and legislative bodies would have almost no legitimacy (Funk 2002).

Legislators generally take one of two approaches to representing their constituents on a particular issue or bill. Some legislators will try to do exactly what they believe the majority of their constituents want them to do, by casting a vote that reflects the position of a majority of the voters in the district. That approach, usually called the delegate approach, is most often used by legislators when they sense a relatively strong majority of support among the people in the legislator's district for the issue under consideration. Legislators who adopt this approach will try to vote the way they believe their constituents would vote, regardless of their personal position on the issue.

FIGURE 2.1   APPROACHES TO REPRESENTATION OF STATE LEGISLATORS

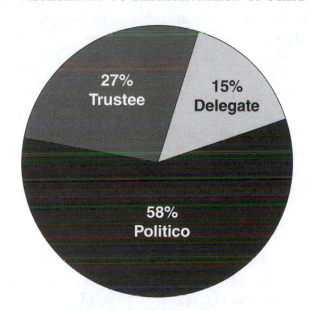

Source: Compiled by authors from an unpublished survey conducted by the Joint Project on Term Limits in 2003, based on responses from 38.1% (2,825 total) of all state legislators.

Delegate-legislators will vote against their personal position and viewpoint if they believe that their position is opposed by a solid majority of their constituents.

While any legislator may adopt the delegate approach to representation, research and common sense suggests that certain legislators are more likely than others to follow it. Legislators from chambers with smaller legislative districts and shorter election terms, as well as less experienced members and members from more competitive districts, are most likely to adopt the approach. Legislative districts with fewer constituents will likely be more homogeneous, with fewer divergent viewpoints and opinions, making it easier for legislators from such districts to gauge and accurately reflect the policy positions of their constituents. Legislators who have to face the voters every two years rather than every four years are likely to be more concerned about accurately reflecting the will of the voters who control their electoral fate, and the constant campaigning associated with two-year terms is likely to provide them with a somewhat clearer understanding of the will of those voters. While legislators with long tenure in their chamber may have built up enough name recognition and "good will" to be reelected without focusing so closely on their districts, less experienced members will often feel compelled to keep a close ear to the feelings of their constituents. Finally, legislators who represent districts in which elections are competitive will be more attuned and responsive to the specific desires of their constituents than will those who represent districts regarded as safe for their party.

Some legislators view representation through a different lens, arguing that legislators are elected not just to mirror the desires of the district but also to act in what they believe to be the best interests of their district. Legislators who hold this view are making use of what is often called the trustee approach to representation, similar to that of the trustee of a bank or a church. Just as lawyers who represent their clients are supposed to draw upon their wisdom, knowledge, experience, and education to steer their clients in the direction of what they feel is their best interest, trustee-legislators believe that they have information by virtue of the legislative positions that will enable them to cast knowledgeable votes in the best interests of their districts. Sometimes a trustee-legislator will cast a vote that does not reflect the will of a majority of the voters in the legislator's district, but the legislator will do so in the belief that the vote is in the long-term interest of the district and would likely be supported by a majority of the district if they were aware of the information that research, discussions, and debate had afforded their legislator.

Not surprisingly, legislators from larger districts who have a longer history of being elected by the district, and who face the electorate less often, are generally more likely to adopt the trustee approach. While most state legislators represent relatively few constituents (compared with members of the U.S. Congress), it is not uncommon for state senators from the nation's more heavily populated states to represent more than a quarter of a million people. Senators in California, Michigan, New York, Ohio, Pennsylvania, and Texas all represent more than 250,000 people (a California state senator actually represents more people than a member of the U.S. House of Representatives). Such districts are likely to include a variety of perspectives and viewpoints, such that a legislator can take a position on either side of an issue and be relatively assured of some level of support. What's more, legislators in thirty-seven state senates and five state houses (Alabama, Louisiana, Maryland, Mississippi, and North Dakota) are elected to four-year terms, distancing them a bit from their voters and giving them somewhat more freedom to cast votes that might not reflect the majority opinions of their districts. Perhaps most significant of all is that legislators who have represented their districts for extended periods may be more likely than relatively new legislators to follow the trustee approach, because they are likely to have established relationships of trust with the residents of their districts; that figures to make them less vulnerable to the wrath of those residents if they vote contrary to a clear majority sentiment.

During the course of any given legislative session, most legislators will move back and forth between the delegate and trustee approaches to representation. On certain types of issues, they may attempt to reflect the positions of their voters, while on others, they may act in what they feel is the best interest of their district—even if it means voting against the wishes of a majority of their constituents. This approach is often called the politico approach. The decision on whether to act as a delegate or a trustee on a given vote can depend on a variety of factors, including the importance of the issue to the district, the degree of consensus on the issue in the district, and the strength of the legislator's convictions regarding the particular issue. Legislators will be more likely to adopt a delegate approach when the issue is important and visible to the district and the position of the district is quite clear. On the other hand, a trustee approach is more likely when the voters in the district are unaware of the issue, or the issue is of little consequence to them, or a legislator's constituents are pretty evenly divided on the issue.

Legislators may take the risk of voting against the prevailing sentiment of their district on issues that they consider matters of conscience or conviction. A recent study of state legislators in six states revealed that when legislators found the positions of

---

DIVERSITY IN STATE LEGISLATURES
1894, A Woman's Place Is in the House (and Senate)

Women have been part of the state legislative scene for more than a century. The first woman state legislators in the United States (Republicans Claire Cressingham, Carrie C. Holly, and Francis Klock) were elected to the Colorado House of Representatives in 1894. The first female state senator appeared two years later, when Democrat Martha Hughes Cannon joined the Utah Senate. That was more than two decades before Jannette Rankin of Montana became the first woman elected to the U.S. House of Representatives in 1916, and Rebecca Latimer Felton from Georgia was appointed to serve a one-day term in the U.S. Senate (1922). It would be another forty years (1963) before a woman of color, Representative Patsy Mink of Hawaii, would be elected to the U.S. Congress.

Source: Center for American Women and Politics, Rutgers University, 2005.

their constituents to be in conflict with their own, a majority said that they would vote their convictions on matters relating to capital punishment, abortion, gun control, and gay rights. However, they were more evenly divided on matters relating to taxes (48 percent said that they would vote their personal view, and 40 percent said that they would vote with the majority viewpoint of their district) and gambling (46 percent their own view, and 39 percent their district) (Rosenthal 2004, 47). Clearly, legislators appear more reluctant to take on their constituents on tax and revenue issues than on matters of conscience and conviction.

How Do Legislators Learn the Views of Those They Represent?

Regardless of the approach that legislators choose to take in representing their districts, they must be keenly aware of the positions and interests of their constituents. Effective legislators must have a thorough understanding of what the voters in their districts would have them do on any given issue, and of how that issue would affect the economic, political, social, or fiscal interest of the district.

On most issues, voters have little interest and seldom express positions. So, on the vast majority of issues, legislators are "free agents," relying more on their own perspectives and understanding of the needs of the district than on the largely nonexistent viewpoint of the voters (Niemi and Powell 2001, 197–200). Most legislators have roots in their state and district. A study of the birthplaces of more than 4,000 state legislators serving in thirty states during 1987 and 1988 reveals that about two-thirds were native to the state in which they served (Thompson and Moncrief 1994, 23–38). Many legislators have deep roots in the very district they represent, having grown up there and lived a significant portion of their lives among the people who are now their constituents. Such a history and affiliation with their community helps to create a belief in many legislators that they know what the voters in their district want or need, simply because they are so much a part of that community. They think, feel, and believe as do the majority of their constituents, and were likely elected to serve in the legislature by those constituents because their viewpoints and positions on important issues are so similar.

Unlike members of the U.S. Congress, members of most state legislatures spend the bulk of their time in their districts, working, living, shopping, and socializing with their constituents. This personal connection with the district was illuminated by a member of the part-time Delaware Senate, whose primary occupation was grounds supervisor of a local community college: "I see these people at the gas station, at the grocery store, and at the school. I have been called an SOB more times than I care to remember by folks who want to know what I was doing down there in Dover!" (Interview with author, August 1991, Dover, Delaware).

Even state legislators who do not work or live full time in their district will get a pretty good feel for how their constituents feel about many issues during campaign periods. More than three-fourths of state legislators must run for reelection and face their voters every two years, and while some legislative campaigns have gone high-tech and professional with large television and radio budgets, most are still low-budget affairs, with large amounts of time spent handing out fliers, knocking on doors, visiting with local merchants, and holding town-hall meetings at churches, clubs, and civic organizations. At these events, candidates are likely to "get an earful" from constituents who will make it perfectly clear what they think is wrong with the legislator, the legislature, the state, the country, and the world (Moncrief, Squire, and Jewell 2001, 86–93).

When legislators do try to determine the positions of their constituents on issues, their sources are often quite biased. Legislators seldom poll their entire district; rather, they tend to seek out those citizens who have shown a propensity to support them in the past. According to a study of the information sources of legislators in six states, the most common source is political supporters in the district, followed by friends in the district and then organized political groups and leaders in the district. These sources, which tend to reinforce the position held by the legislator, are referred to as the legislator's personal constituency (friends and associates) and political constituency (political supporters) (Fenno 1978). Some legislators rely on public opinion polls, usually through their newsletters or on their websites. However, those often will also tend to reinforce the positions of the legislator, because respondents are self-selecting and tend to be supporters; they may well fail to give the legislator an accurate reading of the sentiments of the district (Jewell 1982, 67–72).

Other Components of Representation

While what may be termed policy responsiveness is the aspect of representation most often associated with representative democracy, it is not the only type of representation practiced by state legislators—and perhaps not even the most important one in the eyes of the voters. In addition to attempting to represent the positions of the constituents on matters of public policy, legislators work closely with their constituents in at least three other ways: symbolic responsiveness, service responsiveness, and allocative responsiveness (Eulau and Karps 1977). All three of these may play a more important role in the reelection of an incumbent legislator than the policy responsiveness that is the core of representative government.

Successful state legislators are known by their constituents and are visible in their districts. Legislators ride in parades, speak at civic organizations, show up at the court of honor of the local Boy Scout troop, and participate in the cutting of ribbons when a new plant is opened. They speak on local radio stations, shake hands at high school football games, and are involved in local civic and church activities. While these activities may contribute little to the functioning of state government, they are all part of the symbolic responsiveness component of representation—acts by which legislators show their constituents that they are active and engaged members of their districts. These symbolic activities provide name recognition for the legislators in their districts and often provide them with some latitude to vote against the expressed will of the district on some issues of conscience. If constituents feel as though they know and have some level of comfort with their legislator, they are more likely to be accepting of the legislator's judgment.

Legislators also provide representation by working to ensure that their districts, and groups within them, receive their fair share of government projects and funds (sometimes referred to in a rather derogatory sense as "pork barreling"). All state legislatures fund numerous local projects during each session, ranging from biomedical research at universities to training or equipment grants for volunteer fire departments. To varying degrees, decisions on the distribution of this money, or allocative responsiveness, is determined by the legislature, and particularly by its leaders. Members make use of projects that they bring to their districts to build political support for their party and for their reelection campaigns. Legislators who "bring home the bacon" can point to that success when challengers suggest that they may be out of touch with the policies and needs of the district—particularly when some of their personal policy positions may not reflect that of a majority of the district's voters (Thompson and Moncrief 1988).

Finally, one of the most critical representative responsibilities of any state legislator is "constituent service," or service responsiveness. Legislators are expected to respond to the particular needs of constituents, from the serious to the sublime (an Ohio legislator was once asked to find out if a constituent could have his passport changed from male to female as a result of a recent sex change operation). A 1990s study of casework in four state legislatures suggested that the most common constituent requests focus on providing information about government services (with 72 percent of the respondents indicating requests for such assistance), assistance with the government bureaucracy (72 percent), and requesting assistance in gaining employment with the government (31 percent). To a lesser extent, these requests concerned seeking assistance in easing government regulations (14 percent), intervening in local government disputes (15 percent), and assisting with nongovernmental organizations such as civic groups and businesses. The importance of service responsiveness relative to legislators' reelection efforts is demonstrated by the fact that it is considered of greatest importance by

TABLE 2.1   THE IMPORTANCE OF THE VARIOUS TYPES OF REPRESENTATION TO STATE LEGISLATORS

Representation Activity	% of Legislators Indicating Importance
Symbolic Responsiveness	75.6%
Service Responsiveness	73.0%
Allocation Responsiveness	53.3%
Policy Responsiveness	53.3%

Source: Compiled by authors from an unpublished survey conducted by the Joint Project on Term Limits in 2003. Based on responses from 38.1% (2,825 total) of all state legislators.

LEGISLATURES AND THE PUBLIC

The Sometimes Strange World of Service Responsiveness

The vast majority of constituent requests received by state legislators and legislative leaders are straightforward and serious. A constituent needs help getting a suspended driver's license reinstated or has had difficulty in securing a particular license or permit. However, constituent assistance requests to legislators and particularly to legislative leaders (who have more influence and are usually better known by virtue of their position) are sometimes different and downright strange. A Louisiana legislative leader received a request to assist a constituent in finding a company in the country that would make a particularly large brassiere. A Michigan leader was asked to assist a constituent who was convinced that his neighbor was stealing his thoughts via brainwaves. A Tennessee leader received a request to personally remove a litter of new puppies from the constituent's yard. And a Delaware leader was asked to help a constituent get a new kidney—perhaps, it was suggested, by donating one of his own.

Source: Conversations with chiefs of staff of fourteen state legislative leaders on August 20, 2004.

---

legislators in states with more professional legislatures and more competitive elections (Freedman and Richardson 1996).

The data in Table 2.1 indicate the relative importance of responsiveness. While legislative scholars often cite lawmaking as the most important responsibility for a legislature, individual legislators are clearly more interested in maintaining the representational relationship with their constituents. Activities that involve direct interaction with constituents (symbolic and service responsiveness) and that are likely to show the most direct correlation to reelection were rated important by a significantly higher proportion of the legislators than were the two responsibilities—allocative and policy responsiveness—that relate more directly to the lawmaking side of their job.

LAWMAKING

The responsibility to represent, especially as it relates to policy responsiveness, assumes the performance of the second legislative responsibility: lawmaking. Proposed laws and proposed revisions to existing laws can range from the quality of the water the state's citizens drink, to the nature of the education its children receive, to how fast its drivers can travel on state roads. Every year, state legislators introduce thousands of prospective laws—universally referred to as bills in all legislative bodies—of which many become laws that will affect the lives of citizens and the activities of businesses. Legislatures also approve thousands of resolutions, which do not involve new or amended laws but, rather, are usually noncontroversial citations that recognize groups, industries, constituents, and important events in a legislator's district. Of the more than 44,000 pieces of legislation introduced during the 2003 regular state legislative sessions, almost half were resolutions. Resolutions seldom generate controversy. While fewer than 20 percent of the bills introduced by the legislature ever receive the support of a majority of the legislature, more than 95 percent of resolutions sail right through, often with no discussion and by a unanimous voice vote.

How a Bill Becomes a Law

The formal lawmaking process is examined in detail in Chapter 3, so only a brief overview of the process is included here. While there are particular variations within each state, the general steps are similar across the board. The process begins with the introduction of a bill by an individual legislator, a group of legislators, or a legislative committee. Only sitting members of a legislature can introduce a bill. After its introduction, a bill is sent to a committee for examination and review. Sometimes a bill will fall under the jurisdiction of more than one committee. In such cases, it may subsequently be sent to one or more other committees for additional review if the committee to which it was originally referred finds it worthy of further consideration.

In their review of the bills referred to them, committees go through a "weeding-out" process and decide which ones are deserving of consideration by their full legislative chamber (or, in the case of the Nebraska unicameral legislature or legislatures that operate with joint committees, by the legislature). Some legislatures allow their committees to amend or make changes in bills referred to them. Others permit their committees only to recommend amendments that require approval by the full chamber. Some chambers permit committees to allow a bill to die by taking no action on it, while others require that every bill received be sent to the chamber or legislature with some recommendation, even if that recommendation is to reject the bill.

Bills that committees send to their full chambers with recommendations for passage are debated on the floors of the chamber to which they are sent. A bill passed by the first chamber is sent to the other chamber, where it goes through the same review by its committees (unless the legislature operates with joint committees, in which case the bill is immediately scheduled for consideration by the second chamber). If a bill is passed in identical form in both chambers, it is sent to the governor for signature. If approved (signed) by the governor, the bill becomes law. Should the governor refuse to approve the bill by vetoing it, the bill may still become law if both chambers of the legislature repass it. In thirty-seven states, a two-thirds vote of each chamber's elected membership is required for a gubernatorial veto to be overridden. Seven states require a three-fifths vote of the elected membership in each chamber. In six states (Alabama, Arkansas, Indiana, Kentucky, Tennessee, and West Virginia), gubernatorial vetoes can be overridden by a simple majority vote in each chamber.

This is a generic overview of the process by which bills can become law in the fifty state legislatures. As indicated previously, the specifics of the process vary from state to state. The legislative bill-enactment process is lengthy and highly complex, and the stakes are high. There is a heavy price to be paid for a mistake that harms the people of the state. To help ensure that the process will proceed reasonably smoothly, and to

TABLE 2.2   THE RELATIVE IMPORTANCE OF LAWMAKING ACTIVITIES FOR STATE LEGISLATORS IN 2003

Lawmaking Activity	Legislators Indicating Importance (%)
Studying Legislation	53.3
Building Partisan Coalitions for Legislation	45.3
Building Bipartisan Coalitions for Legislation	39.7
Developing New Legislation	32.2

Source: Compiled by authors from an unpublished survey conducted by the Joint Project on Term Limits in 2003. Based on responses from 38.1% (2,825 total) of all state legislators.

TABLE 2.3   BILLS PASSED BY STATE LEGISLATURES, 2003

Top Five		Bottom Five	
Arkansas	1,816	South Carolina	114
Texas	1,384	Wisconsin	111
Louisiana	1,307	Vermont	78
California	1,156	Pennsylvania	67
Virginia	1,038	Ohio	56

Source: Council of State Governments. 2004. *Book of the States.* Lexington, KY: Council of State Governments, Table 3.19.

avoid costly mistakes, each legislature adopts detailed rules of procedure to regulate each step and every phase of its process for the consideration and enactment of legislation. In addition to those formal rules, there are some informal, unwritten rules of the U.S. legislative process to which legislators are generally expected to conform. And as legislators move toward a decision on whether to support or oppose a particular bill, they are subjected to a myriad of often conflicting factors and influences.

Categorizing Bills

There are many ways of categorizing the thousands of bills introduced and enacted by state legislatures. They can be categorized by the degree of controversy they generate, keeping in mind that most bills generate little or none. Bills might also be categorized according to the breadth of their impact, ranging from those that affect the entire state to those that affect only a few individuals or businesses in one legislator's district

(Rosenthal 2004, 74). Still another approach is to view bills through the eyes of the legislators who have to vote on them. A legislator's response to a legislative proposal will depend on whether the issue the bill addresses is one on which the legislator has some significant knowledge, one in which the legislator's district has a particular interest, one that has national or statewide importance, or one in which the legislator has little concern (Jewell and Patterson 1986, 203–205). Bills might also be categorized according to their source—that is, whether they were generated by a constitutional requirement, a judicial mandate, a gubernatorial proposal, a constituent idea, an interest group's initiative, a national agenda item, or by the legislator alone (Rosenthal 2004, 36–38).

Finally, bills can be categorized according to the area of public policy they address. That is arguably the best way to approach the matter, because it recognizes the wide range of issues that state legislatures are expected to deal with every day. While public policy can be sliced in as many ways as a pie, the public policy agendas of modern state legislatures logically divide into five general areas: economic policy and development, social issues, natural resources, justice and public safety, and government administration and regulation. Each of these represents a distinct and significant realm of public policy, with its own set of unique issues, committees, and key players from within and outside the legislature.

Economic Policy and Development

Much of the legislation proposed by state legislators deals with their state's economy, and efforts to keep it growing and the state's citizens employed. Bills that fall into that area concern tax incentives designed to encourage businesses to expand or settle in the state, efforts to improve the state's transportation and communications systems, matters relating to taxation, and programs to educate, train, or retrain workers. Efforts to improve the state's business climate must address the reality that businesses have to be subject to some level of regulation and oversight if the public is to be treated fairly. Because economic issues are of such extreme concern to voters, they are seen as very important to legislators, who devote a considerable amount of their time to them.

Social Issues

A second area of public policy concerns government efforts to meet the basic citizen needs, such as health care, food, and clothing, of those who are unable to meet those needs on their own. Social issues legislation also includes items such as education, which is deemed beneficial to society. Included in this area of policy are such recognizable programs as public education, Medicare and Medicaid (national programs that are partially funded by the states), children's health insurance programs, food stamps (another federal program, but administered through the states), and unemployment and workers' compensation. These programs are traditionally known as redistributive programs, because their benefits go disproportionately to those who have lower incomes. With the exception of education, legislators often find that redistributive programs have limited public support when they set out to establish spending priorities.

Natural Resources

An area of public policy that is often the focus of state legislators, especially those from districts or states in which agriculture or natural resources are critical to the economy, concerns matters relating to the use and management of natural resources. That would include agriculture (including farming and ranching), environmental matters such as air, land, and water pollution, energy policies, and tourism (because of its relationship to a state's environment and natural resources). Public policy issues in this area often pit those who make a living through the land, such as farmers and miners, against environmentalists whose concerns focus on protecting the natural resources for future generations.

Justice and Public Safety

Still another category of public policy, and one that has taken on increased importance in recent years, concerns government efforts to provide for the safety and security of its citizens. This usually includes the state's criminal and civil justice system. Bills that fall within this public policy area focus on government efforts to ensure that the citizens will be as safe and secure as they can reasonably be in a free society. In recent years legislators have been particularly concerned about the development of homeland security policies that achieve an acceptable balance between the right of the state's citizens to be protected and their right to live free of undue government interference in their daily lives. Issues in the justice and public safety area are of critical importance to voters. But much proposed legislation there can also be very costly, and legislators find themselves constantly grappling with balancing the need to provide a safe society with the costs to that society.

Government Administration and Regulation

Many of the laws passed by state legislatures are designed either to regulate government or to enable government to carry out its constitutional and legal responsibilities. Legislation that falls into that area concerns the state budget, the creation of new government agencies, the regulation of government agencies, and state employees.

A categorization into the five policy areas of nonappropriations bills (that is, bills that did not specifically authorize the expenditure of funds from the state budget) introduced in the Alabama House of Representatives in 2003 shows that well over half concerned government administration and regulation, and justice and public safety.

Many of the policies considered by the Alabama House related directly to how government did its job and how effectively it provided services to the public. Given the importance of both homeland security and public safety, the number of bills introduced on that subject should come as no surprise. Likewise, in light of the economic challenges facing Alabama—as well as the rest of the country in the early part of the twenty-first century—a focus on economic issues (17 percent) was to be expected. Social issues and natural resource programs that are likely to be costly and perhaps of limited political reward (especially in a conservative state like Alabama) were given very limited attention by Alabama House members (13 percent and 5 percent, respectively).

BUDGETING AND APPROPRIATIONS

Nothing that a state legislature does is more time consuming or more challenging than its consideration of the state's budget. While the development of state budgets is a shared responsibility between the legislature and governor, it is the responsibility of every state legislature to adopt a budget for the operations of state government and to provide the revenues to finance that budget. While governors have some limited authority to approve emergency expenditures without legislative authorization, even those emergency expenditures usually come from a discretionary fund appropriated to the governor by the legislature.

State budgets involve huge expenditures. The annual budget of the state of California is larger than the budgets of all but five countries in the world. In 2000, the Golden State's budget exceeded $150 billion. The state of New York spent more than $100 billion. No state budget was less than $2.5 billion in 2000.

How the Budget Process Works

In most states, the development and approval of the state budget is an interactive process involving the legislature, the governor, and the governor's executive branch agencies.

The first stage of the budget process involves the development and formulation of a proposed budget. While governors may anticipate legislative reaction or even involve legislative leadership in the development of the budget, in all but a handful of states this stage is dominated by the executive. The governors of every state have the power

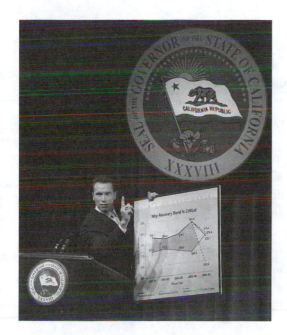

California governor Arnold Schwarzenegger announces his state budget for 2004–2005. Like most governors, Schwarzenegger is required to submit a budget to the legislature. (Ken James/Corbis)

to propose a budget to their legislature. They work with the department heads and their fiscal advisors to develop the proposed executive budget, which will generally reflect the governor's policy objectives.

The next stage of the process, budget review and modification, takes place almost exclusively in the legislature. Once the governor has submitted the proposed budget to the legislature, the legislature undertakes an in-depth examination of its contents. The ball is in the legislature's court from this point on, leading one legislative leader to remind his governor: "You might write the checks, but we have the deposit slips" (State Legislative Leaders Foundation 2005).

While governors can, and almost always do, continue to talk about their budget proposals, the power and responsibility to decide on the final allocation of state funds rests with their legislatures. Legislative authority concerning what changes they can make in the budgets proposed by their governors varies across the states, with most legislatures possessing the power to change the governor's proposed budget by adding or deleting items and increasing or decreasing proposed spending levels. The Maryland, Nebraska, and West Virginia legislatures are limited to only increasing or decreasing their governor's proposed budget. They cannot add or remove programs or items. In Texas, Colorado, and Arizona, the governor's proposals are largely ignored. In Texas, a budget board that includes leaders from the Senate and House proposes its own budget, often quite different from the governor's. In Arizona, senior legislators rank their budget priorities, and those ranked low, regardless of the recommendations of the governor, are unlikely to gain support. In Colorado, state agencies are required to submit their budget requests directly to the legislature, bypassing the governor entirely (Snell 2005a). Most state legislatures have strong professional fiscal staffs that enable their members to effectively challenge the economic and policy assumptions underlying the governor's budget. And, with many legislatures led by long-serving leaders who have been in office much longer than the governor, the legislature often has the institutional knowledge and strength to challenge the governor. Even in states in which the governor traditionally exercises considerable control over the budget, the legislature often finds ways, with assistance from their professional fiscal staff, to influence the governor's budget.

A legislative chamber's in-depth examination of the state budget usually takes place in its Appropriations Committee, and in that committee's subcommittees in which the various parts of the budget are discussed, debated, and analyzed. These committees and subcommittees usually hold hearings in which executive branch officials, and sometimes even the governor, must defend their budget proposals. Once the budget has been debated and discussed in a committee, it comes to the floor of the chamber for final consideration. In thirty-two states, approval of the budget requires a majority of those present, while a majority of all members is required in fifteen states. In Rhode Island, Arkansas, and California, passage of the budget requires approval by more than a simple majority of those elected. Once the budget passes both legislative chambers, it goes to the governor. In all but seven states, the governor can reject individual items in the budget by vetoing them without vetoing the entire budget bill. That is known as a line-item veto. All governors have the power to veto the entire budget document. If either type of veto—line item or regular—is exercised by the governor, the legislature can still approve the budget, or the vetoed budget item, and override the veto by repassing the budget, usually by a two-thirds vote in each chamber.

While the governor usually initiates the budget process, the legislature has ample opportunity to influence it. First, legislators may influence the process during the stage when the governor is developing it, if the governor chooses to permit legislative input. Second, in some states, the legislature tends largely to ignore the governor's budget and prepare its own. Third, once the governor's proposed budget has been presented to the legislature, its committees or subcommittees hold hearings, review the proposals, and make recommendations to change it. Fourth, in order to secure enough votes to pass a budget, governors are generally forced to negotiate with their legislature's leaders and individual legislators, making concessions and agreeing to add items of special interest or concern. Finally, if a governor does veto all or part of the budget, the legislature has an opportunity to repass the budget over that veto.

Not surprisingly, budget votes are often contentious, pitting governors against legislators, Republicans against Democrats, and conservatives against liberals. In most states, the budget vote is the most critical vote taken in a legislative session, and the majority party leadership is almost always heavily involved in building support for the budget. In many states, the budget is one of the few votes on which members are expected to support their party leadership—whether in the majority or the minority—even if the vote might cause some problems for them in their district. It is politically damaging and usually considered a sign of political weakness if the majority party cannot build enough support within its caucus to secure passage of the state's budget. Likewise, if a governor whose political party is in the majority in both chambers of the legislature is unable to gain support for a budget in pretty much the form proposed, it can be a political embarrassment to the governor and the party leadership.

Variations in Budgeting and Appropriations Processes

While the process by which states develop, approve, and administer their budgets is relatively similar, there are, as previously indicated, some important distinctions among state budget processes, including the duration of a state's budget cycle (one or two years) and whether spending levels can exceed revenue.

Relative to the duration of a budget cycle, most state budgets were historically biennial, covering a two-year period. All that began to change in the late 1960s and 1970s, when proponents of stronger and more active state legislatures argued that biennial budgets were not appropriate for increasingly urban, active, and progressive state governments, and also that they allowed governors to exercise excessive influence over government operations at the expense of the legislature (Citizen's Conference on State Legislatures, 1971). By the 1980s, a majority of states had switched to an annual budget cycle. Since the 1980s, some states have reverted back to a biennial budget (among them, Connecticut in 1991 and Arizona in 1999). In 2004, twenty-nine states operated under an annual budget and twenty-one under a biennial budget. All but two of the ten most populous states operated on annual budgets (Ohio and Texas being the exceptions), while many of the less populous states with less professional legislative operations were among the twenty-one biennial states.

Unlike the national government, most state governments cannot pass a budget that is not balanced. That is, they cannot approve the expenditure of more money than they raise through taxes and other sources such as federal grants. However, the definition of balanced budget varies from state to state. According to the National Conference of State Legislatures, thirty-six states have very strict balanced budget requirements, four have weak requirements, and ten are somewhere in between. No state imposes legal penalties for failing to balance its budget, but the fact that most states are not allowed to carry a deficit from one budget year into the next and have strict restrictions on how they may borrow to cover deficit spending, when coupled with the tendency of voters to view deficit spending in a negative light, generally keeps the country's state legislatures from ignoring restrictions on approving unbalanced budgets (Snell 2005b).

TABLE 2.4   NUMBER OF YEARS WITH BUDGET SURPLUSES, 1961–2000

Top Five		Bottom Five	
New Mexico	40 (100%)	*Alaska	27 (67.5%)
Texas	40 (100%)	New Hampshire	25 (62.5%)
Arizona	39 (97.5%)	Rhode Island	24 (69%)
Minnesota	39 (97.5%)	Hawaii	22 (55%)
Ohio	39 (97.5%)	Massachusetts	21 (52.5%)

Source: Council of State Governments. 2004. *Book of the States.* Lexington, KY: Council of State Governments, Table 2.12.

*Connecticut and Delaware also had balanced budgets for twenty-seven of the forty years.

When they were chosen by the members of their caucus to lead their respective chambers, House speakers Larry Householder of Ohio (in 2001) and Franklin "Jake" Flake of Arizona (in 2003) found themselves in similar situations. Both were conservative Republicans with solid Republican majorities (59 to 40 in Ohio, and 39 to 20 in Arizona), large numbers of first term or freshman members in their chambers (almost half in Ohio and more than half in Arizona), and looming budget crises. Further, most of the new members were elected on conservative platforms, opposing any new taxes. Speakers Householder and Flake made conscious decisions to involve all members of their Republican House caucuses in the development of their state's budgets, hoping that such involvement would create a sense of ownership that would lead to broad-based caucus support for the budget.

In Ohio, rather than relying on the Finance and Ways and Means committees, as has traditionally been the case, Householder and his fifty-eight Republican colleagues spent weeks going through the governor's proposed budget, line by line, item by item, looking for places to cut and fees that might be increased. In Arizona, Speaker Flake broke his caucus into five work groups, charged each to find cuts in the governor's proposed budget, and chose two members from among their number to participate in a group of ten to write the final budget. Once the budget was drafted, Speaker Flake met individually with each member of his caucus to encourage support of the final document.

The end results of these efforts were very different. In Ohio, the Republican-developed budget passed with unanimous Republican support for the first time in memory. But in Arizona, a handful of moderate Republicans joined with Democrats to pass a budget far different from the Republican budget they had helped to create, and over the objections of Speaker Flake.

Source: Interview with Brett Buerck, chief of staff; Speaker Larry Householder, February 28, 2002; Interview with Speaker Jake Flake, May 30, 2004, Akron, Ohio; Robbie Sherwood, "House Rebels Pass Budget," *Arizona Republic*, May 21, 2004.

LEGISLATIVE OVERSIGHT

The fourth legislative function is oversight, making sure that funds appropriated by the legislature are spent as intended by the legislature and that they are achieving the objectives they were meant to achieve. State legislatures allocate money to thousands of agencies, departments, and bureaus every year, and they are expected to oversee the expenditure of that money and the implementation of the programs that it funds. While effective oversight of their executives presents legislatures with daunting challenges that will be examined in more depth later, several tools are available to assist them.

First, constituent service activities can provide legislators with good indications of whether government agencies are delivering services to their constituents in a timely and effective manner. Legislators regularly receive requests from constituents for assistance in dealing with state agencies that they do not feel are fulfilling their responsibilities. Constituents frequently call their state legislator to report that they are having difficulty receiving assistance from the state's Department of Human Services, or that they are unable to obtain a particular building permit from a state agency, or that a state regulatory agency is not doing its job effectively. Legislators usually respond to these requests with a telephone call, e-mail, letter, or visit to the agency to gather more information about the complaint. If the constituent's claim is found to have validity, the legislator will seek assurances that appropriate corrective action will be taken by the agency. While inquiries of this sort, handled on a case-by-case basis, will not change the course of the state government, they do have an impact in making executive branch bureaucrats more attentive and responsive to citizen service.

Second, state agency officials must regularly appear before legislative committees to explain and defend their departmental administration and programs and their funding requests. Most legislatures organize their committee jurisdictions to parallel closely those of the executive branch agencies, which enables their members to get comprehensive overviews of the activities of those agencies within the jurisdictions of the committees on which they serve. In committee hearings, legislators have an opportunity to ask questions of agency directors that help them to determine whether programs are being administered effectively and in accord with the basic intent of the legislature.

Once created, government programs and agencies seldom disappear. Ronald Reagan once described government agencies as the nearest thing we will see to eternal life on earth. Legislative action is required to end a government program, while inaction (doing nothing) allows it to stay alive long past its usefulness. In an effort to change that, many states have enacted sunset legislation, placing termination dates on the existence of certain government agencies or programs, and requiring specific action by the legislature to allow the program to continue past its established termination date. In states that have sunset laws, programs covered by the laws must be periodically reviewed by the legislature, with the reviews ranging from every four years in Alabama to every twelve years in Texas. If an agency does not effectively justify its existence and the benefit of its activities to the legislature in that review, or if the legislature elects not to conduct such a review, the agency or program is automatically terminated. Sunset legislation applies to all new government agencies in eight states and to selected agencies in thirteen more. It applies exclusively to regulatory agencies in six states. Seven state legislatures have repealed their sunset acts during the past two decades and now review agencies on a case-by-case basis.

Despite the fact that legislatures are supposed to be the primary lawmaking body in a democratic system, government agencies exercise considerable latitude in determining the specifics of how they administer their programs and activities. For example, a state agency responsible for governing child care exercises significant authority through its issuance of regulations and rules in defining what constitutes a legal child care establishment, a certifiable teacher, space-per-child ratios, and health regulations.

While agencies can issue and enforce regulations that specify how they will administer the authority granted them by the legislature, in most states those regulations are subject to review and repeal by the legislature. Legislative review of administrative regulations takes different forms from state to state. In sixteen states, the legislature, generally with a committee that includes members from both legislative chambers, is empowered to review only proposed regulations, while the legislatures of Colorado and North Dakota can review only existing regulations. New Mexico grants no formal review authority to its legislature. In the remaining states, legislative review power covers both proposed and existing administrative regulations.

As important as legislative oversight is, it is often the responsibility accorded least attention by legislators. There are several reasons for this neglect. First, many government agencies are protected by influential and well-organized constituencies that make it politically risky to challenge their administrative performance. A legislator in a state with a strong agricultural economy who wishes to look closely at the functions and expenditures of the Department of Agriculture risks the wrath of farmers and interest groups that support the agricultural community. Such wrath can mean the withholding of campaign financial support from influential sectors for legislators seeking reelection. Second, astute agency directors are likely to have developed strong supportive relationships with at least some members of the legislative committee charged with overseeing their agency. Many state agency heads are, in fact, former legislators who maintain strong personal relationships with their former legislative colleagues.

Finally, there is usually little political reward to a legislator for conducting effective oversight. Unless the oversight activity uncovers very dramatic and expensive errors or a scandal, neither the news media nor the voters tend to pay much attention to it. While press headlines abound regarding the establishment of a new program or agency, the headline "Program Implemented Effectively" is unlikely ever to grace the front page of a newspaper. Despite the tools available to legislators to enable them to undertake extensive oversight of agencies and programs, these three factors often discourage them from doing so and thereby limit their potential effectiveness.

EDUCATING THE PUBLIC

While the legislature is considered "the people's branch of government," most Americans know little or nothing about their state legislature. Few can name their state senator or representative. Only a small minority know what the legislature does, and even fewer understand how it does it. What little people do "know" is often negative, with many believing that their legislature is under the control of special interests, is overly partisan, and engages in too much bickering (Rosenthal 2004, 3–5).

Public opinion of legislative bodies (as well as of government in general) has been declining precipitously at both the national and state levels in recent years. Among the many factors to which this decline is attributed is that the public has a very limited understanding of the legislative process and even less appreciation for its significance. The legislative process is a complex process that involves intricate rules, compromise, and conflict-resolution—three things that the U.S. public generally neither likes nor understands to be essential to democracy. The reality, however, is that those are the very

Louisiana senator Lydia Jackson visited with fourth- and fifth-grade students at Mooringsport Elementary School in her district. She discussed her service in the Louisiana state legislature and explained to the students how legislators' decisions affect them. (Courtesy Louisiana State Senate)

elements of the legislative process that can, and usually do, lead to decisions that benefit the general public.

To the public, legislative debate that is so essential to representative democracy is viewed as bickering. Ideological divisions that enable the public to choose between different policies are viewed as partisan fighting. Complex rules that make debate manageable and enable legislators to disagree one day and work together the next are viewed by large portions of the public as arcane procedures designed to confuse the public about what its legislators are really doing.

Most of what the public knows about government comes from three sources: the news media, the public education system, and politically biased sources. None of them provide the kind of information necessary to inform the public about the true nature of the legislative process and, more important, its real strengths in what may appear to be its apparent weaknesses. The news media often present the legislature in a negative light, focusing on conflict and scandal to the exclusion of cooperation, while public education teachers and textbooks tend to sanitize the process to the point that students lose interest and don't recognize the political institution they read about in newspapers or see on television. As increasing numbers of legislative candidates respond to this negativism by campaigning against the legislature as a governmental institution, focusing on everything that is wrong with the legislature, more and more voters have come to see their state legislature as something other than the people's branch of government (ibid.).

Educating the public about what legislatures do and how they do it must be an integral part of the job of state legislators as individuals and of legislatures as a whole. They, better than anyone else, understand and appreciate the intricacies of the process and are best equipped and qualified to explain them to the public. Fortunately, there are a number of tools, both traditional and modern, that are available to assist them in undertaking such an effort.

Traditional Communication Tools

State legislators have historically relied on several means of communicating with their constituents. They spend a great deal of their time making public appearances, speaking before community groups ranging from League of Women Voters forums to the local chamber of commerce or Rotary Club to the social studies classes in the schools of their district. Particularly when they are not in session, legislators find themselves speaking before such groups all over their districts. They can use these forums as an opportunity

---

LEGISLATURES AND THE PUBLIC

Public Offers Budget Suggestions in Minnesota

If you have ever wanted to try to balance a state's budget, the state of Minnesota gives you that opportunity. On a website sponsored by Minnesota Public Radio, visitors can raise taxes or cut spending in a budget simulation called "The Budget Balancer." On this site, visitors are charged to eliminate the state's projected budget deficit with a combination of spending cuts or tax increases. They can choose from seven policy areas and five types of taxes or revenues. Each change in expenditure is accompanied with a brief description of the programs that will be cut or increased by that change. Likewise, each proposed tax adjustment is accompanied with a brief description of its effect on the economy, job growth, and the state's revenue structure.

Participants can compare their budget to that proposed by the governor, offer expla-

nations of their choices, and e-mail their proposed budget to state legislators. In addition to allowing the public to make their voices known, this simulation also graphically demonstrates to those who play the simulation some of the difficult decisions that must be made to balance the budget. More than 4,000 people accessed the "Budget Balancer" website during the first two months that it was on line. The Budget Balancer can be found at: http://news .minnesota.publicradio.org/projects/2005/ 03/budget/budget_balancer.php.

Source: Minnesota Public Radio website (http://news.minnesota.publicradio.org/ projects/2005/03/budget/); interview with Andrew Haeg, Minnesota Public Radio, May 5, 2005.

to explain why debate and disagreement are necessary components of democracy and can produce better public policy and services.

Beyond public appearances, many legislators have historically relied on newsletters to convey information to their constituents. In many states, the legislature or the legislator's political party provides resources and assistance to enable legislators to prepare newsletters so as to get their message out to their constituents. In some states, legislative party caucus staffs prepare and distribute newsletters for their members. Newsletters provide legislators with an ideal means of educating the public about what the legislature is doing and what it has done.

Finally, while their "bully pulpit" is not nearly as large or far reaching as that of the state's governor, legislators (particularly legislative leaders and committee chairs) do have access to traditional media outlets, including television, radio, and newspapers. While the news media may focus on the negative and the sensational, legislative leaders are sometimes able to take advantage of the symbiotic nature of the relationship between the media and politicians (neither can be effective without the other) to get their messages out. Legislative leaders can build a positive relationship with journalists that will increase the likelihood of their being able to convey messages as they want to convey them (Ogle, Linsky, and Little 2001).

Modern Methods of Communication

Technological changes of the past decade have made it significantly easier for the public to stay informed about the activities of their state legislatures or their individual members. These changes have made it possible for a legislator literally to be in two places at once, for interested citizens to access the voting records of their representatives instantaneously, and for those who are interested to follow debate on the floor of the legislative chamber or in a legislative committee without ever leaving their homes or offices.

In the past, legislators occasionally had to choose between performing their legislative duties in the statehouse and increasing their exposure in the district by attending an important public function there. They could not be in two places at once. However, with video conferencing, even in states with limited resources, they need face that dilemma no more (Ogden 2002). A legislator can vote on the legislative chamber floor, then, a moment later and at minimal expense, use a computer to appear by video in a town meeting in the district. In the past, such a feat would have required costly video and audio equipment in both the legislator's district and office.

Websites provide an inexpensive and interactive way for legislators to communicate with the public and educate it about the intricacies of the legislative process. With a click of the mouse, citizens can find out how their legislators voted on a bill, check the status of a piece of proposed legislation, find out when committee hearings will be held, and, in some cases, even watch live debate on the floor of one or both chambers.

Web designers Brent Larson, left, and Vaughan Harries review the North Dakota Legislative Branch website at their office in the state information technology department at the capitol in Bismarck, 2005. (AP Photo/Will Kincaid)

Modern technology also enables legislators to establish a communication link with their constituents via electronic communications, including e-mail, chat rooms, discussion groups, and electronic newsletters. All of these methods of communication enable legislators to impart information to their constituents at a fraction of the cost of traditional electronic media or regular mail. Whereas mailing a hard copy of a newslet-

TABLE 2.5   TOP TWELVE DIGITAL LEGISLATURES

1. Nevada	6. Indiana
2. Minnesota and South Dakota (tied)	7. Utah
3. Louisiana	8. Virginia and Washington (tied)
4. Iowa	9. Rhode Island
5. Illinois	10. New Mexico

Source: Center for Digital Government, Legislative Survey, 2003. (http://www.centerdigitalgov.com/center/highlightstory.php?docid=73192.)

ter to constituents can cost a legislator or the legislator's party caucus hundreds or even thousands of dollars, that same newsletter can be sent via e-mail with the click of a button at virtually no cost (see T 2.5). A recent study revealed that "fully 86 percent of state legislatures provide their members with networked laptops to manage . . . constituent contacts while on the capitol campus" (Taylor 2004).

RESOURCES OF STATE LEGISLATURES

Clearly, state constitutions grant state legislatures significant formal power and authority. Every state constitution, in fact, enumerates the powers of the legislative branch before, and usually in a greater degree of specificity, than it does the powers of the executive or judicial branches.

Most state legislatures possess the formal authority to carry out the five responsibilities that have been outlined. The power to propose legislation and create programs helps legislators represent their constituents and has a direct bearing on the lawmaking responsibility. The power to create, expand, or curtail programs and remove officials clearly affects the ability of the legislature to conduct oversight. No legislature could adopt a budget for its state without the power to generate revenue. And the authority to organize and manage its own affairs allows a legislature to develop means of educating and informing the public about how it works and what it is doing.

THE LEGISLATURE AND THE PUBLIC

The South Dakota Legislature Reaches Out

When one thinks of a state on the cutting edge of new policy initiatives, or streamlined political processes, South Dakota is unlikely to spring to the forefront. Its population is smaller than that of all but five other states. Its legislature is one of the least professional and one of only seven that meet only every other year. Its annual budget is smaller than that of most of the nation's major cities. And yet, according to a 2004 study, the South Dakota state legislature stands tall among the states when it comes to using technology to reach out and engage the public. Every legislator is provided with a laptop computer that can access the Internet through a wireless network that covers the capitol grounds. According to James Fry, director of the state's Legislative Research Council: "We try to put information on the website that is integrated with the . . .

process of taking a bill from idea to codification." Each bill is "live" in its current form and also archived in its original form, so that readers can determine the original intent of the legislation. Further, the state's legislative website provides the capability for interested parties to listen to debate on the Senate and House floors and in their committees. Finally, with an application called MyLRC, anyone interested in following particular pieces of legislation can be alerted to changes in those bills. Interested constituents can also request e-mail notification of bill hearings, committee hearings, floor consideration, rules changes, and interim committee activities.

Source: Best of Breed: Top Performing
    Legislative Information Technology Programs.
    Center for Digital Government, 2004.

While the formal power and authority granted to a legislature helps it to carry out its responsibilities, that alone is not sufficient. Formal powers are, in a very real sense, potential powers. They are only as effective as the institution that possesses and exercises them. Fortunately, certain characteristics common to most state legislatures enhance their ability to fulfill their obligations to the people of their states: membership diversity, a well-structured committee system, centralized leadership, and access to information. Each of these characteristics contributes in its own way to helping a state legislature to be an effective representative institution of the public and a strong counterbalance to the state's governor and its courts.

Membership Diversity

Most state legislatures are remarkably reflective of the geographic, ideological, and political diversity of their state. Legislators are elected from every part of a state and they often represent very different constituencies. Some represent conservative districts, others liberal ones. Some represent urban districts and others represent more rural constituencies; still others have districts that reflect the growing suburban population of the United States. This diversity—which is much less likely to be reflected in other branches of government—and the various opinions that it encourages provide a legislature with the opportunity to develop and enact legislation that is reflective of the diversity of its state. Furthermore , this diversity contributes most directly toward the ability of individual legislators to represent their districts and of the legislative branch of the government to represent the variety of needs within their state.

Committee Structure

Every state legislature is organized to process legislation in basically the same way. Each has a system of substantive committees that specialize in particular policy areas and conduct in-depth examinations of legislative proposals relative to their areas of jurisdiction. For example, every state legislature has at least one committee that examines, debates, amends, and recommends legislation relative to education. In 2004, the number of committees in legislative chambers ranged from a low of four in the Maine Senate to a high of forty-seven in the Wisconsin Assembly (see T 2.6). A committee system enables a legislature to work on multiple pieces of proposed legislation at the same time, and to take advantage of the experience and expertise of its members. In addition, given the diversity of the membership, members debating an education bill may be principals, teachers, and superintendents, while those discussing a transportation proposal may have years of experience on the transportation committee or in a transportation-related field. When a bill comes up for final consideration in a legislative chamber, the recommendations of its committees generally hold significant weight and are the primary determinant of its fate (Francis 1989).

TABLE 2.6   NUMBER OF LEGISLATIVE STANDING COMMITTEES, 2004

Top Five		Bottom Five	
Wisconsin Assembly	47	*Alaska Senate	9
Texas House	40	Maryland House	7
New York Assembly	37	Maine House	6
Illinois House	37	Maryland Senate	6
North Carolina House	31	Maine Senate	4

Source: Council of State Governments. 2004. *Book of the States.* Lexington, KY: Council of State Governments, Table 3.23.

*Alaska House, and senates in Massachusetts, Nevada, New Mexico, Oregon, and Tennessee, all have 9 standing committees.

Centralized Leadership

While a decentralized system of substantive committees strengthens the legislature by enabling it to conduct in-depth examinations of numerous pieces of proposed legislation simultaneously, and to take advantage of the diverse experience and expertise of its membership, a centralized leadership structure is necessary if the legislature is to have any chance to speak with a coordinated voice. Every legislative chamber has one member who is considered its presiding officer and who plays a prominent role in assigning bills, appointing committees, naming committee chairs, and managing the flow of legislation. In every state House of Representatives or assembly (except North Dakota), that person is the speaker. In North Dakota it is the majority leader. In state Senates, that leader may be the president, the majority leader, or the president pro tempore; in a few cases, the power is shared among the three. Stable and powerful leadership is necessary if the diverse and often fragmented membership of a state legislature is going to compete with a powerful united executive branch in the battle to determine the direction of state policy. A legislature without strong leadership, no matter how strong its formal powers, will find it difficult to perform its lawmaking, budgeting, and oversight responsibilities with effectiveness (Jewell and Whicker 1994; Rosenthal 2004, 209–230).

Information Resources

To perform its responsibilities with effectiveness, a legislative body must have independent sources of accurate and objective information upon which it can rely in rendering its decisions. Until quite recently, state legislatures had very limited access to independent and unbiased information, and they were often forced to rely on the governor, the bureaucracy, and lobbyists to provide them with information. That is not the case in most legislatures today. If a state legislator casts an uninformed or uneducated vote on a bill today, it is a function of limited time or choice, rather than the lack of information. Even the least professional state legislatures today have strong nonpartisan research staffs that can provide their members and committees with information on the contents and implications of proposed legislation and on its costs. For example, the staff of every state legislature prepares fiscal notes that indicate the immediate and long-term projected cost and, when appropriate, the source of revenue for bills (Council of State Governments 2004, Table 3.18; Chadha, Permaloff, and Bernstein 2001). Every committee that hears and makes recommendations on legislation has at least some professional staff assistance, and every legislature has bill drafting attorneys that prepare bills and amendments for their members. Beyond professional staff assistants, almost every state legislature now provides its members with easy access to the Internet and the web of information that it provides. The Internet opens the door for today's state legislator to a virtually unlimited storehouse of information from government agencies, universities, think tanks, and national organizations (Taylor 2004).

THE LIMITATIONS OF LEGISLATIVE INFLUENCE

It is clear that most state legislatures are granted sufficient power and authority by their state constitutions to enable them to play a dominant policymaking role in their states. It seems equally clear that most legislatures have the membership, organization, and resources to carry out their constitutionally mandated responsibilities. However, many scholars and students of state government suggest that it is governors and sometimes courts that are now the key players in state government (Van Assendalt 1997; Rosenthal 2004; Beyle 2004). How is it possible that an institution with the constitutional power and the necessary resources to be the dominant policymaking body in its state seems to be often lagging behind the other two branches that have, arguably, less impressive constitutional claims to power?

There are many answers to this question. Some lie outside the legislature and concern the expectations and powers of governors and the changing role of the courts. But some of the fault can be found within the modern legislature. We will focus here on the internal challenges faced by the modern legislature and look at the external challenges discussed in Chapter 5, in which the political environment of the legislature is explored. Just as some characteristics commonly found in modern state legislatures serve to enhance their power, others make it difficult for them to exercise fully the authority granted them. Four characteristics in particular—membership and leadership instability, free-agent members, the complexity of the legislative process, and the loss of legislative community—present major obstacles to a state legislature's effective exercise of its constitutional power and authority.

Membership and Leadership Instability

Throughout most of U.S. history, both the membership and the leadership ranks of state legislatures have been marked by high turnover. While there were exceptions, it was not unusual into the mid-1960s for annual membership turnover after each election to be as high as a third in most states, and even up to 50 percent in some. Over a ten-year period, more than 90 percent of the membership of many legislatures would change. Those same heavy rates of turnover occurred with regard to the leadership of these bodies, many of which had traditions of changing their top leadership after each election. While there were exceptions—such as Speaker Jess Unruh in California (1961–1969) and Speaker Solomon Blatt of South Carolina (1937–1946; 1951–1973)—the majority of state legislative leaders served no more than four years. Increased attention paid to state legislatures in the mid-1960s and early 1970s pushed through reforms and ushered in an era that led to reductions in membership turnover and an attendant increase in leadership stability. By the late 1980s, only a few legislative chambers held on to the tradition of changing their top leaders after each election cycle, with some legislators serving in their chamber's top leadership position for six or more years. More than two-thirds of the House and Senate leaders in 1993 had at least two years of experience, and more than a dozen had held their post for more than ten years.

The scandals and recessions that struck a number of states in the late 1980s led to changes that slowed, and in some cases began to reverse, the trend toward long-term stability and began a slow, but steady, increase in the rate of turnover among both members and leaders. The elections of 1994 witnessed a change of party control and leadership in more than a dozen states and the largest general election turnover in decades. And, beginning with Oklahoma in 1990, the early 1990s ushered in the era of state legislative term limits, which, at their high point, were adopted by almost 40 percent of the states. These states experienced dramatic decreases in the tenure potential for both the members and the leaders of their legislatures. By the late 1990s, the trend toward longer tenures in membership and leadership showed a decline for the first time in three decades. By 2002, more than a quarter of all state legislators (32 percent in senates and 26 percent in houses and assemblies) were serving their first legislative term, and more than half of all the leaders were in their first year of leadership.

While new members and new leadership may bring fresh ideas into a legislative chamber, those ideas are purchased at a cost. No matter how smart or able an individual might be, it takes time to become an effective legislator, and even more time to become an effective legislative leader (State Legislative Leaders Foundation 2005). Legislators and legislative leaders are almost never as effective at doing their job in their first term of service as they will be in their second, or their third, or their fourth. This can pose a particular problem for a legislative chamber whose top leader is in the first term in that position and yet is required to contend with a governor and with agency bureaucrats who have extended tenures in office. In states that have adopted the most restrictive legislative term limits, of six years, even the highest ranking leaders will have served no more than one or two terms in their chamber before achieving top leadership status. And once in their positions, they seldom serve more than one term before their state's term limits law bars them from seeking reelection. The leadership vacuum in term-limited states is complicated in that, just as inexperienced leaders find it difficult to lead, inexperienced members often find it difficult to follow. Legislators of limited tenure are more likely than longer-serving legislators—who have often developed a respect and appreciation for the benefits of a legislative hierarchy—to turn their backs on their leaders and be swayed by inducements and flattery from governors, executive branch officials, or lobbyists.

The Free-Agent Legislator

As recently as the 1950s and 1960s, most state legislators were reliant on their local or, sometimes, state political party to help them win their seat in the legislature. Parties recruited candidates, financed much of their campaigns, helped develop campaign messages and literature, mobilized the party faithful to vote, and hosted victory parties on election night. Legal, political, and cultural changes related to the legislative modernization movement of the late 1960s and 1970s changed much of that, and led to the ascendancy of the free-agent legislator. Just as free-agent professional athletes can leave their team and join another that offers a higher salary, free-agent legislators are in a position to walk away from their political parties and leaders if they receive a better offer. Today, many state legislators are self-recruited, or were recruited to run for office by a friend, a lobbyist, an interest group, or leaders from their community rather than their party leaders (Salmore and Salmore 1996; Moncrief, Squire, and Jewell 2001, 40–42). As candidates for office, these legislators raise their own campaign funds, hire their own consultants, conduct their own polls, and establish their own campaign message. Once elected, they feel little or no allegiance to their political party and may, instead, pay more attention to lobbyists, interest groups, or constituents who helped them to win election. Legislative leaders are finding it increasingly difficult to rally these free agents around a common agenda, thereby making it more difficult to initiate and pass major legislation, adopt a budget on time, and generally compete effectively in the policymaking arena with an executive branch that is likely to be united behind the governor (Rosenthal 2004).

A Complex and Slow Legislative Process

In many ways, the greatest strengths of state legislatures are also their greatest weaknesses. The legislative process—the process by which legislatures conduct their business—is a case in point. It is a complex and deliberate process that is designed to make it difficult for bad ideas to become law, and to force cooler heads to prevail in a way that would be far less likely in a more streamlined process, which might yield more reactive policies. In a like manner, George Washington suggested to Thomas Jefferson that the Senate was created so that "we could pour legislation in it to cool," just as tea is poured into a saucer for the same reason.

This slow and deliberate process, which is difficult for the general public (and even some legislators) to understand and is designed to produce good legislation, sometimes does just the opposite when a well-organized minority within a legislative body's membership makes use of the process to block passage of what the majority considers a good bill. Furthermore, research suggests that citizens find distasteful the very type of debate and discussion that the legislative process fosters. In examining the response of Americans to congressional debate, one scholar has written: "As citizens gaze into the fishbowl of elite politics they do not always like what they see. . . .[T]he behavior of political leaders engaged in legislative policy debate contributes to public dissatisfaction with government" (Funk 2002).

The complexities of the legislative process make it difficult for the public to understand and appreciate legislative decisionmaking, and they can also make it difficult for a legislature to compete with the state's governor, who is not encumbered by highly structured operating procedures and is afforded the luxury of acting much more quickly and decisively. When most state legislatures were created, in the eighteenth and nineteenth centuries, news moved at the pace of a horse or a train. People were used to waiting weeks or even months for problems to be addressed. However, in the era in which news and information are instantaneous, the public expects solutions that are just as rapid. While governors can act and react quickly, the deliberative processes of a democratic legislative body make rapid response virtually impossible. Most legislative solutions take weeks, months, or even years to complete the legislative obstacle course. A governor, on the other hand, can issue an executive order and a judge can issue a decision or verdict in a matter of minutes. Speed for a legislature is measured in days, not hours or minutes. In a world in which solutions are often measured by speed rather than quality, the legislative branch of the government operates at a distinct disadvantage.

The Loss of Community and Comity

State legislatures have always been partisan. Republicans vote with other Republicans more than with Democrats, and they always will. Democrats vote more regularly with other Democrats than with their Republican counterparts, and they always will. However, voting records suggest that partisan differences run deeper and are integrated into more issues today than at any time in the country's history. In the past, legislators built strong personal relationships such that they could disagree on the floor of the legislative chamber during the day, but go to dinner and socialize together in the evening. Those relationships allowed legislators to form coalitions, sometimes across party lines, that enabled them to get things done in a timely and efficient manner. Today, for a variety of reasons, legislators seldom build such personal relationships but, instead, view each other in almost purely ideological (liberal or conservative), partisan

(Republican or Democratic), or political (minority party or majority party) terms and seldom take the time or effort to get beyond such boundaries. Many scholars believe that these barriers and labels are making it increasingly difficult for legislators of different political parties or differing ideological viewpoints to work together in the development of bipartisan policy solutions that will meet the needs and expectations of the public (Moncrief, Thompson, and Kurtz 1996; Rosenthal 1998, 40–42).

EVALUATING STATE LEGISLATURES

The efforts of scholars, journalists, researchers, and legislators have produced a great deal of information about the fifty state legislatures of the United States. We know when legislatures meet, the names of their members and leaders, how long they have served in their positions, and whether there are term-limit restrictions on how long they may serve. We know the jurisdictions and chairpersons of their committees and how many members and bills are assigned to those committees. We know the complex and daunting process that a bill must go through to become a law. And, most important of all, we know that each of the fifty state legislatures are unique.

However, all of this information tends to neglect one very important question: are state legislatures doing a good job, and are some doing a better job than others? Like most questions, the answer depends on precisely how the question is asked and what is included in its answer. An evaluation that looks only at the diversity of legislatures' membership will yield a different result than one that examines their power and authority. An evaluation that examines legislatures according to their formal structures will yield different rankings than one that focuses on what those structures actually produce. A glance at previous efforts to rank state legislatures suggests four distinct dimensions on which they can (and have been) evaluated: resources, process, people, and performance.

Institutional Resources

The first comprehensive effort to evaluate state legislatures in a systematic and comparative manner was undertaken in 1971. With a grant from the Ford Foundation, a nonpartisan organization, the Citizen's Conference on State Legislatures (CCSL), composed of former legislators and legislative staff, as well as academics, evaluated the resources available in each state legislature, making the assumption that the legislatures with the strongest personal, financial, legal, and organizational resources would be best equipped and able to carry out their responsibilities.

The CCSL developed a measure based on five criteria that became known as the FAIIR System. A legislature was deemed to be of high quality if it possessed the resources to be Functional, Accountable, Informed, Independent, and Representative. A functional legislature needed strong and stable leadership, a strong staff, and a stable and committed membership. An accountable legislature required competitive elections and the ability to open structures and processes by which voters could evaluate their members. An informed legislature needed independent and autonomous sources of information to compete with the executive and the bureaucracy. To be independent, the legislature had to possess sources of information, leadership, and influence that were not controlled by entities outside the legislature, such as the governor or state political party organizations. Finally, a representative body required a membership that reflected the diversity of the population and possessed a motivation, desire, and opportunity to reflect the interests of their constituents when making policy. Given the emphasis on resources, it came as no surprise that the CCSL study accorded its highest ranking to the legislatures of California, New York, Illinois, and Florida, which were deemed professional, with relatively stable leadership, comparatively higher salaries, full-time staffs, and rather low membership turnover. However, problems that have arisen in these more professional legislatures during the more than three decades since the CCSL study have suggested that an abundance of resources does not necessarily make for an effective legislature (Mathesian 1997; Creelan and Moulton 2004).

The Legislative Process

A second approach to evaluating state legislatures is to examine the various stages of the operational processes. What are the key qualities and characteristics of the process? How well do the legislature's committees function? When and how are key legislative decisions made? How accessible is the legislative process to the public? This approach assumes that an effective legislative process is one that is based on formal rules rather than personal power, encourages input from rank-and-file legislators and the general public, and produces solutions to public policy problems. A study conducted by the Brennan Center for Justice at the New York University School of Law examined the New York legislature relative to other legislatures along five procedural dimensions: committee autonomy, the probability of bills being debated by the Senate and assembly chambers, opportunities for input on the floor, the role of conference committees, and the efficiency of the overall legislative process. Whereas the CCSL study of 1971 had ranked the New York legislature second only to the California legislature, the NYU evaluation of 2004 ranked it among the worst in the country. According to the authors of the study: "New York State's legislative process is broken. . . . [It] limits legislators' consideration of legislation—whether counted in hearings, debate, amendments, readings, conference committees, or even simply legislators' presence when they vote—far more than any other legislature" (Creelan and Moulton 2004).

The People

A third way to evaluate legislative effectiveness is to look at the characteristics of the individual members of a legislative body. What proportion of its membership is male and female? What proportion is black, white, Hispanic, or Asian? How old is the average legislator? To what degree does the legislature's membership reflect the population of the state? This evaluation approach is based on the assumption that an effective legislature is primarily one that represents the needs and interests of its citizens effectively and, further, that membership diversity is a critical element of effective representation (Thomas 1994). In other words, it suggests that a legislature with few women cannot be expected to represent the interests of women adequately, or that a chamber dominated by rural legislators will be unable to recognize and respond effectively to the needs of the state's urban citizens. Rutgers University's Center for American Women in Politics (CAWP) keeps track of the proportion of women legislators and women leaders and ranks states by those proportions. A similar list is kept regarding the proportion of African American and Hispanic members.

Legislative Performance

Finally, Alan Rosenthal (2004) suggests that the most appropriate way to evaluate state legislatures is on their performance—how well they do what they are supposed to do. However, that approach may also face the most difficulties. It assumes that an appropriate set of responsibilities and functions can be established, that acceptable indicators of success can be determined, and that data can be generated to reflect them. There is no unanimity of agreement on how to determine any of these factors. While almost all U.S. legislative scholars agree that legislatures are supposed to make laws, there is limited consensus on their other responsibilities. Wahlke, Eulau, Buchanan, and Ferguson (1962) offer one set of legislative activities, while Crane and Watts (1968) and Rosenthal (2004) offer others. An additional list of responsibilities has been offered in this chapter that tries to incorporate the recommendations of all of these authors. However, even that list of five functions is not comprehensive and is unlikely to generate consensus.

Even if a consensus concerning responsibilities and functions could be achieved, the second hurdle to the Rosenthal approach may prove equally difficult to overcome. How can performance be effectively measured, and how can comparable quantitative data be gathered across fifty states? Many of the functions are complex and somewhat abstract. For example, if it is to be assumed that a legislature is representative in terms of policy responsiveness (just one of four possible definitions), evaluators must be confident that they know the viewpoints of the people of the state, the viewpoints of its legislators, that the state's citizens understand the specifics of legislation under consideration by their legislature, and that the legislators are indeed voting in accord with the viewpoints of their constituents because of their support for them and not purely out of personal conviction or because of some other motivation (such as pressure from lobbyists or their political party). Likewise, to measure effective lawmaking, it is necessary to know what problem a new law is intended to address and the degree to which the law, if approved by the legislature, will solve that problem.

Alan Rosenthal's valiant effort to evaluate the performance of state legislatures in 2004 illustrates both the potential and the difficulty of such an approach. His in-depth analysis of legislatures in five states (Maryland, Minnesota, Vermont, Ohio, and Washington) indicates that it is possible to measure the performance of individual legislatures, at least along his three dimensions (representation, lawmaking, and balancing the executive). He masterfully utilizes observational, quantitative, and qualitative data to paint a thorough picture of the performance of these five legislative bodies. However, the depth of the information that would be needed to undertake evaluations similar to those of Rosenthal suggest that a nationwide evaluation would be virtually impossible without a great expenditure of effort, time, and money. Furthermore, it is highly unlikely that any scholar (or even any group of scholars) could develop the kind of detailed understanding of legislatures and the legislative process that it has taken Rosenthal more than four decades to master.

It may be necessary to conclude that any attempt to evaluate and compare legislatures is destined to be flawed. The methods of evaluation, no matter how well defined, will inevitably be subjective and, depending on which ones the evaluators choose to use, will heavily influence the rankings. There are really no measures that could be used that would reflect with perfect accuracy the complex and abstract concepts that the evaluators would be trying to measure. So it must be considered unlikely that it will ever be possible to design a universally accepted method for the evaluation or ranking of state legislatures. And given the unique qualities and challenges facing each state and its legislature, that may be a good thing.

REFERENCES

Beyle, Thad. 2004. "The Governors." In *Politics in the American States: A Comparative Analysis*, edited by Virginia Gray, Russell Hanson, and Herbert Jacob. Washington, DC: Congressional Quarterly Press.

Bowser, Jennifer Drage, et al. 2003. "Leadership and Term Limits." In *The Test of Time: Coping with Legislative Term Limits*. Lanham, MD: Lexington.

Chadha, Anita, Anne Permaloff, and Robert A. Bernstein. 2001. "The Consequences of Independence: Functions and Resources of State Legislative Fiscal Offices." *State and Local Government Review* 33 (fall):202–207.

Citizens Conference on State Legislatures. 1971. *The Sometime Governments*. New York: Bantam.

Council of State Governments. 2004. *Book of the States 2004*. Lexington, KY: Council of State Governments.

Crane, Wilder, Jr., and Meredith W. Watts Jr. 1968. *State Legislative Systems*. Englewood Cliffs, NJ: Prentice-Hall.

Creelan, Jeremy M., and Laura M. Moulton. 2004. *The New York State Legislative Process: An Evaluation and Blueprint for Reform*. New York: Brennan Center for Justice at the NYU Law School.

Eulau, Heinz, and Paul D. Karps. 1977. "Representation: Specifying Components of Responsiveness." *Legislative Studies Quarterly* 2:233–254.

Fenno, Richard, Jr. 1978. *Homestyle: House Members in Their Districts*. Boston: Little, Brown.

Francis, Wayne L. 1989. *The Legislative Committee Game*. Columbus: Ohio State University Press.

Freedman, Patricia, and Lilliard E. Richardson, Jr. 1996. "Explaining Variation in Casework among State Legislators." *Legislative Studies Quarterly* 21, no. 1 (February):41–56.

Funk, Carolyn L. 2002. "Process Performance: Public Reaction to Legislative Policy Debate." In *What Is It about American Government that Americans Dislike?*, edited by John R. Hibbing and Elizabeth Theiss-Morse. Cambridge: Cambridge University Press.

Jewell, Malcolm E. 1982. *Representation in State Legislatures.* Lexington: University of Kentucky Press.

Jewell, Malcolm E., and Samuel C. Patterson. 1986. *The Legislative Process in the United States.* 4th ed. New York: Random House.

Jewell, Malcolm E., and Marcia Lynn Whicker. 1994. *Legislative Leadership in the American States.* Ann Arbor: University of Michigan Press.

Mathesian, Charles. 1997. "The Sick Legislature Syndrome and How to Avoid It." *Governing Magazine* Volume 11 (February):16–20.

Moncrief, Gary F., Peverill Squire, and Malcolm Jewell. 2001. *Who Runs for the Legislature?* Upper Saddle River, NJ: Prentice-Hall.

Moncrief, Gary F., Joel A. Thompson, and Karl Kurtz. 1996. "The Old Statehouse, It Ain't What It Used to Be." *Legislative Studies Quarterly*, Volume 21, no. 1 (February):51–72.

Niemi, Richard, and Lynda W. Powell. 2001. "United Citizenship? Knowing and Contacting Legislators after Term Limits." In *The Test of Time*, edited by Rick Farmer et al. Lanham, MD: Lexington.

Ogden, Michael R. 2002. "Teleconferencing." In *Communication Technology Update*, 8th ed., edited by August E. Grant and Jennifer H. Meadows. Oxford: Focal.

Ogle, David B., Martin Linsky, and Thomas H. Little. 2001. *Legislative Leaders and the Media.* State Legislative Leaders Foundation. (http://www.centerdigitalgov.com/center/highlightstory.php?docid=73192).

Peery, George, and Thomas H. Little. 2003. "Views from the Bridge: Legislative Leaders' Perceptions of Institutional Power in the Stormy Wake of Term Limits." In *The Test of Time: Coping with Legislative Term Limits.* Lanham, MD: Lexington.

Rosenthal, Alan. 1998. *The Decline of Representative Democracy: Process, Participation, and Power in State Legislatures.* Washington, DC: Congressional Quarterly Press.

———. 2004. *Heavy Lifting: The Job of the American Legislature.* Washington, DC: Congressional Quarterly Press.

Salmore, Stephen A. and Barbara G. 1996. "The Transformation of State Electoral Politics." In *The State of the States*, 3d ed., edited by Carl E. Van Horn. Washington, DC: Congressional Quarterly Press.

Snell, Randall K. 2002. *Annual and Biennial Budgeting: The Experience of State Governments.* (http://www.ncsl.org/programs/fiscal/annlbien.htm.)

———. 2005a. *Annual and Biennial Budgeting: The Experience of State Governments.* (http://www.ncsl.org/programs/fiscal/annlbien.htm.)

———. 2005b. *State Balanced Budget Requirements: Provisions and Practice.* Denver: National Conference of State Legislatures.

State Legislative Leaders Foundation. 2005. *What Have You Gotten Yourself Into? A Guide for New Legislative Leaders.* Centerville, MA: State Legislative Leaders Foundation.

Taylor, Paul W. 2004. "Deliberative and Digital: It Is the Legislature's Turn." *Government Technology Magazine* (January 2004). (http://www.govtech.net/magazine/story.php?id=83623&issue=1:2004).

Thomas, Sue. 1994. *How Women Legislate.* New York: Oxford University Press.

Thompson, Joel A., and Gary F. Moncrief. 1988. "Pursuing Pork in a State Legislature: A Research Note." *Legislative Studies Quarterly* 13, no. 3 (August):393–402.

———. 1994. "Nativity, Mobility and State Legislators." In *Changing Patterns in State Legislative Careers*, edited by Gary Moncrief and Joel Thompson. Ann Arbor: University of Michigan Press.

Van Assendalt, Laura A. 1997. *Governors, Agenda Setting, and Divided Government.* Lanham, MD: University Press of America.

Wahlke, John C., Heinz Eulau, William Buchanan, and LeRoy Ferguson. 1962. *The Legislative System: Explorations in Role Behavior.* New York: Wiley.

Willoughby, Katherine G. 2004. "Tax Revenues in 2004: Governors Look Inward?" *Book of the States, 2004.* Lexington, KY: Council of State Governments.

3

STRUCTURE AND PROCESS

In structure and process, every state legislature is alike—and every state legislature is different. In all but one of the fifty states, the legislature consists of two houses or chambers, a Senate and a House of Representatives or Assembly. The single exception is Nebraska, which has had a unicameral (that is, one-house) legislature since the late 1930s. All state houses of representatives are larger than their state's Senate (meaning that House members represent fewer constituents than their Senate counterparts). The size ratio between the two chambers is smallest in New Mexico, which has 42 senators and 70 representatives, and largest in New Hampshire, which has 24 senators and 400 representatives.

The ratio of constituents to legislator can significantly influence the way a legislator functions. The 40 state senators of California, each of whom represents a district population of almost 900,000, must go about their jobs quite differently than do the 400 members of the New Hampshire House, who collectively represent fewer than 1.3 million people (Rosenthal 2004). But California and New Hampshire legislators have the same ultimate responsibility—to represent and serve the interests of their constituents.

It can be argued that legislatures are the key to making democracy work, precisely because their members are elected by the people to serve as their representatives and agents, responding to their needs and wishes and addressing matters that affect their daily lives. Legislatures establish a process for the enactment of laws that provide for a free and orderly society. This process helps to ensure that funds from the public treasury are spent wisely and productively. It protects the people against abuse or deprivation of their basic human rights. And, most important, it serves as the ultimate restraint on the excessive exercise or abuse of power by a single individual.

A critical element of the U.S. system of representative democracy is a feeling by the people that they have a connection or linkage to their government. The key element of this linkage is the legislature, because the people elect its members to represent them and to make laws that will improve the quality of their lives. When a legislature effectively creates this feeling of connection, the people will see it as *their* representative assembly—a body that understands *their* problems, cares about *their* concerns, and enacts legislation in *their* interest (Jewell 1982).

If representative democracy means the people electing individuals to represent them and make public policy on their behalf, then the legislatures to which those individuals are elected, and the process by which those legislatures conduct their business, constitute the very core of the democratic process. The process by which a legislature makes law and develops policy is the foundation upon which it rests and, therefore, the single most important thing that it does. It is altogether possible to have an elected legislative body that does not conduct its business in a democratic manner. Such is the case, in fact, in a number of countries throughout the world. In these countries, the people feel no connection to the legislature, and representative democracy is a fallacy.

No matter how meticulously a legislature may design and craft the process for the conduct of its official business, how it structures and organizes itself will always be the determining factor in whether that process works effectively and is responsive to the needs and wishes of the people it represents. So, before examining the processes by which U.S. legislatures enact legislation and make public policy, it is necessary first to look at how they structure themselves, organizationally and managerially.

LEGISLATIVE STRUCTURE

It is assumed that for a private company to perform well it must be both well organized and effectively managed. Similarly, in government, no one ever questions the necessity for any of the governor's executive-branch agencies to be well managed and well organized if they are to carry out their responsibilities in an effective manner. However, because the primary responsibility of elected legislators is perceived as being to enact laws, people often lose sight of or downplay the importance of sound management and organization in legislatures. In actuality, the management and organization of a legislative body is the foundation upon which its capacity to make good laws and meet people's needs must be built. A sound managerial and organizational structure will no more guarantee an effective legislature than it will ensure the success of a corporation or executive-branch agency. But without good leadership, management, and organization, effective legislative performance will be virtually impossible (State Legislative Leaders Foundation 2005; Rosenthal 2004).

LEADERSHIP OF THE LEGISLATURE

When legislators are called upon to vote for or against a piece of proposed legislation, no member's vote counts more than that of any other member. In this sense, all members of a legislature are equal. But even a body of equals must have some hierarchy and managerial structure, a system of leadership and management. Certain individuals must be vested with authority to serve as its leaders—to preside over its deliberations, manage its budget, and coordinate its activities. Each legislative body therefore elects individuals from among its membership to serve as its leaders, and it vests these leaders with varying degrees of responsibility for management and coordination of its business and activities.

While democratic legislative bodies are unique entities, one area in which they are very much like an agency of the executive branch of the government—or even like a private business—is that their performance and achievements will be only as good as the quality of their leadership.

While the majority of U.S. state legislators still serve in their positions on a part-time basis, the operation of most of the legislative bodies in which they serve has, over the past thirty years, become very much of a full-time, year-round operation. Modern state legislatures are, with only a few exceptions, complex operations that require strong leadership and sound management to effectively meet the needs of the people they serve. But legislatures are unlike any other body or organization. They are organized and structured differently than any other agency of the government or any private business, and they require their own unique form of leadership and coordination.

LEADERSHIP HIERARCHY

Every state legislature selects leaders from its membership to organize and represent the body and coordinate its activities. Without such people in place, the legislature could not function effectively.

Presiding Officers: Presidents, Presidents Pro Tempore, and Speakers

The speaker of the House is the top institutional leader of the House of Representatives. The individual holding this position presides over floor sessions of the House and is usually viewed as the most powerful individual in a state legislature.

The top institutional leader of the Senate has the title either of president or of president pro tempore, but, in many states, top Senate leaders wield somewhat less power over the operations of their chambers than do the House speakers. The primary reason is that, in twenty-six states, the lieutenant governor serves as president of the Senate and presides over its floor sessions, as the vice president does in the U.S. Senate. Lieutenant governors who serve as president of their state's Senate can usually cast a tie-breaking vote. But with the exception of a few Southern states, they exercise no authority over the internal operation of the Senate. That power usually rests with a president pro tempore, who is a member of the Senate elected to the position by the chamber's membership; in some states, however, operational and managerial authority is shared between the president pro tempore and the chamber's majority leader. In the twenty-four states that do not have a lieutenant governor as their Senate president, the members of the Senate elect one of their members as president.

With rare exceptions, House speakers and Senate presidents or pro tempores are selected by the members of the majority political party in their respective chambers—although they are officially elected by a formal vote of the entire chamber—and, as such, they also serve as their party's leader in that chamber. The position of Senate president (or president pro tempore) or House speaker is almost never handed to a legislator. Legislators who are interested in those positions must seek them—usually by first impressing and then aggressively courting fellow legislators from their political party. While this can be done in many ways, it most often involves establishing an impressive personal record, first as an effective legislator and then usually as a leader in a lower-level leadership position such as deputy or assistant leader, a committee chair, or, most often, as a majority or minority leader.

While the public sees the Senate president or president pro tempore and the House speaker presiding over the floor sessions of their chambers, that is only the most visible of numerous responsibilities that rest upon the shoulders of the top leader of a legislative chamber. A Senate president or president pro tem or a speaker of the House serves as a sort of CEO for that chamber. This usually involves the following areas of responsibility:

- Appointment of deputy and assistant leaders and committee chairpersons, and oversight of those individuals in the conduct of their responsibilities;
- Development of the chamber's schedule for the transaction of business;
- Administrative management of their chamber and its staff and, in coordination with the top leadership of the other chamber, oversight of the legislature's nonpartisan staff and, usually, of its meeting and office facilities;
- Serving as leader and spokesperson of their party in their chamber and ensuring passage of party-supported legislation;
- Taking an active role in the political campaigns of their caucus, perhaps recruiting candidates, raising and dispensing campaign money, and developing an agenda on which candidates from their party can get elected; and,
- Maintaining ongoing communication links with the leadership of the other chamber, with the governor and the executive branch, with the minority leadership in their own chamber, with the news media, and with the public.

Like any CEO, the top leader of the legislature will ultimately be held accountable for everything that goes on under that leader's "watch." But like any other leader of a large organization, the individual in the top leadership position must have a cadre of capable and reliable deputies and assistants to attend to the myriad details that must be dealt with. Some of these are fellow legislators and some are appointed staff.

Floor Leaders: Majority Leaders and Minority Leaders

Directly below the presiding officer of each chamber is the majority leader. In the houses of representatives, the majority leader is usually responsible for steering the majority party's legislative program through the chamber. In those states in which the lieutenant governor presides over the Senate's floor proceedings, that responsibility may be

Women and Minorities Breaking the Glass Ceiling

While the proportion of women and minorities in positions of leadership is not on par with that of their male and white counterparts, they are making some strides. In 2005, some 45 of the 340 top institutional and party leadership positions (presiding officers, pro tempores, and floor leaders in each chamber) were female, including several in the key position in their chamber. In the Vermont House of Representatives, all three of the top posts (speaker, majority leader, and minority leader) were held by women, as was the speaker's post in Oregon and top leaders in Maine, Colorado, and Washington.

Ethnic minorities are rising to leadership as well. In 2003, thirteen of the legislative leaders were African American, including the Senate president pro tempore in Washington and Senate president in Illinois. Hispanic leaders played key roles in California and New Mexico as well, while one Asian leader served outside of Hawaii.

While women and minority leaders have a long way to go, they have come a long way.

divided between the president pro tempore and the majority leader, with the position of greater influence tending to vary from state to state—and within some states even from session to session, depending upon who occupies which position. Being from the same party, the president or president pro tem and majority leader (in the Senate) and the speaker and majority leader (in the House) almost always work closely together to marshal support for passage of their party's agenda in their respective chambers. Because most majority leaders are elected by the members of their party caucus, as are the presiding officers, they have their own independent bases of support within the caucus, and that can, on occasion, cause tension between these two individuals—because of common and potentially clashing aspirations for higher political office, or because of ideological differences. In a few states, the presiding officer appoints the majority leader, making such conflicts less likely.

The minority leader is the leader of the minority party in each chamber. The job can be every bit as demanding, but almost always far less personally satisfying, as that of the top leaders of the majority. The role and influence of a minority leader varies greatly from state to state and is dependent upon the proportion of representation enjoyed by the minority party in the chamber. When the majority party's margin of control over the minority is only a few votes, the minority leader has the potential to wield a great amount of influence every time there are a handful of defections in the majority caucus. When the majority party's margin of control is sizable, the minority leader's role will be much different and almost certainly less influential. It is not uncommon for the minority leader to be from the governor's political party. When that is the case, the minority leader will be expected to be the governor's spokesperson in the chamber. And, if the minority party has the necessary threshold of members to block the override of a gubernatorial veto, the minority leader will be expected to ensure that the chamber will remain veto-proof. When the governor is from the majority party, the minority leader's

---

Minority Leaders Have Varying Impacts

The job of the minority leader is one of the most varied in all of legislative politics. The nature of the position depends on the size of the legislative majority (is the minority party close to being able to win a majority of seats?), the party of the governor relative to that of the minority leader, the relationship between the minority leader and the leaders of the majority party, and the personality and political skill of the minority leader. In the Maryland Senate of the 1990s, Republican minority leader John A. "Jack" Cade was considered a part of the Senate leadership team, invited by the Senate president to sit in on strategy and agenda-setting meetings with leaders of the majority. Republicans held less than a quarter of the seats and did not control the governor's office, but Cade had a strong, positive relationship with Senate president Thomas V. "Mike" Miller. On the other hand, Democrat Dianne Byrum, Michigan's House minority leader during 2003–2004, was not invited to any leadership meetings of the Republican majority and was not privy to strategy or planning sessions in the chamber. Byrum helped to develop a Democratic agenda that was ignored by the House's Republican majority, and voiced the positions of a popular Democratic governor. Although Cade and Byrum both held the title of minority leader, their political environments, and therefore their jobs, were markedly different.

Source: Interviews with leaders in the Maryland Senate and the Michigan House of Representatives.

---

primary responsibility will most often be to serve as an articulate spokesperson for the loyal opposition, effectively making use of whatever influence he or she can muster to shape and modify the majority party's legislative program to the governor's liking.

Second Echelon Leadership: Deputy and Assistant Leaders and Whips

Below the top levels of leadership in each legislative chamber are an array of deputy and assistant majority and minority leaders and party whips. Whereas the presiding officer positions of Senate president, pro tempore, and House speaker are elected by the legislative chamber after being selected by their party caucus, and majority and minority leaders are elected by their respective caucuses, these second echelon leaders are usually appointed by the top leaders. The factors that go into these appointments include a member's strong legislative record and demonstrated leadership potential, a reward for support of the appointing leader in a caucus election, an effort to mend fences by reaching out to supporters of an opponent for the top leadership position, or an effort to build a geographically, ideologically, and ethnically diverse leadership team. In most states a second echelon leadership title carries a higher salary, and appointment to one of these positions is sometimes used as nothing more than a means of rewarding a loyal legislator with a salary increase.

Committee Chairpersons

In the view of many legislative experts and scholars, the most important leadership appointments made by the top leaders of the majority party are the chairpersons of the chamber's committees, because that is where so much of the detail work of the legislature takes place. It is in the committees where the intricate details of legislation are worked out, and a poor or ineffective committee chair can do irreparable damage to all of the majority party's program bills assigned to that committee. While rare, it is not unheard of that a leader will remove a committee chair in the midst of a legislative session. In 2003, for example, the speaker of the Georgia House of Representatives replaced two committee chairmen who refused to support the speaker's request that they release certain bills from the committees they headed.

LEADERSHIP SELECTION

As has been shown, legislative leaders are generally selected in one of two ways: election (by all members of the legislature or by the legislative members of the leader's party, although lieutenant governors who serve as Senate presidents may be selected by the voters), or appointment by the presiding officer, majority leader, or minority leader. The degree of influence and independence that a leader will have is directly related to the way in which that leader achieves a leadership position. A lieutenant governor who serves as Senate president and is elected by the public in an election independent of the governor has an independent base of support and autonomy not afforded one who was elected on a ticket with the governor. In a similar manner, a majority leader who is appointed by the presiding officer is in a very different position than one that was elected to the position by the members of the caucus (Jewell and Whicker 1994).

DID YOU KNOW?
A Whip Is on the Hunt

The title majority or minority *whip*, a leadership position found in many state legislatures, has an interesting history. In theory, the responsibility of a party whip is to ensure that members of the whip's party attend floor sessions and vote in accord with the wishes of their party's leadership. According to Random House (randomhouse.com), the term originated in the British Parliament and is said to stem from the term "whipper-in," the person who served as the assistant to the hunter in an English fox hunt. The responsibility of the whipper-in was to keep the dogs that were to lead the hunters to the fox together in a pack, using a whip if necessary. In most of the state legislatures that have leaders with the title of whip, responsibility involves a variety of activities assigned by the majority or minority leader.

Leaders Elected by the Public

The least common method of selecting legislative leaders is by public election. This occurs only with lieutenant governors who preside over their state's Senate. The public elects no other legislative officer. Of the twenty-six lieutenant governors who serve as president of their state's Senate, fourteen are elected independently of the governor, eleven are elected as part of a team with the governor, and one (in West Virginia) is a state senator elected by Senate members to serve as both its president and lieutenant governor.

Historically, lieutenant governors have often been quite powerful in their roles as president and presiding officers of state senates. But as state legislatures grew more professional and independent, Senate members came to want more control over their own leadership selection and, in all but a few states, stripped the lieutenant governors of all legislative powers not specifically assigned by their state constitution. In most cases, those assigned powers involve only presiding over Senate floor sessions and casting tie-breaking votes. By 2004, only six of the lieutenant governors who presided over state senates had the power to appoint the members of the chamber's standing committees, and only five had the power to assign bills to committees.

Leaders Elected by the Chamber or Their Caucus

In the twenty-four state senates that do not have a lieutenant governor as their president and in all state houses of representatives, the members of the legislative chamber elect the presiding officers. While any member of the chamber is eligible to seek and win the position, barring rare and unique situations of a tied chamber or a bipartisan coup, only members of the majority party are elected as presiding officer. Each political party usually nominates one of its members for the post of president or president pro tempore in the Senate and speaker in the House, although sometimes the minority party does not offer an opposition candidate. Members almost always vote for their party's nominee, thereby electing the nominee of the majority party.

Beneath the presiding officer level, most majority leaders and all minority leaders (sometimes referred to as floor leaders) are elected by the members of their party caucus and are not subject to votes of approval by the entire chamber. In a handful of chambers, the presiding officer appoints the majority leader.

While any member of the legislature is free to seek a leadership post, history suggests that some members will have a better chance than others of being successful. Experience is generally a prerequisite for a leadership position, with more experienced members generally getting the nod over less experienced members. Legislative experience not only gives a legislator time to understand the rules and the legislative process; it also provides the legislator with time to build the relationships necessary to put together a winning coalition among colleagues. And experience in a second echelon leadership position tends to be a prerequisite to election to a top leadership

---

LEADERS IN ACTION

A Rare Bipartisan Coalition Ousts a Presiding Officer

While presiding officers are almost always elected by their chamber on straight party-line votes, on a few very rare occasions, a presiding officer has been ousted through a bipartisan coalition of majority and minority party members. One of the most famous such occurrences took place in the Connecticut House of Representatives in January 1989. Democratic House speaker Irving Stolberg, who had achieved national recognition as president of the National Conference of State Legislatures (NCSL), was seeking an unprecedented third two-year term as speaker, which would end a long-standing Connecticut tradition of no one's holding the speakership position for more than two terms. Two days after the November 1988 election, Stolberg called a meeting of his Democratic caucus, which held an 88 to 63 majority, and was unanimously endorsed for a third term. Soon after the caucus, however, some recalcitrant Democratic House members who disliked what they felt was Stolberg's imperious leadership style and disagreed with his political ideology, which they found too liberal, confidentially approached House minority leader Robert Jaekle about the possibility of forming a bipartisan coalition to oust Stolberg when the House speakership election was held on the opening day of the new legislative term in early January. When the Democratic members suggested to Jaekle that their bipartisan candidate would be Richard Balducci, a low-key moderate Democrat well liked by Republicans, Jaekle indicated that he was receptive. After confidentially polling his caucus members, Jaekle informed the Democratic insurgents that he felt confident he could deliver all sixty-three of his members to the coalition.

Negotiations were held so confidentially that few, other than those directly involved in the planning, had any idea what was happening. Hardly anything appeared in the press, and Balducci surfaced openly as the alternative candidate only on the afternoon before the convening of the legislative session. On the following day, Balducci, pledging to stick to the two-term tradition that Stolberg was trying to end, was elected speaker by a vote of 94 to 57, with his support coming from 31 of the 88 Democrats and all 63 Republicans. Even though his caucus provided more than two-thirds of Balducci's votes, Jaekle refused to ask for anything in the way of a quid pro quo commitment from Balducci in return for the support of his caucus, arguing that he did not want Republican support for the new speaker to appear as part of a political deal.

A similar bipartisan coalition elected Joe Mavaretic speaker of the North Carolina House of Representatives over four-term incumbent Liston Ramsey in the same year.

Source: Jacklin, Michele. 1989. "Conservative Democrats Are Victorious in Connecticut House," *State Legislatures* 15, no. 4 (April); Christensen, Rob. 1989. "Growing Republican Ranks Help Topple Speaker in North Carolina," *State Legislatures* 15, no. 4 (April).

---

post. It is very rare indeed that a legislator elected as Senate president or president pro tempore, House speaker, or majority or minority leader has not previously held a lower-level leadership position (usually that of majority leader or assistant minority leader) (ibid.).

Successful candidates for top leadership positions suggest that their relationship with their fellow legislators was critical to their election to the post. Legislators will want to know and trust the person who will lead them. Once in a top leadership position, the leader's ability to provide campaign assistance to the party's candidates during elections has become an important component of success in recent years, with two-thirds of current leaders indicating in a recent survey of legislative leaders that such activities are an important aspect of their job (State Legislative Leaders Foundation 2004).

Leaders Appointed by Other Leaders

Finally, a few top-level legislative leaders are appointed by a higher-level leader in the chamber, almost always the presiding officer, majority leader, or minority leader. For example, House majority leaders are appointed by the speaker of the House in nine states, and six Senate majority leaders are appointed by their Senate president. The further one moves down the leadership hierarchy (deputy leaders, assistant leaders, whips), the more likely a leader is to owe his or her position to appointment by a higher-level leader—although in some cases, some deputy and assistant leader and whip appointments are subject to a ratification vote of their caucus.

When appointing members of their leadership teams, top legislative leaders generally look for three particular qualities. First, they want leaders who will be loyal to them and to the party. A leader that cannot be trusted is a problem waiting to happen. Second, leaders may be looking to gain the support of particular groups in the caucus, and appointing "one of their own" to leadership may help gain that support. A leader with moderate political views may appoint a floor leader or whip with more conservative views to gain the support of the conservatives in the caucus. Also, leaders often look to achieve regional, ethnic, or gender equity in making their appointments. They want their leadership team to be reflective of the makeup of their caucus.

TABLE 3.1   INSTITUTIONAL SPEAKER POWERS IN STATE HOUSES

Top Five		Bottom Five	
West Virginia	18.5	Hawaii	10.5
Indiana	18	Kentucky	10.5
New Hampshire	18	Washington	10.5
New York	18	North Dakota	7
Delaware	17	Wyoming	5.5

Source: Martorano, Nancy. 2004. "Distributing Power: Exploring the Relative Power of Presiding Officers and Committees in State Legislatures." Paper presented at the annual meeting of the American Political Science Association, September.

Note: Scale of power (0–30) includes determining leaders and members of, and assigning bills to, committees; having longevity as leader; and choosing who speaks about a bill and receives best offices and staff.

TABLE 3.2   INSTITUTIONAL PRESIDING OFFICER POWERS IN STATE SENATES

Top Five		Bottom Five	
Indiana	17.5	Nebraska	8
Maryland	17	Ohio	7.5
New Jersey	17	California	7
West Virginia	17	Hawaii	7
Tennessee	16.5	Michigan	6

Source: Martorano, Nancy. 2004. "Distributing Power: Exploring the Relative Power of Presiding Officers and Committees in State Legislatures." Paper presented at the annual meeting of the American Political Science Association, September.

Note: Scale of power (0–30) includes determining leaders and members of, and assigning bills to, committees; having longevity as leader; and choosing who speaks about a bill and receives best offices and staff.

LEADERSHIP STYLE AND MANAGEMENT

Obviously, top legislative leaders do not all exercise the same amount of control over their chamber's operations and activities. How much formal power and authority a House speaker, a Senate president or pro tempore, or a majority leader has depends primarily on two factors—the historical tradition and practices of their chamber, and the length of time that they have served in their leadership position.

The most time-consuming and demanding part of a top legislative leader's job is administrative management of the chamber and, in cooperation with the leaders of the other chamber, of the legislature as a whole. Very few legislative leaders possess the skill or experience to provide effective day-to-day administrative management in the large, often chaotic, and sometimes volatile environment of a legislature. And for those few who do, the demands are so great and varied that they can almost never allocate the time required for daily administrative management and also tend to their other duties.

Because most legislative leaders are not inclined to get bogged down in the details of legislative administration, and because they also recognize the importance of focusing their attention on the consideration and enactment of legislation in their chambers, they almost always tend to delegate the demanding and time-consuming responsibility for administration of the legislature's budget and supervision of its staff to a staff member. In states such as Massachusetts and New York, where the top legislative leaders are considered among the most powerful in the country and where, by tradition, almost all staff is partisan (that is, responsible for working exclusively for either the majority or minority party), the leader's chief of staff will usually fill this role, with the minority party having its own, smaller-size staff that are exclusively responsible and loyal to the minority leader and the minority party. In those states, the top

Senate leader and the House speaker retain much tighter control over staff operations than do leaders in states with traditions of large nonpartisan professional staffs that serve both legislative houses. In this latter category—the Connecticut, Iowa, and Wisconsin legislatures are prime examples—staff supervision and legislative administrative responsibility often are assigned to a nonpartisan professional (or to several such individuals) who is appointed by a committee of leaders (sometimes including nonleader members) from both chambers. Staff managers who fill these roles almost always enjoy a considerable degree of autonomy in how they operate and generally see their primary allegiance as being to the legislative institution rather than to either political party. In states with such a nonpartisan staff tradition, the administrative and managerial power of the top leaders is more dispersed and much less centralized than in states in which all staff is partisan.

Highly personalized exercise of legislative leadership authority has been the long-standing practice and tradition in only a handful of state legislatures. In Massachusetts, New York, and Texas, the top legislative leaders maintain a tight reign over the administration and management of their chambers, both directly and through loyal assistant leaders and staff. In the past, the most extreme examples of highly personalized leadership control were found in several legislative bodies in the Deep South, where, until the late twentieth century, Democrats enjoyed one-party dominance. The South Carolina legislature until the mid-1970s and the Mississippi House of Representatives until the mid-1980s were two of the most extreme examples. The longer an individual occupies a top leadership position, the more power and influence that leader can be expected to acquire and exercise over the chamber. Even in states without traditions of highly personalized leadership styles, leaders have often, by virtue of longevity in their position, evolved into such a style. That was the case during portions of the 1970s, 1980s, and early 1990s in the California Assembly and the Ohio and Maine houses of representatives, each of which had a speaker who remained in his position for an extended period (Rosenthal 1998).

During the late 1980s and through much of the 1990s, the voters of a number of states adopted—almost always through a voter-initiated referendum—limitations on the number of terms that an individual may serve in their legislature. The most restrictive of these term limits are in the states of Arkansas and California, where senators are limited to a lifetime maximum of two four-year terms and House members to three two-year terms. These limitations, and the somewhat less stringent ones in other term-limited states, have severely hampered the ability of legislative leaders in those states to become effective leaders of their chambers. In states such as Arkansas and California and others with only slightly less restrictive limits, the top legislative leaders must, of necessity, ascend to their positions after only one or two sessions of service. Then, having achieved their positions, they are forced to preside as lame duck, single-term leaders over chambers composed of largely inexperienced and politically unsophisticated members, all of whom know that the ends of their tenures of service are also rapidly approaching. While voters have expressed their support for term limits in the states

Georgia House speaker Tom Murphy, a Democrat, holds his gavel as he watches from the speaker's chair in the House in Atlanta, March 19, 1998. Murphy was defeated for reelection to the House in 2002, after almost three decades as speaker. (AP Photo/John Bazemore)

that have them, very few legislators who have had the experience of serving under these conditions express support for them (Drage Bowser et al. 2003).

Even in states without term limits, top legislative leaders are finding it increasingly difficult to remain in their positions for extended periods of time. Those who are successful have done it by working with, rather than dictating to, their members. When the voters of his district turned Georgia House speaker Tom Murphy out of office in 2002 after more than forty years in the state House of Representatives, the last twenty-eight as its speaker, it likely marked the end of extended leadership tenures of extremely powerful leaders. While a few top leaders may remain in their positions for lengthy periods (the president pro tempore of the Indiana Senate in 2005 was first elected to the post in 1981), neither voters nor modern legislators are likely to accept the heavy-handed tactics or centralized leadership of some past leaders. More and more, state legislators are determined to pursue their own agendas. They find themselves increasingly able to generate their own support and raise all or most of the money they need to fund their reelection campaigns, and do not require assistance from the top leaders of their chambers to get elected or reelected. Moreover, their personal agendas may include moving upward into top leadership positions, and such ambitions will hardly make them supportive of lengthy tenures for those occupying positions on which they have set their sights (Rosenthal 1998).

THE QUALITIES OF AN EFFECTIVE LEGISLATIVE LEADER

Clearly, the leadership of a legislature takes many forms. But, for all their many styles, all legislative leaders have the same basic responsibilities and the same ultimate goal of leading their chamber in the enactment, revision, or repeal of laws that will improve the quality of the life of the people they serve. So, there must be certain qualities that are found to varying degrees in almost every successful legislative leader. But what exactly are they?

There is no precise way to define what constitutes an effective legislative leader. As has been shown, a Senate president or president pro tempore and a House speaker serve as a sort of CEO for the chambers they lead. But a democratic legislature is an entirely different entity than a private corporation, and the qualities that contribute to making a private-sector CEO successful are not necessarily those that make for an effective legislative leader. Perhaps the most important difference between a legislature and a private corporation is that a legislature, unlike a corporation, has an organized opposition whose leaders have as their goal the replacement of the majority leadership—or at the least a reduction in the size of its majority in the next election.

Each legislative body is unique. It has its own personality, its own traditions, its own special practices, and not least its own members. To successfully lead a legislature, a leader must acquire an understanding of the uniqueness of the body's institutional traditions and practices and then determine how his or her personal strengths, skills, and style can be most effectively mobilized and applied. But it is important in doing so that the leader feel completely comfortable with that leadership style. Those who try to transform themselves into something that they are not are almost never successful leaders.

While a legislative leader's style must be compatible with the traditions of the legislative institution, certain qualities are clearly of vital importance to any individual who hopes to lead a body of elected representatives effectively. One respected academic authority has suggested eight qualities and characteristics as being vital to the success of a legislative leader: competence, adaptability, firmness, openness, fairness, tolerance, patience, and stamina (Rosenthal 1981). Slight variations should be added and combined with two of these qualities—flexibility with adaptability, and decisiveness with firmness. And two additional qualities—a combination of honesty and dependability, and humility—should be added to the list. These ten qualities will almost always be evident, to varying degrees, in every successful legislative leader.

Competence

Legislative leaders are selected by their colleagues to lead them because they have demonstrated clear evidence of leadership ability. To be effective in their positions, leaders must, through their performance, demonstrate to those who elected or selected them that their support and trust has been well placed. Leaders must possess a thorough understanding of the workings of the legislative process and an ability to make that process work in behalf of the legislature's constituents—the people who elected them. They must establish solid working relationships with other leaders, committee chairs, and key staff, and must be aware at any given time of the contents, status, and prospects of key legislation. Finally, effective legislative leaders recognize the importance and necessity of setting aside sufficient time in their schedules to tend to the administrative management of the institution.

Flexibility and Adaptability

Legislative leaders must recognize that, in an institution as dynamic as the legislature, circumstances and conditions are in a constant state of flux. An effective legislative leader is always flexible and prepared to reassess and reconsider a previously determined course of action. When circumstances change, the leader is then able to adapt to the new conditions quickly, and adjust tactics and strategies.

Firmness and Decisiveness

As important as it is for legislative leaders to be flexible and adaptable, it is equally important that they be able to act firmly and decisively when circumstances require. Leaders are required and expected to make many decisions and, when they make them, to stand firmly behind those decisions and demonstrate to their colleagues the expectation that they will accept and abide by them. A successful and effective legislative leader must have the respect of the members of the legislative chamber. If a leader is viewed as indecisive, such respect will prove difficult, if not impossible, to attain.

Honesty and Dependability

Effective legislative leaders are honest and forthright with members of the legislature, with the news media, and with the public. When there is bad news to be delivered, whether to colleagues or to the public, a leader must do so in an honest and forthright manner. Likewise, it is often said that a politician is only as good as his word, and that a good legislative leader will take promises made to colleagues with a sense of full obligation. Members must be made to feel that they can depend on their leaders to be completely honest with them. They must feel confident that when their leader makes a commitment to them, that commitment will be honored, and that if they make a request that cannot be granted, they can depend on the leader to clearly tell them so.

Openness

Effective legislative leaders build strong communication links between themselves and the members of the legislature. An effective leader must know at all times what all members of the body are thinking, what is important to each of them, the outside pressures to which they may be subjected, and how they feel about the most important issues before the legislature. Establishment of this communications link requires that a leader take the initiative in reaching out to all members of the legislature, asking both their opinions and their advice, recognizing and making use of their special skills or talents, and letting each member of the body know that the leader's door is open to them.

Fairness

Because all legislative leaders are members and representatives of their political parties, they will, quite appropriately, feel an obligation to use their leadership positions to further the agendas of their parties. But a leader of the legislature has an even greater obligation to the legislature as an institution. Members of the legislature are there because they received a majority or a plurality of the votes in their district. An effective legislative leader will recognize this fact, treat each member of the body fairly, and accord respect and consideration to each member's personal views and priorities. A leader who does this can expect to be viewed by all members of the legislature as a legitimate leader of the institution and can anticipate respect and institutional support from all members, regardless of their party affiliation.

Tolerance

U.S. legislative bodies are inherently "democratic" institutions whose top leaders are in positions of "first among equals." Legislative leaders lead by persuasion, not by dictate. Good leaders understand and accept that members will not be able to support them 100 percent of the time because, on some issues, members of the body may be subject to pressures from their political parties or their constituents. Effective leaders convey this understanding to the members of the legislature and are selective concerning issues on which they attempt to exercise their authority and influence in order to gain support.

Patience

Legislative experts often point out that the deliberative process in a democratic legislature is inherently slow and inefficient. Because the leaders of such a body are essentially leading a group of equals, they are not in a position to force fellow legislators to do something they do not want to do. Legislative leaders must rely on persuasiveness, negotiation, and cajolery to be successful. Progress is always slow in a legislative body. An effective leader accepts this as a by-product of the democratic process and recognizes those times when it is necessary to be patient. A patient leader is always open and available to fellow legislators to discuss any concerns that they might have.

Humility

Effective leaders accept responsibility for their mistakes and do not try to assign blame to others. They display a genuine interest in the views and opinions of their colleagues and constituents. And they do not flaunt the power of their position. Those who do usually antagonize other members of the legislature (including, quite often, those from their own political party) and are seldom treated kindly by the news media; more often than not, they find their stature diminished.

Stamina

A leader of any organization—and certainly one who leads a body of elected legislators—must project a high energy level. An effective legislative leader will take care to convey the image of a dedicated, committed, informed, and hard-working individual who is prepared to lead the legislature—for however long it may take and in whatever ways may be required—in successfully addressing those issues that are of greatest concern to the constituency it serves.

LEGISLATIVE COMMITTEES

It is precisely because a legislature is comprised of a large and diverse group of individuals—each of whom is ultimately accountable to a unique constituency, each of whom possesses knowledge of particular issues, and each of whom has special personal interests and concerns—that it is so ideally suited to carry out its basic responsibility to be responsive to the will and needs of the people it serves.

But the very size and diverse nature of a legislature—elements so vital to democracy—make it impossible for it to exercise its basic functions effectively and tend to the myriad details it must address while acting as a body of the whole. A division of labor is necessary. Given that reality, all state legislatures (and virtually every legislative and parliamentary body in the world) make use of a system of committees as the most effective means by which to discharge their responsibilities. An effective committee system helps a legislature to perform its role as the people's guardian and the protector of their democracy in five specific ways (Ogle 2004). First, committees allow a legislative body to perform several functions simultaneously. These include the careful review of multiple pieces of proposed legislation, the oversight of executive administration and performance, and the examination of special governmental problems.

Second, a legislative committee serves as a screening mechanism for the full legislature by "weeding out" those bills not deemed worthy of consideration by the full chamber. The vast majority of bills that are introduced in a state legislature are not passed and, in fact, never proceed beyond the committee stage. They either die in the committee or, in the handful of legislatures that require their committees to send all bills to the floor of one of its chambers, they die through a committee recommendation that they not be passed. The New York legislature, for example, passed only 693 bills out of 16,892 introduced in its 2002 session. The New Jersey legislature passed only 134 of 5,004, the Hawaii legislature only 263 of 2,249, and the New Mexico legislature only 128 of 900. While some other legislatures have higher rates of enactment, they rely just as much on their committees to carefully review and "weed out" their bills (Council of State Governments 2004).

Third, a committee's deliberation and review process is usually conducted in a much less formal manner than that of the full legislature and allows for an informal discussion and exchange of views among members. This informality creates an environment in which compromises and technical improvements in the details of legislation can be more easily negotiated and agreed to than in a floor session of the full body. It is, in fact, most often in these long, drawn-out meetings of a legislature's committees, not during floor sessions of its Senate or House, that the real details of legislation are worked out.

Fourth, committees enable legislators to acquire a thorough understanding of matters within the jurisdiction of those committees on which they serve. This helps to develop an institutional expertise within the legislature on specific issues. And that, in turn, strengthens the legislature and better enables it to hold executive departments and agencies accountable for their performance.

Finally, committees provide a vital link between the legislature and the public through public meetings and hearings that are covered by the news media and, in some instances, are open to participation by the citizens. Public hearings, in particular, provide a venue for committee members to acquire public input on legislation and to build support for subsequent decisions by the full legislature. Press coverage of these sessions also contributes to greater public awareness and understanding of issues and of the workings of the legislative process.

The Variety of Legislative Committees

Legislative committees are subgroups of legislators that meet regularly to consider legislation, public policy, and internal management issues, but not all legislative committees are the same. They have different purposes, memberships, and permanence. Legislative committees take several forms. They vary according to whether they include members from one or both chambers, whether they review bills, whether they are engaged in oversight of the executive branch or internal management of the legislature, whether they are temporary or permanent, and whether they have the power to make recommendations to their chamber or legislature.

Standing Committees

Standing committees are the most significant and most common of the various types of legislative committees. Standing committees screen and review the bills introduced in their chambers. In all but three of the forty-nine states that have bicameral legislatures, the Senate and House each has its own standing committees that are composed only of members from that chamber. The Connecticut, Massachusetts, and Maine legislatures use joint committees in which Senate and House members sit together, rather than on separate, single-house committees.

In most states, standing committees are authorized to "kill" bills—that is, to decide that they are unworthy of further consideration by the legislature—and make recommendations to their legislative chamber concerning passage or rejection of others. Committee meetings to discuss the specific details of bills, often called "mark-up" sessions, are—in the view of many experts—the very core of the U.S. legislative process.

Standing committees are established for the term of a legislature, although some states limit their activity to periods when the legislature is meeting in regular session. Their areas of responsibility will usually rather closely parallel the basic functional divisions of the state's executive branch. Virtually every bill introduced in a state legislature must be reviewed by a standing committee before the entire body can consider it. The assignment of bills to committee is a responsibility of either the chamber's presiding officer or of a committee of members most or all of whom are appointed by the presiding officer.

The power and authority of standing committees vary from state to state. As indicated, most legislatures allow their standing committees to "kill" a bill in the committee by determining that it is not worthy of consideration. In some legislatures, particularly with the largest numbers of bill introductions, this is the fate of the vast majority of bills. In every state legislature, standing committees make recommendations to their chamber concerning which of the bills assigned to them they feel should be passed, passed in amended form, or rejected. In some states, committees have the power to rewrite bills and send them to the floor of their chambers for consideration in the rewritten form. In others, they must send the bill out in its original form and ask the full chamber to approve the committee's recommended amendments by formal vote.

TABLE 3.3   INSTITUTIONAL COMMITTEE SYSTEM POWER IN STATE HOUSES

Top Five		Bottom Five	
Hawaii	11	Indiana	4
Tennessee	11	North Dakota	4
Texas	11	Pennsylvania	4
Florida	10	Kansas	3
Montana	10	Massachusetts	3

Source: Martorano, Nancy. 2004. "Distributing Power: Exploring the Relative Power of Presiding Officers and Committees in State Legislatures." Paper presented at the annual meeting of the American Political Science Association, September.

Note: Scale of power (0–17) includes receiving, screening, and shaping legislation; gathering information; and influencing passage of bills.

TABLE 3.4   INSTITUTIONAL COMMITTEE SYSTEM POWER IN STATE SENATES

Top Five		Bottom Five	
Florida	10	New York	4
Tennessee	10	Massachusetts	3
Louisiana	9	North Dakota	3
Utah	9	Vermont	3
Arizona	9	New Hampshire	1

Source: Martorano, Nancy. 2004. "Distributing Power: Exploring the Relative Power of Presiding Officers and Committees in State Legislatures." Paper presented at the annual meeting of the American Political Science Association, September.

Note: Scale of power (0–17) includes receiving, screening, and shaping legislation; gathering information; and influencing passage of bills.

The degree to which a full legislative chamber follows a committee recommendation tends to vary by state—and within states even by individual committee. Committee recommendations for the passage of bills in the Ohio, Maryland, Kentucky, and Oregon legislatures have, historically, almost guaranteed passage, with more than 80 percent of the bills reaching the floor with such a recommendation being approved (Rosenthal 1998). On the other hand, in states in which committees cannot "kill" bills and are required to send all bills referred to them to the floor of the chamber, committee recommendations may not carry as much weight. They also tend to be disregarded to a greater degree in states with legislative term limits because the constant turnover hinders the development of expertise within committees, and because legislators who do not serve on a particular committee are often eager to make their mark and have neither the desire nor the institutional respect to defer to the committee's judgment.

Joint Committees

While the Connecticut, Massachusetts, and Maine legislatures are the only legislatures that operate with joint standing committees for the review of their bills, many legislatures make use of joint standing committees for such matters as review of the budget and revenues, legislative management and administration, audit and performance evaluation of executive branch agencies, or review of executive agency regulations. The Wisconsin Joint Committee on Finance is charged with reviewing the budget requests of the governor and the executive agencies. The Mississippi Joint Committee on Performance Evaluation and Expenditure Review is responsible for conducting legislative oversight of executive branch administration. The Maryland Joint Committee on Children, Youth and Families works to coordinate state efforts to improve the health, education, safety, and economic well-being of children in Maryland and oversee the operation of all pertinent agencies. The Michigan Joint Committee on Administrative Rules oversees administrative rules proposed by state agencies. As with standing committees, members of joint committees are appointed by the top leaders of each chamber.

Conference Committees

For a bill to become law, both legislative chambers must approve it in identical form. When the two chambers pass a bill with differing language or provisions, the standard practice is to establish a joint conference committee composed of members of each chamber to try to resolve the differences. Conference committees are the most temporary of legislative committees, existing only to deal with the disposition of a single bill. If the members of a conference committee are unable to resolve the differences and come up with language satisfactory to a majority in both chambers, the bill dies. Conference committees are appointed by the presiding officer, with minority members sometimes appointed by the minority leader. Committee members often include the legislator-sponsors of the bill and the chairs of the standing committees who reviewed the bill in each chamber.

Although conference committees are charged with resolving the differences between two versions of a bill, they do not always do so. Sometimes they never meet, or they meet without having any intention of reaching a resolution. Most legislators, for example, do not like legislative term limits, which have been generally supported by the public. If bills to establish term limits were to be passed by both houses of a legislature but with different limitations on years of service, legislators could vote for their chamber's version (thereby appearing supportive of the popular concept) while knowing full well that the differences will not be resolved in a conference committee and that the bill will not become law.

Special or Select Committees

While standing committees exist for the term of a legislature, special or select committees are established for a brief, specified period within a term. Unlike standing committees, select committees are usually charged with addressing a single matter. Responsibility may involve a policy matter that is felt to require more in-depth review than can be undertaken by the standing committee under whose jurisdiction legislation on the matter would normally fall. Or it may involve an investigation of wrongdoing. The speaker of the Texas House of Representatives, for example, created a Select Committee on Public School Finance during the 2003–2004 term to examine how the state could comply with a court-ordered revision in school funding. In 2004, the Connecticut House of Representatives created a special committee to investigate allegations of wrongdoing by the state's governor. Most special or select committees are charged with providing their chamber with recommendations based on their examination of the assigned matter, with any bills that are proposed as a result of those recommendations usually assigned to the standing committee having jurisdiction over the matter in question.

State representative Johnnie Byrd, Jr. (center), chairman of the House Select Committee on Electoral Certification, Accuracy, and Fairness, listens to testimony during a hearing on whether the Florida legislature should pick its own slate of electors for president of the United States, December 2000, at the state capitol in Tallahassee. (AFP/Getty Images)

Interim Committees

In the more relaxed and less intense atmosphere that exists during interim periods when a legislature is in recess, members of legislative committees have more time to examine problems in depth and to engage in less politically charged discussion of proposed legislation. Some states permit their committees to meet without restriction during interim periods. But in some of the states that place constitutional limits on how long their legislatures are authorized to meet in regular session, standing committees are established only for the duration of each session of the legislative term and do not function during interim periods. In such states, it is generally the practice to create interim committees to meet between sessions to review particular problems or develop recommendations or proposals for the next regular session.

Depending on the practice and traditions of a particular legislature, interim committees may include members from only one or from both chambers. In some cases they are established by resolution of the full legislature prior to the adjournment of its regular session, while in others they are appointed by a constitutional or statutory joint legislative council or legislative research commission that usually includes the top

---

DID YOU KNOW?
Some Committees Are Not Supposed to Work

While the vast majority of standing committees in state legislatures meet regularly and are charged with revising and passing legislation to the floor, most state legislatures have at least one committee that seldom meets and is not expected to review legislation for passage. Every effective legislative leader has at least one committee to which legislation can be sent with the understanding that it will never be voted on or reported out. In many states, that committee has some general name like "Government Affairs" or "State Affairs," so that the leader can claim that any bill may appropriately be sent there. This is a "painless" way to kill legislation that the leaders or the members do not want to have to vote on.

---

leaders of each chamber and is charged with responsibility for coordinating legislative activities during periods when the legislature is not meeting in regular session.

It is during the less demanding and less tension-filled interim periods when legislatures are not meeting in regular sessions that their members are afforded the greatest opportunity to develop a broader and deeper knowledge and understanding of issues; standing or interim committees offer the ideal vehicle for this. However, all but a handful of U.S. state legislatures are considered part time, and most of their members are forced to supplement their meager legislative compensation through private-sector employment when their body is not meeting in regular session. Therefore, few state legislative bodies are able to derive anywhere near full advantage from their interim periods in terms of the extensive standing or interim committee activity that could prove so beneficial to them and to their members.

LEGISLATORS IN ACTION
Standing Committee Meetings Dominate Legislative Day

Schedule for Representative Paul Luebke, North Carolina House of Representatives

May 3, 2005
8:30–10:00: Finance Committee meeting
10:00–11:00: Return phone calls, e-mails
11:00–12:00: Education Committee meeting
12:00–1:00: Environment and Natural Resources Committee meeting

1:00–1:45: Meeting with representatives from governor's office
2:00–3:00: Education Committee meeting
3:00–4:15: House session
5:30–6:30: Reception hosted by NC Council of Community Programs
7:30: Return home

Source: E-mail from Representative Paul Luebke, May 4, 2005.

Committee Structure and Organization

There is no optimum number of standing committees for a legislative chamber. At one end of the spectrum are the 99-member Wisconsin House of Representatives with 42 committees and the 52-member Mississippi Senate with 35. At the other end is the 47-member Maryland Senate with 6.

A number of factors influence how many committees a legislative chamber will have. These include the number of members in the chamber, chairperson commitments that the top leaders have made to their members to secure their support for their leadership position, and the structure of the government's executive branch. Legislators generally express a preference for a smaller number of committees, which helps to minimize conflicts in their meeting schedules, and for jurisdictions that parallel the basic organizational structure of their state's executive branch, which also helps to ensure that all legislation pertaining to a particular executive department will be assigned to the same committee.

Since the beginning of the nationwide legislative modernization movement in the 1960s, committee organization has always been a primary point of focus of organizations and individuals proposing improvements in legislative organization and process. Responding to such calls and pressures, almost every state legislature has undertaken at least one, and often several, examinations of its committee system. Most of these reviews have resulted in findings that concurred with the thinking of both the majority of legislators and of those groups and organizations that had been urging organizational restructuring—specifically, that existing committees should be consolidated and reduced in number, that adjustments should be made in individual jurisdictions to make those jurisdictions more closely parallel the responsibility parameters of executive departments and agencies, and that controls should be placed on when committees are permitted to meet so as to lessen conflicting demands on members' time. Legislatures that have implemented such findings have almost always found that they have improved committee operations and led to a more thorough and productive examination of proposed legislation.

Committee Size and Membership

The number of members who serve on a committee can be a crucial factor in its ability to deliberate effectively. Legislative leaders recognize that to provide an atmosphere conducive to an informal exchange of views and information among committee members, the size of a committee should be kept within reasonable limits.

In most legislatures, the partisan division of a committee's membership is rather closely reflective of the strength of the two political parties in its chamber.

Committee Procedures

Most state legislatures use *Mason's Manual of Legislative Procedure* as a supplementary guide for procedures that are not specifically covered by their own adopted rules. The manual states that the rules of procedure of the full legislature should also be the rules of procedure for its committees insofar as those rules are applicable to committee activities.

Mason's Manual cautions, however, that floor session rules that place limitations on debate or discussion should be relaxed in committee to allow for a maximum of free discussion and exchange of ideas and views, because such frank exchanges will contribute to improvement in the quality of legislation. According to *Mason's*, common floor session rules that are not beneficial to the committee process and should not be required in committee proceedings include the following:

- A requirement that the chairperson vacate the chair to speak on motions;
- A motion to close or limit debate;
- A requirement that a motion be seconded;
- A limitation on the number of times that a member may speak on the same question; and,
- A requirement that a member stand to address the committee.

Each of these represents a relaxation of the more formal debate procedures used on Senate and House floors, and is designed to encourage committee members to engage in informal and open-ended discussions of the contents of the various bills referred to their committee.

A number of legislatures try to minimize meeting and attendance conflicts for their members by placing controls on when their committees can meet. For several years, the Connecticut General Assembly has separated its committees into two groups—those permitted to meet only on Mondays, Wednesdays, and Fridays, and those permitted to meet only on Tuesdays and Thursdays. To further minimize conflicts, members are then assigned to no more than one committee in each grouping. A few other legislatures have adopted variations of this practice, such as permitting certain committees to meet only in the morning and others only in the afternoon. Many legislatures prohibit their committees from meeting when their chamber is meeting in floor session.

It is a generally accepted principle in the United States that citizens have just as much right to attend and directly observe the deliberations of their legislature's committees as they do its floor sessions. Thus almost every state legislature permits public and news media attendance at all of its committee sessions, except for rare instances involving sensitive personnel or investigative matters.

Committee Hearings

All state legislative committees hold hearings, but they are used far more extensively in some states than others. Committee hearings take two forms. In the Congress, information hearings are the practice. These involve receiving testimony from invited experts who are asked to appear before the committee to provide information on issues under consideration, or from cabinet officials who appear to explain and defend their agency's activities and record. In state legislatures, public hearings are the much more common practice. Public hearings have three primary purposes. First, they offer all interested citizens, regardless of whether they have knowledge and expertise about the subject matter of a bill, an opportunity for direct input into the legislative process. Second, they provide a vehicle through which committee members can gauge public sentiment about a bill or bills under their review. And third, they open an avenue for a dialogue and an exchange of ideas and views between legislators and their constituents on issues before the legislature.

Information hearings can be a highly useful tool for any legislature. But they have only limited value to the body in terms of their ability to help it reach out to the public and establish that all-important linkage by actively engaging the people in the legislative process. Public hearings, on the other hand, enable private citizens to participate in the process by speaking directly to the members of a committee concerning matters under its consideration. This enables citizens to feel that they have a venue through which their voices and viewpoints are being heard by their elected representatives (Ogle 2004).

If the benefits that members of a legislature derive from public hearings were to be measured simply in terms of new information on legislation under consideration, it would be difficult to justify the amount of time that many state legislatures spend on them, given their hectic schedules. But, as indicated, their value involves far more than just the acquisition of information.

Particularly in recent years, a number of legislatures have concluded that they can derive maximum value from the public hearing process and reach as many constituents as possible, by "taking the legislature to the people" and moving some of their committee hearings to various locations around their state. This practice has enabled more citizens to participate in the process and has helped to enhance a perception among citizens in all corners of the state that their legislature has a genuine interest in their thoughts and concerns. More recently, some legislative committees have begun taking advantage of modern technology by using closed circuit systems to allow citizens to present hearing testimony from multiple locations simultaneously.

Committees as a Tool for Oversight of the Executive Branch

Second only to working out the details of legislation, the most important activity that a legislature's committees can undertake as a service to its constituents is the exercise of effective oversight of the executive. Under the U.S. "checks and balances" system of

LEGISLATURES AND THE PUBLIC
Citizen Participation in Committee Public Hearings

Many citizens are uncertain of what they need to do if they would like to offer testimony at a public hearing held by a committee of their state's legislature. Most legislatures have some type of public information service that is listed in the telephone directory that can provide a citizen with information on which committee has been assigned a particular bill and when that committee might be holding a public hearing on it. In addition, many newspapers, particularly those in capital cities, print committee meeting and public hearing schedules at least once a week.

And one's senator or representative, who can always be located in the telephone directory or through a call to the legislature, will be pleased to provide a constituent with assistance in finding that information. Some committees ask citizens to sign up in advance if they want to testify at a public hearing, but they seldom prohibit a "walk-in" from offering testimony (although that will usually require the individual to wait to testify until the committee has heard from all who have signed up in advance). Because of time constraints, most committees find it necessary to place a time limit on individual testimony; thus it is best to prepare and time remarks in advance, rather than speaking extemporaneously. Committees will always be pleased to accept additional written materials from citizens who testify before them.

government, legislatures, acting primarily through their committees, are expected to exercise three basic responsibilities with regard to oversight of their executive branch:

- to hold those who exercise executive power accountable for their decisions and actions;
- to make certain that public funds are being spent effectively and in accord with the legislature's intent; and,
- to ensure that the governor and other executive branch officials are properly administering the laws enacted by the legislature, and that those laws are accomplishing their intended purpose.

A legislative committee has an array of oversight tools at its disposal. Probably the most useful and effective is its ability to hold the governor and the governor's department heads accountable for their performance by calling them to appear before the committee to explain and defend their administration and performance.

Every state legislature provides some staff support to its committees, and committee staff can play a major role in helping a legislature to ensure that executive branch agencies are accountable to it. Particularly in legislatures like those of California and New York, which provide substantial staff support to their committees, staff members can make a significant contribution to executive oversight by developing working relationships with counterpart staff in the executive agencies. Through such contacts, committee staff can acquire important information that, once passed on to committee members, will expand their knowledge and understanding of the agency's internal operations and performance. When executive branch officials are scheduled to appear before a committee, staff assistants can help the chairperson and members to frame careful, probing questions that will enable the committee to derive optimum benefit from this special opportunity to elicit information and to make the officials account for their actions.

As important as the oversight function is to a successful checks and balances system, committees recognize that their consideration of bills must take precedence at certain points in the legislative cycle. It is primarily during interim periods—when the legislature is not meeting in regular session, or during session periods when committees are not under pressure to complete the review of large numbers of bills—that they can focus on executive branch oversight. Members of legislatures whose committees make effective use of these periods can be expected to have the most thorough understanding of the internal workings of executive departments and agencies and be best equipped to make informed decisions on legislation relating to those agencies and departments.

LEGISLATIVE STAFF

Members of a state legislature have neither the time nor the specialized skills to undertake the countless support tasks that must be performed with expertise and competence for the legislature to respond to the needs of its constituents effectively. In addition to managerial, administrative, and clerical support, a legislature needs legal and research analysts to help it draft and critique bills, fiscal experts to help it analyze and revise budgets, information technology specialists, librarians, committee staff, staff to assist the political parties or caucuses, and personal staff assistants for members.

Legislative staff fall into three categories: nonpartisan staff who serve all members of the body and whose loyalty is to the legislative institution; party, or caucus, staff who work only for members of one political party and whose primary loyalty is to that party; and, personal staff, who work for a specific legislator and whose primary loyalty is to that legislator.

Scholars of the U.S. legislative and political process have long argued that nonpartisan support staff is the first essential ingredient necessary for a legislature to establish institutional strength as an independent and coequal branch of the government. They point out the importance of skilled professional managerial staff to manage the body's administrative operations and to free up the legislature's leaders to focus their attention on the consideration and enactment of legislation. They further point out that nonpartisan professional research staff can provide members with an independent source of objective and accurate information upon which to evaluate and question executive branch proposals, and with which to develop meaningful alternatives to those proposals when it is found appropriate.

While nonpartisan staffs are most important from the standpoint of a legislature's ability to operate as a coequal partner to the governor in designing public policy, partisan staff enable the legislature to organize effectively on a political basis by providing the majority and minority parties with needed structural support. Personal staffs are the most popular with individual legislators, because they provide them with the most direct assistance in carrying out their responsibilities and in helping them establish a favorable image to present to the voters at the next election.

A movement began throughout the United States in the late 1960s to strengthen and modernize state legislatures in order to enable them to serve as independent and co-equal partners with the executive branch in the policymaking process. Much of the focus of that nationwide movement involved a major expansion of staff services.

Legislative staffs are organized in many ways. Some years ago, the National Conference of State Legislatures conducted an examination of staffing patterns in the fifty state legislatures and found eleven distinct organizational structures, no two of which were exactly the same (National Conference of State Legislatures 2002). The differences are just as great today as they were at the time that survey was undertaken, if not greater. While there is no single preferred manner of organization, it is important that a legislature's staff be organized—first, to respond most effectively to its particular and oftentimes unique processes and activities, and, second, to provide for clear chains of command, with ultimate accountability to the top legislative leaders.

A Functional Breakdown of Legislative Staff Services

As has been shown, staff assistants must perform a whole host of functions and services for members of a legislative body if that body is to perform its responsibilities in an effective manner. Staff service functions can be categorized in various ways, but they most logically break down into eight basic groupings: managerial, document production, and record-keeping; information technology; legal and bill drafting; research and library; budget, fiscal, and audit; committee staff; party and caucus staff; and personal staff (Ogle 1998).

Managerial, Document Production, and Record-Keeping Staff

The critical importance of having competent professional managers to handle a legislature's day-to-day administrative affairs for its leaders cannot be overemphasized. Acting on behalf of the leaders of one or both chambers, these managers or professional administrators manage the legislature's operating budget, personnel administration, meeting and office facilities, and building security. In some states, bipartisan legislative management is the practice, and the top leaders of both parties appoint a nonpartisan executive director or manager to oversee the managerial and financial operation of the entire legislature. The Connecticut General Assembly operates in this way, with all legislative operations including the entire legislative budget under the control of a joint management committee that, chaired by the Senate president pro tempore and the speaker, appoints a nonpartisan executive director. Legislative bodies that operate in a manner similar to Connecticut, but with slightly less centralized control, include Maine, Nevada, Ohio, and Wisconsin. In many states administration is handled in a more diffuse and more partisan manner, with the chief of staff of the presiding officer of each house serving as the chief administrative officer for that chamber. The New York Senate and Assembly operate in that manner.

Document production and record-keeping services are provided by an Office of the Clerk (in many legislatures, the House chamber official is referred to as the clerk of the House and the Senate official as the secretary of the Senate). The clerk is most often elected by the chamber membership, although usually upon nomination of the leader of the majority party. Even when a clerk has a partisan or political background, that clerk is expected to operate in a nonpartisan (or, at least, bipartisan) manner, providing equal service to all members of the body regardless of party affiliation. Clerks' offices are usually responsible for the printing of all bills and official documents, and for the compilation of an accurate and permanent historical record of all proceedings and official actions taken in the chamber. In some legislatures, particularly in states of the Deep South, the clerk is quite powerful and may even have some authority beyond that of document production and record-keeping. In several Northeastern state legislatures, on the other hand, the clerk can be a fairly minor staff figure who serves only on a part-time basis, providing general direction for a full-time clerical staff.

Information Technology Staff

State legislatures have consistently been well ahead of the Congress in utilizing information technology to streamline and upgrade their documentation, record-keeping, and bill drafting processes. In the initial stages of this development, information technology staffers were often assigned to House and Senate clerks' offices. But, as development expanded and became more sophisticated, most legislatures recognized the importance of exercising close supervision and control over their information technology activities to ensure that systems are designed to provide the types of information and documentation that the members most need and want. Today, most legislatures have separate departments or units of information technology and also have partisan staff to maximize use of the information systems within each party caucus.

Legal and Bill Drafting Staff

A legislature's primary activity involves law—adopting it, repealing it, revising it, and amending it. For that reason, staff members trained in the law are an essential support ingredient in every legislature. Legal staff draft bills and amendments to bills and provide legal research and counsel to leaders and members. The most important service provided by legal staff is that of bill drafters. Bill drafting staff are almost always nonpartisan. In the Congress, the Senate and House of Representatives each has its own nonpartisan bill drafting office. But bill drafting services in state legislatures are almost always provided by a central, nonpartisan office that services both chambers. Almost all legislatures require that a bill be drafted, or at least reviewed for proper legal form, by its bill drafting office. Such a requirement ensures uniformity in legislation and serves as a protection against errors caused by inconsistent format. Bill drafting is a special art within the legal profession, and in recruiting bill drafting staff, legislatures generally look not just for individuals trained in the law but also for lawyers with specific training and experience in the writing of legislation—if possible in specialized areas of focus.

Several legislatures also provide that their drafting office or a separate nonpartisan office undertake comprehensive revisions or rewrites of obsolete or antiquated sections of law, although in every instance any such revisions are prepared only in proposal form and are subject to approval by the full legislature.

Research and Library Staff

Accurate objective information is a vital resource for every elected representative. It helps a legislator to cast knowledgeable and informed votes and to develop meaningful alternatives to executive branch or government proposals. Legislators who want to examine issues seriously require assistance from independent professional researchers to provide them with this needed information. Likewise, a legislative library can provide highly useful information, especially because such a library will focus upon the collection of materials that are of particular interest and concern to the members of the body.

Nonpartisan professional researchers are a vital ingredient in the work of a legislative body. Their special value is that their exclusive allegiance and loyalty is to the legislature, and their sole motivation is to provide its members with accurate and objective information. Among the many highly regarded nonpartisan state legislative research offices are those of the California, Colorado, Connecticut, Maryland, New Jersey, Ohio, and Wisconsin legislatures.

Budget, Fiscal, and Audit Staff

The power of the purse is the most important power of a legislative body. And a state legislature's enactment of the state budget is almost always the most important enactment in every legislative session.

Few state legislators have the ability or the specialized training to undertake analysis of a detailed budget plan of billions of dollars. Even those few who possess such expertise do not have the time to pore carefully through the hundreds or thousands of pages of numbers in a complex budget document. For that reason support staff are absolutely essential if members are to cast informed votes on the budget, even when those votes figure to be in support of the governor's proposals.

Some large-state legislatures rely almost exclusively on partisan staff to assist them in analyzing the state budget, with both the majority and minority party having their own assistants. The New York legislature has a sizable number of partisan staff assistants assigned directly to its Senate and Assembly fiscal committees. But other large states, such as California, have partisan staff attached directly to its budget and tax committees, as well as a nonpartisan fiscal research office. The Florida legislature attaches nonpartisan staff directly to its fiscal committees, while the Arizona, Connecticut, Maryland, New Jersey, Ohio, and Wisconsin legislatures have respected nonpartisan fiscal bureaus that service both chambers. Still other legislatures operate like the

Indiana General Assembly, which does not have a separate nonpartisan fiscal office but, rather, includes fiscal and budget experts within its nonpartisan research office.

In almost every legislature, votes on the state budget bill or bills usually break down rather strictly along party lines. When the party of the governor controls both legislative chambers, the budget will usually be close to what the governor has recommended to the legislature. However, when at least one chamber is not controlled by the governor's party, the budget that emerges from the legislature will usually be a negotiated compromise document. But, regardless of such political factors, the more expert the legislature's budget and fiscal staff, the more capable it will be of seriously considering alternatives to executive branch proposals and the more likely it will be to do so.

Legislative audit staff serve a fiscal function different from that of budget review, but one no less important. The legislative audit function is a key aspect of the checks and balances system under which the legislature conducts oversight and examination of executive branch performance and holds the governor and agency officials accountable for their actions. Legislative audit staff are almost always nonpartisan professionals who conduct either fiscal audits in which they review agency books and records for legal and regulatory compliance or performance audits that involve in-depth examination of executive branch programs to determine whether they are accomplishing their objectives. In the latter area, the Virginia General Assembly has long been recognized as having an extremely effective nonpartisan performance audit office.

Committee Staff

State legislatures use a variety of approaches, both nonpartisan and partisan, to provide staff support to their committees. The California and Florida legislatures assign staff directly to their committees. While officially labeled as nonpartisan, these staff provide the bulk of their services to the committee members of the majority party. The New York legislature follows the congressional model, providing each of its committees with both majority and minority staff. In the majority of legislatures, committee staff are provided through a nonpartisan central research office or offices. Among the many states that use this approach with notable success are Colorado, Connecticut, Indiana, Iowa, Kentucky, Maryland, Montana, New Jersey, Ohio, Oregon, Utah, and Wisconsin.

Party or Caucus Staff

Most state legislatures have at least a small number of party staff that serve their majority and minority caucuses. The loyalty of these staff members is to their political party—that is, to the members from their party in the legislative chamber for which they work—rather than to the legislature as a whole. The responsibility of caucus staff that serve the party in the majority is to help the members of their caucus to publicize their accomplishments and to help them create a record that will enable the party to retain its majority. If their party is in the minority, the staff's responsibility is to help their members to create enough public doubts or criticism about the majority's record to enable their party to capture control of the chamber—or at least to increase their party's minority representation in the next election.

The activities of party or caucus staff usually involve the development of party policy positions, research on issues from a political or partisan perspective, and speechwriting. Where members do not have personal staff, the party or caucus staff may also assist them with press releases, constituent services, and clerical assistance. Many legislatures, particularly those of medium-size or small states that lack sufficient resources to provide their individual members with personal staff, have developed strong caucus staffs to provide these services on a pooled basis.

Personal Staff

Depending on their areas of specialty, personal staff provide legislators with clerical, speechwriting, and constituent service assistance. They may also undertake research assignments, prepare press releases, and design and write constituent newsletters. Legislators' personal staff members feel a kinship and responsibility to the legislator they serve rather than to the full legislature, or even to their legislator's caucus. Individuals filling these positions sometimes have a personal friendship of long standing with the legislator and may have their jobs for that very reason. But even if that is not the case, staff members who work directly for a specific legislator know that their personal reputation (and possibly their future) is likely to depend in large part upon the performance and success of that member.

Many legislatures do not provide personal staff for their members but, instead, provide the equivalent of personal staff-type services to their members through centralized caucus staffs that are under the direction of the presiding officer or minority leader or their personal chief of staff. Of those state legislatures that do provide personal staff to members, the number is very small—usually only one or two per legislator—and often

---

DID YOU KNOW?
You Could Work for the Legislature

Most state legislatures operate a student internship program to provide expanded staff support for their members. Internship programs are conducted through a partnership arrangement between the legislature and the state's universities and colleges, which are almost always eager and enthusiastic about the prospect of offering a unique educational opportunity to their students while also providing the legislature that authorizes their budget with information and research assistance. Student interns usually receive course credit for their work and are sometimes provided with a small stipend to cover their travel costs between the university and the capitol. In some states, legislative interns may receive their entire semester's credit for their internship and function as full-time staff members for the legislators or legislative office to which they are assigned. While student interns are no substitute for permanent expert staff, they provide a valuable supplementary source of assistance at a very modest cost.

these individuals serve only part time. Notable exceptions are the California and New York legislatures, whose members have well-staffed offices in both the capital and in their districts.

THE LEGISLATIVE PROCESS

Clearly, a state legislature requires a rational structural makeup if it is to be a policy-making body capable of addressing the myriad problems and issues that affect the people it represents. But to address these problems effectively, a legislature must have sound processes and procedures for the consideration and enactment of legislation and must mobilize its structural capability in support of those procedures.

It is to what is known as the legislative process that focus now shifts. The path by which a bill moves from an idea to enactment as law is long and complex, and it is driven, and controlled, by a combination of both formal rules and procedures and informal practices and traditions.

The Bill-Consideration Process

While the formal process by which a bill moves from an idea to becoming law will have some unique qualities in each legislative body, the basic outline is the same in all fifty state legislatures. The U.S. lawmaking process consists of seven primary steps, with each step comprising several components. To see how this process varies from state to state, see the state summaries in Chapter 6.

Bill Introduction and Assignment

The initial step of the legislative process in every legislature is the formal introduction of a proposed law, or bill. This is done in accord with specific procedures prescribed by the legislative body, but it almost always entails a legislator putting the proposed law into written form and submitting it to the office of the clerk of the chamber in which that legislator serves. Most legislatures require that bills be drafted (that is, written) by professional bill drafting attorneys who put the bill sponsor's ideas into correct legal language.

Legislators receive ideas for bills from numerous sources—personal concerns, constituents, journalists, lobbyists, party leaders, family members. But only a member of the legislature may introduce a bill—although any citizen can certainly request and encourage a legislator to introduce one. Lobbyists, in particular, do this with regularity.

After a bill has been filed with the clerk of the chamber, it is assigned to a standing committee for review. With the exception of a few states, the presiding officer assigns (or refers) bills to committee. While the committee assignment of most bills is routine and logical, based on rather clear committee jurisdictions, presiding officers can sometimes choose between two or more committees that might have reasonable jurisdiction. A bill dealing with education funding for science and math curriculum might reasonably go to the Education Committee (which deals with education curriculum), the Finance Committee (it will require funding), or the Science and Technology Committee (it deals with science courses). In such a situation, the presiding officer would have some discretion in deciding the committee to which the bill will be referred. The bill will most likely be referred to the committee that the presiding officer feels most confident will deal with it in the manner that officer prefers.

Committee Review of Bill

Once the bill has been assigned to a committee in the chamber of its introducer (or in the Maine, Massachusetts, or Connecticut legislatures, to a joint committee), the committee has jurisdiction over the bill. Often, it will hold a public hearing to receive citizen and expert input on the bill and its contents (in a few states, a public hearing is mandatory). After receiving as much information as it feels it needs to render decisions on the bills assigned to it, a committee holds a series of meetings to discuss their contents in detail, sometimes going through some bills sentence by sentence, to determine their fate. Some states refer to these as mark-up sessions. It is these sessions that mark the very heart of the committee process, and, some would argue, of the entire legislative process. A legislative committee has a number of options available to it in these meetings. They generally include:

- *"Kill" the bill.* While a few legislatures require that every bill be voted on by the committee and sent to the floor of the legislature for consideration, the majority allow bills to die in committee by the committee's either taking no action on them or by rejecting ("killing") them through a vote of the committee members. In fact, that is the fate of most bills in that majority of legislatures that do not require their committees to send every bill to the floors of their chambers. Many of the states whose committees are empowered to kill bills have what is called a discharge procedure under which a bill that has been rejected by a committee can be discharged from the committee and brought to the floor of the chamber for consideration through a petition signed by a majority of the chamber's members. But this procedure is seldom used, because the time frames for circulation of the petitions are usually very narrow, and the leadership of the majority party, a number of whose members would have to sign the petition if it is to receive the required number of signatures, is usually capable of exerting enough pressure either to keep their members from signing the petition or to convince the committee chair and members to vote to send the bill to the chamber floor by conventional means.
- *Send the bill to the floor of the chamber in its original form with a recommendation that it be passed.* Sometimes the majority of a committee's members will find the contents of a bill fully acceptable as introduced. In such cases, the

committee will vote to report (recommend) to the chamber that the bill be passed without change.

- *Send the bill to the chamber with a recommendation that it be approved in an amended (altered) form.* Most often, when a majority of the members of a committee approve of a bill's concept, some of that majority will see a need for some amendment to its contents. Some of those proposed amendments will often be incorporated into the bill. In such instances, the committee will favorably report the bill to their chamber with a recommendation that it be approved in its amended form. In some states, bills may be rewritten in committee and sent to the chamber in their revised form, while in others committees are required to send bills to the chamber in their original form and recommend approval of any committee-approved amendments by the full chamber. In legislatures in which committees are authorized to rewrite bills without submitting their amendments for approval by the full chamber, the bill is usually given some designation, such as "substitute bill," to alert the chamber that the committee has amended it from its original form.

- *Send the bill to the chamber without bias.* In some states, committees have the option of sending a bill on to their chamber for consideration without offering any recommendation for passage or rejection. They make no judgment regarding the quality or desirability of the legislation, but simply give the members of the chamber the opportunity to vote for or against it.

- *Send the bill to the chamber with an unfavorable recommendation.* In a few states, committees have the option of sending a bill to their chamber with an unfavorable report, which is a recommendation that the chamber reject the bill. Committees seldom take such an action, even in states in which they are required to report all bills to the floor, and it is almost unheard of in states in which committees are not required to send all bills to the floor. Generally, if a majority of a committee's members believe that a bill should not be passed by the body, they will vote either to kill the bill or agree to take no action on it in the committee. On rare occasions, a committee will report a bill with an unfavorable recommendation, often because a well-respected member of the committee has asked that it be allowed an opportunity for consideration by the full legislative chamber. When a bill comes to the floor of its chamber with an unfavorable report, a majority of the chamber's members must vote to reject the committee's unfavorable report before the bill can be discussed and voted upon.

Floor Action

Once a committee has sent a bill to the floor of the Senate or House, the decision on the bill's fate rests with that chamber. The chamber has four options available to it:

- *Pass the bill.* Because the majority party in the chamber also has a majority of the members in each of its committees, committee recommendations tend to

---

LEGISLATURES IN ACTION
Reconsideration of a Bill (Play It Again!)

The rules of procedure of almost every state legislature require that the Senate and House keep bills in their possession for a short period of time after their passage (usually one day) to allow them to be reconsidered by the chamber. A motion to reconsider can be offered only by a member who was on the prevailing (winning) side of the vote, and it can be offered only while the bill is still in possession of the chamber. Limiting reconsideration motions to legislators from the prevailing side prevents those on the losing side from using the procedure as a delaying tactic. If a motion to reconsider is approved, the bill reverts to the status it had when it came out of committee and is redebated by the chamber. Most legislatures allow a bill to be reconsidered only once.

---

be accepted by the chamber. A committee favorable report means that a bill was supported by a majority of the committee's members, and most legislators will trust the judgment of the committee members from their political party. The most common action that a legislative chamber takes on a bill favorably reported by one of its committees is, therefore, to approve the bill, although some portions may be changed through amendments approved during the course of debate on the chamber floor.

- *Table the bill.* One of the procedures unique to the legislative process is the concept of laying the bill "on the table." Technically, this means that rather than voting on the bill at that time, it will be "laid on the table" for consideration at a later time. But in reality it means that it is highly unlikely that the bill will ever be removed from the table and reconsidered. Rather, it will be left there to die a painless death without coming to a vote. While bills can be removed from the table for reconsideration, a motion to do so usually requires an extraordinary majority (60 percent, or two-thirds of the membership), which can be almost impossible to attain. Tabling a bill allows the bill to die without anyone having to be recorded as voting no. That is particularly useful in the case of bills that might be popular with the public but opposed by a majority of a legislative chamber as bad public policy.

- *Defeat the bill.* The least common occurrence on the floor of a legislative chamber is the outright defeat of a bill—its rejection by a majority vote. That is rare because the chamber's majority party will rarely reject the recommendation of a committee, a majority of whose members are from the majority party. Effective majority party leaders understand the embarrassment and danger to their leadership that can result from having a bill favorably reported by a committee defeated on the floor of their chamber. So the majority leaders will usually counsel their committee chairpersons to take measures to keep bills from coming out of their committees when they do not feel confident that there is enough support in the full chamber to ensure their passage.

- *Take no action on the bill.* While a few chambers require that all bills reported out of committee to be voted upon on the floor, most do not. In the states that do not require their chambers to discuss and vote on every bill, it is not uncommon for some bills to receive no action on the floor. Sometimes this may occur because leaders have belatedly concluded that they cannot muster enough votes for passage, while at other times it may be a result of the chamber's just not having sufficient time to debate and discuss every bill prior to a constitutional or legal adjournment date.

To Other Chamber

Enactment of a bill into law requires its passage in both chambers (except in Nebraska's one-house unicameral system). Once a bill has been passed in the first chamber, it must undergo the same consideration and review process in the second chamber. In all but four states, this means that a bill must be referred to a committee in the second chamber and go through the same review process that it went through in the first chamber. The only exceptions are Nebraska and the three states—Maine, Massachusetts, and Connecticut—that have joint committees and send the bill directly to the floor of the second chamber after passage by the first. Usually, the bill review process takes place in sequence—completed in one chamber before moving to the next. There are occasions, however, in which a legislator in each chamber introduces the same bill, and the bill may be considered in each chamber concurrently.

Passage of a bill by one chamber is no guarantee of its passage in the other. State senates and state houses of representatives are often very different. They have different leaders, different terms (in thirty-four states, senators serve four-year terms and house members two-year terms), their members have different constituencies, and sometimes their respective majority parties are different (in 2003–2004, eleven of the forty-nine bicameral legislatures had different party control of each chamber).

In legislatures in which the chambers are not under the control of the same party, it is not uncommon for each house to pass bills supported by special interest groups that tend to favor the chamber's majority party, even though the bill has no chance for passage in the other house. Such actions serve as an assurance to the interest group that the majority party continues to have its interests at heart—and allows it to blame the other party for blocking passage of the bill.

Conference Committee

Given the many differences that can often exist between the two houses of a state legislature, it is not at all uncommon that a bill is approved by each chamber but with different wording or provisions. If different versions of a bill are approved and neither chamber is willing to adopt the other's version, a conference committee comprised of members from both chambers is appointed to try to come up with a compromise version that can be adopted by each house. A conference committee has three options available to it:

- *Propose a compromise bill.* If the members of the committee can come up with a compromise bill that a majority of the committee members from both houses agree on, they send a conference committee report that includes a redrafted version of the bill to each house. If both approve the conference committee version of the bill, the bill moves to the next stage. If either house fails to support the compromise bill, it can go back to the committee, or to a new conference committee for a further attempt at an acceptable version. Alternatively, the leaders of the two chambers may conclude that further attempts at agreement will be fruitless and allow the bill to die.

- *Meet but fail to reach a consensus on the bill.* Members of the conference committee may meet but fail to reach a compromise on the two differing bills. Conferees (members of the conference committee) are chosen to represent the members and positions of their respective chambers, and they may find that the two bills are just too different to find a middle ground. If that is the case, they will report their inability to reach agreement to their respective chambers. The chamber leaders may appoint another conference committee to try again to work out a compromise, but they are more likely to take no further action and to let the bill die.

- *Never meet to consider the bill.* Sometimes conference committees never meet, and the bill dies without being returned to the two chambers. That outcome may be because the legislature's leaders do not want the bill to become law and the conference committee offers a convenient way kill it, or it may simply be that so many bills are passed in the last weeks, days, or even hours of the legislative session that there is insufficient time for the conference committees to meet and consider the bills.

To the Governor

Finally, if a bill makes it through the challenging and complex legislative process, it goes to the desk of the governor for final consideration. With the granting of the veto to the governor of North Carolina in 1996, all fifty states require that a bill that has been passed by their state's legislature be sent to the governor upon final passage. There are several actions available to a governor with regard to a bill that has been passed by the legislature:

- *Sign the bill.* By far the most common response of governors is to sign a bill, thereby making it a law of the state. With the rare exception of a few partisan or politically charged situations, the vast majority of bills are signed into law by governors with little or no comment.

- *Veto the bill.* If a governor disagrees with a bill, the governor can refuse to sign, or veto, it in which case it does not become law. Most states require their governors to accompany a veto with a veto message explaining why they have decided not to sign the bill into law. While gubernatorial vetoes are relatively rare, they are most likely to occur where there are partisan differences between the legislative and executive branches. In Maryland, Illinois, and New York, where the governor's party was in the minority in at least one legislative chamber in 2003, the governors issued 72, 105, and 153 vetoes, respectively. But that is unusual. In that same year, the governors in thirty-eight states each vetoed fewer than twenty bills (Council of State Governments 2004).

- *Sign the bill, but veto specific portions of it.* In forty-three states, governors are empowered to veto parts of a bill while signing the remainder of the bill into law. The nature of what is called the line-item veto varies from state to state, but governors utilize it most often with regard to provisions of bills that appropriate funds for the operation of the government. Some states limit the line-item veto to only such bills, but about half of the states grant their governors this power on all legislation.
- *Allow the bill to become law without signature.* In most states, a bill becomes law if the governor fails either to sign or to veto it. A governor may allow a bill to become law in this way if the governor does not support the legislation but realizes that it has the support of the people, or if an agreement has been made with a legislator not to veto a particular bill, even though the governor does not support it.
- *Effectively veto the bill by not signing it into law.* In a minority of the states, a bill does not become law if it is not signed by the governor. Governors who have this power may take this action either because they oppose the bill but have some reluctance to cast a veto on it, or because they know that the bill, vetoed or not, will be repassed by the legislature; they may feel that repassage will be less politically and personally embarrassing to them if they are not associated with having formally vetoed the bill.

Final Legislative Action

While the governor signs the vast majority of bills passed by the legislature into law, there are usually a few in every legislature that the governor vetoes. When a bill is vetoed, the legislature has the option of letting the veto stand, in which case the bill does not become law, or attempting to repass it and override the veto. To override a gubernatorial veto, most states require that a bill be repassed in each chamber by extraordinary majorities of between 60 percent and two-thirds. Securing such majorities is not easy, because members of the governor's party are usually reluctant to oppose their governor in such an embarrassing way.

Veto overrides occur most often when the party of the governor is in a substantial minority position in both legislative chambers. But every once in a while, there is a bill about which legislators feel so strongly that even members of the governor's own party will turn their backs on their party leader and support an override. One of the most remarkable veto overrides of the last century occurred in Connecticut in 1969. In that year's legislative session, the General Assembly, which was weak and ineffective and under the domination of the state's party organization leaders, passed a bill to provide for a comprehensive reorganization and modernization of its internal operation. Legislators were caught by surprise when the bill, which was strongly supported by all so-called good government groups, such as the League of Women Voters and the Citizens Conference on State Legislatures, was vetoed by the Democratic governor. In a state in which a veto override was almost unheard of, it was assumed that this would be the end of the matter. But a new breed of legislator that had come to the General Assembly as a result of the Supreme Court's "one man, one vote" decisions was not about to roll over and let the governor dictate how the legislature should organize itself and conduct its business. Legislative leaders of both parties united their forces in support of the bill, and even though the governor's party enjoyed margins of more than two to one in each chamber, the veto was overridden by a unanimous vote in each house—something that had never happened before, and has never happened since, in Connecticut.

The lawmaking process is long and cumbersome. If a bill is defeated at any stage of the process, it does not become law. The path to enactment is made all the more difficult in that a bill must pass through all the steps of the process during a single one- or two-year legislative session. If it fails to do so, it must be reintroduced and begin the process anew.

Formal Rules and Procedures

Each legislature adopts rules that provide for the specific procedures by which it conducts its business. Most legislatures have joint rules that apply to both of its houses, with each chamber having additional chamber rules that have application only to its internal operation. Legislatures also have standardized procedures that they must follow for the documentation of their official actions. And, finally, every state has laws that prescribe what constitutes unethical conduct by their legislators in the performance of their official duties.

Rules Governing the Consideration of Legislation

A legislature's rules of procedure generally spell out in very precise and specific detail how it must consider proposed legislation. While each legislature's rules of procedure are unique and tailored to the legislative and political practices and traditions of the state, they almost always address the following:

- When and how members may introduce bills;
- Committee jurisdictions and authority;
- Deadlines by which committees must complete review of bills referred to them; and
- Procedures for the consideration of bills and the transaction of other business on the Senate and House floors.

Joint rules must be adopted in identical form in each chamber, with each house adopting its own chamber rules. In states that operate primarily with joint committees, the joint rules are likely to be more extensive and detailed than the single-chamber rules.

There is no single, ideal set of rules for the transaction of legislative business. But all legislatures recognize that, to operate with maximum effectiveness, certain provisions are essential. Ample time must be allowed both for committees to review and examine the contents of the bills assigned to them, and for the full chambers to consider those bills favorably reported by the committees. And it is a basic tenet in all democratic legislative bodies that the minority party is afforded the right to debate majority proposals fully and to present and debate alternatives to those proposals.

Documentation of Official Actions

The maintenance of a comprehensive and accurate record of a legislative body's official actions, and as much as possible of the details of its deliberations, is a vital element of the democratic process. Such documentation creates a permanent historical record of the decisions made by a legislature. And a carefully documented record of actions and deliberations helps to clarify legislative intent for current administrative and enforcement officials and for future legislatures. For those reasons, every state legislature has specific procedures for the creation and maintenance of its official records. In most states, these procedures include requirements for the creation and maintenance of a permanent record of each of the following:

- A copy of every bill introduced;
- A record of all official actions, and of all individual legislator votes taken on those actions, on the floor of either chamber;
- A printed verbatim transcript of all Senate and House sessions (or a complete audio- or videotape transcript of each session);
- Minutes of all committee meetings, and in some states, a record of all individual roll call votes taken on the final disposition of a bill in the committee; and
- Written or audiotape transcripts of all testimony presented at committee hearings.

In recent decades, computerized information systems have greatly assisted state legislatures in their design of comprehensive and efficient documentation and record-keeping systems that, in earlier years, they were forced to maintain through less mechanized and more labor intensive means. Modern technology has clearly facilitated the documentation and record-keeping process and has allowed state legislatures to provide future generations with more comprehensive and more accurate records of their activities and decisions.

Legislative Ethics and Conflicts of Interest

All members of a state legislature are under constant scrutiny by the news media, by their political opponents, and by a whole array of other interested groups and organizations. Under such a public microscope, even the appearance of an improper action can do serious, and sometimes irreparable, harm to an individual legislator's reputation and to the public's confidence in its legislature.

It is seldom difficult for a private citizen in everyday life to distinguish correct and appropriate behavior from behavior that is incorrect and inappropriate. But in the complex world of a state legislature, whose members are regularly called upon to make decisions that have great impact on other people's lives—and, in doing so, are subjected to an array of conflicting pressures—there are numerous times when what is appropriate or inappropriate behavior is far from clear. It is particularly in those "gray areas" that legislators require guidance in the form of laws that define parameters for acceptable conduct. Legislative ethics laws prescribe clear and specific standards and guidelines that clarify for legislators what constitutes proper and improper behavior, both in the performance of their official responsibilities and in their nonlegislative activities as private citizens.

There is no set model of ethical standards for all legislative bodies, or even for all state legislatures. Each legislature must tailor its ethical provisions to its state's political culture, traditions, and practices. There are, however, certain guidelines that are included, although in varying forms, in almost every state's legislative ethics laws. These would include the following:

- Disclosure by each legislator of personal and business-related interests and the sources (but not specific amounts) of private income received by themselves, and in some states also by their spouse;
- Voluntary disqualification by a legislator from voting on (or advocating passage or defeat of) any proposed legislation, the passage or defeat of which would result in the legislator's (or a member of the legislator's immediate family) deriving special personal benefit;
- Disclosure of the sources of all campaign contributions to a political party, to a member of the legislature, or to a candidate for election to the legislature;
- Establishment of limits on how much a lobbyist may spend on entertaining any individual member of the legislature (in recent years, a few states have tightened their restrictions in this area to the point that a legislator is prohibited from accepting even so much as a free cup of coffee from a lobbyist); and,
- A means for determining and assigning penalty or punishment for violation or abuse of any of the code's provisions and guidelines.

In addition to these basic provisions, which are found in almost all states, each state addresses various other aspects of ethical behavior that it considers important in maintaining citizen confidence in the integrity of its legislature and its processes. Among the most common are legislator orientation in ethics and conflict of interest laws, which more than forty states include in their orientation programs for newly elected legislators. Thirty-seven states place a limit on the size of financial contributions that individuals, political parties, and political action committees can give to a legislative candidate's election campaign. Twenty-seven states place restrictions on legislators receiving and lobbyists giving campaign contributions when the legislature is in session. Twenty-five states have what are called "revolving door" laws that prohibit legislators from becoming paid lobbyists for a certain period of time after they leave the legislature; nineteen of the states for one year and the other six for two years. Nineteen states either statutorily or constitutionally prohibit, or at least restrict, the relatives of legislators from being compensated with public funds for performing work for the legislator. And twenty-three states prohibit their legislators from accepting an honorarium if it is offered in connection with their official duties (National Conference of State Legislatures 2002).

Informal Rules of the Legislative Process

While a legislature's formal procedures officially control its operations and processes, every legislative body also operates under a series of informal procedures and rules that serve as unofficial guidelines or parameters concerning proper and acceptable conduct. These informal rules are, in their own way, as important as its formal rules in determining a legislature's success or failure, because they directly influence how business is transacted, how decisions are made, and how legislators relate to and with one another.

While the special and sometimes unique traditions, mores, and political culture of a state will dictate some of its legislature's informal rules, there are several rules that are pretty much universally accepted as part of the U.S. legislative process (although, even then, local culture and tradition will determine their relative importance and how strictly members are expected to adhere to them). These include the following:

Your Word Is Your Bond

The first rule of legislative politics is that when a legislator makes a promise or commitment to a colleague—be it to support a bill the colleague has sponsored, to support the colleague in a bid for a leadership position or for another elective office, or to refrain from actively opposing an issue supported by the colleague—that promise should be as "good as gold." Legislators who break their word to fellow legislators or, worse, develop a reputation as being consistently unreliable or undependable quickly lose the respect of their colleagues and are often ostracized. They lose any chance of ever ascending to a leadership position within their chamber, and can almost never be effective lawmakers.

While this rule applies specifically to legislator relations with fellow legislators, any legislator who comes to be viewed by constituents, executive branch officials, or reporters as someone who cannot be relied upon in this way is also almost certainly doomed to ineffectiveness and ultimate failure.

Treat Fellow Legislators with Courtesy and Respect

Legislators are expected to treat one another with courtesy and respect befitting a colleague who has been elected to the legislature. They are expected to address each other respectfully in public, and particularly on the floor of the Senate or House. They are expected to refrain from publicly embarrassing or offending colleagues and to avoid personalizing disagreements on policy issues. Serious personal differences are expected to be ironed out privately, preferably out of view and earshot of colleagues, reporters, and the public.

Do Not Try to "Rock the Boat" Immediately upon Entering the Legislature

The old adage that children are to be seen but not heard also applies to newly elected state legislators. Many first-term (freshman) legislators arrive at their state capitol with a heady feeling, knowing that their constituents have chosen them as the person they want to represent them and serve as their spokesperson. But they are quickly humbled by the realization that every member of their chamber has arrived there under the same circumstances. And, just as quickly, it becomes clear to them that they have a great deal to learn about the intricacies of how the legislative process works and how to master it. It is usually suggested to freshmen legislators, either directly by the leaders of their party caucus or more subtly by their colleagues, that new members of the body are expected to listen more and talk less while they learn the process and earn the respect of their chamber's veteran members. In those states that have adopted term limits on how long their legislators may serve, first-term members are increasingly finding this informal rule to be unrealistic and outdated.

Do Not Try to Appear an Expert on Every Issue

With the host of issues that a modern state legislature must address, it is impossible for any individual member to become an expert on every matter. Newly elected legislators quickly recognize that the most successful veteran members are those who focus on one or two specific areas—the budget, the revenue structure, the environment, transportation, health care, public safety, education—try to learn as much as they can about them, and, in doing so, earn the respect of their colleagues. Legislators who try to pass themselves off to their colleagues as expert in every area almost always come to be recognized as expert in none.

In floor debate, legislators other than the floor leaders and their deputies are expected to be selective in choosing when to speak. Those who develop a reputation for rising to speak too often, on too many different issues, come to be viewed unfavorably by their colleagues.

Do Not Criticize Your Party's Leaders in Public

Legislators who find themselves in serious disagreement with the leadership of their party caucus are expected to discuss such disagreements in private. Legislators who publicly criticize the leaders of their caucus are frowned upon and will usually lose support from within the caucus for bills that they are sponsoring. Public criticism of one's leadership can also result in punitive measures that may range from the leaders' withholding party campaign funds in the legislator's next election campaign to the loss of a desirable committee assignment or staff assistant, or perhaps a preferential parking space.

Always Inform Your Party's Legislative Leadership If You Feel You Cannot Support an Agreed-Upon Position of Your Caucus

As a member of the majority or minority party caucus in their chamber, legislators are expected to support their party's positions on key pieces of legislation. But legislative leaders also recognize that there will be occasions when some members of their caucus will feel that they cannot support a caucus position, perhaps as a matter of conscience or perhaps because there is strong sentiment against that position among those members' constituents. Legislators who find themselves in such a position are expected to take responsibility for ensuring that there will be no unexpected embarrassment for their leader (or their party) by providing notification to their caucus leaders before the matter in question comes up for final consideration on the floor.

Win and Lose Gracefully

The legislative process involves victories and defeats. Even newly elected legislators know—or if not, quickly learn—that they will not be on the victorious side of every issue. Today's winner is often tomorrow's loser. The aphorism of legendary football coach Vince Lombardi, "Show me a good loser and I'll show you a loser," does not apply to legislative politics. Legislators are expected to be magnanimous and gracious in victory and humble and accepting in defeat.

Be Certain about the Accuracy of All Facts in Speeches, Statements, and Press Releases

It is expected that when a legislator makes a public statement it can be assumed that all facts in that statement are correct and accurate. When a legislator is caught in an inaccuracy (or, worse, a lie), that legislator's credibility is immediately brought into question. Opponents will be quick to exploit the mistake. And friends, supporters, and reporters will see the legislator as unreliable and sloppy and may begin to distance themselves. To avoid finding themselves in such a situation, legislators understand that, if they are going to be successful and respected by their colleagues, they must check and double-check all public statements for accuracy before they are made or released in the legislator's name.

Never Lie to or Mislead Constituents, Fellow Legislators, or the News Media

The appearance of deceptiveness or of intent to mislead fellow legislators, constituents, or reporters can cause irreparable damage to a legislator's career. Legislators, constituents, or reporters who suspect that a legislator is deceiving them or withholding information to divert their attention will immediately become distrustful and suspicious. Previously favorable and positive feelings about a legislator found to be dishonest or deceitful can very quickly become negative and skeptical. And an individual who already holds a negative impression of a legislator will only find that attitude reinforced by perceived dishonesty, and may well become openly hostile. In the case of journalists and reporters, any time that they suspect a legislator of being deceitful or untruthful, that suspicion will likely find its way into their story or news report.

There will always be times when a legislator will feel it inappropriate or unwise either to answer a question or to provide a colleague, constituent, or reporter with a comment or information. Successful legislators understand that, on such occasions, rather than giving a misleading or inaccurate response, the correct response is something like: "I'm sorry, but there is nothing that I am able to say about that at this time."

Respect Compromise as the Cornerstone of the Legislative Process

Successful legislators understand and accept that compromise is the essence of the democratic legislative process—a hard give-and-take and exchange of ideas and views that has as its goal the development of public policy decisions that will be acceptable to the largest possible majority of their constituents. They recognize that there is a clear distinction between the *principle of compromise* and the *compromise of principle*. The principle of compromise is the cornerstone of the democratic legislative process. And it is entirely possible (and, in fact, absolutely necessary) for members of a legislative body to operate under that principle without in any way compromising their own basic principles or beliefs. One seldom gets everything one wants in a democratic system, and successful and effective legislators understand and accept that reality.

Stay in Compliance with All Ethics and Conflict of Interest Laws and Guidelines

As previously indicated, every state has laws and guidelines that prescribe the parameters of appropriate and permissible behavior by their elected and appointed officials. Legislators who develop a reputation for casually wandering outside the boundaries of those laws and guidelines are almost certain to lose the respect and support of their colleagues, come under suspicion by the news media, and eventually cause fatal damage to their political careers.

Venerate the Legislature as a Symbol of Democracy

If legislators do not know it when they first arrive in the legislature, they quickly come to understand from their veteran colleagues that, as a member of a democratic legislature, they are a part of something considered very special among those privileged to be part of it. Since ancient Greek and Roman times, the legislature has been considered a symbol of democracy—the branch of government closest to the people, and the one that represents and makes policy on their behalf. Even members who take issue with their legislature's organization, management, or decisionmaking processes understand that they will lose the respect and support of their colleagues if they do not couple their criticism with veneration of the legislature as a democratic institution and with expressions of pride in having been selected by their constituents to represent and serve them in it.

At any given time and in any given legislature, certain of these informal rules will be accorded greater importance than others. And some long-serving legislators and legislative scholars claim that, with heightened partisanship in some states and the establishment of term limits in others, there has been a steady erosion in the respect that legislators accord to all of them. They argue that a decline in civility that has resulted from this erosion has served to cast legislatures in a less favorable light in the eyes of the people they serve and that this, in turn, has contributed to an unhealthy increase in public cynicism about U.S. government and politics.

There is no question that the U.S. political process is a dynamic one that has evolved and will continue to evolve and change. As it does, traditions that are derived from those practices will inevitably be modified or altered. To cite just one example, it is certainly unrealistic to ask first-term legislators to sit quietly and bide their time in term-limited states like Arkansas and California, where their tenure of service is limited to only six years, or in Colorado, Florida, Maine, Nebraska, or Ohio, where they are limited to eight years.

Every legislature has a few so-called maverick members who flout or disregard its informal traditions and rules. News reporters often see maverick legislators as attractive newsmakers; because of that, they may become the recipients of considerable press coverage that can prove helpful to them in advancing their political careers outside the legislature. But they are almost always viewed with suspicion and seen as nonteam players by their colleagues. They seldom, if ever, advance to key leadership positions, and they almost always find it considerably more difficult than do their team-playing colleagues to move their bills through committee and onto the chamber floor.

Factors that Influence Legislative Decisionmaking

Ultimately, the legislative process comes down to individual legislators casting votes on the floor of their chamber. These votes mark the culmination of a long, complex, and often circuitous journey for each bill. While under the U.S. system of representative democracy legislators serve as their constituents' representative, each individual legislator must decide how best to carry out that responsibility when making decisions. Among the considerations that must be weighed are how the legislator views the role and responsibilities of legislative service, involvements that the legislator may have had in the development of a bill prior to its reaching the floor for final vote, personal relationships and priorities, and previous commitments that the legislator may have made. These considerations are influenced by a whole array of forces and pressures—some internal and some external—that affect how legislators finally arrive at their decisions on how to vote.

Personal Feelings

It is highly unlikely that any individual would run for the state legislature without holding strong views on a number of issues of public concern. Obviously, these personal views will heavily influence how that individual will vote if successful in the election campaign. Certainly, a legislator's personal feelings will be the first consideration in determining how to vote on a piece of legislation. And, on matters that the legislator may have made a central issue in the election campaign, or on issues such as abortion and the death penalty, which most legislators see as involving a personal moral judgment, personal feelings may be their only real consideration.

But neither legislatures nor their individual members operate in a vacuum, and there are many external forces and pressures that can also significantly affect how a legislator will vote on a given issue. While there will always be a few issues on which a legislator will be immune to outside pressures, on many others they may have little or no strong feeling. Or, even if they do, they will recognize that they have an obligation as a member of the legislature to listen and respond to the thoughts and opinions of their constituents, their political party and legislative leadership, the governor and executive branch officials, interest groups and lobbyists, and the news media. Each of these has the potential to influence how a legislator votes on a bill.

Constituents

All legislators know and understand that they have been elected by their constituents to serve as their representative at the state capitol. As such, they also know and understand that they need to take this responsibility seriously—first, because it is their obligation under the U.S. system of representative democracy, and, second, because if their constituents perceive them as being unresponsive to their needs and wishes, they are likely to vote them out of office at the next election. Over the past couple of decades, state legislators have gone to increasing lengths to ascertain the attitudes and feelings of their constituents through such devices as regular district office hours, community meetings, and mail or Internet questionnaires. The more heavily that a legislator's constituents come down on one side of an issue, the more pressure—and obligation—the legislator will feel to vote in accord with that viewpoint. On the other hand, when legislators find their constituents pretty much evenly divided on an issue, other factors are more likely to play a role in determining the legislators' decisions.

Political Parties and Legislative Leaders

With only a few minor exceptions, every state legislator is elected as a candidate of a political party. In many instances, the legislator's election campaign will have received financial assistance from the party's legislative leaders who lead the party's legislative caucus. Once in the legislature, the legislator immediately becomes a member of that caucus. If it is the majority party caucus, its role is to try to marshal a majority either to pass the governor's program if the governor is from its party, or to modify and develop alternative and improved approaches to those proposed by the governor if the governor is from the other party. If the caucus is that of the minority party, its role is to support and defend the governor's program if the governor is from its party, or to draw public attention to what it sees as the weaknesses of the governor's proposals if the governor is from the other party.

Whether a legislator is a member of the majority or minority caucus, there is an understood responsibility and obligation to support the caucus's positions, particularly on issues in which the legislative leaders consider party solidarity to be of paramount importance. These will usually include, but are not limited to, votes on the state budget and votes on major gubernatorial initiatives.

As discussed previously, it is the responsibility of the legislative leadership to try to achieve party and caucus solidarity on issues deemed of major importance to their party. They have a number of tools at their disposal that they can draw upon to help them in that effort. The top leadership almost always controls a substantial caucus campaign fund that has been raised through various party and caucus fundraising activities. The leaders selectively distribute these funds. A promise by a Senate president, a House speaker, or a majority or minority leader of either increased or decreased funding support in a legislator's next election campaign can influence that legislator's decision on how to vote, particularly if the legislator expects to be in a tough reelection race in which such funding help might play a decisive role. Another means that legislative leaders can use to influence their caucus members to support a caucus position is the promise of favorable press exposure, perhaps by arranging for the legislator to appear somewhere with the governor, with a member of the state's congressional delegation, or even with the president or vice president if any of them are from the legislator's party. Still other means may involve promises of a desired committee assignment, of secondary leadership posts, of new or additional personal staff assistants, of a larger or better-situated office, or even of a more desirable parking space. For various reasons and to varying degrees, all of these may be important to a legislator. And, when a legislative leader dangles one or more of them before a caucus member, it can have a definite effect on that legislator's decision on how to vote.

Committees

When a piece of legislation comes up for consideration on the floor of the Senate or House, the legislators who serve on the committee to which that bill had been referred should, if they have taken their committee work seriously, be more familiar with the details and specifics of the bill than their colleagues who did not serve on that committee. Information that legislators gather through their work on a committee can prove extremely helpful to them in making their decisions on whether to support or oppose a bill. No matter how issue oriented a legislator may claim to be, it is impossible to be an expert—or even highly knowledgeable—in more than a very few areas. The in-depth, and somewhat less partisan examination that a bill undergoes in a committee affords legislators who serve on that committee a special opportunity to acquire a great deal of information and understanding about the specifics of the bill. Particularly when a legislator does not already hold a strong opinion about a piece of legislation that is referred to committee, information and understanding that the legislator acquires about the bill through the committee can play a significant role in the legislator's eventual decision to support or oppose it.

The Governor and Executive Branch Officials

When a legislator is from the same political party as the governor, it is considered an obligation of the legislator to support most, if not all, of the governor's major program initiatives. This is ingrained in the fabric of the U.S. two-party political system. But it is also seen as advantageous to both the legislator and the legislator's political party to provide such support. The governor is the acknowledged leader of the state, and the creation of a strong positive record of achievement can only help the party to retain the governorship. A strong gubernatorial candidate at the top of a ticket can only help individual members of the governor's party who are running for the legislature on that ticket. So, when the governor, an executive branch agency head, or a key member of the governor's staff asks a legislator for support on a bill, the legislator is sure to listen, especially when the legislator and the governor are from the same political party. Even if they are not, the office of governor carries such stature that a gubernatorial request to a legislator to meet with or discuss the possibility of supporting a particular piece of legislation is something that few legislators are likely to turn down. Whether that will result in the legislator's supporting the legislation is another matter altogether. But the flattery of being personally courted by the governor can, in and of itself, influence a legislator's decision.

Interest Groups and Lobbyists

An interest group may be defined as any organization or organized group of individuals that has a policy agenda and wants to pursue enactment of that agenda actively. Within a legislative body, this active pursuit will involve efforts by individuals representing the interest group to educate and persuade legislators about what they feel is the rightness of their cause. That is the essence of lobbying. While there is a popular perception that lobbyists represent only big business interests, the truth is that somewhere in the halls of every state capitol there are lobbyists representing and advocating various policies and interests that have the support of, and that will benefit, virtually every citizen. Lobbyists therefore constitute a form of communication link between legislators and their constituents.

Lobbyist and former House Speaker Pro Tempore Sherman N. Copelin Jr. (right) speaks with Ed McNeill of the New Orleans Tourist and Convention Commission at the Louisiana State Capitol. (Philip Gould/Corbis)

Few, if any, major issues in any state legislature do not involve lobbyists working on both sides of the issue. Some lobbyists are hired under contract and compensated for focusing on specific issues or bills in which the group or organization has an interest. Others may be full-time employees of the group or organization and have as their specific job assignment to serve as its lobbyist. Regardless of the employment conditions under which a lobbyist operates, successful lobbyists will be thoroughly familiar with the details and specifics of all issues or bills for which they are responsible. As such, they can be a valuable source of information to a legislator on the details of complex issues.

It is common for U.S. legislators to say that they will find time to talk to all lobbyists, because they consider them a potentially valuable source of information on legislation under consideration in their body. But those legislators also usually say that they make sure that each lobbyist they talk to understands that the first time the legislator finds the lobbyist lying to them or providing them with false or inaccurate information will be the last time they will ever speak to that lobbyist.

As valuable a source of information as lobbyists can be for legislators, every state legislature recognizes that there are many skilled lobbyists in their capitol building who represent organizations and interests with large amounts of money at their disposal. And they understand that both the perceived—and the real—potential for lobbyist abuse of these funds to influence outcomes of the legislative process illegally must be addressed through the regulation of lobbying activity. There has been a trend through-out the United States over the past quarter-century to increase and tighten the regula-tion of lobbyists and the activities in which they engage. That trend has been, in large part, a response by legislators to public demands for tighter controls. These demands have been an outgrowth of a decline in public confidence (and a corresponding increase in cynicism) in politics and the democratic process that began with the federal govern-ment's Watergate scandal in the early 1970s.

The News Media

The last but by no means the least important source of influence in legislator decision-making is the news media. The relationship between legislators and the reporters who cover them is often fragile, and it may take quite a while for a newly elected legislator to come to terms with the reality that, while the legislature and the press have a com-mon commitment to the democratic process, reporters do not have a responsibility to make the legislature or any of its members look good in the eyes of their constituents. The news media's only responsibility is to inform the public accurately and fairly on the details of the legislature's decisions, how those decisions were made, factors that entered into them, and the positions, statements, and votes of individual members.

Legislators who understand and accept the role and responsibility of the media will recognize them as providing a valuable source of information that can be of help to leg-islators in making difficult decisions. Good legislative reporters know that the surest path to winning the respect and confidence of legislators is to earn a reputation for ac-curate and thorough reporting on issues under their consideration. And information in the reports of a journalist who has a reputation for accuracy and thoroughness some-times provides insights that play a role in a legislator's decision on whether to support or oppose a piece of legislation. At other times, investigative reporting or a persistent campaign by a news organization in support of a particular course of action can produce a groundswell of public support that can, in turn, influence a legislator to take up that cause.

An Effective State Legislature Makes an Effective State

The organizational and managerial structure of U.S. state legislatures and the processes by which they make decisions provide them with a foundation on which to build the capability to operate as effective and responsive representatives of the people.

A sound legislative structure and process begins with good leadership, particularly at the top level of a legislature's hierarchy. While Senate presidents or presidents pro tem-pore, or House speakers, function as a sort of CEO for their respective chambers, the qualities that are necessary in an effective legislative leader are unique to the position and not necessarily identical to those required of a corporate CEO.

The essential structural components of a legislative body under the U.S. system of government are a committee system for the conduct of the legislature's official business and a professional staff to assist its members. A committee system allows for a division of labor in a legislature's deliberation process and enables it to undertake an examination and review of multiple matters and issues simultaneously. A professional staff gives members of a legislature needed administrative and clerical support and their own independent source of information and legal assistance.

A legislature's organizational infrastructure provides the underpinning for it to undertake its basic responsibility—the enactment, repeal, or amendment of laws that will improve the quality of life for the people it serves. The process by which U.S. state legislatures attempt to carry out this responsibility is quite similar in all states. But the process is also highly complex, and its details vary from state to state. The legislative process is composed of a combination of formal and informal rules that are developed through each legislature's traditions and long-standing practices. The most effective legislators are those who master the formal rules and operate within the framework of the informal ones.

A legislature that has a well-organized and well-managed institutional structure, a well-crafted process for the conduct of its business, and leaders, members, and staff who understand their respective roles and how to perform them, possesses the capacity to serve its constituents effectively. Having all of these elements in place will not guarantee that a legislature will be successful in its mission. But a lack of these elements is a sure recipe for failure.

REFERENCES

Council of State Governments (CSG). 2004. *The Book of the States 2004.* Lexington, KY: CSG.

Craft, Ralph. 1972. *Strengthening the Arkansas Legislature.* New Brunswick, NJ: Rutgers University Press.

Drage Bowser, Jennie, et al. 2003. "The Impact of Term Limits on Legislative Leadership." In *The Test of Time: Coping with Legislative Term Limits,* edited by Rick Farmer, James David Rausch, Jr., and John C. Green. Lanham, MD: Lexington Books.

Hamm, Keith E., and Gary Moncrief. 2004. "Legislative Politics in the United States." In *Politics in the American States: A Comparative Analysis.* 8th ed. Washington, DC: Congressional Quarterly Press.

Hibbing, John R., and Elizabeth Theiss-Morse. 2002. *Stealth Democracy.* Cambridge: Cambridge University Press.

Jewell, Malcolm E. 1982. *Representation in State Legislatures.* Lexington: University of Kentucky Press.

Jewell, Malcolm E., and Samuel C. Patterson. 1986. *The Legislative Process in the United States.* 4th ed. New York: Random House.

Jewell, Malcolm E., and Marcia Lynn Whicker. 1994. *Legislative Leadership in the American States.* Ann Arbor: University of Michigan Press.

Kurtz, Karl T. 1997a. "Legislatures and Citizens: Communication between Representatives and Their Constituents." For National Conference of State Legislatures (NCSL) and Research Foundation of the State University of New York. Research Foundation of the State University of New York. Albany: Research Foundation of the State University of New York.

———. 1997b. "Legislatures and Citizens: Public Participation and Confidence in the Legislature." For USAID National Conference of State Legislatures (NCSL) and Research Foundation of the State University of New York. Research Foundation of the State University of New York. Albany: Research Foundation of the State University of New York.

Lakis, Stephen G. 2001. "The Essential Role of Legislatures and Parliaments in Achieving Global Democracy." Remarks to symposium of German legislators, November. Centerville, MA: State Legislative Leaders Foundation.

———. 2002. "The Operation and Regulation of Lobbying in the Democratic Process." Paper presented to symposium of National Assembly of Bulgaria, Sandanski, Bulgaria, February. Centerville: MA: State Legislative Leaders Foundation.

Linsky, Martin. 1986. "Legislatures and the Press: The Problems of Image and Attitude." *State Government* (spring):40–44.

Little, Thomas H. 1995. "Understanding Legislative Leadership beyond the Chamber: The Members' Perspective." *Legislative Studies Quarterly*, Volume 20 (May):269–291.

———. 2002. "A Systematic Analysis of Members' and Their Expectations of Elected Leaders." *Political Research Quarterly* 47, no. 3.

Little, Thomas H., and Jill Clark. 2002. "National Organizations as Sources of Information for State Legislative Leaders." *State and Local Government Review* 34, no. 1.

Nakamura, Robert T., and John Johnson. 1995. "Legislatures and Legislative Development." Paper presented to Council of Peoples' Representatives, Addis Ababa, Ethiopia. Albany: Research Foundation of the State University of New York.

National Conference of State Legislatures (NCSL). 1979. *A Legislator's Guide to Staffing Patterns.* Denver: NCSL.

———. 1981. *A Chairman's Guide to Effective Committee Management.* Denver: NCSL.

———. 1982. *Legislative Staff Services: 50 State Profiles.* Denver: NCSL.

———. 1989. *Mason's Manual of Legislative Procedure.* St.Paul, MN: West Publishing Company.

———. 2002. *The State of State Legislative Ethics.* Denver: NCSL.

National Democratic Institute for International Affairs (NDI). 1996. "Committees in Legislatures: A Division of Labor." NDI Legislative Research Series paper no. 2. NDI.

———. 1999. "Legislative Ethics: A Comparative Analysis." NDI Legislative Research Series paper no. 4. NDI.

Neal, Tommy. 1996. *Lawmaking and the Legislative Process: Committees, Connections, and Compromises.* Denver: National Conference of State Legislatures.

Ogle, David B. 1970. *Strengthening the Connecticut Legislature.* New Brunswick, NJ: Rutgers University Press.

———. 1972. *Strengthening the Mississippi Legislature.* New Brunswick, NJ: Rutgers University Press.

———. 1998. "Management and Organization of Representative Assemblies." National Conference of State Legislatures (NCSL) and Research Foundation of the State University of New York. Research Foundation of the State University of New York.

———. 2002. "The Administration of the Bulgarian National Assembly." For USAID through State Legislative Leaders Foundation (SLLF) and International Development Group of the State University of New York (SUNY/IDG). SUNY/IDG and USAID.

———. 2004. "Legislative Committees: A Legislative Body's Most Important Institutional Mechanism." Paper prepared for the 2d International Conference on Strengthening Legislatures in Response to Globalization and International Security Issues. Makati City, Philippines. Centerville, MA: State Legislative Leaders Foundation.

Ornstein, Norman. 1992. "The Role of the Legislature in a Democracy." Washington, DC: U.S. Information Agency.

Rosenthal, Alan. 1968. *Strengthening the Maryland Legislature.* New Brunswick, NJ: Rutgers University Press.

———. 1981. *Legislative Life: Process and Performance in the States.* New York: Harper and Row.

———. 1990. *Governors and Legislatures: Contending Powers.* Washington, DC: Congressional Quarterly Press.

———. 1996. *Drawing the Line: Legislative Ethics in the States.* Lincoln: University of Nebraska Press.

———. 1998. *The Decline of Representative Democracy.* Washington, DC: Congressional Quarterly Press.

———. 2001. *The Third House: Lobbyists and Lobbying in the States.* 2d ed. Washington, DC: Congressional Quarterly Press.

———. 2004. *Heavy Lifting: The Job of the American Legislature.* Washington, DC: Congressional Quarterly Press.

Rosenthal, Alan, Karl T. Kurtz, John Hibbing, and Loomis Burdett. 2001. *The Case for Representative Democracy.* Trust for Representative Democracy and the National Conference of State Legislatures. Denver: National Conference of State Legislatures.

———, et al. 2003. *Republic on Trial: The Case for Representative Democracy.* Washington, DC: Congressional Quarterly Press.

Rueter, Theodore. 1994. *The Minnesota House of Representatives and the Professionalization of Politics.* Lanham, MD: University Press of America.

Smith, C. Lynwood. 1970. *Strengthening the Florida Legislature.* New Brunswick, NJ: Rutgers University Press.

State Legislative Leaders Foundation (SLLF). 2001a. *Handbook for Parliamentary Commissions and Committees.* For the regional parliaments of Indonesia through United States-Asia Environmental Partnership Program (US-AEP) and SLLF. Washington, DC: US-AEP.

———. 2001b. *Handbook for Parliamentary Leaders.* For the regional parliaments of Indonesia through United States-Asia Environmental Partnership Program (US-AEP) and SLLF. Washington, DC: US-AEP

———. 2002. *Working with the Media: A Handbook for State Legislators.* SLLF.

———. 2005. *What Have You Gotten Yourself Into? A Guide for New Legislative Leaders.* SLLF.

———. 2004. *Survey of State Legislative Leaders, 2004.* Centerville, MA: State Legislative Leaders Foundation.

U.S. Agency for International Development (USAID), Center for Democracy and Governance. 2000. "Understanding Representation: Implications for Legislative Strengthening." Report on 2d International Conference on Legislative Strengthening. USAID.

Wahlke, John C. 1966. "Organization and Procedure." In *State Legislatures in American Politics,* edited by Alexander Heard. Englewood Cliffs, NJ: Prentice-Hall.

4

THE PEOPLE WHO SERVE

With rare cases in which a state legislator is appointed to fill a vacancy that occurs between scheduled elections, every candidate for the country's fifty state legislatures, incumbent or challenger, must face the electorate. Elections are the heart and soul of representative democracy. Not only are they the method by which citizens choose their representatives in a democracy but they also serve as the primary mechanism to ensure that the will of the public is reflected in the policies that are enacted by those representatives. The awareness of a pending election encourages legislators to keep abreast of the needs, interests, and wishes of their constituents or risk electoral defeat.

Yet, while every state legislator faces the voters and membership in every state legislature is determined by elections, legislative elections differ significantly across the country. In some of the nation's smallest states, candidates can win by spending only a few hundred dollars on their campaign, while others in large states such as California may be required to spend more than a million dollars to get elected. Some candidates face their strongest challenges in the election to secure the nomination of their political party, while others face fierce competition from the opposing party in the general election. Some legislators are elected to serve two-year terms, while others face the electorate every four years. Legislators in a handful of states are allowed to serve in their legislature for a limited number of terms, while the majority of states allow their citizens to serve for as long as the voters see fit to return them to office.

These differences matter, because they have an effect on the kinds of people who serve in the state legislature. First, the differences influence who runs for the legislature. For example, different types of candidates are likely to seek a legislative seat that can be won by spending only a few thousand dollars than will run for a seat in which the campaign will cost half a million dollars. Second, the differences have a dramatic effect on who wins elections. Different types of candidates are likely to win in a state in which the political parties are heavily involved in the elections, than in a state in which the candidates tend to raise their own money and run their own campaigns. The laws passed by a state legislature are a reflection of its membership and its partisan, ethnic, economic, demographic, philosophical, and ideological composition. And that membership is directly reflective of the electoral rules, regulations, and norms that govern that state.

AN OVERVIEW OF STATE LEGISLATIVE ELECTIONS

For the purpose of electing legislators, every state is divided into a number of electoral districts. Each district within a state legislative chamber must contain roughly the same number of people as all other districts in the chamber. In order to gain the right to represent their district in the legislature, most successful candidates run for a two-year term, but about one in five (including a majority in state senates) runs to serve a four-year term. While most state legislators are elected in even-numbered years, legislators in Virginia, New Jersey, Mississippi, and Kentucky run in odd years, when there are no elections for president or the U.S. Congress. More than 80 percent of state legislators run in single-member districts, seeking to be the only representative of that particular district, while legislators in eight states run in multimember districts that elect more than one legislator. Most legislators face an opponent in their election effort, although the challenge is often not a serious one for incumbent legislators who are running for reelection.

In order to serve in their state legislature, successful candidates must meet certain requirements established in their state's constitution, most often relative to age and residency. In most states, candidates for the House or Assembly must be either at least eighteen or twenty-one years old, while Senate candidates generally need to be either at least eighteen or twenty-six. Senators in Kentucky, Missouri, New Hampshire, New Jersey, and Tennessee are required to be at least thirty years old. Residency requirements range from no minimum in a few states to six years for the Kentucky Senate (Council of State Governments 2004, 86–87).

Legislative candidates also have to meet statutory requirements in order to stand for election. They must file for the office and in some states pay a nominal registration fee. Once registered to run, candidates must gain the nomination of a political party in order to compete in the general election. If more than one person from a particular party wants to run for the legislature from a single-member district, the nominee is usually selected in a primary election held in late spring, summer, or early fall, ranging from early March to late September. Those selected to run do so in the general election, which is held in November (ibid., 273–275).

THE CONTEXT OF STATE LEGISLATIVE ELECTIONS

Just as the winner of an athletic contest is determined, at least in part, by the rules, regulations, and environment in which it is played, the winners of election contests for state legislative seats are often a reflection of the environments that define election campaigns in each state and district. The impact and influence of the local environment are evident long before the winning candidate is chosen, usually on the second Tuesday after the first Monday in November. The nature of a pending election season influences who will even consider running for a state legislative seat, as well as who will eventually win it.

Four distinct factors influence the nature and results of state legislative elections: political environment, legal environment, structural environment, and electoral environment (Moncrief, Squire, and Jewell 2001). Each has a significant effect on who will seek and who will win a seat in the state legislature.

The Political Environment

Elections are, by definition, political, and are significantly influenced by the political environment in which they are held. The political environment includes the characteristics of the institutions that are critical to state legislative elections—namely, the state legislature, political parties, and interest groups. Variations in legislative professionalism, partisan competition, political party activities, and interest group strength have a significant influence on state legislative campaigns and elections, influencing who will run for a seat in the legislature, who will vote in a legislative election, and who will win that election.

Professionalism of the Legislature

The amount of time, effort, and commitment necessary to serve in a state legislature varies greatly from state to state. Service in the legislatures of California, New York, Michigan, Ohio, and Pennsylvania is considered full time. On the other hand, one can quite easily serve in the Wyoming, Alabama, or North Dakota legislature—or in those of several other states—while also holding down a full-time job outside of the legislature. In fact, the meager salaries paid to legislators in the majority of states usually necessitate a separate, and primary, source of income.

Most scholars recognize state legislatures as falling into one of three categories—professional, citizen, or hybrid—based on the amount of time that their members are required to commit to service, the nature of their staff support, and the length of time that they meet in session (Morehouse and Jewell 2003).

Higher salaries, substantial professional staff support, and a majority of legislators considering their legislative job to be full time generally characterize professional legislatures. Legislators in California are paid more than $100,000 annually and those in New York, Illinois, Ohio, and Pennsylvania receive compensation that approaches six figures. Legislators in those states also tend to have full-time, professional staff who work directly for them, and they are required to meet in regular session for much of the year. Only about a half-dozen of the fifty state legislatures are considered to fall into the professional category.

On the opposite end of the spectrum from the professional legislature is the citizen legislature—part-time bodies that meet in formal session for relatively short periods each year, with a few meeting only every other year. Most legislators in these states have a private-sector job that provides them with their primary source of income, and they are likely to serve shorter tenures than their counterparts in more professional chambers. The level of staff support is much lower in citizen legislatures than in professional legislatures, with members often having personal staff support only during sessional periods—and, even then, often having to share that staff with other members. The Vermont General Assembly is a true citizen legislature. Its members are paid $600 a month during the legislative session, which is usually no more than five months in odd years and three months in even years. There are fewer than fifty full-time nonpartisan staff members to meet the needs of the 180 legislators, and there is no personal staff support when the legislature is out of session. About 40 percent of state legislatures fall into the citizen legislature category (Rosenthal 2004).

Almost half of the state legislatures are classified as hybrid legislatures, exhibiting some characteristics of a professional legislature but bearing other markings more akin to those of a citizen body. For example, while some legislatures do not meet for an extensive period of time and do not offer high salaries, their committees may meet regularly during the interim (when the legislature is not in formal session), constituent demands on members are high, and their staff support is strong. About two dozen legislatures fall into the hybrid category. The North Carolina General Assembly would fall into this category, with relatively low annual salaries but high time commitments and strong staff support.

Because of the very different levels of commitment and reward associated with professional, citizen, and hybrid legislatures, legislative professionalism has a significant effect on the types of people who seek and win state legislative elections. Professional legislatures often attract candidates and members who are better educated, more politically ambitious, and more able and willing to commit significant time, money, and effort to winning (and keeping) a seat. Historically, legislators in these chambers have been less likely to lose or voluntarily relinquish their seat and more likely to be wealthy and male. Citizen legislatures often have members from a wider variety of occupational backgrounds (more teachers, farmers, ranchers, and the like), but they also have a strong contingent of attorneys and business owners who have the type of private-sector occupation that affords them the flexibility to take time away from their job to commit themselves to the legislature. Historically, women have tended to be better represented in citizen legislatures, but that difference is shrinking. Not surprisingly, election campaigns for seats in professional legislatures are generally more costly than those for less professional legislatures (ibid.).

The Role of Political Party Organizations

Historically, political party organizations, particularly at the state and local levels, have been quite active in state legislative elections. As recently as the 1970s, state political parties played a significant role in candidate recruitment, message development, campaign financing, and voter mobilization (getting voters to their polling places) in many state election campaigns. Up until that time, it was virtually impossible to be elected to the state legislature without the support, or at least without the opposition, of the state party organization in some states (Mayhew 1986; Reichley 1992). For example, it is said that, in Connecticut, nothing happened in electoral politics without the knowl-

Newly elected Democratic National Committee chairman Howard Dean smiles during his acceptance speech at the Democratic National Committee's winter meeting, February 12, 2005, in Washington. (Kevin Lamarque/Reuters/Corbis)

edge, encouragement, and support of Democratic chairman John M. Bailey, who served in his position from 1946 to 1974, or Republican Party chairman J. Henry Roraback, who held his post from 1912 to 1937, and his successors of the following decades (Satter 2004). Such control by the state party leaders and organizations has decreased considerably in recent decades.

This is not to suggest that modern political parties play no role in state legislative elections. There are some states in which the role may be almost as important as ever, but the party organizations today make use of different means to achieve their goals. In some states, the political party organization has begun to focus less on controlling access to the ballot and more on providing support for its preferred candidates. In what is becoming an era of candidate-centered campaigns, candidates today tend, more than in the past, to hire their own consultants, develop their own themes, raise their own money, and often deemphasize their political party affiliation. In such an environment, state party organizations tend to focus more on the provision of services than the manipulation of elections. Modern political parties focus on raising and distributing substantial amounts of money, providing political expertise and technological assistance, assisting in voter registration and mobilization, and helping promising candidates to develop campaign skills (Morehouse and Jewell 2003; Frandeis and Gitelson 1999, 135–153).

In some states, much of the traditional role of the state party organization has, in fact, been co-opted by the party's leaders in the legislature. The past two decades have witnessed the rise of coordinated campaign organizations within legislatures through legislative party campaign committees and leadership campaign committees. The funding for these campaign organizations is raised by the party members and leaders in the legislative chamber and usually coordinated by the legislative leadership with the express purpose of recruiting, supporting, and funding candidates for the legislature. In some states, these committees may raise hundreds of thousands (and, in the most populous states, millions) of dollars to aid their legislative candidates. They also often take an active role in identifying, recruiting, and preparing candidates (Alan Rosenthal 1998, 183–191; Cynthia Rosenthal 1995).

Recent studies suggest that such legislative leadership campaign activities are now among the most important factors in determining legislative leadership elections. Legislative leaders who cannot successfully recruit candidates, raise money, and gain or maintain a majority in their chamber are not likely to keep their jobs, no matter how effective they may be as a manager or legislator (Little 1995; Drage Bowser et al. 2003). State party organizations and legislative leaders are most likely to play major roles in campaigns in states in which the two political parties are competitive and where elections for the state legislature tend to be costly and contested. In states where one party dominates or where state legislative elections can be won with limited resources that the candidates are able to raise themselves, the role of both the state party and the legislature's leaders is likely to be more limited.

The level of party campaign activity significantly affects the nature of state legislative candidates and campaigns. Candidates are much more likely to be recruited and to cite recruitment as a reason for seeking office in states in which the political parties are competitive and take an active role in legislative campaigns (Moncrief, Squire, and Jewell 2001). And in states in which the cost of political campaigning is high, a wider array of candidates will be likely to seek legislative office when political party leaders promise financial, technical, and political support. Finally, there appears to be a strong connection between party support for candidates, especially by legislative leaders and leadership campaign committees, and partisan unity and cohesion on the floor of the legislature (State Legislative Leaders Foundation 2004). Legislators who are recruited and supported by their leaders often tend to feel a sense of obligation and loyalty to those leaders, which results in support both in important votes on the floor of the chamber and when the leaders are faced with internal challenges to their leadership positions.

Interest Group Culture

Special interest groups that focus their attention exclusively on legislation that addresses specific issues play an integral part in democratic elections, often providing much of the financial support for their conduct. However, the interest group culture—the rules, expectations, and norms that govern what an interest group is expected to do, and what it can do relative to the electoral process—varies greatly from state to state. In some states, interest groups and political action committees seem to be almost synonymous with successful elections, whereas their influence in other states seems much less pronounced (Cassie and Thompson 1998). Like any institution trying to exert influence, interest groups are strongest where they have the best opportunity for the greatest payoff with the least investment. The opportunity for influence is greatest where elections are expensive, because candidates need the financial assistance that interest groups can provide. The potential payoff for an interest group is likely to be highest in professional legislatures, because those legislatures generally have the most significant influence on public policy in their states (Dye 1995).

The number of special interest groups active in each state varies considerably, ranging from more than 3,000 in New York, Connecticut, and Arizona to fewer than 300 in Alaska, Delaware, Hawaii, and Wyoming. One recent study of lobbying in the New York Assembly noted: "Government gridlock has proved great for business. The need to hire several firms to do what one once did helps explain why the state's lobbying industry has grown to a $144 million business in 2004, up from $39 million ten years earlier" (Cooper 2005). Furthermore, the amount of money spent by interest groups on campaigns through their political action committees (PACs)—an interest group's financial arm that controls funds received from its members for donation to political campaigns—varies as well. One study revealed that, on average, legislators in professional legislatures receive twenty times as much campaign money from PACs as do their counterparts in less professional legislatures. The same study suggested that restrictions on campaign contributions do less to minimize interest group influence than do low professionalism and low-cost campaigns (Cassie and Thompson 1998). In other words, the campaign money that lobbyists have to offer is less important to legislators who don't have to raise a lot of money to win a seat in a legislature in which their pay and desire to build a legislative career are low.

While it is not clear whether interest group contributions are driving up campaign costs or that higher costs are attracting more interest group contributions, it is evident that elections in states in which special interest groups are very active in campaigns tend to have very costly campaigns. In such states, one would expect to find fewer candidates seeking the office on their own and more candidates running as a result of the encouragement of these influential lobbyists and interest groups. Where interest groups are very active in political campaigns, candidates are likely to find themselves devoting a much larger portion of their time and resources to raising the necessary money to enable them to compete successfully in this high-stakes game. And the lobbyists who represent the interest groups will likely be more than willing to pay the price necessary to "stay in the game."

Institutional Party Competition

While legislative candidates are most interested in the level of competition in their own district, the number of Democrats and Republicans in a given chamber—what scholars call institutional party competition—is an important factor in determining the nature of political campaigns in a state (see T 4.1). For much of history, most state legislatures were not highly competitive. During the late 1800s and for much of the 1900s, Democrats held an almost unbreakable lock on legislatures in the South, and Republicans held a similar lock on legislatures in the Northeast and Midwest. A look at the partisan distribution at the beginning of the twenty-first century reveals a country evenly divided. In 2005, Republicans controlled both chambers in twenty-one states, Democrats in seventeen; each party controlled one chamber in eleven more (with Nebraska a single-chamber, nonpartisan legislature). Republicans have a stronghold in most states in the West (except for the Pacific Coast, where Democrats do well in Washington, Oregon, and California), the South (with the exception of North Carolina, Mississippi, Alabama, and Louisiana), and the Midwest. On the other hand, Democrats tend to dominate legislative chambers in the Northeast and in the Southern states noted above, although Republican strength has been steadily growing throughout those Southern states over the past two decades.

More important than the balance of Republican and Democratic control across the country is their respective margins of majority in individual states. How competitive are the two political parties in the legislature? How many seats would have to change hands for a change of control to occur? In 2005, the majority party held less than 55 percent of the seats in more than a quarter of the state legislative chambers across the country (thirteen House chambers and twelve Senate chambers). In two chambers (the Montana House and the Iowa Senate), both parties held exactly the same number of members. In another quarter of the chambers, the majority party held between 55 and 61 percent of the seats (eleven House chambers and twelve Senate chambers). In the remaining chambers, the majority party held more than 61 percent of the seats, the Mas-

TABLE 4.1   LEGISLATIVE INTERPARTY COMPETITION, 2005–2006*

Top Five		Bottom Five	
Iowa Senate	0	Rhode Island House	45
Montana House	0	Florida House	48
Colorado Senate	1	Maryland House	55
Iowa House	2	New York Assembly	58
Minnesota House	9	New Hampshire House	106

Source: Calculated by authors.

* Number of seats separating majority and minority party.

sachusetts House and the Rhode Island Senate being the most one-sided, with Democratic majorities of 87 percent in each.

The party balance within the legislature has a dramatic effect on political campaigns, because the loss of one or two seats in a close chamber can mean the loss of majority status and the political power and influence that accompany it. As has been indicated, in states in which the two parties are very competitive and control of the legislature hinges on each election, legislative campaigns are usually more expensive and legislative leaders more active in the recruitment and preparation of their candidates. Interestingly, in legislatures in which party competition is strongest and party control is often up for grabs, the majority of individual campaigns are virtually ignored by the party. Instead, party leaders identify the districts that are most competitive and focus the bulk of their resources and attention on them. Thus, even in a state in which the two parties are evenly balanced, a substantial number of candidates are likely to find themselves receiving limited help from their party, because the districts in which they are running are so strongly identified with one party or the other that party assistance will be unlikely to influence the outcome. Party leaders target their money to the vulnerable and winnable districts that are seen as most likely to determine the difference between majority and minority status.

The Legal Environment

Because rules governing state legislative elections are established by each state, within the restrictions of the U.S. Constitution, the rules can and do vary from state to state. While the legal environment might vary on many dimensions, three have proven to significantly influence state legislative elections: the presence or absence of legislative term limits, limitations on campaign donations, and the presence or absence of public financing of state legislative elections.

Legislative Term Limits

For some state legislators, holding their legislative seat is a way of life. For example, Frederick Malkus of the Maryland Senate and Ted Gray of the Ohio Senate each served forty-four years in their respective chambers. While such tenure is rare, it is no longer even possible in more than a dozen states in which legislative term limits have been implemented. In those states, legislators may serve as few as six years in a given chamber (the lower chambers in Maine, California, and Arkansas) or as many as twelve years in each chamber (Louisiana and Nevada). In some states legislators can serve a set number of terms, sit out (or serve in the other chamber) for a session, and then return to serve the same limited number of terms again. In others, the limits are lifetime, such that once a member has served six, eight, or twelve years in a state legislative chamber, it is not possible ever again to seek election to that chamber (or to the legislature in states in which the limitation applies to total legislative service) (see T 4.2).

Legislative term limits have an influence on the types of people who seek to run for and win a seat in state legislatures. They increase opportunity and predictability for those considering a run for the legislature. Everyone knows that within a defined number of years, a particular legislator will have to retire and the seat will be open. This increases the level of competition in that legislator's term-limited year, but it tends to minimize competition in the remaining years as prospective candidates wait for the incumbent to be forced out. While many predicted that term limits would slow the rising cost of state legislative elections, results suggest that this has not happened, with costs rising as fast or faster in term-limited states as in the majority of states, in which terms are not limited (Allenbaugh and Pinney 2003). Individuals seeking a career in politics are, obviously, going to be less inclined to run for the legislature where such a career is made impossible by term limits. That fact has made it more difficult to find quality candidates interested in running for and serving in term-limited legislatures, making candidate recruitment virtually a full-time job for legislative leaders in those states (Finan interview 2002).

While proponents of term limits predicted that they would dramatically increase the percentage of women and minority legislators, evidence suggests the opposite. Overall, states that have imposed term limits have actually experienced a decrease in the number of women running for and winning seats in the state legislature (Bernstein and

TABLE 4.2   STATES WITH LEGISLATIVE TERM LIMITS

| State | Years of Service | | Type |
	House	Senate	
Maine	8	8	Consecutive
California	6	8	Lifetime
Colorado	8	8	Consecutive
Michigan	6	8	Lifetime
Arkansas	6	8	Lifetime
Florida	8	8	Consecutive
Ohio	8	8	Consecutive
South Dakota	8	8	Consecutive
Montana	8	8	Consecutive
Arizona	8	8	Consecutive
Missouri	8	8	Lifetime
Oklahoma	12	12	Lifetime
Nebraska	n/a	8	Consecutive
Louisiana	12	12	Consecutive
Nevada	12	12	Lifetime

Source: National Conference of State Legislatures (http://www.ncsl.org).

Chada 2003). Preliminary research suggests a similar effect with regard to minority legislators. While the nationwide percentage of African American and Hispanic legislators continues to rise, most of that growth is taking place in states without term limits, with California the only exception among the term-limited states (Caress et al. 2003).

Campaign Finance Limitations

All elections cost money and all candidates have to get that money from somewhere. This is a fact that candidates in all state legislative races must understand and accept. However, access to money, and the rules governing that access, vary considerably from state to state. While legislative candidates in Colorado can accept no more than $200 from a special interest group's political action committee during an election cycle, for example, there are no limits on how much a candidate may accept from such groups in Illinois. Likewise, while contributions from labor unions are unlimited in Alabama, they are prohibited in Alaska and Arizona.

In addition to the ability of legislative candidates to tap their own bank accounts for campaign financial support (the U.S. Supreme Court has affirmed that a candidate can contribute to his or her own campaign), there are several other potential sources of money to which they can turn to finance their campaigns. These include individual donors, political parties, political action committees, labor unions, and corporate donors. The degree to which a candidate can seek contributions from each of these sources varies significantly from state to state. Just five states—Illinois, New Mexico, Oregon, Utah, and Virginia—place no limits on contributions from any source. Another seven states—Alabama, Indiana, Iowa, Mississippi, North Dakota, Pennsylvania, and Texas—have minimal contribution limits. These states limit contributions by corporations and unions but permit contributions from most other sources.

Thirty-seven states limit individual contributions to candidates, including those running for the state legislature. The lowest limit is in Montana, where individuals can give no more than $200 to the primary or general election of a state legislative candidate. On the other hand, those wishing to contribute to candidates for the New York Senate can contribute almost $14,000 during each election cycle (National Conference of State Legislatures 2005).

In addition to individual contributors, candidates also turn to political action committees for financial support. PACs are the financial arm of an interest group and control money voluntarily contributed by its members for donation to political campaigns. Thirty-six states limit how much money PACs may give to candidates. In Montana, a PAC can give no more than $200 to a legislative candidate for the primary and general election. On the other hand, they can give up to $7,200 per election cycle in New Jersey.

The least restricted source of money for candidates (other than their personal financial contributions to the campaign) is the political party. In 2005, only twenty-two states restricted contributions from political parties to candidates. And even where such limits are imposed, they tend to be considerably higher than limits on individual or PAC contributions, with some states limiting party contributions in the primary elections but not in the general. In Ohio, candidates for the state House of Representatives may receive more than $50,000 from their political party, while their counterparts in the Senate may receive more than $100,000.

Finally, candidates for public office often turn to labor unions and corporate donors for financial support. Here again, however, legal access to such resources varies considerably across the country. While corporations can still contribute through a PAC, twenty-two states prohibit them from contributing to political campaigns from their corporate accounts. Only five states place no limits on corporate contributions, with the remainder limiting them to between $200 (Vermont) and $5,000 (Nevada) per election cycle. Fourteen states prohibit contributions from labor unions unless they are through a union's PAC, while eight place no limits on union contributions. Limitations in the rest of the states range from $200 (Vermont House) to $13,900 (New York Senate).

Not surprisingly, the nature and amount of money to which candidates have access play a significant role in determining who will run and who will win election campaigns. Candidates with limited resources are less likely to run in states in which contributions are severely restricted, especially if campaign costs are high, as that will give a big advantage to better known incumbents. Likewise, in states in which labor unions may contribute to campaigns but corporations may not, labor-supported candidates are more likely to seek office (La Raja and Kousser 2001). In a similar manner, in states with a high limit or no limit on political party contributions, political parties tend to have a greater role in the selection and election of candidates.

Public Financing

One potential source of campaign revenue, the government, has not been mentioned, because it is a relatively rare source for state legislative campaigns. Only eleven states currently provide for public campaign financing for candidates or political parties. In each of those eleven cases, participation in public financing programs is optional. Candidates who agree to participate are required to agree to abide by spending limits, and either limit or altogether forgo the raising of private contributions.

Public financing of state legislative campaigns falls into two categories. The first, partial public financing, typically relies on a combination of voluntary taxpayer contributions (usually by citizens designating on a state income tax return that a dollar or two of their tax bill should go into a public campaign fund) and government appropriations for their funding. Because voluntary taxpayer participation in public financing programs is declining while the cost of campaigns is rising, many states' public financing programs are unable to fund participating candidates fully, and therefore are declining in popularity. Minnesota and New Jersey are two exceptions. Both states have thriving public finance programs.

"Clean elections" public financing is the most recent reform in state campaign finance. These programs allow candidates to finance their campaigns almost entirely with public funds. Once a candidate qualifies by collecting a specified number of small

LEGISLATURES AND THE PUBLIC
Public Financing under Fire in Arizona

In 1998, Arizona voters approved the Arizona Clean Elections Act in a public referendum. The law was designed to minimize the effects of money and interest groups on Arizona elections and open the opportunity for a wider range of citizens to run for political office. The act established a voluntary system for the funding of campaigns for state offices, created a fund to provide money to candidates choosing to participate, established the Citizens Clean Elections Commission to oversee enforcement of the act, and lowered limits on private campaign contributions. In 2000, in the first election for which candidates were eligible for Arizona Clean Elections grants, fifty-four state legislature candidates accepted the authorized public contribution of $25,000 and the requirements that went with it, each receiving five-dollar contributions from at least 200 constituents to qualify.

Four years later, at the beginning of Arizona's 2005 legislative session, the state's Clean Elections Act was under assault on several fronts. First, a 2004 report by the Goldwater Institute's Center for Constitutional Government revealed that the reform had not significantly increased participation or competition for state legislative seats. It was also revealed that the cost to the taxpayers in the first three elections had been almost $20 million—a significant sum for a state then facing a severe budget deficit. Various members of the 2005 Arizona legislature proposed significant alteration or even repeal of the law, citing its cost and the fact that it had not increased the number of candidates seeking office. In support of their arguments, they pointed out that the 2004 election had witnessed the first case of a candidate exceeding his allowable public campaign limits when it was revealed that Representative David Burnell Smith spent $7,500 more than he was allowed to in his successful election to the state House of Representatives.

Representative David Burnell Smith, ordered to resign his legislative seat for violating campaign spending limits, vowed that he "would never resign." (AP Photo/File)

The Citizens Clean Elections Commission voted that Representative Smith step down from office; Smith was removed from office on January 26, 2006. One day earlier, an Arizona legislator had proposed repealing the Clean Elections Act.

Sources: Diaz, Elvia. 2004. "Overhaul of Clean Elections in Works." *Arizona Republic*, December 19; Sherwood, Robbie, and Chip Scutari. 2005. "Clean Elections Law Faces Big Test: Legislator May Be Tossed Out." *Arizona Republic*, January 23; Francisosi, Robert J. 2004. *Is Cleanliness Political Godliness? Arizona's Clean Election Law after Its First Year.* Goldwater Institute (http://www.goldwaterinstitute.org/article.php/17.html).

contributions (of often as low as five dollars), the candidate agrees to abide by strict spending limits and is prohibited from receiving any additional contributions from private sources. Instead, the candidate receives a grant from the state to finance the campaign. Arizona, Maine, and Vermont have operated clean elections programs since 2000. Massachusetts voters passed a clean elections law in 1998, but it was repealed in 2003, before it took full effect. In Arizona, more than 300 candidates for statewide and legislative office received public money in the 2000, 2002, and 2004 elections at a cost of about $19 million.

While there is as yet little information on the electoral effects of public financing, proponents believe that states that use it, and the restrictions that go with it, will decrease the influence of lobbyists and PACs—and generally of money in politics. Proponents argue that it will slow down or reverse the spiraling costs of political campaigns, decrease unethical behavior by candidates, improve the public reputation of the legislature, and increase political participation. However, tentative findings suggest that public financing of campaigns does not improve the public standing of the legislature (Primo and Milo 2004). And a study of Arizona's Clean Elections Law suggests that the law has not, as its proponents have expected, significantly increased political participation by encouraging more citizens to run for public office (Francisosi 2001).

The Structural Environment

Some factors that influence elections remain relatively stable over time, seldom changing from one election to the next. These factors, which include the number of people in a legislative district, the population density of the district, and the demographic composition of the district's population, are considered part of the structural environment that determines who can and will run, and who will win, state legislative election contests.

Legislative District Population

The population of a legislative district can have a significant impact on the outcome of a campaign for its seat. According to the U.S. Supreme Court, all districts within a state legislative chamber must be similar in population. In other words, the population of a legislative chamber's districts is roughly determined by dividing the population of the state by the number of legislative seats. Obviously, that can create major variations in district size across the country. For example, one of the twelve members of the New Hampshire House of Representatives who has a single-member district represents just over 3,000 people, while a member of the California Senate is elected to represent almost 900,000 people, making that state's senatorial districts considerably larger than those of a member of the U.S. Congress. Vermont House members represent approximately 4,000 people, while Texas senators represent almost 700,000 (see T 4.3).

The cost of a campaign for a state legislative seat is, of course, considerably greater in a state in which the district populations are larger than it is in states such as Vermont

TABLE 4.3   POPULATION OF SINGLE-MEMBER LEGISLATIVE DISTRICTS

Top Five		Bottom Five	
California Senate	846,791	Rhode Island House	10,483
Texas Senate	672,639	Maine House	8,443
California Assembly	423,396	Wyoming House	8,230
Florida Senate	399,559	Vermont House	4,059
Ohio Senate	344,035	New Hampshire House	3,089

Source: Rosenthal, Alan. 2004. *Heavy Lifting.* Washington, DC: CQ.

and New Hampshire with small district populations. In states with large district populations, it is almost impossible to reach enough voters to win election without raising and spending a significant amount of money on advertising, the news media, and direct mail. However, a legislator who represents a small number of voters can often campaign with a lot of handshakes, civic club meetings, and maybe a few direct mail pieces. Campaigns in these smaller districts are generally much more personal and result in a more politically, economically, and demographically diverse group of legislators. It is also easier for legislators to represent lower populated districts because their populations tend to be more homogenous (Rosenthal 2004, 18–19). Legislators in these smaller districts can feel a relationship with their constituents not possible in larger districts.

Population Density

One of the most significant factors influencing politics in the United States is population density—that is, whether an area is urban, suburban, or rural. Within a single state there can often be a huge variation regarding the population density of its legislative districts. For example, even though all of the districts in the Alaska Senate are comparable in population, a district in Anchorage, the state's largest city, may consist of only a few square miles, while a few of the state's most rural districts comprise more than 100,000 square miles. Voters in these districts will have very different policy needs and political expectations.

More than half of the state legislators in the United States represent urban districts, with a high number of citizens in a relatively compact geographic area. While such density makes it easier to "walk" the district, campaigns in these districts also tend to be more expensive because of the higher cost for the purchase of television and radio time in urban areas. In addition, there is significant potential for wasted resources in urban campaigns, because it is difficult to target the advertising to the district when television, radio, or newspaper coverage extends well beyond its confines. Candidates end up paying for contact with voters who are not eligible to vote for them (Shea and Burton

2001, 36–37). Furthermore, legislators who represent urban populations tend to focus on different matters than do their rural colleagues, with a greater interest in social services, public safety, and automobile traffic. Urban districts, therefore, tend to produce candidates who are more interested in addressing these types of issues. Urban populations also tend to have a higher proportion of ethnic minority voters and are more likely to generate and support candidates reflective of their ethnicity.

While the nation's urban and suburban population is growing rapidly at the expense of the country's rural areas, many state legislators still represent districts in which there are as many trees as people (or more). These rural districts are dotted with small towns; also, many residents live in unincorporated areas (part of no town or city). In such districts, "walking" campaigns are seldom possible. More so than in urban districts, whose populations tend to be somewhat more transient, candidates and their families in rural districts often have lived in the community for generations and are seen by their constituents as "one of us." They are likely to campaign by direct mail, by appearances at community events, and by means of newspaper advertisements and local radio stations that are heard almost exclusively in the legislator's district (Hogan and Hamm 1998). Issues that dominate rural districts often involve the declining rural economy, "traditional values," and agriculture. These areas tend to be more conservative and are more likely to nominate and support candidates who are seen as "traditional values conservatives." While rural areas in most parts of the country may be less ethnically diverse than their urban counterparts, many rural Southern districts have a high proportion of African American or even Hispanic voters.

Suburban districts tend to fall between urban and rural districts geographically and politically, as well as in population density. In many cases, such districts include areas just outside a city's "urban core," between the central city and the rural communities. Many suburban areas were considered rural only a few years ago, having become more dense and suburban because of "urban sprawl" (cities growing beyond what are seen as their historical boundaries). With the vast majority of heavily urban citified areas generally safe for Democrats and rural areas trending Republican, suburban districts have become the primary battlegrounds where control of state legislatures is won and lost in states in which the parties are roughly equal in strength. In light of the rapid growth of suburban areas, it is more common for them to nominate and elect someone with relatively short roots in the district than is the case in rural or urban districts. Voters in these areas tend to be concerned about issues revolving around rapid growth, including adequate services, good roads, and "quality of life" issues. The so-called soccer moms tend to define the suburban voter, who wants both low taxes and quality services (Varrus 2000).

Demographic Diversity

Population density is not the only variation in district population that influences state legislative elections. In addition to looking at how many people live in the district, a candidate must also consider who those people are. Do they attend church on a regular basis? How partisan are they, and to which political party, if any, do a majority of the constituents give allegiance? All of these factors are important, because people are, understandably, more likely to select, nominate, and support candidates who have traits similar to their own. Furthermore, the importance of these factors is magnified by the fact that the population of a legislative district defines the pool of its candidates. A district that has a higher proportion of African Americans would, for example, be more likely to produce an African American candidate than a district with fewer African Americans, because there are more African Americans in the pool of potential candidates (Bernstein and Chada 2003).

While it is not clear that voters who are poor or less educated tend to vote for candidates that reflect those qualities, it is clear that they tend to select candidates who are different from those likely to be selected by wealthy or better educated voters. Districts with a lower average income or lower mean level of education are likely to produce and support candidates who are more liberal on social welfare issues and economic incentives and tend to support Democratic candidates. In a similar manner, one can expect different types of candidates to run and succeed in districts in which the education level is higher. In short, the issues, the candidates, the messages, the expenses, and the winners of election contests for the state legislature generally tend to reflect the overall makeup of district (Hill and Hinton-Anderson 1995; Wolfinger and Hoffman 2001).

The Electoral Environment

Finally, there are some factors that are not unique to a given state or a given district but are unique to a given election. These factors, which may vary from one election to the next even in the same district, and will have a significant impact on a candidate's decision to run or not run for a seat in the legislature, might be defined as the electoral environment. They consist of three elements: the electoral status of the incumbent legislator, the anticipated cost of a competitive campaign, and the partisan balance and competitiveness of the district.

Electoral Status of the Incumbent Legislator

It is an accepted fact of political life that it is very difficult to defeat a sitting legislator (an incumbent) who is seeking reelection. An incumbent legislator possesses several advantages. First, incumbents already have significant name recognition among the voters in their district, having won at least one previous election contest. Second, while challengers can talk about what they will do, incumbents can talk about what they are doing or have already done for the district. Finally, because of their proven success and position, incumbents generally are much better able to raise campaign funds. Such daunting advantages often keep potential candidates from challenging an incumbent who plans to seek reelection.

It is possible to get at least a minimal idea of the power of incumbency by looking at the proportion of districts in which one candidate faces no opposition from an opponent of the other major party. Because open seats usually draw more competition between the two major parties, it seems reasonable to assume that many of the seats in which both major parties did not field candidates were districts in which incumbent legislators were seeking reelection. In 2004, more than a third of all contests for state House and Senate seats included a major candidate from only one major party in the general election (see T 4.4).

More than 80 percent of the candidates for the Arkansas Senate ran unopposed in 2004, as did three out of four candidates for the Texas Senate and seven out of ten candidates for the Florida Senate. Likewise, three-fourths of the candidates for the South Carolina and Arkansas houses ran unopposed, as did seven out of ten candidates for the Florida House. That does not even include districts in which both parties fielded a candidate but only one of the candidates had a realistic chance of winning. In California, while both parties contested nine out of ten seats, not a single seat in the Assembly (forty seats) or the Senate (twenty seats) changed parties as a result of the 2004 election.

To defeat an incumbent, barring scandal or a strong national trend away from the incumbent's party, a challenger almost always needs to outspend the incumbent significantly. Given the tendency of both interest groups and political parties (which between them provide a significant amount of campaign contributions) to support incumbents, such a scenario is unlikely (Breaux and Gierzynski 1998, 87). Therefore, most "strategic politicians" (that is, potential candidates who rationally evaluate their chances of victory before deciding whether to run) who consider running against an incumbent legislator will evaluate their chances negatively and decide to sit on the sidelines and wait until the incumbent vacates the seat.

Campaign Costs

One critical factor in the selection of legislators seeking and winning seats in the legislature is the cost—financial and personal—of political success in a given state. How much money must a candidate raise to get elected? How much time must a candidate

TABLE 4.4   PERCENTAGE OF UNCONTESTED SEATES, 2004 ELECTION

Top Five		Bottom Five	
Arkansas Senate	82.4%	New Hampshire House	2.3%
South Carolina House	77.4%	Michigan House	1.8%
Texas Senate	73.3%	Minnesota House	1.5%
Arkansas House	73.0%	Utah Senate	0.0%
Florida Senate*	70.0%	Arizona Senate	0.0%

* 70% of the seats in the Rhode Island House were also uncontested.
Source: Rosenthal, Alan. 2004. *Heavy Lifting: The Job of the American Legislature.* Washington, DC: CQ, p. 18.

commit away from friends and family to be considered a serious candidate? What toll will the campaign have on the candidate's personal life?

The amount of money necessary to win a legislative election varies considerably from state to state, and sometimes from district to district within the state. While most candidates for a state legislative seat spend less than $50,000 on their campaigns, some may spend more than $1 million. A study of state legislative campaign expenditures across ten states during the 1994 election cycle revealed significant variation, with the median expenditures ranging from $219,320 in California to $3,471 in Wyoming. In competitive districts, the difference between these two states was even greater, ranging from $428,290 in California to $4,159 in Wyoming (Moncrief and Thompson 1998). Campaign costs vary for several reasons, including, as previously indicated, the geographic and population size of the district, the density of the state's population, the level of party competition (seats are "worth" more, and therefore more costly, in states in which the loss of a seat or two could mean a change in control of the legislature), and whether the legislature is a full- or part-time operation.

Money is not the only resource that candidates for the state legislature must commit. Successful candidates must also commit a great deal of time and energy to seeking a position in the legislature—time spent raising money, shaking hands, making speeches, meeting voters, and preparing issue positions. This time and energy often come at the expense of the candidate's family. The more time that a candidate has to spend on campaigning, the greater the effect of the effort on the candidate's family members. Individuals who do not have a great deal of wealth, or access to such wealth, cannot realistically seek a position in the legislature in a state that requires major campaign expenditures. In such states, one can expect a higher percentage of candidates who are male, wealthy, and with backgrounds in law or business. Many also believe that candidates who must raise a great deal of money to win their seats are more susceptible to the influences of lobbyists and interest groups that help fund those expensive campaigns than are candidates who can win with limited financial expenditures.

Multimember Legislative Districts

Legislative districts differ not only in size and composition but also in the number of legislators who represent the district. Historically, many states elected legislators from multimember districts. As late as the 1970s, more than 40 percent of all state House members and 20 percent of all state senators were elected from multimember districts (Rosenthal 1981). While a much higher proportion of legislators today are elected from single-member districts, a number of state legislative chambers still elect more than one member from at least some of their districts. As of 2005, only twenty-nine senators (of 1,971) in two states (Nevada and Vermont) were elected from multimember districts. However, about one in six House members (814 out of 5,411) were elected from such districts, with almost half of those (388) elected in New Hampshire. Besides New Hampshire, six states (Arizona, New Jersey, North Dakota, South Dakota, Vermont, and Washington) elect at least some of their House members from multimember districts (see T 4.5).

TABLE 4.5   DISTRIBUTION OF SINGLE AND MULTIMEMBER DISTRICTS,
NEW HAMPSHIRE HOUSE OF REPRESENTATIVES, 2005

Number of Legislators	Number of Districts	Number of Legislators
Single Member	12	12
Two Members	17	34
Three Members	31	93
Four Members	18	72
Five Members	6	30
Six Members	3	18
Seven Members	4	28
Eight Members	6	48
Nine Members	2	18
Ten Members	1	10
Eleven Members	1	11
Thirteen Members	2	26
Total	**103**	**400**

Source: Compiled by authors from New Hampshire House of Representatives website.

In four of the seven legislative chambers with multimember districts, two House members are elected from a district that is represented by a single senator. For example, North Dakota has forty-seven legislative districts, each of which elects one senator and two House members to the legislature. On the other hand, just twelve of the New Hampshire House's 400 members are elected from single-member districts. The remaining members are elected from districts represented by anywhere from two (seventeen districts) to thirteen members (two districts). In a similar manner, only three of the thirty Vermont senators are elected from single-member districts, with the rest elected from districts represented by two (six districts), three (three districts), and six (one district) members.

Whether a legislative district is single- or multimember can influence who its candidates will be, how their campaigns will be conducted, and the outcome of the election. On the one hand, multimember districts provide greater opportunities for challengers wanting to break into the legislature, because they do not have to run directly against a sitting member. Instead, voters vote for as many members as there are seats in the district. Generally, that should make it somewhat easier for a challenger than in a one-against-one campaign against an incumbent legislator (Cox and Morgenstern 1995). Therefore, one can expect a more diverse caliber of challengers in such races.

Multimember districts can also present some unique challenges for candidates. First, the multimember districts will cover a larger population and more extensive geographic area than if the district were divided into several single-member districts. In New

Hampshire, for example, candidates in one of the state's twelve single-member districts must focus their campaign on about 3,000 people, while their counterparts in the state's three six-member districts must campaign among almost 20,000. Candidates running in New Hampshire's two thirteen-member districts must campaign in a district that includes more than 40,000 people and may, in addition, have to campaign against as many as twenty-five other candidates, if each party nominates a full slate of candidates in the district.

Some scholars argue that multimember districts discriminate against both ethnic and minority party candidates, because electing all legislators at-large in a multimember district is likely to result in all of the elected candidates being from the majority party or majority ethnic group. If a multimember district were to be broken into smaller single-member districts, these scholars argue, it would provide minority political party and ethnic candidates a better chance to win because the party or ethnic group that is a district minority might be the majority in the smaller single-member district.

Proponents of multimember districts, on the other hand, suggest that, while they may make it more difficult for minority candidates to win, they actually improve the quality of representation that ethnic minorities may receive in the legislature. If four white candidates are elected to represent a four-member district with a sizable African American population, these advocates argue, all four will be aware that they may need some of the minority votes to be reelected. Therefore, all four will consider the needs of their African American constituents when voting. On the other hand, if the district were carved up, there might be only one legislator representing an African American majority district who would feel compelled to consider the needs of African Americans (Rosenthal 1981).

In states in which two House candidates run to represent the same district as one senator, it is quite common for the Senate and House candidates from the same party to run as a "slate," or team. This can allow candidates to share resources and increase their number of publications, flyers, and mailings. While some suggest that campaigning in multimember districts can be more expensive than in single-member districts, others have found the opposite to be true. A study of 1996 expenditures in North Carolina (which, at that time, had some multimember districts) and Vermont found campaign costs to be lower in multimember districts, both in terms of overall spending and in per candidate average, than in those states' single-member districts (Center for Voting and Democracy).

Finally, supporters of multimember district representation argue that campaigns in multimember districts may be conducted on a higher plane, because it is less likely that a campaign in a multimember district will become personal and negative. Because candidates do not run "head-to-head" against one another in multimember districts but, rather, run to secure one of the several seats available, an attack on an individual candidate may actually hurt the attacker and help other candidates. Therefore, the argument goes, candidates in multimember district races are most likely to try to set themselves apart from the crowd by focusing on policy matters more than on negative personal attacks.

District Competitiveness

Politics is about winning and losing. Electoral competition makes representative democracy work. Legislators are elected to do "the will of the people," and, if they fail to do so, the voters are expected to remove them. However, this assumes that there will be a good alternative to an ineffective legislator. Such is not always the case in U.S. state legislatures. A legislative district that is considered reasonably winnable by either party is considered to be competitive. If one party often fields no candidate or consistently runs weak candidates in a district, that district is considered noncompetitive and safe for the other political party.

A look at a 2003 survey conducted by the Joint Project on Term Limits of state legislators revealed that fewer than two-thirds reported no opposition in a primary election, and just over three in ten reported no opposition in their general election. Combining the two responses, more than a quarter of the respondents faced no opposition in either a primary or general election. For those who did face opposition, the survey suggested that the challenge was seldom serious. On average, legislators who faced primary election opposition in their most recent election garnered almost two-thirds of the vote (65 percent). The numbers are almost identical for those who faced opposition in their general election, with winning candidates receiving an average of almost 64 percent of the vote.

This is not to suggest that there are no close elections for state legislative seats. In fact, in 2004, several elections were still being contested weeks after the polls were closed. Almost two months after the November 2004 election, the Montana Supreme Court declared Democrat Jeanne Windham, the representative of District 12, by one vote! In Texas, Representative Hubert Vo was declared the winner of District 49 by thirty-three votes on February 8, 2005, more than three months after the election. In New York, incumbent senator Nicholas A. Spano was declared the winner of his seat, the next day, February 9, 2005.

The level of electoral competition has a dramatic effect on the nature of the candidates who run for a legislative seat, and on the campaign that they wage for it. The absence of competition by one of the major parties suggests one of two things—either that the district is so strongly tilted toward one party that the other party sees no realistic chance of winning, or that an incumbent is so well established in the district seat that the opposing party would rather wait until the incumbent retires before making a serious effort at winning the seat. In a district in which one party has a significant advantage, it becomes difficult to recruit a candidate to run on behalf of the disadvantaged party; also, when the incumbent decides not to seek reelection, it is almost impossible to narrow down the field for the majority party (Breaux and Jewell 1992).

Obviously, one would expect more primary competition for legislative seats in the party that usually wins a district's general election handily. In such districts, winning the primary election is usually tantamount to winning the general election. On the other hand, in districts in which the two parties are highly competitive, one can expect less competition in primary elections, as candidates and party leaders fear that a bruising primary battle will hurt their party's chance for a victory in a hotly contested general election.

Campaigns in competitive districts and those for open seats tend to generate more interest and tend to be more expensive (Alan Rosenthal 1998, 178–183). But, as has been previously pointed out, a district in which a race is likely to be expensive and competitive will probably limit the number of candidates willing and able to make a run for it.

THE ELECTION PROCESS

While the electoral context is important in determining who will seek, run in, and win elections, it does not, in the end, determine who will win. That determination is made by the voters of the district. Electoral factors merely set the stage for the electoral context, much as rules, strategies, practices, talent, and team chemistry set the stage for a basketball game. While it may appear "on paper" that one team should win the game easily, neither games nor elections are played on paper. Instead, who gets elected to a state legislature is the result of real campaigns involving real candidates and strategists with all of their various strengths and weaknesses. Elections are won and lost in strategy sessions, debates, press coverage, and the ongoing battle to raise adequate revenues with which to fund a campaign.

While an election is often thought of as an event, it is really a process. The state elections that are held every two or four years to determine who will serve in their legislatures are the culmination of a process that usually starts the day after the previous election cycle is concluded. Candidates must decide (or be persuaded) to run for a legislative seat. They must raise the necessary funds to pay for their campaign. They must earn the nomination of their party. And they must organize and run an effective campaign.

The electoral process can be divided into three distinct, yet interrelated stages. The first stage—recruitment—involves determining who is considered a good candidate for state legislative office. During this stage, potential candidates evaluate their resources, opportunities, challenges, and chances of victory in order to decide whether to enter the race. Once the potential candidates have publicly declared their intention to seek office, stage two—the candidate selection process—begins. During this stage, in all but a handful of states, candidates seek the nomination of their party to represent it as its candidate in the general election. The general election campaign to win the legislative seat is the final stage of the process. Again, in all but two states (Louisiana and Nebraska), the general election, if contested, is almost always contested by a Democratic and a Republican candidate, with candidates from minor parties seldom having any realistic chance of victory.

Each stage of the election process plays a unique and significant role in determining who will serve in a state's legislature, ultimately producing a select group of legislators from a large pool of potential candidates, much as a funnel produces a steady and narrow stream of liquid from a much wider opening. Each of the stages is complex.

Stage 1: Candidate Recruitment

While voters choose who will serve in the state legislature, and, in most cases, which candidates will receive the nominations of the major parties to run in the general election, they do not choose who will seek the post. Candidates may be encouraged, recruited, persuaded, and flattered into running, but the final decision is theirs alone. Individuals considering a run for a legislative seat must make the decision to "toss" their hat in the ring.

Why Does Someone Run for the State Legislature?

The most obvious question one might ask is, Why would anyone choose to run for the state legislature in an era when campaigns are time consuming, personal, negative, and expensive? What would motivate someone to consider a run for an office that often pays very little, requires considerable time away from home, and can open the candidate up to ridicule from opponents, the news media, and the general public? Surveys and general research suggest several likely motivations.

Recruitment by a Political Party

In some ways, candidates for the state legislature are no different than any other citizen. They like to be courted and persuaded. A recent study of state legislative candidates revealed that fewer than a third would have run without strong encouragement from others, and one in five had not even considered seeking office until approached by someone else. One of the most common reasons that candidates for a state legislature (or any office, for that matter) seek the position is that they were specifically asked to do so, often by their political party—either their local party, their state party, or their party's leaders in the legislature. According to a 1999 survey of potential state legislative candidates, almost half were encouraged to run by their local party officials, while a third were encouraged by their legislature's leaders or their state party officials (Moncrief, Squire, and Jewell 2001).

Recruitment by a Nonparty Group

While candidates like to be courted by their political parties because parties can usually provide significant resources to assist in their campaigns, parties are not the only influential players involved in candidate recruitment. The same survey cited above found that candidates were also encouraged by family members (32.7 percent), friends (22.7 percent), coworkers (19 percent), interest groups (13.6 percent), and acquaintances from church (12.1 percent). Obviously, family members, friends, and colleagues may be recruiting candidates for a different reason than interest groups. Individuals often encourage someone to seek public office because they know, like, and trust the person, whereas interest group representatives will be looking for a candidate who will support their interests at the state capitol.

Personal Ambition

While candidates for the state legislature like to be courted, that does not mean that they are devoid of ego or ambition. Indeed, many would argue that it is impossible to succeed in electoral politics without both. Many candidates decide to run for the state legislature because it will enable them to achieve some goal that is important to them—to influence public policy, to attain political influence, to further their career outside of politics, or perhaps to use the legislature as a stepping stone to statewide or federal office. A 1960s study of the Connecticut General Assembly found that its members could be divided into four groups, depending on their motivation for seeking office: lawmakers, wanting to make good policy; advertisers, wanting to advance their careers outside of politics; observers, just enjoying being part of the legislature; and reluctants, serving out of a sense of obligation (Barber 1965). In a similar manner, another close observer of the electoral process suggests that many state legislative candidates, especially Democrats, seek the office because of a desire to have a career in politics (Ehrenhalt 1991).

Motivation by a Political Issue

One of the most common motivations for anyone seeking a political office is the desire to influence an area of public policy of particular concern to that candidate. Many legislators whose nonlegislative occupation is as an educator decide to run for office because of their concern for quality education. Longtime Tennessee senator Ben Atchley, an insurance agent in Knoxville, says that he initially ran for the Tennessee House of Representatives because he felt that the policies adopted by the Tennessee legislature were not fair to small businesses (State Legislative Leaders Foundation 1993). Other candidates are motivated more by ideological issues, such as opposition to or support for abortion, school prayer, gay marriage, or gun control.

Who Considers Running for the State Legislature?

Legal requirements make virtually any citizen eligible to run for their state legislature who meets minimum age requirements (18, 21, or 25, depending upon the state and the specific legislative chamber), has lived in the district or state for a prescribed period of time, and does not have a felony arrest record. But that alone does not guarantee a large pool of potential candidates. There are very few eighteen- or twenty-one-year-olds with the desire or the resources to run for their legislature—even if they meet the other requirements. This does not mean that there are no young state legislators. Stacey Hurter and Nick Hacker, members of the 2005 North Dakota House of Representatives, are both twenty-three. Senator and former speaker of the Arkansas House of Representatives Shane Broadway was elected to the Arkansas House at twenty-one, became its speaker at twenty-seven, and was retired from the chamber because of the state's term-limits law at twenty-nine.

People Like You and Me.   The 1999 survey of potential major party candidates for the state legislature reveals that, in some ways, legislative candidates are a lot like the general population of their states. They represent the entire spectrum of ideology, from very conservative to very liberal. They come from a wide variety of occupational backgrounds, with more than half coming from business backgrounds or nonprofessional fields. While most are married, more than a quarter are widowed, divorced, or never married. About half have children living at home.

But Also Different.   While candidates for the state legislature mirror the general citizenry in some ways, the 1999 survey also revealed some marked differences. On the whole, candidates for state legislative seats are more partisan, more male, more Caucasian, and more educated than the general population. According to those candidates responding to the survey, only one in five candidates was female, and more than nine out of ten were Caucasian. On the other hand, while fewer than 6 percent of the candidates did not graduate from college, more than half had at least a four-year college degree.

Political Experience Is Not Necessary.   A decision to run for state legislative office does not require a long political resume. More than three-quarters of the potential candidates who responded to the 1999 survey were not holding an elective office at the time they made their decision to run, and less than one in ten was holding an appointive post elsewhere in government. For more than three-quarters, it was the first time that they had run for their legislature. However, these numbers do mask one distinct difference that was found between the states. While only one in ten candidates in Alabama had previously held political office, almost 30 percent had done so in the term-limited states of Maine and Colorado. A much larger percentage of candidates in those latter two states had previously served in their state's other legislative chamber and had likely been forced to relinquish their seat before they wanted to retire from legislative politics. One particular area of political experience did appear to be quite common across the country. More than 60 percent of candidates indicated that they had previously held a position in their local, state, or national party organization before deciding to run for the legislature.

Strategic Politicians.   While candidates for the state legislature may not be considered professional politicians, nor are they naive to the political game. The 1999 survey found that more than 60 percent had some previous experience in political campaigns, with experience in local campaigns being the most common. These candidates knew (or at least thought they knew) what they were getting into. This is reflected in the fact that a significantly larger percentage of the candidates that had some previous political experience ran for legislative seats that were open rather than for one in which an incumbent legislator was seeking reelection. According to the survey, 60 percent of those candidates with no previous political experience ran against an incumbent, while only 45 percent of the more experienced candidates chose to undertake what would figure to be

---

LEADERS IN ACTION

North Carolina House Leaders Break the Tie that Binds

In January 2005, Democratic representative Jim Black was elected to his fourth term as speaker of the North Carolina House of Representatives, tying him with a previous speaker for the longest tenure in that post. However, Black's has not been an easy tenure. His Democratic majority has never been higher than ten seats, and in the 2003 session, he had to share the post with a Republican cospeaker because there was an evenly divided chamber of sixty Republicans and sixty Democrats. Following the 2004 election, Black and the Democrats picked up three seats, despite the fact that Republican George W. Bush won the state by more than 10 percent and a Republican was elected to fill one of the state's U.S. Senate seats. The Democratic Party's success in the state House of Representatives was no accident, but the result of much hard work by Speaker Black and the House Democratic leadership.

Black raised and contributed more than $700,000 to the House Democratic Caucus Committee and was heavily involved in recruiting, encouraging, and providing support for Democratic candidates. The House Democrats, under the leadership of Speaker Black and Majority Leader Joe Hackney, provided training seminars for candidates, hired consultants in behalf of the party, and managed mail, news media, and polling for their candidates. Both leaders also contributed financial assistance to candidates in competitive districts and traveled the state in behalf of candidates, attending fundraisers, press conferences, and public events. They also provided support for incumbent members to provide effective constituent service. Their hard work paid off. Not a single incumbent House Democrat was defeated in 2004 general election.

Source: Conversations and electronic communications with Meredith L. Norris, political director; Maggie K. Barlow, assistant to the House majority leader; and Julie Robinson, press secretary to the speaker (January/February 2005).

---

a more uphill battle (Moncrief, Squire, and Jewell 2001). Studies of state legislators considering runs for statewide or national office support these findings (Berkman and Eisenstein 1999).

Stage 2: Candidate Nomination

Stage two of the election process—candidate selection—begins as soon as a candidate decides to run for the legislature. It is during this stage that the field of candidates who are seeking a particular legislative seat is usually reduced to two—a Democrat and a Republican—who will compete against each other for the seat in the general election. This stage of the process can often be of little importance, as more than two-thirds of all legislators face no real competition in their effort to secure their party's nomination.

When Are Nominations Contested?

While in the majority of cases only one candidate seriously seeks a party's nomination for a state legislative seat, there are certain conditions that, when they exist, are likely to result in more competition for nomination.

First, races for open seats—in which an incumbent is not seeking reelection—tend to generate more contested primaries in both the party of the incumbent and the opposing party. As has been shown, it is very difficult to unseat an incumbent legislator with all of the advantages that incumbency carries, including fundraising, and the name recognition that is built up through the visibility of holding public office (Hogan 2000). With no incumbent competing, strategic politicians from both parties are likely to view the election as their best opportunity for success, and numerous candidates are likely to seek the nomination.

Second, primary competition is likely to be higher in one-party districts in which the voters generally support candidates from one political party by substantial majorities. With the uneven distribution of population in states and legislative districts often drawn to make districts safe for one party's candidates, it has been estimated that one party or the other has a lock on the vast majority of state legislative districts with "only a tiny fraction" seen as truly competitive (Greenblatt 2004). In districts that are considered "safe" for one party, the real competition for winning the seat takes place in the majority party's primary election. The winner of that election—or, if there is no primary, the consensus nominee of the district's majority party—will, barring some unforeseen political disaster, win election to the seat in the following general election. In such cases, the majority party's nomination contest is likely to draw more interest than the general election.

How Are Nominees Selected?

One of the most important factors in determining who seeks and who gets elected to seats in a state's legislature is the procedure that the state uses for selection of its candidates. For a long period of the nation's history, political party leaders had an almost exclusive role in selecting the candidates who would represent their party in state legislative elections. But that is not the case in most states now. Instead, the vast majority of states select candidates using a direct primary election, with voters rather than political party leaders casting votes to determine the Democratic and Republican candidates. State laws provide for a number of formats for direct primary elections.

A majority of the states use a closed primary, in which only registered members of a political party are allowed to vote in that party's primary election. A closed primary system is currently used in twenty-eight states. Most of the remaining states make use of an open primary election system, in which any registered voter can cast a ballot in the primary election of either party. Republicans can vote in the Democratic primary and Democrats can vote in the Republican primary. An open primary system tends to encourage voting, but it limits the control that parties have over the selection of their nominees.

Until a 1999 Supreme Court decision ruled the procedure unconstitutional, Alaska, California, and Washington selected their candidates through a blanket primary election, in which voters from either party were permitted to vote in either party's primary and to switch back and forth from one party to the other, from office to office. In other words, a voter could cast votes for Republican candidates in that party's primary for governor and state Senate, and then switch to vote for candidates in the Democratic Party's primary for judges and the state House of Representatives.

Louisiana does things differently from everyone else. It has a nonpartisan primary, in which every candidate for an office runs at the same time, with all registered voters eligible to vote in that primary, regardless of party; the two highest vote getters in the primary election, again regardless of their respective party affiliations, face each other in the general election.

Twelve states provide for a runoff primary between the top two vote getters when there are three or more candidates and none receive a majority of the vote in the primary election. (One of those states, North Carolina, provides that a runoff primary election be held if no candidate receives a 40 percent plurality.) All but one of the twelve states that use a runoff primary are in the South (North Dakota being the lone exception). Southern states adopted the runoff system when the Democratic Party was so strong in the then "solid South" that winning the Democratic primary was tantamount to winning the general election, and political leaders wanted to ensure that the winner of an election, who would invariably be a Democrat, would receive a majority of the primary vote. In these twelve states, runoff elections are necessary in only about 10 percent of primary elections, and the candidate who finishes first in the initial primary wins the runoff about 70 percent of the time (Bullock and Johnson 1992).

While most states now use some variation of the direct primary to determine their nominees for the general election, a few states still permit their political parties to choose their nominee in a nominating convention. In South Carolina, Alabama, Georgia, and Virginia, parties have the option of having people vote in a primary election or meeting together in a convention to vote. In New Mexico, Utah, and New York, primaries are held if two or more candidates receive a specified share of the votes at the nominating convention (Bibby and Holbrook 2003).

The nature of the nominating system has a significant influence on who seeks and who gains a party's nomination for a state legislative seat—and on the type of candidate that is likely to emerge victorious in a state's general election. Candidates who win their nomination via a closed primary or a nominating convention are likely to have stronger ties to their political party and are more likely to have been recruited by their party, while those who win in open primaries may be less tied to their political party and better able to appeal to voters across party lines (Moncrief, Squire, and Jewell 2001). In a similar manner, candidates chosen within a closed primary are likely to be more reflective of the values and interests of their party than those selected in open primaries (Morehouse and Jewell 2003, 128–133). Selection through a nonpartisan primary system weakens partisan connections even more.

In an effort to retain control over candidate selection, political parties in seven states make preprimary endorsements, in which party leaders, meeting in convention, publicly endorse a particular candidate. These endorsements—in Colorado, Connecticut, New Mexico, New York, North Dakota, Rhode Island, and Utah—seem to work, with the candidate endorsed by the party convention winning the party's primary nomination more than three-quarters of the time (Bibby and Holbrook 2003, 84; Morehouse and Jewell 2003).

Who Votes in Primary Elections?

While a few states choose their candidates for the general election using a convention process, primary elections are, by far, the most common method of candidate selection. Virtually all legislative candidates who faced opposition for their party's nomination did so in a primary election, whether it was open, closed, or blanket.

Primary elections are generally characterized by lower voter turnout than in the general elections that follow them. In primaries in which a candidate runs unopposed, thereby guaranteeing that candidate the party nomination, the election is a formality; turnout is often less than 10 percent. In many primaries, especially those involving a popular and heavily favored incumbent candidate, the contest will be unlikely to generate much interest among the electorate. Voter turnout in primary elections can also be low because many states hold their primary elections months before their general election, at a time when most voters are paying scant attention to politics. In 2004, for example, Republican primaries in seven states were held before the end of February, more than eight months before the general election. Another twenty-two states held their Republican primary during March. In a similar manner, twenty-four states held their 2004 Democratic Party primary elections before the end of March (Sabato and Scott 2001).

Primary voters in most states tend to be much more partisan and more politically aware than voters who tend to vote only in general elections. Voters in Republican primaries tend to be among the most ardent (and often most conservative) Republican voters, while Democratic primary voters tend to reflect the most strongly Democratic (and often most liberal) members of their party. Along these same lines, studies have shown that larger proportions of primary voters than of voters in general elections tend to be interested in politics and government generally.

Finally, primary voters tend to have a demographic profile that is different from those who do not vote in primaries. Just as general election voters tend to be more educated, more professional, and older than the general public, those who vote in primary elections are even better educated, even more likely to hold professional jobs, and older, on average, than those who usually vote in only general elections. Because primary voters have a distinct profile, the candidates chosen in a party primary may not be those most likely to appeal to general election voters. The Republican Party is generally seen as representing conservative viewpoints, and the Democratic Party as representing liberal viewpoints; thus voters in Republican primaries tend to choose candidates that are more conservative than the general voting public, and voters in Democratic primaries often choose candidates that are more liberal. This can sometimes make it difficult for a primary winner to win the general election, especially if the opposing party's candidate did not have to win a primary to secure the nomination.

What Does It Take to Win a Primary Election?

While nominations for the majority of state legislative seats are won without opposition, more than a third are contested. In a contested nomination, several factors contribute to determining who emerges as the victor.

Usually, the most notable factor in determining how someone will vote in a general election—partisan identification—is of no significance in a primary election, because all of the candidates in a primary are (with the exceptions, previously noted, of Louisiana and Nebraska) of the same party, with Democrats running against Democrats for the Democratic nomination and Republicans running against Republicans for their party's nomination. One possible exception may be open and blanket primaries, in which particular candidates might try to appeal to the members of their own party while others might make an appeal to voters from the other party to cross over and vote for them.

In the absence of partisan identification as a voting cue, voters rely on other factors, most importantly name recognition. Although candidate name recognition may occasionally prove to be disadvantageous, it is generally a positive factor for a candidate. (Consider, for example, the 2004 failed candidacy for the Michigan House of Representatives of John Ramsey, father of child murder victim JonBenet Ramsey. Before he was cleared by authorities, the news media had suggested he was a possible suspect in the murder; he finished last in a five-person primary contest.) When voters have little information about candidates, as can often be the case in primary elections for state legislative seats, any information is better than none. Relatively unknown candidates will try to draw attention to their campaigns to increase their name recognition. A Wisconsin legislator who is an Elvis Presley impersonator considered officially changing his name to Elvis in preparation for a run for governor (Walters 2000).

Previous political experience may also be a factor that can prove to be an asset in a primary election. A candidate who has previously held an elective office will have some campaign experience that should prove helpful. Also, a previous holder of public office may have some established name recognition, although one need not have previously held political office to have name recognition with the voters. Popular athletes, successful business leaders, and local news media personalities all have name recognition that can translate into political success in a primary election. Finally, while primary candidates with no previous experience in elective office must talk about what they will do, candidates who have held office are often able to talk about what they have already done.

Money is necessary for winning primary elections, just as it is for winning general elections. A recent survey of state legislators revealed that the top two candidates in contested primary elections spent an average of $30,000 in their primaries, with one candidate spending $900,000 (Joint Project on Term Limits 2003). It may be argued that, in the absence of partisan identification as a voting cue, money may be even more important in primary elections than in the general elections. Candidates with little or no money may have an extremely appealing message to convey to the voters, but few voters will ever hear it. Money permits candidates to buy name recognition and provides them with the opportunity to get their message out to the voting public. A study of state legislative primary elections in six states over several years in the late 1980s and early 1990s revealed that average campaign expenditures by winning candidates were greater than those of losing candidates in every state in every year (Breaux and Gierzynski 1998).

Stage 3: The General Election

The final step in the electoral process is the general election, which determines who will represent the people in the legislature. Apart from rare occasions when there are serious third-party candidates who have not been required to secure their nominations through the primary process, the general election campaign begins as soon as the Democratic and Republican Party nominees are selected.

What Are the Key Elements of a Successful State Legislative Campaign?

Each election campaign must reflect the political, legal, structural, and electoral environments that characterize the electoral district. However, most successful state legislative campaigns share some common characteristics. First, each successful campaign must include an effective candidate who reflects the concerns, qualities, and character of the voters in the district. Second, successful campaigns need an effective campaign organization. Third, few campaigns will get very far without an effective message or issue strategy. Finally, just as cars run on gas, political campaigns must be fueled by campaign resources—people, information, and money.

An Effective Candidate.   While it is easy to label a candidate for a state legislative seat as an effective candidate after all of the votes are counted and the candidate has won the election, more than two hundred years of U.S. election experience has revealed some characteristics that can indicate before an election whether a candidate is likely to run an effective campaign. In general, effective candidates are those with name recognition, political experience, party support, a significant time commitment, and access to financial support. These qualities are critical for all candidates across all state legislative districts. Some qualities, such as religious affiliation and commitment, marital status, and even physical appearance, can also be important, but those will vary in importance from district to district and, over time, can change even within a district.

Other qualities are more predictable. An effective candidate will almost always reflect the values and ideology of the district. An effective candidate in a rural Texas district is going to have a very different ideology and profile than an effective candidate in an inner-city district of New York City. Conservative Republican districts generally elect conservative Republican legislators, just as liberal Democratic districts usually elect liberal Democratic candidates. In a similar manner, a successful candidate for a seat in the full-time, professional California Senate is likely to be very different from a winning candidate for a seat in the part-time Delaware Senate in terms of the level of time commitment to both campaigning and legislative service. Professional legislatures tend to attract more professional politicians with high educational attainment, more members from professional occupations, and more members with a commitment to "big government," while successful candidates to citizen legislatures tend to represent more diverse vocational backgrounds and to be less interested in making politics a career. These differences are reflected in the types of candidates that run for and win election to a state's legislature.

A Campaign Organization.   While most political campaigns are required by law to have only two people, the candidate and a treasurer, most are more elaborately organized. At minimum, most campaign organizations will include, in addition to the candidate and the treasurer, a campaign manager, a volunteer coordinator, and a fundraising director. Campaigns in districts that tend to require more professional campaigns may also include staff members to oversee polling, media coordination, and research.

The campaign treasurer is responsible for filing all of the financial reports required by the state and for ensuring that all campaign contributions and expenditures meet the state's legal requirements concerning elections. Campaign mangers generally serve as the overall coordinator of the campaign, overseeing its various pieces much as a conductor leads an orchestra, deciding when and how to introduce each "instrument" most effectively into the campaign. Working closely with the candidate, the campaign manager coordinates the message, schedule, staff, and fundraising components of the campaign. Because the majority of state legislative campaigns are low-cost operations, volunteers are critical, and that can make the job of volunteer coordinator, who is responsible for recruiting, organizing, and coordinating volunteers, very important. In many campaigns, particularly those involving citizen or hybrid legislatures, volunteer coordinators are themselves volunteers, receiving no money for their efforts. Sometimes, members of a candidate's family or even candidates themselves will fill some, or even most, of these roles. Candidates may not, however, serve as their own campaign treasurer (Shea and Burton 2001).

While the majority of campaigns for state legislative seats are not elaborate operations, campaigns in some districts can be expensive and organizationally complex. In such cases, campaign organization services may be contracted out to campaign consultants or consulting firms. Among the types of campaign experts that might be employed by a sophisticated state legislative campaign would be a communications director, hired to help develop the campaign's message and see that it is disseminated throughout the district in the most effective manner—perhaps through professionally prepared direct mailings to voters, or through carefully crafted television or radio spots. In order to determine what issues are of greatest concern to a district's voters or how the candidate's ongoing campaign effort is being perceived by the voters, more elaborate legislative campaigns will hire a professional pollster to survey samples of likely voters and provide the campaign with information that can help to enhance the candidate's attractiveness. Pollsters can help candidates to determine what issues are of special concern to the voters and what they see as the strengths and the weaknesses of both the candidate and the candidate's opponent. In highly organized legislative campaigns, candidates also sometimes employ a consultant to conduct opposition research to determine if the candidate's opponent has any special liabilities that could be exploited by the candidate. Oftentimes, the state or legislative party organization also provide, or assist in conducting, this type of research.

An Effective Campaign Theme or Message.   While an effective organization can be of major importance to a candidate's campaign for the state legislature, the candidate must also have something to say to the voters of the district that they will find appealing. As with an effective candidate, an effective message or theme must reflect the problems, concerns, and needs of the district. Candidates in conservative districts generally focus on moral values or limiting the scope and size of government ("Send Your Values to Denver—Vote for Robert Jones," or "Make the Government in Austin Accountable to You!"). On the other hand, candidates in suburban or urban districts will tend to focus on what government can do to improve the quality of life of the voters, with themes such as "Government that Works for You!" or "Vote for Your Children's Education—Vote for Jane Jones."

An effective campaign theme will also need to reflect the strengths of the candidate, relative to the candidate's opponent. For example, if a candidate is young and new to politics and running against an older incumbent legislator, the candidate's theme or message should emphasize youth, vitality, and new ideas ("Vote for Joe Smith—It's Time for a Change!" or "New Ideas for a New Tomorrow!"). On the other hand, the incumbent legislator's campaign will likely focus on contrasting the candidate's experience and record with the opponent's lack of accomplishments.

Oftentimes, effective themes reflect statewide or national campaign trends. Following the terrorist attacks of September 11, 2001, virtually all campaigns in 2002 focused on security and efforts to preserve "our way of life," regardless of the party, or the ideology of the candidates. When the economy is bad, most campaigns will, of necessity, focus on that economy and what can be done to improve it. When politicians as a whole are particularly unpopular (as is the case during and following a high-profile scandal) and incumbent legislators fear that the voters are in a "throw the rascals out" frame of mind, their campaigns will likely back away from placing too much emphasis on the candidate's incumbent status.

Adequate Campaign Resources.   No campaign, regardless of the effectiveness of the candidate, the quality of its organization, the ability of the staff, or the power of the candidate's message, is likely to result in victory if it does not possess the resources to reach the people of the district. Campaigns must have the means to get their message out to the voters. While the most commonly recognized resource is money, people and organizational support can also be of critical importance to a successful campaign.

Jess Unruh, speaker of the California Assembly during the 1960s, once noted that money "is the mother's milk of politics," implying that without money, politics cannot survive. While perhaps that is a bit of an exaggeration, Unruh was not far off. Money is critical for candidates who want to get their message out to the public, whether that public is the almost 1 million people represented by a California senator or the 3,000 or so New Hampshirites in a single-member district in the New Hampshire House of Representatives. A recent study of state legislative campaign expenditures around the country found the cost of a single campaign to be as high as $1.7 million in one California Senate race (primary and general election combined), with an average expenditure of almost $60,000.

The majority of expenditures in most campaigns go to disseminating the candidate's message—through direct mailings, flyers, yard signs, and newspaper, radio, and television advertising. In more elaborate campaigns, money is used to hire professional experts to develop mass-media strategies and campaign themes, and to conduct political polls. Studies have repeatedly shown that, at all levels of campaigning, the candidate with the most money generally wins in both primary and general election contests (Breaux and Gierzynski 1998).

As important as money is to a successful campaign, few if any campaigns can be won with money alone. While state legislative campaigns in California, Ohio, New York, Michigan, and Pennsylvania might be highly professional and expensive, most are still relatively personal affairs with more yard signs than paid advertising (Moncrief, Squire, and Jewell 2001). In these cases, people—most often in the form of volunteers—are critical to getting the candidate's message out to the voters. People are often needed to run phone banks (that is, to telephone prospective voters), to drive voters to the polls, to put up yard signs, to knock on doors, and to stuff envelopes. Evidence suggests that even the best-funded and most "media-centered" political campaigns cannot win without people on the ground making sure that potential voters are contacted, signs are posted, and voters are delivered to the polls (Shea and Burton 2001).

Successful legislative candidates must have significant organizational support from within their district, from such groups as labor unions, professional organizations, and civic and special interest associations. In addition to providing the candidate's campaign with volunteers and money, these groups often provide significant political and technical expertise that can prove invaluable to a candidate. Such information is especially important for first-time candidates for a legislative seat. It can provide the candidate with a history regarding what has or has not worked in the past, which key groups and community leaders must be courted, and which issues have proven to be particularly popular with the district's voters in recent campaigns. Some of these groups may provide invaluable free services that the campaign might otherwise have to hire someone to perform. A supportive telephone company union might, for example, provide a candidate that it supports with free phones, phone lines, and volunteers to operate

TABLE 4.6   LEGISLATIVE TURNOVER, 2004 ELECTIONS*

Top Five		Bottom Five	
Maine Senate	45.7	Illinois Senate	5.1
South Dakota Senate	40.0	Florida Senate	5.1
Nebraska Legislature	39.6	North Dakota Senate	4.3
Oklahoma House	39.0	Arkansas Senate	2.9
Arkansas House	38.4	Delaware Senate	0.0

Source: National Conference of State Legislatures (http://www.ncsl.org).

*Percentage of new legislators.

phone banks. Or members of a fraternity or sorority from a local college might provide hours of volunteer service and invaluable access to young voters on campus for a candidate that they find appealing.

What Determines a Person's Vote?

There are a number of factors, some long term and some short term, that determine how a person will vote in an election contest between two candidates. Long-term factors are characteristics of the voter that are likely to remain stable and unchanged from one election to the next, while short-term factors are associated with the particular election and can be subject to change from one election year to another.

Long-Term Factors.   Long-term factors that influence voter decisions fall into two distinct categories. One category concerns biological characteristics that are unlikely to change, including a person's gender, race, and ethnicity. In most recent elections, a majority of the nation's women and ethnic minorities have been predisposed to vote Democratic for economic, social, and political reasons. Districts that are predominantly Hispanic or African American generally elect Democratic representatives. Women are statistically more likely than men to vote for the type of candidates that are supported by these ethnic groups.

Some nonbiological long-term characteristics that are quite stable from one election to another include income, education, ideology, religious orientation, and partisan affiliation. Again, these variables tend to predispose voters toward candidates of one party or the other. Historical voting patterns suggest that Republican candidates generally fare better than Democrats among voters that are wealthy, better educated (except at the highest levels of educational attainment, with Ph.D.-holders more likely to vote for Democratic candidates), ideologically conservative, and Protestant or fundamentalist Christian. Conversely, recent elections suggest that voters who are less wealthy, less educated, more liberal, Jewish, or Roman Catholic are more likely to support Democratic candidates. These factors, especially a strong psychological identification with a particular party on the part of a voter, tend to be even more important in determining how someone will vote in state legislative election contests than in races for national or statewide offices, because voters often have much more limited information about their state legislative candidates than they do about candidates for national or statewide office. They therefore tend to rely on cues like partisan identification to help them make their decisions in state legislative election contests (Conover and Feldman 1989).

Short-Term Factors.   While these long-term factors predispose a voter to support a candidate of one particular party or the other, short-term factors may cause a person to vote in a way that might not be expected. Some well-educated, wealthy professional men will, for example, vote for a Democratic candidate, while some poor minority women who have not completed high school will vote Republican. Short-term voting factors are determined by a particular campaign—the candidates, the issues, and national trends. By definition, they are much less stable than the long-term factors and are likely to change from one campaign to the next.

Candidate characteristics are very important in state legislative elections. Some voters may have a personal affinity for a particular candidate that will cause them to vote for someone they would not normally be expected to support on the basis of long-term factors. This is particularly true for state legislative and local office races, in which many candidates live near, work with, and even personally know their voters. A lifelong Republican may support a Democratic candidate because he has been a friend of the family or attended the same church or worked in the same office with the candidate, and such personal knowledge overrides all of that voter's normal partisan predispositions. People will often vote for candidates with whom they feel they have something in common, even if that commonality has nothing to do with politics. Women are more likely to vote for female candidates. African Americans tend to vote more often for African American candidates. Youthful candidates do better among younger voters.

Just as a particular candidate may move voters to act contrary to their normal predisposition, particular issues may also move voters out of their comfort zone. If an especially emotional issue, such as abortion, becomes important in a campaign, a person who is generally predisposed to vote Democratic but is pro-life may decide to vote for a pro-life Republican candidate rather than the pro-choice Democratic opponent. Likewise, if the economy is going well while a Democrat is in office, a wealthy Republican voter may be reluctant to vote against the Democratic incumbent for fear of disrupting the economic prosperity; conversely, if the economy is going poorly, that same Republican may vote against a Republican candidate who is seen as to blame for the economic woes. Candidates who can focus their campaigns on issues important to them

can generally be expected to do well (Shea and Burton 2001, 117–129). If the opposition defines the key issues, then its candidate will be the more likely winner. Democrats tend to do better when campaigns are about social issues such as education, the
environment, and government services, whereas Republican candidates tend to fare
better when the focus is on moral, economic, and security issues.

Regardless of such factors, some candidates may win or lose a seat in the state legislature through virtually no fault, or effort, of their own. Because many voters often have
so little information about the specific viewpoints or positions of their state legislative
candidates, the outcomes of state legislative elections are often the result of national
trends. A Republican candidate who is running for a closely contested legislative seat
in a year when Republicans are running well nationwide can expect that the national
trend will increase the chance for victory. Likewise, a Democratic candidate who is engaged in a contested race in a year in which the party's candidates for governor, U.S.
senator, and president are especially popular with the voters is likely to benefit significantly from the popularity of the party's candidates. In recent memory, two elections
stand out as being dominated by national trends. In 1974, following the Watergate scandal and the resignation of President Richard Nixon, Democrats gained a majority in
twenty-four state legislative chambers that had been controlled by the Republicans during the previous term. Twenty years later, in 1994, on the heels of their Contract with
America and the unpopularity of Democratic president Bill Clinton, Republicans cap-
tured control of eighteen legislative chambers that had been under Democratic control
(Little 1997).

Another national trend that is more predictable, but no less important, is legislative
redistricting. After the decennial census that is conducted at beginning of each new
decade, each state is required by law to redraw its state legislative districts to make
their individual populations conform to the new census data. While a handful of states
conduct this process through a nonpartisan or nonlegislative entity, redistricting is
most often done by the state legislature. In a few states, approval of a redistricting plan
requires more than a simple majority, protecting a party that is in the minority from
having the majority draw a plan that will enhance its chances of retaining its majority.
But where one party is in the majority in both chambers and only a simple majority
vote is required to approve a redistricting plan, the majority party will generally redraw
the districts with two things in mind. First, they will protect and even increase their
own majority. Second, they will want to protect their incumbent members from future
challengers. With the advent of sophisticated technology that allows the drawing of districts with the stroke of an electronic pen, a party that controls both chambers of a state
legislature is increasingly able to draw legislative districts to maximize its majority and
its political advantage.

With each decade's redistricting, more and more state legislative districts are being
drawn to be safe for candidates of one party or the other. Even in states in which the
presidential races of 2000 and 2004 were very close (Florida, Ohio, Michigan, and Penn-

The new Texas congressional redistricting map displayed in Austin on August 9, 2003. The map was redrawn by state legislators to allow Republicans to win more congressional seats in the U.S. Congress. (Jana Birchum/Getty Images)

sylvania), the party that controlled both houses of the state's legislature maintained a lock on control of both chambers (Greenblatt 2004). In California, while more than a third of the seats in the state Assembly were open in 2004, not a single seat changed parties. All incumbents seeking reelection were victorious, and, in open contests, every Democratic seat held by a Democrat and every one held by a Republican remained with that party. Following the 2004 elections, a number of efforts were launched around the country to try to reform redistricting processes. It remains to be seen whether any of them will prove successful (Nagourney 2005).

These long- and short-term factors are often arrayed along a "funnel of causality" suggesting that the long-term factors are more subtle and more removed from a voter's decision, while the short-term factors tend to be more immediate. Put another way, the short-term factors at the small end of the "funnel" tend to have more of an impact on the voter's final decision but are often unable to override the historical, social, economic, and political predispositions established by the long-term factors (Campbell et al. 1960).

Who Wins State Legislative General Elections?

At the beginning of an election season, most state legislative candidates believe that they can win or they would not run. However, experience tells us that candidates that possess certain characteristics are much more likely than others to emerge as winners in their election contests. Even running a "perfect" campaign does not guarantee victory, especially if the candidate is running against a candidate who is the incumbent, well financed, and is of the majority party.

Incumbency. The single best predictor of victory in a state legislative race is incumbency. If the candidate is the current holder of the seat, that candidate can be expected to win about nine out of ten times. Incumbent candidates usually have enormous advantages over their challengers, including name recognition, previous experience in running a successful legislative campaign, a track record of constituent service, legislative accomplishments for the district, and better access (by virtue of their incumbency)

LEGISLATURES AND THE PUBLIC
The Power of Legislative Redistricting

Prior to the election of 2004, Democrats had controlled the Georgia House of Representatives for more than 130 years. Going into that election, they had a majority of 35 seats (107 to 72, with one vacancy). On the day following the election, Republicans had an eight-seat majority (94 to 86), which quickly grew to 18 seats (99 to 81) with the defection of five rural conservative Democrats who had won reelection on the Democratic line. How could such a dramatic change—a party shift of 27 seats, a Republican majority for the first time in more than a century—happen in a single election?

Republican president George W. Bush ran extremely well in Georgia in 2004, carrying almost 60 percent of the vote. Republican prospects had already been improving in the state in recent years, with the election of a Republican governor in 2002, the GOP's seizure of control of the state Senate in 2002, and a string of victories in senatorial and congressional elections. But to really understand the dramatic shift, one need only look at the legislative districts created by three federal judges who had struck down a district plan drawn by a Democrat-controlled legislature in 2001.

The district maps drawn in 2001 by the majority Democratic leadership of the Georgia Senate and House had "suppressed the Republican vote," according to Professor Charles Bullock of the University of Georgia. In order to protect the Democratic majorities in the two chambers, the 2001 districts crowded Republicans into a minority of districts, ensuring that they would win in those districts but making it much more difficult for them to win a majority of all districts. The three-judge panel ruled the redistricting plan unconstitutional and drew its own plan. Those maps were the basis for the 2004 elections that completed a switch from the Democrats to the Republicans as the dominant political party in Georgia.

Source: Dodd, Brenda M. 2004. "Election 2004: What Happened and Why." Georgia Public Policy Foundation (http://www.gppf.org/article.asp?RT=7&p=pub/General/bullock041111.htm).

to campaign money and other resources needed for winning a campaign (Morehouse and Jewell 2003, 195).

Candidates from the Majority Party.   As has been explained, the partisan affiliation of voters is the single best predictor of which candidate they will vote for. While this may sound like a contradiction of the importance of incumbency, it is not. Incumbents do well because a large majority of them are elected from districts in which their party has a distinct advantage in partisan identification. Furthermore, incumbents often become incumbents and continue to be reelected because the districts are drawn to provide a big advantage to their party in terms of voter party identification. Even when an incumbent steps down, the candidate of the incumbent's party will usually be the odds-on favorite to win election, with the most hotly contested competition often taking place in the incumbent party's primary rather in the general election (Greenblatt 2004).

Candidates Who Spend the Most.   While most would like to believe that, in a state legislative election as in any election contest, issues matter more than money, campaign results tell a different story. As has been previously explained, the candidate who spends the most money in a state legislative election race wins the vast majority of the contests. That is true in both primary and general elections. It is true in seats in which a challenger is trying to defeat an incumbent as well as seats in which an incumbent is not running. It is true in rural districts and urban districts. It is true in professional legislatures, citizen legislatures, and hybrid legislatures, although it appears to be most true in professional legislatures. A study of campaign expenditures in eighteen states during the early 1990s found that more than 60 percent of candidates who spent more than their opponents were victorious, with the percentage exceeding 90 percent in California, Illinois, Pennsylvania, and Missouri (Cassie and Breaux 1998; Breaux and Gierzynski 1998).

Who Serves in the State Legislature?

Elections legitimize the democratic process and the governments that they produce. They select a group of people who will represent and serve their fellow citizens. Elections provide those who are elected to a legislative body with the authority to make the laws that will govern the lives of the people that elect them. Because of this, it is important to understand exactly who the people are who serve in state legislatures and where they come from.

While state legislators are elected to represent their constituents, legislators cannot (nor, according to many, should they) completely separate themselves from the demographic, economic, and sociological attributes that define them. Men are different from women. Liberals have a different perspective than conservatives. Lawyers will often view the world differently than teachers. Legislators with little or no political experience approach their job differently than do legislators who come from a more political background, just as legislators who view their legislative position as the apex of a political career behave differently from those who have their eyes on the state's governorship or a seat in Congress. In many ways, state legislatures are more diverse now than they have ever been. This is especially true when it comes to the gender and race of their members.

Gender.   Women are, and have always been, underrepresented in state legislatures. In 1969, more than seven decades after the first female state legislator was elected, only 4 percent of the state legislators in the United States were female, with no women legislators in some Southern states. However, by 2005 that percentage had grown significantly, with women constituting 22.5 percent of state legislative members. This aggregate number masks significant differences across the country, with the percentage of women legislators as high as a third or more in six states but less than 13 percent in five. The highest percentage of women legislators to date was in the Washington legislature in 1999, when just over 40 percent of that body was female (see T 4.7).

A Tale of Two Successful Legislative Candidates

Gilda Cobb-Hunter and Lewis R. Vaughn are members of the South Carolina House of Representatives. Both were unopposed in their 2004 reelection bids. Those two qualities may be just about the only thing that Cobb-Hunter and Vaughn had in common.

Representative Cobb-Hunter is a female African American Democrat from an urban district who works as a social work administrator. Representative Vaughn is a white male Republican with roots buried deep in the rural South. He is a retired businessman, a Mason, and a member of the Blue Ridge Ruritan Club. Representative Cobb-Hunter is on the board of directors of Planned Parenthood of South Carolina and is a member of the South Carolina Civil Liberties Union and the Branchville National Association for the Advancement of Colored Persons; she is also a national committeewoman for the Democratic National Committee. In 2004, she received an A++

State Representative Gilda Cobb-Hunter, a Democrat, pumps her fist during a rally to support tougher domestic violence legislation in April 2005 at the statehouse in Columbia, South Carolina. Looking on is Attorney General Henry McMaster. (AP Photo/Mary Ann Chastain)

Historically, women have tended to be less likely to hold seats in state legislatures for a variety of reasons, some within their control but many beyond. On the one hand, there are still cultural barriers that make it less acceptable for women to get involved in politics, particularly if the position requires an extended leave of absence from the home and family. Despite dramatic increases in the proportion of women working outside the home, women are still expected to take a much greater role in raising the family and in household chores (Elder 2004). These expectations are particularly high among both men and women in the South, where the proportion of women is lowest.

from a gay rights organization for her votes on issues important to that community. Representative Vaughn received an F- from that same group.

In South Carolina's 2003–2004 legislative term, Representative Vaughn was a primary sponsor of bills to provide public money for private schools, to define an unborn fetus as a living being, to prohibit cloning, to require that criminals be identified as criminals on their driver's license, to regulate adult businesses, and to limit state spending. On the other hand, Representative Cobb-Hunter sponsored legislation to expand the responsibilities of the State Commission for Minority Affairs, to provide government support for low-income families, to improve awareness and punishment regarding domestic violence, to create an independent commission on women, and to provide for the creation of a breast cancer awareness license plate.

As different as these two members of the same state legislative chamber are, they have both been highly successful candidates. It is expected that both will be able to hold their seats for as long as they wish. They are so different because the districts they represent are so different. Neither could ever be elected in the district of the other. Representative Cobb-Hunter represents a House district that is predominantly poor, urban, and African American. On the other hand, Representative Vaughn's district is predominantly rural, Republican, and conservative.

Source: South Carolina House of Representatives web page (http://www.scstatehouse.net/html-pages/house2.html).

Along similar lines, surveys suggest that women, particularly in some parts of the country, are still conditioned to believe that politics is not their place but, instead, should be left to the men.

Ethnicity.   Historically, ethnic minorities, particularly African Americans, have been underrepresented in state legislatures. While the proportion of minority legislators is increasing, just 8.3 percent of state legislators were African American in 2003, well below the overall African American population (see T 4.8). Still, the percentage is significantly up from under 2 percent in 1970 (Haynie 2001). Just over 2 percent of all state legislators were Latino in 2003, also well below that group's national percentage. Not

TABLE 4.7   PERCENTAGE OF WOMEN LEGISLATORS, 2005

Top Five		Bottom Five	
Maryland	34.0	Pennsylvania	12.6
Delaware	33.9	Mississippi	12.6
Arizona	33.3	Kentucky	12.3
Nevada	33.3	Alabama	10.0
Washington	33.3	South Carolina	8.8

Source: National Conference of State Legislatures, Women's Legislative Network of NCSL (http://www.ncsl.org).

surprisingly, these numbers hide significant differences across the states. While seven state legislatures have no African American legislators, more than one in five legislators are African American in five Southern states—Mississippi (29 percent), Alabama (26 percent), Maryland (23 percent), Georgia (22 percent), and Louisiana (21 percent). Not surprisingly, Mississippi, the state with the greatest percentage of African American legislators, also has the largest percentage of African American citizens of any state—more than 35 percent of its population. Likewise, while four in ten New Mexico legislators are Hispanic, as is one in five in California and Texas, there are no Hispanic or Latino legislators in twenty-six states. Again New Mexico, California, and Texas rank first, second, and third, respectively, among the fifty states in their percentages of Hispanic and Latino residents.

Party and Ideology.   While demographic characteristics influence the attitudes and behaviors of state legislators, they are often overridden by two other more overtly political factors—political party and political ideology—when it comes time for legislators to vote on legislation in their chambers. Male and female legislators vote together in support of their political party more often than they vote with legislators of their gender from the opposing party. Political party affiliation is recognized as the most important predictor of legislator voting behavior in most state legislative chambers. It is interesting to note that, in 2005, the distribution of Republican and Democratic legislators across the country could not have been more balanced, with Democrats holding a 15-seat advantage in the lower chambers (out of 5,411 seats) and Republicans clinging to a 16-seat margin in the upper chambers (out of 1,971 seats)—an overall Republican margin of exactly one seat nationwide!

Along with political party affiliation, political ideology is an important factor in determining how a legislator will vote or what a legislator's priorities are likely to be. A 2003 poll of state legislators found that most considered themselves relatively moderate in their ideological viewpoints. The 2003 poll revealed that just over 5 percent con-

TABLE 4.8   PERCENTAGE OF AFRICAN AMERICAN LEGISLATORS, 2003

Top Five		Bottom Five	
Mississippi	26	Montana	0
Alabama	25	North Dakota	0
Maryland	22	South Dakota	0
Louisiana	22	West Virginia	0
Georgia	21	Wyoming*	0

*There were also no Afrian American legislators in Idaho.

Source: National Conference of State Legislatures (http:/www.ncsl.org).

sidered themselves either extremely liberal or extremely conservative, while more than half (54.1 percent) indicated that they were either middle of the road (22.9 percent), somewhat liberal (10.7 percent), or somewhat conservative (19.3 percent). Almost a third (30.6 percent) indicated that they were conservative, compared with only about 10 percent who identified themselves as liberal.

Where Have They Been?

State legislators do not just emerge one day out of obscurity. They usually bring with them experiences, skills, and interests that contribute to how they will legislate and what policy positions they will take. Just as it is not possible for legislators to separate their gender, race, or ideology from their positions on issues, legislators' actions are also a reflection of their lives. On the whole, state legislators reflect the kind of varied backgrounds common to U.S. society. They have differing levels of education, income, and job experience, and differing views.

Family Income.   On the whole, state legislators are not particularly wealthy. A 2004 survey of legislators showed a wide range of incomes, with about one in seven reporting a family income of less than $50,000 annually. Another quarter reported incomes between $50,000 and $75,000, similar to the percentage of the total population that reported incomes in that range. Almost a third reported incomes between $100,000 and $250,000, but less than one in fifteen reported an income in excess of $250,000. Compared with the income distribution of the U.S. Senate, where almost half of the members report annual incomes in excess of $1 million, the membership of the country's state legislatures seems downright common. Relative to the distribution of incomes in the general population, state legislators appear only a slight bit wealthier than the people they represent.

Occupation.   Advocates of part-time or citizen legislatures argue that one of their benefits is the presence of a wide variety of occupations that are likely to be represented. Legislators who come from varied vocational or occupational backgrounds, these supporters argue, bring their diverse experiences to the legislature and use them in making pubic policy. For example, a teacher or principal may have special insight into educational issues that will assist members of their chamber's education committee. According to a 2004 nationwide survey of legislators, 61.3 percent of state legislators received income from an additional job outside of their legislative service. However, the proportion of legislators with outside incomes varied significantly, ranging from more than 90 percent in Nevada, where the legislature meets in regular session only every other year, to about 15 percent in the full-time California legislature. Obviously, the much greater time demands of professional legislatures such as those of California, Pennsylvania, New York, and Massachusetts mean that those bodies will have more full-time legislators than will those of smaller states (Joint Project on Term Limits 2004).

An analysis of 2002 personal financial disclosure forms of more than 7,000 legislators in forty-seven states revealed that about one in six legislators received additional income from work in a law firm. Another 10 percent reported outside income from real estate or business ventures. Some 9 percent indicated current employment in the field of education and another 4 percent in agriculture, while 10 percent listed themselves as retired from a private-sector occupation (Dagan 2004). Others received significant income from nonprofits and a variety of other sources.

Previous Government Experience.   Vocational or occupational activity is not the only experience that is important in determining how legislators vote and act. Many are also influenced by personal political experiences that they bring to the legislature. It is in political offices held before coming to the state legislature that many members develop the political views, skills, and ideology that will define their legislative careers.

While the majority of state legislators have had some political experience before their election to the legislature, ranging from political activist or volunteer to elected official, only a little more than a quarter have prior service in an elected position. According to the 2004 survey, 53.6 percent held no elected political position prior to their election to the state legislature. Of the remaining legislators, 16.9 percent had come from an elected local legislative position, usually serving as a member of the city council or the county commission. Another 11.4 percent had served in a local executive post, most often mayor or head of their county commission. About 5 percent had served on their local school board, while about 8 percent had served in an elective capacity in their local or state party organization.

DIVERSITY IN THE LEGISLATURE
Membership in a Citizen Legislature

The Maine legislature is often cited as the epitome of a citizen legislature, with members paid low salaries, sessions of short duration, small districts, and most legislators living relatively close to the state capitol of Augusta. A look at the occupations of the legislators who served in the 2003–2004 session of the Maine House of Representatives reveals a very diverse set of occupational experiences. The chamber's membership included eighteen educators (seven active and eleven retired), while another four were in education administration (two active and two retired). There were ten attorneys, two farmers, four members involved in social work (two active and two retired), and ten in the field of health care (nine active and one retired). Six legislators were involved in the pulp and paper industry, while another four were involved in forestry. Nineteen members were businesspeople and five were self-employed. Overall there were thirty-four retirees in the 2003–2004 Maine House of Representatives, many of them having come from the ranks of business and government. Three members formerly served as legislative staff, four members had previous service in the state Senate, and seven of the freshmen members had previously served in the House.

Where Are They Going?

When it comes to the establishment of their legislative priorities, actions, and attitudes, state legislators are not just motivated by where they have come from but also by where they want to go. When determining what position they will take on a critical issue, many state legislators, especially if they have political ambitions beyond their legislative chamber, are conscious of how their decision will affect those future plans. A legislator who hopes someday to run for governor may well react differently to a situation than a colleague who hopes to be speaker of the House or intends to serve a single term in the legislature and then retire from elective politics.

Staying Put.   The most immediately pressing question regarding a state legislator's future plans concerns whether the legislator intends to seek reelection. Those who do not plan to seek reelection may well feel a different level of loyalty and responsibility to their constituents than those who plan to run for reelection or seek another office following the current term. Not surprisingly, most state legislators begin a legislative term with the intention of seeking reelection to their seat. A 2004 survey of legislators found that two-thirds said that they definitely planned to seek reelection, with another 18 percent indicating that they probably would. Just 16 percent indicated that they did not intend to seek reelection, with 5 percent of these respondents in states in which term limits precluded a reelection effort.

Future Office.   Just because most state legislators expect to seek reelection to their seat at the end of their current term does not mean that they have no political ambitions beyond the state legislature. Privately or publicly, most politicians harbor a dream of seeking higher office, given the opportunity and the availability of resources. According to a 2004 survey, more than 85 percent of state legislators indicated that they would consider seeking another political position, either elected or appointed, if the opportunity presented itself. More than one in five expressed interest in serving in the other legislative chamber. A similar proportion expressed an interest in running for the U.S. Congress or seeking a statewide office. About 10 percent indicated that they would consider a future local government position or a career in lobbying.

The Importance of Diversity

As has been shown, modern state legislatures are, in many ways, more diverse than they have ever been. There are more female legislators, and more female leaders in state legislatures, than at any other time in the nation's history. The proportion of African American legislators and leaders has also increased dramatically over the past three decades, and the proportions of Latino and Asian legislators, although still small, can be expected to increase rapidly as those groups become more active in the political arena.

In a number of states, however, occupational diversity has decreased, as more and more of their legislators are coming from legal or business backgrounds, and others give up their nonlegislative jobs to serve full time in the legislature. This trend is exacerbated by the increased costs of political campaigns, which can serve to discourage potential candidates from modest economic backgrounds who might have run for a legislative seat in an earlier era when campaigns were less costly.

The Consequences of Gender.   Women now hold more than one-fifth of state legislative seats, and a comparable proportion of leadership and committee chair positions. These changes are significant because research shows that women state legislators differ significantly from their male counterparts in terms of the committees on which they choose to serve, the issues on which they tend to focus, how they communicate, how they represent their constituents, and how they lead if they achieve a leadership position in their chamber. Surveys show that women are more likely than men to serve on and chair committees that deal with traditional women's interests, such as education, health, and welfare, and are less likely to serve on and chair committees dealing with business and fiscal affairs (Darcy 1996). This patterning has been attributed to both the personal preferences of female and male legislators and to institutional norms that tend to reserve certain committees, particularly committee leadership positions, for men (ibid.; Thomas and Welch 1991). On the policy side, women are more likely than men to focus their policy priorities on issues of women, children, and family, social issues, education, and the environment. On those issues, women legislators tend to be slightly more liberal, and more progovernment, than their male colleagues (Carroll, Dodson, and Mandell 1991).

Interestingly, gender-based policy differences seem to hold steady even as women move up the leadership ladders of state legislatures. Despite all of the gender-neutral pressures and responsibilities associated with a legislative leadership position, differences do clearly exist between men and women in comparable leadership positions. Female leaders are significantly more likely than their male counterparts to emphasize health care and social services, while giving less attention to budget matters and issues relating to criminal justice. Female leaders maintain this distinct perspective even when compared with men of the same party, position, experience, and region (Little, Dunn, and Deen 2001).

Gender differences also manifest themselves in the ways in which women legislative leaders approach their leadership responsibilities. Women in top leadership positions, such as president of the Senate, speaker of the House, majority leader, or minority leader, are more likely to practice consensus-style rather than command-style leadership. They are also more likely to focus on process and policy objectives and less on enhancing the power of their leadership positions (Jewell and Whicker 1994; Cindy Rosenthal 1998). A study of state legislative committee chairpersons revealed a similar pattern of gender-based differences among committee chairs, with female chairs gravitating toward a consensus approach and male chairs opting for a more confrontational and command-oriented style of leadership. This different perspective on leadership tends to generate differences in attitude toward leadership, leadership traits, and leadership behavior (Cindy Rosenthal 1998). The greater "personal touch" frequently associated with women leaders also manifests itself in how female legislators tend to achieve success in gaining leadership positions and getting legislation enacted. Female legislators' success in these areas is more likely to be associated with personal attributes and relationships than is the case for men (Ellickson and Whistler 2000).

Gender differences also appear to influence how women legislators view representation and how they interact with their constituents. Studies indicate that women legislators are much more likely to believe that their legislative position carries a special responsibility to represent women. Male legislators seem to feel no such overt obligation to reflect the interests of men. Female legislators tend to pay more attention to constituent service and the district than do their male counterparts (although, because female legislators tend to have less seniority, those differences may be as much a function of electoral insecurity as of gender) (Thomas 1994).

While it is quite evident that gender influences the behavior, attitudes, and priorities of individual legislators, those differences begin to translate into differences in institutional output only as the number of female members of a legislative chamber increases. Not only do numbers contribute to increased power and influence; they also contribute to increased confidence. Studies suggest that when the percentage of women in a legislature is low, their impact on the institution is limited; perhaps more significantly, the few women who are elected to the chamber do not tend to differ markedly in style or outlook from its male members. As the proportion of women grows, however, the difference between male and female legislators tends also to grow, to the point that gender comes to be reflected in the policy and procedural output of the legislature (ibid.).

Race and Ethnicity.   It has also been shown that, in recent decades, the number of minority legislators has also been increasing dramatically. The proportion of African American legislators has increased twentyfold since 1970, and the proportion of Latino and Asian legislators is also on a steady, though less dramatic, rise. What effect have these increases had on state legislatures?

Research suggests that African American state legislators do differ from their Caucasian colleagues in attitudes, behavior, priorities, and legislative success. First, African American state legislators, both male and female, perceive a responsibility and burden to represent their ethnic group in the legislature in a manner not noted among white legislators. Interestingly, white legislators also expect African American legislators to take on that role (Barrett 1997). African American legislators have tended to pay close attention to issues affecting the black community, including social welfare, economic redistribution, and civil rights. In one study, black legislators in four states were found to be much more likely to introduce "black interest bills." In those states, the percentage of African American legislators that introduced such bills was almost double the percentage of non-black legislators who introduced them in each of three years analyzed (1969, 1979, and 1989) (Bratton and Haynie 1999). This focus by African American legislators remains significant, transcending differences in gender, party, seniority, and district (Haynie 2001).

These issue differences also manifest themselves in committee selection and service. A study of African American legislator committee assignments in five state legislatures revealed a distinct focus on "black interest" committees. According to the study, in 1989, African American legislators were represented on all ten of the black interest committees in the Arkansas legislature and were overrepresented, relative to their proportion in the body, on four of them. The results were similar in Maryland, Illinois, New Jersey, and North Carolina. However, the study also showed that the degree to which African American legislators were overrepresented on black interest committees and underrepresented on other key committees (such as those dealing with budget, revenues, and law enforcement) decreased over time, indicating that African Americans were gradually gaining both more interest and more influence in areas outside of traditional "black interests" (ibid.).

While these findings may be of interest to political scientists and those who study politics, what is really significant for legislators and those they represent is whether race influences the effectiveness of a legislator. One case study of effectiveness in the North Carolina legislature suggests that it does. Looking at a subjective measure of effectiveness, based on the rankings of all of North Carolina legislators by legislators, journalists, and lobbyists, Kerry L. Haynie found that African American legislators were ranked significantly lower than their nonblack counterparts, regardless of seniority, leadership position, party affiliation, the degree of legislative activity, or committee assignments. But perhaps more important, other studies reveal that the effective incorporation of African American legislators into the legislative process has an effect on public policy. In states in which African American legislators are more active on key committees and in leadership positions, policies are different than in states in which such integration has not occurred. Integration of minority legislators into key positions in a state legislature is associated with increased health care, education, welfare, and total redistributive expenditures (ibid.). It appears clear, at least from this study, that ethnic diversity can affect both the internal operations of a state legislature and its policy output.

Occupational Status.   One of the most frequent debates among students of state legislative politics is between advocates of full-time professional legislatures and part-time citizen legislatures. Advocates of a professional legislature suggest that legislators who can dedicate full-time attention to their legislative duties will be more informed on the issues, less influenced by lobbyist claims, more attentive to their constituents, and more proactive in addressing the needs of the state. Proponents of a citizen legislature suggest that legislators who maintain a job outside of the legislature are more attuned to the needs of their constituents and the consequences of laws that they enact, allowing them to be more conscientious stewards of their states' resources. The basic assumption underlying this debate has to do with the occupational status of state legislators—whether they consider themselves essentially employees of the state or whether they consider themselves private citizens who devote a portion of their time to the state's business but see their occupation outside of the legislature as their basic means of support.

Legislators who derive their primary income from legislative service are likely to introduce more legislation, focus on constituent service and securing government contracts for firms in their district, and be predisposed to a more activist government that will provide more services to the people (Owings and Borck 2000). The increase in the number of professional state legislators who do not hold other jobs in their districts is one factor that many associate with the increased growth of government over the past thirty years. Many of this so-called new breed of state legislator have little or no experience outside of government and are quite content to make government—often state legislative service—a career. These legislators generally work hard to stay in their office and, according to critics of professional legislatures, may be more concerned with maintaining their position than with doing what is best for the state (Rosenthal 2004).

On the other hand, many suggest that legislators who do not consider themselves full-time legislators or still derive the largest portion of their financial livelihood from a private-sector occupation will be more effective stewards of the public treasury and will be more attuned to the needs of their district and constituents. Advocates of these citizen-type legislators argue that those who are active in an occupation or vocation outside of the legislature are likely to bring that expertise to their chamber and to the committees on which they serve (Gordon 1994).

A 2002 study provided fodder for supporters of both professional and citizen legislatures. The study revealed that more than a third of state legislators in more than half of the states in 2002 had a financial or vocational linkage to at least one committee on which they served, ranging from a high of 57.2 percent in Kentucky to a low of 5.9 percent in Louisiana. As would be expected, such linkage was much lower in professional legislatures such as California, Michigan, and Pennsylvania than it was in more citizen-oriented bodies, because a much greater proportion of the membership of professional legislatures are full-time legislators with no private-sector occupation. This familiarity with and personal involvement in a policy area can have both positive and negative implications. On the positive side, legislators with an occupational tie to a committee on which they serve can make informed judgments and decisions about legislation that comes before that committee. On the negative side, this familiarity may open them to charges of conflict of interest, suggesting that they may be more concerned with the influence that the legislation will have on their personal situation or profession than on the general population.

Political Ambition.   Several decades ago, prominent political scientists identified three types of ambition that tend to define future options for elected officials: *progressive ambition*, the goal of gaining higher political office; *static ambition*, the goal of retaining one's current political post as a long-term career; and *discrete ambition*, the goal to return to private life after limited public service (Schlesinger 1966). Since that time, a series of studies have applied these categories to political officials at all levels, including members of the U.S. Congress and state legislatures. These studies suggest that legislators' degree of political ambition affects the policy positions that they take, their attention to particular legislative responsibilities, and their attentiveness to their constituents (Maestas 2003).

While the evidence on state legislatures is limited, studies of ambition in the U.S. Congress clearly find that ambitions influence the policy positions of members whose eyes are cast on higher office. Members of the U.S. House of Representatives who plan to run for the U.S. Senate begin to shift their policy positions to reflect the views of their entire state—their prospective constituency in their new office—as long as thirteen years before they make their run for the Senate. If their state is more conservative than their district, they move in the conservative direction. If the state is more moderate to liberal, they go in that direction (Francis and Kenny 1996).

Legislators with an eye on higher office participate more actively in the legislative process, trying to build a public record for their intended future campaign. They introduce more bills, speak more often on the floor of their chamber, give more attention to

---

LEGISLATURES AND THE PUBLIC

Are Citizen Legislators Protecting the Public or Themselves in the Sunshine State?

Advocates of citizen legislatures argue that it makes sense to have legislators with experience in a particular industry or profession analyzing and voting on policy matters relative to that industry. Who better to make that policy, they argue, than someone who is currently involved in the field and directly affected by the policy. However, to others, this smacks of having the fox guarding the hen house.

A recent study of the Florida General Assembly, a decidedly citizen legislature with short sessions, a relatively low salary for the legislature of one of the nation's most populous states, and legislative term limits, found that more than a third of the members who served in the legislature's 2001 session were on committees that regulated the profession or industry from which they derived significant income. The study revealed that the chairman of the Banking and Insurance Committee was on the board of directors of a bank; a practicing chiropractor was the chairman of the Health Regulation Committee; and five of the seven members who

served on the Senate committee responsible for an overhaul of the state's growth management laws had a personal interest in how the state would regulate development.

Tom Feeney, speaker of the Florida House in 2001, argued that such appointments represented an efficient use of resources rather than a conflict of interest. He said: "This is the price you pay for a citizen legislature with term limits. We want to take advantage where we have expertise and experience." Speaker Feeney suggested that his appointment of his colleagues to these positions allowed the House of Representatives to derive the most benefit from the diverse occupational experiences of its members, especially with so many inexperienced members resulting from the state's term limits law.

Source: Fineout, Gary, and Lloyd Dunkelberger. 2001. "Citizen Legislators Keep Eye on Own: Part-time Politicians Serve on Committees that Regulate Their Full-time Businesses." *Sarasota Herald Tribune*, January 15.

their committee activities, and employ more staff members than their colleagues who have no ambition to move beyond their current legislative seat. Interestingly, although legislators aspiring to higher office are more active than their less ambitious colleagues, they are less successful in getting their bills passed, perhaps because they are more interested in appearing busy and productive to the voters than they are in actually passing laws (Herrick and Moore 1993). On the other hand, legislators planning to retire to private life at the end of their current term tend to be less concerned with the policy positions of their district and are less concerned with activity on the floor of their legislative chamber. Such legislators are more likely to miss votes on the floor and in committee, knowing that they will not be facing the voters again (Rothenberg and Sanders 2000).

The effect of political ambition on the amount of attention paid to constituents seems to be mixed. There is some indication that legislators with an eye on higher office are more attentive to their constituents as they try to secure their political base for their planned future run. Legislators who hope to move on to a higher position understand that if they are unpopular in their current district, they may find that climb up the political ladder permanently stalled (Maestas 2003). But there are also contrary indications that suggest that legislators who hope to move on from the legislature to a higher-level position are more interested in the constituency that they will be representing in that next office—often to the detriment of their current constituents. Legislators planning to run for statewide office are likely, for example, to turn their attention to the statewide electorate at the expense of the voters in their district (McAdams and Johannes 1985). Likewise, legislators hoping to receive an appointment from their governor following the end of their legislative tenure may pay more attention to currying favor with the executive branch than with providing representation for their district.

THE LEGISLATIVE LIFE

Once elected, many state legislators find their job considerably more demanding and less financially rewarding than they had expected. In many states, legislators put in long hours, especially during legislative session, for very little financial reward. They find themselves pulled in several directions, trying to balance the demands of constituents, campaign activities, and legislative responsibilities, while also trying to maintain some semblance of a home life.

How Much Compensation and Logistical Support Do State Legislators Receive?

The salaries paid to U.S. state legislators vary greatly, ranging from $100 per year in New Hampshire to more than $100,000 per year in California and New York (see T 4.9). In most states, legislative compensation is separated into two categories: *salary* and *expense allowances*. Salary is the basic compensation that each legislator receives for legislative service, regardless of the length of session or the amount of time spent on the job. In addition to this base salary, most legislators receive some allowance for living expenses, especially if they have to live in the capital during legislative sessions. This allowance helps to cover the cost of an apartment and meals for those who have to re-locate temporarily, or for the daily travel to and from the district for those who com-mute. A number of legislatures also provide their members with lump-sum un-vouchered expense allowances for use on job-related activities within their district.

Salary

In terms of salary, members of the California legislature are the highest-paid state leg-islators. As of 2004, their base salary was $99,000 per year. Michigan was second at $79,650, and New York next at $79,500. On the other end of the scale, legislators in New Mexico receive no salary, only living expenses. Salaries in ten states are based on the length of session, with most paying a set amount for each day that the legislature meets. In Nevada, whose biennial sessions are allowed to run up to 120 calendar days, legislators are eligible to receive a daily salary for only sixty days. The remaining states have set salary levels that are not dependent on session length, with New Hampshire's $100 for each year of a two-year session representing the low end. In twenty of these states, the annual salary is less than $20,000.

Expense Allowances

Some states that have low salary levels for their legislators still compensate them hand-somely through generous expense allowances. For example, although Alabama legisla-tors make only $10 per day in salary, they receive almost $3,000 per month in expenses when the legislature is in session. In Texas, legislators can supplement their $7,200 an-nual salary with a $125 per diem. In seven states, including New Hampshire, which has the lowest salary level, legislators receive no expense allowance (although New Hamp-shire legislators do receive a reimbursement for travel). Apart from New Hampshire, most of these states have a relatively high salary level.

TABLE 4.9   ANNUAL COMPENSATION PACKAGE* FOR STATE LEGISLATORS, 2003

Top Five		Bottom Five	
California	$119,160	Kansas	$14,662
New York	$89,215	North Dakota	$13,400
Michigan	$79,650	South Dakota	$10,400
Pennsylvania	$77,078	New Mexico	$8,400
Massachusetts	$60,879	New Hampshire	$200

Source: Calculated by authors from data provided by National Conference of State Legislatures (http://www.ncsl.org).

*Combining salary and expense allowance based on days in session in 2003.

Total Compensation Package

To understand fully the total compensation packages of U.S. state legislators, it is necessary to look at their combined salary and expense allowances. Again, California legislators lead the way, receiving about $120,000 during a normal session year. New York legislators receive about $90,000. On the other end, New Hampshire remains at the bottom. Even though New Mexico's legislators receive no official salary, the $146 per diem paid to them when their legislature is in session provides them with about $10,000 a year in compensation.

The handful of heavily populated states, such as California and New York, that compensate their legislators well represent the exception. The majority of state legislators in the majority of the states find it necessary to supplement their legislative salaries and expense allowances with private-sector income to provide for themselves and their families.

Office Space and Staff Support

Most, but not all, state legislatures provide their members with free office space—or at least some office space in which to work. Most also provide at least some shared staff support. In many of the less professional legislatures, legislators will share both office space and staff support. In Iowa, only legislative leaders are provided office space, so legislators work at a desk on the floor of their chamber. Each legislator has a secretary who must also work on the chamber floor. Legislators in more than three-quarters of the states have some staff available year-round, even if it is rather limited, but only about a quarter are provided year-round staff in their district.

What Do Legislators Do?

State legislators are saddled with many time-consuming obligations, including reading proposed legislation, attending committee meetings, and attending and participating in floor sessions (Rosenthal 2004). At the same time, they must maintain active ties with their district, responding to district needs and constituent requests for various types of assistance. And, as soon as they are elected, many legislators must almost immediately begin campaigning for their reelection, which requires setting aside time to raise money and plan their next campaign (Salmore and Salmore 1996).

Legislative Activities

A state legislature is supposed to develop and approve legislation that addresses the problems and challenges faced by its state. For a legislature to enact laws, its members must develop and introduce legislation. They must also examine proposed legislation, so that they can cast knowledgeable and informed votes. In a 2004 survey, almost 60 percent of state legislators said that they had devoted a great deal of time to developing legislation and reading materials to prepare for committee and floor debate and votes (see T 4.10).

The development and introduction of a piece of proposed legislation, however, is only the first step in the legislative process. For a bill to become law, it must receive the support of a majority of the members of both houses of the legislature. This requires that legislators spend time building coalitions with other legislators to gain support for bills that they introduce and hope to get enacted. According to the 2004 survey, almost half of state legislators indicated that they devote a great deal of time to coalition-building, both with members of their party and with members of the other party.

Constituent Services

Legislating is only one aspect of the job of a legislator. As the elected representatives of the people of their districts, legislators must spend time addressing the needs of their constituents, both individually and as a group. Individually, they respond to constituent concerns and communications and assist constituents with problems that they may be experiencing with state government agencies. A legislator might, for example, assist a constituent in having a suspended driver's license reinstated by the state's motor vehicle department, or assist another constituent in navigating the state's complex licensing process to enable the constituent to open a child daycare facility. In terms of the district as a whole, a legislator works to ensure that state government money is sent to the district, perhaps to help a local business, to build or repair a bridge, or to expand a local education program. The 2004 survey revealed that three out of every four legislators who responded to the survey spent a great deal of time on constituent-oriented work, ranging from answering letters to securing government money and projects (also known as "pork barrel" projects).

Campaign Activities

Unless they are in a state in which a term-limits provision requires them to leave the legislature, the majority of state legislators have every intention of seeking reelection.

TABLE 4.10   HOW LEGISLATORS SPEND THEIR TIME, 2004

Activity	Some Time	A Great Deal of Time
Developing Legislation	93.5%	58.0%
Building Coalitions	84.1%	48.9%
Constituent Work	96.0%	77.7%
Campaign Activities	58.5%	21.6%

Source: Survey conducted by the Joint Project on Term Limits, 2004.

A recent survey of legislators found that well over 80 percent of all legislators expected to seek reelection (Joint Project on Term Limits 2004). It is therefore not surprising that a number of legislators spend a significant portion of their time working on matters relating to their next campaign, raising money, making speeches in their district, making phone calls, and remaining in close contact with key supporters. While many fewer legislators claimed to spend any significant portion of their time on these types of activities, more than one in five did indicate that they spent a great deal of time on campaign activities, with almost 60 percent indicating that they spent at least some time on them.

THE UNIQUE WORLD OF STATE LEGISLATIVE ELECTIONS

In the late 1980s and early 1990s, there was considerable discussion about the "congressionalization" of state legislative elections, suggesting that elections for state legislatures were moving inexorably along a path toward the professional and expensive elections that characterize campaigns for the U.S. Congress. According to that line of thought, state legislative elections would continue to become more expensive, incumbents would become more secure, and campaigns would become increasingly coordinated by campaign professionals (Salmore and Salmore 1996). A look at elections in states like California, New York, Ohio, Pennsylvania, and Michigan suggests some validity to these predictions, with elections in these states having become increasingly expensive, dominated by incumbents, and professionally managed even in California, Michigan, and Ohio, which have term limits.

However, changes in most of the other states have not supported the "congressionalization" theory. In most states, elections for the state's legislature remain relatively personal and inexpensive. In Vermont, Maine, and New Hampshire, it is rare that a candidate spends more than $5,000 to win a legislative seat, and most candidates spend considerably less. In many states, "media buys" are limited to a few newspaper advertisements, one or two voter mailings, and fans, emery boards, or calendars to hand out at the high school football game or the county fair.

The candidates and the victors of state legislative campaigns will continue to reflect the unique qualities of their particular state or district. Elections in some states will be expensive, professional, and hotly contested, while those in most states will continue to be low-budget, personal affairs, run from the kitchen table with a few friends and close supporters making all of the key decisions. Political parties and interest groups are more active in campaigns in some states than in others, while name recognition, money, and party identification are likely to be of some significance almost everywhere. Legislators in some states will become increasingly full time, while those in other states will continue to be citizen legislators, holding jobs outside their chamber that provide the primary source of their income. The number and influence of women and minority legislators can be expected to become increasingly reflective of the populations of their states. Some state legislators will continue to look at service in the state legislature as a stepping-stone to higher office, while most of their colleagues will view their election to the legislature as the pinnacle of their political career. In the final analysis, it can be expected that state legislative elections and the candidates elected to the country's fifty state legislatures will continue to reflect the particular and unique qualities of each individual state.

REFERENCES

Allenbaugh, Darlene, and Neil Pinney. 2003. "The Real Costs of Term Limits: Comparative Study of Competition and Electoral Costs." In *The Test of Time: Coping with Legislative Term Limits*, edited by Rick Farmer, John David Rausch, Jr., and John C. Green. Lanham, MD: Lexington.

Barber, James David. 1965. *The Lawmakers: Recruitment and Adaption to Legislative Life.* New Haven: Yale University Press.

Barrett, Edith J. 1997. "Gender and Race in the State House: The Legislative Experience." *Social Science Journal* 34 (April):131–147.

Berkman, Michael B., and James Eisenstein. 1999. "State Legislators as Congressional Candidates: The Effects of Prior Experience on Legislative Recruitment and Fundraising." *Political Research Quarterly* 52 (September):481–498.

Bernstein, Robert A., and Anita Chada. 2003. "The Effects of Term Limits on Representation: Why So Few Women?" In *The Test of Time: Coping with Legislative Term Limits*, edited by Rick Farmer, John David Rausch, Jr., and John C. Green, 147–158. Lanham, MD: Lexington.

Berry, Francis Stokes. 1994. "Sizing Up State Policy Innovation Research."*Policy Studies Journal* 22, no. 3 (autumn):442–456.

Bibby, John F., and Thomas Holbrook. 2003. "Parties and Elections." In *Politics in the American States: A Comparative Analysis*, edited by Virginia Gray and Russell L. Hanson, 62–99. Washington, DC: Congressional Quarterly Press.

Blanchette, Rep. Patricia. 2005. Quoted in "Fewer Women in State Politics." *Bangor Daily News*, January 28.

Bratton, Kathleen A., and Kerry L. Haynie. 1999. "Agenda Setting and Legislative Success in State Legislatures: The Effect of Gender and Race." *Journal of Politics* 61:658–679.

Breaux, David A., and Anthony Gierzynski. 1998. "Candidate Revenues and Expenditures in State Legislative Elections." In *Campaign Finance in State Legislative Elections*, edited by Joel A. Thompson and Gary F. Moncrief, 80–114. Washington, DC: Congressional Quarterly Press.

Breaux, David, and Malcolm E. Jewell. 1992. "Winning Big: The Incumbency Advantage in State Legislative Races." In *Changing Patterns in State Legislative Careers*, edited by Gary F. Moncrief and Joel A. Thompson, 87–105. Ann Arbor: University of Michigan Press.

Bullock, Charles S., III, and Loch K. Johnson. 1992. *Runoff Elections in the United States.* Chapel Hill: University of North Carolina Press.

Campbell, Angus, et al. 1960. *The American Voter.* New York: John Wiley.

Caress, Stanley M., et al. 2003. "Effect of Term Limits on Minority State Legislators." *State and Local Government* Review 35, no. 3 (fall):183–195.

Carroll, Susan J., Debra Dodson, and Ruth B. Mandell. 1991. *The Impact of Women in Public Office.* Trenton: Center for the American Woman and Politics (CAWP), Eagleton Institute of Politics, Rutgers.

Cassie, William E., and David A. Breaux. 1998. "Expenditures and Election Results." In *Campaign Finance in State Legislative Elections*, edited by Joel A. Thompson and Gary F. Moncrief, 99–114. Washington, DC: Congressional Quarterly Press.

Cassie, William E., and Joel A. Thompson. 1998. "Patterns of PAC Contributions to State Legislative Candidates." In *Campaign Finance in State Legislative Elections*, edited by Joel A. Thompson and Gary F. Moncrief, 158–184. Washington, DC: Congressional Quarterly Press.

Center for Voting and Democracy. "Bigger Districts Don't Mean More Expensive Campaigns." (http://www.fairvote.org/library/money/seats_costs.htm. Accessed February 2, 2005.)

Conover, Pamela Johnston, and Stanley Feldman. 1989. "Candidate Perception in an Ambiguous World: Campaigns, Cues and Inference Processes." *American Journal of Political Science* 33:912–939.

Cooper, Michael. 2005. "Lobbyists Making Big Money in Albany's Chronic Logjams." *New York Times*, March 15, 2005.

Council of State Governments. 2004. *Book of the States, Volume 36*. Lexington, KY: Council of State Governments.

Cox, Gary, and Scott Morgenstern. 1995. "The Incumbency Advantage in Multimember Districts: Evidence from the States." *Legislative Studies Quarterly* 20:329–349.

Dagan, David. 2004. "Personal Politics: All Too Often, Legislator's Personal Interests Are Hidden from Public View." Center for Public Integrity. (http://www.publicintegrity.org /oi/report.aspx?aid=377&sid=300. Accessed January 26, 2005.)

Darcy, R. 1996. "Women in the State Legislative Power Structure: Committee Chairs." *Social Science Quarterly* 77, no. 4:889–898.

Drage Bowser, Jennie, et al. 2003. "The Impact of Term Limits on Legislative Leadership." In *The Test of Time: Coping with Legislative Term Limits*, edited by Rick Farmer, John David Rausch, Jr., and John C. Green, 119–132. Lanham, MD: Lexington.

Dye, Thomas R. 1995. *Understanding Public Policy*. 8th ed. Englewood Cliffs, NJ: Prentice-Hall.

Ehrenhalt, Alan. 1991. *The United States of Ambition*. New York: Random House.

Elder, Laura. 2004. "Why Women Don't Run: Explaining Women's Underrepresentation in American Political Institutions." *Women and Politics* 26, no. 2:27–47.

Ellickson, Mark C., and Donald E. Whistler. 2000. "A Path Analysis of Legislative Success in Professional and Citizen's Legislatures: A Gender Comparison." *Women and Politics* 21, no. 4:77–100.

Finan, Richard, president of the Ohio Senate, interview by Thomas H. Little, February 28, 2002.

Francis, Wayne L., and Lawrence W. Kenny. 1996. "Position Shifting in Pursuit of Higher Office." *American Journal of Political Science* 40 (August):768–786.

Francisosi, Robert J. 2001. *Is Cleanliness Political Godliness? Arizona's Clean Election Law after Its First Year*. Goldwater Institute (http://www.goldwaterinstitute.org /pdf/materials/17.pdf).

Frandeis, John, and Alan Gitelson. 1999. "Parties, Candidates and State Electoral Politics." Paper presented at the annual meeting of the American Political Science Association, Chicago.

Gordon, Diana. 1994. "Citizen Legislatures—Alive and Well." *State Legislatures* 20:24–28.

Greenblatt, Alan. 2004. "Whatever Happened to Competitive Elections?" *Governing: Magazine of State and Local Government*, Volume 18 (October):22–27.

Haynie, Kerry L. 2001. *African American Legislators in the American States*. New York: Columbia University Press.

Herrick, Rebekah, and Michael K. Moore. 1993. "Political Ambition's Effect on Legislative Behavior: Schlesinger's Typology Reconsidered and Revised." *Journal of Politics* 55, no. 3:765–776.

Hill, Kim, Jan Leighley, and Angela Hinton-Anderson. 1995. "Lower Class Mobilization and Political Linkage in the United States." *American Journal of Political Science* 39:75–86.

Hogan, Robert E. 2000. "Campaign War Chests and Challenger Emergence in State Legislative Elections." *Political Research Quarterly* 54:825–831.

Hogan, Robert E., and Keith E. Hamm. 1998. "Variations in District-Level Campaign Spending in State Legislatures." In *Campaign Finance in State Legislative Elections*, 68. Washington, DC: Congressional Quarterly Press.

Jewell, Malcolm E., and Marcia Lynn Whicker. 1994. *Legislative Leadership in the American States*. Ann Arbor: University of Michigan Press.

Joint Project on Term Limits. 2004. Survey of State Legislators. Unpublished.

La Raja, Ray, and Thad Kousser. 2001. "Campaign Finance Laws Shape Fundraising Patterns and Electoral Outcomes." *Institute of Governmental Studies Public Affairs Report* 42, no. 2 (summer 2001).

Little, Thomas H. 1995. "Understanding Legislative Leadership beyond the Chamber: The Members' Perspective." *Legislative Studies Quarterly* 20:269–289.

———. 1997. "On the Coattails of a Contract: RNC Activities and Republican Gains in the 1994 State Legislative Elections." *Political Research Quarterly* 51:173–190.

Little, Thomas H., Dana Dunn, and Rebecca E. Deen. 2001. "A View from the Top: Gender Differences in Legislative Priorities among State Legislative Leaders." *Gender and Politics* 22: 20–50.

Maestas, Cherie. 2003. "The Incentive to Listen: Progressive Ambition, Resources, and Opinion Monitoring among State Legislators." *Journal of Politics* 65:439–456.

Mayhew, David R. 1986. *Placing Political Parties in American Politics.* Princeton: Princeton University Press.

McAdams, John C., and John R. Johannes. 1985. "Constituency Attentiveness in the House, 1977–1982." *Journal of Politics* 47, no. 4:1109–1140.

Moncrief, Gary F., Peverill Squire, and Malcolm E. Jewell. 2001. *Who Runs for the State Legislature?* Upper Saddle River, NJ: Prentice-Hall.

Moncrief, Gary, and Joel A. Thompson. 1998. *Campaign Spending in State Legislative Contests, 1986–1994.* Livonia, MI: Citizens Research Council of Michigan.

Morehouse, Sarah McCally, and Malcolm E. Jewell. 2003. *State Politics, Parties and Policy.* 2d ed. Lanham, MD: Rowman and Littlefield.

Nagourney, Adam. 2005. "States See Growing Campaign to Change Redistricting Laws." *New York Times*, February 2.

National Conference of State Legislatures.2005. (http://www.ncsl.org/programs/legman /about/ContribLimits.htm. Accessed February 23, 2005.)

Owings, Stephanie, and Rainald Borck. 2000. "Legislative Professionalism and Government Spending: Do Citizen Legislators Really Spend Less?" *Public Finance Review* 28:210–227.

Primo, Jeffrey M., and David Milo. 2004. "Campaign Finance Laws and Political Efficacy: Evidence From the States." Working Papers 0513. Columbia: Department of Economics, University of Missouri.

Reichley, A. James. 1992. *The Life of the Parties: A History of American Political Parties.* New York: Free Press.

Rosenthal, Alan. 1981. *Legislative Life: People, Processes and Performance in the States.* New York: Harper and Row.

———. 1998. *The Decline of Representative Democracy: Process, Participation, and Power in State Legislatures.* Washington, DC: Congressional Quarterly Press.

———. 2004. *Heavy Lifting: The Job of the American Legislature.* Washington, DC: Congressional Quarterly Press.

Rosenthal, Cindy. 1998. *When Women Lead: Integrative Leadership in State Legislatures.* New York: Oxford University Press.

Rosenthal, Cynthia Simon. 1995. "New Party or Campaign Bank Account?" *Legislative Studies Quarterly* 11 (May):249–268.

Rothenberg, Lawrence S., and Mitchell S. Sanders. 2000. "Severing the Electoral Connection: Shirking in the Contemporary Congress." *American Journal of Political Science* 44 (April):310–319.

Sabato, Larry J., and Joshua J. Scott. 2001. "The Long Road to a Cliffhanger: Primaries and Conventions." In *Overtime: The Election 2000 Thriller*, edited by Larry J. Sabato, 15–44. New York: Longman.

Salmore, Stephen A., and Barbara G. Salmore. 1996. "The Transformation of State Electoral Politics." In *The State of the States*. 3d ed., edited by Carl Van Horn. Washington, DC: Congressional Quarterly Press.

Satter, Robert. 2004. *Under the Gold Dome: An Insiders Look at the Connecticut Legislature.* Hartford: Connecticut Conference of Municipalities.

Schlesinger, Joseph A. 1966. *Ambition and Politics.* Chicago: Rand McNally.

Shea, Daniel M., and Michael John Burton. 2001. *Campaign Craft: The Strategies, Tactics and Art of Political Campaign Management.* Westport, CT: Praeger.

State Legislative Leaders Foundation. 1993. "Making the Most of What You Have: The Minority Party Leadership of Senators Harry Meshel (Ohio) and Ben Atchley (Tennessee)." (http://www.sllf.org/pdf/Making-the-Most-of-What-You-Have.pdf.)

———. 2004. "Effective Leadership in the Face of Legislative Term Limits: Larry Householder's Legislative Team." (http://www.sllf.org/pdf/HouseholderCase.pdf.)

Thomas, Sue. 1994. *How Women Legislate*. New York: Oxford University Press.

Thomas, Sue, and Susan Welch. 1991. "The Impact of Gender on Activities and Priorities of State Legislators." *Western Political Quarterly* 44:445–456.

Vavrus, Mary Douglas. 2000. "From Women of the Year to 'Soccer Moms': The Case of the Incredible Shrinking Women." *M.D. Political Communication* 17, no. 2 (April 1):193.

Walters, Stephen. 2000. "Former Legislator Lorge Announces Senate Run." *Wisconsin Journal Sentinel*, June 9.

Wolfinger, Raymond E., and Jonathon Hoffman. 2001. "Registering and Voting with Motor Voter." *PS: Political Science and Politics* 34:85–92.

5

THE POLITICS OF THE LEGISLATURE

Without question, a state legislature has a tremendous impact on the quality of life of the citizens of its state. With the exception of the few laws that are passed through the initiative process (fewer than 1 percent of all laws), every law that governs a state has the undeniable imprint of the state legislature and the legislators who serve in it. Legislators initiate legislation. They debate legislation in committee. They amend, edit, and kill legislation. They vote for and against legislation. Public policy in any given state is a reflection of the ideas, thoughts, values, and efforts of the members of its state legislature.

However, legislatures do not pass laws in a vacuum. Actors outside the formal legislative structure are active at every stage of the legislative process. Legislators look to interest group lobbyists to provide them with ideas and information. They expect the governor to have, and promote, a legislative agenda, working closely with the leaders of the legislature to get that agenda enacted into law. They make laws in accordance with the state constitution and in anticipation of court reaction. Legislators, as well as their constituents, watch the news and take cues from the news media regarding what issues are important enough to warrant legislative attention.

The United States is made up of fifty states, and legislators in one state cannot afford to be ignorant of actions being taken by the legislatures of other states or, in today's global society, even by the legislative bodies of other countries. States compete to retain or recruit businesses, consumers, and tax dollars. Taxes raised or services cut in one state may cause businesses, citizens, or consumers to leave that state in favor of a "greener pasture." Finally, in the federal system of the United States, state legislatures must be aware of the actions taken by the national government because there will always be some federal legislation that will require them to take action, some that will prevent them from acting, and some that will offer their state financial incentives or disincentives for action.

It can be said that there are seven external actors that are critical to the process by which legislatures make public policy. Those seven actors can be separated into three groupings. The first two institutions—governors and the courts—are, like the legislature, entities within the state government. The second grouping—interest groups, political parties, and the press—are outside of the government but have significant influence on public policy. The final grouping concerns actors in the U.S. federal system—other states and the national government—and the impact that their actions have on the actions and policy decisions of individual state legislatures.

THE FOUR BASIC PRINCIPLES OF U.S. GOVERNMENT

Each of the fifty state governments in the United States has its own unique traits and qualities. Some are more professional than others. Some have stronger executives than others. Some are highly partisan, while others divide more along regional or ideological lines. However, all of them share four basic and guiding principles established by the authors of the U.S. Constitution in 1789 and replicated in state constitutions over the decades: separation of powers, checks and balances, republicanism, and federalism. These four principles provide the foundation for government in the United States, and they define the role of legislatures relative to the other political actors that are critical to the public policy process.

Perhaps the most frequently mentioned principle of government structure in U.S. politics is separation of powers. According to that principle, government responsibilities are divided among three independent, yet interrelated, branches—the legislative branch (that is, the legislature), the executive branch (the governor), and the judicial branch (the courts). No one branch is totally and completely responsible for the process of governing. Each is primarily responsible for a particular stage of the governing process. The legislative branch is responsible for making the laws, the executive branch for administering or implementing the laws, and the judicial branch for applying or interpreting the laws.

A second, and almost as frequently mentioned, principle of U.S. government is checks and balances, which means that while each branch of government is responsible for a particular area of activity under the separation of powers principle, the other two branches have a responsibility to ensure that the remaining branch does not acquire or exercise too much power. Each branch of government has some tools, varying in strength from state to state, with which it can limit and constrain the action of the other two branches.

The third basic principle is a republican or representative form of government. Under this principle, the people do not directly make policy, but instead elect individuals to represent them and make policy on their behalf. In order for a representative democracy to be successful, organizations and institutions must be in place (and free from government control) to provide a linkage to legislators to make them aware of the opinions and attitudes of those they represent. Without such linkages, representative government cannot successfully serve the people.

Finally, the overall structure of government in the United States is defined by the fourth principle, federalism, which provides that Americans are represented in and served by three levels of government. Americans find themselves subject to the laws, regulations, and policies of their national government, their state governments, and their local or municipal governments. Under the nation's federal system, the national government can pass laws that override state law or that require state action; state laws that may conflict with federal laws or the U.S. Constitution are subject to review and nullification. Furthermore, laws passed in one state are considered in the political context of laws passed in another, with states always being conscious of the actions of their neighbors.

These four basic principles of U.S. government provide the framework and context within which the various political actors operate. Separation of powers and checks and balances define the responsibilities and limitations of each branch of government and establish the nature of their interaction. The republican form of government establishes the importance of a communication linkage between representatives and those they represent, primarily through the mass media and interest groups. And federalism creates an environment in which state governments make their decisions in the context of relevant decisions in Washington, D.C., and in the capitols of the other forty-nine states.

THE OTHER BRANCHES OF THE GOVERNMENT

While making public policy is the primary responsibility of the legislative branch of government, that responsibility is shared with the executive and judicial branches under the separation of powers and checks and balances principles. The executive and judicial branches each possess some powers that enable them to influence laws passed by the legislature. Not surprisingly, there is an inevitable conflict between the three branches as they try to draw lines demarking where the power of one starts and the power of another ends (Tarr 2004, 230).

The Governor and the Executive Branch

While the primary responsibility of the executive branch, according to the separation of powers principle, is to implement and administer the laws passed by the legislature, the governors of most of the fifty states have become increasingly active in the policymaking process. Governors seldom sit around waiting for the legislature to make policy for them to implement but, rather, take an active role in trying to persuade their legislatures to approve laws and adopt public policy positions that they favor.

The Relationship between the Governor and the Legislature

Constitutionally, the relationship between the legislature and the governor is usually quite simple. According to most state constitutions, governors are to react or respond to actions of the legislature, rather than to initiate proposals. The legislature is supposed to initiate, debate, discuss, and pass legislation, and the executive is supposed to either approve it by signing it into law or reject it by vetoing it. If the legislation

Legislators and governors must work together to pass laws, just as Governor Brad Henry does in Oklahoma. Here, Governor Henry signs legislation to reform that state's worker's compensation system. (AP Photo/File)

becomes law, the governor and the executive branch are responsible for its implementation. If a governor vetoes a piece of legislation passed by the legislature, that legislation does not become law unless the legislature overrides the veto by reapproving the legislation, usually by either a 60 percent or two-thirds majority of each chamber.

According to most state constitutions, governors are required to propose a state budget, but the exact nature of that process varies from state to state and is often expressed in vague terms. In more than half the states, the governor prepares the budget for the legislature to react to, while in some others, the legislature has a much more active role. Governors with a more clearly defined budget power are stronger relative to their legislature than their counterparts who have to share that power. In terms of elections, there is no constitutional link between the legislative branch and the executive, except in those relatively rare occasions in which a candidate for governor and a candidate for lieutenant governor run as a team and the lieutenant governor presides over a chamber of the legislature, as is the case in nine states. However, most state constitutions do establish election terms such that the governor and at least some, and in some states all, legislators are elected at the same time, so that their campaigns are very much linked and influence each other.

Politically, the relationship can be much more complex, depending on the history, partisanship, and political ambition of the governor and the legislative leaders. While the relationship should be symbiotic, with both governors and legislatures benefiting from cooperative effort, that is seldom the case. A governor who has experience in or with the legislature tends to have a much more positive relationship than one who comes to the office from outside of state government or with a limited understanding of the complex legislative process. The political nature of the relationship can be particularly difficult if the governor's political party is not in control of one or both legislative chambers. Generally, legislators in a legislative majority of the same party as the governor will benefit from any gubernatorial successes, while legislators in a majority of the other party may view any success achieved by the governor as an impediment to their party's retention of legislative control in the next election, thereby making cooperation less likely.

If the governor or leaders of the legislature have political ambitions for higher office, the political nature of their relationship with the legislature will reflect those ambitions and can often lead to stalemate. For legislators hoping to advance their own career or political agenda, working with the executive can be either a means to that end or a potential stumbling block, depending on the legislator, the governor, and circumstances within the state. While there is seldom a constitutional reason for a governor to get involved in the legislative process, the political incentives for doing so are many, including a desire to establish a record of leadership, an interest in addressing the challenges facing the state, and a desire to improve the political position of one's political party and supporters.

Tools and Methods of Influence

The ability of a governor to influence the design of public policy in the legislature is a function of both the office and the person. Governors have several official and personal tools at their disposal with which to influence the legislative process. These tools are often described as either institutional or personal in nature. Formal powers are those that are granted to the office by the state constitution or state statutes. The characteristics of the person holding the office are irrelevant in regard to formal or institutional tools of influence. One governor of California will have the same formal powers as another, whether that governor is Gray Davis or Arnold Schwarzenegger. Formal powers of the governor, while varying significantly from state to state, will not vary from one governor to the next within the same state unless the law or the constitution is changed. Informal powers are a function not of the office but of the person who holds the office and the political context in which it is held. For example, a governor who is of the same party as the legislative majority, has experience in the legislature, and is popular and works effectively with the news media is likely to be more influential than a governor who is of the opposite party from the legislative majority, has few personal relationships with legislators, is losing popularity with the public, and has a hostile relationship with press.

Formal Powers of the Governor

Every state governor is granted a certain set of powers and responsibilities initially outlined by Joseph Schlesinger (1966) and since refined by others (for a more thorough discussion of these formal powers, see Chapter 2 in the *Executive Branch of State Government* by Margaret Ferguson (2006). These responsibilities are inherited by the "governor elect" and cannot be changed or altered. In some states, governors have almost exclusive control over preparation of the state's proposed budget, while in other states they share that power with the legislature or with a committee of legislators. In some states governors can serve for as many terms as the voters will elect them to, while other governors are limited to two terms of office (in Virginia, it is only one). Some governors appoint a large number of key statewide officials, while others are restricted to a relatively few high-level appointments. Effective use by a governor of the formal powers of the gubernatorial office increases a governor's ability to work effectively with the legislature.

In addition to dealing with a large number of statewide elected officials, many governors are further hamstrung in their efforts to influence legislative policy because they have a limited period of time in which to achieve their goals. The tenure potential of most governors is limited by the number of terms they can serve in the office, either consecutively or completely. The vast majority of governors (thirty-eight), like the president of the United States, are limited to two four-year terms in office. In a few states (Connecticut, Iowa, Wisconsin, Michigan, New York, and Texas) governors can, if reelected by the voters, serve an unlimited number of terms. In Virginia, the governor is limited to one four-year term. While governors with extended tenure have the opportunity to build personal and political relationships that improve their effectiveness, governors with a fixed tenure find the legislature less responsive during their final term because legislators know that they can just "wait out" the governor (Rosenthal 1990, 21).

Perhaps the most important function of any government is to determine how revenues will be raised and spent. In every state government, the legislature and the governor share this power. But the balance of power and the nature of the relationship between the two branches varies greatly from state to state. The budget power of the governor is a function of how much control that governor has over the process, ranging from two states in which the legislature cannot increase the governor's budget (Maryland and West Virginia), to forty-four states in which the governor has primary responsibility for development of a budget that the legislature is empowered either to increase or to decrease. In one state (Texas), the legislature has an unlimited power to change a budget jointly developed by the governor and the legislature (Beyle 2004, 212–214). While legislatures in most states have the power to change the budget proposed by the governor, the reality is that many do not take the opportunity, in part because many governors skillfully include particular items in their proposed budget that individual legislators want in return for promises of general support for the budget. Governors who are effective in building such coalitions within their legislature can be highly successful in securing legislative approval for much of what they consider most important in their proposed budget.

While some governors are limited in the number of statewide appointments they make, all make a significant number of appointments to boards, commissions, and administrative posts. This power of appointment is critical to a gubernatorial administration's legislative success for a variety of reasons. First, promises of appointments to positions in the state's government are often exchanged for legislative support. Second, because these political appointees are sometimes placed in positions in which they will have to work with the legislature, a governor knows that poor choices can doom legislation. Finally, governors know that if any of their appointees become embroiled in scandal, it will adversely affect their popularity and, therefore, their bargaining position with the legislature. A recent examination of the state appointment authority of administrators in six key policy areas (corrections, education, health, transportation, public utilities regulation, and welfare) revealed a wide range of gubernatorial power across the country, with the governor in Maine having the most independence and governors in Georgia, Texas, and Oklahoma the least (ibid.).

The most direct power accorded governors by state constitutions relative to the legislature is the veto power—the power to refuse to approve a bill passed by the legislature. As previously explained, when governors veto a bill passed by the legislature, that bill does not become law unless the legislature votes to override the veto by repassing the bill, usually with a supermajority of 60 percent or two-thirds. While all governors have the power to veto entire pieces of legislation, governors in forty-three states can exercise a line-item veto—that is, striking parts or sections of legislation passed by the legislature. Some governors also have pocket vetoes, which empower them to kill a bill passed by the legislature by not signing it and by holding onto it until the legislature is no longer in session and is thus unable to override a veto. In a growing number of states, the legislature is empowered to return for a special "veto override session" after its regular session is adjourned to reconsider bills vetoed by the governor after its adjournment. In Arkansas, legislators voluntarily finish their business two weeks before their official adjournment date to prevent their governor from exercising a pocket veto by ensuring that all vetoes will have to be cast early enough to allow them to be reconsidered before adjournment.

A governor's veto power is perhaps most effective when it is not used, but rather held as a threat to encourage the legislature to support particular gubernatorial proposals or to oppose items that the governor wants defeated. Indeed, many view use of the veto as a sign of gubernatorial weakness, indicating that the governor was unable to negotiate an acceptable deal to defeat or modify the bill and was forced to resort to the veto (see T 5.1).

LEADERS IN ACTION

Democratic Leaders and a Republican Governor Make a Deal

In 2005, the Colorado legislature faced what many termed "the perfect storm." New leadership teams led both chambers with the new speaker of the House of Representatives, in which Democrats gained the majority for the first time in more than four decades, having only four years of legislative experience. This meant that no one in the new House majority party had any experience running the chamber. In the Senate, Democrats picked up two seats in the 2004 election to give them a razor-thin one-seat majority, the same margin that the Republicans had had in the previous session, and that the Democrats had the session before that. The new Democratic majority leadership was faced with a popular second-term Republican governor with little history of bipartisan cooperation. Because of requirements in the state's Taxpayers' Bill of Rights (TABOR), the Democrat-controlled legislature and Republican governor immediately found themselves faced with the combination of a mounting budget deficit and a required rebate to taxpayers.

Most Coloradans agreed that dramatic action would be needed to address these challenges, but it was also recognized that the challenges presented by TABOR would be likely to produce a stalemate. However, on March 25, 2005, after weeks of public and private negotiations between the governor, the speaker of the House, and the president of the Senate, the Democrat Senate passed a bill to put TABOR reform before the voters and, it was hoped, ease the financial constraints of the state. The legislation, initially introduced by the Democratic speaker of the House and, later amended in the Senate, was cosponsored by Democratic and Republican leaders in the Senate and endorsed by the Republican governor. The compromise worked out by the legislative leaders and the governor provided some victories for both sides. It lifted the TABOR budget cap for five years, which pleased the governor (the cap had been lifted for ten years in the bill originally introduced by the speaker), but it did not include cuts to education, which were considered victories for the Democrats.

The amended bill passed both legislative chambers with unified Democratic support and a number of Republican votes in the House; some Republican members even cosponsored the bill in the Senate. By working together on a bipartisan basis, Colorado's Democratic legislative leaders and the state's Republican governor were able, along with the support of just enough Republican legislators, to overcome numerous institutional and political obstacles and achieve a compromise solution to a critical public policy problem.

Source: Interviews with House speaker, Senate president, House minority leader, and Senate minority members, April 6, 2005.

Informal Powers of Governors

In contrast to the formal powers, over which new governors have little or no control, and that remain unchanged from one governor to the next within each state, a governor's personal powers are directly reflective of the person elected to hold the office. All governors possess certain character traits that can help or hurt their efforts to influence their legislature. The personal powers of two governors who serve back to back in a state may be markedly different and lead to significantly different levels of success. There are six basic indicators of such personal power: personal and professional character, previous experience, electoral mandate, political popularity, news media skills, and potential tenure. The first five of these qualities mirror those discussed more extensively in the *Executive Branch of State Government* volume of this set. The last one, potential tenure, has, particularly in recent years, been found to be of considerable importance (ibid.).

Governors, like everyone, have their own personalities. Some are personable and friendly. Others are less able to build strong personal relationships. Some find the political process of negotiating with the legislature to be exhilarating and rewarding, while others find it a burden. Some governors may find it much easier to speak to 2 million citizens on television than to sit across the table from the speaker of the House or the president of the Senate. Obviously, those with good interpersonal skills and an appreciation for the legislative process are likely to have more success in dealing with their legislature than will those who lack such qualities. When Republican George W. Bush was governor of Texas, his personality and common ideology with conservative Democratic speaker James L. "Pete" Laney made him much more effective with the Democrat-controlled legislature than had been his Democrat predecessor, Ann Richards.

Each state governor arrives in office with unique skills and experiences. Prior to being elected governor, some have served in the legislature, some in statewide office, some in local government, and others have come directly from the private sector. History indicates that those who have experience working within or with the legislature have an advantage over those who lack such experience. Governors who come to their post with no political experience may find their relationship with their legislature particularly difficult. For example, former New Mexico governor Gary Johnson, who had no prior political experience before his election, battled with his state legislature so often and vetoed so much legislation that he became known as "Governor No."

One rule of democratic politics is quite simple: those elected by larger margins have more political clout and capital than those elected by slim margins. The size of a governor's electoral mandate has significant bearing on how legislators will respond to that governor's proposals and agenda items. Legislators are generally reluctant to oppose a governor who won election by a large margin, fearing that opposition to such a popular executive may result in a loss of support when they come up for reelection. On the other hand, executives who win by slim margins are likely to find their relationships with legislators, especially those from the opposing party, quite challenging.

Because those who govern in a democracy derive their legitimacy from the people, governors who have high levels of popular support are in a better position to negotiate with and influence their legislature than are governors that do not enjoy such support. Legislators have a lot less reason to fear challenging a governor who is unpopular with the public than they do with a popular chief executive. On the other hand, a governor whom the public believes is doing a good job may be able to draw upon that popularity and bring it to bear on legislators who seem to be opposing the governor's agenda.

One of the most effective ways for a governor to persuade a reluctant legislature is to bypass it and to go directly to the public through the news media. A governor that possesses media savvy may be able to persuade the public to put pressure on the legislature to act. Governors who can work effectively with the press may be able to build up the popular support necessary to negotiate effectively with the legislature. They can use the mass media to build public support for particular items of their program and force the legislature to act out of fear of electoral retribution by the public.

Finally, in addition to being a reflection of their past, the powers of a governor are also a reflection of their present—in other words, exactly where they are in their potential tenure as governor. Governors who are in the first year of their first term with the potential to serve another term are almost certainly likely to have more influence with their legislature than are governors in the last year of their final term. Legislators—except those in term-limited states who will eventually find themselves in the same status as a term-limited governor of their state—know that they can outlast a governor who cannot seek reelection and may well feel little incentive to work with that governor. On the other hand, legislators must be concerned about too actively opposing governors who are in a position to seek the office again and to build an electoral mandate that might hurt their own reelection effort.

Where Are Governors Most Powerful?

The most powerful governors are those who effectively combine their informal powers with the formal powers granted them by their state's constitution and laws. While the informal powers and personal qualities of governors depend primarily upon the individual governor, the formal powers assigned to governors are easily quantifiable. Geographically, the states that are considered to have the strongest formal gubernatorial powers are rather evenly distributed across the country (with the strongest considered to be Utah, Alaska, Maryland, and Minnesota). The least powerful tend to be concentrated in the South and Northeast (with Georgia, Alabama, Texas, Vermont, and Rhode Island most often cited as the states with the weakest formal powers).

While formal powers are important, experience suggests that the greatest variation in gubernatorial influence comes from the personalities and personal strengths of those holding the office. For example, when Sonny Perdue became governor of Georgia in 2002, he inherited what was considered to be one of the weakest offices in the country. However, by 2005, Governor Perdue had led a political revolution in the state that transformed the historically Democratic state into one with Republican majorities in both legislative chambers, majorities that passed most of his agenda. On the other hand, when George Ryan, a former legislator and state controller, won the Illinois governor's chair, he was expected to be one of the most effective chief executives in the state's history. Despite a strong effort to reform the death penalty during the final days of his tenure, Ryan's administration was noted more for scandals than for its achievements.

The Balance between the Legislature and the Governor

While state governors and state legislatures each have constitutional, political, and institutional sources of power, most scholars and analysts agree that modern governors

TABLE 5.1   NUMBER OF GUBERNATORIAL VETOES, 2003*

Top Five		Bottom Five	
Maryland	153	Pennsylvania	1
Illinois	105	Delaware	1
New Mexico	85	Tennessee	0
New York	72	Nevada	0
Texas	48	Alaska	0

Source: Computed from Council of State Governments. 2004. *Book of the States.* Lexington, KY: Council of State Governments, Table 3.19.

* Includes pocket vetoes.

have an advantage in the relationship. While that has not always been the case, changes in politics and society in the latter half of the twentieth century have tilted the balance toward the executive. These changes include an increase in the formal powers of the office, especially budget control and tenure power (ibid.), an increase in governors who are willing and able to rally public opinion, the adoption of legislative term limits in a number of states, changes in partisan divisions and leadership turnover that have weakened the capacity of many state legislatures (Rosenthal 1998), and an increase in the quality of individuals being elected to the office of governor (Sabato 1978). In many cases, modern state legislatures and their leaders find themselves looking toward the executive office for guidance and are reacting to their governor's agenda rather than taking the leadership role that their state constitutions assign to the legislature.

Judges and the Judicial Branch

While laws are made in the legislative branch and implemented and administered in the executive branch, neither branch has the final say on what those laws mean. That power is left to the judicial branch and the judges who compose it. Judges decide what laws mean, how they will apply in specific situations, and whether they are in violation of any provisions in the state's constitution.

Relationship with the Legislature

The relationship between the legislative and judicial branches is based primarily upon anticipatory actions and reactive responses. When considering bills, legislators anticipate the response of the courts concerning whether the bill will be in violation of any provisions of the state's constitution. On the other hand, courts act only in response to legislation passed by the legislature, rendering determinations on whether a law is unconstitutional and what the legislators meant and intended when they enacted a law.

Apart from these actions, the legislative and judicial branches also interact in the selection and removal process of judges. In four states, legislators are involved in the selection of state judges. In South Carolina and Virginia, members of the legislature appoint all or almost all of the state's judges. In Rhode Island, they appoint some judges. In almost half of the states, the governor appoints judges subject to the approval of the legislature. In the nine states in which judges are elected in partisan elections, legislators, either directly or indirectly, may take a role in the election of judges. These elections take place at the same time as the legislative elections, and most voters, who have little knowledge of judicial candidates, rely on endorsements from party leaders and interest groups in casting their votes. The ultimate constitutional authority that rests with all fifty state legislatures in their relationship with their state's courts is the power to impeach and remove judges from office.

The legislative and judicial branches operate in very different cultures. Legislatures operate in a political culture in which every decision has political implications and ramifications. They want the courts to do justice in individual cases and uphold their laws. However, they view the courts as just one more political actor in the political process. On the other hand, the courts perceive themselves as very much a coequal branch of government that is independent of both the legislature and the executive and their respective political machinations (Miller 2004). These distinct cultures invariably lead to conflict, with judges seeking autonomy and legislators decrying that same autonomy as antidemocratic.

Tools and Methods of Influence

A state's court system has three limited, but extremely powerful, tools through which it can influence legislative politics and policy: judicial review, judicial intervention, and judicial innovation. The first two are particularly powerful because the judiciary is generally considered the "court of last resort"—meaning that once the courts have spoken, their decision is final. In response to such judicial action, the only recourse available to legislatures is to accept the decision of the court, pass new legislation in an effort to meet the objections of the court, amend the constitution relative to the issues raised by the courts, or, if judges are elected, try to persuade the voters to remove the judges from office when they come up for reelection. None of these options holds much promise for success. In recent years, courts have become increasingly active in using the third, and more controversial, tool of judicial innovation to influence legislative policymakers. Policy innovation involves judges and justices designing policies to deal with new challenges brought about through innovations in such areas as technology, civil liberties, human rights, and medicine. In such cases, legislatures are often left to play "catch up," trying to legislate policy that the courts have already effectively established.

The Power of Judicial Review.   Without question, the most significant tool of the judicial branch, relative to the legislature (and to the executive branch also), is the power of judicial review. Every state constitution grants its state judiciary the power to review acts of both the legislature and the governor to determine if those acts violate the state's constitution. Judicial review can take several forms. The most common involves judicial rulings that find laws passed by the legislature or executive orders issued by the governor in violation of specific provisions of the state's constitution. For example, a state court may find laws requiring minor girls to get permission from their parents in order to obtain an abortion to be a violation of the state constitution's equal rights provisions, or it might rule that localized education funding fails to provide "equal education" for all children as required in the constitution. One study in the early 1990s found that state courts reviewed more than 600 pieces of legislation each year (Emmert and Traut 1992). In great part, legislators themselves are to blame for the large number of laws reviewed and overturned by state courts because, to secure the majority of legislator votes necessary to pass a bill, legislatures often find it necessary to adopt vague language that leaves intent unclear, thereby leaving it to the courts to issue a ruling that will determine intent (Glick 2004).

The power of judicial review, while well established in the constitutions of each state, is still very controversial. While state constitutions establish the power of the courts to review actions of the legislature and the executive, they are much less clear regarding the conditions under which such review should take place. Should judges review legislation and the constitution in light of the current political and social climate of the state, or should they try to interpret the intentions of the authors of the state constitution as well as the legislation? Many see judges and justices who render rulings based on the current political climate as activist judges who are intent on legislating from the bench and violating the will of the democratically elected legislature. On the other hand, critics of the latter original intent approach suggest that judges who use this as the basis for their rulings are abdicating their judicial responsibilities and not providing the proper balance among the three governmental branches that is necessary in an ever-changing society (ibid.; Miller 2004, 214).

Judicial Intervention.   A second power of the judicial branch relative to the state legislature is a function of the increasing level of conflict between the legislature and the governor. As this conflict has escalated in recent years, with both governors and legislatures attempting to take responsibilities from the other, the courts have increasingly been asked to intervene in these controversies. In more than a third of the states, governors have recently asked courts to review and restrain the role of their legislature in the appropriation of federal funds, while legislatures have asked the courts in some states to examine and restrict the extent of their governor's line-item veto authority (Loftus 1994). In other cases, legislative leaders have turned to their state's supreme court to seek an interpretation of the power of their governor to withhold money appropriated by the legislature. History suggests that state courts rule in favor of the governor more than for the legislature in these confrontations (Rosenthal 1990). Clearly, when the judicial branch has to settle these types of disputes, the power of both the legislature and the governor is diminished, while the power and influence of the judicial branch is increased (Frohnmeyer 1989).

Judicial Innovation.   In the eyes of legislators, the most controversial tool of judicial power relative to legislatures is that of judicial innovation—creation by the courts of public policy solutions to problems that have not been addressed through laws passed by the legislature. These innovations often serve as models for both other state courts and other legislatures in their efforts to develop laws in response to new challenges. Judicial innovation differs from judicial review and judicial intervention in that it does not involve court response to legislative or executive acts, but rather initiation by judges in response to specific cases brought to them by civil or criminal litigants. "Right to die" policies and policies requiring equitable funding for state education systems have been two policy areas that, in recent years, were initiated by state courts through case rulings. In both those instances, legislatures were forced to react to judicial branch initiatives arising from judges' interpretation or reinterpretation of state constitutional provisions (Glick 1992; McDermott 1999). Many legislators, both conservative and liberal, express concern that judicial innovation goes well beyond the constitutional responsibility and authority of the courts and violates the separation of powers principle by making judges policy makers rather than policy interpreters (Miller 2004).

Supporters and opponents of gay marriage stand outside the Massachusetts statehouse in Boston, March 11, 2004. The Massachusetts legislature took a first step to amend the state's constitution to ban gay marriage and introduce civil unions for same-sex couples. In November 2003 the Massachusetts supreme judicial court ruled that the state must issue marriage licenses to gay couples. (Brian Snyder/Reuters/Corbis)

Where Are Courts Most Influential?

Just as some state governors are more powerful and influential than their counterparts in other states, judges in certain states are more likely to exhibit traits of judicial activism than are their counterparts elsewhere. State supreme courts are more likely to be asked to review cases in light of constitutionality in those states that have highly detailed constitutions, such as in Alabama, Texas, and some other Southern states. Judges in states that are characterized as more liberal than conservative in voter behavior and whose judges are appointed rather than elected are more likely to adopt an activist approach to judicial review (Wenzel, Bowler, and Lanoue 1997). Understandably, judicial intervention in disputes between the legislative and executive branches is more common in states in which one party controls the legislature and the other holds the governor's office, as well as in states in which one of the branches is trying to expand its power at the expense of the other (Rosenthal 1990).

The Most Common Method

Finally, history suggests that courts in certain states are more likely than courts in others to be policy innovators. Courts in New York; New Jersey; Washington, D.C.; and Massachusetts tend to stand out as policy innovators. These states generally elect more Democrats and liberals than Republicans and conservatives and have large, predominantly urban populations. Close behind those states are three other heavily populated states (Pennsylvania, Minnesota, and Illinois). Most experts suggest that large and urban states are likely to experience new challenges before smaller and more rural states, and that Democrats and liberals are more likely than Republicans and conservatives to view government as the solution to such problems. It should also be noted that most of the more innovative states select their judges through a political process, either elections (New York, Illinois, and Pennsylvania) or gubernatorial appointments (New Jersey and California). Only one of these states (Massachusetts) removes the legislative and executive branches as the primary players in the selection of its judges (Glick 2004), although some suggest that the Massachusetts selection process is really almost as political as the processes in other states whose courts are considered innovative.

The Balance between the Legislature and the Judiciary

In recent years, state courts have become increasingly active in the policymaking process, reviewing more legislative acts and executive decrees, settling more legislative and executive disputes, and offering more policy innovations from the bench. The reasons for the increase in judicial innovation are many. An increase in the number of divided governments, in which the governorship and legislative majorities are of different parties, has escalated conflict between the two branches, necessitating more judicial intervention (Thornburgh 2004, 232). Increased ideological and partisan differences in state legislatures have made it more likely that legislation will be considered as much in light of the political as the legal climate, resulting in legislation that may be more ideological or vague, and more ripe for judicial review. Term limits, which in states that have them have significantly increased the proportion of inexperienced legislators, have led to the passage of more legislation that might not receive adequate scrutiny and may be less likely to meet constitutional muster (Greenblatt 2005). Finally, with rapid advances in technology, society is increasingly encountering issues and problems that legislators have not yet addressed, leaving it to the courts to become policymaking innovators. There have been recent signs that the increase in judicial activism may be producing a backlash in some state legislatures, which are beginning to challenge the autonomy of the courts by cutting their budgets, forcing judicial reorganization, and reducing judicial discretion regarding sentencing (Tarr 2004).

LEGISLATURES IN ACTION

Florida Legislature and Courts Clash Over Right to Die

In 1990, twenty-six-year-old Terri Schiavo suffered a double stroke, leaving her unable to speak, move, or communicate. Four years later, her husband, Michael, initiated efforts to have her feeding tube removed, arguing that she had indicated to him before her stroke that she would not want to be kept alive artificially. Mrs. Schiavo's parents, who became her primary caregivers in 1993 (although her husband remained her legal guardian), contended that she had made no such comments and would have wanted to be kept alive at all costs. Thus began a protracted legal debate that not only pitted a husband against his in-laws but also would pit the Florida judicial system against the Florida legislature.

Citing his spousal rights, Michael Schiavo instructed doctors to remove his wife's feeding tube, but her parents went to court to stop him on the grounds that she was not in a "persistent vegetative state," as Mr. Schiavo indicated, and as required by Florida law before a feeding tube could be removed.

Following a series of judicial decisions supporting Mr. Schiavo, the Florida legislature, at the urging of Republican governor Jeb Bush, became involved in the dispute. In October 2003, almost seven days after Florida circuit judge George Greer found that Terri Schiavo's husband had presented "clear and convincing evidence" that his wife did not want to be kept alive artificially and ordered the feeding tube removed, the Florida legislature passed "Terri's Law." That law, approved by the legislature in less than twenty-four hours, authorized "the Governor to issue a one-time stay to prevent withholding of nutrition and hydration under certain circumstances." Seven months later, in May 2004, another Florida circuit judge found Terri's Law to be unconstitutional because it violated the separation of powers principle as established by the Florida Constitution.

Sources: "Terri Schiavo has Died." Tuesday, March 31, 2005 (http://www.cnn.com/2005/LAW/03/31/schiavo/); "Schiavo's Feeding Tube Removed." Wednesday, March 18, 2005 (http://www.cnn.com/2005/LAW/03/18/schiavo.brain-damaged/).

NONGOVERNMENTAL GROUPS

While state constitutions require that the state legislature interact with and respond to the other two branches of government, governors and courts are not the only entities within a state that influence legislative decisions and activities. Interest groups, political parties, and the news media may not be mentioned in state constitutions, but they are critical to the success of the representative democratic process. They provide the three critical linkages by which the policy viewpoints of the public are translated to its elected legislators and by which the representatives communicate their decisions and actions back to the public.

Interest Groups

Interest groups are not mentioned in the U.S. Constitution or in any state constitution. Those who wrote and defended the U.S. Constitution in the eighteenth century actually derided interest groups as "factions" that should be feared rather than protected.

However, interest groups—associations organized to pursue a common interest by bringing pressure to bear on the political process—and the lobbyists who represent them in the halls of government have existed as long as representative government has existed. They are a natural and necessary outgrowth of this form of government, providing a critical, if often misunderstood, linkage between the representative and the represented. Interest groups are, in fact, an integral part of the legislative environment in every state capitol building.

Relationship with the Legislature

The laws of each state define the relationship between that state's legislature and interest groups. Statutes and legislative rules define what interest groups can do and how they can do it (Ogle and Lakis 2002). In every state, lobbyists who intend to represent an interest group before the legislature are required to register with some governmental agency. The word "lobbyist" was coined many years ago in the United States because of the tendency of individuals working for or against the passage of legislation to congregate in the lobby outside the legislative meeting chamber after legislative bodies had banned them from being on the floor of the chamber while it was in session. Those who intend to represent an interest group before the legislature are required to register with some governmental agency. But the definition of a lobbyist and state requirements for registration vary, with some states severely restricting how much lobbyists can spend in entertaining legislators, while in others there are no limitations as long as all expenditures on legislator entertainment are reported (CSG 2004b).

Politically, the relationship between legislators and lobbyists is marked by the symbiotic relationship between the two, with each benefitting politically from the work and efforts of the other. Neither could do its job as effectively without the other. Legislators gain information and campaign support from interest groups, and interest groups gain access to the public policy decisions critical to their members from legislators.

TABLE 5.2   NUMBER OF REGISTERED LOBBYISTS, 2004

Top Five		Bottom Five	
Connecticut	4,000	Hawaii	250
Arizona	3,413	Rhode Island	300
New York	3,412	Arkansas	302
Illinois	3,824	Vermont	350
Michigan	2,398	West Virginia	350

Source: Council of State Governments. 2004. *Book of the States.* Lexington, KY: Council of State Governments, Table 6.15, pp. 305–306.

While interest groups are generally viewed negatively by the public (Rosenthal 1993), they perform several functions that are critical to the success of representative democracy and the legislature. First, they are a source of valuable information for legislators, especially in states with less professional legislatures in which staff support is limited. Legislators often turn to lobbyists when they have questions about the provisions or financial and political implications of bills. Second, interest groups help to educate and inform the public about the activities of the legislature and state government. Third, interest groups serve as a force for mobilizing public support or opposition to proposed legislation. Such mobilization, which helps to make the voice of the people heard in the legislature, is critical to the success of representative democracy. Fourth, sometimes to the consternation of legislators, interest groups perform a watchdog function, not simply reporting to their members what the legislature is doing but also comparing those activities and policies with what the members had promised to do in their last election campaign. Finally, interest groups, through political action committees that they create, provide a valuable source of campaign support for legislative candidates. As shown earlier, most candidates rely heavily on them for financial and personnel support (Rozell and Wilcox 1995).

Tools and Methods of Influence

Interest groups have a wide variety of tools through which to influence the legislative process. These tools derive from the primary resources that interest groups generally have at their disposal—lobbyists, members, information, and money. Interest group tools and methods can be organized into four different categories: direct lobbying, indirect (or grassroots) lobbying, public relations activities, and campaign activities.

Direct Lobbying.   Direct lobbying involves efforts by a paid representative of the group—its lobbyist—to influence the decisions of individual legislators and, through them, the legislature as a whole. This effort involves personal contact between lobbyists and legislators. Lobbyists employ several methods of direct lobbying. Perhaps the one with which people are most familiar involves face-to-face discussions with legislators or members of their staff to discuss a particular issue under consideration by the legislature. A lobbyist will schedule time to meet with a legislator individually to discuss the merits of a particular piece of legislation. This meeting may take place in the office of the legislator or, in states that do not preclude it, over a dinner or lunch, with the lobbyist picking up the check. The key is that the lobbyist has the attention of the legislator. Another form of direct lobbying involves oral or written presentations by the lobbyist to groups of legislators —most often, at a committee public hearing—on a bill of concern to the lobbyist's client.

While the short-term objective of a lobbyist is to persuade the legislator to support a position on a particular piece of legislation or issue, the long-term objective of the lobbyist is something greater. Over an extended period, a lobbyist wants to build personal relationships with legislators to increase the likelihood that they will support positions favored by the lobbyist's clients unless given a compelling reason not to do so (Rosenthal 1993, 112–118). Relationships of this sort are built on trust and a belief that the lobbyist would suggest nothing that would be contrary to the interests of the legislator. Interestingly, such a relationship occasionally requires a lobbyist to advise a legislator to vote against the wishes or interests of the lobbyist's client if casting a vote with the interest group would not be in the political interest of the legislator. While such advice may cost the lobbyist a vote in the short term, it is likely to gain several valuable votes in the future.

Effective lobbyists abide by a set of unofficial rules or norms. First and foremost, lobbyists must tell the truth. If they are caught in a lie or provide inaccurate information or information that embarrasses or damages the political reputation of a legislator, the credibility and effectiveness of the lobbyist may be damaged irreparably. The most important asset that lobbyists have is their integrity, and once that is gone, so is their influence. Second, lobbyists should never promise more than they can deliver. They should not, for example, promise legislative supporters a certain number of votes for a bill if they are not absolutely certain that they can deliver them. Third, effective lobbyists must know how to listen, making sure that they hear what legislators are really saying to them. Effective lobbyists must know where members stand on legislation and issues of concern to their clients. While lobbyists generally like to talk directly to legislators, they must also understand that staff are there to be worked with, not circumvented, particularly in professional legislatures with large staffs. Staff members often serve as "gatekeepers" for legislators, and lobbyists must know how to "get past the gate" to make their case directly to the legislator. Finally, effective lobbyists never spring surprises on legislators or allow them to be caught off guard. In short, an effective lobbyist is one who understands and responds effectively to the world in which a legislator works (Wolpe and Levine 1996, 13–19).

TABLE 5.3   RANKING OF LOBBY DISCLOSURE LAWS, 2003*

Top Five		Bottom Five	
Washington	85	Tennessee	45
Kentucky	79	South Dakota	42
Connecticut	75	New Hampshire	36
South Carolina	75	Wyoming	36
New York	74	Pennsylvania	34

Source: Center for Public Integrity.

* Out of a possible 100 points, based on a survey of state disclosure. High scores represent greater openness, accountability, and public access.

Indirect (Grassroots) Lobbying.   Lobbyists are not the only resource available to an interest group. In fact, for many interest groups, lobbyists are not their most important asset. That distinction often falls to the individuals that belong to or are actively involved in the interest group. For example, the most valuable asset of a labor union may be its many members who are willing to write letters, make phone calls, and send e-mails to legislators. Such activity, organized and encouraged by the union leadership, is indirect lobbying because no paid lobbyist is in direct contact with legislators. Rather, the contact is indirect, through the group's membership or employee workforce. The objective of indirect lobbying is to influence legislative decisions by making legislators aware of the breadth and intensity of support or opposition to a bill or issue among the members of the interest group. One can divide such efforts into three types: individual personal contact, individual indirect contact, and corporate personal contact.

Often, lobbyists will send out a letter or e-mail to members or employees of organizations or groups they represent, suggesting that they make a trip to the state capitol to meet with legislators face to face. This kind of individual personal contact requires some effort on behalf of a group member, but it is likely to have a significant impact if it is performed by many members of the group. Lobbyists may also contact members and urge them to contact legislators by letter, telephone, or electronic mail. Advances in technology have made such individual indirect contacts much easier to organize, but, ironically, the ease with which such indirect contacts can be orchestrated may also have made them less effective lobbying tools in terms of their ability to influence legislators' thinking. Legislators are less likely to respond to letters or e-mails that appear mass produced and that do not seem to reflect a deep level of commitment to the cause (ibid., 94–98). Finally, lobbyists often find it effective to organize the group's members to descend upon the capitol at the same time, in what we have termed corporate personal contact. This implies that while the contact is personal (face to face), it is corporate in the sense that group members act as a single group. Working with group members, interest group leaders select a day on which group members will come to the capitol and "take to the halls" of the building, meeting with as many legislators as possible. If coordinated effectively, each method of indirect lobbying can effectively demonstrate to legislators that a bill or issue is considered of major importance to the members of an interest group—and that the position they take on the bill or issue could have a significant influence on how they will fare should they seek reelection.

Public Relations Efforts.   While the explicit objective of both direct and indirect lobbying is to persuade legislators how to vote on specific bills, a third method of interest group activity has a broader goal, although the end result may be the same. Some interest group activities are targeted at the general public more than at the legislature—although, obviously, if the general public is moved, the legislature may be compelled to act. The news media are sometimes used as a means of projecting an interest group's image and positions to the public and to public officials. This can appear as a particularly attractive recourse to groups and organizations that lack sufficient funds to employ a lobbyist to engage in direct lobbying, or that may be supporting an issue lacking in public support, which may negate the effectiveness of both direct and indirect lobbying. In other words, the interest group may feel that before it can change the minds of policymakers, it will need to change the mind of the general public. Often groups that have fallen out of public favor for a time (tobacco and cigarette companies since the 1990s, and insurance, health care, and pharmaceutical companies following 2000), rely heavily on this approach to try to influence public policy. Their initial objective is often to soften their image and improve the likelihood that they or their industry as a whole can come to be viewed more sympathetically.

Public relations lobbying relies on publications, advertising campaigns, demonstrations, and community relations. Interest groups often rely on their regular publications to get out their message, distributing newsletters, press releases, or reports to explain all of the good work that a company, organization, or industry has engaged in. In recent years, web pages have also become a significant vehicle for the distribution of information. For example, the website for the R. J. Reynolds Tobacco Company highlights the core values and principles of the company, noting: "We do things right. We treat every person with respect, fairness, and integrity, and we embrace diversity." It also notes the company's efforts to promote responsible uses of its products, to discourage teen smoking, and its many community involvement activities (http://www.rjrt.com/values/resp-Core.aspx·).

Similar themes are also reflected in television and radio advertising strategies. During 2004 and 2005, pharmaceutical companies, faced with growing public discontent over the rising price of prescription medications, launched a series of commercials focusing on the life-saving medications they have developed and programs to sell medications at a discount to the poor. While the effort focused on improving the industry's image in the eyes of the public, and was not directly aimed at legislators, it may have at least indirectly influenced legislators when they were called upon to vote on legislation that affected the pharmaceutical industry. While corporate interest groups may have the money to invest in a nationwide public relations campaign, many other interest groups do not. But many interest groups do not require a national campaign to state their case. Rather, they are looking to draw attention to their issue in a single state or a small group of contiguous states. In such cases, groups may rely on public demonstrations to draw the attention of newspapers and local radio and television stations. In order to bring attention to the negative consequences of drinking, Mothers Against Drunk Driving (MADD) may hold a rally on the steps of the state capitol, complete with thousands of red ribbons, a wrecked vehicle, and speeches by family members of the victims of drunk drivers. The specific purpose of the rally may be to garner support or opposition to a piece of legislation under consideration in the legislature. While members of the legislature may witness this demonstration, the main audience is the news media and the public, who will watch it on the evening news and may follow up by expressing their feelings about the proposed legislation to their legislators.

Campaign Activities.   Finally, many interest groups can provide legislators or candidates for the legislature with at least one of the two resources that they find extremely valuable: money and people. Campaign activities are a critical tool for many interest groups. While the objective of providing campaign assistance may appear to be influencing the selection of policymakers, most campaign assistance, especially financial contributions, is just another effort to influence the decisions of the sitting policymakers, like direct and indirect lobbying. More than two-thirds of all campaign contributions from interest groups are made to incumbent legislators (those already holding office). This is viewed as "part of the game" in order to get access to that legislator. A lobbyist who cannot meet directly with a legislator is unlikely to be able to influence that legislator's decision (Rosenthal 1993, 129–133; Rozell and Wilcox 1995, 86).

Where Are Lobbyists More Influential?

While lobbyists are active in every state legislature, their influence in a particular state and how they attempt to exert that influence are the product of how lobbying is regulated in the state, the specific characteristics of the state and its legislature, and the individual interest group.

Interest groups are generally more numerous and competitive in states in which the economy and the population are diverse. A diverse economy yields more opportunity and resources for interest group activity and generally produces more sophisticated lobbying and more professional lobbyists. However, in states in which the economy is not highly developed, but rather is dominated by one or two prime sectors, interest groups may be less active, even as certain ones may be more influential. When tobacco dominated the North Carolina economy, tobacco interests dominated the legislature (Luebke 2000). In a similar manner, the political environment of a state affects interest groups, with some states, mostly in the South and Midwest, providing less regulation and allowing them the possibility for more influence. In many Southern states lobbyists must register, but they are not limited in how much they can spend on entertaining legislators. In other states, lobbyists can spend a very limited amount entertaining legislators (for example, no money at all can be spent on such activities in South Carolina and Wisconsin). States that have large numbers of competitive state legislative seats in each election present interest groups with good opportunities to influence the development of public policy through involvement in campaign activities.

How legislative lobbying is conducted can vary greatly between professional and citizen legislatures. In professional legislatures whose members are well compensated and well staffed but often face expensive reelection campaigns, campaign contributions are highly valued and are often provided by lobbyists in behalf of their clients. On the other hand, in legislatures in which members are limited in staff and in the time they can commit to the job, information becomes a prized commodity. In such states, direct lobbying can be a lobbyist's most effective tool, with lobbyists being a primary source of information for legislators. In states where the political parties are balanced and very competitive, indirect lobbying and public relations may be as important as direct lobbying, with both parties keeping a close eye on public opinion.

Finally, while all interest groups strive to influence legislative politics, some have a great deal of money but few members while others may have a large, diverse membership but limited funds. Still others may have a small following but a well-connected lobbyist. The characteristics of an interest group determine which of the various lobbying tools it will find most useful. An interest group with a small but well-organized, wealthy, and dedicated following will likely rely on different tools than one with a large, geographically diverse but loosely organized membership. Likewise, a group with an experienced lobbyist (perhaps a former legislator) will rely on a different balance of tools than one that cannot afford a full-time lobbyist.

A 1985 study found that particular types of interest groups tend to have more influence than others in state legislatures. General business organizations—those that do not represent a single company or industry—were ranked as most effective in forty states. Education and teacher's associations were ranked near the top in thirty-seven states. Groups representing particular industries (insurance, utilities, manufacturers) were ranked as very effective in about half of the states, reflecting the states' economies and their most prominent industries (for example, manufacturing would be more important in Michigan than in Wyoming). Finally, groups with limited political clout nationwide (criminal justice groups, and social issue groups), as well as groups representing interests that would be important in a few states (mining, oil and gas, tobacco) were ranked as most effective in very few states (Thomas and Hrebenar 2003).

The Balance between the Legislature and Interest Groups

Since the middle 1970s interest group activity has increased dramatically in state legislatures, but interest group influence has diminished. In other words, many lobbyists find themselves working harder and achieving less. This shift has occurred for several reasons. First, beginning in the late 1960s, most state legislatures began to improve and expand their staff support and organization, thereby providing legislatures with their own independent sources of information and making information provided by lobbyists less important and less valuable to their members. Second, the last half of the twentieth century witnessed economic changes across the country that produced more diverse economies and provided competition for interest groups that once dominated particular states. Third, stung by Watergate and other public scandals, the public became less tolerant of private deals and questionable interest group influence, forcing changes that significantly opened the legislative process and defined acceptable lobbying practices much more restrictively than in the past (Rosenthal 1996).

But two recent trends may be halting and even reversing the decline of interest group influence in some states. First, the increasing cost of legislative elections and the growth of campaign committees managed by the top leaders of many legislatures have made the provision of political contributions a more important and effective tool for interest groups in those states. Second, the limits that more than a dozen states have placed on the number of terms that a member may serve in their legislature have created a large class of new legislators after every election in these states, and these inexperienced members may be more susceptible to the influence directed at them by lobbyists.

Political Party Organizations

While the United States is considered to have a two-party system when it comes to political parties, the reality is that it has a 102-party system. In addition to the national Republican and Democratic parties, there is a developed, organized, and active Democratic and Republican party organization in each of the fifty states. In each state, Democrats and Republicans have paid and volunteer staffs that manage the day-to-day activities of their parties, promote their general positions, and work toward the election of members of their parties to state and local office. At the state level, each party has a chairperson and a state committee. Most hold state conventions in which they elect party leaders, develop a platform of policies and programs that the party supports, and generate momentum for the next election (Morehouse and Jewell 2003, 105–107).

DIVERSITY IN THE LEGISLATURE
Women Gaining Numbers and Influence in Lobby Corps

While the stereotypical image of a legislative lobbyist is a man in a tailored suit, the reality is that the person in that tailored suit is increasingly a woman. While there are no national studies of female lobbyists, two recent studies in North Carolina and Illinois indicate that women are becoming a larger and more significant portion of the state lobby corps in those two states. A 2005 study of lobbyists in the North Carolina legislature found seven women ranked among the forty-eight most influential lobbyists in the state, including two in the top ten. This represents a record high number of women in the twenty years that the study has been conducted.

In Illinois, a 2000 study revealed that female lobbyists are becoming both more numerous in the halls of the state capitol and more influential. A review of the more than 3,000 registered lobbyists in the Illinois legislature in 1999 found that almost 700 (more than 20 percent) were women. A sim-

ilar review of lobbyist registrants twenty-five years earlier had found less than 10 percent to be women. Furthermore, while women historically have lobbied in behalf of "women's issues," the Illinois study revealed that women are now active and successful in all sectors. Two of the most prominent female lobbyists in Illinois include among their clients a major beer distributor, an international communications firm, a major loan institution, and trucking interests. In explaining their success, one female lobbyist noted: "Women are great mediators and facilitators. I think we're naturals."

Sources: Nickel, Heather. 2000. "Spotlight on Women: Winning Her Place at the Rail." *Illinois Issues* (March); N.C. Center for Public Policy Research. 2004. "New Generations of Influential Lobbyists Emerges in Center's Rankings." Press release (http://www.nccppr .org/Lobbyistrankings2004.pdf).

While a state party committee usually elects state political party chairpersons, a state's governor will usually have a significant say in the selection of the state chairman of the party. While policy and ideology clearly matter to those who work in behalf of a political party organization (Shafer 1996, 12–46), the primary objective of a state party organization is to recruit, nominate, and assist party candidates who can win state and local offices. With a few exceptions, state party organizations in the United States are more pragmatic than ideological, and more concerned about winning elections than about maintaining philosophical purity (Morehouse and Jewell 2003, 105–107).

Relationship with the Legislature

Relationships between state party organizations and their state legislatures are defined by law in every state. While twenty-eight states permit political party organizations to give an unlimited amount of money to candidates seeking office, the role that parties play in the actual selection of those candidates is largely determined by how a state provides for candidate selection, with party influence least in states that require candidates to be selected through open primary elections and greatest in states in which candidates are selected in a party convention or parties are allowed to endorse candidates in a primary.

The relationship that matters most between political party organizations and legislatures is based on politics, not on law. While there may be many differences between a state party organization and that party's state legislators, they do have one thing in common. They both want the legislative candidates of their party to defeat the candidates from the other party. Apart from philosophy, ideology, or anything else, that common thread binds the two together.

The modern state party organization is at the service of its state legislative candidates. It does not tell its legislative candidates what to do, but rather provides them with information, organization, and support to help them get elected or reelected. While campaign support activities, party organizations, and the activities of legislative leaders sometimes conflict, the reality of the modern party is that it exists to promote and serve the electoral needs of its candidates for the state legislature and other statewide offices. Seldom will a party organization withhold resources from candidates it believes can win an election to the legislature on the grounds that the candidate does not pass an ideological litmus test, or because the candidate failed to "toe the party line" during a recent legislative vote. Parties generally understand that their refusal to support a candidate of their party is rather counterproductive, because any legislator of their party, no matter how obstinate, is almost certainly going to be more agreeable and more acceptable than a legislator of the opposing party (Coleman 1996; Bibby 1999).

Tools and Methods of Party Organization Influence

The arsenal of tools that state party organizations most often employ to assist their legislative candidates in their campaigns includes the recruitment of candidates, volunteer assistance to candidates, and the contribution of funds to their campaigns. In some states, they also take an active role in the development of a unified party message and statewide coordination of all candidate campaigns.

Recruiting Legislative Candidates.   As has been previously explained, first-time candidates for the legislature seldom choose to run on their own. They are usually encouraged to run by others, most often by friends or by members of their state or local party organization. Because the vast majority of incumbent legislators choose to seek reelection on their own, party leaders generally focus their recruitment efforts on open seats and on seats in which they believe their party stands a good chance of defeating an incumbent legislator from the opposing party. In searching for candidates, party leaders report that they look to people who previously ran for office and did well, for popular local office holders, and for well-known community activists. Although party leaders seek candidates who reflect their party's ideals and are unlikely to recruit a candidate who is completely out of step with the party's platform and views, they are at least as concerned with finding candidates who reflect the predominant views of the district, have a desire to win, and possess the money, time, and name recognition to win. State party leaders will rely on party leaders in the legislature, as well as on county, municipal, and even precinct organizations to assist them in identifying potential candidates. Candidate recruitment has become a particularly important function for party organizations in term-limited states, in which a quarter to a third of the legislature's seats are open every election.

Providing Services to Legislative Candidates.   Candidates for the legislature who are not incumbents seeking reelection are most likely to require help in the development and management of their campaigns. In addition to money, they are likely to need assistance in organization and campaign coordination. Most candidates for the state legislature, particularly nonincumbents, lack the visibility, campaign experience, and staff support that candidates for statewide office and the U.S. Congress can more often draw upon. In most states, political parties step up to assist state legislative candidates with training seminars on everything from message development to fundraising techniques to basic campaign organization. Most state party officials have years, if not decades, of experience in organizing and running campaigns, and that knowledge can be an invaluable resource to first-time candidates. Furthermore, because of their experience and statewide reach, state party officials can often direct candidates to effective pollsters, news media advisors, fundraisers, and political consultants. Many state political parties contract with people to provide these "in kind" types of services to their candidates at no cost to individual campaigns because limited campaign budgets often make it difficult and impractical for individual candidates to hire these experts themselves (Moncrief, Squire, and Jewell 2001).

Funding Legislative Candidates.   Regardless of the power of a candidate's message or organization, every campaign requires money. State political parties have become a critical source of that money for legislative candidates, especially for those who are nonincumbents and have not had time to build up visibility among their voters or extensive contacts and solid relationships with interest groups. While candidates can seek money from individuals and nonparty groups, in most states, political parties have a significant advantage over these other funding sources because there are considerably fewer restrictions placed on party contributions than on contributions by interest groups. As previously indicated, political parties can give unlimited donations to candidates for the legislature and statewide office in twenty-eight states. In the remaining states, parties are allowed to give more than either individuals or interest group political action committees. An advantage to party-provided campaign money is that it is not likely to carry the negative connotations or baggage that might be carried by money received from unpopular interest groups. A legislator may, for instance, be reluctant to take money from a tobacco company, a pharmaceutical lobbyist, or the trial lawyers association, but those groups can give money to the general fund of the political party (usually in higher amounts than to individual candidates); the party can then distribute the money among its candidates, making it almost impossible to tie the candidate to the interest group. This type of financial assistance from their party organizations helps candidates to get their name and message out to the voters and reduces the amount of time that they must devote to raising their own campaign funds (Bibby 1998).

Coordinated Campaigns and Activities.   Because campaigns for state legislatures are usually less well financed and cover much smaller geographical areas than statewide or congressional races, it makes little sense, politically or financially, for most state legislative campaigns to invest large amounts of money in polling, media advertising, or message development and distribution. However, working through their state political party organizations, several legislative campaigns may be able to coordinate efforts and resources to take advantage of those types of services. A state party organization may, for example, conduct an issue poll across several contiguous districts to determine what issues are salient to their voters. Some party organizations promote statewide or regional media buys and messages that are designed to help several, or even all, of the party's candidates for office. In the final analysis, no campaign or campaign message matters unless the voters go to the polls, and state parties generally take an active role in "get-out-the-vote" activities, working with their precinct, district, and county organizations across the state to identify and mobilize voters likely to support the candidates of their party (ibid.).

Where Are Political Parties Most Influential?

The strength and relative influence of political parties vary across the country, with stronger parties usually found in states with diverse populations, less regulation of party activities, and histories of strong competition between the two parties. In states with economically, socially, and racially diverse populations, both political parties have strong bases from which to seek votes. In order to attract voters and prevent the other party from gaining an advantage, both parties have developed strong organizational structures. In these states, the battle for control of the state legislature is likely to be very competitive, even if gerrymandering (that is, drawing the districts to the advantage of one party or the other) has produced large numbers of safe (noncompetitive) seats, with each party working closely with its candidates in the competitive races that determine control of the legislature.

Parties are also strongest and most active in states in which the regulation of parties is the most relaxed. It is difficult for political parties to have a dramatic effect on elections if the amount of money they can raise is restricted, or if they have limited control over how their candidates are chosen. The influence of political parties on legislative politics is likely to be diminished in states that choose their candidates through open primaries, or in primary states in which parties are prohibited from endorsing candidates during the selection process (Morehouse and Jewell 2003).

Finally, some states have historically restricted or encouraged active political parties based on their political cultures and traditions. Parties have historically been most active in states with individualistic political cultures. In these states, most of which are found in the Midwest and West, politics is often considered to be a "business," with the two parties the primary providers in the marketplace. Examples of states with historically strong political party organizations include Ohio, Pennsylvania, New York, Indiana, Connecticut, and Michigan. While Southern states that were, until the past few decades, dominated by the Democrat Party used to be characterized by very weak party organizations, increased party competition has changed this, with active Republican organizations altering the political landscape of most Southern states and forcing Democrats to organize their party organizations to remain competitive. Many rural Western states in which Republican control of the state government is seldom in doubt often have weak state party organizations.

The Balance between the Legislature and State Party Organizations

Fifty years ago, state political parties were viewed as the center of the political universe in most states outside of the one-party South. In Southern states, personal or regional political factions within the Democrat Party, rather than the state party organization itself, tended to assist candidates in legislative campaigns. National party organizations were virtually nonexistent; state party leaders had a strong hand in the selection of gubernatorial and legislative candidates, as well as a significant influence on governance decisions made by both governors and legislatures when the governor was from the party in the majority in the legislature. However, declining party loyalty and identification among voters, the rise of candidate-centered campaigns, and increasingly independent, active, and professional legislators and legislative leaders have, over the past half-century, served to alter the role and influence of state political parties relative to state legislatures. As the number of voters who identify themselves with a party has decreased, parties could no longer credibly promise to deliver votes to candidates, which diminished the influence they could exercise over those candidates. During this same period, the rise of interest groups and political action committees has enabled legislative candidates to manage their own campaigns and messages without support from their party organization. Candidates who get elected with little or no assistance from their party are likely to feel little or no loyalty to their party organization (Salmore and Salmore 1996).

The 1980s and 1990s witnessed the rise of a competing party organization within the legislature—leadership and caucus campaign committees. The same characteristics that tend to produce strong state party organizations (diversity, limited regulation, and individualistic political culture) have given rise to increasingly active campaign organizations within the legislatures of many states. These organizations often compete with the state party organization, but they do so from a position of relative strength. That strength comes because these campaign committees are organized and operate within the legislature, and legislative leaders can promise specific and concrete rewards to candidates that party organizations cannot. Such rewards might include a desired committee assignment, appointment to a secondary leadership position, or the promise of support for passage of personally sponsored legislation. While state party leaders and legislative party leaders sometimes work together, their relationships are often uneasy, and the rise of leadership campaign structures within the legislature has generally weakened the influence and role of state party organizations within state legislatures (Rosenthal 1998, 173–178).

The News Media

Campaign politics in a democracy is about message and getting that message out to the voters. Historically, newspapers and radio and television stations were the public's primary source of information regarding state legislatures and state governments. However, in recent years, as every state legislature has developed increasingly user-friendly websites and the Internet has grown in scope and importance, growing numbers of people have been turning to those sources for news and information about the activities of their state legislature.

The Relationship between the News Media and the Legislature

The relationship between the news media and the legislature is defined by mutual interest and mutual need. Politicians cannot reach the public and the voters who elect them without the media, and journalists cannot get their stories without access to the politicians. In this era in which governors have become adept at using the mass media, this relationship is particularly important for the legislature and those who lead it.

From the perspective of legislators, the news media are a window, even if a somewhat distorted and foggy one at times. It is the window through which most of the public view the state legislature. Few citizens will ever walk the halls of their state's legislative building, sit in on a committee meeting, or watch a debate on the floor of their state Senate or House of Representatives. However, many of them will read an article, see part of a committee hearing on television, or view a story on the Internet. It is through this same window that most legislators learn what the public thinks and wants. Issues covered by the news media today often become legislative proposals tomorrow (State Legislative Leaders Foundation 2005). E-mails received by legislators before a committee or floor vote can often influence an undecided legislator on how to vote on a bill.

Tools and Methods of Influence

The influence of the news media on legislative politics and the making of public policy is very different from the influence exhibited by the actors that have previously been examined. Influence exerted on a legislature by the executive branch, the judiciary, interest groups, and state party officials is intentional—that is, they act purposefully to influence what the legislature will do. Journalists, on the other hand, seldom act with the intention of influencing legislative behavior. Rather, the influence they exert is often a by-product of their primary goal: to sell newspapers, gain listeners, or increase viewers. While a newspaper series about domestic abuse may result in legislative action, the reporter and the reporter's editor are likely to be more concerned about how much the story increases circulation (ibid., 101–105). Although a television report about legislative staff that does campaign work on state time may change the rules and behavior of the legislature, it may also improve the ratings of the station that broadcast the story. Given this distinction, it is important to examine specific effects that news media efforts to maintain and increase the number of their readers, listeners, or viewers can have on decisionmaking in a state legislature.

Bringing Issues to the Attention of the Legislature.   Perhaps the greatest impact that the news media has on legislative politics is its contribution to setting the "legislative agenda." Mass media is one of the most significant agenda setters for public policy in the United States. While it is unclear whether it can effectively persuade viewers, readers, or listeners (or even legislators) to take a particular position on an issue, it is quite clear that it can influence what people think about. If a local television station gives significant attention to a particular issue (often spawned by a newsworthy event, such as the tragic death of a child or the discovery of chemicals in drinking water), that issue will surely be brought to the attention of the legislature by members who either saw the story, or, more likely, were inundated with phone calls, e-mails, letters, and faxes from constituents who did (Rosenthal 2004, 67–71).

Influencing Public Perception of the Legislature and Its Members.   The little knowledge that most citizens have about their state legislators or about their state legislature, they are most likely to have acquired through the news media. The image that most people have of their state legislators is the one portrayed by the media, and that image is seldom flattering (SLLF 2005). In an era of "gotcha" journalism, where journalists are more interested in "catching public officials in seemingly compromising positions" (Brown 1994) than in covering what legislatures do and the legislation they debate and pass, the news media have done considerable damage to the reputations of many legislators and many legislative bodies. A study conducted in the 1990s revealed that the majority of legislators and legislative staff believed that news media coverage of their legislature had become increasingly aggressive, negative, cynical, and biased (Josephson Institute of Ethics 1992). There is no indication that this trend has reversed or abated since that survey was taken.

Effecting Internal Change and Reform.   One of the most critical roles played by journalists in the modern era is that of self-appointed "public watchdog" of state legislatures. The news media, many journalists argue, provide a valuable service by reporting on the internal operations of the legislature, and helping to make sure that legislators individually, and legislatures collectively, uphold the highest ethical standards and democratic ideals. Media stories about a legislator's failure to live up to those standards and ideals often lead to changes in a legislature's process and the rules governing it. This was dramatically demonstrated in the New York legislature in 2004, when an independent study deemed that legislature to be the least representative, least efficient, and least democratic state legislature in country. The study received significant political coverage, especially in the *New York Times* and the *Wall Street Journal* (Creelan and Moultan 2004). Within weeks, the legislature took steps to change many of its rules in accordance with the report's suggestions and, in 2005, approved the state budget prior to the beginning of the state's new fiscal year for the first time in more than twenty years (Baker 2005).

Redefining the Job of Legislators and Legislative Leadership.   Historically, effective legislators and those most often selected to lead their state legislative chambers were those known as "work horses," who eschewed the cameras and worked hard behind the scenes, while those who "performed" for the cameras were labeled "show horses" and received limited respect from their colleagues. However, as governors became more adept at using the news media for their own ends, legislators and legislative leaders were forced to respond. While effective legislative leaders still must spend most of their time on internal matters, the time that most are devoting to external activities is on the rise. The demand for legislative leaders who are "media savvy" is particularly notable among newer and younger legislators (Little 1995). In response, state legislative leaders and most state legislators have changed the way they do business (and, to a degree, the business they do) to take advantage of the significance of both the traditional mass media (television, radio, and newspapers) and modern media innovations (Internet, e-mail, discussion groups, video conferencing, and media streaming) (Moore 2004; Greenberg 2003).

Legislative Actions in Anticipation of Media Responses

As one scholar has noted: "The media [have] become a part of the calculus by which decisions are made and actions are taken in politics and government" (Beyle 2003). As a

---

LEGISLATURES AND THE PUBLIC

"New Media" Bringing the Legislature to the People

There was a time not so long ago when those who wanted to know how their legislator voted on a bill either had to be at the legislature when the vote was taken or had to telephone the capitol afterward. To find out what took place on any given day, one had to be present, speak to someone who had been present, or hope that the local newspaper, radio, or television reporter covered it. Those days are in the past. With the rapid accessibility of the Internet and the almost herculean efforts of most state legislatures to build websites that are useful and informative, citizens with access to the Internet can go on-line and find out how their legislators voted, what their legislature did, and how it did it. They can also be notified when public hearings are scheduled, track legislation, and be made aware when changes are made on bills in which they are interested. Several state legislatures stream video and audio of both floor sessions and committee meetings when they are in session so that constituents can go on-line and listen to live debate and discussion. Full texts of all bills and even amendments are also available on-line on most legislative websites, although their posting is sometimes delayed a bit in some states.

In addition to finding out what is going on in the legislature, this "new media" also makes it easier for constituents to influence what is going on in their legislature. All state legislative websites make it simple for constituents to identify their legislators, and most provide a hotlink to their e-mail addresses. Recent research suggests that legislators respond to electronic mail in a manner similar to the way in which they respond to traditional mail or telephone calls. Many legislators encourage constituent input by placing on-line polling questions on their websites, sending electronic newsletters, or hosting on-line discussion groups or chat rooms on important issues.

Sources: Greenberg, Pam. 2003. "Constituent Communication in Cyberland: Using the Internet to Communicate with Constituents Can Be Very Effective." *State Legislatures* 29, no. 6: 29–30; Alperin, Davida J., and David Schultz. 2003. "E-Democracy: Legislative Constituency Communications in Wisconsin and Minnesota." Prepared for delivery at the annual meeting of the American Political Science Association (2003).

---

result, many legislators consider potential media response before they introduce a bill, announce their position on an important issue, make a speech, or cast a vote.

Where Is the Media Most Influential?

The relationship between the news media and the legislature is so particular to each state that it is difficult to make any determination of the states in which the media might have the greatest influence. However, evidence suggests that certain characteristics of a state are likely to contribute to active and aggressive press coverage of the activities of the legislature and its members. Thus a state with those qualities is likely to experience a more aggressive news media. A key factor is the size and location of the state's capital city. If the capital is not a major city or is not centrally located, news media coverage is likely to be less intense (ibid.). That will be particularly true when the legislature is out of session.

The news media are also more likely to cover controversy than cooperation. A story concerning a disagreement between the governor and the legislature's leaders is more likely to be reported than a story about cooperation between the two. Therefore legislative chambers in which the majority party's margin of control is relatively narrow, and the political climate figures to be more intense and contentious, are likely to receive more coverage than are chambers in which one party dominates. A legislature whose majority party is different from the party of the state's governor can also be expected to receive more coverage than one controlled by the governor's party (Little 1995).

Finally, most legislative observers feel that one of the most important factors that have influenced news media coverage of state legislatures over the past two or three decades has been a tendency by journalists and legislative reporters to make less of an effort than did their predecessors to try to learn and understand the intricacies and complexities of the legislative process, focusing instead on stories about legislative leaders, individual legislators, and final votes on bills (Boulard 1999).

The Balance between the Legislature and the News Media

The relationship between legislatures and the news media is complex and constantly subject to change. In recent years, the relationship has been altered by three trends. First, almost all legislative experts agree that state and national news agencies are offering less coverage of state legislative politics than in times past, with fewer and younger journalists being assigned to cover legislatures (ibid.). Second, while the amount of coverage has been declining, legislatures are becoming more effective at using the coverage they do receive to their advantage. Because it has become a necessary part of effective legislative leadership, legislative leaders have become increasingly adept at working with the news media and using it to the advantage of their caucuses, themselves, and their members. National organizations that assist legislators and legislative leaders offer complete conferences, seminars, and written materials on positive media relations, and legislators are taking advantage of them. A 2002 program on media relations sponsored by the State Legislative Leaders Foundation drew more than fifty legislative leaders from thirty-five states, and media relations seminars are among the best attended at the annual meetings of the National Conference of State Legislatures.

The third trend concerns the changes in technology and the advances of the "modern media" that have given legislators and legislatures tools to coordinate with or even by-pass the so-called mainstream media of newspapers, radio, and television. Today's legislators are using e-mail, video, and audio streaming, as well as user-friendly websites, to provide the news media and the public with information about their personal activities and the activities of their legislature. In 2004, at least two-thirds of state legislatures offered live video or audio feeds, and almost a third offered live coverage of floor proceedings on-line (Moore 2004).

Michigan senator Mark Schauer listens intently at a program sponsored by the State Legislative Leaders Foundation, March 2004. (Courtesy of the State Legislative Leaders Foundation)

AGENTS OF THE FEDERAL SYSTEM OF GOVERNMENT

Perhaps the most striking contribution that America's Founding Fathers made to the organization of government was the development of a federal system with multiple levels of government. They created one country with a national government, but also allowed for independent and somewhat autonomous state governments within that structure. This has allowed for the establishment of both national policies and, where necessary and appropriate, the development of specific state policies. The nation's federal structure has two direct consequences for state legislatures. First, each state makes its policies in the context of similar policies in forty-nine other states. What the Ohio General Assembly does for the people of Ohio affects and is affected by what the Pennsylvania legislature does for the people of Pennsylvania. Scholars refer to this as horizontal federalism. Second, what any state legislature does is limited by and affected by what the national government does. That is referred to as vertical federalism.

Other States

A decision made or an action taken in one of the nation's state legislatures can have ramifications for some or all of the other forty-nine. If the Maryland General Assembly passes a tax increase on businesses, members of the General Assembly of Virginia, which shares a border with Maryland, may pass legislation to make their business climate more business friendly, so as to attract Maryland businesses that want to avoid paying their state's higher taxes. Or, if the Nebraska legislature approves a state lottery, members of the Kansas legislature may feel compelled to do the same to avoid losing potential revenue. Actions taken in every state legislature must be considered in the context of the other forty-nine states.

Relationships among State Legislatures

The relationship between a state legislature and the governments of the other forty-nine states is defined by constitutions, politics, and economics. The U.S. Constitution allows each state to establish its own laws and rules, according to the dictates of its own government. According to the Constitution's full faith and credit clause (Article IV, Section 1), the laws of one state must be recognized as legitimate by the other states. And, further, its privileges and immunities clause (Article IV, Section 2) prohibits a state from treating a person who is a legal resident of another state in a manner different than it would treat its own legal residents.

Politically, the fifty states are linked by a common desire among their respective policymakers to solve problems and be reelected. Therefore, states frequently look to each other for potential solutions to common problems. If Wisconsin creates a program or law that is successful in addressing a policy problem, it will not be long before other states with similar problems take notice and begin to experiment with the Wisconsin program, or variations of it, in their own states. This common need to address problems crosses partisan and ideological lines with conservative Republican states willingly emulating successful programs from liberal Democratic states and vice versa, but with the approach oftentimes modified to make it fully conform to the state's unique conditions and political culture.

Finally, relationships between state legislatures are defined by economics. In one sense, states are like competing markets or companies. If the price of living or doing business in one state is too high relative to other states, its businesses and its citizens may choose to relocate to another state, transferring their tax dollars from their old state to their new one. Legislators in one state must take into consideration the policies of neighboring states in determining whom their state will tax, what rates they will assess, and what services they will provide to their residents. If they fail to do this, they may find their state priced out of the market. For example, two of the five fastest growing states in population between 2000 and 2004 (Nevada and Texas) do not tax corporate income, and the other three (Arizona, Florida, and Georgia) have a tax rate that is low and does not increase as profits grow. This may suggest that low (or no) corporate taxes contribute to population growth.

Tools and Methods of Influence

While the impact of legislation enacted in one state can have a dramatic impact on legislation under consideration in another, interstate relationships are seldom the primary concern of a state legislature when it initiates or approves legislation. Most state laws are enacted to address a problem within the state's borders, and any impact on other states is most often of no more than secondary concern. Nevertheless, the mere existence of the forty-nine other states can and does influence the policy making decisions of a state legislature.

Innovation and Emulation.   Perhaps the most significant positive effect of horizontal federalism is the ability for one or two states to experiment with a particular solution to a problem before it is considered and perhaps adopted by other states with similar problems. The states are often called the "laboratories of democracy," suggesting that each state can experiment with policy solutions on a comparatively small scale (as is done in a laboratory) before they are tested on a larger scale in other states, or nationwide. State legislators often pay attention to the activities of their colleagues in other states, hoping to gain ideas that might work in addressing the problems with which they are faced. Most innovative policies that have swept the nation have begun in one or two states. Included among these are primary elections, child labor laws, equal rights amendments, welfare reform, comparable worth laws, school choice initiatives, and health maintenance organizations. All were started in a few states before moving across the country and, in some cases, to the nation's capital.

There are several organizations and publications dedicated to helping legislators learn what is going on in other states. *State Legislatures* magazine, a monthly publication of the National Conference of State Legislatures, presents numerous stories about policy and procedural innovations and is distributed to every state legislator in the country. Likewise, *Spectrum: The Journal of State Government*, a monthly publication of the Council of State Governments, uses each edition to focus on innovations and solutions in particular policy areas.

Competition.   While horizontal federalism enables state legislatures to learn from, and sometimes emulate, each other in their approaches to common problems, it also often leads to states competing with each other for businesses, jobs, and tax dollars. This competition can take the form of tax breaks for companies, new stadiums for professional sports teams, or increased services for the public. States compete with each other for jobs that will keep their citizens employed and provide a tax base that will generate revenue to fund government programs. A company that is considering expanding or building a new facility will often shop around, playing one state off against another for tax breaks, the provision of special services, and other financial inducements. While some have suggested that such competition sometimes leads states to make bad investments by offering so much in inducements and tax breaks that they lose revenue, there is little indication that states will cease going to such lengths to attract investment.

Collaboration.   Just as horizontal federalism can create competition, it can also contribute to collaboration and cooperation between states. Many of the problems that states encounter do not end at their borders. Polluted water in a shared river cannot be addressed unless all of the states through which the river flows are involved. Likewise, problems with air pollution, child support enforcement, or kidnapping cannot be addressed effectively by a single state. In such cases, states find it necessary to

---

LEGISLATORS IN ACTION
Legislators Meet Regularly to Share Ideas and Information

There are several national organizations that provide state legislators from across the country with opportunities to meet and share ideas about challenges and public policy solutions facing their states.

National Conference of State Legislatures (NCSL). The National Conference of State Legislatures is a bipartisan organization that serves the legislators and staffs of the fifty state legislatures and the legislative bodies in the nation's commonwealths and territories. It provides research, technical assistance, and opportunities for policymakers to exchange ideas on the most pressing state issues. NCSL holds numerous meetings each year for legislators and their staff members. In 2004, more than a quarter of all state legislators attended at least one NCSL event. For additional information, see http://www.ncsl.org.

Council of State Governments (CSG). The Council of State Governments is a nonpartisan organization dedicated to serving the needs of state governing officials, including executives, legislators, and administrators. CSG champions excellence in state government, working with state leaders nationally and regionally to put their best ideas and solutions into practice. More than a fifth of all legislators attended some CSG-sponsored event in

2004. For additional information, see http://www.csg.org.

American Legislative Exchange Council (ALEC). Established in 1975, the American Legislative Exchange Council is a nonpartisan national organization dedicated to the principles of limited government at the state, and especially at the national, level. ALEC holds programs on various political topics, promoting legislative ideas and policies that minimize government intervention and promote responsibility, independence, and autonomy. In 2004, ALEC claimed more than 30 percent of all state legislators among its membership, with almost 2,000 attending some ALEC-sponsored function in 2005. For more information, see http://www.alec.org.

State Legislative Leaders Foundation (SLLF). The State Legislative Leaders Foundation is a nonpartisan, nonprofit organization dedicated to meeting the needs and challenges of state legislative leaders across the country. Established in 1972, it is the only organization in the country dedicated exclusively to presiding officers and floor leaders. SLLF holds meetings on legislative policies and procedures to which all leaders are invited. In 2004, more than a third of all legislative leaders attended some function hosted by SLLF. For additional information, see http://www.sllf.org.

collaborate in forming interstate compacts or agreements to work together to address common problems. In 2005 alone, legislatures in more than thirty states proposed seventy different interstate compacts on various policies, including health care, insurance regulation, crime prevention, pest control, transportation, nurse licensure, tax reform, banking, and waste management. Some compacts, such as the Interstate Compact for Adult Offender Supervision or the Interstate Compact for Juveniles, are relatively national in scope, while others are regional. The Midwestern Higher Education Compact, for example, is a regional compact that includes ten Midwestern states that work together to promote cooperation and share resources relative to higher education.

What State Legislatures Most Influence Their Fellow Legislatures?

While state legislatures may look to other states for policy direction and guidance, some states are more likely to serve as a source of ideas and influence than others. There are generally three different approaches to understanding how policy innovations are shared around the country. First, some suggest that the dispersion of policy innovation follows a regional path. States are more likely to adopt innovations passed in nearby states. A 1960s study found distinctly regional patterns of policy dispersion among the South, the Mid-Atlantic, and the Great Lakes, the Northeast, and the Mid-Atlantic/Great Lakes states (Walker 1969).

A second approach to understanding how policy innovations are shared is the "national dispersion" theory, suggesting that certain states are more likely to be innovators and others more likely to be followers, depending upon their particular political, demographic, and economic characteristics. Historically, those states that are more populous, more economically diverse, and more politically competitive tend also to be the more innovative states. States that are more populous (which invariably means they include a number of highly urban areas) and more economically diverse tend to be faced with policy challenges sooner than the less populous and less diverse states (Rogers

---

DID YOU KNOW?
States Play Follow the Leader

While "follow the leader" may be a popular child's game, it is also a game played by state governments. One state will implement a new policy, and, if it is effective, other states will soon follow. In September 2004, the California Air Resources Board (CARB) voted to implement the nation's strictest auto emissions standards. Within nine months seven other states (Connecti- cut, Maine, Massachusetts, New Jersey, New York, Rhode Island, and Vermont) had followed the lead of the Golden State, and several additional states were considering adoption of the standards.

Source: Maples, Jeff. 2005. "Kulongoski Puts Emissions Plan in Gear." *Oregonian*, April 26.

1995); states with competitive party systems are more likely to seek solutions as both parties try to make use of the policy making process to attract voters (Clark and Little 2000; Dye 1995; Berry 1994; Freeman 1985). At least one student of state government has also suggested that states in which voters and legislators hold a more progressive and liberal view of government tend to be the first to tackle political and social problems (Sabatier and Whitman 1985).

The third approach is the "national interaction model," which presumes that legislators are likely to adopt policies from states with which they regularly have the opportunity to interact, regardless of geographic proximity. It assumes a national communication network among state officials in which they interact freely and mix completely with officials from other states. This approach assumes that the probability that a state that has not yet adopted a policy solution will do so in a particular year is directly proportional to the number of interactions that its officials have had, often through interstate governmental organizations, with officials of states that have already adopted that policy (Berry 1994). Research suggests that those states with limited resources are the most likely to participate in such organizations and, therefore, most likely to benefit from such shared information (Clark and Little 2000).

The Balance between Legislatures and Other States

While legislators and policymakers have always looked across state lines for policy innovations, the trend is stronger now than ever before for several reasons. First, public policy problems have become increasingly complex and more likely to require complex solutions that require interstate and even international cooperation. Second, the explosion of the Internet and other new communications networks in recent years has made it much easier for legislators and their staffs to learn about what is going on in other states. Third, the economic recession that struck most states in the first years of the twenty-first century severely limited expenditures, requiring most states to make the most of every dollar by working harder than ever to find cost-effective solutions to problems. This made it less likely that states would invest in untested reforms, but rather would rely on other states or national policy organizations to develop and test ideas that, if shown to be effective, they would themselves adopt.

Finally, the shift in the United States in the last part of the twentieth century from an industrial economy in which most businesses required machinery, equipment, and buildings to a more flexible, service-oriented approach to business management has enabled companies to move their operations from one state to another virtually overnight and has made it easier for companies to "shop around" for the state that will make them the most attractive offer. In light of economic and technological changes that have internationalized economic decisions, states are increasingly finding that they have to compete not only with other states but also with foreign countries when trying to recruit or retain businesses, factories, and corporate offices.

The National Government

In 1787, when James Madison and the other members of the Constitutional Convention set about to design a government of the United States, they realized from experience that the country could not survive if the original thirteen states were totally independent of one another. The failed Articles of Confederation (the governing structure of the United States from 1783 to 1789) had made that clear. The nation's Founding Fathers therefore created a system in which the states existed within the context of a national government that, like the states, operated under the separation of powers principle, with separate legislative, executive, and judicial branches.

The Relationship between State Legislatures and the National Government

The relationship between state legislatures and the national government is defined by the U.S. Constitution, by politics, and by economics. Constitutionally, the states are severely restricted by the elastic clause (Article I, Section 8, Clause 18), which provides that the U.S. Congress has the power to "make all laws which shall be necessary and proper for carrying into Execution the foregoing Powers, and all other powers vested by this Constitution in the Government of the United States, or any department or Office thereof." In other words, not only does the national government have the powers expressly given it, but it can also exercise such powers as it deems necessary to carry out that expressed authority. This power is buttressed by the supremacy clause (Article VI): "This Constitution, and the Laws of the United States which shall be made in Pursuance thereof, and all treaties made, or which shall be made, under the authority of the United States, shall be the supreme law of the land." The Constitution, it appears, gives the edge to the national government over the states. However, the states are not without recourse in defending their autonomy. The Tenth Amendment to the Constitution, also known as the states' rights amendment, states: "The Powers not delegated to the United States by the Constitution, nor prohibited by it to the states, are reserved for the states respectively, or to the people." This means that the influence of the national government is not total but is limited to those specific powers granted to it within the Constitution.

Politically, the influence of the national government is often limited by the current political environment. While the national government may have the legal power to exert significant control over the states, many members of the national government are reluctant to exercise that power because many of them have served in those state governments; they know that the public generally prefers government "closer to home." Those in office in Washington, D.C., know that, if voters perceive that the national government has become too overbearing, they will be likely to express their feelings through the ballot box by electing candidates who promise to rein in the power and influence that the national government exercises over the lives of the people. Historically, the Republican Party has been the party more associated with favoring limitations on the scope of the national government.

The ability and desire of the national government to influence policies adopted by state legislatures is a function of the economy and the financial and professional resources available to each level of the government. When the national government is experiencing deficits, it tends to exert less influence on state policies, or at least tends to use methods of influence that do not require financial inducements. On the other hand, when the states are strapped for money, they tend to look to the federal government to take on additional financial responsibilities and burdens. When states find themselves flush with money, they tend to focus on the creation of innovative program solutions rather than relying on the national government for support.

One unique aspect of the relationship between the national government and state legislatures is the role played by the legislatures in amending the U.S. Constitution. State legislatures have two potential roles in this process. First, state legislatures can initiate a call for a national convention to propose a constitutional amendment. In order for this to be successful, there must be a call for such a convention in two-thirds (thirty-four) of the states. Throughout the history of the United States, no such convention has ever been called. By the early 1990s, however, twenty-eight state legislatures had approved a call for a national constitutional convention to propose a balanced budget amendment, but the six additional states that were required to make the call valid never materialized.

DID YOU KNOW?

The States Took 200 Years to Ratify the 27th Amendment to the U.S. Constitution.

The 27th Amendment to the U.S. Constitution, which forbids Congress to raise its pay without first facing the voters in a general election, was originally proposed on September 25, 1789, as an article in the original Bill of Rights. It did not receive approval from the required number of state legislatures and did not therefore become part of the Constitution. It sat, unratified and with no expiration date, in constitutional limbo, for more than eighty years until the Ohio legislature ratified it to protest a congressional pay hike. But no other states followed Ohio's lead, and the amendment again languished for more than a hundred more years. In 1978, Wyoming ratified the amendment, but there was again no follow-up by any other states. Then, in the early 1980s, Gregory Watson, an aide to a Texas legislator, took up the proposed amendment's cause. From 1983 to 1992, the requisite number of additional states ratified the amendment, and on May 7, 1992, 74,003 days after it was first proposed, the 27th Amendment became part of the United States Constitution.

Source: U.S. Constitution OnLine.
   (http://www.usconstitution.net/const.html
   #Am27.)

The second, and historically far more meaningful, role that state legislatures play in the constitutional amendment process involves their power to ratify or reject amendments that have been initiated by the U.S. Congress. Such amendments must be ratified by the legislatures of three-quarters (thirty-eight) of the states. State legislatures have ratified twenty-six of the twenty-seven amendments to the U.S. Constitution. The Twenty-First Amendment, repealing the Eighteenth Amendment (a prohibition on the consumption of alcohol), was ratified by individual state conventions rather than state legislatures. In the 1970s, a proposed equal rights amendment was ratified by thirty-five legislatures, three shy of the number required.

Tools and Methods of Influence

The federal government has two primary approaches to influence policymaking in the states. One is money and the other is force. They are often referred to by politicians as "the carrot" and "the stick." On the carrot side, states received more than $260 billion from the national government in FY 2000, more than a quarter of all state revenues (Hanson 2003). On the stick side, states are finding that more and more federal government requirements are either unfunded or underfunded, requiring the states to spend their own money to meet federal government–mandated standards and requirements. When the national budget is in surplus (or at least not in a substantial deficit) and the economy is strong, the national government tends to rely on money, offering financial incentives to states to undertake certain programs or policies favored by Washington. When the federal government is heavily into deficit spending and looking for places to cut expenditures, it tends to rely more on force, telling the states what it wants them to do and threatening to withhold funds or penalize them in some way if they do not respond. There are five tools that the national government uses to influence action by state legislatures and state governments. They range from one that is based almost exclusively on financial inducements to one that relies exclusively on force.

Revenue Sharing.   From 1972 until 1986, the federal government provided a revenue sharing program in which it gave each state a portion of federal revenue to spend in whatever manner it wished, with virtually no strings attached. Each state would receive a certain amount of money—the amount based on the state's population—to spend in policy areas of its choice. One state might spend its money on education, another on public safety, and a third on the environment. The revenue sharing program was ended in the 1980s, victim of a congressional effort to cut federal spending during a recession (ibid.).

Block Grants.   More restrictive than revenue sharing, federal block grant programs involve the federal government giving states money to spend within a specified "block" of programs. A state might, for example, use an education block grant to fund programs in preschool, elementary school, junior high, or high school, but it could not use it for public safety programs. In 2004, the national government authorized seventeen different block grant programs for the states. The amount of a state's block grant is determined by a formula that is intended to identify the degree of a state's need in the particular block grant's policy area. In addition to providing the states with money to supplement the revenues that they raise, the requirement that block grant funds be spent for specified purposes enables the national government to exert influence over how the states spend their own money. If federal block grant funding is available to a state for environmental programs but not education, a state may find itself tempted to spend more of its own funds on the environment, even if it knows that its greatest problems are in the area of education. The ability of the national government to influence state spending is particularly strong if a block grant is a matching grant, in which the amount of federal money a state receives depends on how much money the state is willing to spend on the same purpose.

Categorical Grants.   The most common method by which the national government distributes revenues to the states is by categorical grants. In a categorical grant, federal funds are provided to a state for specific programs and clearly defined purposes. In the early 2000s, there were more than 600 different categorical grant programs distributing money to the states. States and state legislatures have very little say in how categorical grant money is spent, and they must agree to abide by specific regulations to receive it. For example, as a condition for receiving education money for the "No Child Left Behind" program, states had to certify that their schools permitted voluntary religious expression and faith-based student organizations. For a state to receive highway construction or repair funds under a categorical grant, it had to enact a 0.08 blood alcohol level as its legal level of driver intoxication (Kincaid 2004). It is not at all uncommon for the spending decisions of a state legislature to be influenced by the availability of categorical grant funds, with spending sometimes diverted from the state's most pressing problems to what are considered lower-priority matters simply because of the availability of federal categorical grant money.

TABLE 5.4   PER CAPITA NONDEFENSE FEDERAL MONEY TO STATES, 2002

Top Five		Bottom Five	
North Dakota	$9,162	California	$4,848
Alaska	$8,677	Georgia	$4,712
New Mexico	$8,392	Texas	$4,677
Maryland	$7,703	Nevada	$4,367
South Dakota	$7,678	Utah	$4,228

Source: Council of State Governments. 2004. *Book of the States.* Lexington, KY: Council of State Governments, Table 2.12.

President George W. Bush participates in a briefing before touring Hurricane Katrina damage done in the Mobile, Alabama, area, September 2, 2005. From left to right are: Mississippi's Republican governor Haley Barbour, Alabama's Republican governor Bob Riley, and Bush. This disaster brought out both the benefits and challenges of federalism as local, state, and national officials struggled to respond. (Larry Downing/Reuters/Corbis)

There are two types of categorical grants—competitive or project grants, and formula grants. With project grants, states essentially compete against each other for federal funds that are distributed to states on the basis of which ones the federal government feels are operating the most effective programs in the grant area. Formula grants are not distributed on a competitive basis, but rather on a formula designed to determine individual state need. The greatest amount of national grant funding to states is distributed through formula grants. This includes such well-known programs as Medicaid, Medicare, and welfare (Transitional Aid for Dependent Families).

Preemptions. Sometimes, the federal government does not use money or the promise of money to encourage state action. It just tells the states that they are preempted, or prohibited, from doing something. In preempting states, the national government tells them what they cannot do. Preemptions generally take two forms. Historically, they have referred to cases in which the federal government has allowed states to regulate some activity as long as its regulatory standards are equal to or higher than those of federal laws or regulations. For example, states must establish environmental regulations that equal or exceed, but do not fall below, national standards. Or the national government may prevent states from adopting legislation that establishes standards more stringent than those at the federal level. The second type of preemption, which has become more common, involves the federal government's establishing a prohibition on state adoption of any legislation relating to a specific policy area or matter. For example, antispamming legislation passed by the Congress in 2003 preempted state laws that had been adopted in more than two-thirds of the states (ibid.).

Unfunded Mandates. Finally, the federal government sometimes just tells the states to do something, offering no inducements or incentives. It just mandates, or requires, that states take some specific action or adopt some program. Unfunded mandates directed at state and local governments have been increasingly used by the federal government since the 1960s, when federal budget deficits first began to increase. Their use has been somewhat restricted by the 1995 Unfunded Mandates Reform Act (UMRA), which was designed to limit the magnitude of new unfunded mandates by the Congress. According to a 2003 report by the Congressional Budget Office, only two unfunded mandates exceeding the limits established in the 1995 law have been passed since the law's adoption—one concerning the minimum wage, and the other concerning a cut in food stamp assistance. The Congress, however, has been able to circumvent UMRA through what have been termed "underfunded mandates," in which it establishes a program that requires states to take certain actions but does not provide them with enough revenue to cover their costs. For example, while the federal government promised to fund President Bush's "No Child Left Behind" education program at a certain level, the funding that Congress has provided to the states has never approached that level, leaving almost every state to make up the difference in order to avoid the penalties assessed for failing to do so (Jacobson 2005).

When Does the National Government Have More Influence?

It is clear from the U.S. Constitution that the federal government has the upper hand in conflicts between the states and the national government. The "supremacy clause" of the U.S. Constitution pretty much ensures that. However, variations in politics and policy across the states and the national government make the actual application of federal government influence over state policymaking much less clear. The degree to which the national government will exercise a dominant role over the states ultimately comes down to a matter of three things: resources, opportunity, and will. The national government will take a more active role when it has either the financial and organizational resources or a philosophical or political incentive to do so, and when it has the political and fiscal resources to support its action.

The two primary resources that determine the influence of the national government on the states are money and organization. When the federal government has a budget surplus, it is likely to use that money to create programs and encourage the states to act in particular ways. That will be particularly true when the national government has a surplus and the states have a deficit. Organizationally, many of the reforms of the 1960s came about because there was a perception, not just in Washington but also in many state capitols, that the states were not organizationally equipped to handle the growing demands that society was placing on government (Sanford 1967).

From a political standpoint, opportunity is most often the major determinant of the impact of the federal government on states. The federal government is more likely and more able to exert influence on the states when the same party controls both houses of Congress and also the presidency. The 1930s and the 1960s, considered by many to be the two decades during which the financial power of the federal government grew the most, were both marked by unified Democratic control in Washington. The early 2000s, which many see as marked by an increase of mandates and preemptions, was predominantly marked by Republican control of both the Congress and the presidency.

Finally, more than resources and opportunity, the degree to which the national government tries to influence the states comes down to will; that is, the national government will exert its influence on the states when there is political or philosophical reason to do so. Leaders of the national government will take a more active approach toward the states when there is some philosophical difference between their policies and those advocated in many state capitals. For example, Democratic liberals in Washington in the 1960s disagreed with conservative state governments, especially in the South, so they created programs and initiated legislation and programs to exert the federal government's power and influence over the states. This was evident in policies regarding housing, welfare, voting, and desegregation. Forty years later the tables turned, with conservative Republicans in control in Washington sometimes at odds with more liberal Democratic leadership in a number of state governments, and pressuring those governments to change their policies (Krane 2003). These philosophical differences have been evidenced in national policies toward sentencing, the environment, abortion, and education.

While philosophy matters, some usurpation of power by the national government is also purely political. The national government will sometimes act in areas in which the public is demanding action, and where there are perceived political rewards for its doing so. For example, while education policy has traditionally been left to state and local governments, national politicians have taken a more active role since the 1970s because it is seen as such an important political issue. Education matters to voters, so it also matters to politicians. Likewise, while almost all violent crimes are state offenses and therefore of no relevance to national politicians, the national government has increased its role in this area in order to be perceived as "tough on crime."

The Current Balance between Legislatures and the National Government

The current balance between the national government and state legislatures seems to be influenced more by politics and ideology than by history and money. As the budget surpluses of the late 1990s gave way to deficits after the year 2000, Washington has turned to more coercive methods of trying to influence state policymaking. These include preemptions, underfunded mandates, and the adoption of federal regulations that restrict what states can and cannot do.

When the Republican Party found itself in control of both houses of Congress and the White House for the first time in fifty years in 2005, Republican congressional leaders found their desire to influence policymaking in state governments at odds with their party's traditional philosophy of limited national government and the importance of state rights and independence from federal government interference. It appears, at least for a while, that the desire to influence state policies seems to be winning. Under the guidance of President Bush, Republicans have actively pursued policies that restrict state rights in education (No Child Left Behind), energy (drilling in Alaska), the environment (Clean Skies Initiative), public safety (Patriot Acts I and II), and social policy (restrictions on abortion access) (ibid.).

STATE LEGISLATURES CAUGHT IN THE MIDDLE

State legislatures have always been at the center of the policymaking process, interacting with and sometimes coordinating the actions of all other key actors. They have always been "caught in the middle." However, in recent years state legislatures have found themselves constrained by both their constitutional relationships with other actors and by political, philosophical, and economic conditions.

Constitutionally, state governments and their legislatures are caught between their responsibilities to make laws and their obligations to work with and respond to increasingly active governors and courts. In the past half-century, the power of legislatures has, in the eyes of some observers, decreased relative to these constitutional partners. They have seen their constitutional role as key policymaker somewhat diminished as governors have become the center of state government and the courts have taken on an increasingly active and visible role.

Politically, state legislatures are caught in the middle of intense efforts to influence their decisions by their state political parties, interest groups, and the news media. As the responsibilities assigned to state governments have grown, so has the impact of these nongovernmental actors, each of which demands attention and responsiveness from its state legislature. Fortunately, state legislatures are, in many ways, more able to withstand the pressures of these organizations than they were twenty or thirty years ago. With the exception of those hamstrung by term limits, legislatures have the staff, organization, leadership, and membership to respond to them with strength and effectiveness.

Relative to the national government, states seem to be caught in the middle of a conflict between philosophical desires and ideological realities. While the more conservative leadership of the federal government in the first decade of the twenty-first century may believe philosophically in less federal interference in state government decision- and policymaking, they also perceive the leadership of a number of state governments to be more philosophically liberal than they are, and out of step with their own political philosophy. They are caught between adherence to their principle of state autonomy and the reality of increasing federal intervention to extend its influence on policymaking.

Caught in the middle: it is something to which state legislatures are accustomed, and a place in which they can expect to find themselves for the foreseeable future.

REFERENCES

Baker, Al. 2005. "Albany Passes Budget on Time, a First since 1984." New York *Times*, April 1.

Berry, Francis Stokes. 1994. "Sizing Up Judicial Politics Research." *Policy Studies Journal* 22, no. 3 (autumn):442–457.

Beyle, Thad. 2004. "The Governors." In *Politics in the American States: A Comparative Analysis*, 8th ed., edited by Virginia Gray and Russell L. Hanson. Washington, DC: Congressional Quarterly Press.

Bibby, John F. 1998. "State Party Organizations: Coping and Adapting to Candidate-Centered Politics and Nationalization." In *The Parties Respond: Changes in American Parties and Campaigns*, 3d ed., edited by L. Sandy Maisel, 23–49. Boulder: Westview.

———. 1999. "Party Networks: National-State Integration, Allied Groups, and Issue Activities." In *The State of the Parties: The Changing Role of Contemporary American Parties*, 3d ed., edited by John C. Green and Daniel M. Shea, 69–87. Lanham, MD: Rowman and Littlefield.

Boulard, Garry. 1999. "More News, Less Coverage." *State Legislature* 25, no. 6:14–19.

Brown, Peter A. 1994. "Gotcha Journalism." *State Legislatures* 20, no. 5 (May):22–26.

Clark, Jill, and Thomas H. Little. 2000. "When Legislators Meet: National Organizations as Significant and Independent Sources of Policy and Procedural Information for State Legislative Leaders." Paper presented at the annual meeting of the American Political Science Association in Washington, DC.

Coleman, John J. 1996. "Resurgent or Just Busy? Party Organizations in Contemporary America." In *The State of the Parties: The Changing Role of Contemporary American Parties*, 2d ed., edited by John C. Green and Daniel M. Shea, 367–384. Lanham, MD: Rowman and Littlefield.

Council of State Governments. 2004a. "Table 4.10: Selected Administrative Officials: Methods of Selection." In *Book of the States*, Vol. 36, 175–180. Lexington, KY: Council of State Governments.

———. 2004b. "Table 6.15: Lobbying: Registration and Reporting." In *Book of the States*, Vol. 36, 305–306. Lexington, KY: Council of State Governments.

Creelan, Jeremy M., and Laura M. Moulton. 2004. *The New York State Legislative Process: An Evaluation and Blueprint for Reform.* New York: Brennan Center for Justice at NYU School of Law.

Dye, Thomas R. 1995. *Understanding Public Policy.* 8th ed. Englewood Cliffs, NJ: Prentice-Hall.

Emmert, Craig F., and Carol Ann Traut. 1992. "An Integrated Case-Related Model of Judicial Decision Making." *Journal of Politics* 54:543–552.

Ferguson, Margaret. 2006. *The Executive Branch of State Government: People, Process, and Politics.* Santa Barbara, CA: ABC-CLIO.

Freeman, Patricia K. 1985. "Values and Policy Attitudes among State Legislators and Administrators." *Public Administration Quarterly* 7:482–497.

Frohnmeyer, David. 1989. "The Courts as Referee." In *The Courts: Sharing and Separating Power,* edited by Lawrence Baum and David Frohnmeyer, 51–63. New Brunswick, NJ: Eagleton Institute of Politics.

Glick, Henry R. 1992. *The Right to Die.* New York: Columbia University Press.

———. 2004. "Courts: Politics and the Judicial Process." In *Politics and the American States: A Comparative Analysis.* Washington, DC: Congressional Quarterly Press.

Greenberg, Pam. 2003. "Constituent Communication in Cyberland: Using the Internet to Communicate with Constituents Can Be Very Effective." *State Legislatures* 29, no. 6:28–30.

Greenblatt, Alan. 2005. "Term Limits Aren't Working." *Governing Magazine* Volume 13 (April) (http://66.23.131.98/archive/2005/apr/observer.txt).

Hanson, Russell. 2003. "Intergovernmental Relations." In *Politics in the American States: A Comparative Perspective.* Washington, DC: Congressional Quarterly Press.

Jacobson, Lou. 2005. "State Pols Fight Congress on Funding, Mandates." *Roll Call,* April 26, 2005.

Josephson Institute of Ethics. 1992. *Actual and Apparent Impropriety: A Report on Ethical Norms and Attitudes in State Legislatures.* Marina del Ray, CA: Josephson Institute.

Kincaid, John. 2001. "The State of Federalism, 2000–2001." *Publius* 31, no. 3:1–70.

———. 2004. "Trends in Federalism: Continuity, Change and Polarization." In *Book of the States 2004,* Vol. 36. Lexington, KY: Council of State Governments.

Krane, Dale. 2003. "The State of American Federalism, 2003–2004." *Publius* 33, no. 3:1–44.

Little, Thomas H. 1995. "Understanding Legislative Leadership beyond the Chamber: The Members' Perspective." *Legislative Studies Quarterly* 20, no. 2:269–291.

Loftus, Tom. 1994. *The Art of Legislative Politics.* Washington, DC: Congressional Quarterly Press.

Luebke, Paul. 2000. *Tarheel Politics 2000.* Chapel Hill: University of North Carolina Press.

McDermott, Kathleen. 1999. *Controlling Public Education: Localism vs. Equality.* Lawrence: University Press of Kansas.

Miller, Mark C. 2004. "Interactions between Legislatures and Courts." *Judicature,* Volume 18 (March-April): 213–218

Moncrief, Gary, Peverill Squire and Malcolm E. Jewell. 2001. *Who Runs for the Legislature?* Upper Saddle River, NJ: Prentice-Hall.

Moore, Nicole Casal. 2004. "All Star PR: Today's Savvy Legislative Public Information Officers Are Taking Advantage of New Technology to Get Messages Out to the Media and the Public." *State Legislatures* 30, no. 2:26–29.

Morchouse, Sarah McCally, and Malcolm E. Jewell. 2003. *State Politics, Parties & Policy.* 2d ed. Latham, MD: Brown and Littlefield.

Ogle, David B., and Stephen G. Lakis. 2002. "The Operation and Regulation of Lobbying in the Democratic Process." Paper prepared for the National Assembly of Bulgaria, Sofia, Bulgaria.

Rogers, Everett M. 1995. *Diffusion of Innovations.* 4th ed. New York: Free Press.

Rosenthal, Alan. 1990. *Governors and Legislatures: Contending Powers.* Washington, DC: Congressional Quarterly Press.

———. 1993. *The Third House: Lobbyists and Lobbying in the States.* Washington, DC: Congressional Quarterly Press.

————. 1996. *Drawing the Line: Legislative Ethics in the States*. Lincoln: University of Nebraska Press.

————. 1998. *The Decline of Representative Democracy: Process, Participation, and Power in State Legislatures*. Washington, DC: Congressional Quarterly Press.

————. 2004. *Heavy Lifting: The Job of the American Legislature*. Washington, DC: Congressional Quarterly Press.

Rozell, Mark J., and Clyde Wilcox. 1995. *Interest Groups in American Campaigns: The New Face of Electioneering.* Washington, DC: Congressional Quarterly Press.

Sabatier, Paul A., and David Whiteman. 1985. "Legislative Decision Making and Substantive Policy Information: Models of Information Flow." *Legislative Studies Quarterly* 10:395–421.

Sabato, Larry J. 1978. *Goodbye to Goodtime Charlie: The American Governorship Transformed.* Lexington, MA: Lexington.

Salmore, Stephen A., and Barbara G. Salmore. 1996. "The Transformation of State Electoral Politics." In *The State of the States.* 3d ed. Washington, DC: Congressional Quarterly Press.

Sanford, Terry. 1967. *Storm Over the States.* New York: McGraw-Hill.

Schlesinger, Joseph A. 1966. *Ambition and Politics; Political Careers in the United States.* Chicago: Rand-McNally.

Shafer, Bryon E. 1996. "The United States." In *Postwar Politics in the G–7: Order and Eras in Comparative Perspective,* edited by Bryan E. Shafer, 12–46. Madison: University of Wisconsin Press.

State Legislative Leaders Foundation. 2005. *Working with the Media: A Handbook for State Legislators.* Centerville, MA: State Legislative Leaders Foundation.

Tarr, G. Alan. 2004. Comments from panel entitled "Issue at the State Level" at the American Judicature Society midyear meeting, February 27–28, 2004. *Judicature,* Volume 87 (March–April): 230–240.

Thomas, Clive S., and Ronald J. Hrebenar. 2003. "Interest Groups in the States." In *Politics in the American States,* edited by Virginia Gray and Russell L. Hanson. Washington, DC: Congressional Quarterly Press.

Thornburgh, Richard. 2004. Comments from panel entitled "Issue at the State Level" at the American Judicature Society midyear meeting, February 27–28, 2005. *Judicature,* Volume 87 (March–April): 230–240.

Walker, J. L. 1969. "The Diffusion of Innovations among the American States." *American Political Science Review* 63:880–899.

Wenzel, James P., Shaun Bowler, and David J. Lanoue. 1997. "Legislating from the Bench: A Comparative Analysis of Judicial Activism." *American Politics Quarterly* 25:363–379.

Wolpe, Bruce C., and Bertram J. Levine. 1996. *Lobbying Congress: How the System Works.* Washington, DC: Congressional Quarterly Press.

6

THE LEGISLATURE

STATE BY STATE

ALABAMA

● ● ● ● ● ● ● ● ● ● ● ●

THE ALABAMA LEGISLATURE

House of Representatives	Senate
105 Representatives	35 Senators

(334) 242–7600
http://www.legislature.state.al.us

● ● ● ● ● ● ● ● ● ● ● ●

In 1861, Alabama was the heart of the Confederacy and Montgomery its first capital. One hundred years later, it was the heart of the U.S. civil rights movement. Today, Alabama is an increasingly urban state that has developed a diverse economy that includes agriculture, manufacturing, and a growing service sector.

For more than a century following the Civil War, Alabama was a solidly Democratic state, with the Republican Party a nonfactor in elections. Conservatives who would have been Republican in other regions of the United States were bound by history and tradition to the Democratic Party. In 1968 and 1972, Alabama governor George Wallace left the Democratic Party to form the American Party and to run for president. He was paralyzed by a would-be assassin during the 1972 campaign in Maryland.

In the 1970s, the Alabama Republican Party began to flex its muscles, and, by the late twentieth century, the state was electing Republicans to many state positions and most congressional posts. With the exception of 1976, when the state voted for Jimmy Carter from neighboring Georgia, Alabama has not supported a Democratic presidential candidate since 1960. In 2005, the governor of Alabama was Republican, as were its two U.S. senators and a majority of its congressional delegation. However, Democrats retain solid control in both houses of the state legislature, as they have continuously since the Reconstruction era.

On the Steps of History

The Alabama capitol has served as a backdrop for many critical events in the history of the United States. On February 4, 1861, delegates from six Southern states met in the capitol to draft a constitution for the Confederate States of America, and Mississippi senator Jefferson Davis was sworn in as the new nation's president. Just over a hundred years later, in January of 1963, Alabama governor George Wallace stood on the steps of that same capitol building and promised "Segregation today! Segregation tomorrow! Segregation forever!" Just two years later, the Reverend Martin Luther King, Jr., would lead thousands on a march from Selma, Alabama, to those same capitol steps to ensure that everyone in Alabama would be allowed to vote, regardless of color.

Structure and Membership

The Alabama legislature consists of a 35-member Senate and a 105-member House of Representatives. Alabama's House is one of only five lower chambers that elect their members to four-year legislative terms. Alabama senators, like the senators in most states, are also elected for four-year terms. All legislators are elected from single-member districts. While Republicans have made gains in both chambers, they are still a distinct minority in both chambers. Mississippi and Alabama are the only Southern states that have not elected a Republican majority to at least one house of the state legislature since Reconstruction, but Republicans are making gains, particularly in the House.

In 2003, one in ten Alabama legislators was female, including eleven representatives and three senators. However, only three of the legislature's thirty-seven standing committees had female committee chairs. In 2005, almost a quarter of Alabama's legislators were African American, including twenty-seven members of the House, eight members of the Senate, and the speaker pro tempore of the House.

The lieutenant governor, an independently elected official, is ex officio president of the Senate and presides over its sessions. The Senate elects a president pro tempore who is responsible for the chamber's administration. The speaker of the House presides over its sessions and is responsible for House administration.

Professional staff services are provided by a nonpartisan Legislative Reference Service Office and by a Legislative Fiscal Office that operate under the general direction of the Legislative Council and the Joint Fiscal Committee, respectively. Each house also has a small number of partisan staff assistants for leaders and some members. Individual legislators are provided some personal staff during the legislative session and reduced staff during the year.

The Senate has almost as many standing committees (twenty-five) as it does members (thirty-five), and is the only chamber in the country in which the Senate has significantly more committees than the House. The House has sixteen

Alabama State Capitol (PhotoDisc/Getty Images)

standing committees. Committee members and leaders in the Senate are assigned by a committee of senators, while the speaker of the House appoints them in that chamber.

Processes

The Senate president presides over Senate sessions, and the speaker of the House presides over House sessions. Senate committee chairs and members are appointed by a committee on assignments, which is chaired by the president pro tempore and includes the lieutenant governor and three additional members appointed by the president pro tempore. The speaker of the House appoints committee chairs and members in the House of Representatives. The Senate president pro tempore and the House speaker, in consultation with the majority leaders of their respective houses, determine their chamber agendas.

The Alabama legislature meets annually, convening on the first Tuesday in February in the second and third years of its four-year term. In the first year of the term, the session begins on the first Tuesday in March; in the last year of the term, it begins on the second Tuesday in January. Sessions are limited to a maximum of 30 meeting days within a period of 105 calendar days. There are no limitations on bill filing in the House, but senators cannot file bills after the twenty-second legislative day of the session. Legislators may prefile bills in both chambers, but must do so by the first day of the session. All bills require a minimum of five days to pass each chamber. During the 2003 legislative session, Alabama legislators introduced more than 1,300 bills but passed only about 20 percent (258). Of those 258, some 10 were vetoed by the Republican governor.

As is true with most Southern states, the Alabama legislature ranks at the low end on most measures of legislative professionalism. Legislators are paid $10 a day in salary when in session, $50 a day when they are in for more than three days a week, and a $2,280 per month expense allowance. Estimated annual salary for legislators is a little over $30,000. Their session is fixed constitutionally at no more than thirty working days. However, the membership is fairly stable, a turnover rate of 25 percent in the House and 14 percent in the Senate following the 2002 elections. With regular sessions limited to only about three months per year, most members devote the greatest portion of their time to a nonlegislative occupation.

Leadership Structure

The Senate president pro tempore is officially the top leadership position in the Senate. The president pro tempore appoints the majority leader. The speaker of the House is the top leader of the House of Representatives. The Senate president pro tempore and majority leader in the Senate and the speaker and majority leader in the House manage their cau-

cuses. The Senate and House minority leaders are responsible for managing floor debate for their respective parties. Both the majority and minority parties have a number of deputy and assistant leaders.

Leadership, especially in the House, has been quite stable of late. The current speaker (Seth Hammett) has held his post since 1998, and his predecessor held it for twelve years. Speaker Hammett served as majority leader before moving up to speaker. The president of the Senate is the lieutenant governor, and the last two have each served for eight years.

Election Processes

Alabama legislators are elected to their four-year terms in November of nonpresidential even years. The average house district population is about 45,000, and the average Senate district is about 130,000. Legislators take office on the day following their election, and their term ends on the day after the election four years later.

Party nominations are determined by primary.

Key Political Factors

The strength of the Alabama Republican Party can be expected to continue to grow. Republican governor Bob Riley, a former member of Congress, working with the Democratic legislature, proposed a revolutionary tax plan for the state in 2003 but saw it soundly defeated by the public. Conservatives in the state have been energized by their success in defeating the proposal and by the recent actions of a Supreme Court justice who placed a monument to the Ten Commandments in the state judicial building, in defiance of the U.S. and Alabama supreme courts,

While control of the state legislature remains firmly in Democratic hands, this control could be threatened in years to come. Over the past ten years, the number of Republicans in the House has almost doubled (23 in 1993 to 42 in 2002), while the number in the Senate has remained relatively stable. Because legislative elections are held in nonpresidential years, Democratic legislators have tended to be more insulated from the popular Republican presidential candidates that have helped increase Republican representation throughout the rest of the South.

Interest groups play a strong role in the Alabama legislature, providing information and support to part-time legislators with limited staff. There are no limits on how much money any of the almost 600 registered lobbyists can spend entertaining legislators in Alabama. Only expenditures exceeding $250 a day must be disclosed to the state ethics commission.

Further Reading

Bullock, Charles S., and Mark J. Rozell, eds. 2002. *New Politics of the Old South: An Introduction to Southern Politics.* 2d ed. Lanham, MD: Rowman and Littlefield.

Flint, Wayne. 2004. *Alabama in the Twentieth Century.* Tuscaloosa: University of Alabama Press.

Martin, David L. 1994. *Alabama's State and Local Governments.* Tuscaloosa, AL: University of Alabama Press.

Permaloff, Ann, and Carl Grafton. 1996. *Political Power in Alabama: The More Things Change.* Athens: University of Georgia Press.

ALASKA

• • • • • • • • • • • •

THE ALASKA LEGISLATURE

House of Representatives	Senate
40 Representatives	20 Senators

(907) 465–2111
http://www.legis.state.ak.us/

• • • • • • • • • • • •

Alaska is the largest state of the United States, consuming almost 20 percent of the nation's land area. It is twice the size of Texas, the next largest state. It is also the most sparsely populated of the fifty states, but one of the fastest growing. Its citizens derive a unique benefit from the abundance of oil and natural resources found under the ice. In accordance with a 1976 amendment to the Alaska constitution, dividends from the state's oil profits are distributed to every Alaskan— averaging more than $1,000 per year per person.

The state capital, Juneau, has only about 36,000 residents and is not accessible by road. It is distant from Anchorage, the state's population center. The capitol building was constructed in the 1930s, when Alaska was a U.S. territory and Juneau a bustling timber and mining town. In the next few years, the state capital will either be moved to one of the

---

Senate District as Big as Texas

The size and geography of Alaska present some unique challenges for its twenty senators and forty representatives. Take, for example, the senator elected to represent the some 30,000 people in Senate District C. He or she must represent a district that is more than 250,000 square miles in size (just 10,000 square miles less than the state of Texas), which includes 126 small communities (with an average of fewer than 240 people per community), sixteen native languages, nine wildlife refuges, and eight national parks! Or, consider Representative Reggie Joule, whose home in northern Alaska places him more than 2,000 miles from the state capital!

---

more populated areas of the state (probably Anchorage), or a new capitol building will be constructed in Juneau.

The first territorial legislature was elected in Alaska in 1912, and calls for statehood are recorded as early as 1916. Since beating Hawaii by a few months to become the forty-ninth state, in 1959, Alaska has been a politically competitive state that has leaned Republican. The Republican tilt has been decidedly stronger in presidential elections, with Lyndon Johnson, in his 1964 landslide, the only Democratic presidential candidate to carry the state. At the same time, Alaska's voters have demonstrated an independent strain, once electing an independent governor, giving independent presidential candidate Ross Perot 30 percent of its vote in 1992, and giving independent Ralph Nader 11 percent in 2000.

Structure and Membership

The Alaska legislature consists of a twenty-member Senate and a forty-member House of Representatives. Senate terms are four years, and House terms are two years. Legislators are elected from single-member districts in November even-year elections. The twenty-member Alaska Senate is the smallest state legislative chamber in the United States, and the forty-member House of Representatives is the smallest state house chamber.

While Democrats were a force in the early years, Republicans have become an increasingly dominant party since the late 1980s. This trend is likely to continue, as they have a two-to-one advantage in both chambers early in the twenty-first century. As in other states, the proportion of women in the Alaska legislature has risen in recent years. In the 2003–2004 session, they constituted about a quarter of the membership in each chamber. Women held only four of the standing committee positions, but the House had back-to-back female speakers in the 1990s. Given the demographics of the state, it is probably of little surprise that only one member (a senator) of the 2003 Alaska legislature was African American and none of its members were Hispanic.

Like most state legislatures, the primary work in the Alaska legislature is done by the standing committees. There are nine standing committees in the House and nine in the Senate. Assignments to these committees are made by the members of the committee on committees in each chamber, who are appointed by the presiding officer of each chamber. Each standing committee in the Senate has three or five members, and each in the House has seven or nine. Alaska's standing committees always have an odd number of members, to minimize the possibility of a tie.

The president of the Senate is responsible for Senate administration, and the speaker of the House is responsible for administration of that chamber. Most staff services are provided through a nonpartisan legislative services agency that is overseen by a legislative council composed of legislators from both houses.

Processes

The president of the Senate is the chamber's presiding officer. The speaker of the House is the presiding officer of that chamber and controls its agenda. Along with their respective majority leaders, they control their chamber agendas. The presiding officers also appoint the members to the committees on committees, which assign members and chairmanships to standing committees.

The Alaska legislature meets annually, convening on the third Tuesday in January in years following a gubernatorial election, and on the second Monday in January in all other years. Sessions are limited to 120 consecutive calendar days, unless extended for an additional ten days by a two-thirds vote of each house. In order to conduct the state's business in such a limited amount of time, members must abide by a time limit for submitting legislation. Legislators can submit no new legislation after the thirty-fifth day of the second session, unless the members agree to suspend or override the rule. In the 2003 session, 567 bills (proposals) were introduced in the Alaska legislature, but only 154 (just over a quarter) became law.

According to the National Conference of State Legislatures, the Alaska legislature is considered to be almost full time. Its members are paid $24,000 annually and receive an additional $161 per day during session if they do not live in Juneau (for an estimated compensation package of almost $45,000, if the session goes the full 120 days). Members who live in Juneau receive only about $40 per day, for a package of about $30,000 a year. Members also have full-time support staff available in their district office year-round. Turnover is a little higher than average in Alaska, with more than a third of the members being new following each election. Following the elections of 2002, 35 percent of the senators were new and 38 percent of the House members.

Leadership Structure

The president of the Senate and the speaker of the House are the top leaders of their respective chambers. They oversee the appointment of committee chairpersons, the assignment of bills, and the progress of legislation and overall direction of policy in their respective chambers. They are assisted by their majority leaders, who serve as floor managers for the majority parties. The minority leaders lead the minority parties in each chamber. Historically, presiding officers in the Alaska legislature serve no more than four years.

The speaker of the House and the president of the Senate are officially elected by all members of their chamber, but they are generally from the party of the majority. Floor leaders (majority leader and minority leader) are elected by the members of their respective caucuses.

While there are no limits on the tenure of legislative leaders in the state, tradition has it that the speaker and Senate president serve no more than two two-year terms.

Election Processes

Legislators are elected to their two-year terms in the November even-year election. Half of the Senate is elected in each even-year election. The state is divided into twenty electoral districts with about 32,000 citizens in each. Each district elects one senator and two representatives, who run districtwide. The majority of the legislators, like the majority of the population, are in and around Anchorage. Because of the state's size, many of Alaska's legislative districts are larger than most states and, therefore, cause unique campaign problems for candidates with voters few and far between. Contested nominations are decided in party primaries.

Key Political Factors

While Republicans remain the majority party in Alaska, the Democrats are competitive. While the Democratic Party has not achieved any success in presidential elections, it remains highly competitive in other elections and has elected governors and controlled the legislature in the past.

The massive size of the state and of many of its legislative districts, coupled with the fact that the state capital (Juneau) is accessible only by air or boat, presents Alaska's legislators with travel problems unlike those experienced by legislators in any other state.

Because so much of the land in the state is owned by the federal government, and Alaskans receive from the federal government more than $1,000 more per capita each year than citizens in any other state, decisions in Washington are watched very closely by legislators in Juneau. Recent efforts by the president and Congress to open access to Alaskan oil for drilling by oil companies has created considerable political tension in the state.

Furthermore, because of its size and the dispersion of some of its population, Alaska faces unique challenges in delivering government services. Per capita government expenditures in the "Frontier State" are more than $4,000 higher than those of any other state and more than $6,000 higher than the national average.

Further Reading

McBeath, Gerald A., and Thomas A. Morehouse. 2003. *Alaska Politics and Government.* Lincoln: University of Nebraska Press.

Whitehead, John S. 2004. *Completing the Union: Alaska, Hawai'i and the Battle for Statehood.* Albuquerque: University of New Mexico Press.

ARIZONA

• • • • • • • • • • •

THE ARIZONA LEGISLATURE

House of Representatives   Senate
60 Representatives   30 Senators

(602) 542–4900
http://www.azleg.state.az.us/

• • • • • • • • • • • •

Arizona achieved statehood in 1912 and was the last state to join the union before Alaska and Hawaii in the 1950s. Since the 1990s, it has been the nation's second fastest growing state, ranking behind only Nevada.

The influx of out-of-staters that has fueled Arizona's rapid growth has also transformed a state that was predominantly Republican from World War II until the latter part of the century, into one in which—while continuing to lean to the conservative side in outlook—Democrats are a competitive force fully capable of winning statewide races and some congressional seats. Democratic presidential candidates, although competitive, have been successful in carrying the state only once (Bill Clinton in 1996) since the middle of the twentieth century. While Republicans have usually controlled the House since the 1960s, Democrats have won the Senate periodically and the chamber was tied in 2001–2002.

Structure and Membership

The Arizona legislature consists of a thirty-member Senate and a sixty-member House of Representatives. Legislators are elected for two-year terms from single-member districts in November even-year elections. Two house members are elected from each Senate district. Legislators are restricted to a maximum of four consecutive two-year terms in their chamber, but they are eligible to run again after remaining out of that chamber for one term.

Entering the twenty-first century, Republicans maintain control of the House but have a much more tenuous lead in the Senate, having lost that lead in 2000, only to regain it two years later. Women have historically been well represented in the Arizona legislature, never holding less than a quarter of the seats since the mid-1970s. In the mid-1990s, female legislators held more than 40 percent of the seats in the House and more than a third of the Senate positions. Interestingly, that proportion has dropped significantly as the effects of term limits have become more significant, to the point that women held just over 25 percent of the seats in each chamber in 2003. Only one member of the Arizona legislature in 2003 was an African American, but five senators and nine representatives were Hispanic or Latino.

Nonpartisan professional staff services are overseen by a fourteen-member legislative council that is alternately chaired by the Senate president and House speaker. There are also small partisan staffs that serve legislative leaders and individual members. Each standing committee has a Republican staff person and intern, as well as a Democratic staff person and intern. There are just over one hundred full-time staff members working for the two chambers. Each senator can hire year-round staff in their capitol office, and all house members share a staff person with another house member in their capitol office.

The Arizona Senate has about ten standing committees, compared with about fifteen in the more populous House. Members of both chambers serve on three joint standing committees. Each nonbudgetary standing committee in the House has about a dozen members, while each Senate committee has nine or ten.

Processes

The president of the Senate and the speaker of the House appoint committee chairs and members, approve the appointment of legislative staff, and, often in consultation with their majority leaders, determine the chamber agendas. Historically, legislative leaders in Arizona have been quite strong, but the constant turnover created by term limits has limited their influence of late.

The Arizona legislature meets annually, convening on the second Monday of January. The session must adjourn no later than the Saturday of the week in which the 100th session day falls, unless the Senate president and House speaker extend it for up to seven additional days. Thereafter, the session may be further extended by a majority vote of the members of each house. Members of the House can introduce only seven nonbudget bills after the session has begun, and no additional bills can be introduced in either chamber without a suspension of the rules following the first month of the session (the first week of February). Also, each chamber establishes deadlines for reporting bills from either chamber out of committee.

During the 2003 legislative session, members of the Arizona legislature intro-

---

There and Back Again

There and Back Again. That is what Bilbo Baggins titled the report of his travels in J. R. R. Tolkien's *Hobbit.* However, it might just as aptly be the name of the "back again" speakership of Arizona representative Jim Weiers. Prohibited from seeking re-election to the state house in 2002 by term limits, Weiers ran for and won a seat in the Arizona Senate. Because the term limits in Arizona apply only to consecutive years of service in a given chamber, Weiers could run again for the House in 2004—and he did. He was re-elected to that chamber and was immediately selected by his colleagues to serve as speaker of the House once again.

duced more than 900 bills, enacting more than a quarter of them (268). The Democratic governor vetoed 17 of the bills passed by the legislature.

The Arizona legislature is historically a part-time, citizen's legislature. With an annual base salary of $24,000 and a per diem of $35 for the first 120 days of session ($10 after that), Arizona legislators generally receive a little more than $30,000 annually. While term limits have increased legislative turnover in the Arizona legislature, membership in it has always been rather dynamic, averaging between 25 and 30 percent every two years before term limits. It hovers around 40 percent now, with turnover following redistricting reaching almost 60 percent. In 2003, 55 percent of the House members and 57 percent of the senators were in their first term in their chamber.

Leadership Structure

The Arizona constitution prescribes that the president of the Senate and the speaker of the House are the top leaders of their respective chambers. They assign bills, select committee chairs, and appoint members to the standing committees in their chambers. In recent years, because term limits have decreased the number of experienced legislators, committee chairmen are determined more by their support for the presiding officer than by their legislative experience or policy expertise.

The majority and minority leaders of each chamber are responsible for managing floor debate for their respective parties. Because of Arizona's term-limits law, the tenures of legislative leaders are usually one, or at most two, terms. New members begin working toward gaining a leadership position as soon as they are elected to the chamber.

As noted in the opening text, members of the Arizona House found a unique solution to the problem of revolving door leadership. The term-limits law allows Arizona legislators to serve up to eight years, sit out two years, and then start another eight if they get reelected. Jim Weiers, speaker from 2000 to 2002, did just that, taking a break to serve two years in the Senate. Upon reelection to the House in 2004, he was promptly elected speaker again. Should he be reelected to the legislature and the Republicans maintain the majority, he can serve eight years as speaker. Former speaker Franklin "Jake" Flake was elected to the Senate following the forced end to his House service.

Election Processes

Arizona legislators are elected in the November even-year election. Contested nominations are decided in party primaries. Term limits have been accompanied by a small increase in the level of competition for state legislative seats. In 1990, there were an average of 2.1 candidates per seat in the ninety-member House. By 2003, that number had risen to 2.4 candidates per seat. It has also increased the number of House members seeking Senate seats, and vice versa. In 2004, ten of thirty Senate seats had only one candidate, and another seven had competition in the primary but not the general election. Only thirteen of the thirty campaigns had candidates from the two major parties.

The Arizona legislature has thirty electoral districts, with each district electing one senator and two representatives districtwide. Following the 2000 U.S. census, each district included about 171,000 people.

Key Political Factors

The anticipated continuation in Arizona's rapid growth can be expected to further change its political landscape, with the influx of new Arizonans from all parts of the United States likely to make the state increasingly competitive. Even within the rather dominant Republican majority (especially in the House), there are conflicts. The Republican caucus is rather conservative, but there are a significant number of more moderate Republicans who must be kept happy if the party is to govern. In 2003, these moderate Republicans joined with the minority party Democrats and passed a budget over the objections of their own speaker. However, several of them were defeated by more conservative Republicans in the 2004 primary elections, increasing the control of the conservative faction of the Republican Party, especially in the House.

While Arizona's state legislator term-limits law is less restrictive than those of some other term-limited states, it has increased the rate of turnover in both houses of the legislature. In the view of most legislative experts, this has served to weaken the legislature as a policymaking institution by eliminating the possibility of developing long-term institutional expertise within the legislative branch. The law has also weakened the leadership of the legislature, because once elected to leadership, a leader is immediately a "lame duck"—and members know it.

Lobbyists play a significant role in Arizona by providing information to the legislators. Each lobbyist must register in order to influence legislation. In 2003, almost 8,500 lobbyists registered with the legislature. Because of the ethics rules in the state (resulting from a 1989 scandal in which legislators were found to be taking bribes from lobbyists), lobbyists can spend no more than $10 on any legislator per year. This limit is among the most restrictive in the country.

Further Reading

Berman, David R. 1998. *Arizona Politics and Government: The Quest for Autonomy, Democracy and Development.* Lincoln: University of Nebraska Press.

———. 2004. *The Effects of Legislative Term Limits in Arizona.* Tempe, AZ: Morrison Institute of Public Policy.

Reingold, Beth. 2000. *Representing Women: Sex, Gender and Legislative Behavior in Arizona and California.* Chapel Hill: University of North Carolina Press.

Smith, Zachary A. 2002. *Politics and Public Policy in Arizona.* 3d ed. Westport, CT: Greenwood.

ARKANSAS

●●●●●●●●●●●

THE ARKANSAS GENERAL ASSEMBLY

House of Representatives   Senate
100 Representatives   35 Senators

(501) 682–2904
http://www.arkleg.state.ar.us

●●●●●●●●●●●●

While Arkansans tend to be conservative in their political outlook, a longtime Southern loyalty to the Democratic Party has shown only some slight signs of wavering in recent years, particularly in statewide elections. The Republican Party has made significant inroads in presidential voting, with Bill Clinton the only Democrat to carry the state in the last twenty years—including 2000, when Clinton's vice president, Al Gore, failed to carry it.

Republicans have had success at the gubernatorial and congressional levels, but the legislature has remained under solid Democratic control. Legislative term limits of six years in the House and eight years in the Senate have taken their toll in this state, in which the legislature meets for sixty days every two years and legislative influence was historically in the hands of a few senior legislators in each chamber.

Structure and Membership

The Arkansas General Assembly consists of a thirty-five-member Senate and a one hundred–member House of Representatives. Senate terms are four years, and House terms are two years. Legislators are elected from single-member districts in November even-year elections. The Arkansas General Assembly is one of the few Southern legislatures that has remained singularly and strongly under Democratic control since the end of the Civil War. In 2005, they held 72 of 100 seats in the House and 27 of 35 in the Senate. In the election of 2004, Democrats gained two seats, bucking a Republican trend evident in much of the South. Senators are restricted to a maximum of two four-year terms, and House members to a maximum of three two-year terms.

The percentage of female legislators in Arkansas has traditionally lagged behind those in the rest of the country. In 2003, women held seven seats (20 percent) in the Senate and fifteen seats (15 percent) in the House. Furthermore, women chaired only two of the twenty standing committees in the two bodies. The proportion of African American legislators remains even lower. The 2003 Arkansas General Assembly included fifteen African American members (twelve representatives and three senators).

Because the legislature meets in session only sixty days every two years, most members hold jobs outside of the legislature. The membership of a recent Senate included two attorneys, a pastor, the director of a religious foundation, three insurance agents, a rancher, two farmers, two teachers, a pharmacist, an engineer, a contractor, and the owners of a radio station, a nursing home, a funeral parlor, a recycling company, a car dealership, and a real estate company.

Each chamber of the Arkansas General Assembly has ten standing committees. Each House standing committee includes twenty members and each Senate committee seven voting members. Each House member serves on two standing committees. Each of the standing committees has a number of subcommittees that include five to eight legislators. Standing committees may make only three recommendations regarding legislation: Do Pass, Do Pass as Amended, or Do Not Pass (seldom used). They may also fail to act on legislation, allowing it to die in committee (most common).

Each House standing committee includes a large number of nonvoting members added toward the end of the session and who may attend interim meetings of that committee. In a state in which term limits restrict representatives to six years of legislative service, this additional assignment permits them to gain knowledge quickly in several policy areas.

The General Assembly also includes five joint committees, composed of members from both chambers. House and Senate members of the Joint Budget Committee are assigned according to their seniority, with one member from each house representing each of the four re-gional districts that closely mirror the state's congressional districts. Membership on the other joint committees is based on seniority and party, with majority party members selecting first.

Nonpartisan professional staff services are provided to both houses by the Bureau of Legislative Research, which is managed by the Legislative Council, composed of members from both chambers. The House Management Committee is responsible for hiring and supervising House staff and developing personnel policies. The Senate Efficiency Committee supervises staffing in that chamber. There is also a very small partisan staff that serves legislative leaders and individual members who are paid from caucus rather than state funds.

Processes

The lieutenant governor is the president of the Senate, but the president pro tempore is responsible for the legislative process. However, because committee positions and committee chairs are assigned based on legislative seniority in the Senate, the power of the pro tempore is less than that of his counterpart in the House, the speaker. While House standing committee assignments are based on seniority, the speaker does assign their chairs and vice chairs. The president pro tempore exercises primary control of the Senate agenda. Power in the Senate is as much a function of personality as position and often resides in the hands of key chairmen. The speaker of the House presides over sessions of the House of Representatives and, assisted by the speaker

---

Leader Over the Hill at Thirty

Retirement comes early for leaders in the Arkansas General Assembly. When Representative Shane Broadway stepped down from his post as the speaker of the Arkansas House of Representatives in January 2003, he was thirty years old. Elected to the body fresh out of college, Broadway filed for election at twenty-three years of age in the rotunda of the capitol, two days after being married in the same place. In the middle of his second two-year term, Broadway was selected by his colleagues to be the speaker-designate at the age of twenty-six, and he took the post of speaker in January 2001. Forced from the House by term limits in 2003, Broadway successfully won a seat in the Arkansas Senate.

---

pro tempore, has primary control over the chamber's agenda.

The Arkansas General Assembly meets biennially in odd-numbered years, convening on the second Monday in January. Sessions are limited to sixty calendar days unless extended by a two-thirds vote of each chamber. Committee chairs and memberships are determined by seniority. With such a short regular session, special sessions are not uncommon. They are called by the governor and must deal only with legislation relative to the governor's proclamation. However, once such business is concluded, a two-thirds vote of each chamber can extend the session for up to fifteen days to consider other business. The General Assembly has met in four such sessions in the past four years, two in 2001 and two in 2003. In 2003 the Arkansas General Assembly met for a total of ninety-four days, thirty-four days longer than the constitutional limit of sixty.

During the regular session, no budget bills may be introduced after the fiftieth day of the session, and other bills may be introduced after the fifty-fifth day without a special vote of the bodies. In 2003, members of the Arkansas General As-

sembly introduced 2,884 bills, enacting 1,816 of them.

With its short biennial sessions and relatively low legislative compensation, the Arkansas legislature is generally considered among the less professional in the country. Legislators receive less than $13,000 a year in annual salary and $85 per day during session, plus office expenses. This would make their total compensation around $20,000 in session years and $13,000 in off years. Each legislator has shared staff year-round, but the total staff size for the chamber is less than fifty.

Leadership Structure

The Senate president pro tempore, elected by the Senate, is the chamber's top official. The speaker of the House is top leader of the House of Representatives.

The Arkansas House of Representatives and Senate have long maintained a tradition of selecting a new speaker and president pro tempore every two years. This tradition was formalized following the implementation of term limits. A "speaker designate" and "pro tempore designate" are formally chosen a year before taking office as speaker, so that preparation can begin for the transition. The speaker also appoints a speaker pro tempore and four assistant speakers pro tempore, one from each of the states congressional regions. The majority and minority leaders of each chamber are responsible for managing floor debates for their respective parties.

Because of the restrictive nature of term limits in Arkansas, the speaker designate in the House will have, at most, three years of experience in the chamber when taking up the post. This means that positioning for that post begins early in the freshman session of a legislator. Legislators in the freshman and sophomore classes watch closely to see who will rise above the rest and exhibit the abilities and desire to lead.

Election Processes

Arkansas legislators are elected in the November even-year election. Because Senate terms are four years, half of the Senate is elected in each even-year election, except at elections following a reapportionment, when some senators are elected for terms of two years to maintain staggered terms while conforming with the newly apportioned districts. Contested nominations are decided in party primaries.

Key Political Factors

While the Arkansas Republican Party has become a competitive force in presidential, gubernatorial, and congressional elections during the past few decades, it has made only limited inroads in state legislative elections, in which the Democrats continue to win sizable majorities.

The Arkansas term-limits law, which limits senators to two terms and House members to three, and which along with California's law is the most restrictive term-limits law for any state legislature, has led to heavy turnover in both chambers. In the view of most legislative experts, this has served to weaken the General Assembly as a policymaking institution by eliminating the possibility for developing long-term institutional expertise within the legislative branch. The consequences of term limits, however, are greater in the House than in the Senate, with almost all senators having served in the House before moving to the Senate. In the election of 2002, all but one of the newly elected senators had been termed out of the House.

Term limits have also likely increased the influence of the more than 300 lobbyists registered in the General Assembly. There is no limitation on how much lobbyists in Arkansas may spend in efforts at persuasion, although all expenditures must be made public.

Further Reading

Blair, Diane. 1988. *Arkansas Politics and Government: Do the People Rule?* Lincoln: University of Nebraska Press.

Blair, Diane, and Jay Barth. 2005. *Arkansas Politics and Policy.* Lincoln: University of Nebraska Press.

Bullock, Charles S., and Mark J. Rozell, eds. 2002. *New Politics of the Old South: An Introduction to Southern Politics.* 2d ed. Lanham, MD: Rowman and Littlefield.

CALIFORNIA

• • • • • • • • • • • •

THE CALIFORNIA LEGISLATURE

Assembly	Senate
80 Assembly Members	40 Senators

(916) 322–9900
http://www.leginfo.ca.gov/

• • • • • • • • • • • • •

With more than 12 percent of the nation's population and a gross domestic product exceeded by only a handful of countries in the world, California is often likened to an independent nation. The state has something of just about anything that can be found anywhere in the United States—a highly diverse population, a long and scenic coastline, a comfortable year-round climate in its south, mountainous snowy regions in its northeast, a massive high-tech economy—and some things, most notably the Hollywood entertainment industry, that are unique to it.

As its population has become increasingly diverse, California has been transformed from what was considered a "swing" state into one that leans increasingly Democratic in both national and state elections. With the exception of the election of Governor Arnold Schwarzenegger, a Republican, the Democratic Party has, in recent decades, won a majority of the state's presidential contests and statewide elections and maintained consistent control of the state legislature.

For more than three decades, the legislature of the Golden State was considered the "gold standard" for state legislatures. Scholars, legislators, and most journalists suggested that every state legislature should be more professional, with full-time legislators, staff, and funding, as in California. In the late 1980s, the tide began to turn regarding the benefits of a professional legislature, and California, with its partisan membership, high incumbency return rate, expensive elections, and senior and centralized leadership, became a standard of a different sort. It became the symbol of the term-limits movement that swept the nation.

Structure and Membership

The California legislature consists of a forty-member Senate and an eighty-member Assembly. Senate terms are four years and Assembly terms are two years. Legislators are elected from single-member districts in November even-year elections. A citizen-approved initiative, approved in 1990, limits lifetime tenure in the Assembly to three terms of two years and in the Senate to two terms of four years. The president pro tempore of the Senate is responsible for Senate adminis-

---

Wearing Out the Hinges on the Speaker's Door

In the four years following the implementation of legislative term limits in California, the Assembly needed to install a revolving door on the speaker's office. Once known for the long tenure of its leadership, the California Assembly had six speakers from 1995 to 1999. None of those speakers served in that office for more than thirteen months. One Republican was elected speaker by the Democrats and served less than two months in the post before being recalled by angry GOP voters. Another left the post early to seek higher office, and still another was removed only after exhausting all legal efforts to mitigate the effects of legislative term limits.

---

tration, and the speaker of the Assembly is responsible for administration of that chamber.

Although Republicans held a two-seat majority in the Assembly following the 1994 election, Democrats now handily control both chambers, holding about 60 percent of the seats in each chamber. Women have traditionally done well in the California legislature, holding about 20 percent of the positions and significant leadership posts. They generally are not as well represented in the Senate as in the House. African American legislators constitute only about 5 percent of the membership but include former speaker Herb Wesson, Jr., among their ranks. The Hispanic and Latino membership is becoming increasingly influential, making up almost a quarter of the membership in the early part of the twenty-first century. More significantly, Latino legislators have been selected to serve in key partisan, institutional, and committee leadership positions.

Staff services are provided through an extensive network of nonpartisan professional staff, with each legislator also having a number of partisan personal staff assistants. California has one of the largest and most professional legislative staffs in the United States, although its growth has been severely curtailed since 1990 by the same citizen-approved term-limits initiative that also reduced legislative branch spending and imposed a cap on increases.

The California Assembly usually has around thirty standing committees, with the members and chairs assigned by the speaker. Committee membership ranges from seven to fifteen, with the exception of the thirty-member Committee on the Budget. The Assembly often has almost as many select committees (77 in 2004) as it does members. The California Senate has about two dozen standing committees with between seven and thirteen members. Like the Assembly, the Senate has almost as many select committees (35 in 2004) as it does members. There are also about a dozen joint committees, with members from both chambers. In addition to these committees, the California Assembly has a large number of caucuses, or groups organized by party, ethnicity, gender, population density, or sexual preference.

Processes

Under the California constitution, the lieutenant governor serves as the president of the Senate. However, by law and custom, the role of the president is extremely limited, with the lieutenant governor invited to preside only periodically, primarily on ceremonial occasions such as the opening of the legislative session. The Senate president pro tempore is the presiding officer at most sessions and also has primary control over the Senate's agenda. The speaker of the Assembly is the presiding officer of that chamber and controls its agenda.

The California legislature holds a two-year session that begins on the first Monday of December of each even-numbered year and adjourns no later than November 30 of the next even-numbered year. It meets on a continual basis throughout this period. The legislature establishes no limitations on the introduction of bills, but leaves that up to the Rules Committee. Usually, they set the limit at around thirty per session in the Assembly and sixty in the Senate. During the 2003 legislative session, 2,867 pieces of legislation were introduced, with 1,156 passing both chambers. Just over 50 of those were vetoed.

Despite the dramatic decline in membership stability as a result of legislative term limits, the California legislature is still considered among the most professional in the country, with the majority of legislators working full time. There are no constitutional limits on the length of legislative sessions, and members receive a base salary of almost $100,000 a year. Every legislator has a fully staffed district office and year-round staff in a capitol office.

Leadership Structure

The president pro tempore of the Senate and the speaker of the Assembly are the top leaders of their respective chambers. They oversee the appointment of committee chairpersons and members, the assignment of bills, and the progress of legislation and overall direction of policy in their respective chambers. The president pro tempore and speaker are assisted by their chambers' majority leaders, who serve as floor managers for the majority parties, and by a number of deputy and assistant leaders. The minority leaders, assisted by a number of deputy and assistant leaders, lead the minority parties in each chamber.

Since the advent of term limits, the Senate's two-term limit and the Assembly's three-term limit have led to frequent turnover in leadership positions, with most leaders holding their position for only a single term. Members of the majority caucus of the Assembly now select their speaker in the spring of the second year of the legislative session, so that the new speaker can more effectively manage the election efforts of candidates for the fall election. The new speaker will serve the remainder of that session and the first sixteen months or so of that speaker's final session before being replaced. The speaker completes the term as speaker emeritus. Both parties select a rather exhaustive list of party leaders, including floor leaders, assistant floor leaders, whips, assistant whips, and caucus chairs.

Election Processes

Legislators are elected to their two-year terms in the November even-year election. Half of the Senate is elected in each even-year election. Contested nominations are decided in party primaries. Partisan gerrymandering has made virtually all districts safe for one party or the other. In 2004, while term limits forced the retirement of more than a third of the members of the Assembly, not a single district changed hands. Republicans were elected to replace every retiring Republican, and Democrats replaced every Democrat.

California's state Senate districts are by far the most populous in the United States, and its Assembly districts are exceeded in population only by those of the Texas Senate. Senators in the Golden State represent more people than do members of the U.S. House of Representatives. Campaign costs in a contested election can be heavy, sometimes equaling or even exceeding those of congressional elections.

Key Political Factors

The Democrats regularly retain control of both houses of the California legislature, usually by sizable margins. Furthermore, most districts are heavily weighted for one party or the other. Although more than a third of the legislators elected in 2004 were new to the chamber, not a single district in either chamber changed parties.

California's Senate districts are significantly more populous than its congressional districts, and its Assembly districts contain about two-thirds of a congressional district's population (40 Senate and 80 Assembly districts, compared with 53 congressional districts). The cost of running a campaign and the demands on a California legislator's time are considered comparable to those of a congressional candidate. With the recall of Democratic governor Gray Davis and the election of Republican Arnold Schwarzenegger, some predict an increase in popularity for the Republicans. However, the failure of Schwarzenegger's popularity to deliver gains in the legislature suggests that may not happen.

Most experts, both in- and outside of California, believe that the severe term limits established by the voter-approved initiative in 1990 have weakened the effectiveness of the legislature as a policy-making institution by forcing frequent membership turnover and preventing the development of long-term institutional expertise. Others suggest that term limits have increased the influence of the more than 1,000 registered lobbyists.

Further Reading

Clucas, Richard A. 1995. *Speakers Electoral Connection: Willie Brown and the California Assembly.* Berkeley: University of California Press, Institute of Governmental Studies.

Janiskee, Brian, and P. Ken Masugi. 2004. *Democracy in California: Government and Politics in the Golden State.* Lanham, MD: Rowman and Littlefield.

Richardson, James. 1996. *Willie Brown: Style, Power and a Passion for Politics.* Berkeley: University of California Press.

COLORADO

• • • • • • • • • • • •

THE COLORADO GENERAL ASSEMBLY

House of Representatives   Senate
65 Representatives   35 Senators
(303) 866–2904   (303) 866–2316
http://www.state.co.us./gov_dir/stateleg.html

• • • • • • • • • • • • •

Colorado has a number of special distinctions, among them its ski resorts, which receive visitors from all parts of the United States. It is home to the U.S. Air Force Academy, and its capital city, Denver, sits at a higher elevation than any other state capital.

Unlike many of its neighboring states that are usually considered safe for the Republican Party, Colorado is sometimes a battleground state in presidential elections. While the Democratic presidential candidate has carried the state only twice since the middle of the twentieth century (1964 and 1992), the results in elections that have not been national landslides for the Republican candidate have usually been close. Elections for state and congressional offices are often tightly contested, and while Republicans have generally controlled the state legislature, Democrats took control of the Senate in 2002 (by one seat) and have made some gains in the House. Despite GOP strength in the legislature, Democrats held a lock on the governor's office from 1974 to 1998.

Legislative politics in Colorado is dominated by two reforms passed by initiative: legislative term limits and TABOR (Taxpayers' Bill of Rights). As of 1996, legislators were restricted to four two-year terms in the House and two four-year terms in the Senate. The average number of years of service at the beginning of each session has declined by almost two since 1993. These limits have created a revolving door of leadership and committee chairs in the state. TABOR, passed in 1992, severely restricts expenditure growth and severely ties the hands of legislators when it comes to meeting the state's financial obligations.

Structure and Membership

The Colorado General Assembly consists of a thirty-five-member Senate and a sixty-five-member House of Representatives. Senate members are elected for four-year terms and House members are elected for two-year terms from single-member districts. In 2004, Democrats took control of both chambers, gaining a three-seat majority in the House and a one-seat majority in the Senate.

In 2005, just more than a third of the members of the House of Representatives were female, including the speaker pro tempore of the House. Just over a quarter of the senators were female, but those members included Majority Leader Joan

---

The Assembly Has an Extra Member

While the official records (and the state constitution) indicate that the Colorado General Assembly has 100 members, members and staff in Denver know that it really has 101. In 2004, Senate president John Andrews made Clarence Miller an honorary member of the Colorado General Assembly. Mr. Miller, who is developmentally disabled, spends all of his waking hours at the capitol. Everyone knows and likes him. Members, staff, and lobbyists throw him a birthday party every year. He is invited to interest group functions. He knows more about what is going on at the statehouse than most elected members of the legislature. He is the 101st member of the Colorado General Assembly.

Fitz-Gerald. Interestingly, the proportion of women in the legislature has remained constant (just above a third), despite the dramatic turnover caused by term limits. The proportion of African Americans in the legislature is quite low (three in the House and two in the Senate), as it is in the state itself. The proportion of Hispanic members is growing, with four Hispanic legislators in the House in 2003 and two in the Senate.

The Senate elects a president from its membership to preside over its sessions and oversee the chamber's administration. The speaker of the House presides over its sessions and is responsible for House administration.

Nonpartisan professional staff services are provided under an eighteen-member legislative council that consists of the Senate president, the House speaker, the Senate and House majority and minority leaders, and six senators appointed by the Senate president and six House members appointed by the speaker, the Senate president, and the House speaker. The council coordinates most of the General Assembly's work between sessions, and its staff handles general administrative responsibilities for the legislature.

Processes

The president of the Senate and the speaker of the House preside over sessions in their respective chambers. However, much of the business in both chambers takes place in "Committee of the Whole," where other members are selected (by the speaker or the president) to preside.

The rules of the General Assembly limit the number of bills that each legislator may introduce to five per member, excluding appropriations bills. Members of the House cannot introduce legislation after the twenty-second day of the session without special permission. The same goes for senators after the seventeenth day of session. The leadership can, and often does, however, waive those limits and deadlines. The Colorado General Assembly meets annually, convening on or before the second Wednesday of January, with sessions limited to a maximum of 120 calendar days.

During the 2003 session, Colorado legislators introduced 736 bills, passing 449 of them. That is one of the highest page rates of any legislature in the country, suggesting that the limitation on bill introductions works. Since legislators can introduce only a certain number of bills, they don't want to waste those introductions on bills with little chance of becoming law. The governor vetoed fourteen of the laws passed in 2003.

When it comes to legislative professionalism, Colorado is usually considered to be in the middle of the states. The base salary for a legislator is a respectable $30,000 a year, plus a per diem that raises the annual salary to more than $40,000. Members are provided with year-round and session-only staff, but that staff is limited in number. The legislature has about 120 full-time staffers. The personal, full-time staff is quite limited. Legislative turnover in 2003 was 28 percent in the House and 17 percent in the Senate; it has changed very little over the past decade, despite term limits.

Leadership Structure

The president of the Senate and the speaker of the House are the top leaders of their respective chambers. The speaker assigns committee members and appoints committee chairs in the House, while the majority leader (in consultation with the minority leader for minority party appointments) performs those duties in the Senate. The majority and minority leaders of each chamber are responsible for managing floor debates for their respective parties. Both the majority and minority parties have several assistant leaders.

Because of Colorado's term-limits law, legislative leaders usually serve one, or at most two, terms. Prior to term limits, it was not uncommon for legislative leaders to serve multiple terms. Speaker Chuck Berry, the last speaker before term

limits, held the post for eight years, and Senate majority leader Jeff Wells held his post for ten.

In 2003, the Colorado House had eleven standing committees and the Senate had ten. Again, as a result of term limits, committee chairs usually hold their positions for no more than one term, and tenure on any one committee is quite limited.

Election Processes

Colorado legislators are elected in the November even-year election, with eighteen senators elected to their four-year terms in one even-year election and seventeen in the next. Term limits mean that at least a quarter of the House and Senate seats have no incumbents running, for each election cycle. Contested nominations are decided in party primaries.

Key Political Factors

It is impossible to discuss the political context of Colorado without acknowledging the importance of the initiative process. Voters in Colorado have used the initiative process more than voters in any other state (an average of eight initiatives every two years since 1992), and those initiatives have had a significant impact on the legislature. In the last two decades, voters have passed initiatives that have limited how long legislators can serve (term limits), how they conduct legislative business (GAVEL—Give A Vote to Every Legislator), and how they raise revenues (TABOR).

In 2004, legislators fell short in an effort to limit the ability of the voters to pass restrictive initiatives. There have been discussions of efforts to overturn some of the more restrictive initiatives (term limits, the taxpayers bill of rights, and others), but the relatively tight party balance (especially in the Senate) makes it unlikely that either party will step out and risk the wrath of the voters by attempting to overturn "the will of the people."

Colorado can be expected to remain a relatively competitive state. The growing Hispanic population is likely to continue to alter the political landscape of the state, with both parties working hard to recruit Hispanic voters and candidates.

While Colorado's state legislator term-limits law has not significantly increased the rate of turnover in the legislature, it has increased the turnover among the leadership. In the view of most legislative experts, this has served to weaken the legislature as a policymaking institution by eliminating the possibility for developing long-term institutional expertise within the legislative branch. Furthermore, the absence of experienced legislators has opened the door to the significant impact of the more than 500 lobbyists registered with the legislature. There are no limits on how much a lobbyist can spend entertaining legislators in Colorado.

Colorado voters have demonstrated an occasional independent streak in presidential voting. The state gave independent candidates Ross Perot more than 23 percent of its vote in 1992, John Anderson 11 percent in 1980, and Ralph Nader over 5 percent in 2000.

Further Reading

Cronin, Thomas E., and Robert D. Loevy. 1993. *Colorado Politics and Government: Governing the Centennial State.* Lincoln: University of Nebraska Press.
Straayer, John. 2000. *Colorado General Assembly.* 2d ed. Boulder: University Press of Colorado.

CONNECTICUT

• • • • • • • • • • • •

THE CONNECTICUT GENERAL ASSEMBLY

House of Representatives	Senate
151 Representatives	36 Senators
(860) 240–0400	(860) 240–0500

http://www.cg.ct.gov

• • • • • • • • • • • •

Connecticut is a highly urbanized state that, for more than a half-century, has consistently ranked first in per capita income among the fifty states. Long considered a bastion of New England conservatism, the post–World War II years were marked by a rapid growth in ethnic population that have transformed the state's politics from domination by "Yankee" Republicans into a predominantly Democratic state.

Prior to the U.S. Supreme Court's "one man, one vote" decisions in the 1960s, Connecticut's 294-member House of Representatives was the second most malapportioned legislative chamber in the country. The Senate was also malapportioned, although less drastically so. As a result, the House had Republican majorities for all but two years between 1876 and 1968, while the Senate was usually controlled by the Democrats. With the 1965 constitution providing for a Supreme Court–mandated "one man, one vote" legislature, both chambers have been under Democratic control for all but three two-year terms since 1968. Republicans have controlled both chambers during two two-year terms, and there has been one term with split control.

Structure and Membership

The members of the Connecticut General Assembly, 151 in the House and 36 in the Senate, are elected from single-member districts for two-year terms in even-numbered years. Democrats have strong control over both chambers at present. In recent years, the proportion of female legislators in Connecticut has been above the national average, generally around 30 percent. Furthermore, Moria Lyons served as speaker of the House of Representatives from 1999 to 2005, and women have traditionally held significant leadership and committee posts. African Americans usually occupy about 10 percent of the seats.

Administrative responsibility for the operation of the legislature rests with the Joint Committee on Legislative Management, which is jointly chaired by the president pro tempore of the Senate and the speaker of the House. The majority and minority leaders and the top deputy leaders also serve on the committee, which makes all administrative decisions on a bipartisan basis. The committee's nonpartisan executive director is respon-

sible for day-to-day management of legislative operations, administration of the legislative budget, oversight of the capitol and legislative office buildings and their surrounding grounds and parking facilities, and coordination and supervision of staff services. The General Assembly has approximately 500 full-time employees, equally divided between partisan and nonpartisan, with an additional 225 individuals employed during session periods.

Historically, the state party chairs had significant influence on legislative elections and processes. However, that influence began to weaken in the 1970s and has fairly well evaporated.

Processes

Odd-year sessions are limited to five months, with the session convening on the first Wednesday after the first Monday in January and adjourning on the first Wednesday after the first Monday in June. Even-year sessions are one month shorter on each end, with the session convening on the first Wednesday after the first Monday in February and adjourning on the first Wednesday after the first Monday in May.

There are two notable and rather unique features to Connecticut's legislative process. The first is the General Assembly's exclusive use of joint committees. Bills are debated by committee members from both chambers and, when reported favorably, are given a joint favorable report. After a joint favorably reported bill has passed the first house, it immediately goes onto the calendar of the second house, as it has already received a favorable report by the second chamber's

Connecticut State Capitol in 1907 (Library of Congress)

committee members. At any time that a majority of a committee's members from one chamber disagree with a majority from the other, the committee may vote to separate into individual chamber committees. Connecticut's committees operate on a year-round basis.

The second unique feature is the legislature's system for the introduction and consideration of bills, which is designed to focus the efforts of its professional bill drafting staff on those bills that committees find most likely to receive serious consideration. Bills introduced by individual members are called proposed bills and are written in prose form, not in precise legal language. A bill drafter can prepare a proposed bill in only a fraction of

the time that it takes to draft a bill in full legal form. Committees then screen the proposed bills and decide which ones are worthy of serious consideration. Those bills are then drafted into full legal form and given a public hearing.

Connecticut's legislative rules establish strict deadlines for bill introductions. Legislators have only until the tenth day of an odd-year session and the third day of an even-year session to introduce legislation. Committees have later deadlines for the introduction of committee-sponsored bills, and most bills introduced in even-year sessions and a substantial number in odd-year sessions are, in fact, introduced by committees. During the 2003 legislative term, more than 3,000 pieces of legislation were introduced in the General Assembly, but fewer than 200 of them passed both chambers. Twelve bills were vetoed by the governor, but none of the vetoes were overridden.

The Connecticut General Assembly is considered semiprofessional, with some characteristics of a professional legislature and others of a more citizen-oriented body. The annual salary of just over $35,000 is quite low, especially for a state with the highest per capita income in the United States. Odd-year sessions take up almost half of the year, and even-year more than a quarter. Furthermore, interim committee meetings and constituent activities make the time commitment quite significant, even when the legislature is out of session. While most legislators hold other jobs, their legislative time commitment is considerable.

Connecticut's is one of the few state legislatures that can be classified as a commuter legislature. No legislator lives more than a ninety-minute drive from the capitol in Hartford, and for most the drive is less than forty-five minutes. Because of this, Connecticut legislators, unlike the majority of their counterparts in the other forty-nine states, return to their home districts every night and are likely to have more opportunity than most state legislators for dialogue and exchange with their constituents.

Leadership Structure

The lieutenant governor serves as the presiding officer of the Senate but exercises no other power in the chamber except in the case of a tie vote. The chamber's top leadership position is officially the president pro tempore, who automatically succeeds to the post of lieutenant governor if that position becomes vacant. In fact, the president pro tempore and the majority leader are usually seen as a leadership team that jointly fill the Senate's top leadership role. The minority leader leads the minority party caucus. The speaker of the House is the top leader in the House of Representatives, with the majority leader as the floor debate leader. The minority leader leads the chamber's minority caucus.

Both of Connecticut's chambers have traditions of conferring an extensive array of deputy and assistant leadership titles on large numbers of their members. While having a leadership title entitles the legislator to a salary differential over that of a nonleader, many of these positions involve minimal responsibility.

Senate President Sitting on History

In most state legislatures, the chairs in the chamber are merely a place for legislators to sit while they make the laws that govern the state. However, when the lieutenant governor takes a seat to preside over the Senate, that seat is a part of history. The chair is constructed from wood of the state's historic "Charter Oak" tree, which was destroyed by nature in 1856. For seven years (1687–1693), the hollow oak was home to the charter from King Charles II establishing Connecticut as a state, hidden from followers of King James II who wanted to take away Connecticut's independent status.

Election Processes

Until recently, Connecticut used a convention system for party nominations, with candidates receiving a certain percentage of the convention delegate vote entitled to challenge the convention nominee in a primary. While the convention system continues to be the primary means of nomination, recent legislation now permits an individual to bypass the convention altogether and qualify for a primary through filing petition signatures. The average House district contains just over 20,000 people, while the average Senate district contains just under 100,000.

Candidates for both the Senate and the House run in single-member districts for two-year terms, with elections held in November of even-numbered years.

Key Political Factors

The southwestern section of Connecticut (commonly referred to as the Fairfield County area) is the wealthiest part of the state and one of the wealthiest areas of the nation; it is dominated by commuters to New York City. It has long been a bastion of Republican strength. The more rural eastern section of the state is less affluent, has a predominantly Boston orientation, and, along with the urban centers of Hartford, Bridgeport, New Haven, and Waterbury, provides the area of greatest Democratic strength.

The Republican Party has enjoyed some success in gubernatorial elections and in carrying the state for its presidential candidates over the last several decades. But with only two exceptions, Democrats have remained in control of the state General Assembly. The only Republican legislative successes since the "one man, one vote" reapportionment of the mid-1960s were the result of "coattails" from the top of the ticket.

Until 1986, Connecticut had an optional "party lever" on its voting machines that allowed a voter to vote a straight party ticket by simply pulling a party lever. Because it was estimated that as many as four out of five voters used the party lever, there was potential for a significant "coattail effect" in elections in which there was a landslide at the top of the ticket. This coattail effect allowed the Republicans to win control of the legislature in the 1972 and 1984 elections, when Richard Nixon and Ronald Reagan carried the state by huge margins. Those mark the only two times that the Republicans have won control of both chambers since the state moved to its "one man, one vote" apportionment in 1968. With the abolition of the party lever in 1987, the potential for a coattail effect on state legislative elections is now significantly diminished, and Democrats seem to be in solid control of the General Assembly.

Further Reading

Rose, Gary L. 2001. *Connecticut Government at the Millennium.* Fairfield, CT: Sacred Heart University Press.

Satter, Robert. 2004. *Under the Golden Dome: An Insider's Look at the Connecticut Legislature.* Hartford, CT: Connecticut Conference of Municipalities.

Sembor, Edward C. 2003. *Introduction to Connecticut State and Local Government.* Lanham, MD: University Press of America.

DELAWARE

● ● ● ● ● ● ● ● ● ● ●

THE DELAWARE GENERAL ASSEMBLY

House of Representatives   Senate
41 Representatives   21 Senators
(302) 744–4000
http://www.delaware.gov

● ● ● ● ● ● ● ● ● ● ● ●

In land area, Delaware is the nation's second smallest state, after Rhode Island. Originally part of Pennsylvania, Delaware formed its own General Assembly in 1704 and gained its own identity as a state at the start of the American Revolution in 1776. In 1787, Delaware became the "First State" to ratify the U.S. Constitution.

As a border state, Delaware's Civil War loyalties and sympathies were sometimes divided between the North and the South. The state permitted the practice of slavery and had strict laws governing the movements and activities of free blacks. However, Delaware stayed in the Union and raised more troops, per capita, than any other state in the United States. Currently, Democrats enjoy a significant registration edge over Republicans. Despite that, the state has been a fairly good bellwether of the mood of U.S. voters as a whole. Since World War II, the state has generally been won by the successful presidential candidate. With the turn of the century, when Al Gore took the state and its three electoral votes in 2000 and John Kerry did the same in 2004, the state has been trending Democratic, with the voters in the most populous northern county overriding the more conservative voters in the two lower counties.

Delaware's economy is fairly diverse. Banking, agriculture, and tourism are the state's largest economic sectors. The chemical industry also has a strong presence, especially in the northern part of the state. Control of the Delaware General Assembly has been split for more than two decades, with Republicans holding a majority in the House and Democrats holding most of the Senate seats.

Structure and Membership

The Delaware General Assembly consists of a twenty-one-member Senate and a forty-one-member House of Representatives. Senators serve four-year terms and House members serve two-year terms. With redistricting every ten years, half of the senators run for a two-year term following the redistricting each decade. With a total of sixty-two legislators, the Delaware General Assembly has fewer members than all state legislatures except that of Alaska. Politically, Republicans have maintained solid control of the House of Representatives, while Democrats have maintained a similar lock on the Senate.

Women have generally done quite well in the Delaware General Assembly, hold-

Republican? Democrat? Supercandidate!

"It's a Democrat? It's a Republican! No, It's Supercandidate!" That was the headline in a 1994 edition of *Campaigns & Elections*, referring to Delaware senator Margaret Rose Henry. Senator Henry, a registered Democrat, had just defeated fellow Democrat Herman M. Holloway, Jr., and a minor party candidate, with the full and total support of the Republican Party. In the Senate, she sided with the Republicans, voting for their leadership team and meeting with their caucus. A year later, in November 1995, Henry switched her allegiance to the Democratic Party, joining the Senate Democratic Caucus. As of 2005, Ms. Henry still serves in the Delaware Senate as a Democrat.

ing a quarter of the seats for the last decade. During much of the 1990s, former state senator Ruth Ann Minner served as lieutenant governor, and Senator Myrna Bair was Senate minority leader. Hispanic and African American legislators constitute less than 5 percent of the membership of the General Assembly.

The lieutenant governor, an independently elected official in Delaware, acts as the president of the Senate and presides over its sessions. The Senate president pro tempore, who is elected by the members of the Senate, is responsible for general administration of the Senate. The speaker of the House presides over the chamber and is responsible for its administration.

The twenty-two-member Joint Legislative Council Committee comprised of the legislative leaders of each chamber plus ten additional members appointed by the Senate president pro tempore and the House speaker oversees a sizable nonpartisan staff. Each chamber also has a partisan staff that works in behalf of the Republican and Democratic caucuses, with the majority party having larger staff. Legislators have their own offices but, except for the leadership, share clerical and professional staff. The legislature employs about 170 full- and part-time staffers.

Interestingly, the Senate often has more standing committees than it does senators. In 2003, the chamber's twenty-one senators served on twenty-five standing committees. Seven majority-party senators chaired two different committees each. The House is almost as busy, with twenty-six committees for its forty-one members. Two House members chaired two different committees in 2003. Senate committee chairs and members are appointed by the president pro tempore of the Senate. House committee chairs and members are appointed by the speaker of the House.

Processes

The Delaware General Assembly meets annually, convening on the second Tuesday of January; it generally meets three days a week—Tuesdays, Wednesdays, and Thursdays—with a mandatory adjournment by June 30 of each year. A General Assembly session runs for two years. Legislation introduced in the first (odd) year of the session is still active the following year.

One thing that sets the Delaware legislative process apart from that in most other states is that members of the general public often speak from the floor. If invited by a state representative or senator to address the membership, the citizen may proceed to the well of the chamber and address the body.

In its 2003 General Assembly session, Delaware legislators introduced 497 bills. About 40 percent (191) of those measures were sent to the governor to be signed into law. The governor, a former legislator herself, vetoed only one of the bills.

The Delaware General Assembly is usually considered a "citizens' legislature." Most legislators hold full-time jobs, leaving work to attend session. The legislature generally does not go into session until late in the afternoon. Because of the small size of the state, no district is more than an hour's drive from the capitol. Legislators are paid about $34,000 a year. The General Assembly meets approximately fifty-five days annually in a legislative session that begins in early January and ends on June 30. Multiple breaks are built into the legislative schedule to accommodate holidays as well as committee work on the state's annual operating and capital budgets. Turnover is quite low, with about six of every seven legislators returning to the General Assembly following an election.

Leadership Structure

The president pro tempore of the Senate and the speaker of the House are the top leaders in their respective chambers. The majority leader and minority leaders of each chamber are responsible for managing floor debate for their respective parties. The majority and minority leaders of each chamber are assisted by majority and minority whips.

It is not uncommon for Delaware's top legislative leaders to serve more than one term in their position. With his reelection to the post in 2003, speaker of the House Terry Spence—already the longest-serving speaker in Delaware history—became the longest-tenured speaker in the country. Speaker Spence has served as the leader of the House since 1988. The Senate has had only three presidents pro tempore since 1980. Traditionally, the three top leaders from the majority party in each chamber (speaker, majority leader, and majority whip in the House, and president pro tempore, majority leader, and majority whip in the Senate) have been chosen by their caucus with regional balance. Each of the three leaders has been from one of Delaware's three counties.

Election Processes

Delaware legislators are elected in the November even-year election, with approximately half of the Senate membership elected to their four-year term in each even-year election cycle. Party nominations are determined by primary. Each state legislator in Delaware represents a relatively small number of voters. The average Senate district is under 40,000 constituents, and the average House district under 20,000.

Many of the districts in the urban and suburban areas of Newark, Dover, and Wilmington cover a relatively small area. This tends to produce elections that are personal and conducted at the grassroots level. While some legislative races can be expensive, many are won with little money but a lot of shoe leather (walking the district and knocking on doors). Legislators build personal relationships with their constituents, which also goes a long way in explaining how the Senate can be solidly controlled by Democrats and the House by Republicans. Delaware voters tend to vote for people they know and like, regardless of party label.

Key Political Factors

Delaware will likely continue to be a competitive state in the years to come, leaning slightly to the Democrats, particularly in presidential contests. Split-party control of the two houses of the General Assembly will continue to be a possibility in each election.

With its small size, relative informality, and true citizen membership, the Delaware General Assembly harkens back to a type of legislature that many have tried to re-create with term limits elsewhere. While the legislators organize along party lines, few votes are truly partisan, and both chambers seem to maintain a level of collegiality that has been lost in other states. When conflicts arise, they are more regional (upstate-downstate), rural-urban (New Castle County vs. Kent and Sussex counties), or ideological (liberal versus conservative) than partisan.

Delaware is also the only state in which voters do not vote directly on amendments to the state's constitution. Amendments must be approved by both chambers in two consecutive General Assembly sessions. If the amendment passes the second time, it becomes part of the state constitution. Amendments do not require the signature of the governor.

Further Reading

Boyer, William W. 2000. *Governing Delaware: Policy Problems of the First State.* Dover: University of Delaware Press.

Cohen, Celia. 2002. *Only in Delaware.* Newark, DE: Grapevine.

Hoffecker, Carol E. 2001. *Delaware: The First State.* Moorestown, NJ: Middle Atlantic.

———. 2004. *Democracy in Delaware: The Story of the First State's General Assembly.* Wilmington, DE: Cedar Tree.

FLORIDA

• • • • • • • • • • • •

THE FLORIDA LEGISLATURE

House of Representatives
120 Representatives

Senate
40 Senators

(850) 488–1234
http://www.leg.state.fl.us/

• • • • • • • • • • • •

Probably no state has undergone more of a transformation since the middle of the twentieth century than has Florida. An influx of retirees from the North and Latino refugees from Cuba has, over the past fifty years and more, transformed what was an integral part of the Old South composed primarily of residents with family ties dating back for generations into one of the nation's fastest-growing, most populous, diverse, and most cosmopolitan states.

The state's political transformation has been equally dramatic. Unlike the other states of the formerly solid Democratic South that have become heavily Republican—particularly in presidential voting—Florida has become more of a swing state that is almost always hotly contested in presidential and statewide elections. Interestingly, Republicans have made more inroads in state legislative elections in Florida than they have in the other traditional Deep South states, now controlling both the House and Senate by wide margins.

Structure and Membership

Florida's legislature consists of a 40-member Senate and a 120-member House of Representatives. Senate terms are four years and House terms are two years. Legislators are elected from single-member districts in November even-year elections. Members are barred from running for reelection to the legislature if, at the conclusion of their current term, they have served for eight consecutive years.

As in the rest of the South, Democrats controlled Florida politics and the legislature for more than a century, beginning in the 1870s. They controlled the legislature until 1994, when Republicans took control of both chambers for the first time since Civil War Reconstruction. They have not relinquished control since, holding a commanding lead of about two-to-one in each chamber.

Women have traditionally fared quite well in the Florida legislature, with Toni Jennings serving as president of the Senate in the 1990s and others playing prominent roles. Of late, women have held around a quarter of the seats and a quarter of the committee leadership posts in each of the chambers. African American legislators made up more than 20 percent of the Senate (nine senators) and just under 20 percent of the House of Representatives (twenty-nine representatives) in 2004. Latino and Hispanic legislators are taking a more prominent role in the Florida legislature as well, making up just under 10 percent of the membership in each chamber in 2003 (three senators and eleven House members).

The president of the Senate is responsible for Senate administration. The speaker of the House is responsible for House administration. Staff services are provided by a combination of partisan and nonpartisan staff.

Processes

The Senate president serves as the chamber's presiding officer. The president is empowered to appoint members of the Senate's committees. The speaker of the House presides over sessions of the House of Representatives and has primary control over its agenda, as well as assigning members and bills to committees.

The legislature meets for an organizational session to elect officers and form committees two weeks after the November election. Regular annual sessions then convene on the first Tuesday after the first Monday in March and are limited to sixty calendar days, unless extended by a three-fifths vote by both chambers. The legislature's committees

---

Are You Saving This Seat for Anyone?

Reflecting the demographic history of the state, the 1868 Florida constitution provided that the "Seminole Indian Tribe was entitled to one seat in the House and one seat in the Senate with all the rights, privileges, and remuneration, as other members of the Legislature." To date no member of the tribe has held a seat in either chamber, although one white Floridian laid claim to the seat with false claims of being a member of the Seminole Tribe.

---

function on a year-round basis and meet at regular intervals throughout the months when it is not in regular session. In order to make the most of the sixty-day session, all bills must be prefiled—that is, no legislator may introduce a new bill after noon on the first day of the legislative session, unless a majority of the members deem the situation a "reasonable emergency."

Although the Florida constitution limits the legislative sessions to sixty calendar days, it is considered by many to be an almost full-time legislature because of the high level of staffing and regular, year-round committee meetings and obligations. With the state's growing population, each senator represents almost 500,000 citizens, and each House member about 150,000—these are among the largest districts of any state, requiring considerable time and effort to represent. Florida legislators earn $27,900 annually plus a daily allowance of $99 for each day in session. Furthermore, each member has a strong contingent of full-time staff in the capitol and in the district, whether the legislature is in session or not.

Leadership Structure

The president of the Senate is officially the chamber's top leader, although much of the control over daily activity is shared with the majority leader. The speaker of the House is top leader of the House of Representatives. Even before term limits were implemented, Florida had a tradition of rotating House and Senate leaders every two years, with a clearly defined ladder of succession. With the implementation of term limits, however, that process has been formalized in the House, with the designation of a formally selected "speaker designate" chosen more than a year before that member would formally take office as speaker.

The Senate and House majority leaders manage floor debate and organize and develop party positions for their party. The minority leaders do the same for the minority party. The majority and minority leaders are assisted by a number of deputy and assistant leaders.

With the implementation of term limits in Florida, state legislative leadership positions have become a probable launching pad for Florida elected officials. One former speaker is now in the U.S. House of Representatives, and the current speaker is competing with another former speaker for the Republican nomination to run for the U.S. Senate. Former Senate president Toni Jennings is now lieutenant governor of the state.

Election Processes

Florida legislators are elected in the November even-year election. Because Senate terms are four years, half of the Senate is elected in each even-year election, except at elections following a reapportionment, when some senators are elected for terms of two years to maintain staggered terms while conforming with the newly apportioned districts. Contested nominations are decided in party primaries. With term limits and the dramatic partisan shift of the past eight years, legislative leaders have become extremely active in legislative campaigns, raising significant amounts of money and recruiting candidates to run in the races.

While turnover following the 2002 election was more than a quarter in each chamber, the 2004 elections saw only two new senators (5 percent) and nineteen new representatives (16 percent) elected to their respective chambers.

Key Political Factors

Florida is also one of the fastest growing states in the United States, with the population from 1990 to 2000 growing by almost 25 percent. Much of that growth can be attributed to the growing Latino and Hispanic population. In 2000, Hispanics constituted about 8 percent of the state's population, but that percentage is expected to balloon to almost 25 percent by 2025. This shift has been recognized by both parties. Both are actively recruiting Hispanic and Latino candidates and courting Hispanic and Latino voters.

Unlike most of the other states in the Democratic Old South, in Florida, Republicans have achieved more success in state legislative elections than they have at the presidential or gubernatorial levels. Democrats held overwhelming control of the Florida legislature from Reconstruction through the 1960s, when Republican strength began to grow. By the early 1990s, Republican strength had grown to the point where control of both chambers was in question in each election. That strength continued to grow, and, by the early twenty-first century, the Republican Party controlled both chambers by margins approaching two to one.

Historically, interest groups, particularly conservative business groups, have played a significant role in shaping politics and policy in Florida. As the state's population and economy have grown, and the elections have become more competitive, interest groups have become even more important and influential in Florida.

Interestingly, as Republicans were making their dramatic gains in the legislature, Democratic candidates were finding more success in statewide elections, winning several gubernatorial and senatorial contests, carrying the state for their presidential candidates in 1976 and 1996, and finishing in a dead heat in the historic 2000 election in which the eyes of the world were focused on Florida. While the Florida legislature is likely to be Republican for the foreseeable future, because of how the legislative districts are drawn (so that Republicans get the maximum number of winnable seats), the state is likely to be competitive for statewide office and in the national arena for the next few years.

Further Reading

Colburn, David R., and Lance DeHaven-Smith. 1999. *Government in the Sunshine State: Florida since Statehood.* Gainesville: University Press of Florida.
Dye, Thomas R. 1998. *Politics in Florida.* Upper Saddle River, NJ: Prentice-Hall.

Huckshorn, Robert J., ed. 1999. *Government and Politics in Florida.* Gainesville: University Press of Florida.
Prier, Eric. 2003. *Myth of Representation and the Florida Legislature: A House of Competing Loyalties.* Gainesville: University Press of Florida.

GEORGIA

• • • • • • • • • • • •

THE GEORGIA GENERAL ASSEMBLY

House of Representatives	Senate
180 Representatives	56 Senators
(404) 656–5015	(404) 656–5040

http://www.legis.state.ga.us/

• • • • • • • • • • • •

Georgia politics underwent a political revolution in 2002, with the surprising defeat of incumbent governor Roy Barnes and the not unexpected end to the career of Speaker Tom Murphy, who had been in the House of Representatives for more than forty years and had been speaker of the House since 1974. Furthermore, the Republican Party took control of the state Senate when four Democrats changed their party affiliation following the election, giving them a 30–26 majority. Thus a state that had not had a Republican governor or Republican-controlled legislative chamber since the 1800s now had a Republican governor and Republican Senate. The revolution was completed in 2004, when Republicans took a majority in the House. Following defections of several former Democrats, the Republican advantage ballooned to more than a dozen seats. In just more than two years, Georgia Republicans went from no power to almost total control of state government.

Georgia is a state of contrasts with its capital city, Atlanta, and the city's metropolitan area considered probably the most cosmopolitan part of the New South, contrasted to rural areas that retain many characteristics of the Old South. This contrast is reflected in the politics of the legislature as well, with many Democrats from Atlanta and other urban pockets contrasting dramatically with the traditional conservative Democrats from rural Georgia. The Republican Party has found fertile soil in these rural areas, as well as in the suburban areas growing around Atlanta and Savannah.

Like its neighboring states of the Old Confederacy, Georgia has seen itself transformed since the final third of the twentieth century from a bastion of the solid Democratic South into a Republican-leaning swing state. With their gain of the House of Representatives, Georgia Republicans completed a sweep of state government—taking the governorship and both chambers of the General Assembly.

Structure and Membership

The Georgia General Assembly consists of a 56-member Senate and a 180-member House of Representatives. All legislators serve two-year terms and are elected from single-member districts in November even-year elections. As noted earlier, following the 2002 elections, four Democratic senators switched their party identification to Republican (at the urging of the new Republican governor, who had served as a member and leader of the Georgia Senate), giving them a majority in the Senate. With the elections of 2004, Republicans took firm control of the House of Representatives as well.

Like most state legislatures, each chamber of the Georgia General Assembly has a set of standing committees that examine legislative proposals. In 2003 there were twenty-five standing committees in the Senate and thirty-four in the House. Most House committees have between six and fifteen members, with a few (Rules, Appropriations, Ways and Means, and Health and Human Services) having considerably more. In 2005, the new Republican majority created a number of "super committee members" who can vote on any committee at any time. These include the speaker pro tempore, majority leader, and majority whip.

In the early part of the twenty-first century, women hovered around 20 percent of the membership of the two chambers. In 1962, the election of LeRoy Johnson as the first African American elected to the Georgia General Assembly (and the entire Southeast) since Reconstruction raised fears and anxiety across the region. Forty years later, African Americans would hold more than one out of five seats in the General Assembly (18 percent in the Senate and 22 percent in the House) and several committee chairmanships.

The lieutenant governor, who is president of the Senate, the chamber's president pro tempore, and its majority leader share responsibility for Senate administration. The speaker of the House is responsible for House administration. Staff services are provided by a combination of partisan and nonpartisan staff.

Processes

The lieutenant governor, an independently elected official, is the president of the Senate and serves as the chamber's presiding officer. The lieutenant governor's authority over the Senate's process and management was considered among the greatest of any lieutenant governor who presides over a state Senate until 2003. At that time, the new Republican Senate leadership diluted the responsibility of the Democratic lieutenant governor by establishing a committee to appoint chairpersons and members of the Senate's committees, a responsibility that had previously rested exclusively with the lieutenant governor. The speaker of the House presides over sessions of the House of Representatives and manages its legislative activities.

Regular sessions of the legislature convene on the second Monday of January

The Hawks Have Landed in the Statehouse

When Republicans took control of the Georgia House of Representatives following the 2004 elections for the first time since 1870, they made some changes to encourage the success of their agenda and solidify their power. On the first day of the new session, Speaker Glenn Richardson appointed three legislative "hawks," who can swoop in to any committee with the authority to vote the way the speaker wants them to. Senate Republicans, who are solidifying power gained in 2002, have created similar positions, with several members having this authority.

and are limited to forty legislative days. Regular sessions are usually concluded before the end of March but of late have extended into April. All tax bills must be introduced by the twenty-first day of the session. All general bills must be passed in their house of origin (where they were first introduced) during the first thirty-three days of session. This might be reflected in the fact that 1,437 pieces of legislation were introduced in 2003, with some 414 passing both chambers.

The Georgia General Assembly is considered near the bottom according to most measures of legislative professionalism. In 2003, legislators were paid just over $16,000 annually for their services, plus a daily travel allowance of $128 during the forty-day session. Therefore, during a full session, a Georgia legislator will earn just over $20,000. During the legislative session, legislators have shared staff in the capitol and have no staff in the district. Every two years, about one in five (20 percent) of the members of the Georgia General Assembly will be new. Following the revolutionary elections of 2002, 29 percent of the Senate and 22 percent of the House members were new.

Leadership Structure

As president of the Senate, the lieutenant governor is officially the chamber's top leader, although much of the lieutenant governor's control over daily activity was diluted in 2003 when the Republicans took control of the chamber for the first time since Reconstruction and established management by a leadership committee. Following the defeat at the hands of the voters of the state's longest-serving speaker, in 2002, the new speaker promised a more democratic and open legislative process. While he delivered on that promise, he has also found it necessary at times to flex his muscles, removing one committee chair during the 2003 session for failing to work closely with the leadership. The degree to which the Republican speaker, who took over in 2005, will follow his lead remains to be seen; however, changes in the rules that he supported suggest that he will be a strong leader.

The speaker of the House is top leader of the House of Representatives and largely sets its agenda. He also appoints the committee chairs and members of the committees, and if necessary (as it was found to be during the 2004 session) can remove committee chairs and members. The Senate and House majority leaders are elected by members of the caucus; they lead floor debate and organize and develop party positions. The minority leaders do the same for the minority party.

Individuals occupying Georgia's top leadership positions often enjoy lengthy tenures. A recent House speaker held his position for twenty-eight consecutive years, the longest tenure of any top legislative leader in the United States.

Election Processes

All Georgia legislators are elected in the November even-year election. Contested party nominations are decided in party primaries. Until recently, elections, especially for the House, were low key and relatively inexpensive local affairs. However, as the state has become two-party (both parties having a reasonable chance of winning), the level of competition and the cost of winning have increased. Legislative leaders now take an active role in the recruitment and financing of candidates. Furthermore, efforts by the Republican governor to persuade Senate Democrats to switch parties suggest a more active role by the executive in legislative campaigns.

Key Political Factors

While Georgia has been transformed from an overwhelmingly Democratic state into a swing state in national and statewide elections, the state's Democratic tradition remains perhaps a bit stronger at the state legislative election level than it does in the neighboring states of South Carolina, Florida, and Tennessee. Even the big Republican breakthrough to capture control of the Georgia Senate in 2003 required a switch in party affiliation by four senators who had been elected as Democrats in the November election. The defection turned what had been a 30–26 Democratic margin on election night in November 2002 into a 30–26 Republican majority in January 2003. Likewise, the Republican majority that was gained in the House on election day expanded with Democratic defections.

Much of this change can be attributed to the state's growing population. From 1990 to 2000, the state's population grew by 26.4 percent, seventh in the nation and first among Southern states. From 2001 to 2002, it ranked fifth in the country. Much of that population growth is due to migration from other parts of the country, bringing in different political values and political cultures. Interestingly, despite this growth in population, Georgia remains among the lowest states in both voter registration (65.5 percent in 2000, forty-fourth in the country) and voter turnout (43.8 percent in 2000, forty-sixth in the country). Also, with the districts created by Democrats following the 2000 census declared unconstitutional, Republicans drew new district lines for the 2004 elections that were considerably more equitable for Republicans.

Georgia is a year-round, part-time legislature, with short regular sessions but activities continuing on a part-time basis throughout the year. While some members are full-time legislators, many have private-sector occupations. Interest groups have long been considered a powerful force in the Peach State, and there is no reason to anticipate that will change in the near future.

Further Reading

Allen, Lee M. and Richard T. Saeger. 2003. *Georgia State Politics: The Constitutional Foundation.* Dubuque, IA: Kendall/Hunt.

Fleischman, Arnold, and Carol Pierrannunzi. 2003. *Politics in Georgia.* Athens: University of Georgia Press.

HAWAII

• • • • • • • • • • • •

THE HAWAII LEGISLATURE

House of Representatives   Senate
51 Representatives   25 Senators

(808) 586–2211
http://www.capitol.hawaii.gov

• • • • • • • • • • • •

Hawaii is a state with many unique distinctions. The state was annexed by the United States as a territory in 1898. It was the fiftieth, and last, state to join the Union, following Alaska by a few months in 1959. It is the state most distant and isolated from the other forty-nine. And it has by far the largest Asian and smallest white population of any state, excluding the military nonresident population. Its greatest natural resource is the islands, and it has a well-deserved reputation as a vacationer's paradise. Tourism, the state's primary industry, was significantly damaged by the attacks of September 11, 2001. It took more than three years for the state's economy and budget to recover.

Hawaii is a solidly Democratic state that occasionally votes for a Republican presidential candidate and elects a Republican governor. The state legislature has remained under solid Democratic control since the territory became a state in 1959. However, with the 2002 election

of the first Republican governor in forty years and some general dissatisfaction with the Democratic establishment, there appear to be cracks in the Democratic armor. Only two Republicans (Nixon in 1972 and Reagan in 1984) have won the state's four electoral votes since it gained statehood. However, a Republican promise to contest more Democratic seats in 2004 yielded Democratic gains in both chambers.

Structure and Membership

The Hawaii legislature consists of a twenty-five-member Senate and a fifty-one-member House of Representatives. Senators are elected for four-year terms and House members for two-year terms from single-member districts in November even-year elections. Democrats maintain a commanding lead in both chambers, holding a two-to-one majority in each chamber in the early part of the twenty-first century. While Republicans made some gains in the 1990s, those have been wiped out by Democratic gains in the early part of the twenty-first century.

Women are well represented in the Hawaii legislature, holding more than a quarter of the seats in each chamber (13 of 51 in the House in 2004 and 8 of 25 in the Senate), as well as holding key leadership positions in each chamber. African American representation is low in the Hawaii legislature, as is the proportion of African Americans in the population. Several members of the Hawaii legislature consider themselves Hispanic or Latino but also have other ethnic identities as well. More than three-quarters of the members in each chamber are of Asian or Pacific Island descent. Because of the centralized population around Honolulu, more than half of the members represent districts near or in the capitol city.

The House of Representatives has seventeen standing committees, each with between five and fifteen members. Partisan representation on the committees is proportional to the chamber, with committee leadership and majority members appointed by the speaker and minority membership appointed by the minority leader. Committees are divided into two groups, with each member serving on a minimum of two committees, one from each group. The Senate is organized into thirteen standing committees, with five to seven members serving on each committee with the exception of the Ways and Means Committee (sixteen members). Senate committees should reflect the partisan balance of the chamber as much as possible.

Staff services are provided by a combination of nonpartisan and partisan staff. Legislators in both chambers have full-time staff year-round in the capital, but not in the district. The two presiding officers (speaker of the House and president of the Senate) manage the legislative staff.

Processes

The president of the Senate and the speaker of the House preside over sessions and are responsible for general administration in their respective chambers. They appoint committee chairs and members and, in consultation with their majority leaders and majority floor leaders, determine the agendas of their chambers.

The Hawaii legislature convenes annually on the third Wednesday in January. Sessions are limited to sixty legislative days, unless extended by a two-thirds vote of both chambers for up to fifteen additional days. The session usually adjourns the first week of May and includes a mandatory one-week recess in March, by joint chamber agreement. Bills cannot be introduced after the first week of session unless the rules are suspended by a vote of the membership. The rules also include two deadlines by which bills from one chamber must "cross over" to the other and another for "decking"—when a bill is ready for passage and made available to members for consideration in final form at least forty-eight hours before the third or final reading (that is, being on deck, like a baseball player waiting to bat).

Hawaii Legislative Building Is Lesson in History

Hawaii's capitol has more symbolic representation than any other state capitol in the United States. The building rises from its broad base to a narrow opening at the top like the volcanoes that created the island state. The House chamber is colored in earth-tone hues of browns, red, and beige and lighted by a copper and brass chandelier representing the sun. The Senate chamber, colored in various shades of blue to represent the ocean that surrounds the state, features the aluminum and nautilus shell "moon" chandelier. The building is supported by columns that symbolize the palm trees that grace the island.

During the 2003 legislative session, more than 3,400 pieces of legislation were introduced in the Hawaii legislature. Of those, only 269 were passed by the legislature; 50 were vetoed by the new Republican governor.

The Hawaii legislature is generally considered to be a mix of professional and citizen legislators. Members are paid $34,200 a year—a pretty good salary for Iowa, but not much considering the cost of living in Hawaii. The speaker of the House and the president of the Senate get an additional $5,000 annually. Most legislators do have an alternative source of income and live in their districts full time. All members do have full-time staff in the capitol office with a full staff of about 250 for the entire body. Although the legislature is out of session for most of the year, interim committees meet regularly during that time.

One unique feature of the Hawaii General Assembly is its Public Access Room. Established in 1994 and located in the capitol, the PAR serves the citizens of Hawaii by providing equipment, services, and facilities to enhance their ability to participate in the legislative process. PAR staff hold regular sessions to teach the public how to understand and influence the legislative process.

Leadership Structure

The president of the Senate and the speaker of the House are the top leaders of their respective chambers. They preside over their chambers, assign bills to standing committees, appoint committee members and chairs, and prepare their caucuses for the upcoming campaign season. If the Senate president is unable to fulfill his or her duties, those duties are performed by the Senate vice president, a post not recognized in any other state legislature.

The majority leaders and majority floor leaders and the minority leaders of each house are responsible for managing floor debate for their respective parties. Each chamber has a number of deputy and assistant leaders. Leadership in both chambers is relatively stable. The House had only two speakers between 1988 and 2005. Senate presidents serve four-year terms.

Election Processes

Hawaii's legislators are elected in the November even-year election. Half of the senators are elected in each election. Contested nominations are decided in party primaries. Each senator represents about 50,000 people, with each representative about half that. Historically, because of the Democratic dominance of the legislature, the most critical election is often the primary election. However, in the 2002 and 2004 elections, Republicans and Democrats fielded a candidate for each of the state's legislative districts. Despite efforts by the Republican governor to unseat Democratic incumbents, Democrats lost no seats in the Senate and gained six in the House in 2004.

Key Political Factors

Hawaii has been considered a Democratic stronghold from the time it achieved statehood. The Democratic Party has consistently maintained strong and sometimes overwhelming majorities in both houses of the state legislature. With the election of a Republican governor in 2002 and increased numbers of Republicans in the legislature, many anticipated the beginning of significant Republican growth. The Republican governor promised to work for the election of GOP legislators, and there was some thought that George W. Bush might carry the state for the Republicans in 2002. However, in the end, Senator John Kerry won it by almost 10 percent, and Democrats gained six seats in the House. Half of the Senate seats were up for reelection in 2004.

In Hawaii, geography is a much more important political factor than political party. Many of the political disagreements stem from the different needs of Honolulu and Maui and the rest of the state's islands.

Lobbyists have always been considered strong players in this relatively nonprofessional legislature. In 2003, 250 lobbyists were registered with the legislature. There are no limits on how much interest groups may spend in efforts to influence legislators. Individual contributions are limited to no more than $2,000 per election cycle.

Further Reading

Coffman, Tom. 2003. *Island Edge of America: A Political History of Hawaii.* Honolulu: University of Hawaii Press.

Pratt, Richard C., with Zachary Smith. 2000. *Hawai'i Politics and Government: An American State and a Pacific Society.* Lincoln: University of Nebraska Press.

Smith, Zachary A. 1992. *Hawai'i State and Local Government: The Aloha County Situation.* Lanham, MD: University Press of America.

Smith, Zachary A., and Richard C. Pratt, eds. 1992. *Politics and Public Policy in Hawai'i.* Albany: State University of New York Press.

IDAHO

• • • • • • • • • • •

The Idaho General Assembly

House of Representatives
70 Representatives

Senate
35 Senators

(208) 332–100
http://www.state.id.us/legislat/legislat.html

• • • • • • • • • • • •

Idaho is considered one of the nation's most rugged states. Known for its potatoes and its forestry, its economy also includes manufacturing, mining, agriculture, and electronics. The state includes some of the richest mines, farmlands, and forests, as well as some of the most beautiful scenery and diverse wildlife in the United States.

Idaho is a solidly Republican state that consistently gives Republican presidential candidates one of their largest vote percentages. The state's Democratic Party is active and has, on a few occasions, been successful in electing its candidate for governor. The state legislature has remained under Republican control for decades. The Oregon Republican Party has also remained fiercely conservative on fiscal matters, opting to make significant and difficult budget cuts rather than raise taxes during recent economic difficulties.

The Idaho legislature holds the distinction as the only legislature in the United States to repeal legislative term limits that were passed by the voters. In 2002, both chambers overwhelmingly voted to repeal legislative term limits. An effort to reinstate them in the 2002 election was narrowly defeated by the voters.

Structure and Membership

The Idaho legislature consists of a thirty-five-member Senate and a seventy-member House of Representatives. The state has thirty-five legislative districts, each of which contains one Senate district and two House districts. All legislators are elected for two-year terms to single-member districts. Republicans maintain a majority of well over two-to-one in each chamber.

Women have historically been well represented in the Idaho legislature, constituting a third of the membership in 2001–2002 and ranking Idaho as high as fifth among the fifty states. Recently, the proportion of female legislators has dropped a bit to just below 30 percent, ranking the state just inside the top ten. In 2004, four of the seven leaders of the House were women, but none of the top leaders of the Senate. Given the homogeneity of the state's population, the fact that there are very few African American and Hispanic legislators is of little surprise. In 2004 there were no African American members and one Hispanic legislator.

The lieutenant governor, an independently statewide elected official, is president of the Senate and presides over its sessions. The Senate elects a president pro tempore from its membership who assigns members to standing committees and determines who will chair those committees. The speaker of the House presides over sessions of the House.

Legislative administration is the responsibility of a bipartisan fourteen-member legislative council consisting of the president pro tempore of the Senate, the speaker of the House of Representatives, the majority and minority leaders of each house, and four additional members from each chamber (two from each party). All permanent staff are under the council's general supervision. The Legislative Services Office was created by the legislature in 1993 to consolidate the nonpartisan staff support to Idaho's citizen legislators. In an effort to coordinate services, a director of legislative services was named to oversee three formerly separate offices. Functions of the Legislative Services Office include budget and policy analysis, legislative audits, bill research, legislation development, and information technology management.

The Idaho Senate has ten standing committees and the House has fourteen. Each Senate committee is made up of eight to twelve senators, including two from the minority party. In the House, every committee includes ten to fifteen members, including two or three members of the minority party. Each member of the Senate serves on two or three standing committees as does each member of the House. The Idaho legislature has one important joint committee, containing members of both chambers. The Joint Finance Appropriations Committee (JFAC) meets throughout the three-month ses-

sion to develop and propose a budget. This committee is extremely influential.

Processes

The Idaho legislature convenes annually on the Monday nearest January 9 under the direction of the speaker in the House and the lieutenant governor in the Senate. There is no limit on session length, but no member may introduce a bill in the House after the twentieth day of the session. A similar deadline is established in the Senate for the twelfth day. No standing committee can introduce a bill in either chamber after the thirty-sixth day. These deadlines can be extended or overruled with a vote of the body. In the 2003 legislative session, 678 bills were introduced, with 389 passed by the legislature. Eight of those were vetoed by the governor.

The Idaho legislature is historically and proudly a "citizen's legislature." According to the legislative website, "Since statehood in 1890, Idaho's legislators have enjoyed a rich and successful history of charting the state's growth. Much of that success can be attributed to the fact that Idaho's legislators are 'citizen' legislators, not career politicians. They are farmers and ranchers, businessmen and women, lawyers, doctors, sales people, loggers and teachers. Elected for two-year terms and in session at the Capitol just three months each year, Idaho's citizen legislators are able to maintain close ties to their communities and a keen interest in the concerns of the electorate."

Idaho legislators are paid less than $16,000 a year for their services. Those who establish residence outside the district during session are given $99 for each

On Your Mark, Get Set, Go!

On the first day of the legislative session, members of the Idaho Senate stand on each side of the floor, much as their ancestors may have done, waiting to stake claims on land in the frontier state. Legislators wait there as the clerk of the Senate assigns seats. The four top leaders of the Senate choose their seats first, followed by the senior senators, then former members of the House now serving in the Senate. Finally, the names of all senators with no experience in either chamber are put into a hat and assigned the remaining seats in a random fashion. Stake your claim!

day in session, and those who do not establish a second residence receive $38 per day and up to $25 per day for travel expenses. At best, an Idaho legislator could make $22,000 annually. The president pro tempore of the Senate and speaker of the House receive an additional $3,000 annually. During 2003, the Idaho legislature met for 118 legislative days, beginning in January and adjourning the first week of May. The majority of Idaho legislators maintain a job in the private sector. Legislators share staff in their capitol office during the session but do not have support in the district. The legislature employs seventy to eighty support staff members during the legislative session.

Even without term limits, turnover in the Idaho legislature is quite high. In an average election cycle, around a third of the legislators will choose not to seek reelection or be defeated at the polls.

Leadership Structure

The president pro tempore of the Senate and the speaker of the House are the top leaders of their respective chambers. They appoint committees, manage floor activities, and preside over their respective sessions. The majority leader and minority leader of each house are responsible for managing floor debate for their respective

parties. The majority leader and minority leader of each chamber are each assisted by an assistant leader and a caucus chair.

With his reelection as speaker in 2005, Bruce Newcomb became the longest serving speaker in the history of the Idaho House of Representatives. Leaders of the Senate generally serve four or six years, but there is no formal process for rotation of leadership posts.

Election Processes

Idaho legislators are elected in the November even-year election. Contested nominations are decided in party primaries. One senator and two House members are elected from each of the state's thirty-five districts. Each Senate district includes about 50,000 people. Although two representatives are elected from each Senate district, representatives each run in their own district, so that there are no multimember districts and each member represents about 25,000 people.

Because of the dominance of the Republican Party, more than half of the candidates during each election cycle will not be contested by both parties. Oftentimes, the strongest competition occurs during the Republican primary elections. Elections are generally low key and relatively low cost.

Key Political Factors

Idaho can be expected to remain a strongly Republican state, with Republicans continuing to enjoy strong majorities in both houses of the state legislature. Threats were made against legislators who supported the repeal of legislative term limits, but with little impact. While Democrats did gain a few seats in the 2002 election, Republicans picked most of them back up in 2004.

While there is no time limit on Idaho's legislative sessions, sessions are not lengthy. The legislature is a part-time operation, and almost every legislator engages in a private-sector occupation. That fact, plus the limited staff available to legislators, would suggest that the more than 350 registered lobbyists would have a significant impact on policy in the Idaho legislature. What's more, there are no limits on how much money a lobbyist may spend, as long as those expenditures are made public.

Recent economic growth seems to be concentrated in urban areas, while rural Idaho remains affected by recession. In fact the population in the rural areas is shrinking, which fact became evident in the last reapportionment. It is likely that the issues addressed and the powers distributed in the legislature will change accordingly.

Further Reading

Duncombe, Sydney, and Robert Weisel. 1984. *State and Local Government in Idaho and in the Nation.* Moscow: University Press of Idaho.

Stapilus, Randy. 1988. *Paradox Politics: People and Power in Idaho:* Boise, ID: Ridenbaugh.

Stapilus, Randy, and James B. Weatherby. 2005. *Governing Idaho: Politics, People, and Power.* Boise, ID: Claxton Press.

ILLINOIS

● ● ● ● ● ● ● ● ● ● ● ● ●

THE ILLINOIS GENERAL ASSEMBLY

House of Representatives   Senate
118 Representatives   59 Senators
(217) 782–2000
http://www.legis.state.il.us

● ● ● ● ● ● ● ● ● ● ● ● ●

Illinois, which gave the nation Abraham Lincoln, epitomizes in many ways what Americans refer to as Middle America. Dominated by cosmopolitan Chicago bordering on Lake Michigan in the northeast and by typically rural Midwestern communities in most of the rest of the state, Illinois has corporate headquarters in manufacturing, insurance, retail trade, and health care, as well as a large agricultural sector.

Politically, Illinois has historically been a competitive state that was often seen as a battleground state in presidential elections. However, no Republican presidential candidate has carried the state since 1988. The state's voters tend to elect roughly equal numbers from each political party to statewide and congressional offices, with both parties having shown themselves capable of

---

Welcome to Your Capitol, Kaskaskia

The Illinois General Assembly meets in Springfield, but that has not always been the case. Springfield was the third capital in the history of the state. The first was Kaskaskia, which was eventually flooded by the Mississippi; the second was Vandalia. In 1837, nine legislators, known as "the long nine" because of their cumulative height of 54 feet, successfully lobbied to make Springfield the capital city. One of the "long nine" legislators was a young Whig legislator and attorney named Abraham Lincoln.

---

winning elections by landslide margins when they have offered a popular candidate. Statewide elections usually come down to who is more successful in getting out the vote—the Democratic stronghold of Cook County includes Chicago; there are heavily Republican areas in the "collar counties" surrounding Cook County, as well as the downstate rural communities. Republicans in the state tend to nominate candidates that are more moderate than national Republican candidates, and that fact has helped them stay competitive.

With the exception of a two-year period in the mid-1990s, Democrats have held the House for more than two decades. The Senate has been a bit more competitive, but it has generally been controlled by the Republican Party. However, Democrats took control of the Senate in 2004 and are not likely to relinquish control anytime soon. The most important political characteristic of the Illinois General Assembly is the virtual total control by the central leadership. By virtue of formal power and longevity (all four of the key leaders in 2005 had been in leadership for more than two decades), they control virtually every aspect of legislative life in Illinois.

Structure and Membership

The Illinois General Assembly consists of a 59-member Senate and a 118-member House of Representatives. Each Senate district contains two single-member House districts. Illinois senators are elected for four-year terms, and its House members are elected for two-year terms. In 2005, Democrats held a twelve-seat advantage in the House (65 to 53) and a five-seat majority (32 to 27) in the Senate.

While women have historically been underrepresented in the more professional legislatures, that is not the case in the Illinois House. More than a third of those elected to the House since the late 1990s have been women. They have not done as well in the Senate, however, where their membership has remained under 20 percent. About one in seven members of each chamber is African American, mostly from Chicago and Cook County. The longtime minority leader, who became president of the Senate when the Democrats gained control in 2004, is the African American Emil Jones, Jr. Women have recently served in high leadership posts in the House. Hispanic legislators make up a small but growing caucus in the legislature (ten legislators in 2003).

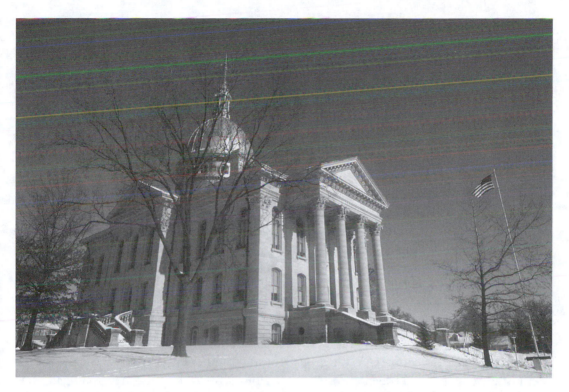

Old Illinois State Capitol, Springfield (Richard Hamilton Smith/Corbis)

Illinois has a combination of partisan and nonpartisan professional staff, most of whom are appointed to serve only the members of their chamber. The Illinois General Assembly employs more than 1,000 full-time staff persons, and legislators are provided year-round staff in Springfield and in the district. All of the professional staff (for individuals, parties, and committees) are controlled by the leadership and can be hired or fired by the leaders.

The Senate usually has about twenty standing committees, while the larger House of Representatives generally has about forty (there were thirty-seven in 2003). Committee members are assigned by the speaker and the minority leader in the House, and the president and the minority leader in the Senate. The speaker and the president of the Senate have the final say.

Processes

The president of the Senate and the speaker of the House preside over sessions in their respective chambers and appoint committee chairs and majority party committee members. The minority leaders of each chamber appoint minority party committee members. In consultation with the majority leaders of their respective houses, the president and speaker determine their chamber agendas.

The Illinois General Assembly convenes annually on the second Wednesday in January. There is no limitation on session length. Legislators generally introduce around 6,000 pieces of legislation in a regular annual session. However, they pass only about 10 percent (around 600) into law. In 2003, the new Democratic governor vetoed 105 of the 600 bills passed by the legislature. Obviously, there are no limits on how many bills an individual legislator can introduce.

The legislature is considered to be full time and year-round, generally ranked behind New York and California (before term limits) in terms of professionalism. The base salary of more than $55,000 a year makes Illinois legislators among the highest paid in the country. With a per diem living expense and travel allowance, their annual salary can exceed $70,000. Few Illinois legislators hold full-time jobs outside the legislature, but many do have alternative sources of income selling insurance, providing legal services, or serving in a local government. While some unusual events led to a turnover rate of almost a quarter in 2002 (scandals and redistricting), membership in the Illinois legislature is generally very stable.

Leadership Structure

The president of the Senate and the speaker of the House are the top leaders of their respective chambers. The Senate and House majority leaders and the Senate and House minority leaders are responsible for managing floor debate for their respective parties. The "leadership teams" go quite deep in each party. For example, House Democrats and Republi-cans each have two deputy leaders and six assistant leaders, as well as a chairperson of the caucus. All of these posts are elected by the party (usually at the will of the top leaders) and serve to help the party gain or maintain their majority status. Because legislators in leadership get an additional salary, more than a third of the members of the Illinois Senate hold some formal leadership title. Many of these leaders get a significant increase in salary for their leadership efforts. For example, the speaker of the House, Senate president, and floor leaders in each chamber get more than $20,000 on top of their legislative salaries.

It is not uncommon for an Illinois legislator to hold a top leadership position for a number of terms. The speaker of the House in 2003, Michael Madigan, had been at his post since 1983, with the exception of one term as minority leader. Senate president Emil Jones, Jr., is in his first term as Senate president after more than a dozen years as minority leader. In addition to having a strong say in the legislative activities, legislative leaders in Illinois are active in the recruitment, development, and financing of party candidates for legislative elections.

Election Processes

Illinois legislators are elected in the November even-year election, with each senator elected to two four-year terms and one two-year term in each ten-year cycle, and all senators elected in the first election following a decennial reapportionment. Because of partisan redistricting, most Illinois legislators face little or no competition in the general election.

The vast majority of districts are safe for one party or the other. When competition does arise, the elections can be rather expensive and bitter. Contested nominations are decided in party primaries.

Prior to 1980, the Illinois House of Representatives had 177 members, each elected from three-member districts using a cumulative voting method whereby voters could cast ballots for three of the four on the ballot. Each of the parties could then put only two of those four candidates on the general election ballot. Therefore, every district usually elected two members from one party and a third from the other. Voters changed that system in 1980 with the only statewide initiative ever passed in the state, called the Cutback Amendment. In 2005, each Senate district included about 210,000 people, and each House member represented about 105,000.

Key Political Factors

While Illinois has historically been a competitive state, the Democratic Party seems to be gaining the upper hand. The state has not supported a Republican president since 1988, and most analysts don't see a change in that trend. In 2002, Democrats took the governor's office and won a majority in the state Senate for the first time in more than a decade. They have controlled the statehouse for all but two of the last twenty years. Cook County and Chicago are strongly Democratic areas and will likely continue to dominate state politics. In 2005 both U.S. senators from Illinois were Democrats, including the first black male since Reconstruction.

On many issues, coalitions revolve around geography more than party. Many issues focus on the distinct needs and problems of the more liberal and urban upstate areas (Chicago and Cook County) and the more conservative suburban areas around Cook County and downstate. Like most everything in Illinois, elections are very partisan. Legislators spend a lot of money running for and winning their offices. Legislative leaders maintain their positions by raising money, recruiting candidates, and making sure that incumbents from their party get reelected. Most contentious votes in the legislature divide along party lines. Even votes that appear regional are often partisan, because Democrats dominate Cook County and the Chicago area, while Republicans do much better in the more rural parts of the state.

Lobbyists are active and important in the Illinois General Assembly. The almost 3,000 registered lobbyists are a primary source of funding for the increasingly expensive campaigns.

Further Reading

Banovetz, James M. 1999. *Governing Illinois: Your Connection to State and Local Government.* 2d ed. Springfield: University of Illinois at Springfield.

Gove, Samuel K., and James D. Nowlan. 1996. *Illinois Politics and Government: The Expanding Metropolitan Frontier.* Lincoln: University of Nebraska Press.

Mooney, Christopher Z., and Barbara Van Dyke-Brown. 2003. *Lobbying Illinois: How You Can Make a Difference in Public Policy.* Springfield, IL: Abraham Lincoln Presidential Center for Governmental Studies.

Van Dyke-Brown, Barbara. 2004. *Almanac of Illinois Politics—2004.* Springfield, IL: Institute for Public Affairs.

INDIANA

● ● ● ● ● ● ● ● ● ● ●

THE INDIANA GENERAL ASSEMBLY

House of Representatives   Senate
100 Representatives   50 Senators
(317) 232–9400
http://www.in.gov/legislative/

● ● ● ● ● ● ● ● ● ● ● ●

From its suburban Chicago northwest, to its Lake Michigan dunes, to the fertile rolling plains in its central portion, to its hilly south bordering the Ohio River and Kentucky, Indiana is one of the most physically diverse of the fifty states. The state has a manufacturing base with influential labor unions, a sizable agricultural sector, and rural southern areas that are closer in lifestyle and perspective to border states than to Indianapolis and Chicago.

While strongly Republican in their presidential preferences (the last Democratic presidential candidate was Lyndon Johnson in his 1964 landslide), Hoosier voters tend to elect almost equal numbers of governors, senators, and congressmen from each party. While the state Senate has remained under Republican control since the 1970s, the state House of Representatives has been very close in partisan breakdown, with Democrats enjoying narrow majorities more often than Republicans in recent decades; on two occasions, there has been an even split in the partisan membership, with the parties sharing leadership positions.

Structure and Membership

The Indiana General Assembly is composed of a 50-member Senate and a 100-member House of Representatives. Following the 1989 session, in which a 50–50 split in the House resulted in stalemate, a move was initiated to add one more member to the chamber so that a tie would not be mathematically possible. However, that effort failed, and the chamber remained at 100 members. Legislators in both chambers represent single-member districts and are elected in the November even-year elections. Senate terms are four years and House terms are two.

While the Senate has remained Republican for more than three decades, the House has been quite balanced since the mid-1980s, with an equal number of each party following the elections of 1988 and 1996. Republicans regained control in 2004.

While women tend to be better represented in lower chambers, that is not the case in the Hoosier State, in which 24 percent of the members in 2003 were female, versus 14 percent in the House. While women held none of the top leadership posts, four of the nineteen committees in the Senate were chaired by women, as were two of the twenty in the House. In 2003 four senators and seven representatives were African American, and one member of the house was Hispanic.

The president pro tempore of the Senate and the speaker of the House have primary responsibility for legislative administration. There are large nonpartisan staff offices (the Legislative Services Agency) that provide bill drafting and budget analysis services to both chambers. Each party caucus also has substantial partisan staff support. The number and competence of both the partisan and nonpartisan staffs have grown significantly in recent years, providing a potential independence from the executive that was not possible in the past.

Although the House has twice as many members as the Senate, the two have a similar number of standing committees. In 2005, the House had nine standing committees and the Senate ten. Each nonbudget standing committee in each chamber has between eight and fourteen members. The majority party usually maintains a majority of two on each standing committee in the closely contested House.

Processes

The first regular session of each two-year General Assembly term convenes on the third Tuesday after the first Monday of November of each even-numbered year. The session must adjourn by April 29 of the following odd-numbered year. The second session of the term commences on the third Tuesday after the first Monday of November in each odd-numbered year and must adjourn by March 14 of the following even-numbered year. Under the rules of the chambers, bills must be introduced by mid-January. In 2003, Indiana legislators introduced almost 1,600 pieces of legislation, while passing fewer than 300. The governor vetoed only 6.

The Indiana General Assembly has historically been, and remains proudly, a rather nonprofessional or "citizen's" legislature. According to the state constitution, the legislature must adjourn by the end of April in odd years and the middle of March in even years. With a base salary of $11,600 annually and a per diem of $112, Indiana legislators make about $20,000. Membership is relatively stable, with the 2002 election yielding a change of 15 percent in the House and 6 percent (3 new members) in the Senate.

Leadership Structure

The lieutenant governor, who is elected on a ticket with the governor, presides over the Senate and has the title of president. But control over the agenda is in the hands of the president pro tempore, who also makes appointments to committees with assistance from the majority leader. The speaker of the House presides over the chamber and makes committee appointments. The speaker and majority leader control the House agenda.

In case of a tie in either chamber, party control will go to the party that wins the governor's race in that year, or the winner of the secretary of state race if there is no election for governor. In 1996, Democrats controlled the tied House because Democrat Frank O'Bannon was elected governor of the state.

Because the lieutenant governor, who is elected with the governor and is not necessarily of the majority party in the Senate, presides, the president pro tempore and the majority leader jointly lead the floor debate and organize and develop

---

Got Government? No, Thank You

For two years, 1863 to 1864, constitutional government in Indiana did not exist. As the Civil War continued and dissatisfaction with Governor Oliver P. Morton grew, he and the legislature were unable to work together. The legislature stopped meeting as taxes went uncollected and funds unappropriated. Governor Morton used his own personal credit to finance state and military operations from 1863 to 1864. However, neither the legislators nor the public seems to have held a grudge. The front of the capitol building today has a large statue of Morton, flanked by two Union soldiers.

---

party positions. With the speaker presiding, the House majority leader handles the primary in the coordination of floor debate.

The Senate and House minority leaders are the leaders for their respective parties and coordinate floor debate and the development of party positions. The majority and minority parties in each chamber have a number of assistant and deputy leaders who assist their chamber's top leadership.

For the last twenty years of the twentieth century, leadership in the Indiana Senate has been defined by stability. Robert D. Garton was first elected president pro tempore in 1981 and remained in that post in 2005. He was selected to the post following scandals in the leadership office of previous Senate leaders. As a result of the partisan turnover in the House, leadership has been much less stable, with five different speakers since 1990.

Election Processes

The Senate's four-year terms are staggered, with half of the senators elected in each November even-year election. With House members serving two-year terms, the entire House of Representatives is elected in each November even-year election. The average Senate district is just over 120,000 people, and the average House district is about half that number. Contested nominations are decided in party primaries.

Campaigns for the Indiana House and Senate have become significantly more costly in recent years, and the ability to get members of their party elected has become a critical component of leadership, especially in the House. Legislative leaders have become more and more concerned with recruiting and providing financial support for legislative candidates. Republican and Democratic caucuses in both chambers raise and distribute a significant amount of money in efforts to get their candidates elected.

Key Political Factors

The recent history of Indiana's state legislative elections has been quite consistent, with Republicans enjoying substantial majority control of the Senate, and control of the House almost always up for grabs. Most experts see Hoosier political views as being moderate to conservative, and many Democratic legislative leaders attribute their party's success in legislative elections to advocating positions and policies somewhat more conservative than those of the national party and taking care of the local constituents.

Partisanship is very important in Indiana legislative politics, especially in the House, where neither party has enjoyed a majority of more than eight seats for almost two decades. The Indiana Democratic coalition of urban legislators from Indianapolis and Ft. Wayne and rural legislators from southern Indiana has, at times, been difficult to hold together. The Republican caucus faces a similar challenge in trying to unite its legislators from the suburbs around Chicago, Ft. Wayne, and Indianapolis with some more conservative rural members in the small towns and less populated southern parts of the state. In the end, the close party balance has provided the incentive for party members to put aside geographic and ideological differences in the name of party unity.

While lobbyists do have to register if they intend to attempt to influence legislation, Indiana does not limit how much lobbyists can spend on legislators during a session. However, the more than 1,400 registered lobbyists are restricted from making campaign contributions during the legislative session.

Further Reading

Borst, Lawrence William. 2003. *Gentlemen, It's Been My Pleasure: Four Decades in the Indiana Legislature.* Indianapolis: Emmis.

Eisenstein, Maurice, ed. 1999. *Indiana Politics and Public Policy.* Needham Heights, MA: Simon and Schuster.

IOWA

● ● ● ● ● ● ● ● ● ● ● ●

THE IOWA GENERAL ASSEMBLY

House of Representatives	Senate
100 Representatives	60 Senators
(515) 281–5381	(515) 281–5307

http://www.legis.state.ia.us

● ● ● ● ● ● ● ● ● ● ● ●

Perhaps best known for its fields of corn and its "field of dreams," more recently, Iowa has become one of the nation's leaders in the insurance industry, with the corporate headquarters of a number of large insurance companies now located in the state. The state also has two major research universities in Iowa State and University of Iowa. ISU is an international leader in the field of biotechnology, developing technologies that are changing the world.

Politically, Iowa is more competitive than one might expect. In many ways it is a microcosm of the country as a whole. The Democratic presidential candidate carried the state in 1988, 1992, 1996, and 2000. During that period, Republicans were more successful in state and congressional elections. Both parties have controlled the legislature, which has also, at times, been under split control. In 2004, Democratic governor Tom Vilsack, a former state legislator, was reportedly

---

Legislator Meets Secretary on the Chamber Floor

Apart from the elected leaders, members of the Iowa House and Senate do not have office space in the capitol. Instead, legislators conduct their business on the floor at their chamber desk. Each senator is provided one clerical staff person during session who has a smaller desk beside the senator on the floor. Beside each of the 100 desks in the House and 50 desks in the Senate is a file cabinet with a pull-out top and a chair. Lobbyists also are tight for space—their briefcases can be seen piled on two large tables outside the chamber or under benches or in cubicles in the law library.

---

strongly considered as a possible vice presidential nominee. In 2004, Democrats gained a tie in the Senate and moved within two seats of the Republicans in the House.

Structure and Membership

The Iowa General Assembly consists of a 50-member Senate and a 100-member House of Representatives. Senate members are elected for four-year terms, and House members are elected for two-year terms from single-member districts. Increasing Republican strength in the General Assembly was halted and reversed with Democratic gains in 2004. As the 2005 session began, the Senate had an equal number of Democrats and Republicans, and Republicans held a two-seat margin in the House.

A quarter of the house members are female, but only 14 percent of the Senate membership. Still, leaders such as past president of the Senate Mary Kramer have made strides. In light of the homogeneous population, it is of little surprise that there are few (less than 3 percent) African Americans in the Iowa General Assembly and no Hispanic members.

Iowa is one of a growing number of states in which the lieutenant governor has no formal role with the legislative branch. The Senate elects a president from its membership to preside over its sessions and oversee the chamber's administration. However, the most significant decisions are made by the majority leader, who is elected by the majority caucus. The speaker of the House presides over its sessions and is responsible for the chamber's administration. Each chamber has a similar number of committees to facilitate its lawmaking. In 2005, there were seventeen standing committees in the House and sixteen in the Senate. Committees in Iowa are not required to act on every bill.

Nonpartisan professional staff services are provided by a legislative services agency that operates under the general direction of the Joint Legislative Council. Each party caucus also has a small number of professional partisan staff. Staff to support individual legislators is provided during session only.

Processes

There are no constitutional limits on the length of session, but per diem compensation is limited to 110 days in odd years and 100 days in even-numbered years. Seldom does the legislature go beyond those limits. In 2003, the legislature was in session for 109 calendar days. The legislature may be called into a special session, called an "extraordinary session," by the governor or a two-thirds vote of each chamber.

Committee appointments are made by the majority and minority leaders, for their respective parties in the Senate, and by the speaker in the House of Representatives. The Senate majority leader and the speaker determine the agendas for their respective houses.

The Iowa General Assembly meets annually, convening on the second Monday of each January, with no limitations on session length. There are no limits on the number of bills that individual legislators can introduce, nor dates by which they must be introduced. However, both chambers set deadlines by which bills must be voted out of committee, a specific period when chambers will consider bills generated in their own chamber, a date by which bills from one chamber must be submitted to the other chamber for consideration, and a period during which each chamber will consider only bills submitted by the other chamber. Legislators in Iowa refer to this narrowing down process as "the funnel."

During the 2003 legislative session, members of the Iowa General Assembly passed only 183 of the 1,160 bills introduced by its members. Most of the bills never made it out of committee, much less to the other chamber. The Democratic governor vetoed 12 of the bills passed by the Republican chambers. The 2004 session was a bit more contentious, with the Republican legislature overriding more than a dozen vetoes in one day.

When it comes to legislative professionalism, the Iowa General Assembly is generally in the middle. Its salaries are reasonable—a base salary of about $20,000, with per diem and travel allotments that can push the annual total above $30,000 annually. The speaker and floor leaders in the House, as well as the president and floor leaders in the Senate, make an additional $10,000 annually. While individual staff is limited, the institutional and nonpartisan staff is quite strong. The legislature employs about 180 full-time staff each year, including the Legislative Services Bureau, the Fiscal Services Bureau, the Computer Services Bureau, and a citizen's aide, or ombudsman. However, turnover is generally quite stable, except following a round of redistricting. Following the last redistricting (the election of 2002) almost 40 percent of the legislators were new.

On another positive note, the Iowa General Assembly is on the cutting edge of legislative technology. With this system, legislators have at their fingertips up-to-the-minute information on bill status, bill analysis, employee salaries, and bill amendments, as well as daily deposits and withdrawal activity from all Iowa General Fund accounts. One application, called Billbook, allows the user to see the bill and amendments together with the amendments linked to the appropriate part of the original bill. All legislators are supplied with laptops, and the entire building has a wireless network.

Leadership Structure

The president of the Senate and the speaker of the House preside over their respective chambers. However, the president of the Senate shares significant power with the majority leader. Indeed, the majority leader of the Senate has the final say on committee member and chair assignments as well as bill assignment. In the House, the speaker has the power to make these decisions, although he or she generally consults with the leader of the minority party on committee assignments.

The majority and minority leaders of each chamber are responsible for managing floor debate for their respective parties. The majority and minority parties in each chamber each have several assistant leaders. These assistant leaders generally assist with vote counting, floor management, agenda development, coalition building, and campaign-related activities.

Election Processes

Iowa legislators are elected in the November even-year election, with half of the members of the Senate elected to their four-year terms in each even-year election. Contested nominations are decided in party primaries. Each senator represents about 60,000 constituents and each House member about 30,000. Each senatorial district includes two House districts, because the constitution states that each House district must exist wholly in a senatorial district.

Unlike almost every other state, Iowa's decennial reapportionment is undertaken with no political considerations concerning incumbents or current district lines. This produces a larger than normal turnover for a non–term limited state in the first election under each new apportionment plan. The Legislative Services Board gets three tries at developing districts that will gain the support of the legislature. If that is not completed by December 31 of the year following the census, the districts are drawn by the Iowa supreme court.

Key Political Factors

Iowa can be expected to remain a barometer state in presidential elections, and a highly competitive state in elections for all offices. Control of the legislature can be expected to be up for grabs in most elections. While the Republicans hold a comfortable lead in both chambers, Democrats, with a strong presence statewide (governor and senator in 2004), will make the elections competitive.

Within the legislature, both caucuses struggle with unity. The Republican caucus includes many members from traditionally rural and conservative areas of the Hawkeye State, as well as a growing number of members from suburban districts. Democrats sometimes find it difficult to balance the demands of their urban, more liberal members and those of the old-line rural Democrats.

While lobbyists play a critical informational role in Iowa because of the limited staff, there are important restrictions on their activities. According to the rules of the General Assembly, they must register with the secretary of the Senate or the chief clerk of the House. Furthermore, they must indicate the issues of importance to them or their clients, as well as the identification numbers of the bills they expect to lobby. Also, no former member, staff person, or other government official can serve as a lobbyist for two years after leaving a government job. Apart from a few exceptions (plaques, funeral flowers, wedding or anniversary gifts, for example), gifts that lobbyists give to legislators cannot exceed a value of $3 per day!

Further Reading

Schenken, Suzanne O'Dea. 1995. *Legislators and Politicians: Iowa's Women Lawmakers*. Ames: Iowa State University Press.

Schweider, Dorothy. 1996. *Iowa: The Middle Land*. Ames: Iowa State University Press.

KANSAS

• • • • • • • • • • • •

THE KANSAS LEGISLATURE

House of Representatives
125 Representatives

Senate
40 Senators

(515) 281–5011
http://www.kslegislature.org/

• • • • • • • • • • • • •

Kansas first became famous as a bloody battleground territory between pro- and antislavery settlers in the years leading up to the Civil War. It eventually entered the Union as a free state in 1861. Today, the Kansas economy is dependent primarily on manufacturing and services rather than agriculture.

Like most of its neighboring Great Plains states, Kansas leans strongly Republican. It has voted for the Democratic presidential candidate only once since the middle of the twentieth century (Lyndon Johnson in his 1964 landslide victory). Democratic candidates have fared much better in other elections, however, winning a number of gubernatorial elections and control of one or both chambers of the state legislature on occasion.

Structure and Membership

The Kansas legislature consists of a 40-member state Senate and a 125-member House of Representatives. Senators serve four-year terms and House members serve two-year terms. Republicans retain strong control over both chambers, generally holding at least a two-to-one majority in both. In 2003, they held a 35-seat majority (80 to 45) in the House and a 20-seat advantage (30 to 10) in the Senate.

The president of the Senate is elected by the membership and presides over its sessions. The speaker of the House presides over House sessions. The Kansas legislature also has an increasingly strong and important committee system. The fourteen Senate and twenty-one House standing committees take significant actions on bills and seldom send a bill to the floor without an expectation that it will pass. Increasingly, committees are completely redoing bills and submitting them to the floor as "committee substitutes," sponsored by the committee rather than the individual legislator who initially submitted the bill.

Women have historically done well in the Kansas government, with the election of female governors, senators, and a significant portion of state legislators. In recent

The Tricameral Legislature

The Kansas legislature once had three chambers: a Senate and two Houses. After thirty years of Republican domination in Kansas, the Populists were swept into office in the election of 1892. Both parties claimed control of the House. Rather than compromise, the floor leaders of each party called the House to order. In effect, Kansas had two Houses meeting in the same room.

On the morning of February 15, 1893, the Republicans marched from their headquarters to find the House chamber locked. It was soon smashed open with axes and sledgehammers. The governor called out the state militia to restore order. In two days the hostilities subsided. The Republicans continued to meet in Representative Hall, while the Populists found a different room in the capitol. On February 25, 1893, the Supreme Court held that the Republican House was the legal body.

years, women have held about a quarter of the seats in the Kansas legislature and a comparable number of committee chair posts. In 2003, they held 28 percent of the seats in the House and 22 percent in the Senate. Historically, the proportion of minority legislators in Kansas has been very low. However, that is gradually changing. The 2003 legislative session witnessed nine minority legislators in the House and three in the Senate.

Professional staff services are provided by a nonpartisan legislative research department and revisor office for bill drafting that operates under the direction of the Joint Legislative Coordinating Council, which is also responsible for legislative administration. The Senate president and the House speaker alternate as chair and vice chair of the council, whose other members are the majority and minority leaders of each house and the speaker pro tempore of the House.

Processes

The Kansas legislature convenes annually on the second Monday in January. In odd-numbered years, there is no limitation on session length, although they seldom extend past ninety days. Even-year sessions are limited to ninety calendar days unless extended by a two-thirds vote of each house.

Leaders of the Kansas legislature establish various deadlines for bill introduction during the session, including dates by which members must prefile legislation, by which bills must be considered in the house of origin, and dates by which bills must be considered by the second chamber. During the 2003 session, Kansas legislators introduced 758 bills, passing a little under 20 percent of them (160). The Democratic governor vetoed 14 of the 160.

Relative to other states, the Kansas legislature is considered rather nonprofessional. When you combine a daily salary, per diem living expenses, and travel expenses, Kansas legislators are unlikely to earn more than $20,000 a year. Their legislative session seldom lasts longer than three months, and there are more legislators in the House (125) than full-time staff members (120) in the entire legislature. Individual legislators are provided staff support during the legislative session, and freshman House members have to share one staff person among three legislators. These office managers are hired on a full-time basis, but only for the length of the legislative session. Individual legislators rely heavily on legislative staff members from caucus leadership offices for support. Interns, normally college students or law students, also assist in the legwork necessary to make a legislative office function. House turnover is usually around a quarter each election cycle, more the result of voluntary retirement than electoral defeat.

Leadership Structure

The Senate president presides over Senate sessions, and the House speaker presides over House sessions. The speaker controls the size, number, and composition of standing committees and can create and appoint select committees for special circumstances that may arise. The speaker also directly appoints committee chairs in that chamber. The House speaker and majority leader determine the House agenda.

Senate committee chairs and members are appointed by the Committee on Organization, Calendar and Rules (OCR). When the majority party meets to caucus and elect leaders in December of each election year, before session, they also vote on members running for OCR. The president and majority leader determine the Senate agenda.

The majority and minority leaders of each house are responsible for managing floor debate for their respective parties. There are several majority and minority assistant leaders in each chamber. The leadership team for each party consists of at least six legislators in each chamber.

While neither leaders nor members are term limited, House and Senate majority party leaders generally serve no more than two terms at any given post. This also may reflect the conflict between the two party factions, in that there is more turnover among Republican leaders than among the minority Democratic Party leaders, who have not followed the two term and out approach.

Election Processes

Kansas legislators are elected in the November even-year election. Members of the state House of Representatives are elected in each even-year election. Members of the state Senate are elected to their four-year terms in the presidential election years. Contested nominations are determined in party primary elections. Because of the partisan redistricting process, most legislative districts are generally safe for one party or the other, with the significant competition taking place in the primary.

Compared with other states, legislators in Kansas represent rather small legislative districts. Legislative districts in the House contain about 20,000 citizens, and senators represent around 50,000. This small size makes it possible for legislators to win elections with relatively limited resources. Furthermore, it enables legislators to build a pretty positive and personal relationship with the district, fending off electoral competition with personal popularity. However, because of the low pay, legislators do not traditionally make legislative service a career, but voluntarily retire, leaving a significant portion of open seat elections each election cycle.

Key Political Factors

While Kansas is a predominantly Republican state, the state's Democratic Party remains competitive and capable of winning elections. With occasional exceptions, the Republican Party continues to win control of the state legislature. However, because of a growing division within the Republican Party between the moderates and conservatives, dominance of the Republican Party in the legislature can be exaggerated.

This dynamic has led some to describe Kansas as a "three-party state." Indeed, following the 2000 census, a coalition of conservative Republicans and Democrats in the Senate formed a coalition to defeat the redistricting plan proposed by the moderate leadership and pass one of their own. This intraparty conflict appears in the Republican primaries for statewide offices, state legislative races, and campaigns for state legislative leadership.

Even though there is no limit on session length in odd-year sessions of the Kansas legislature, session periods are not extensive. Members receive only a modest per diem compensation when the legislature is in regular session, and almost all members devote the majority of their time to a private-sector occupation.

While the limited staff and resources available to legislators in Kansas would suggest a strong role for lobbyists, that does not appear to be the case. Lobbyists in Kansas are limited to giving each individual legislator gifts of no more than $40 value each year, recreation activities valued at no more than $100 a year, and honoraria or financial gifts of no more than $200 per year. All lobbyists must also register with the legislature before each session in which they intend to attempt to influence legislation.

Further Reading

Frederickson, H. George. 1994. *Public Policy and the Two States of Kansas.* Lawrence: University Press of Kansas.

Kansas Legislative Research Department. 2004. *Legislative Procedure Manual.* (http://skyways.lib.ks.us/ksleg/KLRD /about/legproc.pdf).

Loomis, Burdett. 1994. *Time, Politics and Policy: A Legislative Year.* Lawrence: University Press of Kansas.

KENTUCKY

• • • • • • • • • • • •

THE KENTUCKY GENERAL ASSEMBLY

House of Representatives	Senate
100 Representatives	38 Senators

(502) 564–8100
http://www.lrc.state.ky.us

• • • • • • • • • • • •

Kentucky was the first state west of the Alleghenies to be settled by American pioneers. While the state remained part of the Union during the Civil War, it was a slave-holding state with conflicting loyalties. Parts of the state remain very "Southern" in economy, culture, and manner. While much of the state's economy has diversified from its agricultural and mining roots, the mountain regions struggle with lower education levels and high unemployment.

Politically, Kentucky has, over the past half-century, been slowly transforming itself from a heavily Democratic state to one that is predominantly Republican. Democrats have been able to retain control of at least one house of the state's legislature and the congressional delegation through seniority, leadership, and effective redistricting. However, Republicans have made significant gains in statewide races, particularly for governor and the U.S. Senate. In 2005 it had a Republican governor, a Republican majority in the state Senate, two Republican U.S. senators, and a congressional delegation with one Democrats and five Republicans.

Structure and Membership

The Kentucky General Assembly consists of a 38-member Senate and a 100-member House of Representatives. Senators are elected to four-year terms and House members serve two-year terms. Both are elected from single-member districts.

The president of the Senate presides over Senate sessions and is responsible for the chamber's administration. The speaker of the House presides over its sessions and is responsible for House administration. Republicans took the majority of the Kentucky Senate in 2000 for the first time, after more than a century of Democratic control. Democrats continue to hold a majority in the House of Representatives.

While Kentucky has had a female governor, and a female legislator, as early as 1922, women continue to be very underrepresented in the state legislature. In 2003 only 11 of the 100 house members were female, and just 4 of the 38 senators. In the same year only 1 of the 16 top leaders in the House and Senate was female (the majority whip of the Senate), but they did chair four of the Senate's thirteen committees and one of the seventeen committees in the House. An African American legislator was first elected to the Kentucky General Assembly in 1963, and African Americans serve in both chambers.

The bipartisan, sixteen-member Legislative Research Commission composed of Senate and House leaders oversees a staff that provides professional nonpartisan services to both chambers. They are responsible for committee staffing, bill drafting, oversight of the state budget and educational reform, production of educational materials, maintenance of a reference library and Internet site, and the preparation and printing of research reports, informational bulletins, and a legislative newspaper. Leadership offices are fully staffed year-round, and rank-and-file legislators also have access to shared clerical staff, which is increased during the session. Each standing committee also has full-time staff support. Each house has a small number of partisan staff assistants.

The House usually has around sixteen standing committees and the Senate about a dozen. Members and chairs in both chambers are assigned by the respective Committee on Committees in each chamber, which consists of the presiding officer pro tempore, floor leaders and majority whips, and the majority caucus chair in each chamber, plus the minority

---

Have Gun, Will Not Travel to Kentucky Legislature

Like legislators in every state, newly elected members of the Kentucky legislature take an oath of office on the first day of the legislative session following their election, in which they swear to support and uphold the state constitution and faithfully execute the duties of their office. However, the oath in the Blue Grass State is a bit unusual. Since 1850, Kentucky legislators have had to swear that they "have not fought a duel with deadly weapons within this state nor out of it, with a citizen of this state" or "acted as second in carrying a challenge nor aided or assisted any person thus offending." In 1891, the oath was amended to remove the condition that the duel not involve another Kentuckian. Apparently, between 1850 and 1891, it was alright to duel with someone from outside the state!

---

floor leader. From the time that the General Assembly adjourns (usually late spring) until it reconvenes is called the Interim. During that period the work of the General Assembly is conducted by interim joint committees, formed from the standing committees of both chambers, and special committees appointed by the LRC to study particular issues during the Interim. The special and interim joint committees may profile bills for the pending legislative session and make recommendations to the body, but they cannot act on any legislation.

Processes

The Kentucky General Assembly meets annually, convening on the first Tuesday after the first Monday in January. According to the state constitution, sessions in even-numbered years may not last more than sixty legislative days and cannot extend beyond April 15. In odd-numbered years, sessions may not last more than thirty legislative days and cannot extend beyond March 30. That is quite rare, with the "short" session immediately following the election and the "long" session" in the year of the next election. This dif-

ference stems from the days when the Kentucky legislature met biennially (every two years), meeting one year after the election so that new members could "get their feet wet" before tackling the budget.

While these dates may vary a bit, in even-numbered years (sixty-day session), all bills usually must be introduced by the fourteenth day in each chamber. The fifty-seventh and fifty-eighth days are reserved for consideration of concurring amendments and conference committee reports. The fifty-ninth and sixtieth days are reserved for considering executive vetoes. During the 2005 (short) session, members of the Kentucky General Assembly introduced 741 pieces of legislation. Of those, 159 were enacted, with 14 vetoed by the Republican governor. None of those vetoes were overridden. In 2004 (long session), 999 bills were introduced, with 165 passing and 13 vetoes. Again, none were overridden.

The Kentucky General Assembly is usually considered to be closer to a part-time legislature than to a professional full-time one. During the sixty-day session, legislators are paid a little over $250 in salary and living expenses for each calendar day (if the legislature meets Monday through Friday of a week, legislators are also paid for Saturday and Sunday). During the long session, that would equate to a little over $20,000 a year. During the short session, it would be half that amount. While the Legislative Research Council provides strong and professional institutional staff, the total staff for the entire legislature is about 350. Individual legislators share clerical staff year-round that is increased during the session. Most legislators in Kentucky of necessity have additional sources of income outside the legislature.

Leadership Structure

The Senate president is officially the top leadership position in the Senate, and the speaker of the House is the top leader of the House of Representatives. The speaker of the House and president of the Senate do not possess sole power to appoint committee members and assign committee chairs, however, as is common in most states. They share these responsibilities with their majority leaders, majority whip, pro tempore, caucus chairs, and minority leaders as members of the Committee on Committees.

The Senate president and the speaker of the House preside over sessions in their respective chambers and, in consultation with the majority floor leaders of their houses, determine their chamber agendas. House and Senate leadership also includes a caucus chair and whip for each party.

The Senate majority floor leader, the House majority floor leader, and the Senate and House minority floor leaders are responsible for managing floor debate for their respective parties. Kentucky's top legislative leaders often hold their positions for several terms.

Election Processes

Kentucky legislative (odd-year) elections are generally low-cost contests with the vast majority of incumbents winning re-election handily, with a few exceptions. In selective competitive elections, candidates for the House can spend more then $80,000. All one hundred House seats are up for election every two years, with half of the thirty-eight Senate seats up every two years. Senators serve four-year terms. Kentucky Senate districts usually include just over 100,000 people, while House districts include about 40,000. Candidates for state legislature must live in the state for six years prior to seeking the office. This provision seldom matters, but in 2004 the residency of one Republican candidate who received more votes than his Democratic opponent was challenged. The case set off a battle between the courts and the Senate that challenged the traditional separation of powers associated with representative democracy in America.

Key Political Factors

Kentucky can be expected to continue its movement toward becoming a predominantly Republican state, with Republicans posing greater challenges for control of the once Democrat-dominated legislature. As in most Southern states, Kentucky Democrats have struggled to piece together a coalition of urban Democrats (Lexington and Louisville) and traditional conservative Democrats from the more rural towns and communities in the state. Republicans have made significant gains in recent years as rural conservative voters have increasingly voted, and sometimes registered, Republican.

Democrats have managed to maintain control of the House, while Republicans now control the Senate and other statewide offices. Once controlling both legislative chambers, Democrats were able to control the process of legislative redistricting and had used that power to their advantage. Republicans have now seen their star rise, while many of the Democratic legislators are conservative in views, values, and politics, with little resemblance to their national Democratic counterparts.

Given the limited personal staff available to legislators in Kentucky, one can expect that the more than 600 registered lobbyists will play an active role in the policymaking process. They provide information to legislators but are restricted to spending no more than $100 on entertaining any single legislator during a given year; all expenditures must be fully disclosed.

Further Reading

Jewell, Malcolm K., and Penny M. Miller. 1988. *The Kentucky Legislature: Two Decades of Change.* Lexington: University of Kentucky Press.

Miller, Penny M. 2003. *Kentucky Politics and Government: Do We Stand United?* Lincoln: University of Nebraska Press.

LOUISIANA

• • • • • • • • • • • •

THE LOUISIANA LEGISLATURE

House of Representatives
105 Representatives

Senate
39 Senators

(225) 342–2456
http://www.legis.state.la.us/

• • • • • • • • • • • •

Louisiana, the land of Mardi Gras, Cajun cuisine, and Huey Long, is a state unlike any other. But it is also very unlike the state that fought as part of the Confederacy a century and a half ago. While the Civil War shattered the state's plantation economy, the rise of forestry and the discovery of sulfur in the postwar period—and the later discovery of oil and natural gas, of which Louisiana is today a major U.S. producer—have given the Louisiana of today a very diverse economy.

While Louisiana's Republican Party has grown from a nonfactor in state politics to a major force that wins its share of state and congressional contests, the state has become highly competitive rather than predominantly Republican as have a number of its neighbors. In the nine presidential elections between 1968 and 2000, the state voted for the Republican candidate five times. The other four times it supported Southern candidates—independent George Wallace from Alabama in 1968, Georgian Jimmy Carter in 1976, and Arkansan Bill Clinton in 1992 and 1996. Louisiana Republicans have been least successful in making inroads into the long Democratic domination in the state's legislature, in which the Democrats have

Louisiana State Capitol (Richard Hamilton Smith/Corbis)

held strong majorities in both chambers since the Reconstruction era. In 2004, Louisianans elected their first Republican U.S. senator in the history of the state.

Structure and Membership

The Louisiana legislature consists of a 39-member Senate and a 105-member House of Representatives. All Louisiana legislators are elected from single-member districts for four-year terms. While Republicans have made significant inroads in the state, Democrats hold comfortable margins in both legislative chambers.

While female legislators make up just less than a sixth of the membership in each chamber, they are well represented among the leadership. In 2003, the pro

tempores of both chambers were female, as was one of the House committee chairs. About one in five members of the Louisiana legislature is African American (22 percent in 2005), but there are no Hispanic members.

The president of the Senate presides over Senate sessions and is responsible for that chamber's administration. The speaker of the House presides over its sessions and is responsible for House administration. Each house of the legislature has a nonpartisan staff office that provides professional staff services to its members. The House Legislative Staff (HLS) serves the members and the standing committees of that body, as does the Senate Legislative Services in that chamber. Individual legislators are budgeted

---

Only in Louisiana

For a variety of political, historical, and geographic reasons, politics in Louisiana is perhaps unique. While all other legislatures hold spring or summer primaries or caucuses to narrow the field of candidates before the general election, Louisiana holds bipartisan primary elections in November and then holds runoffs a month later if no candidate gets more than 50 percent of the vote. Most states elect their members in even-numbered years, but Louisiana voters go to the polls in odd-numbered years. While leaders in other legislatures often compete with the governor, governors in Louisiana are actually very involved in leadership elections. The Louisiana capitol, unlike almost all other state capitols, has no dome; instead, it is a thirty-four-story skyscraper.

$2,000 to $3,000 a month to hire as many staffers as they wish, and each regional caucus is allocated one full-time staff member for its members. Each house also has a small number of partisan staff assistants for leaders and individual members.

The Louisiana Senate usually has fewer than twenty standing committees. Each committee includes six to ten senators. The Louisiana House is organized into a similar number of standing committees, with each committee including between ten and twenty members. Each chamber has a number of select committees appointed each session by the speaker in the House and the president in the Senate.

The Louisiana legislature also has several organized caucuses, including a Women's Caucus, a Black Caucus, a Rural Caucus, and an Independent Caucus. Each of these caucuses is provided a room to meet, one full-time staff person, and one intern by the legislature. With the exception of the Independent Caucus, each meets regularly and takes positions on various issues each session. The Rural Caucus, with its increasingly Republican membership from northern Louisiana, is particularly active and influential. The

House of Representatives is also provided space and clerical support if requested for three regional delegations: the Orleans Delegation, the Acadiana Delegation, and the Jefferson Delegation.

Louisiana legislators are limited to serving a maximum of three consecutive terms in their chamber. Term-limited legislators who have been out of office for one four-year term are eligible to run again. The first class affected by term limits will be forced out in 2008.

Processes

The Louisiana legislature meets annually. Even-year sessions convene on the last Monday in March in those years, with the session limited to a maximum of sixty legislative days within a period of eighty-five calendar days. Odd-year sessions convene on the last Monday in April and are limited to a maximum of forty-five legislative days within a period of sixty calendar days. Odd-year sessions are limited to consideration of fiscal matters.

In 2003, members of the Louisiana legislature introduced 3,166 pieces of legislation, passing 1,307 of them in both chambers. Fifteen of those bills were vetoed by the governor.

The Louisiana legislature is generally considered to be in the middle of the legislative professionalism scale. With its relatively high turnover rate of about 30 percent each cycle and constitutionally restricted sessions, it has some qualities of a part-time legislature. On the other hand, with base salary, per diem, and expense allowance, members earn in excess of $30,000 in a long session year, and the legislature has a highly effective professional staff of more than 400 people. These qualities are often associated with a more professional legislature.

Leadership Structure

The Senate president is officially the top leadership position in the Senate and the speaker of the House is the top leader of the House of Representatives. They are the primary architects of the agenda in each chamber. The bodies elect a Senate president pro tempore and a House speaker pro tempore to preside in the absence of the president or speaker. There are no majority or minority leaders in either house of the Louisiana legislature. Neither chamber formally elects floor leaders, whips, or assistant leaders. Partisanship has little, if any, impact on the nature of leadership in the Louisiana legislature.

Since the days of Huey Long, Louisiana's governor has exercised perhaps more influence than any other state governor in the selection of the top leaders of the legislature. It is the regular practice when a new governor takes office for an incumbent Senate president or House speaker to be replaced by a member of the chamber more to the governor's liking. Some Democratic governors have even been successful in securing the election of a Republican president or speaker even in the face of overwhelming Democratic majorities.

Because of the influence that Louisiana's governors wield over leadership selection, the tenures of the state's Senate president and House speaker tend to be short, often lasting for only a single four-year term, depending on the gubernatorial election.

Election Processes

Louisiana has a unique election system. Candidates from both parties as well as independent candidates run in an open primary, with the top two vote-getters (assuming no one receives more than 50 percent) facing each other in a run-off. It is not uncommon for the run-off to include two candidates of the same party. Candidates' party affiliations are listed on the ballot. All Louisiana legislators are elected to their four-year terms in the November nonpresidential odd-year election preceding the presidential election year. Their terms run concurrently with that of the governor, who is elected at the same time.

Each Louisiana senator is elected from a district of just under 120,000, while each member of the House represents about 45,000 people.

Key Political Factors

Historically, politics in this one-party Democratic state have been defined much more by values and the culture of voters in each region than by political party. Legislators were more likely to divide along regional lines (New Orleans versus northern Louisiana, for example) than by partisanship. Northern Louisiana tends to be more conservative, traditional Bible-belt Southerners, while voters in Acadiana Parish and New Orleans tend to be more ethnically diverse and moderate in their views. Neither legislative party formally selects floor leaders or whips, and Republicans and Democrats are selected to be chairs and vice chairs of standing committees, regardless of who holds the majority.

However, this bipartisanship (or nonpartisanship) is changing. The strength of the Louisiana Republican Party can be expected to continue to grow. While control of the state legislature remains firmly in Democratic hands, that control could be threatened in years to come. House Republicans began to meet as an organized caucus a few years ago, but the Democrats organized for the first time in 2005.

While the state has undergone a great deal of change since Huey Long could change the votes of legislators from his desk in the governor's office, most of Louisiana's governors continue to exercise as much or more influence over decisionmaking in the state's legislature as any of their counterparts in the other forty-nine states.

While the legislature is well staffed, lobbyists still play a significant role in educating and informing members of the Louisiana legislature. The more than 500 registered lobbyists are not limited in how much they spend to influence the decisions of legislators.

Further Reading

Bullock, Charles S., and Mark J. Rozell, eds. 2002. *New Politics of the Old South: An Introduction to Southern Politics.* 2d ed. Lanham, MD: Rowman and Littlefield.

Parent, Wayne. 2004. *Inside the Carnival: Unmasking Louisiana Politics.* Baton Rouge: Louisiana State University Press.

MAINE

• • • • • • • • • • • • •

The Maine Legislature

House of Representatives
151 Representatives

Senate
35 Senators

(207) 624–9494
http://www.janus.state.me.us/legis

• • • • • • • • • • • • •

Maine, the nation's easternmost state, consumes almost half of the land area of New England while providing less than one-tenth of its population. Renowned for its seafood and potatoes, the state abounds in natural assets. Its seacoast, lakes, and inland mountains make it a popular vacation spot.

The "District of Maine" was initially part of the Commonwealth of Massachusetts until granted her charter in 1819. Statehood was considered as early as 1786, when a delegation from the region considered, but rejected, a proposal to petition for statehood. From 1786 until 1806, citizens of the region voted three times to reject statehood. Finally, they voted in the affirmative in 1816, putting in motion the wheels for statehood three years later. Finally free of Massachusetts, the members of the Maine legislature decided to build a capitol much like the one they had just broken away from, going so far as to hire the very architect who had designed the Boston masterpiece.

Until the second half of the twentieth century, Maine was a conservative Republican bastion (it was one of only two states won by Republican Alf Landon in his landslide loss to Franklin Roosevelt in 1936). That has decidedly changed over the past half-century, as Maine has become a swing state in which Republicans and Democrats enjoy roughly the same electoral success. The state's voters have demonstrated a penchant for independence in recent years, electing an independent candidate as its governor three times since the mid-1970s and giving Independent Ross Perot his largest state vote percentage in 1992.

Structure and Membership

The Maine Senate is composed of 35 members, and its House of Representatives of 151. Legislators are elected from single-member districts for two-year terms in even-numbered years and are limited to serving a maximum four terms in each chamber. Legislative term limits were passed in 1993 and took effect with the 1996 election. Administrative responsibility for the legislature rests with the Legislative Council, which is composed of the ten elected members of the legislative leadership (five from each chamber). The chair of the council rotates between the Senate and House for each two-year term. The Legislative Council is responsible for all aspects of legislative administration, including the legislature's budget and facilities and nonpartisan staff services, which are coordinated by an executive director.

A unique feature of Maine's legislative process relates to its committee system. Like its New England neighboring legislatures in Connecticut and Massachusetts, Maine uses a joint committee system with members of both chambers sitting together to consider legislation. Each committee has two chairs, one from the House and one from the Senate. In 2003, the Maine legislature had seventeen joint standing committees.

Following the 1994 elections, Democrats held a one-seat majority in the House and Republicans a one-seat majority in the Senate. Since then Democrats have gained solid control of the House but have found getting a handle on the Senate a bit more tricky. For much of the last decade, the Senate has been relatively balanced between Republicans and Democrats, with Democrats holding a significant majority (20 Democrats to 14 Republicans and 1 Independent) only in the 1999–2000 legislative session. Following the 2002 elections, Democrats held a sixteen-seat majority (82 Democrats to 66 Republicans) in the House, but a one-seat lead (18 Democrats to 17 Republicans) in the Senate.

Women have historically done well in the Maine legislature. During the 1997–1998 session, women held four of the top six leadership posts. However, the proportion of female legislators has gradually declined since the implementation

The People's House

One of the proposed benefits of a "citizen's legislature" is the possibility that it will be a more accurate reflection of the general public than a more "professional" legislature. That was clearly the case with the 2003–2004 Maine legislature. Its membership included twenty-two educators, ten attorneys, four farmers, four social workers, ten health care professionals, six representatives of the pulp and paper industry, and another four involved in forestry. Nineteen members were businesspeople, three were former legislative staffers, and there were also some former federal and local government officials.

of term limits, to less than a quarter of the membership in 2005. Like the population of the state, the Maine legislature is overwhelmingly white, with no African American or Latino members.

Even before term limits, legislative turnover was quite high in Maine. However, term limits have pushed it even higher. Following the 2002 election, 45 percent of House members and 31 percent of senators were new. Maine is truly a citizen legislature, with the current membership including ten attorneys, ten in the forestry or timber business, seven active educators, two farmers, and thirty-four retirees.

Processes

The legislature's first-year session convenes on the first Wednesday of December following the general election, and its second-year session on the first Wednesday after the first Tuesday of January. The business of the second regular session of the legislature is limited to budgetary matters and bills carried over from the first regular session, legislation of an emergency nature admitted by the legislature, legislation referred to committees for study and report by the legis-

lature in the first regular session, and legislation presented to the legislature by written petition of the electors. The state constitution requires the legislature to enact "appropriate statutory limits" on the length of each session. In order to facilitate legislative action, legislators are prohibited from introducing legislation after the first day of the first session!

Members of the seventeen joint standing committees sit together and debate bills in a joint setting that affords an opportunity for an interchamber exchange of ideas and views on the merits of legislation at an early stage of the process before positions become hardened. Standing committees can make one of several recommendations regarding a bill when reporting it to the floor: ought to pass, ought to pass as amended, ought not to pass, refer to another committee, or unanimous ought not to pass. If a committee recommends a "unanimous ought not to pass," no further action can be taken without a special order from the floor.

Leadership Structure

The Maine legislature operates with ten leadership positions, five in each chamber. The Senate is headed by the president, who is first in line to succeed the governor in the event of a vacancy in that office. The Senate's other leadership positions are the majority floor leader, assistant majority floor leader, minority leader, and assistant minority floor leader. The House of Representatives is headed by the speaker, with the remaining leadership positions being the majority leader, assistant majority floor leader, minority leader, and assistant minority floor leader.

Even before the institution of term limits, leadership turnover was frequent. The longest tenure of any Senate president since 1900 has been seven years, with most presidents holding the position for only a single two-year term. With the single exception of one individual who served as speaker of the House for nineteen years from 1975 to 1994, no other speaker has held the post for more than five years since 1900. Indeed, it was the long, and some suggest dictatorial, service of this speaker that was used to promote the cause of legislative term limits in Maine. As with Senate presidents, most speakers have served only one two-year term.

Even before term limits, Maine was considered a "model" citizen legislature, with most of its members either retired, students, or working other full-time jobs. With base salary and per diem combined, a member of the Maine legislature is unlikely to make more than $20,000 for the two-year session. The 2003 regular session lasted for 130 days, or a little more than four months, and legislators have only shared staff, with a total staff of 151 for the entire legislature.

Election Processes

All Maine legislators are elected from single-member districts for two-year terms in the November even-year election. Nominees are selected in party primaries.

The most unusual aspect of Maine's election process is its voluntary program of total public financing of political campaigns for the legislature and for the office of governor. Adopted in 1996 and in effect since the state legislative election of 2000, the Maine Clean Election Act (MCEA) allows candidates running for the state Senate and state House of Representatives the option of financing their campaigns with public funds. Candidates who choose to participate in MCEA may accept limited private contributions—called "seed money contributions"—only at the beginning of their campaigns. After candidates receive an initial payment of public funds, they are prohibited from accepting or using any further private contributions—including their own personal funds. All subsequent campaign expenditures must be made exclusively with funds provided through MCEA.

Participation in the MCEA is purely voluntary. The program does not prohibit any candidate who chooses not to participate from raising campaign funds in the traditional manner through private contributors and publicly reporting them in compliance with state law.

Key Political Factors

Because of legislative term limits and the relatively strong competition for them, legislative seats and the legislative majority are usually quite contested. Interestingly, while Maine is the one state with term limits that could overturn them with legislative action (Idaho and Utah already have), the relative partisan balance in Maine makes it unlikely that the legislature will take such an action. If the Democratic majority supports such a move, the Republicans will most surely use it in the campaign and take the majority in the Senate and probably in the House.

While Maine has, over the past half-century, become a "swing" state and has elected roughly equal numbers from each party to statewide and congressional offices, the Democrats have fared somewhat better than the Republicans in state legislative elections. While control of the Senate has fluctuated between the two parties, the House has remained under exclusive Democratic control since the mid-1970s.

Further Reading

Barringer, Richard, ed. 2004. *Changing Maine, 1960–2010.* Gardiner, ME: Tilbury House.

Moen, Matthew C., Richard J. Powell, and Kenneth T. Palmer. 2004. *Changing Members: The Maine Legislature in the Era of Term Limits.* Lanham, MD: Rowman and Littlefield.

Potholm, Christian. 1998. *The Insider's Guide to Maine Politics, 1946–1996.* Lanham, MD: Madison.

MARYLAND

● ● ● ● ● ● ● ● ● ● ● ●

THE MARYLAND GENERAL ASSEMBLY

House of Delegates	Senate
141 Delegates	47 Senators
(410) 841–3999	(410) 841–3908

http://www.mlis.state.md.us

● ● ● ● ● ● ● ● ● ● ●

Maryland serves as a buffer state between the southernmost point of the Northeast and the northernmost point of the Southeast. During the Civil War, it was a slave-holding state that declined to join the Confederacy and remained part of the Union. The state is often considered a microcosm of the United States because of its geographic diversity. The western part of the state includes the Allegany Mountains and reflects mountain values and ways. Southern Maryland is rural and reflects the traditions of the Old South, while the economy and culture of the Eastern Shore is tied to the ocean and the Chesapeake Bay. Baltimore and the counties around Washington, D.C., are as urban and urbane as anywhere in the country.

Politically, Maryland is much closer to its neighbor states to the north than to those to its south. It is a predominantly Democratic state that occasionally elects a moderate Republican to Congress and, more rarely, to state office. The state legislature remains under firm Democratic control. However, the eastern and western portions of the state are increasingly Republican, and those changes are beginning to show up in the legislature. The state elected a Republican governor in 2002 for the first time in almost three decades.

Meeting for the first time in 1637, the Maryland General Assembly has the dis-

Maryland State Capitol ca. 1840s (Library of Congress)

tinction of being the longest continually sitting legislative body in the United States. The Maryland statehouse, completed in 1779, is the oldest statehouse in continuous use; it served as a meeting place for the Continental Congress (1783–1784) and was the site of George Washington's resignation as commander-in-chief of the Continental Army on December 23, 1783.

Structure and Membership

The Maryland General Assembly consists of a 47-member Senate and a 141-member House of Representatives. All Maryland legislators serve four-year terms. Maryland is divided into forty-seven legislative districts. Democrats have long maintained solid majorities in both chambers, and there is no indication to suggest that will change in the near future. In 2005, Democrats held majorities of more than two-to-one in each chamber.

With four-year terms in each chamber and no legislative term limits, membership is fairly stable. Approximately a quarter of the members are new every four years. Women have traditionally been well represented in the Maryland General Assembly, usually constituting around 30 percent of the membership. In 2005, a third of the members of the House of Delegates were female, as were more than 30 percent of the senators. The Black Caucus is active and represented in the Maryland General Assembly as well, with African Americans holding more than a fifth of the seats in each chamber. Women and African American leaders are generally well represented in leadership and committee chairs as well.

In the Maryland House, Mace Is a Good Thing

When the Maryland House of Delegates convenes in January of each year, its members observe a 300-year-old tradition. The chief clerk of the House enters the chamber carrying a two-foot-long "speaker's mace" of wood and silver that dates back to 1698. In that year, the colonial governor presented the mace to the House, recognizing the legislature's independence from the executive branch of government. The mace is placed in a felt-lined holder to the right of the speaker's chair. It is the oldest such symbol of legislative autonomy used in the world.

The president of the Senate presides over Senate sessions and is responsible for the chamber's administration. The speaker of the House presides over its sessions and is responsible for House administration.

The Maryland General Assembly is notable for having the fewest number of standing committees of all state legislatures. The Senate usually has no more than six standing committees and the House of Delegates generally as no more than seven. Few legislators serve on more than one standing committee. Each House committee has twenty to twenty-five members, and each Senate committee seats ten to fifteen members. Standing committee recommendations wield a great deal of influence on the floor of both chambers, and committee recommendations are almost always followed. Standing committees are not required to report bills out, but they can, if they desire, let them stay in committee.

Maryland has a nonpartisan Department of Legislative Services that serves under the general direction of the Senate president and House speaker and provides professional staff services to both chambers. Each house also has partisan staff assistants for leaders and individual members. In total, the Maryland General Assembly employs more than 500 full-time staff members. Each standing committee is provided year-round staff and hires additional staff during session.

Members of the House of Delegates do not sit by party but, rather, sit by seniority, with the most junior members at the back of the chamber, regardless of political party affiliation. Seating in the Senate is by party, with the respective leaders of each party making the seating assignments.

Processes

The Senate president presides over Senate sessions, and the speaker of the House presides over House sessions. They also appoint committee chairs and members and, in consultation with the majority leaders of their respective houses, determine their chamber agendas.

The legislature convenes annually on the second Wednesday in January. Sessions are limited to a maximum of ninety calendar days but may be extended for up to thirty additional calendar days by a majority vote of the membership of each house. No bills may be introduced in the last thirty-five days of session without a suspension of the rules, which requires agreement by 60 percent of the members of the chamber. During the 2003 legislative session, Maryland legislators introduced 1,959 bills, passing 476 of them. Some 153 of the bills passed by the Democratic-controlled legislature were vetoed by the Republican governor.

The Maryland General Assembly is considered a part-time legislature, because it meets formally for about three months each year. However, committees and other legislative groups continue to meet throughout the year. Maryland legislators earned $31,509 in 2003. Members are also entitled to reimbursement for expenses up to $130 per day for lodging and meals while in session or while attending scheduled legislative committee meetings. With the ninety-day session and regular interim committee meetings, legislators whose district is not close to Annapolis may make more than $40,000 per year. However, most Maryland legislators do hold jobs outside of the legislature.

Leadership Structure

The Senate president is officially the top leadership position in the Senate, and the speaker of the House is the top leader of the House of Representatives. Both are considered among the most powerful legislative leaders in the country. Each appoints committee members and chairs, as well as the other party leaders in their chamber. In the House of Delegates, both parties have a rather extensive list of leaders, including floor leaders, assistant floor leaders, whips, and assistant whips.

With an unusually small number of standing committees, committee chairs in Maryland are more powerful than in most states. The seven committee chairs in the House and the six chairs in the Senate are considered part of the leadership team, meeting regularly with the presiding officers and party leaders. If you include party leaders and committee chairs, more than a quarter of the members hold a leadership post.

The Senate majority leader, the House majority leader, and the Senate and House minority leaders are responsible for managing floor debate for their respective parties. Both the majority and minority parties have a number of deputy and assistant leaders

Maryland's top legislative leaders usually hold their positions for several terms. Recent leaders in both chambers have had tenures of more than ten years, including Thomas V. Mike Miller, who began his fifth four-year term as president of the Senate in 2005.

Election Processes

Maryland legislators are elected to their four-year terms in the November non-presidential even-year election. Voters elect one senator and three House members from each of the districts. The average district includes about 112,000 people. For the House of Representatives, some of the districts are divided into three single-member districts (about 38,000 people each), while, in others, members are elected at-large from multi-member districts. Historically, Democratic candidates in each district have run as slates, with the three candidates for House of Delegates and the candidate for Senate running as a team. That has become less common in recent years.

Because of the strong Democratic control of both chambers, Maryland has witnessed little of the partisan and leadership influence on elections that has been so prominent in most other states. While each legislative caucus (Republicans and Democrats in each chamber) does raise and distribute some campaign money, legislators in the Old Line state tend to manage and coordinate their own campaigns. Most campaigns are relatively low profile, and incumbents are seldom seriously contested. Party nominations are determined by primary.

Key Political Factors

Maryland can be expected to remain a predominantly Democratic state, with control of the state legislature remaining in Democratic hands. However, the 2002 election of a Republican governor suggests opportunity for the GOP.

Much of the politics of Maryland is defined by the geographic distribution of its population. Democrats tend to do very well in Baltimore City and in Prince George's and Montgomery counties, which border the District of Columbia. Republicans tend to do better along the state's Eastern Shore (on the Chesapeake Bay) and in its western and southern rural counties.

Lobbyists are an important part of the legislative process in Maryland. The more than 700 registered lobbyists provide information and campaign support for the Maryland legislators. There are no statutory or constitutional limits on how much money a lobbyist may spend on efforts to persuade legislators, but they are limited in their ability to raise campaign contributions for elected officials.

Further Reading
Smith, C. Fraser. 1999. *William Donald Schaefer: A Political Biography.* Baltimore: Johns Hopkins University Press.

MASSACHUSETTS
• • • • • • • • • • • •

THE MASSACHUSETTS GENERAL COURT
House of Representatives   Senate
160 Representatives   40 Senators
(617) 722–2000
http://www.mass.gov/legis/

• • • • • • • • • • • •

Few legislative bodies or chambers are as steeped in tradition as the Massachusetts General Court. The 1629 charter establishing the Massachusetts Bay Colony allowed for regular meetings of a governing body, and by the 1630s that body had become quite autonomous, including representatives from every town. The capitol, or statehouse, was completed on January 11, 1798, and was designed by Charles Bulfinch, one of the first great architects of the United States. The historic chambers of the statehouse have witnessed the oratory of John Adams, Samuel Adams, John Hancock, Paul Revere, John F. Kennedy, and Thomas P. "Tip" O'Neil.

Massachusetts has a population almost equal to that of the other five New England states combined. The state is quite diverse, encompassing Boston, New England's largest city, with its rich history, the popular Cape Cod tourist area, the manufacturing and industrial southeast, and the more rural central and northwest sections. Once more of a "Yankee" Republican state, Massachusetts has become one of the nation's strongest Democratic bastions, although Republicans continue to enjoy occasional successes in gubernatorial elections. An effort by the Republican governor to increase the number of Republicans in the General Assembly backfired, however, with Democrats gaining seats in 2004 in both chambers.

Structure and Membership

The Massachusetts legislature is known as the Great and General Court. The name dates from colonial times, when the legislature also had judicial powers. It consists of a 40-member Senate and a 160-member House of Representatives. All Massachusetts legislators serve two-year terms and are elected from single-member districts in November even-year elections.

The president of the Senate is responsible for Senate administration, and the speaker of the House is responsible for administration of that chamber. Staff services are provided to each individual chamber, and all appointments, including those of the minority party, are subject to the approval of the Senate president in the Senate and the speaker in the House.

Along with its neighboring Northeastern legislatures in Connecticut and Maine, the Massachusetts General Court operates with joint committees. Each house does have a number of single-chamber committees that are empowered to review legislation, but bills that come out of those committees must still go to the appropriate joint committee and receive a favorable report before they come before either full chamber. In 2003, there were twenty-one joint standing committees.

Democrats hold an overwhelming majority in both chambers, usually of about six Democrats for each Republican. Women make up just above a quarter of the membership of the Massachusetts General Court (26 percent in each chamber) and hold a quarter of the leadership posts in the joint committees. Only 6 members of the General Court are African American, but their 3 percent is not too far below their 5 percent of the general population. Only 4 of the 200 legislators are Hispanic.

The Massachusetts General Court is considered one of the more professional state legislatures in the country. The majority of the legislators report that they spend more than 80 percent of their professional time on their legislative activities. Their base annual salary exceeds $50,000, and supplemental salaries range from $10 to $100 per day, depending on distance to the capitol. Members of the House and Senate both have full-time, year-round staff in their statehouse office.

Processes

The General Court essentially holds a two-year session, convening on the first Wednesday in January in the odd-numbered year. Legislative sessions usually end by the third Wednesday of November in odd years and late July of even-numbered years.

The Fish that Did Not Get Away

A 220-year-old wooden codfish hangs in the rear of the chamber of the Massachusetts House of Representatives, a 1784 gift from merchant John Rowe, signifying the importance of fishing and sea-related industries to the economy of the Commonwealth of Massachusetts. It is considered a good luck symbol and must hang above the House chamber for the session to be held. Tradition has it that the head of the codfish points toward the majority party.

Bills must be introduced by the first Wednesday in December of the even-numbered years. Legislation filed subsequent to that deadline requires approval by the rules committees of both houses. Only matters filed by the governor and matters that have local approval of a city or town are exempt from this provision. However, legislators may "late file" a bill at any time with unanimous consent of the body.

Massachusetts is one of the few states that permit its citizens to introduce legislation. Called the "right of free petition," the process allows a citizen to introduce a bill if a legislator files the petition on the citizen's behalf. If the petition is filed "by request," it means that the legislator does not endorse the idea; its chances of becoming law are very slim. Because of this procedure, the Massachusetts legislature consistently has the highest rate of introduced bills per citizen of any state legislature.

The rules that govern the Massachusetts General Court place very few limitations on bill introductions. Legislators may not introduce any bill after the first Wednesday in December of odd-numbered years, or after the first Wednesday in November of even-numbered years. The relatively weak limitations are reflected in the number of bills introduced. During the 2003 legislative session, members of the Massachusetts General Court introduced more than 6,000 bills and resolutions. They make no distinction between a bill that changes or creates a law and a bill that recognizes the local high school football team for winning the state championship. Only 168 of those bills introduced were enacted; 5 were vetoed.

Leadership Structure

The Senate president and the speaker of the House are the presiding officers of their respective chambers and have primary control over their chamber agendas. Both are considered very strong leadership positions. Indeed, little, if anything, gets done without their approval.

They appoint their chamber's majority and assistant majority leaders, the cochairs and members from their chamber to joint committees, and chairs and members (majority and minority) of their own chamber committees. In addition, they determine the daily calendar and hire all staff for their chambers.

While turnover among leaders was quite common for much of the history of the General Court, recent presiding officers have had longer tenure. Senate president William Bulger held his post for eighteen years, until 1996, and the two most recent former speakers served for eight years each. The minority leader leads that party in each chamber, although the speaker approves and hires all minority staff appointments.

Legislative leaders in Massachusetts are well compensated for their efforts. The speaker and the president of the Senate each receive an additional $35,000. Majority and minority leaders earn an additional $22,500, with other leaders receiving between $7,500 and $15,000 for their additional work.

Election Processes

Massachusetts legislators are elected to their two-year terms in the November even-year election. All districts are single member. Each House member represents about 35,000 people, and each senator about 140,000. Given the relative security of the Democratic majority in both chambers, many of the battles occur in the Democratic primary. Republican governor Mitt Romney promised to challenge Democratic legislators in the 2004 election in an effort to increase the number of Republican legislators. The effort failed, however, with Democrats actually adding to their majorities in both chambers.

Key Political Factors

The Democrats have enjoyed overwhelming control of the Massachusetts General Court for years. Their majority margins, which normally run four or five to one over the Republicans, usually rank second only to those of neighboring Rhode Island among the fifty state legislatures. Over the past half-century, however, Republicans have achieved some successes at the state level, electing a few moderate to liberal governors and carrying the state for Ronald Reagan in his 1980 and 1984 landslides.

Even though the Massachusetts legislature meets on a continuous basis, the heavy concentration of population in the eastern half of the state, where the capital, Boston, is located, means that most legislators reside no more than an hour's drive from the capitol. While Massachusetts legislators are among the nation's better compensated state legislators, the ability of most of them to move back and forth between their home and the capital with relative ease allows many also to have a private-sector occupation. Massachusetts is one of the few states whose state capital is also its largest and most inviting city. This means that members who have to travel from the western part of the state or the Cape don't mind staying for long sessions and sampling life in "the big city."

While the state and the legislature are overwhelmingly Democratic, many of its legislators, particularly those who are Roman Catholic, are not very liberal. That fact is most evident on social issues.

Further Reading

Leading the Way. 2001. Boston: Office of the Secretary of State of Massachusetts.

The Massachusetts Political Almanac. 2005. Centerville, MA: State Legislative Leaders Foundation.

McDonough, John E. 2000. *Experiencing Politics: A Legislator's Stories of Government and Health Care.* Berkeley: University of California Press.

Schulz, John A. 1997. *Legislators of the Massachusetts General Court, 1691–1780: A Biographical Dictionary.* Boston: Northeastern University Press.

Taymor, Betty. 2000. *Running against the Wind: The Struggle of Women in Massachusetts Politics.* Boston: Northeastern University Press.

MICHIGAN

• • • • • • • • • • • •

THE MICHIGAN LEGISLATURE

House of Representatives   Senate
110 Representatives   38 Senators
(517) 373–0135
http://www.michigan.house.gov

• • • • • • • • • • • •

Best known as the home of the U.S. automobile industry, Michigan has many other notable features, including nonautomotive manufacturing, agriculture, a long Lake Michigan coastline, and a northern peninsula noted for its harsh winters that is separated from the rest of the state by the convergence of three of the Great Lakes. In an effort to diversify its economy, the state has also increased investments in its technology sector and public education in recent years.

Politically, Michigan is a highly competitive state that is almost always seen by both political parties as a battleground in presidential elections. Between 1952 and 2004, it voted for the Democratic presidential candidate eight times and for the Republican candidate six times. Control of the state was quite competitive in the 1980s and 1990s, with Democrats and Republicans tied for control of the House during one session. However, the Republicans have held control of both chambers since 1998.

Structure and Membership

The Michigan legislature consists of a 38-member Senate and a 110-member House of Representatives. Senators are elected for four-year terms and House members

for two-year terms from single-member districts in November even-year elections. Members of the Michigan Senate are limited to serving a maximum of two four-year terms, and members of the state House of Representatives are limited to serving three two-year terms. Terms need not be served consecutively, but the overall limits last a lifetime.

With term limits "kicking in" for the first time in the Senate in 2002, three-quarters of the Senate class of 2003 were in their first term. Turnover in the House, when term limits took effect in 1998, was well over 50 percent, with 64 of the 110 members taking their positions in 1999 for the first time. However, despite the dramatic turnover, it appears that Republicans are in rather firm control. They lost only one seat in the Senate and gained five in the House following the 2002 elections.

Generally, about a quarter of the members of the Michigan legislature are female. However, in the years following the implementation of term limits, that proportion declined to about 20 percent. The proportion has not changed dramatically in recent years. In 2005, 19 of the 110 House members were female, as were 11 of the 35 senators. Women also have held some leadership posts and about a quarter of the committee chairs.

African Americans hold about 15 percent of the positions in the Michigan legislature, while only one member in 2003 was Hispanic.

The lieutenant governor is president of the Senate and presides over its sessions. Senate administration is the responsibility of the majority leader and president pro tempore. The speaker of the House presides over its sessions and is responsible for House administration.

Michigan has a sizable nonpartisan professional staff that serves both chambers under the general direction of the Legislative Council. Each house also has its own nonpartisan staff, as well as partisan staff assistants for leaders and individual members. However, a significant portion of the staff is partisan, serving the majority and minority caucuses exclusively. That is particularly true of policy staff, with each caucus using partisan staff to develop legislation.

The Michigan legislature has a strong standing committee system. Each chamber has about twenty standing committees (in 2005, there were seventeen committees in the Senate and twenty-two in the House). Michigan also has five statutory standing committees created by law rather than rules.

Processes

The Michigan legislature convenes annually on the second Wednesday in January under the watchful eyes of the speaker of the House and the lieutenant governor. There is no limitation on session length. Annually, Michigan legislators introduce more than 2,000 bills, but usually pass just over 10 percent of them. In 2003 the Democratic governor vetoed fourteen of the 322 bills passed by the legislature.

The Michigan legislature is considered among the four or five most professional state legislatures in the country, along with California, New York, Ohio, and Illinois. It meets year-round, and there are no limits on how many bills a Michigan legislator may introduce. Michigan legislators are among the best paid in the United States, with an annual salary of almost $80,000 plus an annual expense allowance of $12,000. Combined, this puts salaries at more than $90,000 annually, second only to California. Furthermore, senators and House members have year-round, full-time staff members. The Michigan legislature employs more than 1,300 full-time staff members.

Leadership Structure

The Senate president pro tempore is officially the top leadership position in the Senate, but the chamber's majority leader is its most influential member. The speaker of the House is the top leader of the House of Representatives. The Senate majority leader, the House majority leader, and the Senate and House minority leaders are responsible for managing floor debate for their respective parties. In addition to the presiding officers and floor leaders, Michigan leadership teams also include a number of assistant and associate leaders. The Senate majority leader and speaker appoint committee chairs and members and, in consultation with the president pro tempore in the Senate and the majority leader in the House, determine the chamber agendas. Leaders and members of the minority party have very little influence in the schedule,

---

Hit the Deck!

From the visitors' gallery, the Michigan House of Representatives looks like mass chaos, with members running around and periodically "hitting the deck," almost crawling across the floor. However, there is a method to the madness. While it is appropriate for members to speak to each other while a colleague is addressing the body, they will be gaveled to order should they obstruct the line of vision between the person speaking and the presiding officer. Therefore, rather than standing tall while walking around, legislators will duck down rather than risk obstructing the line of vision between their colleague and the chair.

---

agenda, or output of the Michigan legislature. Top party leaders are paid a significant stipend in addition to their base salary. For example, the speaker of the House and the majority leader were paid an additional $27,000 in 2003.

Until the imposition of term limits, Michigan legislators sometimes held top leadership positions for a number of terms. With the advent of term limits, however, leadership tenures have generally been one term in the Senate and no more than two terms in the House of Representatives. Historically, gaining leadership was almost exclusively a function of tenure—serve long enough and, if you wanted to, you could become leader. However, with term limits, no one has a long career. Now, leadership elections come down to which candidate for leadership can recruit candidates and raise enough money to get party members elected. Because term limits have been in place for less time in the Senate, their effect on leadership is unclear.

Election Processes

In Michigan, contested nominations are decided in party primaries. Legislators are elected in November of even-years. All senators are elected to four-year terms in the same year in which Michigan voters choose their governor. Senate and gubernatorial terms are therefore concurrent. With more than 260,000 people, Michigan Senate districts are among the largest in the country. House districts include about 90,000 Michiganers, a more manageable number.

Contested and competitive elections to the Michigan House are costly. On average, it costs more than $100,000 to compete for an open seat. Senate races can be more costly. Term limits ensure that the seats will remain contested (either in the primary or general election) and expensive. The legislative leaders of both parties raise and distribute large amounts of money to the campaigns of legislative candidates in their party. Interest groups also play a very active role in Michigan campaigns, providing significant campaign contributions.

Key Political Factors

Michigan can be expected to remain a highly competitive state, especially at the national level and for statewide offices. However, effective redistricting by the Republicans following the 2000 census has created a relatively safe Republican majority, especially in the House. Legislative term limits create a large number of open seats in any given election, but the real contest for those seats is often in the primary, because partisan control is ensured by the partisan composition of the district. Many experts feel that the state's term limits law will reduce the power and influence of the legislature in state policymaking by discouraging the development of long-term expertise within its membership. Since the establishment of term limits, the rate of turnover in the legislature has been significantly greater than in the past.

Perhaps the dominant political feature of the Michigan legislature, apart from term limits, is partisanship. The four party caucuses (House and Senate Republicans and House and Senate Democrats) are each well-funded, organized, and proactive organizations. Each has its own budget, staff, public agenda, and website. Few, if any, controversial votes in Michigan do not fall along party lines, with Democrats opposing Republicans.

Partisanship in Michigan is very much a function of geography. While there are few rural Democrats, their main base of power is in Detroit and the surrounding area. On the other hand, Republicans tend to dominate in rural areas and the Upper Peninsula.

Lobbyists are also an integral part of the legislative process in Michigan. More than 2,400 lobbyists register to lobby the legislature each session. They are prohibited from spending more than $49 per month on any given legislator.

Further Reading

Brown, William Paul, and Kenneth VerBurg. 1995. *Michigan Politics and Government: Facing Change in a Complex State.* Lincoln: University of Nebraska Press.

Grummon, Phyllis T., and Brendon Mullin, eds. 1995. *Policy Choices: Creating Michigan's Future.* East Lansing: Michigan State University Press.

Loepp, Daniel. 2000. *Sharing the Balance of Power.* Ann Arbor: University of Michigan Press.

Saurbaugh-Thompson, Marie, Charles D. Elder, Richard Elling, and John Strate. 2004. *Political and Institutional Effects of Term Limits.* Basingstoke, UK; New York: Palgrave Macmillan.

MINNESOTA

● ● ● ● ● ● ● ● ● ● ● ●

THE MINNESOTA LEGISLATURE

House of Representatives	Senate
134 Representatives	67 Senators
(651) 296–2146	(651) 296–0504

http://www.leg.state.mn.us/

● ● ● ● ● ● ● ● ● ● ● ●

Minnesota is a state whose economy involves manufacturing, agribusiness, mining, and forest products. Known as "the land of 10,000 lakes," it is also a popular warm-weather vacation spot. More than half of the state's population resides within and around the "twin cities" of Minneapolis and St. Paul.

Politically, Minnesota is a competitive state that tilts slightly more toward the Democrats in presidential and congressional elections than it does in elections for state office and the state legislature. It has historically been known as a very progressive state, with even the Republican leaders holding rather moderate views. From 1998 to 2002, Minnesota officially had a three-party government, with Democrats controlling the Senate, Republicans leading the House, and Independent Party member Jesse Ventura serving as the state's governor. The state has produced Democratic presidential candidates and liberal standard-bearers Hubert Humphrey, Jr. (1968), and Walter Mondale (1984). Republicans have made steady gains over the past decade to the point where they elected a Republican senator to replace liberal Democrat Paul Wellstone. Republicans have a majority in the state House and are drawing close in the state Senate. The difference between the statewide elections and local state House/Senate elections is best explained by legislative district concentrations of votes.

Structure and Membership

The Minnesota legislature consists of a 67-member Senate and a 134-member House of Representatives. Senators are elected for four-year nonstaggered terms and House members for two-year terms from single-member districts in November even-year elections. Minnesota is divided into sixty-seven legislative districts. Voters elect one senator from each of the districts. Each Senate district is then divided into two sections, and voters elect one House member from each section. After regaining the majority in the House in 1998, the Republican Party saw that majority grow to almost thirty seats in 2000 (81–53) while Democrats saw

their majority in the Senate decrease from a high of thirty-one in 1977 (49–18) to only four seats (35–31) in 2003. However, the 2002 election brought a dramatic shift in the lower chamber, with Democrats pulling within two seats of the Republicans (68–66). No Senate seats were up in 2004.

The first woman was elected to the Minnesota legislature in 1923, and at least one woman has served in the legislature since that time. Since the middle 1990s, the proportion of female legislators has exceeded 25 percent, including an all-time high of 28 percent in 1999. Unlike many states, the proportion of women is higher in the Senate (34 percent in 2003) than in the House (23 percent in 2003). Representative Dee Long served as speaker of the Minnesota House of Representatives from 1991 to 1993. Like the population of the state, the proportion of minority members in the Minnesota legislature is quite low. In 2003, there were only two African American legislators and one Hispanic legislator in the Minnesota legislature.

The president of the Senate presides over Senate sessions. Senate administration is the responsibility of the majority leader and president pro tempore. The speaker of the House presides over its sessions and is responsible for House administration. Minnesota has nonpartisan professional staff that serves both chambers. The staff of the Minnesota legislature exceeds 600 people. Each committee has full-time, year-round staffing, and each member has year-round staffing at the capitol. Each house also has partisan staff assistants for leaders and individual members.

O Brother Where Art Thou? I'm in the Legislature.

Service in the Minnesota legislature, especially the House, is a family affair. Eleven of the 201 members of the 2003 membership were the children or grandchildren of former legislators. Ten members of the House and one member of the Senate are serving in the chamber once occupied by their father. One member, Representative Aaron Peterson, is the son (Doug Peterson, 1991–2002) and grandson (Harry Peterson, 1965–1973) of former members of the House. From 1993 to 2002, Andy Dawkins and his wife, Ellen Anderson, served in the House and Senate, respectively! Two brothers, Doug and Howard Swenson, served together in the 1990s until Doug became a judge.

The Senate operates with about a dozen committees, with membership ranging from nine to eighteen members. Each Senate committee has a professional staff of at least four. The House, with twice as many members, usually has twice as many (about two dozen) standing committees. With the exception of the smaller Ethics Committee (five members), each House committee has between ten and twenty-seven members and two full-time staff persons.

Processes

The legislature convenes in regular session each odd-numbered year on the first Tuesday after the first Monday in January. In even-numbered years, it convenes on a date set by joint agreement of both bodies. The state constitution places a limit of 120 legislative days during each two-year term. In addition, the legislature may not meet in regular session after the first Monday following the third Saturday in May of either year. There are no limitations for the introduction of bills in either chamber, but bills must be reported from their respective committees about a month before the scheduled end of the legislative session. In 2003, Minnesota legislators introduced 1,658 pieces of legislation, enacting 131 of them. The governor vetoed only two.

The Minnesota legislature is considered semiprofessional. With a base salary of more than $30,000 annually and per diem allowance of $66, Minnesota legislators make almost $40,000 annually. The legislative session is limited to 120 legislative days and must adjourn by late May of each year. While legislative turnover was almost a third in 2003, turnover in years not following redistricting is about 15 percent. Legislative staffing is strong in Minnesota.

Leadership Structure

The Senate president is officially the top leadership position in the Senate and the speaker of the House is the top leader of the House of Representatives. But the majority leader is considered the most influential leader in the Senate. Both are elected by the members of their caucus. The Senate majority leader, the House majority leader, and the Senate and House minority leaders are responsible for managing floor debate for their respective parties. The speaker of the House and the majority leader of the Senate also assign committee chairs, while the members of the Senate committees are determined by a Committee on Committees.

The role of legislative leader has become increasingly important in recent years as the legislative chambers have been controlled by different parties and the office of governor by a third party for four years. The leaders have taken on additional importance in representing their institutions in negotiations with the executive and his or her counterpart in the other chamber.

Historically, House speakers have seldom served more than two terms (only two since 1900 have served longer). With his reelection as speaker in 2005, Steve Sviggum will begin his fourth two-year term. On the other hand, Roger Moe served as majority leader of the Senate for more than twenty years, leaving in 2002 to seek the office of governor.

Election Processes

Minnesota legislators are elected in the November even-year election. All senators are elected to their four-year terms in the same even-year election. Senators represent just over 50,000 people, while House districts include about 25,000 Minnesotans.

The state's constitution provides that all senators be elected in the November even-year election following the decennial census, which means that over any given ten-year cycle, senators serve two four-year terms and one two-year term. Legislative leaders are expected to raise money and recruit candidates for their caucus, as well as be the spokesperson and agenda setters in their respective caucuses. Party nominations are determined by primary.

Key Political Factors

Minnesota can be expected to remain a highly competitive state, with control of the state legislature up for grabs in every even-year election and split control always a possibility. However, following the last redistricting, it would seem unlikely that the Democrats will regain control of the House anytime soon.

The 2003–2004 sessions proved to be a difficult one for all parties concerned. While Steve Sviggum was in his third term as leader of the House, Republican governor Tim Pawlenty and Democratic majority leader Dean Johnson were new to their posts and spent considerable time trying to "get their footing." The result was a remarkably contentious session, especially between the Republican governor and the Democrat-controlled Senate. The Senate ultimately decided not to act on important legislative issues, given that no senators were up for election and the entire House was up for election on November 2, 2004. As a result, Democrats made significant gains in the Republican-controlled House in 2004. While there is no Senate election in 2004, many expect a strong battle for control of the chamber in 2006.

The Minnesota legislature is recognized for setting a high standard of ethics for its members and those who try to influence legislation. Indeed, a speaker in the 1990s was forced from office because she mishandled a case in which one of her members charged state-related calls to his state calling card. This infraction would be minor in most states, but it ended a promising political career in Minnesota.

More than 1,200 lobbyists registered with the legislature in 2003. In Minnesota, a lobbyist is defined as anyone who generates more than $3,000 from lobbying efforts, or someone who spends more than $250 in any given year in an attempt to influence legislation pending before the Minnesota legislature. Lobbyists must report their total expenditures by category.

Further Reading

Elazar, Daniel Judah, Virginia H. Gray, and Wyman L. Spano. 1999. *Minnesota Politics and Government.* Lincoln: University of Nebraska Press.

Reuter, Theodore. 1994. *Minnesota House of Representatives and the Professionalization of Politics.* Lanham, MD: University Press of America.

MISSISSIPPI

● ● ● ● ● ● ● ● ● ● ● ●

THE MISSISSIPPI LEGISLATURE

House of Representatives	Senate
122 Representatives	52 Senators

(601) 359–3770
http://www.ls.state.ms.us

● ● ● ● ● ● ● ● ● ● ● ●

A bastion of the solid Democratic south for more than a hundred years following the Civil War, Mississippi has become a strongly Republican state in federal elections, having supported the Democratic presidential candidate only once since 1956 (Georgian Jimmy Carter narrowly carried the state in 1976). For state offices, generations-old family loyalties to the Democrats have been slower to fade. While the Republican Party has become highly competitive and has won gubernatorial, lieutenant governor, and mayoral elections, Democrats have continued to control the legislature, as they have since Reconstruction. But even here, Republicans have slowly chipped away at what, as late as the end of the 1960s, was a virtually unanimous Democratic membership.

Mississippi has the largest percentage of African Americans of any state and, since the end of the Jim Crow era, the two political parties have become somewhat polarized—with the largely conservative white population gravitating to the Republican Party and the more liberal African Americans providing a solid base for the Democrats. Despite economic gains and economic diversification, Mississippi remains near the bottom of the states in terms of income, education, and health care. These challenges, along with a public desire for low taxes, is likely to continue to vex the Mississippi legislature in the near future.

Structure and Membership

The state Senate is composed of 52 members, and the House of Representatives of

122. Legislators are elected from single-member districts for four-year terms. As of 2005, Mississippi, Louisiana, and Alabama were the only Southern legislatures to have remained in united Democratic control since the end of Reconstruction. The election of Governor Kirk Fordice in 1991 ended their control of the executive office, but Democrats maintain a strong hold on the House and a more tenuous hold on the Senate.

Women have not fared particularly well in the Mississippi legislature. Just about one out of eight (13.7 percent) of the members of the legislature are women, and they held only two of the thirty-four committee chairs in the House and only three of thirty-five in the Senate in 2004. However, Lieutenant Governor Amy Boynton Tuck, only the second woman in the history of the state to be elected statewide, presides over the Senate and appoints all standing committees and all committee chairs and vice chairs. Reflecting the population, more than a quarter of the members of the Mississippi legislature are African Americans (28 percent in the House and 26 percent in the Senate in 2003). However, those proportions are still below those of the general population, where African Americans constituted 36.3 percent of the population in 2000. There are no Hispanic members of the Mississippi legislature.

Administratively, each chamber operates autonomously, with the lieutenant governor and the speaker of the House as the officials primarily responsible for administrative oversight. All staff that service the Mississippi legislature are nonpartisan.

The Mississippi legislature has a large number of standing committees, usually more than thirty per chamber. In the Senate, well over half of the membership are likely to chair a committee. Almost a third of the House will likely chair a committee in that body. Because there are so many committees in the Mississippi legislature, their autonomy and influence on the floor is below average compared with committees in other states. Instead, the power lies mostly in the hands of the speaker and the lieutenant governor.

Processes

The lieutenant governor, an independently elected statewide official, has the title of president of the Senate and presides over that chamber's sessions. The speaker of the House is the dominant leader in the House of Representatives. The speaker exercises primary control over the chamber's agenda and proceedings.

Annual regular sessions convene on the Tuesday after the first Monday in January and are limited to 90 calendar days, except in the first year of a new gubernatorial administration, when the limit is 125 calendar days. In order to accomplish its legislative goals in such a limited time, Mississippi's legislature abides by several deadlines for legislative activity, including dates for the introduction of bills and constitutional amendments, committee reports, revenue and appropriations bills, committee reports from the other chamber, and passage of bills from the other chamber. There are several joint committees, the most important of which is the Joint Legislative Budget Commission, which is the primary author of the state's

---

Taxes Due

The Mississippi capitol, which houses the House and Senate chambers as well as office space for support staff and its 174 legislators, was paid for by back taxes owed the state by the Illinois Central Railroad. The building was constructed from 1901 to 1903, just under four decades after the city was burned to the ground following the Civil War.

---

budget. It includes seven members from each chamber.

The Mississippi legislature is considered one of the less professional state legislatures in the country. Its members are paid $10,000 per year and $85 per day while in session and during out-of-session committee hearings. In light of Mississippi's ninety-day session and relatively limited committee schedule out of session, a legislator is unlikely to make more than $20,000 per year. The 174 Mississippi legislators share a staff of around 130 people during the legislative session but have no formal support in the district or when the legislature is out of session. Legislators cannot introduce any legislation after the fourteenth day of the session. During the 2003 session, Mississippi legislators introduced 2,696 pieces of legislation and passed 323, with the governor vetoing three bills.

Leadership Structure

Two individuals in each chamber carry a leadership title. The lieutenant governor serves as president of the Senate, and a member of the chamber serves as its president pro tempore. The power that the Mississippi lieutenant governor exercises over the Senate is among the most considerable exercised by any of the lieutenant governors in the country, with the most important power being to make committee appointments.

The speaker of the House appoints all committee members and committee chairs and is a dominant player in the chamber. The only other House member with a leadership title is the speaker pro tempore. In terms of formal power, the speaker of the House is considered by many to be the most important post in the state, more powerful than the leader of the Senate or the governor. Over the past half-century, the tenures of Mississippi's House speakers have been among the lengthiest of any state legislature.

Despite the steady growth in Republican representation in the legislature, the party's members have never formally elected a minority leader in either chamber. However, that seems likely to change in the near future.

Election Processes

All Mississippi legislators are elected for four-year terms from single-member districts in the odd year immediately preceding a presidential election. Mississippi is one of only a handful of states that hold their elections in odd years, enabling conservative Mississippi Democrats to avoid the often negative effects of more liberal national elections in even-numbered years. Contested nominations are decided by direct primary. Mississippi elections are traditionally low key and inexpensive, with name recognition and incumbency being the most important factors in success. However, campaigns in more expensive mass-media markets (around Jackson; in and around Tupelo; and near Memphis, Tennessee, or New Orleans, Louisiana); can run as high as $50,000 for House races and $100,000 for Senate seats.

Mississippi legislators can seek an unlimited number of terms to the legislature, thanks to the defeat of term limits in 1995 and 1999. Led by House speaker Tim Ford, Mississippi voters are the only voters twice to defeat an effort to limit the terms of state legislators and other governing officials. Reflecting on the politics of the state, the opponents of term limits made the case that term limits would be bad for the people of Mississippi and were being pushed on them by "outsiders." Even without term limits, however, more than one in five legislators who took their seats following the 2003 election were beginning their first terms.

Key Political Factors

Two factors have dominated Mississippi politics since the late 1960s: the increase in the African American vote and influence, and the rapidly growing strength of the Republican Party.

African American voters have been credited with tipping the balance in favor of Democratic candidates in almost all of the recent close statewide elections that the party has won. The increasing strength of the African American caucus in the legislature and the African American vote in the state has caused some concerns in the legislature and the state. Traditional white conservative Democrats from rural areas are clashing with the more urban and liberal African Americans on various issues of policy.

During this same period, as the long shadow of the Civil War has finally begun to fade, the Mississippi Republican Party has transformed itself from a nonfactor in state politics into a competitive growing force that has elected governors, U.S. senators, and congressmen, and has become a cornerstone of the new Republican South. The state legislature is the last remaining bastion of Democratic dominance in Mississippi, but, even there, Republican representation continues to show steady growth.

Historically, interest groups have played a significant role in shaping politics and policy in the Magnolia State. While the one-party nature of the state enabled them often to have more power than the political parties, increased party competition is not likely to dampen their influence. With minimal staff and limited resources, Mississippi legislators rely heavily on lobbyists for information.

Further Reading

Bullock, Charles S., and Mark J. Rozell, eds. 2002. *New Politics of the Old South: An Introduction to Southern Politics*. 2d ed. Lanham, MD: Rowman and Littlefield.

Coleman, Mary Delorse. 1994. *Legislators, Law and Public Policy: Political Change in Mississippi and the South*. Westport, CT: Greenwood.

Krane, Dale, and Stephen D. Shaffer. 1992. *Mississippi Government and Politics: Modernizers vs. Traditionalists*. Lincoln: University of Nebraska Press.

MISSOURI

• • • • • • • • • • • •

The Missouri General Assembly

House of Representatives	Senate
163 Delegates	34 Senators
(573) 751–3829	(573) 751–3766

http://www.moga.state.mo.us

• • • • • • • • • • • • •

The midpoint of the continental United States is located in Missouri, a state that may mirror the United States as a nation as much as, or more than, any of the other forty-nine states. It has dense urban areas in and around St. Louis and Kansas City, as well as very conservative rural sections in the rest of the state. The rural economies are governed by agriculture and natural resources, while the urban and suburban centers are dominated by a service-oriented economy. The rural areas are primarily white, while the urban and suburban areas represent a melting pot of cultures and ethnic groups. More than half of the legislators are elected from one of three metropolitan areas: St. Louis, Kansas City, or Springfield. Because of the rural nature of parts of the state, one Senate district includes sixteen counties!

The presidential preferences of residents of the Show Me State come close to being a microcosm of the nation as a whole. The state last voted for a losing presidential candidate in 1956, and its percentages in the ten elections since then have almost invariably been close to the nationwide percentages. In state and congressional elections, the state had leaned to the Democratic Party in the middle of the twentieth century, but the two parties are now virtually even. However, that strength is defined by geography, with Democrats strong in and around the two urban centers of St. Louis and Kansas City and Republicans gaining support in the rest of the state.

Structure and Membership

Democrats controlled both chambers of the Missouri legislature as recently as the late 1990s. However, beginning with control of the Senate in 2001, Republicans began to gain and solidify control of the legislature. Within the first years of the new century, they seem to have a strong hold on both chambers now, with a majority of more than 2 to 1 in the Senate and a more than 25-seat majority in the House, of a total of 163 House and 34 Senate members.

While Catherine Hanaway recently served as the first female speaker of the Missouri House of Representatives, women have not historically faired very well in the Missouri General Assembly. Only in recent years have they reached the 20 percent threshold of membership, and their proportion has actually declined as the number of Republicans has increased. They tend to hold between 15

A House Divided against Itself

The American Civil War caused great strife in every state, but perhaps none more so than the "Show Me State." Considered a border state and namesake of the infamous Missouri Compromise, which legally divided the United States into slave and nonslave regions, the state found itself divided in 1861. While the people voted to remain in the Union, Governor Laiborne Jackson fled the capitol with a handful of legislators and attempted to establish a new capital, voting to secede from the Union. Eventually, Jackson was removed from office and the rightful government restored in Jefferson City, the state capital.

and 20 percent of the committee chair posts. Historically, African Americans have made up about 10 percent of each body, and 2004 witnessed the election of the state's first Hispanic and first Latino legislators, both Republican.

The lieutenant governor, an independently elected official, is the president of the Senate. The Senate elects a president pro tempore from its membership to preside over its sessions and oversee the chamber's administration. The speaker of the House presides over its sessions and is responsible for House administration.

Legislators in both chambers are assigned to standing committees. There are usually sixteen or seventeen such committees in the Senate, with ten to fifteen members on each committee. Each Senate committee has a chair and vice chair, appointed by the president pro tempore. The House organizes itself into almost thirty-five standing committees, including five different appropriations committees, each responsible for a particular area of the budget. Each committee includes fifteen to eighteen members of the House, including a chair and vice chair, appointed by the speaker of the House.

Nonpartisan professional staff services are provided under the direction of the twenty-member Joint Legislative Research Committee. Altogether, the Missouri General Assembly is staffed by nearly 500 full-time employees. Members of the House and Senate are provided with year-round staff in the capitol but are not provided with district staff.

Processes

The president of the Senate and the speaker of the House preside over sessions in their respective chambers. The Senate president pro tempore and the speaker of the House appoint committee chairs and majority-party members of committees in their respective chambers. Minority leaders appoint minority-party members. The president pro tempore and the speaker, in consultation with their majority leaders, determine the agenda for their respective houses.

The Missouri General Assembly meets annually, convening on the Wednesday after the first Monday in January. Sessions must adjourn by the first Friday following the second Monday in May. In addition to the regular session, the Missouri General Assembly may meet in extraordinary (special) sessions as called by the governor. The governor also determines the issues to be covered during the special session.

In 2003, the House met for seventy-five legislative days (excluding holidays and other days in recess), and the Senate met for seventy-six legislative days. They also had two special sessions in June and September to address budget differences between the Democratic governor and the Republican legislature.

In 2003, the Republican governor vetoed 30 of the 254 bills enacted by the General Assembly. Missouri legislators had introduced 1,464 pieces of legislation. In order to expedite the legislative process, House members can begin prefiling bills on December 1, before the January session begins. Senators can begin prefiling on July 1! All bills must be pre-filed prior to the first day of session. The deadline for filing bills during the legislative session is set by rule in the House and is March 1 in the Senate. Leaders in both chambers set deadlines for when bills can cross over from one chamber to the other and when particular types of bills must be disposed of.

The Missouri General Assembly is usually considered a part-time legislature, with its sessions restricted to about four months. However, recent extraordinary or special sessions have extended the time that legislators need to spend in the capitol. Furthermore, with a base salary of just over $31,000 and per diem allowances of $78 a day plus travel reimbursements, Missouri legislators can earn more than $40,000 a year. That, along with full-time, year-round staff in the capitol, moves the Missouri General Assembly along the path toward a full-time legislature. However, most members of the legislature, who can serve no more than eight years, do maintain an occupation or profession outside of the legislature.

Leadership Structure

The president pro tempore of the Senate and the speaker of the House are the top leaders of their respective chambers. The lieutenant governor, elected statewide, presides over the Senate but has limited other legislative powers.

The majority and minority leaders of each chamber are responsible for managing floor debate for their respective parties. Both the majority and minority parties have several assistant leaders, including assistant floor leaders, whips, caucus chairs, and caucus secretaries.

Because of Missouri's term-limits law, the tenures of legislative leaders are usually one, or at most two, terms. Prior to legislative term limits, it was not unusual for Missouri leaders to serve more than one term.

Election Processes

Missouri legislators are elected in the November even-year election, with half of the members of the Senate elected to their four-year terms in each even-year election. Senate districts include about 163,000 people and range in size from a few miles to sixteen counties. Each House district, on the other hand, includes fewer than 34,000 people.

Because of term limits, legislative turnover is quite high. Following the 2002 elections, more than half of the members of the House were new to their post, as was over a third of the Senate. Following the 2004 elections, about a quarter of the House members were new and a third of the senators. Contested nominations are decided in party primaries.

Key Political Factors

Missouri can be expected to remain a barometer state in presidential elections, and a highly competitive state in elections for all offices. Control of the General Assembly will be up for grabs in most elections. One can also expect the battle lines to develop along geographic lines, with Republicans claiming the rural areas, Democrats the urban areas, and much of the battle taking place in the suburbs.

Missouri's state legislator term-limits law has increased the rate of turnover in both houses of the legislature. In 2002, just fewer than half of the members of the House of Representatives and more than two-thirds of the senators whose districts were up for election were ineligible to seek reelection. Three-quarters of the General Assembly members who will convene in January 2005 will have two or fewer years of previous legislative service. In the view of most legislative experts, this has served to weaken the legislature as a policymaking institution by eliminating the possibility for the development of long-term institutional expertise within the legislative branch.

While legislators have full-time clerical staff, the number of their policy or issue-oriented staff is restricted. Therefore, the more than 1,000 lobbyists who register each year with the Missouri Ethics Commission are likely to be a significant source of information. There are no limits regarding how much they can spend in their efforts to persuade legislators to act.

Further Reading

Hardy, Richard A., Richard Dohm, and David A. Leuthold. 1995. *Missouri Government and Politics.* Columbia: University of Missouri Press.

MONTANA

• • • • • • • • • • • •

THE MONTANA LEGISLATURE

House of Representatives
100 Representatives
(406) 444–4822

Senate
50 Senators
(406) 444–4844

http://www.state.mt.us

• • • • • • • • • • • •

Montana, the nation's third least densely populated state after Alaska and Wyoming, has elements of both the Midwestern Great Plains and the Western Rocky Mountains, with its eastern two-thirds gently rolling plains and its western third mountainous. Its economy depends heavily on timber, mining, and agriculture.

Politically, Montanans tend to be conservative and to lean toward the Republican Party—but not so strongly as to prevent them from electing a number of Democratic governors and members of Congress, and sometimes putting one or both houses of their state legislature under Democratic control. Indeed, unlike the rest of the West, Republicans do not have a lock on the "Treasure State." In 2004, they elected a Democratic governor who ran on the ticket with a Republican lieutenant governor, giving the Democrats a tie in the House and a slim (two-seat) majority in the Senate.

Structure and Membership

The Montana legislature consists of a 50-member Senate and a 100-member House of Representatives. Each Senate district includes two House single-member districts. Senate members are elected for four-year terms, and House members are elected for two-year terms. While Republicans had controlled both chambers of the Montana legislature since 1995, 2004 saw significant changes, with Democrats gaining a two-seat majority in the Senate and a split in the House.

Not surprisingly, the state that sent the first woman to the U.S. Congress (Congresswoman Janette Rankin) has a relatively high proportion of women in its state legislature. The proportion of women in the Senate tends to be about 15 percent, and the proportion in the House between 25 and 30 percent. Women have seldom held leadership posts in either chamber, but they often chair significant standing committees, particularly in the House. Given the homogeneity of the Montana population, it is little wonder that there are no Latino, Hispanic, or African American legislators. Members of the Montana legislature are restricted to a maximum of eight years of service in their chamber within any sixteen-year period.

Nonpartisan professional staff services are provided under a twelve-member legislative council. This powerful body includes the speaker of the House, president of the Senate and minority leaders of both chambers, and four additional members appointed by the speaker (House members) and the Senate president (Senate). The council coordinates most of the legislature's work between sessions, and its staff handles general administrative responsibilities for the legislature.

The Legislative Council oversees the operation of the Legislative Services Division, which provides research, information, and technical support to members. Other important staff bodies are the Legislative Audit Division (which makes sure that government agencies are working effectively and efficiently) and the Legislative Fiscal Division (which provides information regarding budgetary matters). A joint legislative committee manages each of those units.

The Montana legislature organizes the House and Senate into standing committees, usually seventeen or eighteen in each chamber. House committees include between thirteen and eighteen House members and generally meet on either a Tuesday–Thursday schedule or a Monday-Wednesday-Friday schedule. Each member generally sits on two committees, one T–TH committee and one M-W-F committee. Senate committees include about ten members and are organized along a similar schedule. However, with fewer members in the Senate, most members serve on more than two committees. The speaker appoints House members, but senators are assigned by the Committee on Committees.

Every Vote Counts

Following the election of 2004, Republican efforts to maintain control of the Montana House depended on the status of seven ballots in which voters appeared to have voted for two candidates for the same House seat. The Montana supreme court ruled that at least one of those ballots was invalid, giving the seat to Democrat Jeanne Windham by a single vote and creating a 50–50 tie in the House. Under rules designed to avoid a shared-power situation in case of a tie vote for control of the House, control shall go to the party holding the governorship, giving control to Democrats for the first time in more than a decade.

Processes

The president of the Senate and the speaker of the House preside over sessions in their respective chambers. The Senate president and the House speaker, in consultation with their respective majority leaders, determine their chambers' agendas.

The Montana legislature meets biennially, convening on or before the first Monday in January in odd-numbered years, with sessions limited to a maximum of ninety legislative days. All general bills must be introduced by the tenth day of the session and all revenue bills by the seventeenth legislative day. All committee bills must be to the floor by the thirty-sixth legislative day, and committee bills implementing general appropriations (budget bills) must be to the body by the seventy-fifth day of the ninety-day session.

In the 2003 Legislative Session, Montana legislators introduced 1,360 bills. Of those, both chambers passed 612 and the governor only vetoed two. The legislature voted to override one of those two vetoes.

With the exception of its very strong professional staff, the Montana state legislature is the classic citizen's legislature. It meets only three months every two years, and it adjourns by the end of April. Many of its farmer/rancher members return home to manage the livestock or the farm, returning for relatively few meetings during the interim. Legislators receive no annual salary. They receive a daily salary of about $72 a day for each day the legislature convenes during the regular session and an additional $58 living allowance. That adds up to little more than $10,000 for the two-year session! Not surprisingly, between low salaries and term limits, turnover is quite high, with more than a third of the legislators usually being replaced over each election cycle.

Because the Montana legislature is in general session only three months out of every twenty-four, interim committees are very important. These committees meet as needed when the legislature is not in session, gathering information, evaluating the performance and effect of legislation, and making recommendations that will be considered by the body at the beginning of the biennial session. Those recommendations take the form of legislation that has been approved by the committee and its members and is presented by September 15, prior to the regular session. There are usually about ten interim committees each session. Interim committees include members from both chambers.

Leadership Structure

The president of the Senate and the speaker of the House are the top leaders of their respective chambers. The majority and minority leaders of each chamber are responsible for managing floor debate for their respective parties. The Senate majority and minority leaders each have an assistant leader, and the House majority and minority leaders each have two assistants.

A Committee on Committees elected by the Senate appoints Senate committees. The speaker who consults with the minority leader on minority appointments appoints House committees.

Although Montana has had relatively stable leadership (one person served as speaker for eight years in the 1990s), term limits are likely to increase turnover among both leaders and members.

Election Processes

Montana legislators are elected in the November even-year election, with half of the senators elected to their four-year terms in each even-year election. Elections in Montana are often low-key and low-expense events. With small districts (about 18,000 for senators and 9,000 for House members), elections are personal. With term limits, many more legislators lose to retirement than to defeat.

Republicans attribute strong Democratic gains in 2004 (taking over the Senate and gaining a tie in the House) to successful gerrymandering by the Democrats, who controlled the last round of legislative districting. Contested nominations are decided in party primaries.

Key Political Factors

Although Montana has leaned more toward the Republican Party since the late 1980s, it can be expected to remain a competitive state. While the Republican Party has controlled the state legislature most of the time since the mid-1980s, the Democrats controlled one or both chambers more often than the Republicans during the 1970s and into the mid-1980s. Montana voters have demonstrated an occasional independent streak in presidential voting. The state gave Independent candidate Ross Perot 26 percent of its vote in 1992 and almost 14 percent in 1996.

The environment is such a critical issue in the state of Montana that, in 1971, the legislature created a separate administrative arm to ensure environmental quality. The Environmental Quality Council, consisting of members of both chambers, is charged to research environmental issues, monitor environmental quality in the state, and advise the legislature on environmental policy. This permanent, constitutionally created committee is the only one of its kind among the state legislatures of the United States. Many people believe that the focus on the environment established in the 1972 constitution has shaped politics and policy in the state since that time.

Because of the part-time nature of the Montana legislature, lobbyists and interest groups are an invaluable source of policy information. Although the population is small and the legislative session short, more than a thousand lobbyists usually register each session.

Further Reading

Legislative Branch: Mission, Goals and Objectives. Montana Legislature. (http://leg.state.mt.us/content/about/goalsandobjec_2005.pdf.)

Rules, Procedures and Guidelines for Interim Committees. Legislative Services Council, Montana Legislature. (http://leg.state.mt.us/content/committees/interim/2003_2004/int_com_rules_proc_guidelines_%20011604.pdf.)

NEBRASKA

● ● ● ● ● ● ● ● ● ● ● ●

THE NEBRASKA UNICAMERAL LEGISLATURE
Senate
49 Senators
(402) 471–2311
http://www.unicam.state.ne.us

● ● ● ● ● ● ● ● ● ● ● ●

Once an almost exclusively agricultural and livestock state, Nebraska now has a more diverse economy, particularly in the eastern part of the state where Omaha and Lincoln, its largest cities, are located.

In addition to being unicameral, the Nebraska legislature is also the only state legislature in the country where its members run in nonpartisan elections. Candidates are not allowed to list their party affiliation on the ballot. Furthermore, the legislature is not formally organized by political party. However, partisan tendencies are quite evident in the voting behavior and leadership votes of the members.

During the 1960s, when Supreme Court decisions indicated that state legislatures had to be based on population, many people suggested that bicameralism was no longer necessary. Many states, including California, Connecticut, Florida, Hawaii, Illinois, Kansas, Kentucky, Minnesota, Montana, New York, Oklahoma, Rhode Island, Tennessee, and Texas, considered the Nebraska model. Nebraska legislators visited several states promoting the benefits of unicameralism. However, in the end, no states made the move to replicate the Nebraska revolution.

Nebraska is a predominantly conservative and strongly Republican state that usually elects Republicans to statewide and federal office and has not supported the Democratic presidential candidate since Lyndon Johnson narrowly carried the state in his 1964 landslide victory. While the legislature is nonpartisan, three of the last four speakers of the legislature have been Republican.

Structure and Membership

Although the official name of the body is the "Nebraska Legislature," it is most commonly known as the Nebraska unicameral legislature. Legislators have the title of senator. The Nebraska unicameral legislature includes forty-nine members, each elected from a single-member district or constituency. Senators are chosen for four-year terms, with one-half of the seats being up for election every even-numbered year. Since the adoption of a constitutional initiative in 2000, legislators in Nebraska are restricted to two four-year terms.

Policies regarding services and personnel matters of the legislature are under the control of the legislature's executive board. The board includes a chairperson, a vice chairperson, six senators selected by caucus, the speaker, and the chair of the Appropriations Committee, who serves as a nonvoting ex officio member. This executive board supervises all staff (all of whom are nonpartisan) and refers bills to committees. The chair and the vice chair of the executive board are elected by the membership of the entire body in a secret ballot. The remaining members, other than the speaker and appropriations committee chair, are appointed by caucus. The legislature has three executive board caucuses, the geographical boundaries of which primarily coincide with the geographical boundaries of Nebraska's three congressional districts. Each executive board caucus selects two of its members to serve on the board. While the speaker has generally been a Republican, several Democrats have served in the post of chairman of the executive board.

A number of women and minorities have served in the Nebraska legislature. In 2005 there were twelve female senators (almost a quarter of the membership), one African American senator, and one Hispanic senator. The limited number of minority members is a slight underrepresentation of the state's population. The Nebraska legislature has fourteen standing committees, with between seven and nine members.

Processes

The Nebraska legislature convenes annually on the Wednesday after the first Monday in January. Sessions are limited to ninety legislative days in odd-numbered years and to sixty days in even-numbered years. Each session may be extended by a four-fifths vote of the legislature.

In order to facilitate an efficient legislative process, all bills, with a few exceptions, must be introduced within the first ten days of the legislative session. Bills are held over from one year to the next in the biennial session. In other words, a bill that is introduced in 2003 but does not complete the legislative process will be held over for consideration in the 2004 session. During the 2003 session, more than 800 bills were introduced. The legislature passed 259 bills, 4 of which were passed notwithstanding a gubernatorial veto. An additional 343 bills were held over for action in 2004.

Because of its unicameral nature, the Nebraska legislature has no need for conference committees. Once a bill passes out of one of the fourteen standing committees, it is considered on the floor by the full membership. If at each of three stages of consideration a bill receives the necessary number of votes on the floor

All for One and One for All

The Nebraska legislature is the only state legislative body with only one chamber. Its members are called senators, but their presiding officer is called a speaker. From the time Nebraska joined the Union in 1867 until 1933, it had a House and Senate, just like the other states. However, in the depths of the Depression, in order to save money and at the urging of "New Deal Republican" George Norris, the voters overwhelmingly (286,000 to 193,000) approved a constitutional amendment to abolish the House of Representatives. Senators abandoned their chamber, taking over the more spacious House chamber and removing more than half of the chairs.

(usually a simple majority), it goes to the desk of the governor for signature. The governor may sign a bill, veto it, or let it become law without a signature. In order to prevent decisions that are too hasty in the single chamber, all bills (except for a few housekeeping bills) must receive a public hearing, and a minimum of five days must elapse between the time that a bill is introduced and the time it passes the chamber. Also, each bill can address only one subject.

The Nebraska legislature is generally considered to be a traditional citizens legislature, with most members holding full-time jobs in addition to their legislative service. To some degree, that is necessitated by the low salaries. Legislators in Nebraska receive an annual salary of $12,000 plus a daily allowance during session. Although the expenses are based upon a per diem, legislators must verify that their actual expenses incurred are equal to or exceed their per diem reimbursement. For those senators who live within 50 miles of the capitol, the daily per diem rate is $31. If a senator lives farther than 50 miles from the capitol, the rate is $86 per day.

Each legislator has two full-time staff members, and leadership have three or four. Relatively short legislative sessions do permit many legislators to pursue outside occupations, primarily farming, law, or business pursuits. Legislative turnover is generally about 15 percent every two years. However, given that only half of the members are up for election every two years, that means that each election results in a replacement of about 30 percent of the positions being elected.

Leadership Structure

Because legislators are nonpartisan, the legislature does not have majority or minority leaders. The speaker presides over the proceedings, and the chairperson of the executive board presides over administrative details. Both officials and the vice chairperson of the executive board are elected by the full body. Historically, the two were chosen to reflect the urban-rural distribution of the state's population, with one leader from each area. However, this balance has not been as much of a concern in recent years. All leadership elections, whether for speaker, chairperson of the executive board, or committee chairs, are conducted by secret ballot of the forty-nine senators on the first day of the first session of the two-year legislative session.

The speaker of the legislature is allowed to select up to twenty-five bills each session to be priority legislation. Such priority legislation is generally considered ahead of other bills. Each rank-and-file legislator can identify one priority bill, and each committee can assign the designation to two bills referenced to it. The speaker can also designate up to five pieces of legislation as "major proposals," but each of these must be designated already as a senator's priority bill or be a general appropriations bill. Also the speaker must receive approval for a major proposal designation by two-thirds of the membership of the executive board. These major proposals move to the top of the state's legislative agenda.

Election Processes

The Nebraska unicameral includes forty-nine members, each chosen by a single-member district or constituency. Senators are chosen for four-year terms in the November even-year elections, with one-half of the seats being up for election each even-numbered year. Senators are limited by constitution to two four-year terms. Each legislative district includes about 35,000 people. Because Nebraska legislators are nonpartisan, there are no party primaries for state legislative seats. Rather, the state holds a single nonpartisan primary, in which the top two vote getters in each district primary run-off against each other in the general election.

Key Political Factors

While Nebraska legislators are officially nonpartisan, their ideological and political sympathies are rather well known. The legislature's speaker and executive board leadership indicate that they are aware of the party affiliation of each member of the chamber. Voting coalitions generally are issue driven, but they may run along ideological lines, in which case they often reflect partisan differences. The coalitions also tend to reflect the states urban-rural distinctions, with legislators from Omaha and Lincoln coming together against those from the more rural parts of the state.

Some critics of the Nebraska system—almost all of them from outside Nebraska—argue that the lack of formal Democratic and Republican Party caucuses within the legislature leads to the creation of de facto factions that can, at times, make it difficult to build coalitions for the passage of legislation. Almost all Nebraska legislators take strong issue with this criticism and vocally defend the effectiveness and desirability of both the legislature's nonpartisanship and its unicameral structure.

Some state party officials, especially Republicans, have suggested that the state should get rid of its nonpartisan elections. Indeed, some state and local parties have begun to contribute money to candidates they believe will support the positions of their party. However, support for the position that Nebraska senators elected and organized on a nonpartisan basis are able to focus more on issues than party politics is strong among Nebraska senators.

Further Reading
Berens, Charlyne. 2005. *One House: The Unicameral Progressive Vision for Nebraska*. Lincoln: University of Nebraska Press.

NEVADA

• • • • • • • • • • • •

THE NEVADA LEGISLATURE

Assembly   Senate
42 Assembly Members   21 Senators
(775) 684–8555   (775) 684–1401
http://www.leg.state.nv.us

• • • • • • • • • • • •

Nevada has been the fastest growing state in the United States over the past four decades. Its population currently increases by about 4 percent each year. The state's population is heavily concentrated in Clark County, where more than 70 percent of the state's citizens reside. The city of Las Vegas in Clark County contains almost a quarter of the state's total population. The linchpin of Nevada's economy is its gaming industry, which attracts tourists from around the world and generates much of the state's revenues.

Politically, Nevada is a highly competitive state that, as the influx of new residents from all parts of the United States continues, has increasingly become a microcosm of the country as a whole. It has supported the winning presidential candidate in all but one election (1976) since the middle of the twentieth century, and its victory margins are usually reflective of the country as a whole. This was also true in the close 2004 general election, in which George W. Bush won in Nevada and the rest of the country. In state and congressional elections, Nevadans elect almost equal numbers of Democrats and Republicans, and the state legislature has on a number of occasions been under split control.

Structure and Membership

The Nevada legislature consists of a twenty-one-member Senate and a forty-two-member Assembly. Senate members are elected for four-year terms, with seventeen elected from single-member districts and four representing two two-member districts. Assembly members are elected for two-year terms from single-member districts. In recent years, the legislature has mirrored the politically divided state, with Democrats controlling the Assembly and Republicans holding a majority in the Senate.

Women have traditionally fared quite well in the Nevada legislature. In recent years, they have held about a third of the seats in each chamber, including the posts of majority leader, minority leader, and committee chair. While there have been few Hispanic members elected to the Nevada legislature, about 10 percent of the membership is African American, which is above the statewide ethnic population of 7 percent.

The Legislative Counsel Bureau provides central, nonpartisan staff support for the legislature through its Fiscal Analysis, Legal, and Research divisions. It also includes the Audit Division, whose job consists of auditing the accounts of state agencies, and an Administrative Division, which provides accounting, security, and operating and technical support to the other divisions and to the legislature. The Legislative Counsel Bureau is supervised by the Legislative Commission, a body of twelve legislators, six from each chamber. The commission meets periodically to take action on behalf of the legislative branch of government and provide guidance to the staff of the Legislative Counsel Bureau.

Processes

The lieutenant governor, an independently elected official, is the president of the Senate. The president of the Senate and the secretary of the Senate oversee Senate sessions. The Senate elects a president pro tempore from its membership to preside over its sessions in the absence of the lieutenant governor. The speaker of the Assembly presides over its sessions and is responsible for the chamber's administration in cooperation with the chief clerk of the Assembly.

The Nevada legislature meets biennially, convening on the first Monday in February in odd-numbered years. At the 1998 general election, Nevada voters approved a constitutional amendment limiting future biennial sessions to 120 days. Since that time, there have been five special sessions, one in 2001, one in 2002, two in 2003, and one in 2004. In order to complete their business, legislators must abide by a series of introduction deadlines established at the start of each session. During the 2003 regular session, Nevada legislators considered 1,064 bills, of which 516 were approved. The governor signed 514 bills into law and allowed two to become law without his signature.

Because of the biennial nature of the Nevada legislative session, meeting in regular session every two years, the period between sessions (the twenty-month interim) is very important. The Interim Finance Committee, composed of the members of the Senate Committee on Finance and the Assembly Committee on Ways and Means from the preceding session, makes fiscal decisions for the legislature during the interim. In addition to their ongoing representational duties, members of the legislature are also involved in committee work between sessions. Members are assigned to various permanent and interim study committees to investigate a wide range of issues and make recommendations to the next session of the legislature. These committees hold public hearings, direct research, and deliberate on proposed legislation for the next regular session of the legislature.

The Nevada legislature is considered a "citizens' legislature," with its biennial sessions and absence of an annual salary. Furthermore, there is a permanent institutional staff that legislators share during the legislative session and the interim. The legislature also employs such staff as is necessary to its operations, expanding by approximately 250 session employees over its normal staffing level. When the legislature is not in session, only a small support staff is provided in both houses.

Huck and Tom Are in the House

While Nebraska is the only state that has a unicameral legislature, Nevada may be the only one that is tricameral! The "Third House" is a mock legislative body established in the 1860s to make fun of the Nevada legislature. It was originally held in local saloons, public buildings, and even the real legislative chambers. The first governor of the Third House was a young reporter with the *Territorial Enterprise* known as Josh, but whose real name was Samuel Langhorne Clemens. He would go on to international fame as Mark Twain. The tradition of the "Third House" has been continued as members of the press who cover the legislature gather at the end of each session to perform skits and mock the other two "houses" of the legislature.

The legislature depends primarily on the permanent staff of the Legislative Counsel Bureau.

Compensation for the sixty-three legislators includes salary, per diem allowance, travel expenses, postage, and telephone expenses. During the regular legislative session, legislators receive up to $7,800 in salary. Legislators' salaries are paid only for the first sixty days of the session. Many legislators maintain private-sector employment when the legislature is not in session.

Leadership Structure

The most visible leader in the House is the speaker; in the Senate, it is the lieutenant governor, who is elected with the governor. The Senate majority leader and the speaker of the Assembly determine the number of standing committees, their chairs, and the number of members on each according to political party. The Senate majority leader and the Senate minority leader appoint committee members from their own political parties. In the Assembly, the minority leader nominates committee members from the minority party, but the Assembly speaker makes all final appointments. The majority and minority leaders of each chamber are responsible for managing floor debate for their respective parties. The majority and minority parties in each chamber also have assistant leaders and majority/minority whips.

Each chamber of the Nevada legislature is organized into standing committees to analyze and process legislation. The Assembly usually has ten or eleven standing committees, typically ranging from ten to fifteen members in size. The Senate usually has nine standing committees, each with seven members. Committees in each chamber are chaired by members of the majority party. These committees may recommend that a bill pass as it is written or pass with amendments, or be amended and rerefered to another committee; committees may also indefinitely postpone consideration of a bill, or may take no action at all. Indefinitely postponing consideration of a bill effectively kills the bill, thereby keeping it from a floor vote.

Election Processes

Nevada legislators are elected in November even-year elections, with approximately half of the members of the Senate elected to their four-year terms in each even-year election. Assembly members must run for election or reelection every two years. Members of the Nevada Senate are restricted to a maximum of three four-year terms, and members of the Assembly are limited to a maximum of six two-year terms. Voters amended the state constitution in 1998 to provide term limits for legislators and certain other elected public officials. Legislators with twelve or more years in their house are not permitted to seek reelection in that house starting in 2010. The limits are for a lifetime, so members cannot sit out a term and return to the same chamber.

Based on current population estimates, the average Assembly district now includes about 56,000 Nevadans. The seventeen single-member Senate districts contain an average of 112,000 people, while the two districts with two senators average twice that number. The average district size increased in population by about 66 percent between 1991 and 2001, reflecting the state's rapid population growth.

Key Political Factors

Nevada can be expected to remain a barometer state in presidential elections, and a highly competitive state in elections for all offices. Control of the legislature can be expected to be up for grabs in most elections, with the recent history of a Republican-controlled Senate and a Democratic-controlled Assembly continuing to be likely.

Because of the distribution of the state's population, all but ten of the state's sixty-three legislators come from two counties. More than two-thirds (forty-three legislators) come from Clark County, which includes Las Vegas. Another ten come from Washoe County, which includes Reno. This distribution often pits the Clark County legislators against the rest. Obviously, representatives of the gaming industry have a keen interest in the activities of the Nevada legislature and are considered quite influential. The more than 800 lobbyists registered with the legislature are not limited in how much they can spend in their efforts to influence legislation. However, all expenditures made in behalf of a legislator or legislative caucus must be reported to the Administrative Division of the Legislative Counsel Bureau.

In terms of technology, the Nevada legislature is one of the most professional in the United States. It is the most digitally advanced legislature in the country. Its legislative website is considered among the most informative and user friendly in the United States, with easy access to information on legislators, schedules, legislation, and general information. Most of the legislative meetings are available online, and many are videoconferenced between Carson City and Las Vegas.

Further Reading

Bowers, Michael Wayne. 2002. *Sagebrush State: Nevada's History, Government and Politics.* Reno: University of Nevada Press.

Driggs, Donald E., and Leonard Goodall. 1996. *Nevada Politics and Government: Conservatism in an Open Society.* Lincoln: University of Nebraska Press.

NEW HAMPSHIRE

•••••••••••

THE NEW HAMPSHIRE GENERAL COURT

House of Representatives   Senate
400 Representatives   24 Senators
(603) 271–1110
http://www.state.nh.us/gencourt/gencourt.htm

•••••••••••

Every state is unique and every legislature has its own unusual qualities. However, perhaps no state legislature has more unusual qualities than the New Hampshire General Court. With 424 state legislators, it has the distinction of having the largest state legislative membership of the fifty states. The state's House of Representatives, with 400 of those members, calls itself the fourth largest legislative body in the world after the British House of Commons, the U.S. House of Representatives, and the Indian House of People. The dozen House members from single-member districts represents about 3,000 people, the smallest district population of any national or subnational legislative body in the world. The majority of House districts elect no more than four members to the House.

In addition, the New Hampshire General Court is the only state legislative body in the country that must contend not just with an executive but also with an elected executive council, a body established and retained in the Granite State as a check on the governor. This five-member board was created more than two centuries ago in the state's 1784 Constitution, but its origins go back another century, to a 1679 commission created by King Charles II. Each member is elected by the voters from one of five electoral districts across the state. The council has the power of approval over gubernatorial appointments, pardons, and state contracts in excess of $500,000.

Structure and Membership

The official name of New Hampshire's legislature is the New Hampshire General Court. Legislators are elected to the 24-member state Senate from single-member districts, while members of the 400-member House are elected from a mix of single- and multimember districts. All New Hampshire legislators serve two-year terms following November even-year elections. Republicans hold a two-to-one advantage in the Senate and a five-to-three majority in the House.

The president of the Senate and the speaker of the House have primary responsibility for legislative administration. There are nonpartisan staff offices for bill drafting and budget analysis that serve both chambers. Each chamber has its own nonpartisan research office.

Despite their dramatic difference in membership, the House and Senate have similar numbers of standing committees.

In 2005, there were sixteen standing committees in the Senate and twenty-one in the House. Each Senate committee is composed of a chairperson, a vice chair, and three members. On the other hand, because of the membership of the House, each House committee includes about twenty members. No House member serves on more than one committee, whereas each senator serves on a minimum of four.

Women are well represented in the New Hampshire General Court, particularly in the House of Representatives. The proportion of women in the House generally exceeds a quarter of the membership, while women senators seldom make up more than 20 percent of that body. The number of women in the House (usually well over 100) makes it among the largest contingent of women legislators in any single national or subnational legislature in the world. However, leadership has generally been in the hands of men. The House elected its first (and only) female speaker in 1996, the same year in which it appointed its first female speaker pro tempore. There have also been two female Senate presidents. In light of the limited ethnic diversity of the state, it is no surprise that there are usually few minority legislators.

Given the limited salary, it is no wonder that legislative turnover is quite high. Indeed, with turnover of at least a third every two years (33 percent in the House following the 2004 elections, and 25 percent in the Senate), the rate of membership turnover is higher than many of the states that constitutionally limit the terms of their legislators.

The New Hampshire General Court is considered one of the least professional legislatures in the country, with its very low salary and limited staffing. The 424 legislators share a permanent staff of fewer than 140. New Hampshire's state legislators must be considered perhaps the closest thing to pure citizen legislators that can be found in the United States. The annual salary of the members is only $100, and this level is set by the state constitution, which can be amended only by a two-thirds vote of the people. Citizens and legislators alike view their "citizen's legislature" with pride. The legislative website encourages constituents to contact their legislators at home, listing their home numbers on the web page.

Processes

The two-year term of the New Hampshire General Court begins (and ends) on the first Wednesday in December of the even-numbered year when both houses of the newly elected legislature organize, elect their leaders, and announce committee assignments before the regular session begins. The legislature reconvenes on the first Wednesday following the first Monday in January. The legislative session is limited to forty-five legislative days, but it may be stretched out over several months. For example, while they met for only twenty-two days in 2003, those days were stretched out over a eight-month period with the first on January 8 and the last on September 4.

There are no formal or constitutional limitations on how many bills a legislator

---

Like Father Like Son, and Son Again

When W. Douglas Scamman, Jr., was elected speaker of the New Hampshire House of Representatives in 2005, he made history on two counts. First, he was elected to the speakership after a fourteen-year absence from the post and from the chamber. He was speaker of the House from 1987 to 1991, before stepping down from the legislature to run for the U.S. House of Representatives and pursue other positions. Second, he took the post that had been held by his father, W. Douglas Scamman, Sr., almost fifty years earlier. Interestingly, speaker Scamman's wife, Stella, is also a member of the House, representing the same multimember district as her husband.

---

can introduce or when those bills must be introduced, although legislative rules require that bills must be introduced early in the session. All bills introduced must have hearings, and all bills must be reported from their respective committees to the floor of the chamber of origin. The more than 400 legislators introduced only 988 bills during the 2003 session, passing 318 of them.

Surprisingly, given their emphasis on limited government and the nobility of government service, there are very few restrictions on lobbyists in the Granite State. While they do have to register with the secretary of state, there are few limitations on activities in which they can engage and no limits on how much money they can spend lobbying legislators.

Leadership Structure

The president of the Senate is the chamber's top leader. Because New Hampshire has no lieutenant governor, the Senate president is first in line to assume the governorship in the event of a vacancy in the office. The speaker of the House is the top leader of the House of Representatives. The speaker, who ranks second in line for the governorship after the Senate president, does not vote except to create or break a tie. Both of these leaders preside over their respective chambers, manage floor debate, and assign members and chairmen to the legislative committees. They also determine which legislative committee will evaluate the bills introduced by their members.

Senate and House majority leaders lead floor debate and organize and develop party positions. They also serve as a communications link between the speaker and the large membership. The minority leaders lead floor debate and organize and develop party positions for the minority party. The majority and minority leaders are assisted by deputy leaders, especially in the House.

Election Processes

New Hampshire legislators are elected to their two-year terms in the November even-year election. Nominees are selected in party primaries. New Hampshire voters vote for one Senate candidate in their single-member district. However, most House members are elected to multimember districts, with only a dozen elected to single-member districts. Two districts elect thirteen legislators, while two others elect eleven and ten, respectively. The remaining districts elect anywhere from two (sixteen districts) to nine (two districts) legislators.

Because of this arrangement, selecting House candidates is rather complex. Each party can nominate a number of candidates equal to the number of representatives from that district. Because a number of districts are not considered competitive, it is not uncommon for one party—more often, the Democrats in rural, heavily Republican parts of the state—to list fewer candidates on the ballot than the number of seats from the district. Voters vote for a number of candidates equal to the number of seats from the district.

Campaigns in New Hampshire, especially the House, are usually low key and very personal. The New Hampshire House may be one of the few state legislatures left in which you can run a successful campaign by printing a few brochures, knocking on doors, and handing out football schedules or fans with your name on them!

Key Political Factors

Since the latter part of the twentieth century, New Hampshire has been transformed from a predominantly conservative, Republican state into a much more competitive state that has supported presidential candidates and elected governors from both political parties. Much of this competition comes from the large number of independents, who outnumber those registered either Republican or Democrat. Unlike those who claim no

party affiliation in many states, being independent in New Hampshire does not signal a lack of interest in politics, but truly a willingness to vote for either party.

One reason for this shift toward the Democratic Party has been an influx of out-of-staters into the most southern part of the state, some parts of which have become commuting suburbs of Boston. Lower real estate prices than in the immediate Boston metropolitan area continue to attract new residents to this part of the state. While the strength of New Hampshire's Democratic Party has been growing in recent years, the Republican Party remains the stronger of the two parties, particularly in elections other than those for president and governor, in which Democrats have found their greatest success. While the 400-member House has remained under continuous Republican control, the Democrats have been able to win control of the much smaller Senate a few times.

Because of its size, small districts, low salaries, and limited legislative session, the New Hampshire House of Representatives is like stepping back in time, where legislators are truly part of "the people," going home every night to live, eat, and work among them. With such small districts, legislators know most of their constituents, and constituents know their legislators.

Further Reading
New Hampshire General Court Ethics Booklet: Ethics Guidelines and Procedural Rules. November 2004. (http://gencourt.state.nh.us/misc/ethics.pdf.)

NEW JERSEY

•••••••••••••

THE NEW JERSEY GENERAL ASSEMBLY

Assembly	Senate
80 Assemblymen	40 Senators
(609) 292–5135	(609) 292–6821

http://www.njleg.state.nj.us

•••••••••••••

In many ways, New Jersey is a state of contradictions. It is the most urban state in the nation, but more than 20 percent of its land is productive farmland; it ranks among the top nationally in the production of most garden vegetables. Its diverse economy is sandwiched between chemical and oil refineries to the north and tourism along its southern coastal areas, anchored by Atlantic City. It is one of the wealthiest and most economically diverse states in the country, but it often gets crowded out by its neighbors to the east (New York) and the west (Pennsylvania).

Politically, New Jersey is also a contradiction in today's world of strongly Republican or highly Democratic states. It is an extremely competitive state, with the governorship and control of the legislature frequently switching back and forth between Democrats and Republicans. The national Republican Party has recently been seen as more conservative than the state party, and moderate Republican candidates have generally enjoyed the greatest success against Democrats.

Structure and Membership

The New Jersey legislature consists of a forty-member Senate and an eighty-member General Assembly. Senate terms are four years (except for the first election in each decade, when they are two), and Assembly terms are two years. Partisan control of the two chambers has been quite balanced, although it tends to be trending Democratic in the early part of the twenty-first century. The 2001 elections yielded a tied Senate, but Democrats regained the majority in 2003.

The percentage of women legislators in the Garden State historically lags behind the rest of the nation, hovering around 15 percent. While women chair committees, there have been few women in high-ranking leadership posts. The proportion of African American legislators also stays around 15 percent, which is quite similar to their proportion in the general population. At less than 10 percent, the percentage of Hispanic legislators is a bit below their state proportion.

The legislature has a large staff, both partisan and nonpartisan. Nonpartisan staff services are provided by the Office of Legislative Services, which operates under the jurisdiction of the Legislative Services Commission, a sixteen-member bipartisan panel with equal representation from each house. The office, which is headed by an executive director appointed by the commission, provides administrative, bill drafting, and general and fiscal research services.

Like all other state legislatures, the New Jersey General Assembly organizes itself into standing committees, with each chamber selecting a number of well-staffed and informed committees. However, relative to most other states, committees in the Garden State have relatively limited power, with limited influence on shaping the agenda or influencing the floor passage of legislation. The Senate usually organizes into about a dozen standing committees, while the larger House usually has about twice that many. The speaker selects committee members and chairs in the Assembly. In the Senate, the president selects them.

Processes

With no limitation on session length, the New Jersey legislature meets on a year-round basis, usually only one or two days per week (usually Mondays and Thursdays), with committee meetings and hearings often held on the nonsession days. Because the session extends for two years, bills not acted upon during the first (even year) are automatically carried forward to the second year. Because of the full-time nature of the institution, there are no limitations on bill introduction. The failure to limit introductions is evident in the number of bills introduced. In 2003, New Jersey legislators introduced more than 11,000 pieces of legislation! Of those, fewer than 500 passed both chambers; the governor vetoed nineteen.

Only the legislature's leaders and a handful of senior members have personal offices at the state capitol in Trenton, but all legislators are provided with funds for a district office and personal staff assistants. Given the legislature's one- or two-day-a-week meeting schedule, the state's small size geographically, which permits members to commute to Trenton on session days, and the state-funded district offices, most legislators and their personal staffs operate primarily out of their district offices.

New Jersey legislators are paid an annual salary of around $50,000 per year, placing them in the top five in legislative compensation. The General Assembly employs more than 1,500 employees in the legislators' Trenton and district offices. The salaries, staff, and lack of session limits make the New Jersey General Assembly one of the more professional in the country. Legislative turnover is generally around 10 to 15 percent every two years, with most attributed to voluntary retirement rather than electoral defeat.

Leadership Structure

The Senate is headed by its president, who presides over its operation. With no lieutenant governor, the Senate president is first in line to succeed the governor in the event of a vacancy in the position. The General Assembly is headed by the speaker, who presides over its activities and is second in line, after the Senate president, for governor. Each chamber also has a majority leader, a minority leader, assistant leaders, and whips. The speaker and Senate president appoint committees and committee chairs in their chambers.

What Separation of Powers?

Richard Codey, acting governor and Senate president of New Jersey, may well be the envy of legislative leaders and governors across the country. As acting governor (taking over when the governor resigned), he can propose legislation with the full force of his executive office. As Senate president, he can preside over one of the two legislative chambers that must pass the legislation he proposed as acting governor! As of 2005, New Jersey was the only state whose acting governor remains the Senate president when he or she ascends to the office of governor. In 2005, voters chose to create an office of lieutenant governor. Candidates for this office will run with their party's nominee for governor and would take over in case of resignation or death of the governor. The change takes effect in 2010.

Leadership tenure used to be very brief, usually limited to one term. Beginning in the latter part of the twentieth century, however, tenures became longer; it is now not uncommon for a Senate president or Assembly speaker to serve more than one term in the position. The speaker of the General Assembly and the president of the Senate receive one-third above the regular salary for their positions, while the other elected leaders receive no additional compensation. Both are considered among the most powerful legislative leaders in the country, with very strong powers relative to committees, agenda setting, floor management, and the ability to serve long terms in leadership.

Election Processes

With two assembly members and one senator in each of the state's forty legislative districts, all New Jersey legislators represent the same size constituency. The average district includes more than 200,000 people. New Jersey is one of four states that hold their state legislative elections in November of odd-numbered years. The others are Mississippi, Virginia, and Louisiana.

The state is divided into forty legislative districts, with each district electing one senator and two assembly members. Sessions convene on the second Tuesday in January in even-numbered years for a two-year term, with no limitations on length. Each party nominates two General Assembly candidates and one senatorial candidate per district. Voters vote for two General Assembly candidates. Senators are elected for four-year terms except in the first election of a decade, when they are elected for two years to conform to the decennial reapportionment.

Because of the urban nature of most of the legislative districts and their proximity to the expensive mass-media markets of New York City and Philadelphia, legislative elections can be very costly. It is not unheard of for a legislator to spend more than $100,000 on a seat in the New Jersey General Assembly. In the relatively few highly competitive districts (about ten out of the forty), it is not unusual for the two parties to spend up to $2 million trying to elect the senator and two representatives for the district.

In 2004, the New Jersey legislature adopted the Fair and Clean Elections (FACE) Pilot Program, providing public financing in two legislative districts in

2005. Candidates in these two districts (selected by the parties) agree to various conditions, including raising a certain amount of money in the district and accepting only money donated through the NJ Clean Elections Fund up to $100,000. In 2007, the program will expand to include four of the state's forty legislative districts. The impact of the reform will depend on which districts are chosen for the program—if the districts are chosen from the thirty or so that are considered safe for one party or the other, the effect is likely to be small.

Key Political Factors

Because of the unique nature of the state's legislative process, which allows members to spend the greatest portion of their time in their state-funded district offices, New Jersey legislators have greater opportunities for constituent contact and interaction than do their counterparts in most other states.

Because New Jersey holds its state elections in odd-numbered years, its elections are sometimes seen by national party leaders as barometers of how a president is faring in the first year of a term and of what voters may be thinking in the year preceding an upcoming presidential election.

Politics in the Garden State are often fought along demographic lines, with Democrats controlling the urban areas in Newark, Jersey City, and Paterson but Republicans staking claim to the more rural southern communities. The political "brass ring" is the growing suburban areas around the cities and bordering Philadelphia and New York City.

Further Reading

Salmore, Barbara G., and Stephen A. Salmore. 1998. *New Jersey Politics and Government: Suburban Politics Comes of Age.* 2d ed. Lincoln: University of Nebraska Press.
Stonecash, Jeffery M., and Mary P. McGuire. 2003. *Emergence of State Government: Parties and New Jersey Politics, 1950–1999.* Madison, NJ: Farleigh Dickinson University Press.

NEW MEXICO

• • • • • • • • • • • •

THE NEW MEXICO LEGISLATURE

House of Representatives	Senate
70 Delegates	42 Senators
(505) 986–4751	(505) 986–4714

http://www.legis.state.nm.us

• • • • • • • • • • • •

New Mexico was the next to last of the forty-eight continental states to become a state, joining the Union one month ahead of Arizona in 1912. It has the largest Hispanic population of any state, with more than four out of every ten New Mexicans of Hispanic origin. It is famous for the Los Alamos scientific laboratory, where the atomic bomb was developed during World War II.

Unlike many of its neighboring states, which tend toward the Republican Party, New Mexico is a highly competitive state that leans Democratic. The state's elections for state and congressional offices are usually tightly contested, while the state legislature is most often under Democratic control. In recent elections it has become a battleground state for the presidential election. The large Hispanic population sets the state apart from many of the other Western states, which are consistently Republican. However, recent political trends indicate that the Hispanic community may provide an opportunity for Republican growth.

Structure and Membership

The New Mexico legislature consists of a forty-two-member Senate and a seventy-member House of Representatives. Senate members are elected for four-year terms, and House members are elected for two-year terms from single-member districts. The state has the smallest population ratio between House and Senate districts of any state legislature. New Mexico and Delaware are the only states in which the House or Assembly membership is not at least twice the size of the state's Senate membership. Democrats hold a substantial but declining margin over Republicans as we enter into the first part of the twenty-first century.

As in many of the Western states, women tend to do quite well in the New Mexico legislature, holding about a third of the seats in the House and a quarter or so of the seats in the Senate. They also chair a significant proportion of the House and Senate standing committees. Reflecting the population of the state, the New Mexico legislature has few African American members, but the nation's highest proportion of Hispanic members. The proportion of Hispanic members usually exceeds or approaches 40 percent of each chamber. Furthermore, most of the key leaders (speaker, pro tempore, and floor leaders) are usually Hispanic.

The Senate president pro tempore and the House speaker provide nonpartisan professional staff services under a twenty-nine-member legislative council that is cochaired. The council coordinates most of the legislature's work between sessions, and its staff handles general administrative responsibilities for the legislature.

New Mexico's legislative committee system is generally considered to be among the weakest committee systems in all the fifty state legislatures. Both the House and Senate organize themselves into standing committees to conduct the business of the state. The House traditionally has about fifteen standing committees, with between eight and eighteen members. All committee chairs and vice chairs are members of the majority party. The Senate normally has nine or ten standing committees with ten to twelve members. As in the House, chairs and vice chairs of all Senate standing committees are from the majority party. New Mexico's legislative committees have limited ability to shape, screen, or affect the passage of the legislation referred to them for review, relative to the power of committees in most other states.

Because the New Mexico legislature's regular session cannot exceed sixty (odd years) or thirty (even years) days, interim committees are extremely important. Traditionally, the legislature will have at least twenty such committees that meet regu-

What's in a Name?

"A rose by any other name," wrote William Shakespeare, "would smell as sweet." Such was not true for Raymond Sanchez, longtime speaker of the New Mexico House of Representatives. In 2000, Democratic speaker Raymond L. Sanchez was defeated for reelection to the House by the relatively politically unknown Republican John Sanchez. Most blame the defeat, at least in some part, on confusion over the names. Ray Sanchez returned to private law practice, and John Sanchez ran as the Republican candidate for governor in 2002, losing to former U.S. ambassador Bill Richardson. In 2004, the members of the New Mexico Senate elected Raymond Sanchez's brother, Michael Sanchez, majority floor leader.

larly between legislative sessions. They include between ten and thirty members, with members from each chamber being appointed by the president pro tempore of the Senate and representatives being appointed by the speaker of the House.

Processes

The president of the Senate (lieutenant governor) and the speaker of the House preside over sessions in their respective chambers. The president pro tempore and the speaker, in consultation with their majority leaders, determine their chambers' agendas.

The New Mexico legislature meets annually, convening on the third Tuesday in January. Odd-year sessions are limited to sixty calendar days, and even-year sessions to thirty calendar days. Even-year sessions are primarily limited to consideration of budgetary matters. In order to meet this very tight schedule, no legislation can be introduced after the thirtieth day of the sixty-day session, or beyond the fifteenth day of the thirty-day session. There is no provision for introducing legislation after that point in each session.

Legislation not acted on by the governor within twenty days of adjournment is considered "pocket vetoed." In 2003, New Mexico legislators introduced 1,902 pieces of legislation, enacting 439. The governor vetoed 84, 12 by signed veto and 72 by pocket veto (he failed to sign them, so they were considered vetoed after twenty days).

The New Mexico legislature is a true "citizen's legislature," with members receiving no annual salary. They do receive a per diem and travel allowance for the days they are in session and when their committees meet during the interim (the period between legislative sessions). These payments may reach as high as $10,000 during the sixty-day session and half that during the thirty-day session year. Leaders receive no additional pay for their efforts. Legislators have staff support only when the legislature is in session. All legislators rely on an additional source of income outside of the legislature.

Leadership Structure

The president pro tempore of the Senate and the speaker of the House are the top leaders of their respective chambers.

However, the speaker is considerably more powerful in his chamber. The speaker appoints all committee members and committee chairs, whereas the Committee on Committees makes the Senate committee decisions. While the president pro tempore appoints and chairs that committee, he does not have control over its decisions.

The majority and minority floor leaders of each chamber are responsible for managing floor debate for their respective parties. The majority and minority leaders of each house have one assistant floor leader.

Although legislative leaders in New Mexico receive no additional salary for their service, it is quite common for leaders in the New Mexico legislature to serve extended terms. One recent speaker served eighteen years, and his counterpart in the Senate served fourteen.

Election Processes

New Mexico legislators are elected in the November even-year election. House members run every two years, and all senators are elected to their four-year terms in the same election. Each senator represents about 44,000 people, and each House member about 26,000. Because of the sparse population in some areas of the state, some legislators, especially in the Senate, represent geographically large districts that create unique campaign challenges. Contested nominations are decided in party primaries.

Key Political Factors

Much of the politics of New Mexico is driven by the conflicts between Albu-

querque and its surrounding area, while more than a quarter of the state's population resides in the smaller communities around the state. Of late, the northern parts of the state have tended to vote Democratic, while the eastern and southern parts have tended to be more supportive of the Republican Party.

The Democratic legislature has had some political clashes with some of the state's Republican governors that verge on legendary. When Republican businessman Gary Johnson (1995–2003) was governor, he became known as "Governor No" for his constant vetoing of legislation passed by the Democratic-controlled legislature.

New Mexico can be expected to remain a highly competitive state that leans toward the Democratic Party. Increased efforts by the Republican Party to appeal to Hispanic voters using social issues in 2004 likely tipped the state in the Republican column for President Bush. It remains to be seen if that Republican shift can be replicated in future elections.

Because of the less professional nature of the New Mexico legislature, lobbyists are a significant source of information. More than a thousand lobbyists registered their intentions to lobby the legislature during the most recent session. They are not limited in how much they can spend in efforts to influence legislation.

Further Reading

Hain, Paul L., F. Chris Garcia, and Gilbert K. St. Clair. 1994. *New Mexico Government*. Albuquerque: University of New Mexico Press.

NEW YORK

• • • • • • • • • • •

The New York Legislature

Assembly	Senate
150 Assembly Members	62 Senators

(518) 455–2800

http://www.assembly.state.ny.us   http://www.senate.state.ny.us

• • • • • • • • • • • •

Given its historical prominence in the colonies, the roots of legislative governance came a bit later in New York (1683) than one might expect. It came more than sixty years after the establishment of such a body in Virginia and after their establishment in the New England states of New Hampshire, Connecticut, and Massachusetts. However, despite this late start, the New York legislature has become one of the most professional state legislatures in the United States.

The New York legislature, once held up alongside the California General Assembly as the model legislature to which all others should aspire, has found its image tarnished a bit as public interests and ideologies across the country have shifted. Its full-time status, high salaries, and professional staff that were once the envy of most are now accused by some of being "too professional." Its progressive policies, which led the way for other states in a variety of policy areas, are now decried in some quarters as "big government." However, despite these criticisms, or perhaps because of them, the New York legislature remains one of the most professional, well-funded, and well-staffed legislative bodies in the world.

Because of the cosmopolitan makeup of its population, there is a natural base of support for each party in the state. Democrats generally do well in and around New York City, while Republicans draw more support upstate. In recent years, however, with more population growth in New York City, the state has trended more Democratic.

Structure and Membership

The state Senate is composed of 62 members and the State Assembly of 150. Legislators are elected from single-member districts for two-year terms. With rare exceptions relating to landslide presidential or gubernatorial victories, the Senate has been under Republican control and the Assembly under Democratic control since the mid-1970s. However, in recent elections, Democrats have closed the gap in the Senate. In 2005 the margin was eight seats, so that a shift of only four seats would yield a tie.

Annual regular sessions convene on the Wednesday after the first Monday in January and have no limitation on length, although legislative leaders generally try to limit each one to no more than six months. Each chamber is

---

Leaders Everywhere

While leadership may be rare, leadership positions are not, at least not in the New York legislature. More than a third of the members of the Senate (thirty members) and the Assembly (forty-one members) are assigned some leadership title and considered a part of the leadership team. Not a very exclusive club!

---

dominated by its top leader—the majority leader (who also carries the title of president pro tempore) of the Senate and the speaker of the Assembly. Administratively, each chamber operates autonomously, with the staff of the Senate majority leader and the Assembly speaker providing coordination. The majority of the legislative staff members are appointed on a partisan basis, with minority staff subject to supervision by the minority leadership.

Both chambers generally have more than thirty standing committees that review and act on all of the legislation introduced in the legislature. In 2003 the Senate had thirty-three such committees, compared with thirty-eight in the House. All major legislation is reviewed by the standing committee to which it is assigned by the speaker (House) or the majority leader (Senate).

Women fare reasonably well in the New York legislature, making up at least 20 percent of the membership in recent years. In 2003, about 22 percent of the legislators were women. However, only three of the thirty-three Senate committees are chaired by women. They do better in the Assembly, with seven of the thirty-eight positions now held by women. Since its establishment in 1981,

the New York State Assembly Task Force on Women's Issues has reviewed legislation and identified issues that affect women, initiated new legislation, and promoted pending legislation concerned with the specific problems of New York State's women.

African Americans also have a relatively strong presence in the New York legislature, making up about 15 percent of the membership. The minority leader of the Senate is African American, as are several committee chairs in the Assembly. As the Latino population of New York City has gone up, so has the number and influence of Latinos in the legislature. In 2003, they constituted 15 percent of each chamber.

Processes

The lieutenant governor, who is elected on a ticket with the governor, has the title of president of the Senate and presides over its sessions. However, the lieutenant governor exercises no power in the Senate other than the right to preside and to break a tie vote. The speaker presides over Assembly proceedings.

New York's legislative process is dominated by the Senate majority leader and speaker of the Assembly, who maintain strict control over the agendas of their respective chambers. Along with the governor, they are considered the most powerful people in New York state government, and the three officials are often referred to as the Big Three. Like any elected officials, New York legislative leaders must listen to their members or risk losing their support. However, the formal powers assigned to each places them among the most powerful in the country.

Because the state's fiscal year begins on April 1—less than three months after the convening of the session—the legislature is seldom able to adopt a state budget prior to the commencement of the fiscal year. In an attempt to alleviate what has become an almost annual crisis, the legislature has been looking for some time at the possibility of moving the beginning of the fiscal year to June 1 or July 1.

With a base salary of almost $80,000 and a per diem rate of reimbursement that varies by location of the district, it is not unusual for New York legislators to earn more than $100,000 per year. Furthermore, all legislators have a full-time staff in the capitol, as well as in their district office. With a full-time legislative staff in excess of 3,500, New York's permanent staff is larger than that of any other state, and larger than the permanent staffs of the twenty-seven least staffed legislatures in the country added together.

In 2003, members of the New York legislature introduced more than 14,000 pieces of legislation, but enacted only 697 of them. Seventy-two of these bills were vetoed by the governor.

Leadership Structure

The legislature's leadership structure consists of the Senate majority leader (also called the temporary president) and the Senate minority leader, the Assembly speaker, Assembly majority leader, and Assembly minority leaders. While there are many people on the "leadership teams" in each chamber, including the chairs and vice chairs of the Senate Finance and the Assembly Ways and Means Committees, the real power resides with the two top leaders.

The speaker of the House and the majority leader of the Senate are considered among the most influential in the country. In addition to the traditional roles of presiding, managing the debate, setting the agenda, and making committee and chair assignments, leaders in New York also handpick most of the other leaders on their team and have access to large amounts of campaign money to assist in the elections of their members. All of this translates into so much influence on the legislature that most consider the speaker, the Senate majority leader, and the governor (one of the most powerful in the United States) to be on equal footing.

The speaker of the Democrat-dominated Assembly almost always comes from New York City, from which more than 40 percent of the state's legislators are elected. The majority leader of the Senate, which most recently has been under Republican control, usually represents an upstate district but, on occasion, comes from Long Island or Westchester County. The legislature does not have any tradition of limited leadership tenures, and individuals who ascend to the position of Senate majority leader and Assembly speaker usually remain in their respective positions for several terms.

As of the early part of the twenty-first century, New York senator David A. Paterson, who is legally blind, serves as the minority leader of the Senate. While not the first or only legally blind state legislator in the United States, he is believed to be the first to rise to the pinnacle of power of his legislative party.

Election Processes

New York legislators are elected from single-member districts for two-year terms in the November even-year election. Contested nominations are decided by direct primary. While most districts in New York City and rural upstate areas are considered safe for one party or the other, the few closely contested elections in either chamber can have some of the most costly state legislative campaigns in the country. However, because of partisan districting and incumbent security, elections to the New York Assembly and Senate are seldom competitive.

Key Political Factors

Geographically and politically, New York has three rather distinct political subdivisions: New York City, which is overwhelmingly Democratic; the New York suburban areas (primarily Long Island and Westchester County), which might be termed "swing" areas; and the upstate areas, in which, with the exception of a few urban Democratic enclaves, Republicans are generally dominant.

With the Senate usually under Republican control, the Assembly almost always controlled by the Democrats, and the governorship as likely to be controlled by one party as the other, the so-called Big Three are required to negotiate and compromise on most major issues. This has, on occasion, led to protracted deadlocks over the past few decades. Split control of the chambers also allows each political party to appease its support groups by passing bills in the chamber it controls with the knowledge and understanding that the legislation will never be passed by the other chamber.

Further Reading

Creelan, Jeremy M., and Laura M. Moulton. 2004. *The New York State Legislative Process: An Evaluation and Blueprint for Reform.* New York: Brennan Center for Justice at NYU School of Law.

Liebschultz, Sarah F., Jane Shapiro Zacek, and Joseph F. Zimmerman. 1998. *New York Government and Politics: Competition and Compassion.* Lincoln: University of Nebraska Press.

Pecorella, Robert F., and Jeffrey M. Stonecash, eds. 2005. *Governing New York.* 5th ed. Albany: State University of New York Press.

Schneier, Edward V., and Brian Murtaugh. 2001. *New York Politics: A Tale of Two States.* Armonk, NY: M. E. Sharpe.

NORTH CAROLINA

• • • • • • • • • • • •

THE NORTH CAROLINA GENERAL ASSEMBLY

House of Representatives
120 Representatives

Senate
50 Senators

(919) 733–4111
http://www.ncga.state.nc.us

• • • • • • • • • • • •

North Carolina is a state that has a little of everything—an Atlantic coastline whose Outer Banks are one of the Eastern Seaboard's most popular vacation spots, a mountainous western region that signals the beginnings of Appalachia, and a great intellectual center in the Raleigh/Durham/Chapel Hill Triangle. The state has a diverse economy, featuring manufacturing, agriculture, financial services, and high technology.

For a century following the Civil War, North Carolina was a solidly Democratic state in which the state's Republican Party was a nonfactor in elections, even though some of the counties in the western part of the state voted consistently Republican. In the late 1960s, North Carolina's generally conservative electorate began to look more and more to the Republican Party, and it experienced a period of rapid growth that led to success, particularly in federal elections.

As in a number of other Southern states, Democrats have been most successful in fending off the Republican expansion in state legislative elections. Republicans finally won control of the state House of Representatives for the first time since the Reconstruction era in 1994, but Democrats regained the majority four years later. The Democrats have maintained control of the state Senate for more than 130 years.

Structure and Membership

The North Carolina General Assembly consists of a 50-member Senate and a 120-member House of Representatives. All legislators serve for two-year terms and represent single-member districts. Democrats have maintained control of both chambers since Reconstruction, with the exception of two sessions in the 1990s, when the Republicans held a slim majority of the House seats (1995–1999) and the 2003 session, in which each party had sixty seats in the House at the beginning of the session.

The proportion of female legislators is gradually growing in the state but still lags behind that of many others. Women usually hold 10 to 15 percent of the seats in the Senate and around a quarter of the seats in the House. In recent sessions, women legislators have also chaired key committees and subcommittees. African American legislators hold 12 to 15 percent of the seats in each chamber. From

The Black and Decker Coalition

Selecting a speaker is usually simple and takes a matter of minutes. In 2003, it took the North Carolina House a matter of days, not minutes, to achieve that feat. Following the 2002 elections, Republicans held a one-seat majority in the legislature. However, that majority was wiped out prior to opening day when one Republican dissident decided to join the Democratic Party, giving each party sixty members. Former Republican Michael Decker agreed to support Democrat Jim Black for speaker in what became jokingly known as the Black and Decker Coalition. After five intense days, the parties agreed on a power sharing agreement whereby North Carolina would have two speakers for the first time in its history.

1991 to 1995, Representative Dan Blue, and African American legislator, held the post of speaker of the House. Historically, the North Carolina General Assembly has had few Hispanic members, but demographic changes in the state are likely to change that.

Professional staff services are provided by nonpartisan divisions that operate under the direction of the fourteen-member Joint Legislative Services Commission, which is cochaired by the Senate president pro tempore and House speaker. Each house also has a small number of partisan staff assistants. The Legislative Services Commission oversees the five divisions: Bill Drafting, Fiscal Research, Legislative Research and Library, Administration, and Information Systems. These nonpartisan units serve the needs of all legislators. The offices of principal clerk in the House and Senate are vital to each chamber's administration and are also overseen by the Legislative Services Commission.

Each chamber of the North Carolina General Assembly includes standing committees, approximately twenty in the Senate and approximately thirty in the House. While seniority is important in the appointment of committee membership and chairs, the relationship with the speaker (in the House) and the president pro tempore (in the Senate) is even more important.

Each House committee, with the exception of Appropriations and Finance, has fifteen to twenty members. Traditionally, every member of the House serves on either Finance or Appropriations, with about eighty members sitting on House Appropriations. In the Senate, most committees have around ten members, but more than 80 percent of the senators serve on Appropriations, as do about two-thirds on Finance.

Processes

The lieutenant governor, in that office's capacity as Senate president, presides over Senate sessions, and the speaker of the House presides over House sessions. The Senate president pro tempore and the House speaker, in consultation with their majority leaders and rules chairmen, determine their chamber agendas.

The North Carolina General Assembly meets biennially, convening on the third Wednesday after the second Monday in January in odd-numbered years, called the "long session." There is no limit on session length, but it generally concludes by mid- or late July. The General Assembly meets in even-numbered years for its "short session," usually beginning in May and meeting for about eight weeks. The primary goal of the short session is adjustment of the two-year budget passed in the long session. Introduction of legislation is severely curtailed during the short session.

In the House, members must meet certain deadlines for introduction. For example, in the 2003 session, all bills with no financial impact had to be introduced by April 9, while "money bills" had to be in by April 16. All bills referred from the Senate had to be introduced in the House by May 1. During the 2003 legislative session, members of the North Carolina General Assembly introduced 2,302 pieces of legislation, passing 433 of them, and saw 2 vetoed by the governor.

The North Carolina General Assembly is considered to be a hybrid of a professional legislature and a part-time, or citizen, legislature. While many of its members hold jobs in the private sector, the fact that recent "long sessions" have lasted eight or nine months makes it difficult for those legislators to continue to serve in their private jobs. With an annual base salary of just under $14,000 and a per diem allowance of just over $100, a North Carolina legislator will typically make more than $30,000 during the long session year and around $20,000 during the short session.

Leadership Structure

The president pro tempore is the top leadership position in the Senate. Until 1988, when a Republican lieutenant governor was elected, along with a heavily Democratic Senate, that honor went to the lieutenant governor; the pro tempore position was primarily an honor afforded the most senior senator. Following the 1988 election, leaders in the Senate shifted much of the appointment, assignment, and agenda-setting powers to the president pro tempore.

The lieutenant governor and the speaker preside over their chambers and make committee assignments. The Senate president pro tempore and majority leader, the House majority leader, and the Senate and House minority leaders are responsible for managing floor debate for their respective parties. There are a number of assistant majority and minority leaders in each chamber, referred to as whips.

When North Carolina's governor was restricted to one four-year term, legislative leadership traditionally rotated every two or four years. However, when North Carolina voters in 1977 allowed governors to seek two consecutive terms, legislative leaders began to serve longer terms as well.

Election Processes

North Carolina legislators are elected in the November even-year election. Each senator and representative is elected from single-member districts. The average Senate district has about 170,000 people, and the average House district includes about 70,000. Historically, state legislative campaigns were relatively inexpensive, but the increasing partisan balance of the legislature and the importance of each seat has increased the cost and the party involvement in each legislative race. Party nominations are determined by primary, which is usually held in May preceding the November general election.

Key Political Factors

The strength of the well-organized and well-funded North Carolina Republican Party can be expected to continue to grow, making it increasingly difficult for Democrats to retain control of the state General Assembly, which they dominated for more than 125 years following the Civil War. However, state Democrats have maintained control by distancing themselves from the national Democratic Party and taking the correct position on issues important to the state, including agriculture, textiles, and outsourcing.

Politics in the Tar Heel State have often been divided along regional lines, with each of the state's three regions focusing on different issues and needs. The mountainous western region includes the part of the state that did not support secession during the Civil War and has traditionally supported the Republican Party. The central, or Piedmont, region of the state is more progressive and includes the state's major urban centers, institutions of higher education, and well-educated and professional population. Democrats and Republicans fight hard for votes in this region. For decades, eastern North Carolina and its coast was the state's bastion of conservative, "yellow-dog" Democrats, who focused on agriculture and traditional values. In recent years this area has become increasingly Republican, with the exception of several more urban areas. These regional differences sometimes override partisan differences on legislative votes.

Because individual legislators are provided rather limited policy staff, the more than 500 registered lobbyists are a significant source of policy information. As campaigns have become more expensive and competitive, lobbyists have become increasingly important sources of campaign support.

Further Reading

Bass, Jack, and Walter De Vries. 1995. *The Transformation of Southern Politics: Social Change and Political Consequence Since 1945.* Athens: University of Georgia Press.

Beyle, Thad, and Merle Black, eds. 1975. *Politics and Policy in North Carolina.* New York: Irvington.

Fleer, Jack D. 1994. *North Carolina Politics and Policy.* Lincoln: University of Nebraska Press.

Leubke, Paul. 2000. *Tar Heel Politics, 2000.* Chapel Hill: University of North Carolina Press.

NORTH DAKOTA

● ● ● ● ● ● ● ● ● ● ●

THE NORTH DAKOTA LEGISLATIVE ASSEMBLY

House of Representatives	Senate
94 Representatives	47 Senators
(701) 328–2916	(701) 328–2916

http://www.state.nd.us

● ● ● ● ● ● ● ● ● ● ●

North Dakota is the nation's third least populated state, after Alaska and Vermont. Agriculture, particularly wheat, barley, and oats, is a major part of the state's economy. But the manufacturing sector has become increasingly important, with farm equipment, processed foods, and fabricated metal among its most important products. It also has a growing tourism industry, built around the Badlands and the state's scenic natural wonders.

In presidential voting, North Dakota is a strongly Republican state, having voted for the Democratic candidate only once since the middle of the twentieth century (Lyndon Johnson in his 1964 landslide victory). Democratic candidates have fared much better in other elections, winning their share of congressional and state elections. While the state legislature has remained under fairly regular Republican control, the Democrats have, on occasion, enjoyed majorities in one of the chambers.

Structure and Membership

The North Dakota Legislative Assembly includes the Senate, which has forty-seven members, and the House of Repre-

sentatives, with its ninety-four. The state is divided into forty-seven legislative districts, with each district electing one state senator and two state representatives districtwide. Prior to redistricting following the 2000 census, the Senate had forty-nine members and the House ninety-eight.

Women have historically made up a relatively small portion of the membership of the North Dakota Assembly, seldom reaching more than 15 percent of that body. In 2005, there were eighteen women in the House and five in the Senate. Reflecting the homogeneous population, there are no African American or Hispanic legislators in the Assembly.

The lieutenant governor, who is elected on a ticket with the governor, is president of the Senate and presides over its sessions. The Senate elects a president pro tempore and majority leader from its membership. The Senate majority leader holds the bulk of the legislative power in the Senate. The speaker of the House presides over House sessions. However, unlike every other statehouse in the United States, the speaker of the House has limited power apart from presiding. The power to appoint committees and to set the agenda lies squarely

---

Taking It to the (State) Bank

When North Dakota legislators talk about "taking it to the bank," they mean it literally! In 1919, the North Dakota Assembly created the Bank of North Dakota. It is, to this day, the only state-owned bank in the United States. It is the fifth biggest contributor to the state's general fund. Between 2001 and 2003, the bank transferred almost $80 million to the state's general fund to help balance the state's budget.

---

on the shoulders of the House majority leader rather than the speaker.

Professional staff services are provided by nonpartisan staff that operate under the direction of the seventeen-member Joint Legislative Council, which includes the majority and minority leaders of both houses and the speaker of the House. The majority and minority caucuses select the other council members. Generally, the majority leader of the Senate and the speaker of the House take turns chairing it each session.

Like virtually all other state legislatures, the North Dakota Assembly divides itself into standing committees in order to analyze and process legislation. In each chamber, the dozen or so standing committees apart from the Appropriations Committee are identified as A committees or B committees, depending on when they meet. Each member not appointed to the Appropriations Committee is assigned to one A committee and one B committee—except for the floor leaders, who may, if they desire, serve on more than two committees. Each Senate committee usually has six members and is reflective of the partisan balance of the body. House committees usually have about a dozen members.

Processes

The president of the Senate (lieutenant governor) and the speaker of the House preside over sessions in their respective chambers. The Senate elects a president pro tempore to preside in the absence of the president. The Senate majority leader is responsible for determining the Senate agenda. The House majority leader determines the House agenda.

Members of the North Dakota Assembly take office on December 1 of even-numbered years and convene in regular session on the first Tuesday after January 3, or no later January 11 in odd-numbered years. Sessions are limited to a maximum of eighty legislative days during a two-year period.

In order to make the most efficient use of the short biennial session, leaders of the North Dakota Assembly have established several deadlines. Executive agencies and the state's supreme court can submit bills to the Legislative Council for consideration but must do so a month before the beginning of session. Legislators may profile bills before the session begins, but representatives can introduce only five bills after the fifth day of the legislative session. They may not introduce any bills after the tenth legislative day, and senators may introduce only three bills after that deadline. No senator may introduce a bill after the fifteenth day. All bills must be reported out of committee by the thirty-first day, and any bills that are going from one house to the other must "cross over" by the thirty-fourth day.

During the 2003 legislative session, North Dakota legislators introduced 924 bills, with 570 passing both chambers. The Republican governor vetoed 6 of them, including two line-item vetoes, in which he vetoed only part of the legislation. Activity during periods when the Assembly is not in regular session is limited but is under the control of the Legislative Council.

The North Dakota Assembly is a classic part-time legislature with almost all of its members holding a full-time post in the private sector. With its constitutional limit of eighty calendar days, the legislature usually finishes its business by the end of April, leaving legislators twenty months in which to earn a living, with occasional interim committee meetings. Legislators receive no annual salary, but rather $125 per calendar day during session and up to $650 per month during session for lodging expenses for those who must maintain an additional residence during the session. All legislators receive $250 per month for other expenses. All told, a North Dakota legislator is likely to make no more than $20,000 over the two years, including living expenses.

Leadership Structure

The majority leader is the top leader of the Senate. The speaker of the House and the majority leader are the top leaders of the House of Representatives. The majority leader and minority leader of each house are responsible for managing floor debate for their respective parties. The majority leader and minority leader of each chamber each have one assistant leader. A Committee on Committees in both chambers appoints committee chairs and members. The Senate Committee on Committees is chaired by the majority leader. Leaders of each party make additional appointments. The House committee is chaired by the House majority leader, with the speaker as vice chair and three additional members from each party appointed by the leaders.

The majority leader of the House, elected by the majority caucus, is the central leader of the House of Representatives. By tradition, the office of speaker is rotated every two years. While the speaker does have the power to preside and to assign bills to committee, speakers generally work closely with the majority leader. The majority leader determines committee positions and committee chairmanships. The majority leader position does not rotate every two years.

Election Processes

Approximately half of the membership of each house of the North Dakota Assembly is elected to its four-year term in each November even-year election. The North Dakota House of Representatives is one of only a few houses or assemblies that elects its members to four-year terms. Generally, members from odd-numbered districts are elected in nonpresidential years and seats from even-numbered districts are filled in presidential years.

Two House members and one senator run districtwide in each of the forty-seven legislative districts. Because of the relatively small population of the legislative districts (about 13,000), campaigns are relatively inexpensive. It is rare for a campaign to exceed $25,000, and many successful candidates spend less than $10,000. Party caucuses are active in recruiting candidates and providing some financial assistance for candidates. Contested nominations are determined in party primary elections.

Key Political Factors

While the North Dakota Democratic Party has enjoyed some successes in congressional and statewide elections, the state's legislative Assembly has, with a few exceptions, remained under Republican control.

Interestingly, the economy of North Dakota is often a reverse of the rest of the nation. Because of the importance of natural gas and oil to the economy of the state, low energy prices, which fuel the national economy, depress the North Dakota economy. On the other hand, high energy prices help to fill the coffers of the Peace Garden State, fueling economic booms when other states are going bust. During the early part of the twenty-first century, when other states were experiencing significant debt, a conservative legislature and rising fuel prices kept North Dakota in the black.

Native Americans play an important role in North Dakota politics, with the state encompassing all or part of four different reservations. Hidatsa, Mandan, Sioux, Arikara, the Spirit Lake Nation, and other tribes make up more than 5 percent of the state's population. These reservations are part of eight of the state's forty-seven legislative districts. Native Americans are one of the few segments of the North Dakota population that traditionally vote Democratic.

The North Dakota Assembly is a part-time citizen legislature. Members receive only a modest per diem compensation when the Assembly is in regular session, and almost all members devote the majority of their time to a private-sector occupation.

Further Reading

Michels, Greg. 2000. *Governments of North Dakota.* Austin, TX: Municipal Analysis Services.

OHIO

• • • • • • • • • • • •

THE OHIO GENERAL ASSEMBLY

House of Representatives   Senate
99 Representatives   33 Senators
(614) 466–2000
http://www.legislature.state.oh.us/

• • • • • • • • • • • •

Ohio is in most ways a microcosm of the United States. It has industry, manufacturing, agriculture, large cosmopolitan cities like Cleveland, Cincinnati, and Columbus, small rural towns, tobacco farmlands, poor Appalachian communities, major military bases, a long Lake Erie coastline, and a diverse population.

Politically, Ohio also mirrors the country in many ways. It is a highly competitive state that is invariably seen as a battleground state in presidential elections. However, parts of the state, like the country, lean heavily toward one party or the other. Northern Ohio and parts of central Ohio tend to vote Democratic, while Cincinnati, Dayton, and southern Ohio tend to line up behind the GOP. The state has voted for the winning presidential candidate in every election except two since 1900. While the state tends to tilt to the Republican Party in state and congressional elections, it is highly contested at the presidential level.

The state legislature is one of the most partisan and most professional in the country. While the Democrats usually controlled the House from the 1960s to the 1990s, the Senate was closely divided for much of that period, with neither party holding a majority of more than three seats in the 1980s. In 1994, Republicans took control of the House and solidified their hold on the Senate, and the chambers have become solidly Republican since that time.

Structure and Membership

The Ohio General Assembly consists of a thirty-three-member Senate and a ninety-nine-member House of Representatives, with House districts nested inside Senate districts. Senators are elected for four-year terms, and House members for two-year terms from single-member districts in November even-year elections. The Republican Party seems to be solidly in control of the Ohio General Assembly as we head into the twenty-first century, with majorities of almost two-to-one in both chambers.

The Senate elects a president from its membership to preside over its sessions and oversee the chamber's administration. The Senate president is elected as part of a team, including the president pro tempore, the majority leader, and the majority whip. The speaker of the House puts together a similar team in that chamber. The speaker presides over

Where Did the Senate Go?

In creating a bicameral legislature, Thomas Jefferson noted that the two chambers would work much like a cup and saucer: passions and ideas might "boil over" in the House, only to be cooled and let mellow in the saucer, or the Senate. Historically, that was true in the Ohio House and Senate as well, with calmer Senate heads often prevailing over more radical House proposals. However, with the imposition of legislative term limits in 2000, many see the "Housification" of the Senate, with many of the mores and norms of the Senate going away as term-limited House members bring their passions, rules, and approaches to the Senate. In 2004, ten of the eleven new senators came from the House.

House sessions and is responsible for House administration.

Ohio has a large and highly regarded nonpartisan professional staff that serves both chambers. Each house also has partisan staffs that serve legislative leaders and individual members. Changes in recent years have shifted much of the emphasis to the partisan staff, taking resources away from the more professional nonpartisan staff, especially in the House of Representatives. In the House, the partisan staff serves at the pleasure of the speaker.

Since the 1980s, women have fared quite well in the Ohio General Assembly, with JoAnn Davidson serving as the speaker of the House from 1995 until 2001, when she was forced from office by term limits. During the 2005 legislative session, five women served in the Senate (12 percent) and twenty-one in the House (21 percent). Interestingly, the influence and proportion of women in the Ohio General Assembly have decreased under legislative term limits, contrary to popular expectations. African Americans constitute about 12 percent of the membership, with most of the African American legislators elected from Cincinnati or Cleveland, the largest urban centers of the state. During the late 1990s, African American legislators served as leaders of the Democratic Party in both chambers (Ben Espy in the Senate and Jack Ford in the House). In 2003, there were no Latino legislators in the General Assembly.

Processes

The Ohio General Assembly convenes on the first Monday of January in the odd-numbered year (or on the next succeeding Monday if the first Monday is a legal holiday) and on the same date in the following year. There is no limitation on session length, nor is there any limit on the number of bills a legislator can introduce or the point in the session at which they can be introduced. In practice, members of the Ohio General Assembly usually meet on Tuesday, Wednesday, and Thursday, with periodic week-long recesses. During the 2003 session, the House met for 130 days and the Senate for 128.

During that time, they introduced 532 pieces of legislation, enacting only 56.

The number of bills proposed and enacted, quite low relative to other professional legislatures, can be attributed to two factors. First, the parties and party leader control the agenda and "screen" the bills before introduction. Second, many of the bills address numerous issues within the bill, whereas other states require that each bill be restricted to one issue.

Leadership Structure

The president of the Senate and the speaker of the House are the top leaders of their respective chambers. Both offices have traditionally been very powerful, especially the post of speaker of the House. Indeed, one speaker who served from 1974 to 1992 is said to be the primary reason that Ohio has legislative term limits. When he was speaker, his control was such that the House was called the House of Representative (singular, no "s"), because if you got his vote, you did not need anyone else!

The president of the Senate and the speaker of the House preside over sessions in their respective chambers. The Senate president is also the majority leader of the Senate. The president and speaker appoint committee chairs and members and, in consultation with the president pro tempore in the Senate and the majority leader in the House, determine the chamber agendas. The Senate president, majority leader, and president pro tempore, the House majority leader, and the Senate and House minority leaders are responsible for managing floor debate for their respective parties. As a team, each is responsible for recruiting legislative candidates and raising money for the caucus campaigns. In Ohio, getting members of your caucus elected is a critical part of successful leadership.

Until the imposition of term limits, it was not uncommon for an Ohio legislator to hold a top leadership position for a number of terms. With the advent of term limits, however, leadership tenures have generally been one term in the Senate and no more than two terms in the House of Representatives. With the election of Larry Householder, only in his second term in the House, as the first House leader elected after the full impact of term limits, the Ohio House appears to have established a practice of electing speakers for two four-year terms. The speaker chosen to succeed him when Householder is termed out is also ending his second term in the House.

The role of interest groups and lobbyists has always been significant in the Ohio General Assembly. However, 1990s reforms have changed the dynamic by limiting the amount that any lobbyist can spend on a legislator to $75 per legislator per year. Because the limitation is per lobbyist rather than per firm or interest group, firms with more lobbyists tend to be more effective and have greater access.

Election Processes

Ohio legislators are elected in the November even-year election, with sixteen Senate members elected in one election and seventeen in the next. Members of the Ohio Senate are limited to serving a maximum of two consecutive four-year terms, and members of the state House of

Representatives are limited to serving four consecutive two-year terms. Term-limited legislators are eligible to run again after a break of four years.

Given the generally competitive nature of the state and the large populations of the districts (especially in the Senate), as well as the urban nature of many of the districts (in expensive media markets), Ohio legislative elections have generally been very expensive. By the mid-1990s, some Senate campaigns were exceeding $1 million, and it is not unusual for house races to exceed $500,000. The passage of legislative term limits has decreased neither the competition nor the cost of elections in the Buckeye State. With partisan redistricting in place, even when legislative seats are open, they seldom change parties. Contested nominations are decided in party primaries with plurality votes.

Key Political Factors

Legislative term limits have dramatically altered the political landscape of politics in Ohio and the General Assembly. It has dramatically increased the turnover of members and leaders in the legislature. It has also significantly altered the responsibilities associated with effective leadership. While leaders in the highly partisan state have been responsible for caucus elections for more than two decades, the ability to raise money, recruit candidates, and manage the caucus campaign now seems to be the prime and often only requirement for being elected into leadership. The most recent speaker required that each of his leaders and committee chairs commit to raising a certain amount of money for the campaigns of their fellow Republican House members.

Under term limits, the influence of the speaker seems to have increased, but that may be based more on the abilities and personality of the person holding the post than on the powers of the position. The past speaker was actively involved in the election of more than half of the members of the Republican caucus, and they feel an allegiance to him. On the Senate side, leadership appears to have become more dispersed under the current leader, and it appears that the Senate will not follow the lead of the House in trying to elect a Senate president in his or her sophomore term.

Political success in the Buckeye state really comes down to two things: money and mobilization. Because each party has enough potential loyalists to win an election, the winner is usually the one that can raise enough money to get out the message and mobilize key constituencies. If voter turnout in Cleveland, Akron, and Columbus is high, Democrats do well. If it is higher in and around Cincinnati and southern Ohio, Republicans tend to do better.

Further Reading
Curtin, Michael F., and Julie B. Bell. 1996. *Ohio Politics Almanac*. Kent, OH: Kent State University Press.

OKLAHOMA

• • • • • • • • • • • •

THE OKLAHOMA LEGISLATURE

House of Representatives
101 Delegates
(405) 521–2711

Senate
48 Senators
(405) 524–0126

http://www.lsb.state.ok.us

• • • • • • • • • • • •

Almost exclusively a ranching and agricultural state when it joined the Union in 1907, Oklahoma has diversified itself into a state that includes manufacturing and industry. Ranching and farming remain an important element of the state's economy.

During its first several decades as a state, Oklahoma's Democratic Party dominated its politics. Since the middle of the twentieth century, however, the state's leanings have become predominantly Republican in national elections, with the only Democratic presidential candidate to carry the state being Lyndon Johnson from neighboring Texas, who won narrowly in 1964. Democrats have fared better in state elections, electing a number of governors and other statewide officials and retaining control of the legislature. In recent elections, the state has also moved in a more conservative direction.

Structure and Membership

Oklahoma's legislature consists of a 48-member Senate and a 101-member House of Representatives. Senate terms are four years and House terms are two years. Legislators are elected from single-member districts in November even-year elections. Members are limited to twelve years of state legislative service, regardless of the chamber of service. The first state to pass state legislative term limits, in 1990, Oklahoma did not feel their impact until 2004, because of the twelve-year maximum.

With the election of 2004, the first under term limits, Republicans took control of the state House for the first time in more than eighty years (the last Republican House majority had been elected in 1922). Republicans held on to the Senate, losing two members but maintaining a four-seat (26–22) majority. It appears that Republicans are in solid control of the House and have a very realistic shot at the Senate majority in the years to come.

Women are not elected to the Oklahoma legislature in large numbers, with the proportion of female legislators hovering between 10 and 15 percent, although the 2004 election following term limits did increase the number of women (by two in the Senate and three in the House). Had the Republicans not gained control, a senior female Democrat had been poised to take over as speaker of the House. There are just a small number of African American members and no Hispanic legislators.

Black Gold, Texas Tea

Every state legislative building and complex or grounds reflects the history and industry of the state it represents. That may be even more true of the Oklahoma capitol complex: the state seal, which is prominently displayed in the capitol building, features a five-pointed star, representing the five established Native American tribes that settled the territory. Paintings in the rotunda tell the story of the state's history. Outside the capitol building, an active oil well pumps oil, the historic lifeblood of the state, from deep under the building and capitol complex.

The president pro tempore of the Senate is responsible for Senate administration. The speaker of the House is responsible for House administration. Staff services are provided by a combination of partisan and nonpartisan staff.

During sessions, the Oklahoma legislature employs more than 200 full-time staff. This includes staff for committees, personal staff, communications staff, staff to support the technology infrastructure, fiscal staff, and support staff. Individual legislators have very limited staff support when the legislature is not in session.

The Oklahoma Senate organizes itself into eighteen standing committees. With the exception of Appropriations, which includes all forty-eight members of the Senate, each committee has between twelve and twenty-two members, including a chair and vice chair. The Appropriations Committee is divided into seven subcommittees. The House historically organizes into more than two dozen standing committees. Many scholars consider legislative committees in Oklahoma to be among the most powerful in the country in terms of institutional powers, with significant abilities to screen, shape, and affect the passage of the legislation the committees receive.

Processes

The legislature holds a one-day organizational session in January of odd-numbered years. Its regular sessions convene on the first Monday in February and must adjourn by the last Friday in May. All bills must be introduced more than two weeks before the legislative session begins, unless exempted by a two-thirds vote of each chamber. Two and a half weeks after the beginning of session, all bills must be reported out of the committee in the house they started in. A month later, they must be read on the floor of that chamber. One month before the legislature adjourns, all bills must have received their final reading.

Bills that are introduced in the odd-year session and not acted upon are automatically carried over to the even-year session, and committees continue to review them during the interim period between the sessions. During the 2003 legislative session, Oklahoma legislators introduced 1,655 bills. Fewer than a third (486) made it through the maze of deadlines to reach the desk of the governor. The Democratic governor vetoed 12 of them, including one line-item veto.

The Oklahoma legislature is generally considered to be a "citizen's legislature," with constitutionally limited sessions and relatively small full-time professional staffing. However, there is a base salary of almost $40,000 per year plus per diem allowances of more than $100 while the legislature is in session. With the legislative session usually running at least seventy legislative days, an Oklahoma legislator can earn close to $50,000 annually. Nevertheless, the limited length of session means that most members do hold another job in the private sector.

Leadership Structure

The lieutenant governor is designated by the state's constitution as president of the Senate but, in fact, presides only over joint sessions with the House of Representatives. The president pro tempore serves as the chamber's presiding officer. The president pro tempore also appoints members of the Senate's committees in consultation with the minority leader. The speaker of the House presides over sessions of the House of Representatives and has primary control over its agenda. The Senate and House majority leaders lead floor debate and organize and develop party positions. The minority leaders do the same for the minority party. The majority and minority leaders are assisted by a number of deputy and assistant leaders.

Historically, leaders have served relatively long terms in Oklahoma. Recent speakers have served four or six years, as have recent Senate presidents pro tempore. However, the implementation of legislative term limits is likely to alter that pattern. The speaker of the House and the president pro tempore of the Senate are paid an additional $18,000 each year beyond the regular legislative salary. The majority leaders and minority leaders of the respective chambers receive an additional $12,000 annually for their efforts.

Election Processes

Oklahoma legislators are elected in the November even-year election. Because Senate terms are four years, half of the Senate is elected in each even-year election. Senate districts include about 72,000 Oklahomans and House districts about 35,000. Historically, elections have been relatively low key and inexpensive. However, recent efforts by the Republican Party to gain control and the Democratic Party to maintain control have increased the level of competition and the level of expense. They have also increased the pressure on legislative leaders to recruit and fund effective candidates.

Electoral turnover in Oklahoma has traditionally been around 15 percent every two years. However, the year 2004, the first election under term limits, witnessed a turnover of more than 40 percent in the House, with several Democratic seats going Republican. Contested nominations are decided in party primaries.

Key Political Factors

While Republicans made huge strides in Oklahoma over the past several decades, particularly in presidential and congressional elections and to a slightly lesser extent in gubernatorial and other statewide elections, the state legislature remained under continuous Democratic control. In fact, since Oklahoma became a state in 1907, Republicans have never controlled the state's Senate and have controlled its House of Representatives for only one two-year term, in the 1920s. However, the 2004 election changed that, with the takeover of the House by the Republicans. Democrats still hold a slim majority in registration, but Republicans get more votes.

While Democrats do well in and around the metropolitan areas of Tulsa and Oklahoma City, the traditional small town and rural areas of the state have become increasingly Republican. Many of the old "yellow dog" Democrats that once dominated these areas and rural areas in the southeast are dying off and being replaced by morally and socially conservative Republicans. Traditional conservative Republicans dominate northwest Oklahoma, while southern Oklahoma, once the

stronghold of conservative Democrats, is becoming more Republican. This geographic party split results in many urban-rural battles that also appear partisan.

Because of the limited staff provided to Oklahoma legislators, many rely heavily on lobbyists for information. The almost 400 lobbyists registered with the legislature can spend no more than $300 each year to try to influence or persuade legislators to act in their behalf. Not surprisingly, agricultural, cattle, and oil-related industries tend to have a significant influence on public policy in the Sooner State.

Further Reading
Markwood, Chris. 1998. *Oklahoma Government and Politics.* Dubuque, IA: Kendall/Hunt.
———. 2000. *Oklahoma Government and Politics: An Introduction.* Dubuque, IA: Kendall/Hunt.

OREGON

• • • • • • • • • • • • •

THE OREGON LEGISLATIVE ASSEMBLY

House of Representatives	Senate
60 Delegates	30 Senators
(503) 986–1870	(503) 986–1851

http://www.leg.state.or.us

• • • • • • • • • • • • •

Tucked between California, its southern neighbor, and Washington to the north, Oregon is one of the three states in the continental United States that borders the Pacific Ocean. While the state has a diverse economy that includes high technology, manufacturing, finance, and tourism, it also has an exceptionally large amount of forested acreage and a large timber and lumber industry.

Politically, Oregon is a highly competitive state in which either party is capable of electing candidates to statewide office or winning control of the state legislature. In presidential elections, Oregonians have favored the Democratic candidates in the majority of statewide elections since the 1970s.

Like many Western states, Oregon imposed term limits on its state legislators in the 1990s. However, the Oregon supreme court found that those limits violated the state's constitution because they limited the terms of other officers apart from legislators. This application to multiple offices violated the constitutional requirements that initiatives (legislation proposed and passed by the public) not amend more than one part of the constitution.

Structure and Membership

The Oregon Assembly consists of a thirty-member Senate and a sixty-member House of Representatives. Senators are elected for four-year terms and House members for two-year terms from single-member districts in November even-year elections. In the 1990s, Republicans controlled both chambers, but with declining margins. In 2002, Democrats gained a tie in the Senate and then control in 2004. Following the 2004 elections, Republicans found that their majority in the House was down to six seats.

As in most Western states, women legislators have been elected to the Oregon legislature at a rate higher than the national average. This reflects the progressive nature and history of the state, where women received the right to vote (1912) seven years before the passage of the Twentieth Amendment to the U.S. Constitution. Furthermore, it is quite common for female legislators to be elected to leadership, with women holding key positions (speaker of the House, floor leader) in the early part of the twenty-first century. Given the demographic makeup of the state, it should be of little surprise that African Americans and Hispanic legislators do not constitute a significant portion of either chamber.

The Senate elects a president from its membership to preside over its sessions and oversee the chamber's administration. The speaker of the House presides over its sessions and is responsible for House administration. General administration of the legislative Assembly is under the supervision of the joint Legislative Administration Committee (LAC), which includes the Senate president and House speaker as well as four other senators and four other House members, appointed by the president and speaker, respectively.

Nonpartisan offices that serve legislators in both chambers provide professional staff services. There are also small partisan staffs that serve legislative leaders and individual members. The LAC includes the Committee Services Office, which provides research of issues and measures and legislative oversight assistance to members of the Senate and House of Representatives. The office provides professional staff for session and interim committees, task forces, and work groups. Other duties include assistance with the committee process as well as clerical support and official record-keeping duties. The "money committees" are supported by the Legislative and Fiscal Revenue Office, which provides information regarding the economy and the fiscal impact of legislation.

The House and Senate, like all other state legislative bodies, organize themselves into standing committees, with about a dozen such committees established in each chamber. There are usually

---

All in the Family

Representative Karen Minnis, speaker of the Oregon House of Representatives, maintains strong and positive relations with the members of the Oregon Senate—or, at least, with one member of that body. Since 1972, Speaker Minnis has been married to John Minnis, who was a member of the Oregon Senate during the first year of Minnis's tenure. Prior to her election to the House in 1998, when her husband was forced out by term limits, Speaker Minnis served as his administrative assistant.

---

four to six senators on each committee in that chamber, while each House standing committee includes seven to ten House members. One unique feature of the Oregon committee system is the Joint Ways and Means Committee, which includes ten members from each chamber and is responsible for putting together the state's biennial budget.

Processes

The Oregon Assembly meets in a biennial session, convening on the second Monday of January in odd-numbered years. There is no limitation on session length, although most sessions conclude within six months. No bills can be introduced after the thirty-sixth day of the legislative session without a two-thirds vote of the chamber. During the 2003 legislative session, members of the Oregon legislature introduced 2,769 bills, with only 158 (less than 10 percent) passing both chambers. The Democratic governor vetoed 7 bills.

Because the legislature is officially biennial, committees operate throughout the term of the legislature, organizing as interim committees when the legislature is not in session, and continue to examine legislation and issues after adjournment.

Although the Oregon legislature technically meets every other year, many consider it to be a hybrid professional and citizen's legislature. While it is in session only about six to eight months every two years, its interim committees meet actively and regularly during the "off months." Legislators receive a base annual salary of about $16,000 plus a daily allowance of around $85 while the legislature is in session or when members have to come in for interim committee business. During the session year, an Oregon legislator may earn more than $30,000. During the off year, that amount is likely to be closer to $20,000. Most Oregon legislators have sources of income outside of the legislature. Members of both chambers are provided staff year-round, and the standing committees are all fully staffed. The legislature employs more than 250 staff members.

Leadership Structure

The president of the Senate and the speaker of the House are the top leaders of their respective chambers. The majority and minority leaders of each chamber are responsible for managing floor debate for their respective parties. Furthermore, both parties elect a number of assistant leaders and whips. In 2005, eleven of the eighteen Democratic senators held some leadership post, including two deputy majority leaders and five assistant majority leaders.

The president of the Senate and the speaker of the House are clearly the key leaders in their respective chambers. Elected by the members of their caucus, they each preside over their chambers, establishing the chamber agenda, appointing committee members and committee chairs, and assigning bills to the appropriate standing committees. The Senate president and speaker of the House are considered among the more powerful legislative leaders in the country, considering their potential for extended tenure and influence over floor and committee actions.

Election Processes

Oregon legislators are elected in the November even-year election, with half of the Senate membership elected in each election. House members, who serve two-year terms, are up for reelection every cycle. The average Oregon senator serves about 120,000 citizens, while the average House district includes about 60,000. Campaigns remain rather low key. Contested nominations are decided in party primaries.

Key Political Factors

Oregon can be expected to remain a highly competitive state, although recent elections suggest a subtle shift toward the Democratic Party. The state is quite divided politically, with the rural areas in the east and south tending to go Republican and the more urban and suburban areas in and around Portland, Lane County, and Benton County leaning more toward Democratic candidates. Most of the recent population growth has been in and around the urban areas, giving the nod to the Democrats. In recent years, Republicans have tended to nominate rather conservative candidates for statewide office that do not fare well against more moderate Democrats.

Oregon has a long history of political activism that defines its present as well as its past. It was the first state to use the initiative process (1902), allowing the public to initiate and pass legislation. It is considered easier to get an initiative on the ballot in Oregon than in most any other state, and voters have made use of that option, with more than 300 initiatives reaching the ballot since 1902. More than 60 have made it to the ballot since 1996. Both numbers represent highs among all fifty states. Legislators in the Beaver State know that if they don't act, or they act inappropriately or without forethought, the voters can and will take matters into their own hands. Everything Oregon legislators do is tempered by that reality.

Supporters of state legislator term limits were embittered by the state supreme court's overturn of their voter-initiated term-limits amendment to the state constitution and have vowed to continue to work to get term limits reinstituted through a new voter initiative.

More than 500 lobbyists usually register their efforts to influence the Oregon state legislature during each session. Lobbyists in Oregon may spend no more than $100 per event on a legislator and no more than $250 for the year. However, those limits do not apply to food and beverage consumed in the presence of the provider or purchaser.

Further Reading

Clucas, Richard A., Mark Henkels, and Brent S. Steel, eds. 2005. *Oregon Politics and Government: Progressives versus Conservative Populists.* Lincoln: University of Nebraska Press.

Heider, Douglas, and David Deitz. 1995. *Legislative Perspective: 150 Years of the Oregon Legislatures, from 1843 to 1993.* Portland: Oregon Historical Society Press.

PENNSYLVANIA

● ● ● ● ● ● ● ● ● ● ● ●

THE PENNSYLVANIA GENERAL ASSEMBLY

House of Representatives	Senate
203 Representatives	50 Senators
(717) 787–2372	(717) 787–5920

http://www.legis.state.pa.us

● ● ● ● ● ● ● ● ● ● ● ●

Some of the most significant events in U.S. history have taken place in Pennsylvania. Both the Declaration of Independence and the Constitution were signed in Philadelphia; Washington's army encamped at Valley Forge in the bitter winter of 1777–1778; and the Battle of Gettysburg, which marked the turning point of the Civil War, was fought on the state's soil. Benjamin Franklin once served as speaker of the Pennsylvania House of Representatives.

Bordered by the Northeastern states of New Jersey and New York on its east and north and by the Midwestern state of Ohio on its west, Pennsylvania, not surprisingly, features characteristics of both the Northeast and the Midwest. The state has industry, manufacturing, and agriculture, with the large cities of Philadelphia on the east and Pittsburgh in the west separated by rural farming lands. The eastern part of the state, surrounding and including Philadelphia, is more attuned to the politics and philosophy associated with the liberal Democratic Northeast, and the more mountainous and rural west is more reflective of the Republican and conservative Midwest.

Politically, Pennsylvania is a highly competitive state that is usually seen as a battleground state in presidential elections. While the state tends to tilt to the Democrats in closely contested presidential elections, the state's voters tend to elect relatively equal numbers of Democrats and Republicans in statewide and congressional contests. Either party is capable of winning control of the state legislature in any election, according to the numbers, although Republicans have managed to craft a small but stable majority in both chambers, having held the majority in both chambers since the early 1990s.

Pennsylvania State Capitol (Richard T. Nowitz/Corbis)

Structure and Membership

The Pennsylvania General Assembly consists of a 50-member Senate and a 203-member House of Representatives. The House of Representatives is the second largest state legislative chamber in the United States, after the 400-member New Hampshire House of Representatives. Pennsylvania's state senators are elected for four-year terms, and its House members are elected for two-year terms from single-member districts in November even-year elections.

The two chambers have remained quite evenly divided along partisan lines in recent years, with Republicans opening a small but consistent lead since gaining control of both chambers in 1993. Both legislative parties are fully staffed with pollsters, media consultants, and in-house television studios.

The proportion of women in the Pennsylvania legislature hovers around 10 to 15 percent. Women have seldom cracked the ranks of leadership in the legislature of the Keystone State. The percentage of African American legislators is even lower, staying just above 5 percent in each chamber, with most of those being elected from districts in and around Philadelphia. Interestingly, the representation of Hispanic legislators is almost nonexistent, with one or two legislators of Hispanic origin serving each year.

Pennsylvania has a combination of partisan and nonpartisan professional staff, most of whom are appointed by the

Hollywood Goes to Harrisburg

The story line of the 1992 comedy *The Distinguished Gentleman,* starring legendary comedian Eddy Murphy, is that Murphy's character goes to Washington as an "accidental" congressman. However, a close look at the scenes in the movie will suggest that Murphy actually went to Harrisburg, Pennsylvania. Shots of Murphy walking down the corridors of power reveal that he is walking in the ornate and elegant corridors of the Pennsylvania state capitol, built in the early 1900s in the image of the U.S. Capitol Building.

individual chambers to serve only the members of that chamber. Each party caucus is fully staffed and controls staffing for its members. Each caucus also maintains its own staff for the purpose of legislative communications.

The committees of the Pennsylvania General Assembly are among the best-staffed legislative committees in the country. Usually, the Senate has around twenty standing committees, while the leaders of the House usually assign members to about twenty-five. Each House committee has about two dozen members, with a majority from the majority party, but each party elects a chairman and vice chairman from its caucus. Each Senate committee has about a dozen members, including a chair and vice chair from the majority party and a minority chair from the minority party.

Processes

The Pennsylvania General Assembly convenes for a two-year session on the first Tuesday in January in odd-numbered years. There is no limitation on session length. There are no limits on how many bills a legislator may introduce or deadlines during the session by which certain types of bills must be introduced. This absence of limitations is reflected in the 2003–2004 session, when more than 3,000 bills were introduced; only 308 were passed by both chambers and sent to the governor.

The Pennsylvania General Assembly is considered to be one of the most professional state legislatures in the country, generally ranked with or near California, New York, and Michigan. However, now that California and Michigan have implemented term limits, it is likely to move up in the rankings. Legislators in Pennsylvania make more than $60,000 a year, in addition to a daily allowance during session of up to $125. A rank-and-file legislator in Pennsylvania will easily receive more than $70,000 a year. Legislators have full-time, year-round staff in their capitol and district offices. The General Assembly employs almost 3,000 people to support the effort of the legislators. While the Pennsylvania General Assembly is usually in session for fewer than one hundred "legislative" days each year, their job and responsibilities are full time.

Leadership Structure

The president pro tempore of the Senate and the speaker of the House are the top leaders of their respective chambers. They set the agenda, preside over the chambers, assign bills to committee, and make committee and chairmanship assignments in their respective legislative chambers. The speaker of the House and the president pro tempore of the Senate are among the most powerful legislative leaders in the country. The Senate and House majority leaders and the Senate and House minority leaders are responsible for managing floor debate for their respective parties as well as presiding over caucus meetings. Both parties elect several other leadership posts, including a whip, caucus chair, caucus secretary, caucus appropriations chair, and a Policy Committee chair. The lieutenant governor, who is elected with the governor, presides over the Senate but has a very limited legislative role beyond that constitutional duty.

It is not uncommon for a Pennsylvania legislator to hold a top leadership position for a number of terms. Leaders in the Pennsylvania General Assembly are handsomely rewarded for their service with additional salaries (on top of the $60,000 salary for all legislators). Leaders receive stipends ranging from about $6,000 for the caucus secretaries to almost $35,000 for the speaker and president pro tempore.

Election Processes

Pennsylvania legislators are elected in the November even-year election, with half of the members of the Senate elected to their four-year terms in each even year. Turnover in the state legislature is very low, because incumbent legislators tend to seek reelection and can build up significant campaign war chests to fend off all but the most ardent opposition. Open

seat elections to the Pennsylvania Senate or House can well generate campaigns in excess of $1 million. Leaders and members of the House and Senate caucuses raise and donate significant amounts of money to recruit and support candidates in open seats or in seats in which one candidate or the other is considered vulnerable. Contested nominations are decided in party primaries.

Although the state is the fifth most populous in the United States, the large number of representatives in the House makes the district size quite manageable. Each house member represents about 60,000 Pennsylvanians. On the other hand, the smaller membership of the Senate means that the average senator must represent almost 250,000 people. This makes the districts among the largest in the fifty states (behind California, New York, Florida, Ohio, and Michigan).

Key Political Factors

Pennsylvania can be expected to remain a highly competitive state, with both parties competing for control of the state legislature. However, with effective redistricting, fundraising, and candidate recruitment, Republicans are likely to stay in control of the statehouse for quite some time. Much of the politics of the state is defined geographically, pitting Pittsburgh against Philadelphia, or the central and western parts of the state against the more moderate eastern areas anchored by Philadelphia.

The Pennsylvania General Assembly is defined by two qualities. First, it has strong and stable leadership. At one point early in the twenty-first century, no top leader in either chamber had fewer than eight years of experience. Second, partisanship is critical. If things get difficult, party overrides district, region, and ideology.

Lobbyists play a central role in politics in the Keystone State, providing information for policy development and money for political campaigns. The more than 700 lobbyists usually registered with the General Assembly are not restricted in how much they may spend on legislators during a given session.

Further Reading

Caffin, Charles Henry. 2001. *A Handbook of the New Pennsylvania Capitol.* Harrisburg: Pennsylvania Capitol Preservation Society.

Kennedy, John J. 1999. *The Contemporary Pennsylvania Legislature.* Lanham, MD: University Press of America.

Martin, Jere. 1996. *Pennsylvania Almanac.* Mechanicsburg, PA: Stackpole.

RHODE ISLAND

• • • • • • • • • • • •

THE RHODE ISLAND GENERAL ASSEMBLY

House of Representatives
75 Representatives
(401) 222–1478

Senate
38 Senators
(401) 222–6655

http://www.rilin.state.ri.us

• • • • • • • • • • • •

Rhode Island is the nation's smallest state in land area, measuring just over 1,200 square miles. One of the original Thirteen Colonies, it was originally opposed to joining the Union and was the last of the colonies to ratify the U.S. Constitution. With a popular Atlantic coastline of more than 600 miles, tourism and manufacturing are the primary elements of its economy. More than 12 million tourists visit this state with a population of less than a million every year.

In the early twentieth century, Rhode Island was under the domination of the Republican Party. But the Democrats moved into a permanent ascendancy during the Great Depression of the 1930s. Since that time, there is no state in which the Democratic Party has consistently enjoyed more success in both federal and state elections than it has in Rhode Island.

Structure and Membership

Rhode Island's legislature consists of a thirty-eight-member Senate and a seventy-five-member House of Representatives. All Rhode Island legislators serve two-year terms and are elected from single-member districts in November even-year elections. Because the population of the state is low, just over 1 million, legislative districts are geographically small and politics quite personal. Democrats hold a commanding lead in each chamber, usually outnumbering Republicans by at least five-to-one.

The president of the Senate, assisted by the majority leader, is responsible for Senate administration. The speaker of the House is responsible for House administration. Staff services are provided by a combination of partisan and nonpartisan staff.

The proportion of female legislators in Rhode Island is generally a bit below the national average. In 2005, eleven of the seventy-four members of the House were female (14.8 percent), as were eight of the thirty-eight senators (21 percent). Women often chair committees in both chambers but are less likely to serve in institutional leadership posts. Reflecting the population of this Northeastern state, the legislature has generally few African American or Latino legislators.

In order to conduct business, each chamber of the Rhode Island General Assembly usually organizes itself into about a dozen standing committees. Each House committee has between ten and eighteen members, with one chair, one secretary, and two vice chairs. Each Senate standing committee has between seven and eleven members, with a chair, vice chair, and secretary. Standing committees in Rhode Island are considered quite strong, making well-informed decisions and having significant impact on floor outcomes.

Processes

Until 2003, the lieutenant governor served as presiding officer of the Senate. Beginning with that year's new legislative term, however, the Senate elected a president from among its members to serve as its presiding officer. The president is empowered to appoint members of the Senate's committees, although the chamber's rules allow the president to delegate that responsibility to the majority leader, who is responsible for leading and managing the members of the majority party in floor debate. The speaker of the House presides over sessions of the House of Representatives and has primary control over its agenda

The General Assembly meets in annual regular sessions, with each year's session convening on the first Tuesday in January. There is no limitation on session length, but they generally adjourn in June or July. The legislature also takes one week's recess in February (the winter recess) and another in April (the spring recess). All public bills must be introduced by the first Tuesday in February unless permitted by a simple majority vote of the chamber. Committees must complete action on bills introduced in their own chamber by the first week of April, prior to the spring recess.

During the 2003 legislative session, members of the Rhode Island General Assembly introduced 2,121 pieces of legislation. About a quarter of those (547) were passed by both chambers and sent to the governor's desk. The Republican governor vetoed 11, with one of those vetoes overridden by the legislature.

The Rhode Island General Assembly is a traditional "citizen's legislature," with low pay, limited staffing, and high turnover. The base annual salary is just over $11,000, and members receive no per diem or lodging allowances. Legislators share office staff year-round with one staff person for every seven or eight members. They have no district staff. The General Assembly employs just over 200 staff persons for the entire legislature. About a third of the legislators are new every two years.

Leadership Structure

The president of the Senate is officially the chamber's top leader, although much

An Independent State

The state of Rhode Island (officially Rhode Island and Providence Plantations) was established almost exclusively on the basis of independence. Roger Williams, fleeing from religious persecution in Salem, Massachusetts, established the Providence Plantation in 1636 as a refuge for those seeking religious independence. And they came: Protestants, Catholics, Jews—all wanting to practice religion free from government intervention. In honor of that search for independence, the dome of the Rhode Island capitol is topped by the "Independent Man," a gold-plated figure, clad in a loincloth and holding a staff, as a symbol for the independent spirit that led Roger Williams to settle there.

of the control over daily activity is shared with the majority leader. The speaker of the House is top leader of the House of Representatives. Because of the stability and institutional power associated with the post, many people consider the speaker of the House to be the most powerful political leader in the state. The speaker of the House and president of the Senate are responsible for assigning members and chairs to the standing committees.

Senate and House majority leaders lead floor debate and organize and develop party positions. The minority leaders do the same for the minority party. The majority and minority leaders are assisted by a number of deputy and assistant leaders.

Historically, leadership in the Rhode Island General Assembly has been strong and stable. However, scandals and potential conflicts of interest that forced the resignation of top leaders in each chamber in 2002 and 2003 affected both the stability and power of the General Assembly. In the House, the speaker selected to succeed his predecessor of ten years agreed to run the House in a more open and democratic fashion than his predecessor had. In the Senate, a leader

stepped down from his post rather than reveal some information he considered personal, paving the way for a new leader.

Legislative leaders in Rhode Island do not receive additional compensation for their efforts. Recent studies have placed leaders of both chambers in the lower half of the rankings relative to formal power.

Election Processes

Rhode Island legislators are elected to their two-year terms in the November even-year election. All districts are single-member. The average House district is just over 13,000, and the average Senate district about twice that size. In the urban areas of Providence, it is not at all uncommon for House districts to cover only a few city blocks. Given the small size and low population of the districts, campaigns are usually relatively inexpensive and very personal. A senior House member may well know virtually every family in the district.

Contested nominations are decided in party primaries. Because the state is so overwhelmingly Democratic at the state and local level, the Democratic primary is often more contested and significant than the general election. In 2004, several incumbent Democrats, including the former speaker of the House, were defeated in the Democratic primary election.

Key Political Factors

Over the past half-century, Democrats have enjoyed overwhelming control of the Rhode Island General Assembly. Their majority margins, which normally run five or six to one over the Republicans, are almost always their largest in any of the fifty state legislatures. This is not to say that Republicans have not had their own successes in Rhode Island, having elected three of the last four governors, and mayors of the second- and third-largest cities, in addition to holding on to one U.S. Senate seat through two generations. Nixon (1972) and Reagan (1984) even managed to carry the state.

It can be argued that part of this phenomenon of having a Republican governor in such an overwhelmingly Democratic state can be traced to the increased number of voters who chose not to identify themselves with a party. This lack of affiliation or personal attachment to particular party platforms allows many to proclaim their independence and split their vote, which in their minds assures a type of balanced power. This was caused in part by the exodus of manufacturing from the state and the migration of many to the suburbs. Both diminished the base that had spurred the party to power in the first place.

Others would claim that poor party discipline among the Democrats is the cause, along with contentious primaries that result in many longtime Democrats voting Republican and against the person who defeated their original choice in the primary. Since Rhode Island even allows voters to disaffiliate immediately after voting in the primary, or up to ninety days prior to the primary, in other cases it has been the failure of the party to deliver during the primary. The move to open primaries with its root in discouraging voting strictly by party and creating a better informed and intelligent electorate has had some unintended consequences. It allows for the supporters of a candidate without a primary opponent to vote in the other party's primary and diminish the chances of the strongest candidate from advancing to the general election. In 2004, the mayor of Cranston accused the Democrats of doing that very thing. They were not successful. Ironically, the method has had a greater effect on the majority Democrats than on the Republicans, as Republicans used the new system to their advantage in 1976 to ensure that a Democratic governor did not win his primary election for U.S. Senate.

Based on the success of the party on the national level and the election to some high-profile positions within the state, Republicans made a concerted effort in 2004 to increase their numbers in the General Assembly. Although they increased their overall numbers in the Assembly, their success was limited. In the House, Republicans increased their numbers by three but lost a seat that they had traditionally held and remain at a disadvantage of almost four to one. In the Senate they lost a seat, giving the Democrats a six-to-one advantage.

Further Reading
Conley, Patrick T. 1999. *Neither Separate nor Equal: Legislature and Executive in Rhode Island Constitutional History.* Providence: Rhode Island Publications Society.

Moakley, Maureen, and Elmer Cromwell. 2001. *Rhode Island Politics and Government.* Lincoln: University of Nebraska Press.

SOUTH CAROLINA

●●●●●●●●●●●●

THE SOUTH CAROLINA GENERAL ASSEMBLY

House of Representatives
124 Representatives
(803) 734–2010

Senate
46 Senators
(803) 212–6200

http://www.leginfo.state.sc.us

●●●●●●●●●●●●

South Carolina was the first state to secede from the Union following the election of Abraham Lincoln in 1860. It is also the home of Fort Sumter, where the first shots of the Civil War were fired, in February 1861. Today's South Carolina is far different than the state of a century and a half ago. It has a diverse economy that includes manufacturing, agriculture, and tourism, particularly along its popular Atlantic coastline.

For more than a century following the Civil War, South Carolina was a solidly Democratic state in which the state's small Republican Party was a nonfactor in elections. In the late 1960s, however, the South Carolina Republican Party began to flex its muscles when U.S. senator Strom Thurmond left the Democratic Party and became a Republican. Republican momentum built rapidly after the Thurmond switch, and by the late twentieth century, the state was electing the party's candidates to many state and congressional offices and even giving it majorities in both houses of the state legislature. With the exception of 1976, when

the state voted for Jimmy Carter from neighboring Georgia, South Carolina has not supported a Democratic presidential candidate since 1960. Following the 2004 election, South Carolina's governor and both U.S. senators were Republican, as were a majority of the state's congressional delegation and both chambers of the state legislature.

Structure and Membership

The South Carolina General Assembly consists of a 46-member Senate and a 124-member House of Representatives. Senators serve four-year terms and House members serve two-year terms. All legislators represent single-member districts. The lieutenant governor, an independently elected official, is ex officio president of the Senate and presides over Senate sessions. The Senate elects a president pro tempore who is responsible for the chamber's administration. The speaker of the House presides over its sessions and is responsible for House administration.

After more than a century of control by Democrats, Republicans gained control of the House in 1994 and the Senate in 2000 and have built up solid majorities in each chamber. Following the 2004 elections, they held a twenty-four seat majority in the House and an eight seat majority in the Senate.

South Carolina, like many of its counterparts in the southeastern United States, has relatively few female legislators. Following the 2004 elections, only one member of the South Carolina Senate was female, and fourteen (12 percent) of the South Carolina House members were women. Historically, women have chaired few key standing committees in the Palmetto State. The proportion of African American legislators serving in the South Carolina General Assembly tends to stay between 15 and 20 percent. However, because Republicans control both chambers and most of the African American members are Democrats, there are few African American legislators in leadership or committee chair positions. As of the 2005 legislative session, there were no Latino legislators serving in South Carolina.

Professional staff services are provided by a nonpartisan staff that operates under the direction of a legislative council that includes the speaker of the House and the lieutenant governor. Each house also has a small number of partisan staff assistants for leaders and individual members.

Each chamber of the South Carolina General Assembly regularly organizes itself into standing committees for the purpose of conducting legislative review. The Senate usually has about a dozen standing committees, with seniority of membership determining both committee membership and leadership. Each Senate standing committee has between ten and twenty senators. In the House, members serve on any of about a dozen committees as well, with committees having between six and thirty members. Some House committees have a chair and vice chair, while others have two vice chairs to assist the chair. There are also about twenty joint committees, with members of both chambers.

Processes

The South Carolina General Assembly meets annually, convening on the second Tuesday in January. Sessions must conclude by the first Thursday in June unless extended by a two-thirds vote of the membership of each chamber. All House bills must be introduced by April 15 of the second year of a two-year session, and all Senate bills must be reported to the House by May 1 of the second year. Likewise, all House bills must be reported to the Senate by May 1 of the second year. During the 2003 session, South Carolina legislators introduced 1,330 bills, passing just 114 on to the desk of the governor. Thirty-nine of those bills were vetoed by the governor, only to see the legislature overturn twenty of them.

The South Carolina General Assembly is generally considered to be a part-time legislative body, with most legislators holding jobs outside the chamber. This is necessitated by the annual salary of less than $11,000 with a per diem of about $100 for meals and lodging during

Three Decades as Mr. Speaker

For more than three decades, the South Carolina House of Representatives could rightly be called the House of Representative—no "s." From 1937 to 1946, and then again from 1951 to 1973, Representative Solomon Blatt served as speaker of the South Carolina House of Representatives. Working closely with his tight-knit circle of rural legislators (called the "Barnwell Ring," after Blatt's hometown), he ruled the House and the state with an iron fist. The longest serving state speaker in the United States, he served with eight different governors and several Senate leaders, controlling state government for almost a half-century. A sign in his office read: "No man, his life or liberty is safe while the legislature is in session!"

session. For a legislator who must live in the capital during the session, the per diem may actually exceed the base salary, but the total financial benefits seldom exceed $20,000 per year. Legislators do have minimal year-round staff at the capitol but are not provided district staff. The General Assembly has a full-time staff of less than 300.

Leadership Structure

The president pro tempore is the top leadership position in the Senate. The speaker of the House is the top leader of the House of Representatives. The speaker of the House is considerably stronger in the House than is the Senate president pro tempore in that body. With considerable control over floor debate and agendas, many consider the speaker of the House to be the most powerful position in South Carolina state government.

Senators select their own committee assignments, with seniority the determining factor in the event of a conflict. The senior member of the majority party automatically becomes committee chair. The speaker of the House appoints House committee members, but the committee chairs are determined by the membership of the committee. The Senate's president pro tempore and the House speaker, in consultation with the majority leaders of their respective houses, determine their chamber agendas.

The Senate president pro tempore and majority leader, the House majority leader, and the Senate and House minority leaders are responsible for managing floor debate for their respective parties. The speaker of the House and the president pro tempore of the Senate each receive an additional $11,0000 annually for their leadership service. The speaker pro tempore receives an additional $3,600.

Election Processes

South Carolina legislators are elected in the November even-year election, with all senators elected to their four-year terms in the presidential election year. Historically, as in other Southern states, the Democratic primary has been the most important election. However, partisan shifts over the past twenty years have made the Republican Primary more important, often determining who will win the seat in Republican-controlled districts well before the general election. The average Senate district has about 90,000 people, while each House district houses about 35,000 South Carolinians. Turnover in South Carolina is relatively low, with about one in six legislators retiring or being defeated every election cycle. Party nominations are determined by primary.

Key Political Factors

Unlike the case in several other states of the Old Confederacy (Alabama, Mississippi, and Louisiana), the South Carolina Democratic Party has been unable to retain control of the state's legislature in the face of the growing strength of the state Republican Party. Indeed, since taking control of the House in 1995 and the Senate in 2001, Republicans have seen their majorities grow to margins that are quite safe. Following the 2000 election, they used their power of districting to solidify and expand their gains.

The strength of the South Carolina Republican Party can be expected to continue to grow, and that will make it increasingly difficult for Democrats to win control of the state legislature, which they dominated for more than a hundred years following the Civil War.

As is the case in most Southern states, the governor's office of South Carolina is relatively weak. When Democrats controlled everything, many of the power struggles were between the legislative and executive branches, rather than between parties. Now that the Republican Party seems to have a pretty firm grasp on most of the offices, that same institutional battle continues.

Because of the limited support staff provided individual legislators in South Carolina, lobbyists are a valuable source of political and policy information. Following a federal investigation in the late 1980s and 1990s that led to the indictment and conviction of several South Carolina legislators, the state enacted one of the strongest ethics laws in the country. Individual South Carolina legislators are prohibited from accepting so much as a cup of coffee from a lobbyist.

Further Reading

Bryan, John Morrill. 1999. *Creating the South Carolina State House*. Columbia: University of South Carolina Press.

Bullock, Charles S., and Mark J. Rozell, eds. 2002. *New Politics of the Old South: An Introduction to Southern Politics*. 2d ed. Lanham, MD: Rowman and Littlefield.

Graham, Cole B., Jr., and William V. Moore. 1994. *South Carolina Politics and Government*. Lincoln: University of Nebraska Press.

Poole, W. Scott. 2004. *Never Surrender: Confederate Memory and Conservatism in South Carolina Upcountry*. Athens: University of Georgia Press.

SOUTH DAKOTA

• • • • • • • • • • • •

THE SOUTH DAKOTA LEGISLATURE

House of Representatives	Senate
70 Representatives	35 Senators
(605) 773–3851	(605) 773–3821

http://www.state.sd.us

• • • • • • • • • • • •

South Dakota is perhaps best known for the Mt. Rushmore presidential memorial and for its Native American heritage (primarily the Sioux tribes). The Native American influence is prevalent in the rotunda of the capitol, including Native American flags and staves displayed along with the flags of France, Spain, the Dakota Territory, the United States, and South Dakota. The economy of South Dakota, which was long focused on agriculture, has become somewhat more diversified over the past half-century, adding banking/finance, tourism, real estate, and insurance to its economic base.

South Dakota is a strongly Republican state that nevertheless has elected several prominent Democrats such as 1972 presidential candidate George McGovern and U.S. Senate majority and former minority leader Tom Daschle. The state has voted for the Democratic presidential candidate only once (Lyndon Johnson in his 1964 landslide) since the middle of the twentieth century. The state legislature has remained under almost exclusive Republican control throughout the state's history. The state legislature is governed by a solid Republican majority.

Structure and Membership

The South Dakota legislature consists of a thirty-five-member Senate and a seventy-member House of Representatives. All legislators are elected for two-year terms. South Dakota legislators are limited to serving a maximum of four consecutive two-year terms in their legislative house. The lieutenant governor, who is elected on a ticket with the governor, is president of the Senate and presides over its sessions. The Senate elects a president pro tempore from its membership. The speaker of the House presides over its sessions.

Republicans have quite consistently, with rare exception, maintained a solid majority in both chambers of the South Dakota legislature. In 2005 they outnumber Democrats by more than two to one in each chamber.

The first female legislator was elected to the South Dakota legislature in 1922 (Gladys Pyle), and there has been at least one female legislator in the chamber since that time, with the exception of five legislative sessions. By the beginning of the twentieth century, women consistently held about 15 percent of the legislative positions, as well as several committee chairmanships. There are usually no African American or Hispanic legislators in the South Dakota legislature.

Staff services are provided by a nonpartisan legislative research council office directed by an executive board consisting of the speaker of the House and the president pro tempore of the Senate and thirteen legislators (six senators and seven representatives) that are elected by their respective houses.

There are thirteen standing committees in each house. In the Senate most committees consist of seven or nine senators. The majority leader, president pro tempore, and minority leader select the members of each committee and the chair and vice chair. In the House, most committees consist of thirteen or fifteen representatives. The speaker of the House, with advice from the minority leader, picks the members and the chair and vice chair of the committees. Most legislators are members of two committees. Some serve on more than two committees, but that is often impossible because two or three committees are usually meeting at the same time.

From a political standpoint, the composition of each standing committee mirrors the composition of the house as a whole. If the Republican Party holds a two-thirds majority in the Senate, they would also hold a two-thirds majority in each of the Senate standing committees, and the chair and vice chair of the committees would likely all be Republicans. The Democrats would not be in the majority on any committee. Standing committees must take action on every bill assigned to them, but that action can include tabling the bill so that it will not be considered, or postponing consideration until the body is adjourned, in effect killing it. Whatever action the committee takes must be reported to the whole body.

Probably the most important committee in the South Dakota legislature is not a traditional standing committee but a joint committee. The Joint Appropriations Committee includes members from both chambers and is responsible for developing the state's budget, in light of the economic and budget forecasts made by the executive branch and the legislature.

Processes

The South Dakota legislature convenes annually on the second Tuesday in January. Sessions are limited to forty legislative days (excluding weekends and days not in session) in odd-year sessions, and thirty-five days in even-year sessions. During the forty-day session, all member bills must be introduced by the fifteenth legislative day and all committee bills and resolutions by the sixteenth legislative day. During the thirty-five-day session, the same bills must be introduced by the tenth and eleventh legislative days, respectively. Legislators may also prefile bills up to thirty days before the start of the legislative session.

There are also limits on how often and how long members may speak on a bill. Unlike in the committees, where there are no limits on debate, the joint rules limit legislators in their debate of bills on the Senate and House floors. First of all, every member is entitled to speak on a

Everything Is Looking Down (and Blue)

If you notice everyone in the South Dakota capitol looking down, that is not because things are bad. They are not feeling blue—they are looking for blue! Blue stones, that is. The floor of the South Dakota capitol is inlaid Italian terrazzo, individually laid by sixty-six Italian artisans. Legend has it that as a way of "signing" their work, each artisan was given a blue stone to place somewhere in the floor. To date, only fifty-five blue stones have been found.

particular subject before any member of the body speaks on it more than once. Additionally, no member of the Senate or House may speak on the same subject more than twice or longer than ten minutes without the consent of a majority of the members present. If a member wishes to speak beyond the time limit, other members not desiring to speak on the issue may yield up to twenty minutes of their time to the member speaking.

In 2003, South Dakota legislators introduced 520 pieces of legislation, with 258 passing both chambers. The governor vetoed 3 of those bills, one of which the legislature passed over the veto. Historically, South Dakota governors veto an average of ten to fifteen bills each session.

The South Dakota legislature is truly a part-time institution. Indeed, if you dial the capitol phone number of the speaker of the House, it rings through to a local hotel where he stays during the session, rather than an office in the capitol!

The "long" session seldom extends beyond May, and legislators cannot live off the salary and per diem. South Dakota state legislators are paid $12,000 for the two-year session, plus $10 per legislative day, not to exceed forty days in odd years or thirty-five days in even years. Even if there are a few special sessions, a member

of the South Dakota legislature will earn no more than $13,000 for the two-year session. Legislators tend also to be farmers, ranchers, or businesspersons, or to hold other professional posts. Legislative turnover has stayed around 25 percent since the implementation of term limits in 1992. Legislators have only minimal staff support during the legislative session and minimal Legislative Research Council support once the session has ended. The legislature has about sixty full-time staff members.

Leadership Structure

While the lieutenant governor presides over the Senate as its president, the president pro tempore of the Senate and the majority leader are the top leaders of the Senate. They are responsible for determining its agenda, managing the flow of legislation, appointing committees, and assigning committee chairs. Those tasks are all performed by the speaker of the House in that chamber.

The majority leader and minority leader of each house are responsible for managing floor debate for their respective parties. The majority and minority leaders are each assisted by an assistant leader, and the Democrats also have a caucus chair.

Election Processes

South Dakota legislators are elected in the November even-year election. Contested nominations are decided in party primaries. Because of the general dominance of the Republican Party, many seats are more likely to be determined in the primary rather than the general election.

There are thirty-five legislative districts in South Dakota. Voters in each of those districts elect one senator and two representatives from the district. The average district has just over 20,000 South Dakotans. While the cost of winning a legislative race in South Dakota is generally low (around $15,000), races in the more urban areas (primarily in Sioux Falls and Rapid City) can exceed $25,000. In 2004, one candidate in Rapid City spent more than $100,000 to win a position that pays well under one-fifth that amount over two years.

Key Political Factors

While the South Dakota Democratic Party has enjoyed some successes in congressional and statewide elections, the state's Republican Party has, with a few rare exceptions, held strong majorities in both houses of the state legislature. Democrats controlled the House of Representatives for only four years, during the mid-1930s. The Democrats have been a bit more successful in the Senate, holding the majority for most of the 1930s, for two years in the late 1950s, from 1973 to 1976, and from 1993 to 1994. However, it is safe to consider South Dakota a strongly Republican state.

Further Reading

Farber, William O., Thomas C. Geary, and Loren M. Carlson. 1979. *Government of South Dakota*. 3d ed. Vermillion, SD: Dakota Press.

TENNESSEE

● ● ● ● ● ● ● ● ● ● ● ●

THE TENNESSEE GENERAL ASSEMBLY

House of Representatives	Senate
99 Representatives	33 Senators
(615) 741–2901	(615) 741–2730

http://www.legislature.state.tn.us/

● ● ● ● ● ● ● ● ● ● ● ●

Tennessee is a Southern state that is nevertheless not as completely Southern as its neighbors to the south. While it did join the Confederacy, Tennesseeans were far from united in their support, as more than 30,000 of them fought in the Union army. After the war, Tennessee was the only Confederate state that did not undergo military occupation. Today, Tennessee is perhaps best known as the home of the country music industry in Nashville and the Elvis's Graceland in Memphis, but it also has a diverse economy that includes manufacturing, finance, insurance and real estate, and agriculture.

For almost a century following the Civil War, Tennessee politics was dominated by

---

This Capitol Is a Real Political Graveyard

While all state capitols have given witness to the deaths of many promising political careers, the Tennessee capitol may be the only one that holds the physical remains of a politician. James K. Polk, governor of Tennessee, member of the U.S. Congress from Tennessee, and the eleventh president of the United States, is interned in the Jackson Garden at the foot of the Tennessee capitol. His wife, Sarah, is buried there as well.

---

the Democratic Party. That began to change when Republican Dwight Eisenhower narrowly carried the state in both his 1952 and 1956 presidential victories. From that point, Tennessee's small Republican Party grew quickly, and by the early 1970s both of the state's U.S. senators were Republican. But Tennessee's Democrats have remained a formidable force, and today the state is highly competitive. As with a number of its neighboring states, the state legislature is where Democrats have achieved their greatest recent success. However, with gains in 2004, Republicans took control of the state Senate for the first time since Reconstruction.

Structure and Membership

The Tennessee General Assembly consists of a thirty-three-member Senate and a ninety-nine-member House of Representatives. Senators serve four-year terms and House members serve two-year terms. All legislators are elected from single-member districts.

Until Republicans recently gained a majority in the Senate, Democrats had held a majority in both chambers since Reconstruction in the 1870s. However, their majority in both chambers has grown gradually smaller since the 1970s, finally culminating with the Republican majority in the Senate in 2004. Following that election, Democrats maintained a slim seven-seat majority in the House.

The proportion of female legislators in the Tennessee General Assembly is, as in the rest of the South, below the average for the rest of the country, usually hovering between 15 and 18 percent. However, that is among the highest percentages in the South. Furthermore, the Honorable Lois DeBerry, an African American woman legislator from Memphis, has served as president pro tempore since 1988. Female legislators have also held significant committee chair positions as well as other leadership posts in both chambers. African American legislators also play a significant role in the Tennessee General Assembly, generally holding 10 to 15 percent of the seats and significant leadership posts and committee positions.

The Joint Legislative Services Committee (JLSC) chaired by the two speakers oversees nonpartisan staff services. The JLSC includes the Office of Legal Services, which provides bill drafting and committee support, the Office of Legislative Administration, which oversees personal and budgetary administration, and the Office of Legislative Services, which provides for the printing and distribution of bills and resolutions. Each house also has a small number of partisan staffers for leaders and individual members.

The Tennessee General Assembly has a well-organized, active, and well-staffed standing committee system. Each chamber usually has approximately a dozen standing committees that are responsible for reviewing all legislation and making recommendations to the whole body. The General Assembly also has about a dozen joint committees composed of legislators from both chambers and chaired alternately by senators and representatives. Given the fact that all bills must be assigned to a standing committee, but that the committee is not required to act on all bills, standing committees in the Tennessee General Assembly are considered among the most powerful state legislative standing committees in the country.

Processes

The Tennessee General Assembly meets annually. It convenes in an organizational session for a maximum of three days on the second Tuesday in January in odd-numbered years and then takes a two-week break before beginning the session work. The regular session must then convene no later than the Tuesday following the conclusion of the organizational session and is limited to a maximum of ninety legislative days over a two-year period. General bills must be introduced in each chamber by the end of the tenth legislative day, unless approved

by two-thirds of the members present or a unanimous vote of the Committee on Delayed Bills. Legislators may also pre-file legislation before the January start of the session.

During the 2003 session, Tennessee legislators introduced more than 2,000 bills, with a little under 20 percent (483) passing both houses. The Democratic governor vetoed none of the legislation that reached his desk.

Most people consider the Tennessee legislature to be a hybrid between a part-time and a full-time legislature. While they are officially in session for fewer than fifty legislative days each year, the session can stretch into five months. The 2000 session went until the end of June, the longest in the state's history. Legislators also have personal and support staff year-round. The General Assembly employs more than 200 full-time, year-round staffers. Legislators are paid less than $17,000 annually, plus $144 per legislative day during session. Legislators can expect to earn about $22,000 annually, so most do hold private-sector jobs. Turnover is usually between 15 and 20 percent every election cycle.

Leadership Structure

The Senate and House speakers are officially the top leaders in their respective houses. The speakers of the Senate and House, elected within their respective chambers, preside over sessions in their chambers. Senate committee chairs and members are appointed by a committee on assignments, which is chaired by the president pro tempore and includes the lieutenant governor and three additional members appointed by the president pro tempore. The speakers of each house appoint committee chairs. Each chamber has a committee composed of leaders that determine their respective agendas.

While party control has always gone to the majority party in both chambers, a Republican majority elected in 2004 chose to keep Senator John S. Wilder, a Democrat, in place as the speaker of the Senate. Speaker Wilder has recently governed the Senate in a bipartisan manner, giving Republicans equal status on committees and splitting committee chair positions equally between the parties.

The majority leader and minority leader of each chamber are responsible for managing floor debate for their respective parties. Both the majority and minority parties have a number of deputy and assistant leaders.

Tennessee has a tradition of relatively long leadership tenures. With his reelection to be speaker of the House in 2005, Jimmy Naifeh entered into his eighth two-year term at the helm, and Senate speaker John Wilder began his seventeenth two-year term in that position, making him the longest serving Senate leader in the country.

Election Processes

Tennessee legislators are elected in the November even-year election, with approximately half of the Senate membership elected every two years. Even-numbered districts run one year, and senators from odd-numbered districts run two years later. Every seat in the House is contested every two years. Each Senate district has about 175,000 people, and each House district about 60,000. Party nominations are determined by primary elections.

Key Political Factors

With two strong and stable political parties, Tennessee can be expected to continue as a highly competitive state in the years to come, with control of the state's General Assembly up for grabs in most elections. However, Republican growth in some suburban areas and in the eastern part of the state may suggest that the GOP will eventually gain a consistent majority in the Volunteer State. Geographically, Republicans tend to do better in the eastern part of the state, while Democratic strongholds are in the west, particularly in and around Memphis. The central part of the state tends to be competitive.

Tennessee is one of only nine states in the country that do not have a state income tax, and if the voter response to recent efforts to impose one is any indication, it will stay that way. In June 2000, Tennessee legislators met to consider implementing a state income tax on citizens making more than $100,000 a year. They were greeted by honking cars around the capitol complex and jeering constituents outside their doors. The capitol building was locked down as protestors broke windows, and a rock was tossed through the office window of the governor (who was not in the office at the time). Legislators were escorted from their offices by state police officers. The state budget passed without the proposed tax.

Lobbyists play a significant role in legislative politics in the Volunteer State. During 2003, 450 were registered to influence public policy. A recent study finds regulations on lobbyists in Tennessee to be among the weakest in the country.

Further Reading

Lyons, William, John M. Scheb, and Billy Stair. 2001. *Government and Politics in Tennessee.* Knoxville: University of Tennessee Press.

Vile, John R., and Mark Byrnes, eds. 1998. *Tennessee Government and Politics: Democracy in the Volunteer State.* Nashville: Vanderbilt University Press.

TEXAS

• • • • • • • • • • • •

THE TEXAS LEGISLATURE

House of Representatives	Senate
150 Representatives	31 Senators

(512) 463–4630
http://www.capitol.state.tx.us

• • • • • • • • • • • •

The nation's second largest state in both population and land area, Texas historically has combined key elements of the independent Western culture and the traditional patrician South. The western part of the state (the panhandle) reflected the "cowboy culture" of the Western United States, with its belief in limited government and personal responsibility. The eastern side of the Lone Star State reflected the traditional Southern culture, with its cotton-based economy (before the discovery of oil in the early 1900s), large plantations and ranches, efforts to discourage voting among the poor, and historical loyalty to the Democratic Party.

By the twenty-first century, Texas had transformed itself into a diversified cosmopolitan state in which one can find just about anything that can be found in any other part of the United States, with more than 80 percent of the population living in metropolitan areas. Long known for its oil and its large ranches, today's Texas is also known for large, modern cities like Dallas and Houston, its high-tech corridor between Austin and Dallas–Ft. Worth, and a popular Gulf of Mexico coastline.

Texas has also experienced dramatic change in its political makeup. Once a predominantly Democratic state, it is now viewed as a strong Republican bastion in presidential elections. By electing majorities to the state House and Senate, Republicans have completed their sweep of the state. Republicans in 2005 controlled both chambers of the state legislature, all six of the statewide offices (including governor), both U.S. Senate seats, the state supreme court and the Court of Criminal Appeals, and a majority of the congressional delegation. Forty-five years earlier, they had controlled none of these posts!

Texas State Capitol (Richard Cummins/Corbis)

Structure and Membership

The Texas legislature consists of a 31-member Senate and a 150-member House of Representatives. Senate terms are four years and House terms are two years. Legislators are elected from single-member districts in November even-year elections. The lieutenant governor, an independently elected official, is responsible for Senate administration. The speaker of the House, elected by the majority party of the House, is responsible for House administration.

Following historic state legislative gains in 2002, Republicans took control of the state House for the first time since Reconstruction, and they did it in convincing fashion: when the dust had settled, Republicans had turned a 78 to 72 Democratic majority into an 88 to 62 Republican majority and ousted an eight-year Democratic speaker. Turning from a bipartisan tradition established by previous Democrats, Republican leaders in the House did not appoint members of the opposing party to chair key committees. Republicans have held a majority of the seats in the Texas Senate since the election of 1996.

Women have traditionally been well represented in Texas politics, electing a governor, U.S. senator, comptroller, and several statewide commissioners. One in five Texas legislators in the 2005 session was female, including the Senate president pro tempore and three of thirteen committee chairs. Interestingly, three of

Texas Legislature Moves to New Mexico

In a failed effort to stall a Republican effort to redistrict Texas's congressional districts to benefit Republican candidates in 2003, Democratic members of the Texas House of Representatives spent several days in a Howard Johnson's in Oklahoma so that the legislature could not conduct business. Several weeks later, once the plan was in the Senate, Senate Democrats headed west and spent several days in New Mexico for the same reason. In the end, the redistricting plan passed.

the four female senators are Republicans. While the African American population in Texas is about 10 percent, African American legislators make up only 6 percent of the Senate (two senators) and 9 percent (thirteen representatives) of the House. On the other hand, one in five members of the Texas legislature is Hispanic. Most of the Hispanic members represent districts along the Mexican border and the Gulf of Mexico, but a growing number are being elected from metropolitan areas such as Houston and Dallas.

Nonpartisan professional staff services are provided to both houses through a fourteen-member legislative council cochaired by the lieutenant governor and House speaker. Partisan staff serve legislative leaders and individual members.

Processes

The Texas legislature meets biennially in odd-numbered years, convening on the second Tuesday in January. Sessions are limited to 140 calendar days. In order to complete its legislative task in one 140-day session every two years, rules require that no new bills be introduced after the sixtieth day of the session unless approved by 80 percent of the chamber.

Many have suggested that Texas is too large and too metropolitan to be governed with a biennial session, but most have resisted the move to an annual session. However, the number of supplemental special sessions has grown considerably in the last two decades, perhaps to make up for the failures of a biennial session. During the 2003 regular session, Texas legislators introduced more than 5,000 bills (5,592), enacting about a quarter of them (1,384). That works out to more than thirty pieces of legislation introduced per member!

The Texas legislature is considered semiprofessional by most scholars. Its members are poorly paid ($7,200 a year plus a daily allowance during session that pushes their total to about $24,000 a year during the year they are in session). Thus legislators must be independently wealthy, retired, financially dependent on someone else, or must work another "real job" to make ends meet. Furthermore, the fact that the legislature does not meet in even-numbered years suggests a nonprofessional legislature. However, with almost 2,000 full-time staff members and year-round staff in the district and in the capitol, Texas legislators are supported like professionals.

Leadership Structure

As president of the Senate, the lieutenant governor is the chamber's top leader and, even though not a member of the chamber, exercises a great deal of influence in shaping state policy and influencing legislation. The lieutenant governor appoints committee chairpersons and individual members and determines the order in which bills will be considered. The president pro tempore serves as the chamber's presiding officer and assists the president in the appointment of committee members.

Because he is not officially a member of the Senate, the lieutenant governor can vote only when a tie occurs or when the Senate is not meeting as a formal voting body. The Senate president pro tempore, elected by the Senate, is the top official from among its membership, but the post is largely honorific, boasting little or no power, except in the absence of the lieutenant governor.

The speaker of the House is top leader of the House of Representatives. The speaker pro tempore is the second-ranking leader. In recent years, Texas speakers have served several terms. However, prior to the constitutional change allowing governors to succeed themselves, tradition held the speaker to two two-year terms. In 1975, that tradition was abandoned. While House leaders have historically been bipartisan, recent leaders have been reluctant to appoint members of the opposing party to key positions.

Texas is one of the few states in which the lieutenant governor is considered more powerful than the speaker of the House. While both appoint committees, the speaker of the House is subject to seniority rules, which require that half of the appointments to most committees made be based on seniority.

Election Processes

Texas legislators are elected in the November even-year election. Because Senate terms are four years, half of the Senate is elected in each even-year election—except at elections following a reapportionment, when some senators are elected for terms of two years to maintain staggered terms while conforming with the newly apportioned districts. Because of the small number of Senate districts (thirty-one) and the large population of the state, Texas Senate districts are similar in size to congressional districts. Each Texas senator represents almost 800,000 Texans. In recent years, elections for the Texas Senate have become quite expensive, sometimes topping $500,000. Members of the Texas House represent around 150,000 Texans. Contested nominations are decided in party primaries.

Key Political Factors

While the Texas Republican Party has steadily built its strength since the 1960s, particularly in presidential and congressional elections, it was not until 2003 that it won control of both houses of the state legislature. Democrats continue to enjoy considerable grassroots strength that enables the party to remain competitive at all levels. The greatest changes in the state have come in the eastern part, which was once solidly Democratic but has seen most of the old-style conservative Southern Democrats replaced by Republicans.

The rapid growth of the Hispanic population will continue to have a significant impact on politics in the Lone Star State as both parties seek to recruit Hispanic voters and candidates. Furthermore, the rapid rise in the proportion of Hispanics, making them the "majority minority," has caused some significant rifts between Hispanic and African American leaders, presenting challenges for the Democratic Party.

Further Reading

Halter, Gary. 2005. *Government and Politics of Texas* 5th ed. Boston: McGraw-Hill.

Jones, Nancy Baker, and Ruthe Winegarten. 2000. *Capitol Women: Female Texas Legislators, 1923–1999.* Austin: University of Texas Press.

Kraemer, Richard H., Charldean Newell, and David F. Prindle. 2002. *Texas Politics.* 8th ed. Belmont, CA: Wadsworth/Thompson Learning.

Maxwell, William Earl, et al. 2003. *Texas Politics Today.* 11th ed. Belmont, CA: Wadsworth/Thompson Learning.

Tannahill, Neal R. 2005. *Texas Government: Policy and Politics.* New York: Pearson/Longman.

UTAH

• • • • • • • • • • • •

THE UTAH LEGISLATURE

House of Representatives	Senate
75 Representatives	29 Senators
(801) 538–1029	(801) 538–1035

http://www.le.state.ut.us

• • • • • • • • • • • •

Utah was largely settled by the Mormons in the late 1840s and requested admission to the Union as early as 1850. But it did not achieve statehood until 1896, after the Mormons had abandoned their doctrine of polygamy. Today, Utah's population and culture remain heavily Mormon; the state is a popular tourist spot for skiers in the winter and for visitors to its spectacular rock structures in the warmer months.

Utah is one of the most heavily Republican states in the country. It consistently gives the Republican presidential candidates some of their largest percentages. In line with its Mormon moral tenets, the Utah Republican Party is quite conservative. The state's Democratic Party is active and has won some statewide and congressional races, although the Republican Party has maintained consistently large majorities in the state legislature.

Structure and Membership

The Utah legislature consists of a twenty-nine-member Senate and a seventy-five-member House of Representatives. Senate members are elected for four-year terms, and House members are elected for two-year terms from single-member districts. The Senate elects a president from its membership to preside over its sessions and generally oversee the chamber's administration. The speaker of the House presides over its sessions and is responsible for House administration. As has been the case for much of the state's history, Republican legislators held a dominant lead (about 2-1/2 to 1) in each chamber in 2005.

Despite being the second territory in the United States to grant women the right to vote (1870), the percentage of women in the Utah legislature is slightly below the national average. While women hold just above 22 percent of seats nationally, they hold just above 20 percent of the seats in the Utah legislature. They generally chair a similar proportion of standing committees. Given the rather homogeneous nature of the ethnic population, it is little wonder that a very low proportion of Utah legislators are Hispanic or African American. In 2003, there was one African American in the Utah Senate and one African American House member, who served with one Latino representative.

Nonpartisan professional staff services are provided under a bipartisan Legislative Management Committee. The Senate president and the House speaker serve as chair and vice chair of the committee in alternating terms.

The House of Representatives does the bulk of its work in its standing committees, which usually number more than a dozen. Each House committee includes ten to fifteen House members, appointed by the speaker. The Senate usually has just under a dozen standing committees, with each committee having between seven and nine senators. Apart from these standing committees, the legislature has ten appropriations subcommittees, which include members from both chambers. The president of the Senate and the speaker of the House appoint members of these powerful subcommittees.

While most bills are considered by a standing committee, the Rules Committee in the House may prevent some bills from being considered by a standing committee. These standing committees often meet in the interim, and they have significant power to shape legislation, standing committees in Utah being among the most powerful in the country. Standing committees in Utah may refer bills to the floor favorably, favorably as amended, substituted (basically a new bill), or they may table a bill—keeping it in committee and taking no further action. Interim committees meet jointly (with members from both chambers) on the third Wednesday of every month between April and November to discuss issues of public policy and to accept public opinions on those matters. In addition to their service on standing committees, members are usually assigned to two interim committees and one appropriations subcommittee.

Processes

The president of the Senate and the speaker of the House preside over floor sessions and appoint committees in their respective chambers. The president and the speaker, in consultation with their majority leaders, determine their chambers' agendas.

The Utah legislature meets annually, convening on the third Monday in January, with sessions constitutionally limited to forty-five calendar days. According the joint rules of the House and Senate, each legislator may designate up to and no more than three pieces of legislation as "priority bills." The rather small legislative staff will draft those bills, but additional bills will be drafted as time and staff permit. Usually, most bills in which legislators have an interest are drafted. Priority bills must be identified a month before the beginning of session. These bills will be the first numbered and the first to receive legislative attention. Individual legislators may request no bills after the eleventh day of the session, unless permission is granted by two-thirds of the chamber.

During the 2003 legislative session, Utah legislators introduced 628 bills, sending 343 to the desk of the governor for a signature. The governor vetoed a line item on one of these bills, and the rest were signed into law.

The Utah legislature is most definitely considered a part-time legislative institution. According to the state constitution, its legislative session cannot exceed forty-five calendar days, and its members do not receive a set annual salary. Instead, they receive a salary of $120 for every day the legislature is in session, plus about $110 daily allowance for lodging and living expenses. During a full forty-five day session, a member of the Utah legislature will earn less than $10,000, including salary, lodging, and living expenses. They also receive the per diem, lodging, and living allowance for days that they must come to Salt Lake City during the interim, but no additional salary. Legislators share staff members during the session, and most are assigned one student intern during session. There is no personal staff when the legislature is out of session. The legislature employs just over a hundred staff members to support the work of the legislators. Legislative turnover is about 20 percent every two years. Most legislators hold a job in the private sector.

Leadership Structure

The president of the Senate and the speaker of the House are the top leaders of their respective chambers and, in consultation with their majority leaders, determine the agenda of their house. They also preside over their respective chambers, enforce the rules of order during debate, appoint members to committees, and represent their chamber in negotiations with the other chamber or the executive. They also determine who will chair standing committees. Each is elected by the members of his or her chamber and is from the majority party.

The majority and minority leaders of each chamber are responsible for managing floor debate for their respective parties. They also conduct their party caucus meetings, inform their members of the pending schedules and votes, mobilize party support, and communicate with each other regarding partisan floor activities. Each party also selects whips and assistant whips to help the majority and minority leaders fulfill their obligations and responsibilities.

Legislative leaders in Utah usually serve no more than two or three two-year sessions in their posts. The presiding officers, floor leaders, and whips each receive some additional compensation for their work, ranging from $1,500 to $2,500. The formal leadership powers of leaders in the Utah legislature, particularly regarding committee activity, floor management, and tenure potential, are considered among the strongest in the country.

Legislators Fire Themselves

In 1994, Utah legislators voted themselves out of a job. Utah is the only state legislature to vote for legislative term limits, effectively limiting their own ability to serve in the legislature. However, it is not as silly as it may sound. With an eight-year, lifetime initiative on the ballot in 1994, Utah legislators promised to pass a more reasoned limit in the legislature if the voters would defeat the ballot initiative. In 1995, they voted for a limit of twelve consecutive years of service in the legislature. Eight years later, when term-limits momentum had died down, Utah legislators passed a repeal of the term-limits law.

Election Processes

Utah legislators are elected in the November even-year election. Approximately half of the members of the Senate are elected to their four-year terms each even-year election. Each Senate district has about 77,000 Utahans in it, and each House district about 30,000.

Contested nominations are decided in party conventions or primaries. Given the strong partisan makeup of most individual districts, the primary election is often more important than the November general election.

Key Political Factors

Utah is expected to remain a Republican-dominated state that will on occasion spring a surprise by electing a Democrat to state or congressional office. The state's voters have demonstrated an occasional independent streak in presidential voting. The state gave Independent candidate Ross Perot 27.4 percent of its vote in 1992, which was more than the 24.7 percent that it gave to Democrat Bill Clinton.

Politics and the political institutions in Utah remain quite conservative. Because of the overwhelming presence of the Mormon Church in the population and among elected officials, there is a strong relationship between the philosophical views of the church and the activities of the government.

As in most Western states, Utah citizens have the power of initiative and referendum. In fact, Utah was the first state to approve of the initiative process, doing so in 1900. Voters in Utah can initiate and implement law, but they cannot initiate changes to the state's constitution. The initiative process in Utah is established by the legislature, which has created detailed if difficult procedures for initiative approval for the ballot. Twenty-one initiatives have been adopted in Utah since 1900.

Further Reading

Bickmore, Jean White. 1970. "The Gentle Persuaders: Utah's First Women Legislators." *Utah Historical Quarterly* 38, no. 1: 31–49.
Haymond, J. Brent, Janet L. Geyser, and Pamela R. Benzon. 1996. *The Utah State Legislature Centennial History, 1896–1996.* Salt Lake City: Office of the Third House.

VERMONT

●●●●●●●●●●●●

THE VERMONT GENERAL ASSEMBLY

House of Representatives	Senate
150 Representatives	30 Senators
(802) 828–2247	(802) 828–2241

http://www.leg.state.vt.us

●●●●●●●●●●●●

With a ranking of forty-ninth among the fifty states in population, its largest city (Burlington) having only 40,000 residents, no other municipality with even 20,000 and a state capital with less than 10,000, Vermont is unlike any other state. The most popular ski areas east of the Mississippi, lush green mountains in the spring and summer, gorgeous foliage in the fall, and a rustic rural setting make Vermont a popular all-season vacation spot.

Contrary to what might be expected of a state composed almost exclusively of small towns and virtually no minority population, Vermonters have, over the past several decades, shown a surprisingly liberal strain in their political preferences. Indeed, Vermont generally ranks among the top five states in terms of policy liberalism, tax progressivity, and public financial support for the poor.

In recent years, Vermonters have elected and reelected a moderate Democratic governor followed by a moderate Republican governor, along with a socialist congressman to fill the statewide seat (the state's only seat) in the U.S. House. A Republican U.S. senator from Vermont left his party to become an independent because he found the national party too conservative for his liking. The Republican Party has achieved its most success in recent years in the state legislature, control of which is considered to be up for grabs in almost every state election.

Structure and Membership

There are 30 members of the Vermont Senate and 150 members in its House of Representatives. All legislators serve two-year terms, with elections held in November of even-numbered years. In 2004, Democrats regained the majority they had held in the House from 1986 to 2000, replacing a slim Republican majority with a majority of more than twenty seats. With the six progressives and one independent, who usually support the Democratic leadership, the majority balloons to almost thirty.

Women have historically done quite well in the Vermont General Assembly, usually holding about a third of the seats in each chamber, as well as key committee and leadership posts. In 2005, members of the Vermont House elected their second female speaker, the first since 1953. In light of the nature of the state's population, it is little surprise that the number of Hispanic and African American legislators is usually very low (two

---

Janitors and Sergeant-at-Arms, Artists in Residence

A fourteen-foot statue called *Agriculture* looks out proudly from atop the gold dome of the Vermont Statehouse in Montpelier. The statue was not carved by a famous sculptor, but by an eighty-six-year-old sergeant-at-arms aided by his janitorial staff. When the old statue and dome had to be replaced in 1938, during the last stages of the Great Depression, Sergeant-at-Arms Dwight Dwinell carved a replica of the statue carved decades earlier (1861) by internationally renowned sculptor Larkin Mead, Jr.

African American and no Hispanic members in 2005).

An eight-member legislative council consisting of four members from each chamber is responsible for employing and overseeing a nonpartisan staff that provides bill drafting and research services to both chambers. Senate members include the president pro tempore and three senators appointed by the Senate Committee on Committees. House members include the speaker and three members appointed by the speaker. A similarly appointed and organized joint fiscal committee appoints and oversees the staff of a nonpartisan fiscal office that provides budget review and analysis for the appropriations and revenue committees in each house.

Vermont's legislative committees receive only minimal staff support. The House usually has fifteen standing committees, with membership ranging from seven to eleven. The speaker of the House appoints all members to committee, with the exception of the Rules Committee. The speaker serves as a member of that committee, appointing two additional members. The remaining four members are appointed by the majority and minority caucuses. The Senate usually organizes into about a dozen standing committees, with between five and seven members sitting on each. The Senate president pro tempore appoints and chairs the Senate Rules Committee.

Processes

The Vermont General Assembly has a regular two-year session that convenes on the first Wednesday following the first Monday in January of odd-numbered years. While there is no limitation on session length, the odd-year session usually adjourns between the middle of April and the middle of May. The legislature then reconvenes to continue the adjourned session in the even-numbered year, usually on the first Tuesday of the year.

During sessions, legislators meet Tuesday through Friday. Bills can be drafted prior to session but cannot be introduced until the first day of session. All bills in the House during the first session (odd year) must be introduced by the end of February. All bills in the House during the second session (even year) must be introduced by the end of January. On the

Senate side, bills must be introduced by the fifty-third calendar day in the first session and the twenty-fifth calendar day of the second session. These deadlines can be extended by a vote of the rules committees in each chamber.

During the 2003 legislative session, members of the Vermont General Assembly introduced 559 pieces of legislation. Of those, 78 were enacted by the legislature and 2 were vetoed by the governor. Both vetoes were sustained.

The Vermont General Assembly is often cited as the classic "citizen's legislature," with its members coming from all walks of life and most living and working in the district during their relatively limited legislative service. Legislators receive no salary when they are not in session and receive just under $600 per week during session (that includes a pay raise enacted for the 2005 session). Given that the first session usually goes about four to five months, a Vermont legislator will earn no more than $12,000 per year. The legislature usually adjourns by mid-May in the first session and mid or late April in the second. Virtually all legislators hold a job or are retired from a job in the private sector. Legislators share personal staff during the legislative session, and the General Assembly employs fewer than fifty full-time staff members for the 180 members.

The rather informal and part-time nature of the Vermont General Assembly is evidenced in the weekly "Farmer's Night Concert Series," which is held for three months during the legislative session in the state capitol. The free events, open to the public as well as to legislators, feature statewide or local acts ranging from the Vermont Symphony to local historians, magicians, and dancers. The events are free, and all participants (including the acts) are voluntary.

Leadership Structure

The lieutenant governor, an independently elected official who is president of the Senate, and the president pro tempore, who is elected by the Senate, share some administrative and appointment responsibilities in their chamber, while the speaker of the House has more centralized control in the House. Senate committee appointments are made by a three-person committee composed of the president, president pro tempore, and a third senator elected by the members of the chamber. The president presides over the legislative session of the Senate but shares power with the president pro tempore, who is elected from the body.

The speaker of the House is top leader of the House of Representatives and makes House committee appointments. The Senate and House majority leaders lead floor debate and organize and develop party positions. The minority leaders do the same for the minority party. The majority and minority leaders are each assisted by an assistant leader. The six-member Progressive Party also elects a floor leader.

Election Processes

Vermont legislators are elected to their two-year terms in the November even-year election. The Senate has a combination of single- and multimember districts.

The House of Representatives has a combination of single- and two-member districts. The House contains sixty-six single member districts and forty-two districts with two members. The Senate has three single-member districts, six districts with two members, three districts with three members, and one district with six members. Members in the multimember districts run districtwide, so the district in and around Burlington would include more than 120,000 voters, and a legislator representing a two-member district in the House will represent about 8,000 Vermonters.

The small size of the state and the small population of most of the electoral districts makes politics in the Green Mountain State very personal. Most legislators, especially members of the House, are known by, and know, most of the people in their districts. Most House seats are winnable with less than $5,000, according to one legislative leader. Most campaign expenditures go toward direct mail, adds in local newspapers, and yard signs.

Key Political Factors

While continuing to be a competitive two-party state, Democrats have enjoyed more success than Republicans in statewide elections over the past few decades. The Republican Party has been somewhat more successful in state legislative elections, gaining control in 2000 as voters reacted negatively as Vermont became the first state in the Union not only to recognize same-sex partnerships but also to make sure that every single right outlined in the Vermont constitution and Vermont laws applied equally to heterosexual and homosexual Vermonters. Democrats lost control of the House for the first time in fourteen years as Republicans put together a majority of almost twenty seats. By 2005, Democrats had retaken control by a similar count.

Regional and local ties are much more important in the Vermont General Assembly than party affiliation or ideology. This is particularly true in the Senate, where districts are assigned names based on the towns and counties or communities included, rather than numbers. Furthermore, Senate seat assignments are established in the Senate rules and ensure that members will sit by region rather than party or at the whim of the president or president pro tempore. Approximately half of all legislators commute from their homes to the capitol on a daily basis during session periods.

Further Reading

Bryan, Frank M. 2003. *Real Democracy: The New England Town Meeting and How It Works.* Chicago: University of Chicago Press.

Dean, Howard. 2003. *Winning Back America.* New York: Simon and Schuster.

Moats, David. 2004. *Civil Wars: A Battle for Gay Marriage.* Orlando: Harcourt.

Sherman, Michael, ed. 1999. *Vermont State Government since 1969.* Burlington: University of Vermont, Center for Research on Vermont.

VIRGINIA

•••••••••••••

House of Delegates	Senate
100 Delegates	40 Senators
(804) 698–1619	(804) 698–7400

http://www.legis.state.va.us/

••••••••••••••

Virginia is a much different state than it was as late as the midpoint of the twentieth century. Until that time, it had retained many of its characteristics from the time when its current capital, Richmond, served as the capital of the Confederacy. Contemporary Virginia is a cosmopolitan state with a diversified economy that is the only state in the United States to have elected an African American governor (Doug Wilder, 1989–1993). Its economy, once driven by agriculture, tobacco, and textiles, is now very diverse.

Politically, Virginia has been transformed from a solid Democratic state in which the Republican Party was a nonfactor into a competitive state that leans increasingly Republican. In presidential elections the state has become a Republican stronghold, having narrowly voted for a Democrat only once, in the Lyndon Johnson landslide of 1964, since the middle of the twentieth century. Republicans now have solid control over the state House and Senate.

Structure and Membership

The Virginia General Assembly consists of a 40-member Senate and a 100-member House of Delegates. Senators are elected for four-year terms and House members for two-year terms from single-member districts in November odd-year elections. All senators are elected at the same election.

The legislative business of the Virginia Senate is conducted primarily by its twelve standing committees. The same is true of the House of Delegates, which has fourteen standing committees. Professional staff services are provided by a nonpartisan Division of Legislative Services, which operates under the supervision of the Joint Rules Committee. This committee consists of a small number of members from each chamber, appointed by the chair of the Rules Committee in their respective chamber. The membership usually includes a member of the minority party from each chamber and is chaired by the speaker of the House and the chair of the Senate Rules Committee on an annual rotating basis. There are also small partisan staffs that serve legislative leaders and individual members.

Historically, the Virginia General Assembly has been the dominion of male legislators. The proportion of women in the General Assembly remains quite low (about 15 percent), and only in Virginia and two other states (South Carolina and

Virginia State Capitol (Library of Congress)

New Jersey) has the proportion of female legislators declined in the last election. Furthermore, women chaired no standing committees in either chamber during the 2003–2004 session and held no partisan or institutional leadership posts. African Americans have fared somewhat better in the state that boasts the capital of the Confederacy, but not much. They constitute almost 20 percent of the state's population but just over 11 percent of the House and Senate. Because Republicans control both chambers and there are no Republican African American legislators, they chair no committees.

Turnover in the Virginia General Assembly is quite low. Following the 2003 elections, only one in eight legislators was new to the post.

Processes

The president of the Senate and the speaker of the House preside over sessions in their respective chambers. Senate committee chairs are elected by the senators from the majority party, and standing committee members are confirmed by the full Senate. The speaker makes House committee appointments. The Senate president pro tempore and the House speaker, in consultation with their majority leaders, determine the agendas for their respective chambers.

The Virginia General Assembly meets annually, convening on the second Wednesday of January, with odd-year sessions limited to thirty calendar days and even-year sessions to sixty calendar days. Each session may be extended for up to thirty additional calendar days by a two-thirds vote of the members of each chamber. It has become tradition that the odd-year "short" sessions are regularly extended to forty-five days. In order to complete the state's business in a timely manner, Senate and House leaders often set deadlines for the introduction of various types of bills. During the 2003 regular session, Virginia legislators introduced 2,124 bills, enacting almost half of them (1,038). The Democratic governor vetoed only 7 of the bills passed by the Republican Assembly.

The Virginia General Assembly is considered to be a part-time, nonprofessional legislature, with its sixty- and thirty-day sessions and limited staffing. Members are allocated about $30,000 annually with a benefits package for one full-time staffperson. They are also allotted a per diem salary for one additional staff person during session. Also, each senator is provided a receptionist during the session. Two delegates share a receptionist during the session. Some legislators hire an additional staff person out of their campaign funds. Delegates and senators are each paid about $18,000 a year for their legislative services, plus a daily rate of $115 while the legislature is in session. Given the short length of session, average annual salary is unlikely to exceed $25,000.

Leadership Structure

The Virginia constitution provides that the lieutenant governor is president of the Senate, but the only powers that the lieutenant governor has are to preside and break a tie vote. When the lieutenant governor and the Senate majority are of the same party, he or she does play an advisory role in policy development. The president pro tempore of the Senate and the speaker of the House are the top leaders of their respective chambers.

Legislative leaders in Virginia generally serve long tenures, including the legendary A. L. Philpott, who served as speaker of the House for more than a decade and Senate leader Stanley Walker, who served as president pro tempore for twelve years. The majority and minority leaders of each chamber are responsible for managing floor debate for their respective parties.

The speaker of the House is considerably more powerful than his or her counterpart in the Senate. In the House, the speaker appoints committees and assigns committee chairs. In the Senate, committee assignments as proposed by the Committee on Committees and are voted on by the body. The Committee on Committees is composed of senior members, generally appointed by the majority leader, who also chair the committee. Chairmanships are assigned to the senior member of the majority party on the committee.

Election Processes

Like fellow Southern state Mississippi, Virginia holds its statewide and state legislative elections in off years (1989, 1993, 1997, and so forth). This practice was established so that conservative Virginia Democrats would not have to run with more liberal national Democrats. As the state has gained a Republican majority, many Republicans may wish to have the

---

This Old House

The Virginia General Assembly dates from the establishment of the House of Burgesses at Jamestown in 1619, making it one of the oldest continuing legislative bodies in the world. It was the first representative assembly in the new world. One hundred years before the American Revolution, Nathaniel Bacon of the Virginia House of Burgesses led the first uprising against the British, running the colonial governor out of town and sowing the seeds that would one day grow into the American Revolution and earn Virginia the nickname the "Mother of Rebellion."

coattails of the popular Republican presidential candidates.

Delegates are elected every two years, while senators are elected to four-year terms. All Senate seats are up every four years. Statewide offices are up during the year that senators are not. Senators represent around 180,000 Virginians, while delegates represent about 75,000.

Contested nominations are decided in party primaries or conventions. In such cases, the incumbent determines the nature of the nominating process. He or she can choose between a traditional primary, a firehouse primary, or a convention.

Key Political Factors

Virginia is becoming a predominantly Republican state, but one in which the Democrats remain competitive and very capable of winning statewide elections. However, politics in the Old Dominion are often as governed by geography as they are by party. Democrats find themselves struggling to find a common message for urban Democrats in Richmond and some of the more urban areas around the District of Columbia, and the traditional rural Democrats that have long dominated the southern region of the state. However, as some of these conservative voters in southern and western Virginia have turned toward the Republican Party, they have found themselves clashing with the more urban and less morally conservative Republicans in wealthy and metropolitan northern Virginia (Fairfax and Prince William counties). It is this split that has prevented Republicans from taking control statewide,

as they have in some other Southern states.

Unlike the situation in a number of other Southern states, Virginia's Republican Party has achieved as much success in state legislative elections as it has in gubernatorial races, having won control of both houses of the state legislature for the first time since the Reconstruction era in the late 1870s. Since taking control of the legislature in the 1990s, Republicans have used control of the legislative districting process to solidify their majorities. While the Republican Party swept all statewide offices in 1997, Democrats regained the top two posts (governor and lieutenant governor) in 2001. Growth in the Republican Party has also resulted in more intraparty division, with suburban "Main Street" Republicans being challenged more by conservative "anti-taxers."

Because Virginia is one of the few states that holds its state elections in odd-numbered years, the state's elections attract an inordinate amount of nationwide attention as potential barometers of national trends.

Further Reading
Bullock, Charles S., and Mark J. Rozell, eds. 2002. *New Politics of the Old South: An Introduction to Southern Politics*, 2d ed. Lanham, MD: Rowman and Littlefield.

Fox, William F. 2004 (Reprint). *Civil Government of Virginia*. Whitefish, MT: Kessinger.

Kidd, Quinton, ed. 1999. *Government and Politics in Virginia*. Upper Saddle River, NJ: Pearson.

Porter, William Earl. 1993. *Virginia State Government: Fun, Frustrating and Frightening*. Lanham, MD: University Press of America.

WASHINGTON

● ● ● ● ● ● ● ● ● ● ● ●

THE WASHINGTON LEGISLATURE

House of Representatives	Senate
98 Representatives	49 Senators
(360) 786–7750	(360) 786–7550

http://www1.leg.wa.gov/legislature

● ● ● ● ● ● ● ● ● ● ● ●

Washington is the linchpin state of the Pacific Northwest. Best known as a long-time center of the aerospace industry, the state economy also includes international trade, advanced technology, agriculture, and forestry.

Politically, Washington is a highly competitive state that, since the late 1980s, has leaned toward the Democratic Party in presidential elections. Congressional and statewide elections and elections for the state legislature are won almost equally by both parties. The 2004 gubernatorial election, decided by fewer than 200 votes after a state hand recount, was one of the closest in U.S. history. The party breakdown in the state legislature is usually close. It also was the state that ushered in the era of state legislative term limits, even if in defeat. In 1991, Washington voters defeated legislative term limits by 54 to 46 percent, making it the first state to defeat that proposal.

Structure and Membership

The Washington legislature consists of a forty-nine-member Senate and a ninety-eight-member House of Representatives. The state has forty-nine legislative districts, each of which contains one Senate district and two House districts. Senators serve four-year terms and House members serve two-year terms. The lieutenant governor, an independently elected official, is president of the Senate and presides over its sessions. The Senate elects a majority leader from its membership who is the primary leader of that chamber. The speaker of the House presides over sessions in the House unless delegated to the speaker pro tempore.

Partisan control of the two legislative chambers has been hotly contested over the past decade. As in many states, Republicans made significant gains in 1994, taking control of the House by a large margin and coming within one seat of gaining the Senate. They gained a majority in the Senate in 1996. From 1999 to 2001, the House was evenly split between the two parties. The Republicans held a slim majority in the Senate during that time but relinquished that control in the 2004 elections.

The proportion of female legislators in Washington is historically among the highest in the country. Indeed, Washington state usually establishes the benchmark by which the other states are measured, with membership of female legislators recently approaching 40 percent of the legislative membership in the Evergreen State. In 1998, Washington

The Tie That Binds

The more things change, the more they stay the same—or so it seemed in Washington state following the 2000 election. In 1998, Washington voters had sent forty-nine Republicans and forty-nine Democrats to their state House of Representatives, forcing a power-sharing system in Olympia. In 2000, Republicans gained two seats previously held by Democrats. However, Democrats gained two seats previously held by Republicans, so that "after the smoke cleared," the chambers were tied once again! The Washington House of Representatives became the only state in U.S. history to have a tied chamber for two consecutive sessions.

became the first state to have more than 40 percent of its legislature composed of female members. In 2005 the membership of women declined to 33 percent, but women remain active in leadership and as the chairs of key legislative committees. Generally, the proportion of African American and Hispanic legislators in the Washington General Assembly is quite low, seldom exceeding 3 or 4 percent. In 2005 there were three African American legislators, three Hispanic members, and one Native American legislator.

Senate administration is the responsibility of the Facilities and Operations Committee, chaired by the majority caucus chair. The speaker chairs the Executive Rules Committee, similar to Facilities and Operations in the Senate, and is responsible for House administration. With the exception of bill drafting, most professional staff services are provided separately by each house.

The Washington legislature operates with about twenty standing committees in the House and sixteen or seventeen in the Senate. Each House standing committee has between seven and twenty-five members, while each Senate standing committee has between four and sixteen senators. Members of the House committees are appointed by the speaker, with the consent of the members of each caucus. Committee chairs are appointed by the speaker with the approval of the majority caucus and based on recommendations from the Committee on Committees. In the Senate, committee members are appointed by the lieutenant governor with the approval of the Senate. Senate committee chairs are appointed by a Committee on Committees. Committees in either chamber can report a bill favorably, report it favorably as amended, report a committee substitute for the bill, refer it to a different committee, or take no action.

Processes

The Washington legislature convenes annually on the second Monday in January, with odd-year sessions limited to 105 calendar days and even-year sessions limited to 60 calendar days. In odd-numbered years, they generally complete their work by the end of April. In even years, they adjourn by mid-March. The only deadline in either chamber regarding bill introduction indicates that no bill may be introduced during the final ten days of the session, unless approved by a two-thirds majority in each chamber. However, while the limitations on introductions are few, there are deadlines for the reading of committee reports, reports on budget bills, and the reading of bills from the other chamber. In 2003, Washington legislators introduced 2,363 pieces of legislation, with some 418 passing both chambers. The governor vetoed 8 of the bills outright and exercised a partial veto on 28 more.

The Washington legislature is generally considered a hybrid mix of professional and citizen's legislature, although in recent years it has shifted more toward professional. Washington legislators are relatively well paid, with an annual salary of more than $30,000 plus a per diem of about $80. In an odd-year session, Washington legislators can expect to earn well over $40,000. Washington legislators are provided full-time staff year-round and may move some of that staff to the district office when the legislature is not in session (the interim). The Washington legislature employs more than 500 people to assist its members. Generally, turnover in Washington is quite low, hovering at or below 15 percent. Although most legislators do hold other jobs outside of their legislative work, the Washington legislature would probably be considered professional, except for the strict constitutional limit on session length (105 days in odd years and 60 days in even).

Leadership Structure

The president of the Senate (lieutenant governor) and the speaker of the House appoint chairs and members of their chambers' committees, with the consent of the party caucuses. Each house has a rules committee, chaired by the lieutenant governor in the Senate and by the speaker in the House of Representatives, that determines the agenda for the chamber. The lieutenant governor, by virtue of chairing the rules committee, exercises some influence over Senate activity. The president pro tempore of the Senate presides over Senate sessions in the absence of the lieutenant governor, but the majority leader is the most influential member in the chamber. The majority leader is elected by and directs the members of the majority caucus. The speaker is the top leader in the House of Representatives.

The majority leader and minority leader of each house are responsible for managing floor debate for their respective parties. The majority leader and minority leader of each chamber are each aided by an assistant leader. Each House and Senate party also elects a caucus chair to preside over caucus meetings. The majority and minority leaders in the Senate and the speaker of the House receive additional compensation for the leadership efforts not afforded leaders who hold other positions.

Leadership in the Washington legislature tends to be quite stable, with most recent leaders serving three to four terms. One recent Senate majority leader was selected for that post after only six years as a member of the Senate. However, he had worked in the legislature for more than forty years, beginning as an elevator operator in 1949!

Election Processes

Washington legislators are elected in the November even-year election, with twenty-five senators elected in one even-year election and twenty-four in the other. All House seats are up every two years. There are forty-nine electoral districts in the state, with one senator and two representatives from each district. Both House members are elected districtwide, creating dual-member districts in the House, with each member representing the same constituency as the senator from that district. Each district includes about 120,000 people. Contested nominations are decided in party primaries.

Key Political Factors

While Washington has leaned to the Democrats in presidential elections since the late 1980s, Democrats and Republicans have been victorious on an almost equal basis in other elections. Control of the state legislature is up for grabs in almost every November even-year election. On one occasion, the Senate was split 25–24; when the minority party won a special midterm election, party control of the Senate switched in the middle of a two-year term. A similar situation occurred in the House when a special election gave the Democrats a majority, breaking a tie between the two parties.

Democrats continue to gain strength in the more urban and suburban areas, particularly in and around Seattle (King County), Tacoma, Everett, and Olympia. Republicans gain most of their strength from the more rural and small-town areas in the central and southern parts of the state.

Ethics rules regarding lobbyists are quite strong in the Evergreen State. Lobbyists are required to register with the Public Disclosure Commission and are prohibited from making campaign contributions to legislators during session. Legislators cannot solicit contributions or gifts. They must also register with the Public Disclosure Commission and follow strict ethics rules as governed by the Legislative Ethics Board and House and Senate rules.

Further Reading

Seeberger, Edward. 1996. *Sine Die: A Guide to the Washington State Legislative Process.* Spokane: University of Washington Press.

WEST VIRGINIA

• • • • • • • • • • • •

THE WEST VIRGINIA LEGISLATURE

House of Delegates	Senate
100 Delegates	34 Senators
(304) 340–3200	(304) 357–7800

http://www.legiss.state.wv.us

• • • • • • • • • • • • •

West Virginia has not undergone nearly as much change over the past half-century as has Virginia, its sister state to the east. However, its economy has changed significantly and sometimes painfully in recent years, as coal mining and manufacturing, once the bedrock of its economy, have declined dramatically. The state and its leaders have struggled to replace the jobs and income stream once provided by those industries.

Politically, West Virginia has been and continues to be a predominantly Democratic state, although the Republican Party has made significant gains in recent elections. The state legislature has remained under continuous Democratic control for decades. However, many of those Democrats reflect the basic conservative values of most West Virginia citizens.

Structure and Membership

The West Virginia legislature consists of a 34-member Senate and a 100-member House of Delegates. When the state was established, the House had forty-seven members and the Senate eighteen. Senators are elected for four-year terms and House members for two-year terms in November even-year elections. Two senators are elected from each of seventeen senatorial districts, with one senator from each district up for election every two years. The House of Delegates is composed of a combination of single- and multimember districts.

The bulk of the legislative business takes place in the standing committees. There are usually about fifteen such committees in the House and a few more in the Senate. There are also about a half-dozen joint committees, with members from both chambers. Legislators serve on multiple committees, and professional staff services are provided by a nonpartisan staff that operates under the supervision of a joint committee co-chaired by the Senate president and House speaker.

The West Virginia legislature is not particularly well balanced regarding gender or ethnicity. Usually less than one in five of the members are women, and the proportion of Latino or African American legislators is traditionally very low, though not out of line with the minority portion of the population, which is below 5 percent.

Let's Retire to the Lounge

Talk to many old-time legislators and they will lament the loss of the friendship and collegiality that was part of the legislature in the "old days." Legislators fought on the floor during the day but went out to dinner in the evening. Now, say many, that feeling is gone, because legislators of different parties or ideologies never come together. Not so in the West Virginia Senate, which has a room just off the Senate chamber set aside for senators and former senators. No one else is allowed. After a long, hard day of arguments, debates, and discussions, senators sit around in the quiet and privacy of the "lounge," away from the eyes and ears of the lobbyists and the news media, and rebuild personal relationships.

Processes

The president of the Senate and the speaker of the House preside over sessions in their respective chambers. They appoint committee chairs and members and, in consultation with their majority leaders and other senior legislators, determine the agendas for their respective chambers. The West Virginia constitution requires that each bill be read on three separate days in each chamber before it can become law. The first reading occurs when the bill is reported to the floor from the committee. The second reading usually occurs the next day. At that point, amendments or changes might be offered by members of the chamber; these changes must be voted on. If the bill receives enough support during the second reading, it is engrossed, or formally recorded. Finally, the bill goes to third reading, usually the next day, at which it is debated, discussed, and voted on. If it receives a majority of the votes, it goes to the other chamber for three more readings.

The West Virginia legislature meets annually, convening on the second Wednesday of January, except in the year following a gubernatorial election, when the session is delayed until February. Sessions are limited to sixty calendar days unless extended by a two-thirds vote of the members of each chamber. In order to keep bills from piling up at the end of the session, no bills may be introduced after the forty-first day in the Senate and after the forty-fifth day in the House. During the 2003 legislative session, 1,882 bills were introduced and 259 were passed. Five bills were vetoed by the governor.

The West Virginia legislature is generally considered among the less professional in the country. Its sessions are limited to sixty days, and combined salary and per diem compensation is about $20,000 a year. West Virginia legislators estimate that they spend about half of their time on legislative activities and the other half on their "real job." Furthermore, with only 170 staff members for 134 legislators, there is just barely one staff person per member. Each senator is provided with one full-time staffer during session, and each member of the House of Delegates shares a staff person with several colleagues. Generally, between 20 and 25 percent of the West Virginia legislators are freshmen members, or in their first term. However, without term limits, some remain in the legislature for extended periods of service.

Leadership Structure

The president of the Senate and the speaker of the House are the top leaders of their respective chambers. According to legislation passed in 2000, the president of the Senate also serves as the state's lieutenant governor and becomes governor in the event of a vacancy in that office.

The majority and minority leaders of each chamber are responsible for managing floor debate for their respective parties. Both parties also have whips, or assistant leaders. The House Democrats also have six assistant whips, or assistants to the assistants. All West Virginia leaders are elected by their party members in their chamber, except for the majority leader, assistant majority leader, majority whips, and assistant whips in the House—all of whom are appointed by the speaker.

The president of the Senate is the dominant player in that chamber. The president presides over the chamber, assigns all bills to committees, determines which members will be on which committees, and decides who will chair those committees. However, he does not appoint the other members of leadership in the Senate. On the other hand, the speaker of the House possesses all of the aforementioned powers of presiding, bill assignment, and committee control, and also appoints all of the leadership posts for the House Democrats. This makes the speaker of the House one of the most powerful political leaders in the state, along with the president of the Senate and the governor.

Leaders in the West Virginia House and Senate generally serve extended tenures. Earl Ray Tomlin, the president of the 2003–2004 West Virginia Senate, has held the post since 1995, and Robert Kiss, the speaker of the House of Delegates, has held his post since 1997.

Election Processes

West Virginia holds its state elections in even-numbered years, with one of the two senators from each of the seventeen senatorial districts elected in each election. Most members of the House of Delegates run in single-member districts, but a few run in multimember districts, meaning that more than one person is elected from that district. Senators are elected from districts with about 110,000 citizens, and House members from single-member districts represent about 20,000 constituents. These small numbers and the relatively safe Democratic status of most of the seats means that the campaigns are generally low key and relatively inexpensive, although there are some exceptions in each election cycle. Contested nominations are decided in party primaries.

Key Political Factors

West Virginia remains a predominantly Democratic state, but one in which the Republicans have become increasingly competitive and capable of winning statewide elections. While Republicans have had victories in presidential, statewide, and congressional elections, they have not been able to win control of the state legislature, which has remained under Democratic control.

West Virginia's response to the transformation of its economy has become a central political battle. Unemployment in the state has remained among the highest in the country for the last decade or more, and government revenues among the lowest. Efforts to improve that economic picture with corporate incentive packages, improvements to the state's infrastructure, and a more diversified economy (tourism is now more important to the state's economy than coal!) have been the focus of campaigns and elections for the past decades and are likely to continue so.

Because of the legislature's low level of staff support and low salaries, legislators in West Virginia have always relied on lobbyists to provide information and to enhance the social environment around the capitol. However, as a result of recent reforms, all lobbyists must register with the state's Ethics Commission and report any lobbying effort in which they engage, the amount of money they spend, and the compensation they receive for their efforts. Furthermore, each lobbyist is limited to spending no more than $25 per year to entertain each member of the legislature. In 2003, there were 350 lobbyists registered with the Ethics Commission.

Further Reading

Brisbin, Richard A., et al. 1996. *West Virginia Politics and Government.* Lincoln: University of Nebraska Press.

Forrester, James R., ed. 1992. *Government and Politics in West Virginia: Readings, Cases, and Commentaries.* 2d ed. Needham Heights, MA: Ginn.

WISCONSIN

• • • • • • • • • • • •

THE WISCONSIN LEGISLATURE

Assembly	Senate
99 Representatives	33 Senators
(608) 266–1501	(608) 266–2517

http://www.legis.state.wi.us

• • • • • • • • • • • •

Wisconsin is bordered by two of the Great Lakes (Superior and Michigan) on its eastern and northern borders and by the Mississippi River on part of its western border with Minnesota. There are more than 14,000 lakes in the Badger State. The state has a diverse economy, ranging from its famous dairy products to increasing high-tech sectors. The largest city, Milwaukee, is three times larger than the next largest city, Madison, and much of the state is quite rural and dominated by small farming and timber towns.

Politically, Wisconsin generally trends Democratic in congressional elections, but Wisconsin elections are always competitive. Since 1976, Wisconsin has supported every Democratic presidential candidate (although usually by close margins), except for Ronald Reagan's two landslide Republican victories in 1980 and 1984. In elections for state offices and for the state legislature, the parties are virtually equal in strength. It was considered a battleground state in the 2004 election, with Democrat John Kerry eventually winning by a slim margin.

Structure and Membership

The Wisconsin legislature consists of a thirty-three-member Senate and a ninety-nine-member Assembly. Each Senate district contains three Assembly districts. Senators serve four-year terms and House members serve two-year terms. All legislators are elected from single-member districts. While Democrats controlled the Senate as recently as 2000, Republicans seem to be in firm control of both chambers. Despite ethical questions that forced the retirement of several Republican leaders following the 2003 session, Republicans lost only two seats in the Assembly and gained one in the Senate in 2004.

Perhaps in reflection of its history as an early advocate for women's suffrage, the Wisconsin legislature is generally above the national average in the proportion of female legislators, with women usually holding about a quarter of the seats. Women also generally hold significant positions in both leadership and committee posts. The proportion of African American legislators hovers around 5 percent, while there are usually no more than one or two Hispanic or Latino legislators.

The Senate president is a member of the chamber and presides over its sessions. The speaker of the Assembly presides over Assembly sessions. The Senate president and majority leader and the Assembly speaker are responsible for general administration of their respective chambers.

A twenty-two-member joint legislative council committee composed of the legislative leaders of each house plus ten additional members appointed by the Senate president and Assembly speaker oversees a sizable nonpartisan staff. Each house also has partisan staff assistants.

Since the 1980s, the Wisconsin Assembly has experienced a gradual increase in the number of standing legislative committees to more than forty such committees in 2004. However, a looming budget deficit forced a reduction of both staff and committees in 2005. Committee members are appointed by the speaker of the House in consideration of recommendations from the minority leader regarding appointments from members of the minority party. Senate standing committee assignments are made by the Committee on Senate Organization, which is chaired by the majority leader and includes the president, the minority leader, and the assistant minority and majority leaders. The Committee on Senate Organization also determines which members will chair the Senate committees. Committees in the Wisconsin legislature are considered among the weakest in the country.

After the first (odd-year) session of Wisconsin's two-year legislative term, the Legislative Council establishes study committees to examine problems and issues identified by the legislature during the recent session. These study committees include legislators and informed and concerned citizens and are charged to examine a particular problem and prepare a report for the entire legislature. In June 2004, twelve such committees were established, addressing such topics as adoption, parental rights, transportation, and violent sex offenders.

The Roots of a Progressive Legislature

The progressive roots of Wisconsin politics run deep. The initial constitution proposed in 1848 included such radical ideas as rights for married women, elected judges, and a prohibition on banks. Over the years Wisconsin has been the first state to regulate utilities, provide for workman's compensation, end discrimination against women, start kindergartens, and adopt an income tax. Internally, it was the first legislature to use electronic voting machines so that votes could easily be recorded for the public to review.

Processes

The president of the Senate and the speaker of the Assembly preside over sessions in their respective houses. They control the agenda and the flow of debate on the floor of their respective chambers.

The Wisconsin legislature convenes a two-year term on the first Monday in January of odd-numbered years. There are no limitations on session length, and the legislature meets in floor session at scheduled intervals throughout the two-year term. In 2003, the session ran from January 6 through November 13. However, the Senate recorded that it met for seventy-three legislative days during that ten months, and the Assembly met for sixty-seven legislative days. The legislature divides its time during session between floor debate (called floor period) and committee and other legislative activity. The rules of operation do not allow for prefiling of legislation before the beginning of the session.

In 2003, Wisconsin legislators introduced 1,074 pieces of legislation, with both houses passing just 111. The Democratic governor vetoed 22 of the bills passed by the Republican legislature; all of the vetoes were sustained.

Budget bills in Wisconsin do not pass through the same bicameral committee process facing other legislation. Instead, the legislature has a Joint Finance Committee in which Senate and Assembly members sit together to review and respond to the governor's proposed budget. However, the budget they propose must be approved by the respective legislative bodies and the majority caucuses. The members of the Joint Finance Committee are appointed by the speaker (House members) and the Committee to Organize the Senate (Senate).

The Wisconsin legislature is considered one of the most professional in the United States, usually ranked in the top five with California, New York, Michigan, and Illinois. Its members are paid more than $40,000 annually plus a per diem of just under $90 for time spent in the capital on legislative business. This per diem is not limited to days the legislature is in session. Most Wisconsin legislators earn well over $50,000 annually and few hold other full-time positions. Members also have full-time, year-round staff to support their legislative efforts. The Wisconsin legislature employs almost 700 full-time staffers.

There is no limit on the length of the legislative session in the Wisconsin legislature. Legislative turnover tends to hover around 15 percent every two years.

Leadership Structure

The president of the Senate presides over the chamber's floor sessions, but the majority leader is considered the most powerful leader in the Senate. The speaker of the Assembly is the top leader in the Assembly. The majority leader and minority leaders of each chamber are responsible for managing floor debate for their respective parties. Both the majority and minority parties have a number of deputy and assistant leaders. Legislative leaders in Wisconsin do not receive additional compensation for their efforts.

It is not uncommon for Wisconsin's top legislative leaders to serve more than one term in their position. However, recent ethics concerns and investigations in the early part of the first decade of the twenty-first century caused the early departure of leaders in both the House and the Senate.

Election Processes

Wisconsin legislators are elected in the November even-year election, with approximately half of the Senate membership elected every two years. Senators and Assembly members are elected from single-member districts, with senators representing about 160,000 people and members of the Assembly a third of that. As in most states, incumbent legislators tend to win. In 2004 no incumbent senator seeking reelection was defeated, and in the Assembly only two incumbents were defeated. Party nominations are determined by primary.

Key Political Factors

Wisconsin seems to be a state in transition. On the one hand, it is a state with a proud history of progressive policies and public service, producing such leaders as progressive Governor and Senator Robert LaFollette and leading the nation in the implementation of workers' rights, women's rights, and rights for the disabled. On the other hand, the state of late has found itself increasingly controlled by a Republican Party more focused on keeping the states taxes low than maintaining its place as a leader in policy development.

Citizens in the state's urban centers in Milwaukee and Madison remain steadfast to the old view of the state, while the rural and small-town Wisconsin residents tend to lean more toward the Republican Party. While the state still shows flashes of policy innovation, including the welfare reforms initiated by Republican governor Tommy Thompson in the late 1980s, such efforts have become fewer in recent years.

With both political parties strong and well organized, Wisconsin can be expected to continue as a highly competitive state in the years to come, with control of the state legislature up for grabs in most elections.

Lobbyists play a significant role in the state, with more than 750 registered to lobby members of the legislature annually. However, they are highly regulated. They are prohibited from making campaign contributions during the legislative session and cannot spend any money directly on legislators for perishable items or gifts.

Further Reading

Mead, Lawrence M. 2004. *Government Matters: Welfare Reform in Wisconsin.* Princeton: Princeton University Press.

Weber, Ronald E. 2004.*Crane and Hagensick's Wisconsin Government and Politics* New York: McGraw-Hill.

Weisberger, Bernard A. 1994. *LaFollettes of Wisconsin: Love and Politics in Progressive America.* Madison: University of Wisconsin Press.

WYOMING

•••••••••••••

THE WYOMING LEGISLATURE

House of Representatives	Senate
60 Representatives	30 Senators
(307) 777–7852	(307) 777–7725

http://legisweb.state.wy.us/

•••••••••••••

Wyoming is the nation's least populous state and its second most sparsely populated after Alaska. A favorite statistic is "500,000 people, 350,000 antelope"! It is mountainous, averaging 6,100 feet above sea level, making its land best suited for cattle grazing. However, the land also possesses a tremendous wealth of minerals, including oil, uranium, natural gas, coal, trona, and gold.

While the state is generally viewed as conservative in its political outlook, it has, throughout its history, demonstrated an independent streak. Its territorial legislature granted women the right to vote in 1869, twenty-one years before the state joined the Union and fifty-one years before approval of the Nineteenth Amendment to the U.S. Constitution. In the 1992 presidential election, Wyoming gave Ross Perot more than a quarter of the vote, well above his national percentage, and in 2002 it elected a Democratic governor who had been a district attorney in the Clinton administration.

Wyoming is a solidly Republican state that nevertheless occasionally elects a Democratic governor. In 2002, Wyoming voters elected a Democrat and former member of the Clinton administration to serve as their governor.

Structure and Membership

The Wyoming legislature consists of a thirty-member Senate and a sixty-member House of Representatives. Senators are elected for four-year terms and House members for two-year terms, from single-member districts in November even-year elections. Two House districts are nested in each Senate district. Republicans maintain in solid control of both legislative chambers, with a three-to-one majority following the 2004 election cycle.

The Senate elects a president from its membership to preside over its sessions and oversee the chamber's administration. The speaker of the House is similarly elected and then presides over its sessions and is responsible for House administration.

Although the Wyoming Territory was the first governmental unit in America to grant women the right to vote, participation in the legislature has not kept pace. The proportion of the Wyoming legislature that is female stays around 15 percent, well below the national average of more than 20 percent. However, women often hold key leadership positions in both chambers, including the most recent Senate presidency. The percentage of legislators who are nonwhite, as with the population in general, is very low. In 2004 there was one Hispanic legislator, and there were no African American members. In 2005, a Native American legislator joined the House, representing the Wind River Indian Reservation as part of his district.

The nonpartisan Legislative Services Office (LSO), which serves both chambers, provides most staff services, and is the full-time central staff agency of the Wyoming legislature. Services provided by the LSO include research; bill and amendment drafting; revision and recompilation of statutes; legislative budget and accounting; and personal staff services for legislators.

The House and Senate employ temporary session staff (including chief clerks, staff supervisors, committee secretaries, and so forth) to assist during each legislative session. Session staff are responsible for many of the day-to-day operations of the legislature and work under the general direction and control of the presiding officer, chief clerk, and staff supervisor in the House and Senate. During the session, standing committees and many legislators also use student interns and legislative aides to assist with research, filing, correspondence, and the like.

The House and Senate of the Wyoming legislature have twelve parallel standing committees. Senate committees have five members, and each House committee has nine, with the exception of Appropriations, which has only eight House members. The speaker of the House and the president of the Senate assign committees and chairs in their respective chambers. When the legislature is not in session, the twenty-four standing committees combine to form twelve "joint interim" committees charged to study problems identified by the legislature. During the 2004 interim, for example, the twelve joint interim committees were charged to study more than forty issues, ranging from the legal representation of children to tort reform, from split estates to water rights. The president of the Senate and the speaker of the House may also appoint special and select committees to study issues during the interim.

Processes

The president of the Senate and the speaker of the House preside over sessions and are responsible for general administration in their respective chambers. They appoint committee chairs and members and, in consultation with their majority floor leaders, determine the agendas of their chambers.

The Wyoming legislature convenes on the second Tuesday in January in odd-numbered years and on the second Monday in February in even-numbered years. Odd-year sessions are limited to forty legislative days and even-year sessions to twenty legislative days. Even-year sessions are limited to consideration of

---

Two Thousand Pound Bison in the Capitol

The capitol complex in Cheyenne, Wyoming, is a reflection of the state that its members represent. As people enter, they are greeted by a statue of Esther Hobart Morris to remind them that Wyoming gave women the right to vote more than a half-century before the United States did. Once inside, a 2,000-pound bison and an elk, reflective of the vastly undeveloped lands of the state, greet you. In the chambers, you will find murals representing the colorful history of the Cowboy State, including Indians, cowboys, ranchers, homesteaders, and trappers. The desks in the chambers were designed by a Wyoming firm and built using Wyoming wood and Wyoming granite. This truly is the people's branch!

---

budget bills and nonbudget bills approved for consideration by a two-thirds vote of a chamber.

In order to complete the legislature's business in less than forty days, members abide by several deadlines. All bills must be introduced in the House by the eighteenth legislative day and in the Senate by the fifteenth legislative day. Deadlines are also set during the session, by which bills must be reported out of committee and reported from the floor in the House in which they originated; there are similar deadlines regarding bills that originated in the other chamber. In 2003, Wyoming legislators introduced 455 pieces of legislation, passing 165 of them through both chambers. The governor vetoed 5.

As of 2003, the legislature can call itself into special session. Prior to that time, only the governor could issue a call for a special session of the Wyoming legislature. The legislature took advantage of that change in 2004, calling itself into special session to address issues regarding insurance and medical malpractice, and related judicial system reforms.

The Wyoming legislature prides itself on its status as a "citizen's legislature." Legislators receive $125 for each day the legislature is in session, plus $80 per day for meals and lodging. In the "long" forty-day session, Wyoming legislators can expect to make no more than $8,000 dollars. Almost all legislators have other employment. Legislators do not have individual staff and have limited office space. Except for a few officers of the House and Senate, members of the legislature are not provided offices in the capitol, nor do they maintain full-time offices in their districts. While in session, the "office" of a typical Wyoming legislator consists of the legislator's desk on the floor of the House or Senate and one or two filing cabinet drawers in a committee meeting room.

Leadership Structure

The president of the Senate and the speaker of the House are the top leaders of their respective chambers. They preside over the session, manage the flow of legislation, appoint committees (standing, special, and conference) and committee chairs, and generally maintain order in their respective chambers. The speaker and Senate president receive an additional $3 per day for their efforts!

The majority floor leader of each chamber, in consultation with the speaker of the House and the president of the Senate, are responsible for managing the floor agenda and debate. Minority leaders manage the affairs of the minority caucus. The minority leader of each house is responsible for managing floor debate for their respective parties. Each party also selects a floor whip that assists the floor leader and makes sure that party members are on the floor for important votes. Party caucus chairpersons are elected by their respective caucuses to preside over meetings of the party caucuses. These leaders do not receive additional pay for their work.

Election Processes

Wyoming legislators are elected in the November even-year election. Half of the senators are elected in each election. Because of the low pay and the part-time nature of the job, legislative turnover is fairly high, averaging about a quarter in the House every two years, but substantially less in the Senate, partially because only half of the Senate seats are contested in each election. While the geographic size of Wyoming legislative districts varies greatly, Senate districts include fewer than 17,000 people and House districts just over 8,000. The largest district, however, encompasses nearly 20,000 square miles.

Term limits for the legislature were adopted by the voters in 1992 but were overturned by the Wyoming supreme court in 2004. Contested nominations are decided in party primaries.

Key Political Factors

Wyoming has experienced rather limited political change relative to other states and can be expected to remain a Republican stronghold for the foreseeable future. Despite the fact that the state elected a Democratic governor in 2002, most anticipate a continued dominance by the Republican Party.

While the time demands on members of the Wyoming legislature are intense, given increasing interim committee work and the grind of keeping up with issues and correspondence, the state prides itself on having a true part-time citizen legislature. Sessions are short, compensation is small, not even top leaders have any personal staff assistants, and only a few top leaders have offices in the state capitol building. Almost every legislator devotes the majority of his or her time to a private-sector occupation.

Between 100 and 200 lobbyists usually register to lobby members of the Wyoming legislature during their brief sessions. One recent study suggests that registration and reporting requirements for lobbyists in Wyoming are among the weakest in the country.

Issues tend not to break along partisan lines. Rather, shifting coalitions reflecting regional differences (north versus south, or east versus west) or specific interests (urban versus rural, small school versus large school) dominate voting patterns. The legislature is known for tough fights and deep friendships.

Further Reading

Miller, Tim R. 1985. *State Government: Politics in Wyoming.* 2d ed. Dubuque, IA: Kendall/Hunt.

Walter, Oliver. 2000. *Equality State: Government and Politics in Wyoming.* 3d ed. Peosta, IA: Eddie Bowers.

GLOSSARY OF COMMON LEGISLATIVE TERMS

Absent: Not present at a session.

Act: Legislation enacted into law. A bill that has passed both houses of the legislature, has been enrolled, ratified, signed by the governor or passed over the governor's veto, and published. It is a permanent measure, having the force of law until repealed.

Adhere: A step in parliamentary procedure whereby one house of the legislature votes to stand by its previous action in response to some conflicting action by the other chamber.

Adjournment: Termination of a daily session, with the hour and day of the next meeting being set prior to adjournment.

Adoption: Approval or acceptance; usually applied to amendments, committee reports, or resolutions.

Advise and Consent: The process by which a legislative body is required to review and approve executive and judicial appointments.

Agenda: Schedule of business for a legislative day or a committee meeting.

Amend: To alter formally by modification, deletion, or addition.

Amendment: An addition, deletion, or revision in the wording of a bill. A substantive amendment changes the content of the bill. A technical amendment makes grammatical or format changes that do not alter its substantive content.

Appeal: A parliamentary procedure for testing (and possibly changing) the decision of a presiding officer.

Apportionment: Establishment of the legislative districts from which members are elected.

Appropriation: A legislative authorization to make expenditures and incur obligations for specific governmental purposes; usually limited as to the time when it may be expended. One of the prime responsibilities of the legislature is this power to appropriate moneys.

At-large Election: An election in which multiple candidates are elected to represent a large geographic area rather than dividing that area into smaller units in order to elect individual candidates to represent each part. At-large elections are not common, but they may be used in cases where it is difficult to divide an area into smaller districts.

Author: The person (usually a legislator) who presents a bill or resolution for consideration; may be joined by others, who are known as coauthors. See also: Introducer, Patron, Sponsor.

Baker vs. Carr, 1962:   Ruling in which the Supreme Court applied the Fourteenth Amendment to the U.S. Constitution and decreed that equal protection and the one-person, one-vote principles required that there be the same number of people in each of the legislative districts within a single state legislative chamber.

Balanced Budget Requirement: The prohibition against appropriating funds in excess of the amount of available revenue.

Bicameral: Literally, having "two rooms"; the term is used to refer to legislative bodies having two houses. Each serves as a check on the other's power.

Biennial Budget: State budget that covers a two-year cycle.

Biennium: A two-year period of legislative activity.

Bill: A proposal created for the enactment of a new law, the amendment or repeal of a law already in existence, or the appropriation of public money. Draft of a proposed law presented to the legislature for consideration.

Bill History: A record of all action on any legislative measure.

Bill Limit: A limit imposed by a House or Senate rule limiting the number of bills and joint resolutions that members may introduce in a regular or special session.

Bipartisan: Having an affiliation or association with (or representatives of) both political parties or caucuses in a two-party system. Usually associated with an issue in which members from both parties set aside political differences to support the issue.

Blanket Primary: A primary in which voters may cast ballots in either party's primary (but not both) on an office-by-office basis.

Bloc: A group of legislators with common interests who may vote together on matters affecting that interest.

Block Grant: Broad grant with few strings attached given to states by the federal government for specified activities, such as secondary education or health services.

Budget: A plan for expending funds by program for a given fiscal year or biennium and the means of financing the expenditures. A suggested allocation of state money presented to the legislature for consideration

Calendar: Printed list of measures or other matters, arranged according to the Order of Business, scheduled for consideration by a chamber on a legislative day.

Call of the Senate or House: Procedure used to compel the attendance of members who are missing from the chamber and to compel those members already in attendance to remain in the chamber.

Call to Order: The action of the presiding officer that brings the legislature officially into session. It may also be used to call a disorderly member to order.

Candidate-Centered Campaigns: Political campaigns in which candidates make the critical decisions regarding their own campaign, including hiring consultants, raising and spending money, and developing themes. Further, it implies that ballots are cast for or against candidates rather than political parties.

Capital Expenditures: Expenditures for durable items such as furniture, roads, buildings, and infrastructure.

Carry-Over Bills or Legislation: Legislation that is held over from the first year of a legislative biennium to the second year.

Categorical Grant: Financial grant for which Congress appropriates funds to states or communities for a specific purpose.

Caucus: An informal meeting of a group of members; most commonly based on political party affiliation, but may have other bases, such as gender, race, geographic location, or specific issue. Can also be used as a verb meaning "to meet."

Caucus Chair: Person selected by a caucus (see definition above) to organize the caucus and to preside over its meetings.

Censure: An action by a legislative body to officially reprimand an elected official for inappropriate or illegal actions committed by that official while in office. The act of censuring is an official condemnation for inappropriate or illegal actions committed by a public official while holding a position of trust.

Chair: Presiding officer of a committee or the chamber.

Chamber: Official hall for the meeting of a legislative body.

Checks and Balances: A governmental structure that gives each of the three branches of government some degree of oversight and control over the actions of the others.

Christmas Tree Bill: Informal nomenclature for a bill containing a wide variety of amendments providing benefits for members, interest groups, or members' districts.

Clerk of the House or Assembly: A nonlegislator officer who is appointed or elected by the members of the House of Representatives or Assembly to perform and direct the parliamentary and clerical functions of the chamber. Also may be titled "chief clerk" or "principal clerk."

Closed Primary: A primary election in which only a party's registered voters are eligible to vote.

Coauthor: Member of either house added as a sponsor to a measure after it has been introduced. See also: Author.

Code: A compilation of laws and their revisions according to subject matter (usually arranged by title, chapter, and section); the official publication of a state's statutes.

Codification: The process by which newly enacted law is systematically numbered.

Commit: To send or return to a committee. Synonymous to "refer" or "recommit."

Committee: A body of members appointed by the presiding officer (or another authority specified by the chamber) to consider and make recommendations concerning the disposition of bills, resolutions, and other related matters.

Committee Amendment: An amendment that is attached to a measure by a standing committee and made part of the committee's report.

Committee of the Whole: Either house of the legislature sitting in its entirety as a committee to consider bills or issues.

Committee Report: The official report of the members of the standing, special, or conference committee on any measure, which is transmitted to one chamber of the legislature or the full legislature in the case of a conference committee report. The document usually states findings of facts and conclusions, together with a distinct recommendation as to the disposal of the matter. Official release of a bill or resolution from committee with (or without) a specific recommendation, such as "pass," "pass as amended," or "do not pass."

Committee Substitute: A bill offered by a committee in lieu of another bill that was originally referred to the committee for consideration; technically, the committee substitute is an amendment to the original bill.

Companion Bill: Two bills identical in wording that are introduced in each house. They will most likely not have the same number. Some companion bill sponsors feel that such bills increase the chances for the passage of the bill.

Competitive Grant: A type of categorical grant in which states must compete with each other to receive money from the federal government.

Concurrence (to concur): Action by which one house agrees to a proposal or action of the other house.

Conferees: Legislators appointed to serve on a conference committee.

Conference Committee: An ad hoc or temporary committee, with members from each house, appointed to reconcile differences in a measure that has passed both houses.

Conference Committee Report: A document submitted to both houses containing the agreements of a conference committee resolving the differences of the two chambers or indicating that conferees could not reach agreement.

Confirmation: The process by which the Senate considers a nomination submitted by the governor.

Conflict of Interest: Any interest, financial or otherwise, any business or professional activity, or any obligation that is incompatible with the proper discharge of a legislator's duties in the public interest.

Consent Calendar: Bills placed on this calendar are normally noncontroversial and not subject to debate or amendment on the floor.

Consider: To take up a measure, motion, or matter for the purpose of action.

Constituent: A citizen residing within the district of a legislator.

Constituent Service (Case Work): The work done by legislators to help those in their voting districts.

Constitution: A written instrument embodying the fundamental principles of the state that establishes power and duties of the government and guarantees certain rights to the people.

Constitutional Majority: More than half of the members of a deliberative body; the actual number may be defined in the state constitution.

Convene: The assembling of either house of the legislature.

Cracking: A method of *gerrymandering* whereby members (and therefore votes) of the group that you hope to minimize are distributed across many districts.

Crossover: Deadline for bills or resolutions to move, or cross over, to the other house for consideration.

Debate: Discussion of a matter according to parliamentary rules.

Decorum: Proper order, etiquette, and conduct of members during a floor session.

Delegate Approach: Legislators who see their role primarily as voting according to their constituents' beliefs, as they understand them.

Died in Committee: The defeat of a bill by not returning it from committee to the house for further action. (Permitted only in certain states.)

Direct Democracy: Means by which the people can act as a legislative body. The most common are the initiative (voters place on the ballot and vote), the referendum (voters cast ballots on an issue placed on the ballot by the legislature), and the recall (voters decide whether to remove an elected official from office before the end of the term).

Direct Lobbying: Actions by individuals, usually lobbyists, who contact legislators or policy-makers directly (phone calls, visits, dinners, hearings, presentations, and so forth) in an effort to influence the political process.

Discrete Ambition: Describes legislators who have chosen not to seek re-election to their current post or to seek election to another political position.

Dissent: Difference of opinion; to cast a negative vote.

District: That division of the state represented by a legislator, distinguished numerically or by geographical boundaries.

Division: A method of voting, or a motion requesting a show of hands or other action when the outcome of a voice vote is unclear or in dispute.

Effective Date: A law generally becomes effective, or binding, either upon a date specified in the law itself or, in the absence of such a date, a fixed number of days (depending on the state) after the final adjournment of the session during which it was enacted, or on signature by the governor. Provisions may specify when the entire act or portions thereof become effective as law. Synonymous to "operative date."

Elastic Clause: A statement in the U.S. Constitution granting Congress the power to pass all laws necessary and proper for carrying out the enumerated list of powers (Article I, Section 8).

Election: Act of selecting a person to fill an office.

Engrossment: The preparation of an exact, accurate, and official copy of a measure passed in the house of origin, along with amendments and proper signatures; then dispatched to the other house. Engrossment of a measure in the originating house results in the "engrossed" measure. The opposite house's amendments to an engrossed measure will also undergo engrossment.

Enrollment: The process by which a measure is proofed and certified as passed by both houses of the legislature for signature by the presiding officers for presentment to the governor or secretary of state. This is the last legislative action taken on a bill unless it is reconsidered after objection by the governor.

Excused: Absent with the permission of the body or the presiding officer.

Executive Order: A document issued by the governor regarding the operations of state government.

Executive Session: A session for the purpose of confirming executive nominations, considering personnel matters, or conducting other business. During this session all persons other than members and essential staff personnel are excluded.

Ex Officio: Holding another office by virtue of or because of the holding of the first office.

Federalism: Political system in which national and regional governments share powers and are considered independent equals.

Filibuster: The prolonged discussion of a bill to delay legislative action.

Final Action: Most frequently means Third or Fourth Readings, but it can also refer to the situation provided by House rules that defeats a measure and prohibits consideration of a similar measure during the remainder of the legislature in the House.

First Reading: The first presentation of a bill or its title for consideration. In some states, the first reading is done at the time of introduction.

Fiscal: Dealing with state revenues and expenditures.

Fiscal Impact: The additional or reduced costs or revenues of a measure to the state or other parties.

Fiscal Note: A fiscal note seeks to state in dollars the estimated amount of increase or decrease in revenue or expenditures and the present and future implications of a piece of pending legislation.

Floor: That portion of the legislative chamber reserved for members and officers of the assembly or other persons granted privileged access. Reference to the interior of the chamber of either house. Floor action suggests consideration by the entire House or Senate rather than committee action.

Floor Amendment: An amendment offered to a legislative document, or to modify another amendment, presented by a legislator while the document is on the floor of that legislator's house.

Floor Leader: Legislators designated by the majority (majority floor leader) and minority (minority floor leader) caucuses to manage and schedule the business of the House

Floor Substitute: A floor amendment proposing a substitute to the entire printed bill.

Formula Grant: A form of categorical grant in which every state receives a certain amount of financial assistance from the federal government based on a particular distribution formula.

Free-Agent Legislators: Legislators that feel little loyalty or obligation to their political party and are quite willing to support their district, ideology, or a lobbyist at the expense of their political party affiliation.

Full Faith and Credit Clause: A reference to Article IV, Section I of the U.S. Constitution, which indicates that each state must fully recognize the "public acts, records, and judicial proceedings of every other state."

Gerrymander: To design election districts to give one political party or group an electoral advantage.

Hearing: Scheduled committee meetings to receive testimony on proposed legislation or other legislative matters. See also: Public Hearing.

Held in Committee: The defeat of a measure by the decision of a standing committee not to return it to the full house for further consideration.

House: Generally, either body or chamber of the legislature. Usually the body in a bicameral legislature that has the greater number of members. (If capitalized, the House of Representatives.)

House Rules: Rules of procedure adopted by the House of Representatives governing procedures in that body, such as duties of House officers, rights and duties of members, and floor procedures.

Impeachment: Procedure to remove from office a public official accused of misconduct.

Incumbent Candidate: Candidate who currently holds the office that he or she is seeking.

Incumbent Seat: Election for a seat in the legislature in which the incumbent is seeking re-election to the position.

Indirect (Grassroots) Lobbying: Efforts to influence public policy in which a lobbyist encourages others, usually employees or supporters of the interest group, to contact policy-makers and express a particular position.

Initiative: The means by which the electorate can propose a law or constitutional amendment. If properly drafted and with sufficient signatures, the petition will result in a state question that is placed on the ballot for the vote of the people.

Interest Group Culture: The rules, expectations, and norms that govern what an interest group is expected to do and can do relative to the electoral process; varies greatly from state to state.

Interim: The interval between regular sessions of the legislature. The period from adjournment sine die of one regular legislative session to the commencement of the next regular legislative session.

Interim Committee: A committee created to study legislative proposals or other legislative matters during the time the legislature is not in session and to make recommendations to the next regular session of the legislature.

Introducer: The legislator who presents a bill or resolution for consideration; may be joined by others, who are known as cointroducers.

Item Veto: An action taken by the governor to prevent the enactment of an item of an appropriation bill; also may be called line-item veto.

Joint Committee: A committee composed of a specified number of members of both houses.

Joint Resolution: Resolution passed by both houses; has the force and effect of law. It may be used when a law of a temporary character is proposed. Joint Resolutions are also used to propose amendments to the constitution and to ratify amendments to the U.S. Constitution.

Joint Rules: Rules adopted by both houses governing the procedure of the legislature in matters requiring their concurrent action.

Joint Session: A combined meeting of the Senate and House in one chamber.

Journal: The official chronological record of the proceedings (including motions and votes taken) of the Senate and House, corrected, certified, indexed, printed, and bound at the close of each session.

Killer Amendment: An amendment that might lead to the defeat of a measure somewhere in the legislative process or when it is considered by the governor.

Lame Duck: Jargon for an elected official who has not been re-elected or did not seek re-election and who is serving out the balance of the term.

Lay on the Table: A postponement of the matter before the house that may be brought up later for consideration by a motion to "take from the table." Synonymous to "tabling."

Leadership: A group of members recognized by other members to negotiate or devise policy and strategy on behalf of the larger membership.

Leadership Campaign Committees (LCCs):   Campaign committees organized and managed by state legislative leaders to elect members of their party to the legislature.

Legislative Day: A day on which either chamber convenes (or both chambers convene) to conduct official business.

Legislative History: Information on the background of legislation that may be used to determine "intent."

Legislative Immunity: Members' constitutional protection from lawsuits and arrests associated with their legislative duties.

Legislative Party Campaign Committees (LPCCs):   Political action committees organized by the leaders of the various legislative parties. They exist to raise and distribute money to legislative candidates representing their party.

Legislative Term Limits: Legislation designating that state elected legislators may serve only a specified number of years.

Legislative Veto: A procedure permitting the legislature or legislative committee, by joint or concurrent resolution, to disapprove an administrative rule.

Legislator: Elected member of a legislative body.

Legislature: The branch of state government responsible for enacting laws.

Line-Item: Numeric line in an appropriation or budget bill.

Line-Item Veto: The power to veto specific provisions of a bill by the governor without vetoing the bill in its entirety.

Lobbyist: A person who, voluntarily or for a fee, works to oppose or promote legislation or other official acts.

Logrolling: Jargon for a legislative tactic in which members build support for their legislation by promising to support the issues of other members or by adding related or nonrelated provisions to a measure.

Long-Term Voting Factors: Characteristics of individual voters that predispsose them to vote for candidates of one party or the other. Usually include party identification, race, religion, gender, age, education, and income.

Majority Leader: A legislator from the majority party who is a leader of the party in that house. The procedure for designating the majority leader and other officers varies from state to state.

Majority Party: The political party having the greatest number of members in the legislature or in either chamber.

Mandate: A requirement from a higher to a lower level of government forcing certain actions, often without any provision for funding of the activity, making it an "unfunded mandate." Also, popular sentiment for or against some issue.

Markup: A meeting or series of meetings by a committee during which a measure is amended.

Member Elect: Member who has been elected, but who has not yet taken the oath of office or who is not yet officially serving.

Minority Leader: A legislator from the minority party who is its leader in that house. (Process of designation varies from state to state.)

Minority Party: The political party having fewer numbers of members in the legislature or in either chamber.

Minority Report: A report that reflects the thinking of the members not favoring the majority position or action on an issue.

Motion: A formal proposal offered by a member for a procedural action, such as to consider, to amend, to lay on the table, to reconsider, to recess, or to adjourn.

Multimember Districts: Electoral districts from which more than one person is elected to represent them in the legislature.

Nested Districts: Refers to more than one geographic House (or Assembly) district drawn within and covering all of a Senate district.

Nonpartisan: Having no association or affiliation with a political party or caucus.

Oath of Office: Oath taken by members elect of the legislature prior to being seated and embarking upon official duties.

Open Primary: A primary in which party members, independents, and sometimes members of the other party are allowed to vote.

Open Seat: A campaign in which neither candidate is the current officeholder.

Order of Business: The sequence of events during a legislative day.

Order Reported: A committee's formal action of agreeing to report a measure to its house for floor consideration.

Organizational Session: A usually one-day legislative session at the beginning of each new legislature designed to allow for election of legislative officers and other matters in preparation for the first regular session.

Out of Order: Conduct or activity not in accord with appropriate parliamentary rules and procedures.

Override: A legislature's repassage of a bill after the governor has vetoed it.

Oversight: Legislative review of state agency operations.

Package Veto: The veto of an entire measure just prior to the end of a session.

Packing: Method of gerrymandering in which members of the group one is trying to minimize are put predominantly in one or two districts where they will be in a minority, relative to the other members of the legislature.

Parliamentarian: Advisor to the presiding officer on the interpretation of the chamber's rules and procedures.

Parliamentary Inquiry: Question posed by a member to the presiding officer for clarification of the procedure or business before the house.

Partisan: Associated or affiliated with a single political party or caucus.

Partisan Staff: Legislative staff hired by the party or the legislature to work for members of either the Democratic or Republican party, but not for both.

Party-Centered Elections: Political elections in which campaigns are, to a large degree, controlled by the political party organization. Parties have a significant influence on candidate recruitment, selection, and campaign message, and voters cast their ballots more along party lines than candidate attributes.

Patron: The person (usually a legislator) who presents a bill or resolution for consideration; may be joined by others, who are known as copatrons. See also: Author, Introducer, Sponsor.

Per Diem: Literally, per day; daily expense money rendered to legislators or staff.

Personal Privilege: An act by which a member delivers comments before a legislative body that do not subject the member to libel or slander charges.

Petition: Formal request submitted by an individual or group of individuals to the legislature.

Pocket Veto: Failure of the governor to sign a measure passed during the last five days of a regular or a special session. See also: Veto.

Point of Order: A question by a member to the presiding officer calling attention to a breach of order or of the rules.

Political Action Committee (PAC):   The financial arm of an interest group. It is the PAC that raises and distributes political contributions for candidates.

Politico Approach: Role played by elected representatives who act as trustees or as delegates, depending on the issue.

Popular Title: An unofficial name for a bill or act such as the "Make My Day" act.

Pork or Pork Barrel: A pejorative term for government appropriations for a district, designed to garner political support for the elected representatives of the district.

Postpone Indefinitely: A means of disposing of an issue by not setting a date on which to consider it again.

Precedent: A previous ruling on a parliamentary matter or a long-standing practice or custom of a house.

Prefiled Bill: A bill filed with the appropriate chamber by a member prior to the official convening of a session.

Presentment: A requirement that a bill or joint resolution be sent to the governor for action prior to the bill's being enacted.

President: Usually, the title given to the person elected (or designated by the constitution) as the presiding officer of the Senate.

Presiding Officer: The individual, designated in a formal meeting, who is vested with the responsibility of presiding over the legislative session. The presiding officer is authorized to maintain order and decorum, recognize members to speak or offer motions, and apply and interpret the house's rules, precedents, and practices.

Previous Question: A nondebatable motion that, if approved, cuts off further debate, additional amendments, and brings the pending matter to an immediate vote.

Printed Bill: The version of a measure prepared for final action of a house.

Privileges and Immunities Clause: Section 1 of the Fourteenth Amendment to the U.S. Constitution, which states: "No State shall make or enforce any law which shall abridge the privileges or immunities of citizens of the United States."

Professional Legislature: An informal category of state legislature usually characterized by membership stability, professional staff, high salaries, and extended legislative sessions.

Professional Staff: Staff hired by legislature to provide support for all legislators equally, regardless of party affiliation.

Progress: As a parliamentary motion in committee, a "report progress" vote generally denotes the committee's will to defeat the measure or to defer final consideration of the measure to a later date.

Progressive Ambition: Describes legislators who are seeking higher office rather than re-election or retirement.

Pro Tempore (Pro Tem):   The designated officer of the Senate or House acting in the absence of the regular presiding officer.

Public Campaign Financing: Public money given to candidates running for public office. In order to be eligible for the money, candidates must abide by particular spending and fundraising limits.

Public Hearing: A formal session of a legislative committee wherein interested members of the public are invited to present testimony on a proposal; distinguished from an informational briefing, at which the public is usually allowed to attend but not present testimony.

Public Relations: Describes efforts of interest groups to influence public policy by trying to influence public opinion.

Question: Any matter on which there is a vote, such as passage of a bill or amendment.

Quorum: The minimum required number of members of a house, committee, or other group that must be present before the group may conduct official business.

Quorum Call: A method used to establish the presence of a majority for the lawful transaction of business.

Ratify: To approve and make valid.

Reading: A presentation and vote by the entire House or Senate on a bill or resolution. A formal procedure required by constitution and rules that indicates a stage in the enactment process. Most often, a bill must receive three readings on three different days in each legislative body.

Reapportionment: The allocation of seats in a legislative body among established districts, in which the district boundaries do not change but the number of members per district does. Done to provide equality of representation.

Recall: The procedure by which any bill referred to a committee may be removed from that committee's jurisdiction after referral.

Recess: An interruption in a legislative day or session that does not end it.

Recognize: The presiding officer recognizing a member to speak. At that point, the member "has the floor."

Recommittal: The sending of a measure back to the committee that reported it out for further consideration.

Reconsideration: A second consideration by a chamber of a bill before it has been sent to the other chamber or the governor. Only a member who voted on the prevailing side in the original vote may offer a motion to reconsider, and a bill may only be reconsidered once.

Recorded Vote: A vote in which the ayes and nays are kept by name.

Redistricting: The drawing of new political district boundaries.

Referendum: The principle or practice of submitting a law to popular vote after the filing of a petition expressing the wish of the people to vote on such law (in whole or in part).

Referral: The sending, assigning, or referring of a measure to a committee or committees.

Regular Session: The annual (or biennial) meeting of the legislature required by a state's constitution.

Regular Veto: The formal, constitutional authority of the governor to reject bills passed by both houses of the legislature, thus preventing their becoming law without further legislative action.

Repeal: A method by which a legislative action is revoked or annulled. Legislative measures will provide only statutory citations for laws being repealed in the "repealer clause," found near the end of the measure.

Report: To approve by committee.

Representation: When individual legislators act as the voices of their constituencies within the House or Senate.

Republican (Representative) Government: A form of government in which citizens exercise power indirectly by choosing representatives to legislate on their behalf.

Re-Referral: The act of reconsidering the referral of a measure to a committee or committees.

Rescind: Annulment of a previous action.

Resolution: A document that expresses the sentiment or intent of the legislature or a chamber, that governs the business of the legislature or a chamber, or that expresses recognition by the legislature or a chamber.

Revenue-Raising Measure: A measure whose principal object is to raise revenue or levy taxes.

Revenue Sharing: Federal money "shared" with the states based on the population of the states between 1972 and 1983. Larger states received more money, and there were few restrictions on use of the money.

Revolving Fund: Sometimes called special, continuing, or earmarked fund. It is a statutorily created fund to which monies that are deposited can be spent on a continuing basis without a specific annual appropriation by a specific agency and for a specific purpose.

Reynolds vs. Simms, 1962:   A Supreme Court Case that extended the "one man, one vote" principle to state legislative elections, requiring that districts must be similar in population and signifanctly altering the power structure in many state legislatures.

Roll Call: Names of the members being called in alphabetical order and recorded.

Roll-Call Vote: A vote in which members' votes are recorded.

Rules: Regulating principles or methods of legislative procedure.

Ruling of the Chair: A decision by the presiding officer concerning a question of order or procedure.

Runoff Primary: A second primary election between the two candidates receiving the greatest number of votes in the first primary.

Secretary of the Senate: A nonlegislator officer appointed or elected by the members of the Senate to perform and direct the parliamentary and clerical functions of the Senate; also may be called "clerk," "chief clerk," or "principal secretary."

Senate: A legislative body; usually the body in a bicameral legislature having the fewer number of members.

Seniority: Recognition of prior legislative service.

Session: (1) Period during which the legislature meets; (2) the daily meeting of the Senate or House.

Session Laws: The published compilation of bills and resolutions that have passed as a result of action by the current legislature.

Short-Term Voting Factors: Characteristics of a particular election that influence the way in which a person votes, such as the issues, candidates, or national trends relative to a particular election. Such factors may cause a voter to cast a vote that seems to be out of line with that person's long-term characteristics—race, gender, party, religion, and so forth.

Show of Hands: When a voice vote is called into question by the chair or a member, the member presiding may ask for members, either for or against a question, to raise their hands in order to conduct a count.

Simple Majority: One more than half of those voting on a question.

Simple Resolution: A measure similar to a joint resolution, but passed by one house of the legislature. Simple resolutions do not affect the laws of a state but are used primarily to express appreciation of the legislature to companies, individuals, and the like, or to make a point on some subject more definite than debate on the floor.

Sine Die: Adjournment on the last day of a regular or special legislative session. A date is not set for reconvening.

Single-Member Districts: Electoral districts from which only one legislator is elected to the legislature.

Speaker: Usually the title given to the person elected as the presiding officer of the House or Assembly; in some states, the title given to the presiding officer of the Senate. The individual presiding over the House of Representatives while in session is addressed as Mr. or Madam Speaker, even if that person is not the elected speaker.

Speaker Pro Tempore: A representative elected by the members to preside in the absence of the speaker.

Special and Local Laws: While a formal deliberative process is in place by which most bills must be considered, some laws are allowed to bypass this often cumbersome and generally slow process. Such is the case with special or local laws, which often can be passed with much more limited discussion or debate.

Special Committee: A committee created for a limited purpose or time.

Special (or Extraordinary) Session: A special meeting of the legislature that is called by the governor (or the legislature itself) and limited to specific matters.

Special Order: (1) To set consideration of a bill or measure for a specific, future time of the session; (2) matter of business set for discussion at a special time, on a designated day, or both.

Sponsor: The legislator who presents a bill or resolution for consideration; may be joined by others, who are known as cosponsor. See also: Author, Introducer, Patron.

Standing Committee: A committee established in a house for consideration of legislation.

States Rights Amendment: Tenth Amendment to the U.S. Constitution, which states: "The powers not delegated to the United States by the Constitution, nor prohibited to it by the states, are reserved to the States respectively, or to the people."

Static Ambition: The desire of a legislator or other public official to seek re-election to that legislator's current position.

Status: The location of a measure in the legislative process.

Status of Bill: The progress of a bill at any given time in the legislative process. It may be in committee, on the calendar, in the other house, and so forth.

Statutes: Compilation of all state laws presently in effect.

Stricken Title: The amendment of a bill to eliminate its title, thereby leaving the bill available to be completely rewritten, often on a completely different subject matter.

Strike Out: The deletion of language from a bill or resolution.

Substantive Bill: A measure not containing fiscal matters.

Substitute: An amendment proposing the replacement of the entire text of a measure or amendment.

Sunset Review: The automatic termination of the existence of numerous boards, commissions, and agencies, already provided for by statute, unless the legislature decides to continue their existence. States that have enacted sunset laws have utilized a variety of methods to administer and enforce them. In some states the enforcement process is largely ineffective.

Supplemental Appropriations: A midyear appropriation.

Supremacy Clause: Portion of Article VI of the U.S. Constitution that mandates that national law is supreme to (that is, supersedes) all other laws passed by the states or by any other subdivision of government.

Suspension of the Rules: Parliamentary procedure whereby a legislative chamber votes to allow actions that would otherwise be out of order.

Table (a Bill or Amendment):   To end consideration of a matter, usually with the intention of postponing or shelving it indefinitely.

Task Force Committee: Small number of legislators appointed to meet during the interim with state boards to learn about the activities and problems of state agencies.

Term of Office: Period of time for which a person is elected.

Title: A concise statement accurately expressing the contents of a bill, prepared as a preface to the bill.

Trustee Approach: Role played by elected representatives who listen to constituents' opinions and then use their best judgment to make final decisions.

Unanimous Consent: A motion to approve unanimously when there appears to be no opposition to the action before the body, thereby not requiring a formal vote.

Unfunded Mandate: The imposition of legal requirements from a higher level of government without funding for their costs.

Unicameral: A legislature with only one chamber.

Unopposed Seat: A legislative seat for which only one candidate is running.

Veto: A power vested in the governor to prevent the enactment of measures passed by the legislature by returning them, with objections, to the legislature.

Veto Override: Vote by the legislature to pass a bill over a governor's veto.

Voice Vote: Oral expression of the members when a question is submitted for their determination. When asked by the presiding officers, members respond "aye" or "nay." The presiding officer then decides which side has prevailed.

Vote: Formal expression of a decision by the body.

Voting Record: A member's voting history on one or more issues.

Well: The area in which the center podium is located in the House chamber. This podium is used for presentations and momentous occasions.

Whip: A legislator, usually selected by the members of that legislator's party, assigned to ensure that members of the party vote the way they are expected to on particular votes. The whip is to "whip" members into line.

Yeas and Nays: Recorded vote of members on an issue.

Yield: To relinquish the floor to another member to speak or to ask a question.

ANNOTATED BIBLIOGRAPHY

GENERAL

Barber, James David. 1965. *The Lawmakers: Recruitment and Adaption to Legislative Life*. New Haven: Yale University Press.

A fascinating look at the motivations and lives of state legislators in the 1960s. While it focuses on the Connecticut legislature, the adaptations and motivations that Barber discusses could apply to most legislatures of that era.

Crane, Wilder, Jr., and Meredith W. Watts Jr. 1968. *State Legislative Systems*. Englewood Cliffs, NJ: Prentice-Hall.

A brief (118-page) but comprehensive look into the state legislature of the 1960s, before the reform era that would change the institution.

Hamm, Keith, and Peverill Squire. 2005. *101 Chambers: Congress, State Legislatures and the Future of Legislative Studies*. Columbus: Ohio State University Press.

An outstanding summary of the historical origins of the U.S. legislature, as well as a basic description of key legislative structures, functions, membership, and careers. This book is a "must read" for anyone trying to understand state legislatures. Available in print and electronic format.

Loftus, Tom. 1994. *The Art of Legislative Politics*. Washington, DC: Congressional Quarterly Press.

Written by a former speaker of the Wisconsin House of Representatives, an insider's perspective to legislative life, with outstanding case studies of legislative action on some critical issues, including abortion, education, gun control, child welfare, and ethics.

Rosenthal, Alan. 1974. *Legislative Performance in the States*. New York: Harper and Row.

In this classic, Rosenthal gives the first comprehensive analysis of variations in legislative processes across the fifty state legislatures.

———. 1998. *The Decline of Representative Democracy: Process, Participation and Power in State Legislatures.* Washington, DC: Congressional Quarterly Press.

Rosenthal discusses the challenges facing the modern state legislature, especially direct democracy, increasingly independent legislators, weakening leaders, and a decreasingly effective legislative institution. He also offers a good overview of the legislative process.

———. 2004. *Heavy Lifting: The Job of the American Legislature.* Washington, DC: Congressional Quarterly Press.

Focuses on the three primary tasks of the modern state legislature: representing the people, making laws, and balancing the executive branch. Using interesting examples, Rosenthal explains how the modern state legislature approaches each of these responsibilities and the challenges that it must overcome to fulfill them.

Wahlke, John C., Heinz Eulau, William Buchannan, and LeRoy C. Ferguson. 1962. *The Legislative System.* New York: Wiley and Sons.

A classic, the first book to take a systematic and in-depth look at the lives of state legislators. The authors look at the state legislature as a "system" with many interactive parts and pieces.

BIOGRAPHIES

Bulger, William M. 1997. *While the Music Lasts: My Life in Politics.* Boston: Houghton Mifflin.

An entertaining look at how one gets to and manages the state legislature, with great insight into the internal politics of the Massachusetts legislature through the eyes of William M. Bulger, president of the Massachusetts Senate for almost two decades.

Clucas, Richard. 1995. *The Speaker's Electoral Connection: Willie Brown and the California Assembly.* Berkeley: University of California Institute of Government Studies Press.

Explores the life and sources of power of the Honorable Willie Brown, speaker of the California Assembly from 1980 to 1994. Speaker Brown was one of the most colorful and powerful individuals ever to hold that office.

National Conference of State Legislatures (http://www.ncsl.org).

LEGISLATIVE CAMPAIGNS

Gierzynski, Anthony. 1992. *Legislative Party Campaign Committees in the American States.* Lexington: University of Kentucky Press.

An exploration of the fundraising and distribution patterns of the relatively (at the time) new phenomenon of legislative party campaign committees, which have since become key players in state political processes.

Moncrief, Gary F., Peverill Squire, and Malcolm E. Jewell. 2001. *Who Runs for the Legislature?* Upper Saddle River, NJ: Prentice-Hall.

Uses a survey of first-time candidates for the state legislature to explore who runs for the state legislature, why they run, and how they manage their campaigns.

Shea, Daniel M., and Michael John Burton. 2001. *Campaign Craft: The Strategies, Tactics, and Art of Political Campaign Management.* 2d ed. Westport, CT: Praeger.

Basically a "how-to" manual for running a successful political campaign, including discussions of organization, strategy, and effective methods for reaching the voters that will help the candidate win.

Thompson, Joel A., and Gary F. Moncrief, eds. 1998. *Campaign Finance in State Legislative Elections.* Washington, DC: Congressional Quarterly Press.

A variety of perspectives on the nature and importance of campaign finance regulations and contributions across the states, including discussions of where campaign money comes from, how it is spent, and when it matters.

GENDER AND ETHNIC DIFFERENCES

Center for American Women and Politics (http://www.cawp.rutgers.edu).

Haynie, Kerry L. 2001. *African American Legislators in the American States.* New York: Columbia University Press.

A look at the attitudes, behaviors, and impact of African American legislators in Maryland, New Jersey, North Carolina, Illinois, and Arkansas, finding significant differences between white and black legislators in terms of the issues that are important to each and to legislative success.

Joint Center for Political and Economic Studies (http://www.jointcenter.org).

Rosenthal, Cindy Simon. 1998. *When Women Lead: Integrative Leadership in State Legislatures.* New York: Oxford University Press.

A consideration of the differing leadership styles of male and female legislative leaders, particularly committee chairs, and the factors shaping the practice of each style. Includes useful case studies.

Thomas, Sue. 1994. *How Women Legislate.* New York: Oxford University Press.

Thomas examines differences between male and female leaders regarding their behaviors, their attitudes, their support, and their influence on public policy.

LEGISLATIVE LEADERSHIP

Jewell, Malcolm E., and Marcia Lynn Whicker. 1994. *Legislative Leadership in the American States.* Ann Arbor: University of Michigan Press.

A singular and systematic look at what state legislative leaders do and how they do it. One unique contribution is a scale by which leadership power can be compared across states and leaders.

State Legislative Leaders Foundation. 2005. *What Have You Gotten Yourself Into? A Guide for New Legislative Leaders.* Centerville, MA: State Legislative Leaders Foundation.

A booklet examining the qualities of effective leadership in the modern state legislature. It focuses on steps that new leaders must take in order to be successful in their new positions.

State Legislative Leaders Foundation (http://www.sllf.org).

GOVERNORS AND BUREAUCRATS

Baum, Lawrence. 2002. *American Courts: Process and Policy*. Boston: Houghton Mifflin.

One of the country's leading texts on U.S. judicial politics and judicial process. In a comprehensive manner, it covers such topics as judicial selection and the role and function of trial courts, appellate courts, and lawyers in U.S. society.

National Governors Association (http://www.nga.org).

Rosenthal, Alan. 1990. *Governors & Legislatures: Contending Powers*. Washington, DC: Congressional Quarterly Press.

Although now more than a decade old, still the best and most interesting discussion of the relationship between the legislature and the governor, and the powers and advantages of each, with numerous interesting examples.

INTEREST GROUPS AND POLITICAL PARTIES

Morehouse, Sarah McCally, and Malcolm E. Jewell. 2003. *State Politics, Parties, Policy*. 2d ed. Lanham, MD: Rowman and Littlefield.

While this book focuses on the relationship between political parties and all three branches of government, the information on the relationship with the legislature is particularly strong.

Rosenthal, Alan. 2001. *The Third House: Lobbyists and Lobbying in the States*. 2d ed. Washington, DC: Congressional Quarterly Press.

A view into the world of legislative lobbying, this book offers a great context for understanding what lobbyists do and how they do it in the states. It is full of lively and entertaining stories and examples.

Rozell, Mark J., and Clyde Wilcox. 1999. *Interest Groups in American Campaigns*. Washington, DC: Congressional Quarterly Press.

Discusses the growing importance of interest groups and their political action committees (PACs) in political campaigns. While the examples are often taken from the national level, the lessons can be applied to the states.

ETHICS

Rosenthal, Alan. 1996. *Drawing the Line: Legislative Ethics in the States.* Lincoln: University of Nebraska Press.

The only book in recent years to specifically address questions of what is ethical and what is not in state legislatures. Rosenthal uses interesting examples to explore the ethical regulations and limits in state legislatures, as well as the processes by which they are established and their violations dealt with.

POLICY AND REFORMS

Farmer, Rick, John David Rausch, Jr., and John C. Green, eds. 2003. *The Test of Time: Coping with Legislative Term Limits.* Lanham, MD: Lexington.

Discusses the impact of legislative term limits on different aspects of the legislative process, including the effects of term limits in four states.

Nice, David C. 1994. *Policy Innovation in State Government.* Ames: Iowa University Press.

Nice examines state policy innovation and diffusion in several substantive policy areas, including teacher competency testing. He treats policy innovation as a product of three factors: state resources, problems, and attitudes toward change (political culture).

Rosenthal, Alan. 1974. *Legislative Performance in the States.* New York: Harper and Row.

In this classic, Rosenthal gives the first comprehensive analysis of variations in legislative processes across the fifty state legislatures.

———. 1998. *The Decline of Representative Democracy: Process, Participation and Power in State Legislatures.* Washington, DC: Congressional Quarterly Press.

Rosenthal discusses the challenges facing the modern state legislature, especially direct democracy, increasingly independent legislators, weakening leaders, and a decreasingly effective legislative institution. He also offers a good overview of the legislative process.

Rosenthal, Alan, et al. 2002. *The Republic on Trial: The Case for Representative Democracy*. Washington, DC: Congressional Quarterly Press.

Outlines many of the challenges facing the modern state legislature, including term limits, direct democracy, and declining public support. It extols the virtues of representative government in the face of these challenges.

Index

ABOUT THE AUTHORS

Thomas H. Little, Ph.D., is an adjunct instructor at the University of North Carolina at Greeensboro. He has published numerous articles and book chapters on state legislatures, leadership, and elections as well as publications designed to help legislative leaders perform their jobs more effectively.

David B. Ogle is an independent consultant on legislative process and organization and democracy development with more than 35 years of experience working with legislative and parliamentary bodies. He is the author of two books on American state legislatures, has written numerous monographs, articles, and reports on legislative organization, management, and process and civic education. He served as a consultant to seven American state legislatures and to legislative and parliamentary bodies in eighteen countries.